Modern War in an Ancient Land

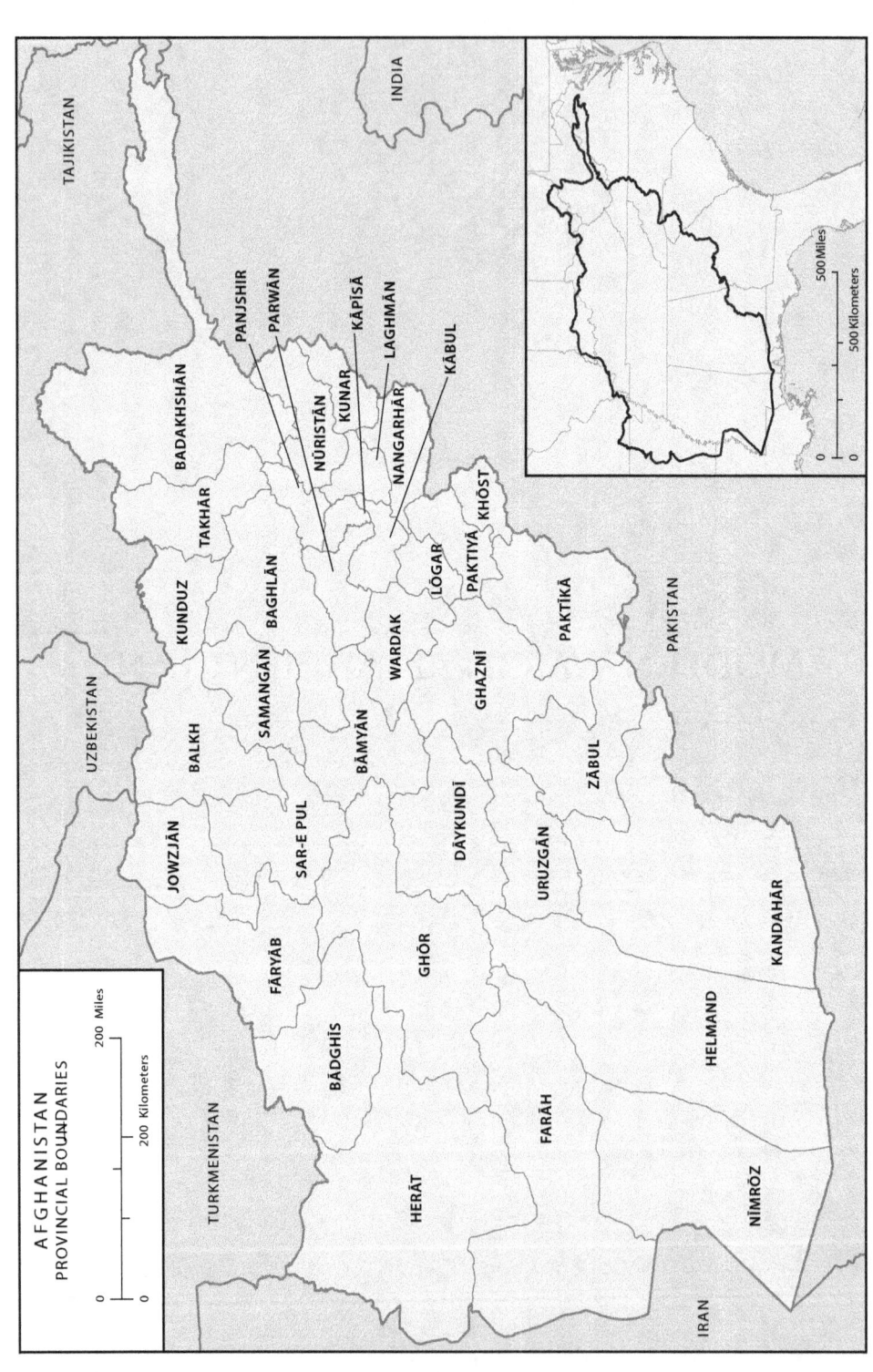

Modern War in an Ancient Land
The United States Army in Afghanistan
2001–2014
Volume I

by

Edmund J. "E. J." Degen

Mark J. Reardon

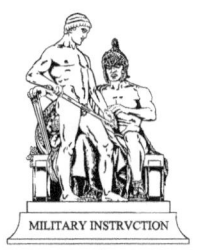

CENTER OF MILITARY HISTORY
UNITED STATES ARMY
WASHINGTON, D.C., 2021

Prepared by the Chief of Staff of the Army
Operation ENDURING FREEDOM Study Group

Col. (USA Ret.) Edmund J. "E. J." Degen
Study Director and Editor

Lt. Col. (USA Ret.) Mark J. Reardon
Senior Historian and Editor

Study Group Research and Writing Team
Col. Adrian A. Donahoe
Col. Bryan R. Gibby
Dr. Brian F. Neumann
Col. Francis J. H. Park
Dr. Gregory G. Roberts
Lt. Col. (USA Ret.) Matthew B. Smith
Lt. Col. (USA Ret.) John R. Stark
Maj. Miranda M. Summers-Lowe
Col. Victor H. Sundquist
Dr. Colin J. Williams

Foreword by
Former Secretary of Defense Dr. Robert M. Gates

... to Those Who Served

Contents

Chapter	Page

Foreword xiii
Preface xvii

Prologue 1
    The Taliban 2
    The Birth of al-Qaeda 8
    U.S. Army Operations from the Post–Cold War Era to
    11 September 2001 12
    The Institutional Army before 11 September 2001 18
    Factors Influencing U.S. Strategic Views in 2001 24
    Arrayal of Forces in September 2001 28

SECTION 1: LIBERATION

Introduction 33

1. The American Response to 11 September 2001 35
    The Global War on Terrorism 36
    The Bush Doctrine 41
    Coalition Building 47
    Planning for OEF-Afghanistan 50
    The September 11th Attacks and the U.S. Army 64
    Preparing for Battle 66
    Fleshing Out the Theater Framework 68
    Initial Deployment of Conventional Forces 70
    Opening Moves 71

2. Initial Combat Operations 79
    The First Shots 79
    Into the Heart of Taliban Country 81
    Bringing the United Front into the Fight 84
    The United Front 87
    More Americans Join the Fight 93
    Catastrophic Success 95
    Second Foray into the Taliban's Heartland 99
    Adapting to a Dynamic Operational Environment 102
    The Conflict Goes International 112
    All Roads Lead to Kandahar 117
    Expanding the Hunt for al-Qaeda 119

Chapter	Page

3. Path to Victory 127
    The U.S. Army Enters in Force 130
    Success Creates Growing Complexity 134
    Playing the "Long Game". 136
    New Boots on the Ground for Evolving Missions 141
    Planning for the Shahi Kot 143
    Into the Shahi Kot 151
    Day Two and Beyond 157
    Pushing South 162
    Winding Up ANACONDA 165
    Securing the High Ground 168
    Operation POLAR HARPOON. 169

4. A Campaign in Transition 171
    Creating the Afghan National Army 173
    CFLCC Prepared to Hand Over 176
    The Last Enclave: MOUNTAIN LION. 180

Conclusion 185

SECTION 2: SEARCHING FOR A SOLUTION

Introduction 191
    Political Setting as of May 2002. 194
    The Operating Environment. 198
    Enemy Situation as of May 2002 201
    The Emergence of Drone Strikes in Pakistan 204

5. Counterterrorism as an Operational Approach 207
    Planning Collides with Reality 208
    Counterterrorism 212
    From Civil Affairs Task Forces to Reconstruction Teams... 222
    Replacing Warlords with Government Security Forces 228
    The Army Adapts to the Campaigns 233
    Denying Sanctuary in Eastern Afghanistan. 243
    General Vines in Command 248
    Apparent Success 253

6. Counterinsurgency as an Operational Approach ... 257
    Political Setting as of September 2003. 259
    Enemy Situation as of September 2003 263
    A New Operational Approach 266
    General Barno's First Three Months 273
    Accelerating Success 276
    Election Preparations 287
    Measuring Success 302

Chapter	Page

    The U.S. Army Meeting Unanticipated Strategic Needs 305

7. Afghan and ISAF Expansion as an Operational Approach 319
    Political Setting as of May 2005 321
    Enemy Situation as of May 2005 324
    Posturing for a Long War 326
    Developing Afghan Government Security Forces 330
    The End of the Bonn Process 339

Conclusion 345
    Forward Deployed in Afghanistan 345
    Back in the United States 347

Bibliographical Note 351
    Documents and Publications 351
    Oral History Interviews and Manuscript Sources 352
    Secondary Sources 353

Operation Enduring Freedom Study Group Biographies 357

Appendix: U.S. Military Terminology and Definitions 361

Acronyms, Abbreviations, and Key Terms 381

Map Symbols and Note Terms 383

Index 387

Number	Page

MAPS
        Afghanistan, Provincial Boundaries .... *Frontispiece*
  1.1. Operation Enduring Freedom Service Arrivals,
       September 2001–February 2002 72
  2.1. Northern Theater, 19 October–10 November 2001 90
  2.2. Qala-i-Jangi, 25 November–1 December 2001 109
  2.3. Fall of Kandahar, 14 November–9 December 2001 112
  2.4. Tora Bora, 30 November–19 December 2001 121
  2.5. Pakistan's Federally Administered Tribal Areas, 2002 124
  3.1. Operation Anaconda: The Plan, February 2002 149
  3.2. Operation Anaconda, 27 February–20 March 2002 166
  5.1. Area of Operations, April 2002–January 2003 215
  5.2. Area of Operations, September 2002–August 2003 244
  5.3. Area of Operations, August 2003–May 2004 252
  6.1. Area of Operations, May 2004–March 2005 293
  6.2. Area of Operations, March 2005–March 2006 299

| Number | Page |

FIGURES

- 6.1. Barno's Campaign Model 269
- 6.2. Army Force Generation Model 313
- 7.1. Note on U.S. Military Tactical Terminology 327

PHOTOGRAPHS

The Damaged Pentagon on 11 September 2001 36
Firefighters at the World Trade Center Ruins on
 14 September 2001 39
Afghan Mountain Range near the Pakistan Border,
 South of Tora Bora 59
Paktiya Province, near the Pakistan Border 62
Afghanistan's Agricultural Valleys 68
B–52 Stratofortress Providing Close Air Support to
 Ground Forces 73
U.S. Air Force C–17 Globemaster 74
ODA 595 "Horse Soldiers" with General Abdul Rashid
 Dostum's Forces 85
ODA 595 Calling in Close Air Support of United Front
 Forces near Kunduz 87
Defense Secretary Donald H. Rumsfeld and
 General Tommy R. Franks 103
Qala-i-Jangi Fortress 108
Defense Secretary Donald H. Rumsfeld and
 Hamid Karzai 115
Cave Complex in the Tora Bora Area 123
Detention Operations at Kandahar 133
Senior U.S. Military Leaders Overseeing
 Operation ANACONDA 147
Soldiers Scanning a Nearby Ridgeline for Enemy Movement
 during Operation ANACONDA 158
The A–10 Thunderbolt II (Warthog) 160
Soldiers Dig into Fighting Positions during
 Operation ANACONDA 162
A Soldier Scans the Countryside for Enemy Targets during
 Operation ANACONDA 165
A Soldier Manning a .50-Caliber Machine Gun during
 Operation ANACONDA 167
U.S. Navy SEALs Conducting Operations in Afghanistan's
 Dzadzi Mountains 172
U.S. Navy SEALs Interacting with Local Villagers in the
 Dzadzi Mountains 177
Lt. Gen. Dan K. McNeill with Governor Hakim Taniwal 179
Soldiers on a Search-and-Attack Mission during Operation
 MOUNTAIN LION 213

	Page
Soldiers Securing an Ordnance Cache Found during Operation Mountain Lion	218
Soldiers Destroying a Weapons Cache during Operation Alamo Sweep	220
An Army Civil Affairs Unit in Uruzgan Province	223
Lt. Col. Najibullah Sadiqi, ANA, Presents Kandaks to President Hamid Karzai	231
Soldiers Searching for Arms Caches during Operation Alamo Sweep	241
Air and Ground Force Coordination during Operation Alamo Sweep	247
Troops Preparing to Enter a Residential Compound during Operation Alamo Sweep	251
Lt. Gen. David W. Barno	259
Brig. Gen. Lloyd J. Austin and General John P. Abizaid	270
The Kajaki Hydroelectric Plant	279
Providing Medical Care during a Combined Medical Assistance Mission	283
Soldiers Preparing to Destroy Cases of Ammunition and Various Weapons	284
An Afghan Voter in Khost Province	296
Local Afghan Guards Securing Road Construction in Paktiya Province	299
Defense Secretary Donald H. Rumsfeld Addressing Troops at Bagram	317
Maj. Gen. Karl W. Eikenberry and Ambassador Zalmay Khalilzad	321
ANA Trainees at the Kabul Military Training Center	332
A CH–47 Chinook on an Airstrip near Khost	340
An AH–64, Guarded by ANA Soldiers, Collecting Afghan Presidential Election Ballots	342

ARTWORK

Overwatch	xvi
Army Horse Soldiers	31
"I'm OK, Guys"	190
Close Air Support	350

Note on the Images

The majority of the photographs contained in these volumes were taken by U.S. Department of Defense service members and selected specifically to portray Afghanistan from the perspective of those who served. The authors appreciate the U.S. Agency for International Development for the photographs on pages 59, 62, 296, and 299

M. Sgt. Juan C. Munoz, the 2015–2019 Army Artist in Residence, painted the artwork in these volumes based on photographs taken in Afghanistan by military personnel. The U.S. Army thanks Sergeant Munoz for his evocative work and its valuable contribution to the long history of soldiers expressing themselves through their art.

Foreword

Operation ENDURING FREEDOM, the American intervention in Afghanistan in response to the terrorist attacks of 11 September 2001, was the opening campaign of an era in which extremist groups vied with nation-states to gain territory and followers throughout the world. Initiated during a period when post–Cold War viewpoints still influenced U.S. strategic deliberations, ENDURING FREEDOM achieved its initial goals of removing both the safe haven for the terrorist organization al-Qaeda and the Taliban government protecting them. At the same time, however, it exposed shortfalls in the U.S. military's ability to provide security and its accepted but unwarranted assumptions about ends, ways, and means as the conflict progressed. The U.S. military's experiences in Afghanistan reinforced hard-earned lessons about the complexity of coalition warfare and also revealed the fault lines— and resource disparities—between the U.S. government agencies that export influence and those that compel submission. Moreover, ENDURING FREEDOM raised important questions about how to intervene militarily against stateless organizations while shedding new light on the relationships between global terrorists and their nation-state sponsors.

Taking place between 7 October 2001 and 31 December 2014, Operation ENDURING FREEDOM was the longest named military operation in American history. It spanned eighty-five months of President George W. Bush's two terms in office and seventy-one months of President Barack H. Obama's tenure, as well as the entirety of my four-and-a-half years as secretary of defense. Almost 100,000 Afghan, American, and coalition lives were lost during the campaign, and a significantly greater number were wounded. Those stark figures include more than 2,300 killed and 20,000 wounded American service members, with most deaths occurring after 2007 mainly because of the increase in Taliban insurgent activity and the larger number of U.S. forces on the ground. The violence migrated with the deposed Taliban regime into neighboring Pakistan, where another 21,500 civilians, 6,000 government security personnel, and 29,000 militants died in fighting between 2001 and 2014, as transplanted extremist groups sought to gain power and influence there. In addition to the thousands of Americans killed or wounded in Afghanistan, the United States expended a staggering $718 billion in direct costs. That total includes $104 billion spent on Afghan reconstruction and almost $20 billion in aid to Pakistan. Our North Atlantic Treaty Organization allies also spent tens of billions in aid for the Afghan people and International Security Assistance Force efforts. The conclusion of ENDURING FREEDOM in December 2014 signified transformation rather than termination, as the conflict in that region continues unabated. The ongoing fighting, and the grim statistics associated with the conflict, justify the efforts of this account to shed additional light on the U.S. Army's role in Operation ENDURING FREEDOM.

The conflict in Afghanistan had far-reaching external and internal ramifications, affecting not merely Afghanistan itself but also its relations with neighboring countries. Extremists operated from sanctuaries in adjacent Pakistan, generating forces in training camps and sending supplies into Afghanistan with virtual impunity. American efforts to deny safe havens to these extremists, through actions that included drone strikes, training for Pakistani security forces, and economic and military aid to Islamabad, had uneven and inconsistent success. More than a decade of continuous conflict also produced numerous changes within Afghan society, many of which proved so profound that they influenced events in remote areas previously considered inaccessible. In fact, some observers argue that Afghanistan now only faintly resembles the country that the United States and its allies liberated from the Taliban in 2001.

The conflict also affected the U.S. Army in a similarly thorough fashion. Mindful of the tremendous logistical difficulties of operating in Afghanistan, as well as the experiences of the Soviet forces defeated by irregular Afghan forces during the 1980s, the United States did not send Cold War–era armored and mechanized divisions to fight against the Taliban and al-Qaeda. Instead, the Army's participation in the opening phase of the Afghan conflict consisted of a Special Forces Group, elements of two downsized brigades of the 10th Mountain Division plus a portion of the divisional headquarters, two Marine Expeditionary Units, and a downsized brigade from the 101st Airborne Division.

From 2002 onward, as planning for the proposed invasion of Iraq gained momentum, U.S. commanders in Afghanistan found themselves competing for supporting assets, including space-based surveillance; fixed- and rotary-wing aviation; and fire, logistics, engineer, and transportation units. Responding to administration priorities, the Army leadership devoted the bulk of available resources to the Iraq conflict from 2003 through 2009, while Afghanistan managed with whatever remained. That operational dilemma dominated the Army's overall approach to Afghanistan for several years; from 2003 onward, mechanized and armored units were sent exclusively to Iraq, while light infantry and Special Forces participated in both conflicts.

On the domestic political front, the Bush administration twice sought to minimize its military commitment to Afghanistan to provide more resources for the Iraq conflict. Taking advantage of the success of the Iraqi "surge" authorized by his predecessor, President Obama authorized the deployment of tens of thousands of reinforcements to Afghanistan, with a firm withdrawal timeline announced in advance to assuage domestic concerns about prolonging a stalemate. Although the Afghan "surge" achieved a great deal, it did not end the fighting. Our enemies simply retired to their sanctuaries to recoup their losses and reconstitute—and wait us out. The final years of ENDURING FREEDOM thus witnessed American forces providing more assistance to their Afghan counterparts as we prepared to hand over responsibilities to them. At the same time, we began shipping troops and materiel out of theater in anticipation of the campaign's projected December 2014 end date.

By consulting primary evidence and interviewing key participants, the Chief of Staff of the Army's Operation Enduring Freedom Study Group has produced the most authoritative account of the conflict yet written. The team's unprecedented access to such vital sources enabled it to make informed observations about counterinsurgency, insurgent sanctuaries in Pakistan, the in-theater coordination of conventional and Special Forces, advisory and operational partnerships with Afghans, and the debate between protecting forces and sending them into harm's way. It is my sincere desire that the insight gained by readers of these volumes will help our military and civilian leadership to understand, fight, and prevail in future conflicts.

DR. ROBERT M. GATES
22d United States Secretary of Defense, 2006–2011

PREFACE

President George W. Bush and his National Security Council viewed the invasion of Afghanistan in October 2001 as far more than retaliation for the 11 September 2001 terrorist attacks. Even as they were still defining the threat they faced, Bush and his advisers felt that the American way of life was under assault. To confront this threat, they launched Operation ENDURING FREEDOM to oust the Taliban regime that had sheltered Osama bin Laden's al-Qaeda network in Afghanistan and replace it with a representative government permanently hostile to international terrorism. By sending military forces to take down the operating base of the extremists responsible for the deadliest terrorist attack in American history, the Bush administration initiated Operation ENDURING FREEDOM expressly to prevent another such occurrence.

However, the opening phase of Operation ENDURING FREEDOM drew heavily from misconceptions of recent history. Senior administration officials, overly mindful of the negative public perceptions of failed U.S. military operations—exemplified by recent nonfiction and film accounts of the "Black Hawk Down" incident in the Battle of Mogadishu in 1993—sought to avoid similar problems in their forthcoming campaign. The Department of Defense and other government agencies also had relatively little in-depth knowledge of the dynamics affecting the region. As a result, the United States initially considered the Taliban as militarily capable as the *mujahideen* fighters who defeated Soviet troops in the 1980s.[1] Based on that erroneous comparison, the campaign plan envisioned a much harder and lengthier fight than actually occurred. Consequently, the U.S. military was not prepared to exploit the dramatic success it achieved early on. Furthermore, because the Pakistani government had aided American efforts to supply Afghan insurgents during the Soviet-Afghan War, the Bush administration continued to view Pakistan as a stalwart ally when in reality its strategic interests clashed with those of the United States. Unfortunately for the trajectory of the campaign, this pervasive lack of comprehensive knowledge persisted as America turned its sights on other strategic goals.

OVERVIEW

Modern War in an Ancient Land: The United States Army in Afghanistan, 2001–2014 examines the U.S. intervention in Afghanistan in October 2001 and

---

1. *Mujahideen* is the plural form of the Arabic term *mujahid*, meaning one who is struggling or striving for a praiseworthy aim. In English, it is used primarily to describe the Afghan guerrillas who fought against Soviet troops throughout the Soviet-Afghan War (December 1979–February 1989).

the thirteen-plus years of conflict that followed. Whether sent to Afghanistan to counter terrorists, defeat an insurgency, develop institutions, or support a democracy, Army commanders operated under the assumption that by securing Afghans and their fledgling national government, the U.S. military was protecting America and the Western way of life. For more than a decade, Army formations deployed to Afghanistan to forge a country that would remain unified, at peace with its neighbors, and inhospitable to terrorists who expressed their hatred of the American homeland through violence.

Modern War in an Ancient Land is the result of historical thinking by the Army's senior leadership. In the summer of 2014, General Raymond T. Odierno, the 38th Chief of Staff of the United States Army, formed the Operation ENDURING FREEDOM Study Group to research and write an operational history of the U.S. Army's involvement in Afghanistan from October 2001 to December 2014. The book was carried to completion by his successors, Generals Mark A. Milley and James C. McConville, officers with multiple combat tours in Afghanistan. All three understood that history must be both accurate and timely if it is to inform government officials and military officers facing the problems of the present. By giving a diverse team of historians the latitude to pursue primary documents and interview key leaders, Generals Odierno, Milley, and McConville promoted the spirit of independent inquiry needed to uncover the reasons why events happened as they did. By placing the team under the leadership of an accomplished war planner and operator, Col. E. J. Degen, the Chiefs of Staff ensured that any present-day utility offered by this history would not be lost to the passage of time.

Befitting its sponsors, *Modern War in an Ancient Land* is a history of the United States Army. Although Special Forces, joint headquarters, North Atlantic Treaty Organization (NATO) troop-contributing nations, unaligned third parties, and the United States Marine Corps are all integral to the story, its interpretative scope focuses on what the U.S. Army did in theater, how and why those actions occurred, and what effect those actions had on both Operation ENDURING FREEDOM and the U.S. Army as an institution. These two volumes are a narrative of how the U.S. Army formed, trained, deployed, and employed combat power overseas to prevent a repetition of the terrible events of 11 September 2001. The narrative is focused at the operational level of war and will discuss policy and strategy only as needed to illuminate the operational story. At the same time, it will delve into the tactical realm only when such insights amplify the implications of operational decisions or occurrences.

Although *Modern War in an Ancient Land* is Army-centric, it gives full credence to the multiple causal factors that determined events throughout the campaign. As the theater of operations, Afghanistan's dynamic environment and unique characteristics inherently shaped the nature of the conflict. Its topography, political leadership, security forces, lack of historic unity, economic dependence on opium poppy production, endemic poverty, and persistent corruption all exerted immense influence on what the U.S. Army could and could not do in Operation ENDURING FREEDOM. At the same time, Afghanistan's neighbors, particularly Pakistan, weighted the conflict with transnational aspects that often fell beyond the purview of operational commanders. Finally, a number of tenacious enemies—not merely the Taliban, but also the Hezb-e-Islami Gulbuddin (HIG) militant group, the guerrilla insurgent forces of the Haqqani Network, and various criminal networks—impeded the U.S. Army's efforts to protect Afghanistan and its indigenous population during the conflict. All of these factors required the U.S. Army's strategy to evolve and adapt to the constantly changing conditions on the ground.

These factors influenced the organization of *Modern War in an Ancient Land*. After a prologue highlighting the ongoing missions of the United States Army at the time of the September 11th attacks, the history proceeds with five chronological sections divided across two volumes. Section 1, Liberation, covers the Bush administration's decision to invade Afghanistan, its plan for the campaign, and the ways in which initial combat operations supported campaign objectives. Its four chapters examine how the Army built up forces during this phase of the conflict, deploying first Special Forces to partner with the anti-Taliban United Front and topple Afghanistan's ruling government, and then conventional forces from the 10th Mountain Division and the 101st Airborne Division to reduce Taliban concentrations in the country during Operations ANACONDA and MOUNTAIN LION.

Section 2, Searching for a Solution, starts with the Department of Defense decision to deploy a three-star joint task force to impose control over combat operations and ends with the conclusion of an international process to install a new Afghan government. The three chapters in this section evaluate the factors that hindered multiple attempts to achieve end-state objectives during this period. A few examples of these problems include nongovernmental organizations unwilling to operate outside the Afghan capital, the near impossibility of discriminating the opposition from the citizenry, the emergence of enemy sanctuaries in western Pakistan, and vacillating interest from a presidential administration intent on overthrowing Saddam Hussein's dictatorial rule of Iraq. This volume closes with some observations and conclusions from the first few years of the war in Afghanistan.

Volume II opens with Section 1, An Economy of Force, and covers the nadir of American military efforts in Afghanistan, one of the most consequential three-year periods in Army history. It begins with an attempt to refocus combat power on the country's eastern provinces, which had been shortchanged in 2006 and 2007 by the need to aid NATO forces ensnared in deadly combat in the southern provinces. The first three chapters of the section explain how the Taliban, HIG, and the Haqqani Network challenged NATO's assumption of operational responsibility for the theater, while its final chapter specifies how intervening forces tried to blunt the opposition's rise by developing Afghanistan's security forces. The section also describes how America's war in Iraq from 2003 onward further complicated matters by severely degrading the U.S. Army's ability to provide trained, combat-ready forces at this stage of the conflict, leading to changes in mission, force structure, and readiness.

The final two sections of *Modern War in an Ancient Land* relate America's attempt to reassert political, strategic, and operational initiative in Afghanistan following the 2009 inauguration of President Barack H. Obama. Under President Obama's leadership, the scope and intensity of Operation

Enduring Freedom would increase temporarily. This growth would limit enemy aggressiveness, creating the necessary time and space to reduce troops to a level deemed acceptable to the American public. Section 2, The Surge in Afghanistan, begins with a strategic reassessment of Operation Enduring Freedom meant to align the new administration's policies with theater objectives. Recommendations from the military focused on personnel end strength. To solve the problems highlighted in the review, President Obama directed a temporary surge in U.S. forces. Commanders used the increased forces available to them to conduct counterinsurgency operations on the northeastern and southwestern peripheries of NATO-controlled Afghanistan. Although occasional tactical setbacks reversed operational gains, they did not alter the Obama administration's intent to reduce force strength starting in late 2011. Section 3, End of Campaigns, describes how the U.S. Army began removing its active components from an environment hostile to foreign forces while forming and conducting aggressive security force assistance operations. The retrograde focused on developing indigenous security forces, accelerating Western efforts to improve Afghan governance, and setting up an ambitious program to ship more than a decade's worth of stockpiled war materiel out of the country. The final section of these volumes presents the overarching lessons learned at the operational level across more than thirteen years of campaigning in Afghanistan. These lessons include the critical balance of ends, ways, and means; the value of force innovation and agility; and the benefits and challenges of force structure transformation in a time of conflict. They also highlight the importance of unity of command and effort, the vital role of information operations on the modern battlefield, and the need for security as a precursor to stability. As always, war is a marathon, not a sprint.

Modern War in an Ancient Land is not the final word on the U.S. Army during Operation Enduring Freedom. Even when viewed through the lenses of the U.S. Army and the operational level of war, Operation Enduring Freedom was an incredibly complex conflict. More work needs to be done to evaluate its broader legacy in American military history. To that end, the U.S. Army Center of Military History (CMH) is now assembling historians to write a series of "Tan Books" covering all facets of the Global War on Terrorism. Not to engage in this comprehensive effort would be to slight the importance of campaigns not mentioned and units not detailed in *Modern War in an Ancient Land*.

Acknowledgments

In writing this book, the authors have benefited from numerous experts. Although it would be impractical to list them all, any attempt must begin with our review board: Dr. David E. Johnson of the RAND Corporation; General (Ret.) Charles H. Jacoby Jr. of the U.S. Army; Dr. Jack D. Kem of the U.S. Army Command and General Staff College; Dr. Brian M. Linn of Texas A&M University; Dr. Brian Glyn Williams of the University of Massachusetts, Dartmouth; Dr. Robert M. Citino from The National World War II Museum; Paul W. Westermeyer from the Marine Corps History Division of the Marine Corps University; and Dr. William Shane Story from

CMH. The insight and knowledge of these distinguished gentlemen saved the Study Group from errors both large and small. Any errors remaining are the fault of the authors alone. In addition, Dr. Donald P. Wright at Army University Press (Fort Leavenworth, Kansas) and Genoa Stanford at the Maneuver Center of Excellence's Donovan Research Library (Fort Benning, Georgia) contributed documents that greatly expanded the study group's research archives.

The authors also owe considerable gratitude to the staffs of both U.S. Central Command and U.S. Special Operations Command. From hosting and assisting the research team to fast-tracking the declassification of critical documents, their timely and friendly support was second to none and a clear reflection of the commands. The team also owes much to Generals John F. Campbell and John W. "Mick" Nicholson Jr. at NATO's International Security Assistance Force headquarters, who ensured that their staff provided anything and everything we requested from them. And finally, we offer a special thanks to then Maj. Gen. John M. Murray and the staff of the 3d Infantry Division, who allowed the writing team to access the servers of the National Support Element Command–Afghanistan in Bagram, Afghanistan, from which they siphoned multiple terabytes of critical historical data.

Closer to home, Directors of the Army Staff Lt. Gen. Gary H. Cheek, Lt. Gen. Joseph M. Martin, and Lt. Gen. Walter E. Piatt and Vice Director Mr. Steven J. Redmann deserve special thanks for the constant "top cover" they provided the team. They eagerly gave support when and where it was needed. General Raymond T. Odierno, General Mark A. Milley, and General James C. McConville empowered and guided the team and critiqued its work as necessary. Their sage guidance and consummate support were invaluable. The former Administrative Assistant to the Secretary of the Army Mr. Gerald B. O'Keefe, and CMH's Executive Director Mr. Charles R. Bowery Jr. and Chief Historian Mr. Jon T. Hoffman, provided the Study Group with administrative support as well as a wonderfully collegial place in which to conduct the serious work of history. As always, Chief of Historical Services Mr. Frank R. Shirer, and all the historians who deposited and maintained data in the CMH library, proved invaluable. The CMH Historical Products Division, under the intrepid leadership of Ms. Cheryl L. Bratten, the rigorous editorial direction of Ms. Shannon L. Granville, and the dedicated editorial review of Ms. C. Sarah Castle, Ms. Margaret J. McGarry, and Ms. Karla Moon, excelled at preparing *Modern War in an Ancient Land* for publication. Mr. Matthew T. Boan and Mr. Ramon L. Perez, the branch's cartographers, prepared all of the maps in this book. CMH visual information specialists Mr. Timothy J. Mazurek and Mr. Michael R. Gill provided the critical design and production work to see both volumes into print. Their collective skill and expertise are all integral to the value of the finished product.

Finally, this history has benefited from leaders who entertained our questions. From President George W. Bush to platoon leaders, they all met willingly with members of the writing team and answered questions to the best of their recollections. A special thanks is due to former Secretary of Defense Robert M. Gates, who graciously consented to provide an in-depth interview and to write the foreword for Volume 1.

Prologue

In late December 1979, Soviet leader Leonid I. Brezhnev dispatched troops to Afghanistan to prop up a failing communist government in Kabul. Yet instead of strengthening a faltering ally, the Soviet intervention only further destabilized the country, sparking a nationwide Islamist insurgency that led to a decade-long war for the Soviet Union in Afghanistan. After initially deploying massed tanks, artillery, and airpower against the Afghan guerrilla movement known as the mujahideen, the Soviet military began relying on Special Operations Forces (SOF), heliborne infantry, and Afghan proxy fighters. The adoption of more sophisticated tactics, however, did not deliver victory. The insurgency grew in scope and ferocity. Years of inconclusive combat, coupled with a growing need for domestic political and economic reforms, prompted the Soviet Union—now led by Mikhail Gorbachev—to announce a plan to withdraw its troops from Afghanistan in October 1985. That process required four years to complete, as Moscow reduced its troop commitment while transferring responsibility for the ongoing conflict to its communist Afghan allies.

As the Soviets withdrew, Western nations that had been funneling weapons to the Afghan resistance through Pakistan also pulled out of the conflict. The flow of American aid to Pakistan, its main ally in the region, had come under scrutiny in August 1985 after Congress passed the Pressler Amendment to the U.S. Foreign Assistance Act of 1961. The amendment stipulated that no military or technology equipment would be sold or transferred to Pakistan unless the American president certified that Pakistan did not possess an assembled nuclear bomb or all of the components necessary to make a bomb.[1] Although President Ronald W. Reagan's administration obtained evidence that Pakistani scientists were violating the amendment, it deferred enforcement of it until the Afghan-Soviet conflict ended.[2] Once the United

---

1. The 1985 amendment was a compromise measure worked out in Congress after Democratic senators John H. Glenn Jr. and Alan M. Cranston proposed a more stringent change to the act in March 1984. Some evidence suggests that Pakistan was informed about the Pressler Amendment in advance. See Rabia Akhtar, "The Correct Narrative on Pressler," *Dawn*, 29 May 2017, https://www.dawn.com/news/1335979, Historians Files, Chief of Staff of the Army Operation Enduring Freedom Study Group (hereinafter Hist Files, OEF Study Grp).

2. Available evidence suggests that Pakistani scientists were doing so without official backing or approval. These sanctions were not permanent, as the U.S. government lifted and reimposed them several times before 11 September 2001. Even though the United States eased the sanctions after the September 11th attacks, U.S.-Pakistan relations remained problematic. See "A. Q. Khan's Nuclear Network," *History Commons*, 2009, https://www.historycommons.org/timeline.jsp?timeline=aq_khan_nuclear_network_tmln&aq_khan_nuclear_network_tmln_us_

States began enforcing the Pressler Amendment in October 1990, relations with Pakistan deteriorated. The end of U.S. aid hurt Pakistan both financially and militarily, but it freed Islamabad to pursue its own aims in Afghanistan without Washington's interference.

Even after the Soviets departed in 1989, the Afghan conflict continued as mujahideen fighters battled the communist regime and each other. Afghanistan's weak proxy government, mountains of surplus weaponry, and panoply of insurgent bands formed along various ideological and ethnic lines combined to sustain chaos on a national scale. This constant instability motivated a group of religious students to form an armed movement to end the fighting. These students, known as the Taliban (students of Islam), shared a strong ideological bond with a number of volunteers from Arab countries who had traveled to Afghanistan to join the mujahideen and fight the Soviets. In an effort to increase its influence within Afghanistan and thus gain strategic depth against India, the Pakistani government began providing weapons and advisers to the Taliban. In addition, Saudi Arabia provided cash, weapons, and thousands of vehicles to the Taliban as part of its plan to surround Shia-dominated Iran with Sunni-dominated governments.[3] This influx of outside aid helped convince many Afghan warlords to ally with the Taliban.

Imbued with a single-minded dedication that many of its opponents lacked, the Taliban eliminated virtually all opposition before it. After securing control of most of Afghanistan by late 1995, it offered sanctuary to extremist groups such as al-Qaeda (the foundation or the base) and the Islamic Movement of Uzbekistan in return for assistance in defeating local political leader Ahmad Shah Massoud, whose collection of Hazara, Tajik, and Uzbek militias had been resisting Taliban rule in the Darya-ye Panjshayr Valley of northern Afghanistan. To prevent the Taliban from taking control of the entire country, the U.S. Central Intelligence Agency (CIA) funneled some aid to Massoud in the late 1990s. That aid, however, did nothing to prevent terrorist organizations from establishing camps in Afghanistan. Nations targeted by these groups had limited retaliatory options unless they wanted to risk war with the Taliban.

THE TALIBAN

Even though the Soviets ended their troop presence in Afghanistan in February 1989, they continued to provide substantial military and economic assistance to the Afghan communist regime in Kabul. The government forces of President Mohammed Najibullah sorely needed that aid, because the Afghan mujahideen turned against them as soon as the Soviet troops departed. Najibullah's regime clung to power for almost three more years, largely with the help of Soviet weaponry and funds. In addition to

---

intelligence_on_pakistani_nukes=aq_khan_nuclear_network_tmln_us_sanctions, Hist Files, OEF Study Grp.

3. Celia W. Dugger, "Indian Town's Seed Grew into the Taliban's Code," *New York Times*, 23 Feb 2002, https://www.nytimes.com/2002/02/23/world/indian-town-s-seed-grew-into-the-taliban-s-code.html, Hist Files, OEF Study Grp.

furnishing Najibullah's troops with firepower, Soviet aid allowed the Afghan communists to buy the allegiance of local mujahideen militias.[4] Although their outside funding sources made the Pakistan-based mujahideen bands less susceptible to bribery, they were unable to muster enough strength to overcome Najibullah because they were as politically or violently opposed to each other as they were to the communists.

The most effective foes of the Najibullah regime during this period included Gulbuddin Hekmatyar's Hezb-e-Islami Gulbuddin (HIG) and Massoud's Tajik militia.[5] Hekmatyar mobilized support among fellow ethnic Pashtuns, while Massoud attracted non-Pashtun ethnic groups including Tajiks, Uzbeks, and Hazaras.[6] When Najibullah's regime began disintegrating as the Soviets withdrew their aid, the communist-armed forces dispersed into the various militias depending on which one made them the best offer. In many ways, this situation benefited Massoud most, as it allowed him to occupy Kabul days ahead of Hekmatyar's troops in April 1992. The fall of the communist regime, however, did not bring peace to war-torn Afghanistan. After efforts to form a unity government failed, various armed factions attempted to take by force what they could not cajole by *shura* (a local consultative council or assembly).[7]

The post-1992 conflict differed from the Afghan-Soviet conflict in that other regional powers were willing to invest significant resources to influence the metamorphosing Afghan civil war. Russia, Iran, and Turkey all had proxies and interests in northern and western Afghanistan. The Central Asian republics, now freed from Soviet control, also had their preferred strongmen: Abdul Rashid Dostum, an ethnic Uzbek, and Massoud, an ethnic Tajik, looked to the newly independent Uzbekistan and Tajikistan, respectively, for support and sanction. At the same time, Pakistan focused its energies on promoting Hekmatyar's HIG forces.[8] The Saudis aided Islamabad's efforts by funding recruitment and training infrastructure in Pakistan and Afghanistan and by purchasing Pakistani factories to manufacture small arms and ammunition, explosives, and other weapons.[9] The end product was an overall stalemate and general misery. Afghanistan would not achieve peace or stability until something, or someone, broke the deadlock.

As the Afghan civil war stagnated into factional violence, Islamabad started looking for other options to bring down the Tajik-dominated seat of government in Kabul. Elements within Pakistan's government quietly began

---

4. Thomas J. Barfield, *Afghanistan: A Cultural and Political History* (Princeton, N.J.: Princeton University Press, 2010), pp. 241–49.

5. Peter Tomsen, *The Wars of Afghanistan: Messianic Terrorism, Tribal Conflicts, and the Failures of Great Powers* (New York: PublicAffairs, 2011), pp. 303–20.

6. Husain Haqqani, "Insecurity along the Durand Line," in *Afghanistan: Transition under Threat*, eds. Geoffrey Hayes and Mark Sedra (Waterloo, Ontario: Wilfrid Laurier University Press, 2008), pp. 228–29.

7. Barfield, *Afghanistan*, pp. 249–50.

8. Tomsen, *Wars of Afghanistan*, pp. 454–55; Ahmed Rashid, *Taliban: Militant Islam, Oil and Fundamentalism in Central Asia* (New Haven, Conn.: Yale University Press, 2000), p. 21.

9. Tomsen, *Wars of Afghanistan*, p. 464.

shifting support from Hekmatyar to the increasingly influential Taliban.[10] Hailing from the fertile triangle between the two branches of the Arghandab River in the Panjwa'i District west of the provincial capital city of Kandahar, the Taliban represented a large group of familial and tribal interests firmly committed to the principles of Islam. Because most Taliban members were Pashtuns from southern Afghanistan and western Pakistan, they had an immediate constituency in those regions, even though much of the local population did not embrace the movement's strict interpretations of *sharia* (Islamic religious law) and Islamic theology.[11]

Led by Mullah Mohammed Omar, a reclusive one-eyed preacher from the rural district of Maywand in Kandahar Province, the Taliban emerged onto the world stage in late autumn of 1994 when a few dozen former *talibs*—as individual members of the Taliban were known, from the Arabic word for "student"—gathered to attack highway brigands that had been preying on innocent travelers.[12] Taliban mythology claims that Omar personally led a group of no more than thirty talibs, half with rifles, to rescue two teenage girls who had been abducted by a local warlord. Omar's prestige grew following this successful raid and other actions that his followers took to confront warlords and petty criminals in the province. The Taliban's growing reputation for timely Islamic justice, charitable work, and the empowerment of Pashtuns also improved its local standing. All these threads combined to enhance Omar's appeal to ethnic groups on both sides of the Afghanistan-Pakistan border who were looking to end Afghanistan's internal turmoil and divisions.[13]

An important dimension of Omar's world view was his adherence to an Islamic school known as Deobandism, a late-nineteenth-century revivalist and anti-imperialist movement. Even today, it remains one of the more influential schools of sharia legal interpretation prevalent in south and central Asia.

---

10. The U.S. Embassy in Islamabad was aware of fissures in Pakistan's policy of supporting the "Peshawar Seven"—the alliance of seven mujahideen parties that had come together in the 1980s to fight the Soviets. Afghan sources revealed anxiety over any overt Pakistani influence in Afghanistan's internal affairs. Pakistani sources indicated that support for the Taliban was problematic and just as likely to harm Pakistan as to benefit it. The confused reporting likely contributed to a fundamental misreading of the situation as the Taliban emerged from an unknown group to the region's most potent military movement. Fax, U.S. Embassy Islamabad [Redacted] to Ron McMullen, 5 Dec 1994, sub: Developments in Afghanistan, The National Security Archive, George Washington University (hereafter NSA GWU), https://www2.gwu.edu/~nsarchiv/NSAEBB/NSAEBB227/1.pdf, Hist files, OEF Study Grp; Fax, Islamabad 11584, U.S. Embassy Islamabad to Sec State, 6 Dec 1994, sub: [Redacted] Believe Pakistan Is Backing Taliban, NSA GWU, https://www2.gwu.edu/~nsarchiv/NSAEBB/NSAEBB97/tal5.pdf, Hist Files, OEF Study Grp; see also Fax, Islamabad 003466, U.S. Embassy Islamabad to RUEHC/Sec State, 22 Apr 1996, sub: A/S Raphel Discusses Afghanistan, NSA GWU, https://www2.gwu.edu/~nsarchiv/NSAEBB/NSAEBB97/tal15.pdf, Hist Files, OEF Study Grp.

11. Rashid, *Taliban*, pp. 25, 33.

12. Fax, Islamabad 01792, U.S. Embassy Islamabad to Sec State, 20 Feb 1995, sub: Finally, a Talkative Talib: Origins and Membership of the Religious Students' Movement, NSA GWU, https://www2.gwu.edu/~nsarchiv/NSAEBB/NSAEBB97/tal8.pdf, Hist Files, OEF Study Grp.

13. Rashid, *Taliban*, p. 25; Fax, U.S. Embassy to Sec State, 20 Feb 1995, sub: Finally, a Talkative Talib; Tomsen, *Wars of Afghanistan*, p. 536.

Prologue

Highly structured and legalistic, Deobandism also promoted a sense of Muslim national identity in conflict with the West. The Taliban fused this vision of Islamic purity with Salafist orthodoxy and Pashtun nationalism to glorify armed resistance to foreign influences. It was a short step for this philosophy to evolve into a movement that promoted *jihad* (struggle, in the sense of a holy war waged on behalf of Islam) against infidels, apostates, and modernity.[14]

A charismatic and trusted leader, Omar decided to spread the Taliban's sharia-based mandate throughout Afghanistan.[15] Flush with growing popular support, he reportedly went as far as to take the cloak of the Prophet Muhammad from a Kandahar shrine, wrap himself in it, and extract the *bayat* (an oath of personal allegiance) from his followers. He also accepted the title of *Amir al-Mahmunen* (Commander of the Faithful).[16] It was a masterful political stroke that brought him supporters from Uzbek, Tajik, and other ethnic groups who were willing to subscribe to his military and political objectives.[17] Reports of the Taliban's deeds also breathed credibility and impetus into the new movement, and motivated an increasing number of veteran mujahideen to side with Omar.

Finally, in the fall of 1994, Pakistan's Inter-Services Intelligence agency blatantly threw its weight behind the new movement. On 4 October—though some sources suggest that the attack took place in late September—200 Taliban militants, Islamic *madrassa* (religious educational institution) students, and Arab fighters attacked Spin Boldak, a port of entry on the Afghan side of the border with Pakistan. In addition to its role as a major transportation hub (and therefore revenue producer), the Spin Boldak border crossing was controlled by Gulbuddin Hekmatyar's followers. American diplomatic sources believed that Pakistan's military supported the attack with "artillery shelling . . . from Pakistani Frontier Corps positions."[18] Hekmatyar's men fled after a brief firefight, abandoning a large weapons store that added thousands of small arms, dozens of artillery pieces, and large quantities of ammunition, explosives, and vehicles to the Taliban's inventory. The victory at Spin Boldak convinced many lesser warlords and militias to join the Taliban as repeated military successes allowed the new movement to consolidate Afghan political and social authority under Omar's banner.

---

14. Hassan Abbas, *The Taliban Revival: Violence and Extremism on the Pakistan-Afghanistan Frontier* (New Haven, Conn.: Yale University Press, 2014), pp. 13–17; Abdul Salam Zaeef, *My Life with the Taliban* (New York: Columbia University Press, 2010), pp. 22–26; Mark Silinsky, *The Taliban: Afghanistan's Most Lethal Insurgents* (Santa Barbara, Calif.: Praeger, 2014), pp. 13, 17. For Deobandi ideas and proliferation, see Ira A. Lapidus, *A History of Islamic Societies*, 2d ed. (Cambridge, UK: Cambridge University Press, 1988), p. 465.

15. Mustafa Hamid and Leah Farrall, *The Arabs at War in Afghanistan* (London: C. Hurst & Company, 2015), p. 250.

16. Rashid, *Taliban*, pp. 42, 86–93. The Kandahar shrine that held the Prophet Muhammad's cloak had been built by Ahmed Shah Durrani, Afghanistan's first Pashtun king (r. 1747–1772).

17. Hamid and Farrall, *The Arabs at War in Afghanistan*, pp. 250–51.

18. Fax, U.S. Embassy Islamabad to Sec State, 6 Dec 1994, sub: [Redacted] Believe Pakistan Is Backing Taliban.

A few weeks after seizing Spin Boldak, a Taliban unit marched on Kandahar, capturing it with little effort on 5 November. Thousands of Afghan refugees returned from Pakistan to join the Taliban colors. They were young and lacked combat experience, but they knew how to handle guns and were completely detached from Afghanistan's traditional tribal network and traditions, which made them loyal to the Taliban alone. Veteran journalist Ahmed Rashid believes that as many as 20,000 Afghan refugees and "hundreds" of Pakistani Pashtuns crossed into Afghanistan following the fall of Kandahar.[19] With this influx of fresh manpower, Mohammed Omar's lieutenants surged into neighboring Helmand Province, overrunning it by February 1995. Twin drives then reached the cities of Herat in the west and Kabul in the east.[20]

Herat's provincial governor, Ismail Khan, fled the provincial capital in early September, allowing the Taliban to seize the city on 4 September 1995 and cement its hold on the western side of the country. In Kabul, Massoud's forces fought with more skill and firepower, giving the Taliban its first rebuff. Taliban forces, now augmented with tanks, artillery, and rockets, besieged the city, using their indirect fire assets to bombard Kabul in much the same way as Hekmatyar's men had a few years earlier. Massoud's limited resources were fully committed to retaining control of the embattled capital as the Taliban sent men and munitions from the Pashtun south into the fight in a bid to overwhelm its Tajik defenders.[21] In the summer of 1996, Pakistan broke the impasse by allowing Taliban forces in South Waziristan to launch an assault on the eastern city of Jalalabad, which fell on 10 September. Additional Taliban columns swept north, scooping up Kunar, Nangarhar, and Nuristan Provinces, thus sealing Kabul's fate. Massoud withdrew on 26 September. The Taliban flag now flew over Afghanistan's hollowed-out capital city.[22]

The 40,000 to 50,000 combatants serving with the Taliban were nominally under a corps headquarters in Kabul commanded by Mullah Mohammed Fazl. Air defense assets included about a dozen MiG jet interceptors, as well as three batteries of Soviet-made SA–3 radar-guided surface-to-air missiles, 300 to 550 antiaircraft guns of varying calibers, and several hundred SA–7 man-portable surface-to-air missiles. In addition to jet fighters, the Taliban possessed transport planes and helicopters. The Taliban inventory also contained about 200 operational artillery pieces, as well as multiple truck-mounted rocket launchers, all of which were distributed piecemeal in accordance with battlefield needs. Additionally, it had an armored brigade equipped with 250 tanks and other armored vehicles. Like the rocket launchers, most armored fighting vehicles were distributed in platoons or smaller formations to assist infantry units that required additional fire support to gain a local advantage.

---

19. Tomsen, *Wars of Afghanistan*, p. 536.

20. Ibid.; Rashid, *Taliban*, pp. 29–32.

21. Fax, Islamabad 08185, U.S. Embassy Islamabad to Sec State, 6 Sep 1995, sub: Afghanistan: Heavy Fighting Rages West of Kabul; Herat Calm after Taliban Takeover, NSA GWU, https://www2.gwu.edu/~nsarchiv/NSAEBB/NSAEBB97/tal11.pdf, Hist Files, OEF Study Grp; Rashid, *Taliban*, pp. 35–40.

22. Rashid, *Taliban*, pp. 48–49.

Prologue

As Omar formed a new national government, it became clear that Pashtuns—who represented less than half of the country's twenty-seven million citizens—would be dominant in Afghan affairs. The lesser ethnic groups, all of whom practiced less-stringent versions of Islam, deeply resented being dominated by predominantly Sunni Pashtuns. The combined Tajik and predominantly Shia Hazara populations, which matched the Pashtuns in numbers, were excluded from the new government. As a result, Hazari, Tajik, and Uzbek communities and former mujahideen commanders continued to resist Taliban expansion. Despite fierce fighting, by 1998 the Taliban had captured the cities of Bamyan and Mazar-e Sharif, along with the Hazarjat region in central Afghanistan. The fighting grew more vicious as Omar's followers pushed north and northwest from Kabul, with Hazaras and Taliban each committing atrocities against their opponents.[23] Each new success further energized Taliban efforts to persecute their enemies.[24]

In addition to condoning the torture and execution of captured fighters, the Taliban imposed a harsh brand of justice—one which drew heavily from the Pashtuns' pre-Islamic tribal code and Wahhabi interpretations of sharia—on the general population. Policies designed to suppress un-Islamic behavior, such as banning music and television, jailing men whose beards were considered to be too short, and forcing women to wear the head-to-toe covering known as the *burqa*, appalled Western observers.[25] In 1998, the United Nations (UN) Security Council passed two resolutions admonishing the Taliban for its abusive and restrictive treatment of women and issued formal sanctions on the regime.[26] These sanctions diplomatically isolated the Taliban with only Pakistan, Saudi Arabia, and the United Arab Emirates recognizing the regime's legitimacy.

By 1999, Massoud, living in exile in Tajikistan, had assembled the remaining opposition elements into a shaky coalition called the United Islamic Front for the Salvation of Afghanistan—known in the West as the United Front.[27] The United Front proved so adept at keeping its opponents at bay that Omar continued to feed troops into the fight until the bulk of the Taliban's field forces were committed in the north. The resultant stalemate led Pakistan to send in advisers who could provide technical advice and support planning. Although a highly trained and motivated unit of Uzbek, Chechen, and Arab

---

23. Brian Glyn Williams, *Afghanistan Declassified: A Guide to America's Longest War* (Philadelphia: University of Pennsylvania Press, 2012), p. 38.

24. Donald P. Wright et al., *A Different Kind of War: The United States Army in Operation ENDURING FREEDOM (OEF), October 2001–September 2005* (Fort Leavenworth, Kans.: Combat Studies Institute Press, 2010), p. 12.

25. Ibid., pp. 23–24.

26. Zachary Laub, "The Taliban in Afghanistan," Council on Foreign Relations, 4 Jul 2014, https://www.cfr.org/afghanistan/taliban-afghanistan/p10551, Hist Files, OEF Study Grp.

27. Pakistan chose to use the term "Northern Alliance" in order to portray the anti-Taliban coalition as a narrow, Tajik-dominated resistance without broad national appeal. Henry A. Crumpton, *The Art of Intelligence: Lessons from a Life in the CIA's Clandestine Service* (New York: Penguin Group, 2012), p. 127.

extremists—known as Brigade 055—aided the Taliban, decisive battlefield success in the north remained elusive.

The Taliban regime presented the international community with a dilemma. It had delivered stability and Islamic justice to a war-weary nation. Although the regime was not universally accepted, particularly by non-Pashtuns, it did have enough Afghan support to give it legitimacy. However, it appeared to show little respect for international norms. Its human rights policies were abysmal, and its crude enforcement of sharia law made it appear to encourage gratuitous violence and domestic oppression.[28] Moreover, the Taliban's international stature suffered greatly from the regime's willingness to offer protection to some of the world's most wanted terrorists. Although the United States made several diplomatic efforts during the latter half of the 1990s to close the gap between Taliban words and actions regarding international terrorism, those overtures produced little progress and few tangible results.[29]

THE BIRTH OF AL-QAEDA

The Soviet invasion of Afghanistan attracted thousands of young Arab men who pledged to defend Islamic lands from the invading infidels. Many of these individuals were also angry at the corrupt and secular nature of many Arab governments in the Middle East. For them, joining the anti-Soviet jihad was one way to express pan-Islamism, and Afghanistan became the epicenter of a growing idealistic vision that would redeem the heritage of the Prophet Muhammad.[30] One of these religious zealots was Osama bin Laden, the son of a Saudi billionaire who headed a construction conglomerate. Under the mentorship of a Palestinian cleric, Abdullah Azzam, bin Laden initially supported and advised Arab and other Islamic fighters through his association with an Islamic charity, the Services Office (Maktab al-Khidamat).[31] Dissatisfied with remaining on the sidelines as others fought, bin Laden sought more active participation as well as a leadership role in the field. The young Saudi expatriate's path to martyrdom began when he provided funds and equipment to strengthen logistical sites, including Tora Bora and Zhawar Kili, in remote eastern Afghanistan. After upgrading the mujahideen fortifications, bin Laden took to the field in 1987, where he personally participated in a defensive battle against a strong Soviet attack near Dzadzi (Jaji) in Paktiya Province in 1987.

In the wake of this and other intense battles against communist forces, bin Laden's view of jihad broadened from a defense of Islamic lands to encompass

---

28. Zaeef, *My Life with the Taliban*, pp. 77–78, 84.

29. Rashid, *Taliban*, p. 80; John R. Ballard, David W. Lamm, and John K. Wood, *From Kabul to Baghdad and Back: The U.S. at War in Afghanistan and Iraq* (Annapolis, Md.: Naval Institute Press, 2012), pp. 24–26; U.S. Department of State Cable 203322, Sec State to U.S. Embassy Islamabad, 28 Sep 1996, sub: Dealing with the Taliban in Kabul, NSA GWU, https://www2.gwu.edu/~nsarchiv/NSAEBB/NSAEBB97/tal17.pdf, Hist Files, OEF Study Grp.

30. Hamid and Farrall, *The Arabs at War in Afghanistan*, pp. 21–23.

31. Peter L. Bergen, *The Osama bin Laden I Know: An Oral History of al-Qaeda's Leader* (New York: Free Press, 2006), p. 24.

direct confrontation and overthrow of Muslim governments that failed to follow traditional Islamic ways. This approach was a significant break from accepted thought, which defined jihad as the liberation of former Muslim lands from non-Muslims. As a result, bin Laden broke with Abdullah Azzam and began to form al-Qaeda, a multinational group of Sunni Islamist fighters in Pakistan dedicated to continuing the war and overthrowing the Afghan communist regime.[32] Al-Qaeda differed from other Afghan mujahideen groups in its intensity. Its training camps were known as tough, austere, disciplined, and effective at transforming civilians into guerrilla fighters.

Like-minded individuals, such as the Egyptian Islamic Jihad's Ayman al-Zawahiri, found their way to western Pakistan to meet with bin Laden. In 1988, they organized a loosely structured military elite to give Islamic direction, tactical training, financial resources, and networked leadership to potential mujahideen. According to one of its founding members, al-Qaeda's goals were simple: to be "an organized Islamic faction . . . to live the word of God, [and] to make his religion victorious."[33] In addition to a military function, bin Laden promoted his organization as the vanguard "to spread the soul and the idea of jihad among Muslims . . . their idea of jihad, which means fighting infidels and to establish a truly Islamic government all over the world." Foreign recruits came from many countries, not merely from Middle Eastern nations such as Egypt, Iraq, Jordan, and Saudi Arabia, but also from Western nations such as Canada, Great Britain, and the United States. The newcomers were divided into two groups: one would support the Afghan mujahideen for the duration of the war, while a second would join the international crusade against apostates, heretics, and infidels.[34]

Afghanistan proved an ideal battlefield for al-Qaeda to establish its roots and to nurture its internationalist vision. Bin Laden benefited directly from Pakistan's sanctuary and from Saudi and Gulf States' largess. Despite the influx of men and money, al-Qaeda suffered some humiliating defeats that caused severe internal fractures and decreased bin Laden's prestige among those who valued military proficiency over martyrdom. The Soviet-backed Afghan government's victory at the Battle of Jalalabad, fought between March and June 1989, was a disaster for al-Qaeda, and bin Laden shouldered most of the blame for his reckless, self-promoting rush into battle. His subordinates subsequently worked to change their approach to training, specifically by deemphasizing direct combat. The transition heightened bin Laden's appeal as an international visionary of means who could lead a worldwide jihad, and downplayed the problems he had faced as a battlefield commander.[35]

The end of Soviet operations and the eventual collapse of Najibullah's regime made bin Laden and other foreign Islamists a liability for Pakistan.

---

32. Hamid and Farrall, *The Arabs at War in Afghanistan*, pp. 76–79; Bergen, *The Osama bin Laden I Know*, pp. 27, 51–55, 74.

33. Seth G. Jones, *Hunting in the Shadows: The Pursuit of Al Qa'ida Since 9/11* (New York: W. W. Norton & Company, 2012), p. 38.

34. Bergen, *The Osama bin Laden I Know*, pp. 80–81, 99. Jamal Ismail, a Palestinian who knew bin Laden, is the source of the quotation. Idem, p. 82.

35. Hamid and Farrall, *The Arabs at War in Afghanistan*, pp. 158–60.

In 1990, bin Laden's attention turned away from Afghanistan when Saddam Hussein's Iraq overran neighboring Kuwait and posed a direct threat to Saudi Arabia. Bin Laden approached the Saudi royal family soon after the invasion of Kuwait with an offer to lead thousands of mujahideen fighters against the Iraqis in defense of his native land. Yet the Saudi government spurned his offer, and instead invited non-Muslim military forces into the kingdom to eject the Iraqis from Kuwait. Bin Laden interpreted these developments as an insult to his faith and began agitating against the Saudi royal family. In 1991, officials in Riyadh forced bin Laden to leave Saudi Arabia permanently. He briefly returned to Pakistan to reconstitute and reestablish his leadership over a much-reduced al-Qaeda organization before relocating to Sudan the following year. From the safety of Khartoum, bin Laden nurtured contacts, established training camps, and supported regional jihad, mostly against President Hosni Mubarak's Egypt.[36]

Osama bin Laden's plans for toppling Muslim governments that failed to follow Islamist ways included attacking the interests of the Western nations that supported them. Al-Qaeda began spreading influence from its base in Sudan, initially by supporting Muslim militants engaged in conflicts in Bosnia, North Africa, Chechnya, and Yemen.[37] The failure of the U.S.-led UN effort to subdue Somali warlords in late 1993 convinced bin Laden that "Americans were soft and that the United States was a paper tiger that could be defeated more easily than the Soviets had been in Afghanistan."[38] Driving America from the Middle East now seemed an attractive prospect because it would deprive Israel of its main Western backer and separate "the head of the snake" from "its many tails"—namely, the region's authoritarian Arab governments. However, before bin Laden translated those thoughts into action, in 1996 an assassination attempt by a rival group forced him to relocate to Afghanistan, where the Taliban now ruled in place of the defunct mujahideen regime.[39]

Years of Western neglect and festering internal conflicts had allowed the Taliban to turn Afghanistan into a sanctuary state for Islamic extremists. Bin Laden and his followers brought with them money, credibility, and religious influence that blinded Mullah Mohammed Omar's organization to the dangers that al-Qaeda posed to regional stability.[40] On 23 February 1998, bin Laden, al-Zawahiri, and three other prominent jihadists published a *fatwa* (a deliberate call to arms for believers). The legal opinion of the fatwa, which quoted the Quran, commanded "every Muslim who believes in God and wishes to be rewarded to comply with God's order to kill the Americans and plunder their

---

36. Ibid., pp. 177–79; Bergen, *The Osama bin Laden I Know*, pp. 112–13.

37. Osama bin Laden's influence in Somalia may have been aimed more at sparking jihad in Yemen than at confronting the American and United Nations (UN) efforts there. Hamid and Farrall, *The Arabs at War in Afghanistan*, pp. 184–94, and the chart "Activities of bin Laden in Sudan, 1992–5," p. 195.

38. George Tenet with Bill Harlow, *At the Center of the Storm: My Years at the CIA* (New York: Harper Collins, 2007), p. 103.

39. Bergen, *The Osama bin Laden I Know*, pp. 116, 132–36; Hamid and Farrall, *The Arabs at War in Afghanistan*, pp. 204–05.

40. Rashid, *Taliban*, pp. viii, xi.

money wherever and whenever they find it."[41] In doing so, it placed al-Qaeda and its Taliban hosts on a collision course with the United States and its allies.

The CIA first took note of bin Laden in 1993 when a financial analysis cell identified the Saudi expatriate, then living in Sudan, as an active backer of terrorist networks.[42] The al-Qaeda bombings of the U.S. embassies in Kenya and Tanzania on 7 August 1998, which killed 224 people (including 12 Americans), brought bin Laden to the attention of the American public. Thirteen days later, President William J. "Bill" Clinton announced Operation INFINITE REACH, a series of cruise missile strikes against al-Qaeda targets in Sudan and Afghanistan.[43] Because the United States lacked detailed targeting information, the retaliatory attacks did little more than damage some terrorist training facilities. Nevertheless, the CIA's covert fight against al-Qaeda gained momentum in the wake of the much-publicized missile strikes. Although most U.S. government departments were under budgetary pressures at the time, funding for counterterrorism efforts rose more than 50 percent over the next four years.[44] The CIA utilized some of the additional funding to develop human assets within Taliban-controlled southern and central Afghanistan while strengthening its ties with opposition groups in the northern part of the country. This increased funding convinced some Afghans to work for the Americans, but none of the new informants were highly placed within the Taliban, and so their contributions were less helpful than their handlers desired.

As a consequence of the al-Qaeda attack on the U.S. embassies and the less-than-effective American response, bin Laden's prestige soared within the Muslim world, particularly among those Islamists who already subscribed to the ideology of global jihad. Around this time, bin Laden also seemed to deepen his relationship with Mohammed Omar and the Taliban.[45] A source close to bin Laden later revealed that Operation INFINITE REACH actually helped steel the Taliban leadership's resolve to provide refuge to al-Qaeda, which had been in doubt because of bin Laden's refusal to keep his actions discreet. Some reports suggest that al-Qaeda's bellicose rhetoric and fatwas against the United States had discomfited the Taliban. The U.S. missile strikes dispelled this tension, and bin Laden began to enjoy greater freedom of movement and influence in Taliban-controlled Afghanistan.[46] As Sami ul-Haq, headmaster of a prominent Islamic madrassa near Peshawar, told American journalist

---

41. Osama bin Laden, "Al-Qaeda's Second Fatwa," *PBS NewsHour*, 23 Feb 1998, https://www.pbs.org/newshour/updates/military-jan-june98-fatwa_1998/, Hist Files, OEF Study Grp.

42. Tenet with Harlow, *At the Center of the Storm*, p. 100.

43. William J. Clinton, "Address to the Nation by the President" (National Address, The White House, 20 Aug 1998), https://clinton6.nara.gov/1998/08/1998-08-20-president-address-to-the-national.html, Hist Files, OEF Study Grp.

44. Tenet with Harlow, *At the Center of the Storm*, p. 21.

45. Hamid and Farrall, *The Arabs at War in Afghanistan*, pp. 243–45.

46. U.S. Department of State Cable 177309, Sec State, 25 Sep 1998, sub: Afghanistan: Taliban Convene Ulema, Iran and Bin Laden on the Agenda, NSA GWU, https://www2.gwu.edu/~nsarchiv/NSAEBB/NSAEBB97/tal26.pdf, Hist Files, OEF Study Grp; Bergen, *The Osama bin Laden I Know*, pp. 224–27.

Peter Bergen in September 1998, "Osama bin Laden has become a symbol for the whole Islamic world. All those outside powers who are trying to crush Muslims interfering with them; he is the courageous one . . . he is a hero to us, but it is America itself who first made him a hero."[47] It was an object lesson that Omar and his Taliban followers would remember.

Throughout the late 1990s and into the first year of President George W. Bush's administration, the United States attempted to communicate with the Taliban through intermediaries on more than thirty occasions. U.S. officials urged the Taliban, among other things, to shut down all terrorist networks, control illicit narcotics trafficking, and expel bin Laden from Afghanistan. The Taliban responded by assuring the Americans that Afghanistan would dismantle infrastructure that supported terrorism and energize drug eradication efforts, but Omar manifestly refused to abandon bin Laden, even as Taliban emissaries reported that the al-Qaeda leader's activities had been "restricted."[48] To some extent, bin Laden may have hijacked the Taliban ideologically by successfully expanding his worldview to Central Asia, Palestine, and the United States.[49] His real genius, though, was channeling ethnic and religious discontent into violence against the West. He was a sponsor for extremists—not necessarily a terrorist himself, but a facilitator and a lodestone for like-minded individuals. For al-Qaeda and the Taliban, it was an unholy alliance of mutual assistance. The symbiotic relationship between the two organizations would become starkly clear in the fall of 2001.[50]

U.S. Army Operations from the Post–Cold War Era to 11 September 2001

The U.S. Army underwent significant changes following the end of the Cold War. In 1988, as the Soviet economy continued to falter, the Pentagon Joint Staff commissioned a study examining U.S. strategy in the absence of a Soviet Army. The report concluded that communism had failed, that the Cold War had ended in May 1988, and that the world would soon witness a second Russian revolution.[51] Although the United States and its fellow members of the North Atlantic Treaty Organization (NATO) rejoiced as they watched the Warsaw Pact (Eastern Europe's Soviet-led military confederation) disintegrate, celebrations soon gave way to calculations as U.S. defense

---

47. Bergen, *The Osama bin Laden I Know*, pp. 227–28.

48. Rpt, U.S. Department of State, [ca. 16 Jul 2001], sub: U.S. Engagement with the Taliban on Usama bin Laden, NSA GWU, https://www2.gwu.edu/~nsarchiv/NSAEBB/NSAEBB97/tal40.pdf, Hist Files, OEF Study Grp.

49. Bergen, *The Osama bin Laden I Know*, pp. 235–36.

50. Fax, Islamabad 04450, U.S. Embassy Islamabad to Sec State, 12 Jun 1998, sub: Afghanistan: Taliban Said to Loosen Grip on Bin Laden as They Increasingly Turn to Him for Financial Support and Advice, NSA GWU, https:// www2.gwu.edu/~nsarchiv/NSAEBB/NSAEBB389/docs/1998-06-12%20-%20Haqqani%20as%20 UBL%20Advocate.pdf, Hist Files, OEF Study Grp.

51. Lorna S. Jaffe, *The Development of the Base Force, 1989–1992* (Washington, D.C.: Joint History Office, 1993), p. 8.

budget projections were reexamined to discern a potential post–Cold War peace dividend. Fewer troops and less equipment would be needed to confront regional threats than those required to deter Soviet ambitions.

As the leader of the NATO alliance, the United States contributed large numbers of modern tanks, aircraft, and ships. Keenly aware that defense cuts would invariably bite deeply into the U.S. armed forces, Chairman of the Joint Chiefs of Staff General Colin L. Powell (1989–1993) sought to prevent immediate large-scale drawdowns, preferring a 20 to 25 percent reduction spread over four to five years. President George H. W. Bush approved Powell's plan, which called for 442,000 personnel to be culled from the 2.1 million men and women then on active duty.[52] The U.S. Army shouldered the bulk of the personnel cuts as it shrank from 760,000 personnel in eighteen divisions to 525,000 personnel in four corps and ten divisions.[53] In addition, many of the units remaining on the rolls would also move from overseas locations back to the continental United States.

On 2 August 1990, President Bush announced his decision to reduce military expenditures by 25 percent over the next five years. That same day, however, Iraq's dictatorial President Saddam Hussein ordered his army into Kuwait, an act that temporarily postponed the planned drawdown. In a response dubbed Operation DESERT SHIELD, the United States assembled a sizable military coalition in neighboring Saudi Arabia. Following thirty-eight days of preparatory airstrikes, the American-led effort to liberate Kuwait began in February 1991 with a massive ground assault involving seventeen division-sized formations, known as Operation DESERT STORM. In just over four days, the coalition defeated the Iraqis, while suffering only minimal losses. Although many of the coalition forces returned to their own countries after the conflict ended, a residual U.S. presence remained in Kuwait and northeastern Saudi Arabia to deter future Iraqi aggression.

The first post–Cold War Army Chief of Staff, General Gordon R. Sullivan (1991–1995), assumed his duties just before the start of Operation DESERT SHIELD. Sullivan viewed the end of DESERT STORM as an opportunity to make more far-reaching changes than merely reducing the Army's manpower and materiel reserves. The most pressing issue from the conflict with Iraq involved the high number of incidents in which coalition aircraft or ground troops fired on friendly units. As a result, the Army began relying on space-based technology to mitigate human errors in target identification with digital devices such as the Enhanced Position Location Reporting System. The system employed satellite positioning technology similar to the Global Positioning

---

52. Associated Press, "25% Cut Will Save $8.6 Billion, Cheney States," *Los Angeles Times*, 20 Jun 1990, https://articles.latimes.com/1990-06-20/news/mn-238_1_cheney-states, Hist Files, OEF Study Grp.

53. Eric V. Larson et al., *Defense Planning in a Decade of Change: Lessons from the Base Force, Bottom-Up Review, and Quadrennial Defense Review* (Santa Monica, Calif.: RAND Corporation, 2001), p. 25.

System used by American troops in the Kuwaiti and Iraqi deserts to broadcast the location of friendly vehicles to other U.S. units.[54]

The Army's decision to leverage satellite information drew inspiration from a theoretical military hypothesis about the future of warfare known as the Revolution in Military Affairs (RMA). RMA proponents believed that during certain periods of history, innovations in military doctrines, strategies, tactics, and technologies irrevocably change the conduct of warfare. Citing the enormous damage inflicted by precision airstrikes, backers of the RMA theory claimed that DESERT STORM showed how decisive information operations, guided weapons, and space-based surveillance technology had become. Following that line of reasoning, militaries that exploited those technologies better than their opposition would prevail on any future battlefield. All of the services embraced the RMA concept to varying degrees, but it exerted considerable influence on the post–Cold War Department of Defense (DoD), which sought new ways to meet strategic responsibilities in a constrained fiscal environment.[55]

Although a post–DESERT STORM Air Force survey provided instances of an adaptive enemy instituting countermeasures to limit the impact of coalition bombing, RMA adherents dismissed these findings by claiming that technologically superior nations could always dictate the ultimate trajectory of a conflict.[56] Enthusiasm for adopting the means to wage decisive war from air and space grew stronger after the United States became involved in a series of controversial international peacekeeping and peace-enforcement missions. The first of these took place in December 1992, just before President Clinton entered office, when U.S. Army troops landed near the Somali capital of Mogadishu to support humanitarian aid efforts in Operation RESTORE HOPE. When the dire situation in Somalia began to improve the following spring, President Clinton allowed UN peacekeepers to assume most of the American responsibilities, ordering all but a 3,000-strong logistical, aviation, and quick-reaction force home.[57]

---

54. John S. Brown, *Kevlar Legions: The Transformation of the U.S. Army, 1989–2005* (Washington, D.C.: U.S. Army Center of Military History, 2011), p. 120.

55. Following the publication of the Office of the Joint Chiefs of Staff Revolution in Military Affairs (RMA)-inspired operational concept, *Joint Vision 2010*, the Army unveiled *Army Vision 2010* in November 1996. To quote *Army Vision 2010*, "In the theater of operations, information-age technologies will facilitate *shaping the battlespace* to set the conditions for *decisive operations*, resulting in the successful accomplishment of all missions." [Emphasis in the original.]. Yet the enemy is never mentioned, except in passing, and all of the accompanying illustrations show U.S. troops in a sterile desert environment. Headquarters, Department of the Army (HQDA), *Army Vision 2010*, p. 18, https://webapp1.dlib.indiana.edu/virtual_disk_library/index.cgi/4240529/FID378/pdfdocs/2010/varmy.pdf, Hist Files, OEF Study Grp.

56. A 2007 assessment of Donald H. Rumsfeld's tenure as secretary of defense lauds his qualifications while asserting that his embrace of RMA blinded him to the influences exerted by the enemy, allies, and politics during a conflict. Bradley Peniston, "Why Did Donald Rumsfeld Fail?," *Armed Forces Journal* (1 Jan 2007), https://armedforcesjournal.com/why-did-donald-rumsfeld-fail/, Hist Files, OEF Study Grp.

57. Richard W. Stewart, *The U.S. Army in Somalia, 1992–1994* (Washington, D.C.: U.S. Army Center of Military History, 1994), pp. 8–15.

Prologue

Somalia's improved domestic conditions, coupled with a decreasing number of foreign military forces, convinced warlord Mohammed Farah Aideed to seize the opportunity to gain ascendency over his rivals. In a bid to burnish his image as the most powerful figure in Mogadishu, Aideed ordered his followers to ambush a convoy of Pakistani peacekeepers on 5 June 1993. The following day, the UN adopted a resolution authorizing offensive operations against the rogue warlord. Subsequent efforts to bring Aideed to justice led to a battle in Mogadishu between his fighters and U.S. Special Forces personnel on 3 and 4 October 1993. Hundreds of Somalis and eighteen U.S. soldiers were killed in the clash. Photographs of Somalis dragging a downed U.S. helicopter crewmember's corpse through the streets of Mogadishu turned U.S. public opinion against further involvement in the region. On 7 October, Congress demanded that the Clinton administration develop an exit strategy for American troops in Somalia. Paradoxically, the chosen strategy involved temporarily sending 1,700 additional Army troops, including mechanized forces, and 3,600 marines to Somalia to safeguard the withdrawal.[58] On 20 October, President Clinton ordered the withdrawal of the Army Rangers and Special Operations personnel who had been sent to bring Aideed to justice.[59] Over the next five months, U.S. forces disengaged in a deliberate, systematic fashion, with the last marine security element departing Mogadishu on 25 March 1994.[60]

The negative experience in Somalia did not quench White House interest in peacekeeping. Presidential Decision Directive 25, published by the White House on 3 May 1994, stated that multilateral peace operations were a legitimate means of advancing American national interests. To the Clinton administration, these interests included maintaining regional stability and relieving suffering. Although the directive noted that U.S. forces could be employed under the operational control of a competent UN commander, it envisioned the United States taking a leading role in planning, executing, and supporting peacekeeping operations.[61]

---

58. "The Somalia Mission; Clinton's Words on Somalia: 'The Responsibilities of American Leadership,'" *New York Times*, 8 Oct 1993, https://www.nytimes.com/1993/10/08/world/somalia-mission-clinton-s-words-somalia-responsibilities-american-leadership.html, Hist Files, OEF Study Grp.

59. Art Pine, "Clinton Orders Army Rangers Home from Somalia," *Los Angeles Times*, 20 Oct 1993, https://articles.latimes.com/1993-10-20/news/mn-47764_1_clinton-orders, Hist Files, OEF Study Grp.

60. Approximately 100,000 U.S. service members were deployed to Somalia between December 1992 and March 1994. American casualties totaled 30 killed and 175 wounded. Donatella Lorch, "Last of the U.S. Troops Leave Somalia; What Began as a Mission of Mercy Closes With Little Ceremony," *New York Times*, 26 Mar 1994, https://www.nytimes.com/1994/03/26/world/last-us-troops-leave-somalia-what-began-mission-mercy-closes-with-little.html, Hist Files, OEF Study Grp.

61. Presidential Decision Dir, NSC-25, William J. Clinton, 3 May 1994, sub: U.S. Policy on Reforming Multilateral Peace Operations, pp. 1–3, https://clinton.presidentiallibraries.us/items/show/12749, Hist Files, OEF Study Grp.

The White House released an updated National Security Strategy two months after Clinton signed Presidential Decision Directive 25. The new guidance asserted that the United States possessed unparalleled military capabilities as the only nation on the globe capable of conducting large-scale operations far beyond its borders. This belief was the basis for embracing a new approach that emphasized American participation in military coalitions designed to preserve regional security. The National Security Strategy noted that the U.S. military also needed to be prepared to deal unilaterally with threats such as global terrorism and the proliferation of weapons of mass destruction.[62]

Less than a year after its release, President Clinton's national security vision would be tested in a region far from America's borders. Since April 1992, ethnic strife between Orthodox Christian Serbs and Muslim Bosnians had dominated Bosnia and Herzegovina, a province of the former Yugoslavia. The killings and forced expulsions continued for two more years, chiefly because the United States and its European allies, particularly Great Britain and France, hesitated to do more than send token peacekeeping contingents or launch small-scale airstrikes in retaliation for Serb atrocities. The May 1995 massacre of 8,000 Bosnian men and boys in Srebrenica, which took place despite the presence of Dutch peacekeepers, finally spurred NATO into pursuing a more aggressive stance toward this internal conflict.

In mid-August 1995, U.S. diplomat Richard C. Holbrooke was designated as a special envoy and opened negotiations among concerned parties in Bosnia and Herzegovina with the goal of brokering a permanent peace. Talks stalled until NATO airstrikes against Serb artillery surrounding the besieged city of Sarajevo broke the impasse. Following the December 1995 General Framework Agreement for Peace, NATO dispatched a substantial military presence, which included more than 24,000 Germany-based U.S. troops headed by the 1st Armored Division of the V Corps, to Bosnia and Herzegovina over a three-month period.[63] RMA proponents viewed developments in the Balkans with favor, noting that precision munitions were effective in environments other than featureless desert. The Serbs, like the Iraqis in 1991, responded by developing countermeasures to lessen the impact of future NATO air attacks on their ground forces.

The prospect of maintaining a sizable contingent of ground troops in Bosnia for a decade or longer prompted Army leadership to examine the use of reserve component units for that mission. To implement such an approach, however, the existing mobilization process would need to be changed significantly. Congress proved receptive to amending those laws, in large part because Reserve and National Guard leaders supported the initiative. Although the Balkans commitment pushed the Army to rely on its reserves for a growing number of peacetime missions, it also furthered a closer bond

---

62. William J. Clinton, *A National Security Strategy of Engagement and Enlargement* (Washington, D.C.: The White House, Jul 1994), pp. 8–9.

63. R. Cody Phillips, *Bosnia-Herzegovina: The U.S. Army's Role in Peace Enforcement Operations, 1995–2004* (Washington, D.C.: U.S. Army Center of Military History, 2005), pp. 11–13, 16–20.

among all components and helped prepare reserve units for short-notice and nontraditional overseas deployments.[64]

Tensions in the Balkans rose again in 1998 as Serbian troops led by Yugoslavian president Slobodan Milošević initiated a program to expel almost 1.8 million ethnic Albanians from the province of Kosovo. Hundreds of homes were destroyed and thousands more were looted in an orgy of violence, during which 12,000 Albanian Kosovars met their deaths at the hands of Serb security forces. Ethnic Albanians responded in turn, perpetuating a cycle of violence as each killing led to further reprisals. NATO extended its original deadline for both parties to reach a diplomatic resolution three times, but to no avail. On 24 March 1999, a series of NATO airstrikes hit Serbian military, communications, and industrial sites throughout Kosovo and Serbia. Yet Serb air defense systems and passive countermeasures, such as dispersing military units to prevent them from being detected and attacked by high-flying fixed-wing jet aircraft, minimized the effect of the NATO bombing.[65] The Serbs, emboldened by President Clinton's assurances that ground troops would not be employed in Kosovo, refused to concede as they had earlier in Bosnia.

Faced with Serb intransigence, NATO jets began striking targets south of the 44th parallel in Serbia proper instead of focusing on Milošević's military forces in Kosovo. Inclement weather and coordination problems within the multinational air forces conducting the attacks prevented this second effort from producing the desired results. Those unwelcome developments forced the NATO forces to modify their plans yet again. By the end of the campaign's third week, coalition aircraft had switched to hitting strategic targets, including industrial and national infrastructure, though this change in tactics did not mitigate the existing coordination issues.[66] In addition to intensifying the air campaign, NATO put into motion a contingency plan that added American attack helicopters, rocket artillery, and mechanized units to the fight. The movement of U.S. ground troops from Germany to Albania took place under grueling conditions that produced unexpected delays and considerable negative press coverage. Despite its embarrassing debut, Task Force (TF) Hawk's AH–64 Apache helicopters, M270 Multiple Launch Rocket Systems, M1A1 Abrams tanks, and M2A3 Bradley infantry fighting vehicles sent to Albania were set to initiate operations in neighboring Kosovo by the first week of May. Although the precise reasons remain unclear, Milošević announced his decision to pull Serb troops from Kosovo on 9 June 1999.[67] Shortly afterward, American

---

64. Brown, *Kevlar Legions*, p. 161.

65. Capt Gregory Ball, "1999 – Operation Allied Force," Air Force Historical Support Division, 23 Aug 2012, https://www.afhistory.af.mil/FAQs/Fact-Sheets/Article/458957/operation-allied-force/, Hist Files, OEF Study Grp.

66. One particularly embarrassing and controversial failure for the North Atlantic Treaty Organization (NATO) coalition forces was the accidental bombing of the Chinese Embassy in Belgrade on 7 May 1999. "DCI Statement on the Bombing of the Chinese Embassy," Central Intelligence Agency, 22 Jul 1999, https://www.cia.gov/news-information/speeches-testimony/1999/dci_speech_072299.html, Hist Files, OEF Study Grp.

67. Although the NATO commander, U.S. General Wesley K. Clark, noted in his memoirs that "[p]lanning and preparations for ground intervention were well under way by the end of

ground forces entered Kosovo as part of a multinational contingent to take part in what promised to be yet another lengthy peacekeeping mission.[68]

Events during this period heartened RMA proponents within the DoD. The department allocated $1.2 billion in emergency supplemental funds to upgrade 624 land attack versions of Tomahawk Cruise Missiles, convert 321 Tomahawks from nuclear to conventional delivery platforms, and procure 11,000 Joint Direct Attack Munitions kits that used Global Positioning System technology to convert unguided bombs into precision weapons.[69] However, the DoD overlooked the possibility that potential U.S. opponents would use the Kosovo experience as a model for their own ambitions. Taking to heart the bitter lessons of Bosnia, the Serbs demonstrated in 1999 that poor weather, harsh terrain, dispersal, camouflage, limited use of electronic emitters, and positioning high-value military assets in civilian areas could degrade or render ineffective even the most advanced military technology.[70]

THE INSTITUTIONAL ARMY BEFORE 11 SEPTEMBER 2001

The first major challenge to the Army's post-Vietnam organizational approach, known as the Abrams Doctrine or Total Force Policy, occurred two decades after the concept was first created.[71] The origins of the challenge

---

the campaign, and I am convinced that this, in particular, pushed Milosevic to concede," he also informed NATO Secretary General Javier Solana that 175,000 to 200,000 ground troops were needed to secure Kosovo. Task Force (TF) Hawk, however, had only 6,200 personnel, a fact that appears to undercut Clark's assertion. However, senior U.S. Air Force leaders believed that Milošević quit because of rising domestic political opposition following bombing attacks on Serb infrastructure. See David E. Johnson, *Learning Large Lessons: The Evolving Role of Ground Power and Air Power in the Post–Cold War Era* (Santa Monica, Calif.: RAND Corporation, 2007), pp. 68–81.

68. R. Cody Phillips, *Operation Joint Guardian: The U.S. Army in Kosovo* (Washington, D.C.: U.S. Army Center of Military History, 2007), p. 19.

69. The report also requested $178 million to address intelligence, surveillance, and reconnaissance shortfalls that emerged during the NATO efforts. Rpt, Department of Defense (DoD) to Congress, Jan 2000, sub: Message from Secretary William S. Cohen and Chairman of the Joint Chiefs of Staff Henry H. Shelton, Kosovo/Operation Allied Force After Action Report, p. 3, https://archive.org/stream/ReporttoCongressKosovoOperationAlliedForceAfterActionReport/Report%20to%20Congress-Kosovo%20Operation%20Allied%20Force%20After-Action%20Report_djvu.txt, Hist Files, OEF Study Grp.

70. Lt Gen H. R. McMaster, "Continuity and Change: The Army Operating Concept and Clear Thinking About Future War," *Military Review* 95, no. 2 (Mar–Apr 2015): 8.

71. The end of the draft, coupled with a major post-Vietnam drawdown, led Secretary of Defense James Schlesinger to reissue the Total Force Policy in 1973. Schlesinger's directive led Army Chief of Staff General Creighton W. Abrams to realign the active and reserve component force structure to ensure the former could field the sixteen divisions it needed to meet current global strategic requirements, despite a presumed ceiling of 785,000 troops. However, some have since suggested that Abrams consciously transferred the majority of theater- and corps-level combat support and combat service support force structure to the reserve component to curb the executive branch's ability to commit major military forces for sustained periods without congressional consent. In reality, the force structure transfer began in 1969, three years before Abrams became chief of staff, and the first mention of the Abrams Doctrine did not occur until

stemmed from a 1973 decision to replace the third maneuver brigade in active component divisions based in the continental United States with a "roundout" National Guard or Army Reserve brigade or armored cavalry regiment. The displaced active brigades became three additional active component divisions. Although the decision made sense from a fiscal and administrative perspective, some Army leaders felt it overlooked the need to synchronize force structure with doctrine. The dissenters believed that active component divisions might find themselves deploying to a combat situation without their "roundout" brigades, which meant that they would be forced to fight in accordance with doctrine based on three brigades, not two, until the reserve component units arrived.[72]

RESERVE COMPONENT READINESS ISSUES

Concerns about the time required for reserve units to mobilize and improve combat readiness before overseas deployment proved to be highly relevant in 1990–1991 during Operations DESERT SHIELD and DESERT STORM. Two active component divisions—the 24th Infantry Division (Mechanized) from Fort Stewart, Georgia, and the 1st Infantry Division (Mechanized) from Fort Riley, Kansas—had to be filled with active component separate brigades from Germany and Fort Benning, Georgia, before deploying to Saudi Arabia because their designated roundout National Guard brigades were not ready. A third active component unit, the 1st Cavalry Division from Fort Hood, Texas, had to deploy to Kuwait without its roundout brigade, which relegated the division to the VII Corps reserve for most of the conflict. The National Guard roundout units—the 256th Infantry Brigade (Mechanized) from Louisiana, the 155th Armored Brigade from Mississippi, and the 48th Infantry Brigade (Mechanized) from Georgia—were mobilized in late November and early December 1990. Although each received three to five months of predeployment training, only the 48th Infantry Brigade met the readiness ratings necessary for overseas service. The brigade, however, achieved this status only on the last day of the conflict, which meant that none of the brigades left the continental United States.[73]

1986, more than a decade after his death. As historians Conrad C. Crane and Gian Gentile contend, if Abrams actually sought to curb executive power, a review of U.S. military activity since the adoption of the Total Force approach would reveal that he failed to achieve that alleged goal. Conrad Crane and Gian Gentile, "Understanding the Abrams Doctrine: Myth Versus Reality," War on the Rocks, 9 Dec 2015, https://warontherocks.com/2015/12/understanding-the-abrams-doctrine-myth-versus-reality/, Hist Files, OEF Study Grp.

72. Col Roland R. Rollison, *Are Roundout Brigades a Viable Concept for the Future?* (Carlisle Barracks, Pa.: U.S. Army War College, 1990), p. 1.

73. Col Clifford G. Willis, *Forward Deployed, Separate Brigades as Roundout Units for Partial Divisions* (Carlisle Barracks, Pa.: U.S. Army War College, 1992), pp. 1–3. This report details how the brigades in question were unable to deploy owing to a combination of legislative limits on mobilized reserve personnel, late mobilization call-up, overstated readiness reporting, and insufficient home station training facilities.

These negative experiences with roundout brigades during Desert Storm meant that partnering relationships among full-time soldiers, guardsmen, and reservists attracted significantly more oversight and funding. On 1 November 1991, the National Guard instituted Project Standard Bearer, designed to keep high-priority units designated as the Contingency Force Pool at the highest level of personnel readiness through increased retention and recruiting programs as well as the implementation of an overstrength policy.[74] The number of personnel affected by the project expanded as the Contingency Force Pool grew to 389 units, 97 percent of which were deployable for domestic and international missions by 1993.[75]

In response to the Army National Guard's inability to contribute maneuver units to Operation Desert Storm, Congress passed the Army National Guard Combat Readiness Reform Act in 1992. Known as Title XI because of its location in the 1993 National Defense Authorization Act, the act paired National Guard units deemed necessary for the execution of the National Military Strategy with an equivalent active component unit.[76] In addition to pairing similarly organized units, the Army National Guard Combat Readiness Reform Act authorized active component divisional headquarters training oversight for three designated high-priority reserve units, termed Enhanced Separate Brigades.[77] These brigades were designated as Force Package 3 units, the highest rating obtainable in peacetime for the reserve component.[78] These changes produced National Guard units that could operate alongside active component units in the near term. However, the initiative also had negative long-term consequences: the high-priority units received better training and support than the traditional reserve units, creating an unequal two-tier structure, and the plan did not have the resources to maintain that capability through multiple deployments over a sustained period.[79]

In addition to the actions mandated by Congress, internal efforts to reshape reserve components produced an "Offsite Agreement" by Army senior leaders that realigned the mix of units within both the Army Reserve and National Guard. At the macro level, the Army National Guard retained a balanced mix of combat and combat support units while the Army Reserve focused exclusively on fielding combat service support units, with special emphasis on

---

74. Steven E. Everett and L. Martin Kaplan, *Department of the Army Historical Summary, Fiscal Year 1993* (Washington, D.C.: U.S. Army Center of Military History, 2002), pp. 77–78.

75. Michael Doubler, *I am the Guard: A History of the Army National Guard, 1636–2000*, Pamphlet 130-1 (Washington, D.C.: Department of the Army, 2001), p. 341.

76. *Army National Guard Combat Readiness Reform Act of 1992*, 10 U.S.C. § 10542(b) (1992), Hist Files, OEF Study Grp.

77. Ellen M. Pint et al., *Active Component Responsibility in Reserve Component Pre- and Postmobilization Training* (Santa Monica, Calif.: RAND Corporation, 2015).

78. Ofc of the Deputy Ch of Staff for Opns and Plans, *The United States Army Modernization Plan* (Washington, D.C.: Department of the Army, 13 Apr 1998), p. A–13.

79. Dennis P. Chapman, *Planning for Employment of the Reserve Components: Army Practice, Past and Present*, Land Warfare Papers No. 69 (Arlington, Va: The Institute of Land Warfare, Sep 2008), pp. 2–6.

those organizations normally found at echelons above division and corps.[80] In practical terms, the agreement resulted in the Army Reserve transferring its Special Forces Groups and nearly all of its aviation forces to the National Guard, thereby divesting itself of its combat arms force structure.[81] The new structure postulated that early-deploying active component units would be self-sufficient for thirty days, at which point responsibility for theater sustainment shifted to mobilized reserve component units. This force structure shift made the Army more dependent on the Total Force (meaning active, guard, and reserve components). Army forces would flow into theater led by active component units, followed by Army Reserve support units whose main role would be to relieve early deploying units of theater logistical responsibilities. More troops, including additional National Guard and active component combat units, would follow as needed.

Partnership initiatives and improved readiness among reserve units, coupled with the growing number of peacekeeping responsibilities assumed by the United States, fundamentally shifted the employment of National Guard and Army Reserve personnel during the Clinton administration. The change stemmed from the Army's decision to use reserve component units for overseas peacekeeping tasks. The earliest example occurred in 1993 when General Sullivan authorized the deployment of ad hoc units of reserve component volunteers to participate in the Multinational Force and Observers mission in Sinai.[82] Because the Army had fewer troops available to support the growing number of peacekeeping missions, it sought to commit progressively larger reserve organizations to those missions. By November 1997, more than 15,000 personnel from the Army Reserve and the National Guard had participated in the Bosnia peacekeeping mission.[83] Reserve component involvement, both as entire units and as individual augmentees assigned to active organizations, had expanded to such a degree that guardsmen and reserve soldiers were deployed in more than a hundred countries by 2001.[84] That process culminated with a decision by General Eric K. Shinseki, the 34th Chief of Staff of the U.S. Army (1999–2003), to use National Guard division headquarters to command and control the Balkans peacekeeping rotations. He intended not only to relieve growing pressures placed on active component units, but also to provide reserve units with an opportunity to gain valuable experience in a relatively benign operational environment.

---

80. Andrew Feickert and Lawrence Kapp, *Army Active Component (AC)/Reserve Component (RC) Force Mix: Considerations and Options for Congress*, R43808 (Washington, D.C.: Congressional Research Service, 5 Dec 2014), p. 6.

81. Doubler, *I am the Guard*, p. 346.

82. Ruth H. Phelps and Beatrice J. Farreds, eds., *Reserve Component Soldiers as Peacekeepers* (Alexandria, Va.: Army Research Institute for Behavioral and Social Sciences, 1996), p. xv.

83. United States Gen Accounting Ofc, *Reserve Forces: Cost, Funding, and Use of Army Reserve Components in Peacekeeping Operations*, GAO/NSAID-98-190R (Washington, D.C.: U.S. Gen Accounting Ofc, 15 May 1998), p. 3.

84. Bfg, Army G-3 Staff to Sec Def, Apr 2002, sub: War on Terrorism: A War of Wills, slide 9, Hist Files, OEF Study Grp.

Active Component Readiness Issues

With the dissolution of the Soviet Union and the subsequent reorganization of American military spending throughout the 1990s, the U.S. Army received far fewer dollars than it needed to sustain high levels of combat readiness. To avoid an overall reduction in readiness throughout the entire force, the Army adopted a policy of tiered resourcing by dividing units into four categories, also known as Force Packages, based on existing contingency plans and strategic deployment timelines. It determined Force Package readiness levels by the priority placed on fielding new equipment or maintaining existing equipment, as well as staffing level percentages.[85] Force Package 1 units were the highest priority and Force Package 4 units, the lowest. Most active combat units were in Force Packages 1, 2, or 3—reflecting the fact that they would be required in theater sooner rather than later—and the majority of reserve component combat units were in Force Packages 3 and 4. Regardless of component, combat support and combat service support units were placed in the Force Package that corresponded with wartime mission requirements, which meant that many reserve support units were maintained at higher readiness levels than reserve combat units.

The Army's Major Contingency Response Force, consisting of the 82d Airborne Division, 101st Airborne Division (Air Assault), 1st Cavalry Division, 3rd Infantry Division (Mechanized), and 3d Armored Cavalry, formed Force Package 1. These forces were responsible for preparing and planning for a major regional conflict in either Southwest Asia (XVIII Airborne Corps) or Northeast Asia (III Corps). Force Package 2 units making up the Regional Rapid Response Force included the forward deployed 2d Infantry Division in Korea as well as stateside-based combat units with wartime responsibilities in the Pacific region. Force Package 3 included active units forward deployed in Europe, active units within the continental United States designated as reinforcements for overseas contingencies, and Army National Guard enhanced brigades. Force Package 4 consisted of National Guard divisions, active combat units making up the strategic reserve, and any remaining National Guard combat units.[86]

To varying degrees, tiered resourcing produced a culture of haves and have-nots within the Army as a whole. Fully staffed and equipped Force Package 1 units had their full allocation of operations and maintenance funding, whereas lower priority units received personnel, equipment, and funding only after all higher priority needs were met. Force Package 2 through 4 units were uniformly resourced through a process known as cascading, whereby higher priority units received new equipment and passed down their older equipment to lower priority units. The reserve component

---

85. Force Development Directorate, Ofc of the Deputy Ch of Staff for Opns and Plans, *The United States Army 1995 Modernization Plan* (Washington, D.C.: Department of the Army, 1995), p. 13.

86. The National Guard and Army Reserve also fell under the categories of Force Support Packages 1 through 3, which established the readiness levels of early deploying and reinforcing combat support and service support units. Col (Ret.) John R. Brinkerhoff, "The Army National Guard and Conservation of Combat Power," *Parameters* 26, no. 3 (Autumn 1996): 4–16.

PROLOGUE

in particular felt the negative effects of cascading, as it resulted in major commands and sometimes even the same unit having multiple generations of equipment.

In addition to complicating routine logistical and training responsibilities, tiered resourcing made it more difficult to deploy guard and reserve units during peacetime. The practice of passing down displaced older equipment to lower priority units created growing interoperability issues as more reserve units took part in peacekeeping rotations in the Balkans. Outgoing active component units often found themselves being replaced by reserve component forces that did not have the same equipment. As a result, the Army had to maintain overseas stockpiles of repair parts and replacement equipment to support differently equipped units.

Given the resource-constrained environment of the 1990s, it is not surprising that by 2001, some Army units were fully prepared and equipped for twenty-first-century warfare while others were significantly less capable.[87] The interoperability of light and heavy forces was a particular concern. Although the force structure included both heavy and light units, the Army did not actively create opportunities for both types to work together. In fact, it had separate training centers for heavy and light units at Fort Irwin, California, and Fort Polk, Louisiana, respectively. More problematically, although heavy units had been experimenting with new aspects of digital command and control, the technology had not been miniaturized to the point at which light units could readily use it in combat conditions. Thus, light units could not benefit from the technological experiences and lessons learned by heavy units. Even when the Army took its first belated steps to introduce digitization into the light force, it did not fully appreciate the potential of man-portable information technology. The initial light force digitization trials involved a two-day Joint Contingency Force Advanced Warfighter Experiment exercise at Fort Polk in September 2000. Troops from the 1st Brigade, 10th Mountain Division, along with a company from the 2d Marine Division, battled the defending Joint Readiness Training Center opposing force in an urban combat setting.[88] In spite of exercises such as this, the Army's digitization interests remained overwhelmingly centered on the heavy force.[89]

When General Shinseki became chief of staff, he sought to redress the balance problems and gaps within the active component. Soon after taking office in 1999, he informed other Army senior leaders that "we will begin to erase the distinctions between heavy and light forces."[90] The first tangible

---

87. Brown, *Kevlar Legions*, pp. 99–100.

88. Pvt James Strine, "Final JCF-AWE Attack Shows Equipment Works," *Army News Service*, 20 Sep 2000, https://fas.org/man/dod-101/sys/land/docs/man-la-land_warrior-000920.htm, Hist Files, OEF Study Grp.

89. Jean L. Dyer, Richard L. Wampler, and Paul N. Blankenbeckler, *After Action Reviews with the Ground Soldier* (Washington, D.C.: U.S. Army Research Institute for the Behavioral and Social Sciences, Sep 2005), pp. v–vii.

90. Ofc of the Ch of Staff, *The Army Vision: Soldiers on Point for the Nation; Persuasive in Peace, Invincible in War* (Washington, D.C.: Department of the Army, 1999), p. 6.

bridges between operational cultures were the Interim Brigade Combat Teams established at Fort Lewis, Washington. Those units, equipped with the Stryker wheeled personnel carrier, came from the armored and light infantry brigade located there. Shinseki wanted the Interim Brigade Combat Teams to validate the organizational and operational model for medium-weight units. His ultimate goal was to field a strategically mobile future force equipped with lighter, highly lethal, and survivable weapon systems linked by digital networks that would be fully compatible with those used by other services.[91]

Factors Influencing U.S. Strategic Views in 2001

As the United States sought to respond to the September 11th terrorist attacks, senior administration officials and military leaders relied on past experience and shared beliefs to devise appropriate strategic goals and operational plans. For example, the George W. Bush administration's views on postconflict involvement in Afghanistan drew heavily on the fact that thousands of American troops were still on peacekeeping duty in the Balkans. In addition, perceptions of the Soviet experience in Afghanistan influenced U.S. Central Command's (CENTCOM) decision to open its campaign using Afghan proxies and SOF. Similar concerns motivated transformation proponents touting aerially delivered precision-guided munitions and space-based surveillance assets as the weapons of choice.

As the Clinton administration reached the end of its second term, military readiness was a key issue during the presidential campaign between Democratic candidate Vice President Albert A. Gore and Republican challenger George W. Bush, then governor of Texas.[92] As president, Bush's campaign rhetoric claimed, he would restore the rightful function of the U.S. military, in contrast to the Clinton administration's years of systematic neglect and misuse of defense resources. In a September 1999 campaign speech at the Citadel, Bush criticized Clinton for sending American troops on "vague, aimless, and endless deployments" and promised that "we will not be permanent peacekeepers, dividing warring parties."[93] Condoleezza Rice, who was heading Bush's foreign policy team, told reporters during the campaign that long-term peacekeeping operations were not an appropriate use of the United States military power: "Carrying out civil administration and police functions is simply going to degrade the American capability to do the things America has to do. We don't need to have the 82d Airborne escorting kids to kindergarten."[94]

---

91. Thomas K. Adams, *The Army After Next: The First Postindustrial Army* (Stanford, Calif.: Stanford University Press, 2008), pp. 82–84.

92. Victoria K. Holt and Michael G. MacKinnon, "The Origins and Evolution of U.S. Policy Towards Peace Operations," *International Peacekeeping* 15, no. 1 (Feb 2008): 18–34.

93. George W. Bush, "A Period of Consequences" (Speech, The Citadel, 23 Sep 1999), https://www3.citadel.edu/pao/addresses/pres_bush.html, Hist Files, OEF Study Grp.

94. Michael R. Gordon, "Bush Would Stop U.S. Peacekeeping in Balkan Fights," *New York Times*, 21 Oct 2000, https://www.nytimes.com/2000/10/21/us/the-2000-campaign-the-military-bush-would-stop-us-peacekeeping-in-balkan-fights.html, Hist Files, OEF Study Grp.

The political rhetoric drew a response from the DoD shortly before Americans went to the polls. On 3 September 2000, Chairman of the Joint Chiefs of Staff General H. Hugh Shelton publicly rebutted Bush's declaration that Clinton-era defense polices had left two out of ten active army divisions unready for combat. Shelton explained that the combat readiness of the units that Bush had cited—10th Mountain and 1st Infantry—had been downgraded because large segments of both were deployed to Bosnia and Kosovo for peacekeeping duties rather than training for combat.[95] The exchange took place as decreasing numbers of U.S. troops were involved in peacekeeping. Although NATO peacekeeping forces in Bosnia and Kosovo each originally numbered nearly 50,000 personnel in June 1999, at the time of the 2000 U.S. presidential election, the security situation had improved enough to dramatically reduce the size of the participating contingents.[96] By January 2001, more than 9,000 active component U.S. soldiers were stationed in the Balkans, along with another 1,000 soldiers with the Multinational Force and Observers in the Sinai. However, those figures reflected units actually conducting peacekeeping and not others preparing for peacekeeping deployments or training to regain warfighting skills after redeploying to their home stations. The constant rotation of active units to the Balkans had such an impact on readiness that Army leaders spent the latter half of the 1990s obtaining congressional approval for National Guard units to assume those responsibilities.[97]

On 11 October 2000, in his second debate with Gore, Bush stated unequivocally: "I don't think our troops ought to be used for what's called nation-building. I think our troops ought to be used to fight and win war. I think our troops ought to be used to help overthrow the dictator when it's in our best interests."[98] One day later, the United States received a stark reminder of the significant global threat posed by extremism, when two suicide bombers rammed a motorboat full of explosives into the destroyer USS *Cole* as it refueled in Aden, Yemen. The blast ripped a gaping hole in the vessel's hull, killing seventeen crewmembers and wounding thirty-nine others. Osama bin Laden's al-Qaeda terrorist network took credit for the attack.[99] It occurred only three weeks before Americans cast their votes for the next president.

---

95. Gen (Ret.) Hugh Shelton with Ronald Levinson and Malcolm McConnell, *Without Hesitation: The Odyssey of an American Warrior* (New York: St. Martin's Press, 2010), pp. 415–16.

96. Steven Lee Myers and Craig R. Whitney, "Crisis in the Balkans: Peacekeeping Force of 50,000 Allied Troops to Enter Kosovo as Yugoslav Forces Withdraw," *New York Times*, 4 Jun 1999, https://www.nytimes.com/1999/06/04/world/crisis-balkans-nato-peacekeeping-force-50000-allied-troops-enter-kosovo-yugoslav.html, Hist Files, OEF Study Grp.

97. Steven Lee Myers, "Army Will Give National Guard the Entire U.S. Role in Bosnia," *New York Times*, 5 Dec 2000, https://www.nytimes.com/2000/12/05/world/army-will-give-national-guard-the-entire-us-role-in-bosnia.html, Hist Files, OEF Study Grp.

98. George W. Bush, "The Second Gore-Bush Presidential Debate" (Debate, Winston-Salem, N. C., 11 Oct 2001), Commission on Presidential Debates, https://www.debates.org/?page=october-11-2000-debate-transcript, Hist Files, OEF Study Grp.

99. "USS Cole Bombing," 9/11 Memorial, https://www.911memorial.org/uss-cole-bombing (page discontinued), Hist Files, OEF Study Grp.

As a result of the November 2000 election, George W. Bush became president-elect of the United States by the narrowest Electoral College margin in more than a century. Bush entered office pledging to give the men and women in uniform "clear missions with attainable goals."[100] Within a short time, however, campaign rhetoric succumbed to political realities. Governor Bush had spoken of drawing down the U.S. commitment in Bosnia, but as president he heeded pressure from NATO allies and made only a slight cutback.[101] In July 2001, the Bush administration authorized U.S. military support for NATO's Operation ESSENTIAL HARVEST, intended to disarm ethnic Albanian rebels in Macedonia, though the U.S. contingent drew only on resources already stationed in Kosovo.[102]

Bush's efforts to wean the U.S. military from its outdated "industrial age" outlook on warfighting encountered resistance from both familiar and unexpected quarters. Soon after taking office, Bush signed Presidential National Security Directive 3 tasking his new secretary of defense, Donald H. Rumsfeld, with transforming and modernizing the armed forces.[103] Rumsfeld sought to leverage the upcoming Quadrennial Defense Review to shift the military toward a new mindset in which force structure requirements would be defined by joint capabilities rather than regional needs. Several key military leaders, including General Shelton, opposed Rumsfeld's initial efforts, warning him of the dangers of compromising readiness for modernization. Shelton and other Army generals also believed that any approach founded on deploying air and naval assets from the continental United States would be a less effective regional deterrent than an enduring U.S. ground presence overseas.[104]

Anticipating considerable resistance within the Pentagon, the new secretary placed transformation-oriented thinkers in critical DoD, Joint Staff, and service billets. Longtime associates, including Deputy Secretary of Defense Paul D. Wolfowitz and special assistant Dr. Stephen A. Cambone,

---

100. "Text: Bush Names Rumsfeld Defense Secretary," *Washington Post*, 28 Dec 2000, https://www.washingtonpost.com/wp-srv/onpolitics/elections/bushtext122800.htm, Hist Files, OEF Study Grp.

101. Steven Erlanger, "Europeans Say Bush's Pledge to Pull Out of Balkans Could Split NATO," *New York Times*, 25 Oct 2000, https://www.nytimes.com/2000/10/25/world/europeans-say-bush-s-pledge-to-pull-out-of-balkans-could-split-nato.html, Hist Files, OEF Study Grp; Steven Erlanger and Michael R. Gordon, "Allies, Questioning Bush Stand, Say U.S. Kosovo Role Is Crucial," *New York Times*, 16 Jan 2001, https://www.nytimes.com/2001/01/16/world/allies-questioning-bush-stand-say-us-kosovo-role-is-crucial.html, Hist Files, OEF Study Grp; Keith B. Richburg, "Rumsfeld Worries Europeans on Bosnia; Allies Warn US Against Withdrawal," *Washington Post*, 23 May 2001, Hist Files, OEF Study Grp; Michael R. Gordon, "NATO Plans Only Modest Bosnia Cutback," *New York Times*, 27 May 2001, https://www.nytimes.com/2001/05/27/world/nato-plans-only-modest-bosnia-cutback.html, Hist Files, OEF Study Grp.

102. John Diamond, "U.S. Offers Limited Help to NATO in Macedonia," *Chicago Tribune*, 6 Jul 2001, https://articles.chicagotribune.com/2001-07-06/news/0107060191_1_nato-force-nato-mission-european-troops, Hist Files, OEF Study Grp.

103. Bradley Graham, *By His Own Rules: The Ambitions, Successes, and Ultimate Failures of Donald Rumsfeld* (New York: PublicAffairs, 2009), p. 208.

104. "14th Chairman of the Joint Chiefs of Staff, General Henry Hugh Shelton," Joint Chiefs of Staff, https://www.jcs.mil/About/The-Joint-Staff/Chairman/General-Henry-Hugh-Shelton, Hist Files, OEF Study Grp.

figured prominently in Rumsfeld's inner circle.[105] The new administration selected Army, Navy, and Air Force secretaries who had corporate experience with reputations for revitalizing underproducing business enterprises.[106] The secretary of defense also selected replacements for the chairman of the Joint Chiefs of Staff, vice chairman, and Joint Staff chief operations officer (J-3).[107]

The baseline premise for Rumsfeld's transformational vision drew heavily from earlier work on network-centric warfare; Effects-Based Operations; and, most significantly, the notions of "dominant maneuver" and "dominant battlespace awareness." All of these concepts had been unveiled in *Joint Vision 2010*, the Department of Defense's 1990s-era concept for future warfare.[108] Rumsfeld oversaw his transformation efforts out of the Office of Force Transformation under Vice Admiral (Retired) Arthur K. Cebrowski, which was formed in October 2001. Transformation combined the notions of dominant maneuver and dominant battlespace awareness to arrive at a new concept known as Rapid Decisive Operations. Developed by the U.S. Joint Forces Command, Rapid Decisive Operations envisioned a force that could deploy and engage quickly in combat operations in the pursuit of American national interests. It suggested the possibility of a comparatively bloodless campaign (at least for the United States) and quick victory achieved through the use of technical intelligence, information technologies, and stand-off precision strike systems to meter force discriminately and end conflicts at times and places of American choosing. Because such operations would not need as many ground forces, the United States would not need to establish a large theater logistics infrastructure to support them.

Although this infusion of new blood undoubtedly would support the Pentagon's transformation and modernization efforts, departing Chairman of the Joint Chiefs of Staff General Shelton pointed out the danger of pursuing a single-minded agenda: "Units undergoing transformation, and those involved in experimentation, may not be available or ready to respond to crises within required operational timelines."[109] Indeed, Rumsfeld's pursuit of reform proved so focused that many questioned whether the secretary of defense's

---

105. Both Wolfowitz and Cambone served on the bipartisan Rumsfeld Commission formed by the Republican-controlled Congress in 1998 to examine the growing threat of nuclear proliferation by rogue states. As of the end of 2019, Cambone still served on the board of the Rumsfeld Foundation. Bradley Peniston, "Who Is Steve Cambone? A Look at Rumsfeld's Right Hand Man," *Armed Forces Journal* (1 Apr 2006), https://armedforcesjournal.com/who-is-steve-cambone/, Hist Files, OEF Study Grp.

106. Jeffrey M. Borns, "How Secretary of Defense Rumsfeld Sought to Assert Civilian Control over the Military," Course Material, The Interagency Process Seminar C, Course 5603, National War College, National Defense University, 2002, p. 7, https://www.dtic.mil/dtic/tr/fulltext/u2/a442491.pdf, Hist Files, OEF Study Grp.

107. Shelton et al., *Without Hesitation*, pp. 425–27.

108. Frederick W. Kagan, *Finding the Target: The Transformation of American Military Policy* (New York: Encounter Books, 2006), pp. 229–30.

109. Donald H. Rumsfeld, *Quadrennial Defense Review Report*, DoD, 30 Sep 2001, pp. 68–70, https://archive.defense.gov/pubs/qdr2001.pdf, Hist Files, OEF Study Grp.

preference for technological solutions obscured other types of answers to strategic challenges.

Arrayal of Forces in September 2001

On 30 September 2001, the U.S. Army numbered 1,038,258 soldiers, which included 480,801 on active duty or attending the U.S. Military Academy at West Point; 351,829 National Guardsmen, and 205,628 reservists.[110] On any given day, 125,000 soldiers were stationed outside the continental United States in Europe, the Pacific, Kuwait, Qatar, Alaska, and Hawaii. An additional 26,000 soldiers, including some normally assigned to bases in the continental United States, participated daily in military exercises in dozens of countries around the world. Europe boasted the largest overseas Army presence, which included an active component armored division and a mechanized infantry division, an airborne infantry brigade, and theater support elements capable of sustaining a large number of reinforcing units. Most European-based personnel were stationed in southern Germany, with smaller contingents assigned to the Supreme Headquarters Allied Powers Europe in Belgium and the Southern European Task Force in Italy. In the Pacific, forces available to the U.S. Army Pacific and the Eighth Army in Korea included an infantry division, a light infantry division, two separate infantry brigades, an air cavalry brigade, and a robust theater-level support infrastructure. Army troops in the Pacific region were based primarily in South Korea and Hawaii, with some based in Alaska and Japan. In the Middle East, a small number of Army headquarters and logistics personnel were based in Kuwait, Saudi Arabia, and Qatar, all of which reported to CENTCOM.

Active component units in the continental United States under U.S. Army Forces Command (FORSCOM) at Fort McPherson, Georgia, included an armored division, two mechanized infantry divisions, a light infantry division, an air assault division, an airborne division, and two armored cavalry regiments. These forces were assigned various training and planning responsibilities in the event of a war, such as responding to unforeseen contingency missions, reinforcing forward deployed troops in Europe and the Pacific, and defending Kuwait against Iraqi aggression. Most Army Special Operations units—four active and two National Guard Special Forces groups, a Ranger regiment, a Special Operations aviation regiment, four Army Reserve civil affairs commands, and their associated support units—were stationed in the continental United States, although two of the active Special Forces groups had battalion-sized forward presences in Germany and Japan.

Some Army National Guard units had been temporarily deployed overseas, but normally they were stationed in the continental United States, Hawaii, Puerto Rico, the Virgin Islands, and Alaska. These forces consisted of seven infantry divisions, one armored division, twelve separate infantry brigades, one infantry group, three separate armored brigades, one armored cavalry regiment, seventeen field artillery brigades, three air defense artillery

---

110. Christopher N. Koontz, *Department of the Army Historical Summary, Fiscal Year 2001* (Washington, D.C.: U.S. Army Center of Military History, 2011), p. 13.

brigades, six aviation brigades or groups, and six engineer brigades, among other elements. The Army Reserve, based similarly to the National Guard, consisted of mobilization-oriented training organizations and combat service support units totaling eleven regional support commands, three regional support groups, four training support divisions, seven institutional training divisions, one theater army area command, three theater support commands, and two theater signal commands.[111]

Army Chief of Staff Shinseki thus found himself balancing Army transformation efforts—which included fielding a division-sized "digitized" force furnished with networked information systems and several highly deployable but untested medium-weight brigades equipped with wheeled-armored vehicles—with operational challenges worldwide. Digitization efforts focusing on improving the capabilities of light forces, however, were still in the formative stage. Although enabling transformation and maintaining readiness were high on Shinseki's list of priorities, daily reminders of post–Cold War regional instability also occupied his thoughts, as evidenced by remarks he made during the summer of 2001 when visiting U.S. troops in Kuwait: "There will most certainly be another war in our future. If history is any indicator, it will happen sometime in the early decades of this century."[112]

---

111. Unit deployment data and strength figures derived from *The 2001–02 Army Green Book* 51, no. 10 (Arlington, Va.: Association of the United States Army, 2001): pp. 208–34.

112. In his end-of-tour interview with the U.S. Army Center of Military History (CMH), General Shinseki detailed the circumstances behind these remarks. They are also quoted in the Association of the United States Army's annual *Green Book* issue published after 11 September 2001. See Gen Erik K. Shinseki, "The Army Vision: A Status Report," ibid., p. 33.

SECTION I
LIBERATION

Section I

Introduction

The September 11th attacks orchestrated by Osama bin Laden were the deadliest hostile act on U.S. soil since the Japanese strike against the U.S. naval base at Pearl Harbor, Hawaii, on 7 December 1941. An often overlooked but nonetheless equally applicable comparison is that neither al-Qaeda nor the Japanese felt that the American people possessed the will necessary to prevail in the coming struggle. Yet the memory of Pearl Harbor did not resonate within President George W. Bush's cabinet as it mapped out the U.S. response to the attacks. An examination of subsequent policy decisions reveals that events of the past twenty years—including the Soviet experience in Afghanistan, the UN intervention in Somalia, and the NATO operations in the Balkans—dominated thinking within the White House. The decision to assemble an international coalition to wage war on global terrorism, for example, owed more to the Balkans experience than to dimly remembered World War II policies.

Comparisons between Pearl Harbor and September 11th also fail to account for the different situations facing the U.S. military before and after each attack. In the decades before the attack on Pearl Harbor, war planning, doctrinal development, training, and weapons procurement anticipated the real possibility of armed conflict between the United States and Japan. The impending German conquest of France in the summer of 1940 convinced President Franklin D. Roosevelt that American involvement in the ongoing European conflict would be inevitable. To that end, Roosevelt summoned William Knudsen, president of General Motors, to the White House on 30 May 1940 to oversee the reorganization of the American economy to produce war materiel. This transformation progressed significantly over the next eighteen months, allowing American industry to switch rapidly from manufacturing consumer goods to airplanes, tanks, and ships soon after the Japanese attack on Pearl Harbor in December 1941.[1]

In sharp contrast, with the exception of a few experts in the Special Operations community, military planners paid scant attention to al-Qaeda prior to 11 September 2001. At the time, it was U.S. policy to consider terrorists as a criminal threat and not a danger to national security. As a result, the CIA and the Federal Bureau of Investigation shared responsibility for protecting American interests from terrorism abroad and at home. The unexpected attacks on the World Trade Center and the Pentagon caught the U.S. military

---

1. Charles K. Hyde, *Arsenal of Democracy: The American Automobile Industry in World War II* (Detroit: Wayne State University Press, 2013), pp. 7–15.

ill-prepared to mount a global war on terrorism. Although certain U.S. military units could perform counterterrorism operations, memories of U.S. involvement in the UN response to the Somali Civil War—specifically, the disastrous Battle of Mogadishu in 1993, captured in both journalism and film as the "Black Hawk Down" episode—hindered the willingness of senior military leaders to employ ground troops against terrorist strongholds prior to 11 September. Moreover, a substantial percentage of available conventional forces, which were required to defeat state sponsors of terrorism, were already committed to preserving regional security around the globe, with large commitments in Europe and East Asia. Transitioning these committed units to wartime readiness following a decade of budget cuts would prove to be a major task.

In spite of these challenges, the U. S. military succeeded in gathering the intelligence needed to develop plans, obtain basing and overflight rights, form alliances of indigenous allies, and deploy forces into theater. CENTCOM commander General Tommy R. Franks initiated the U.S. retaliatory campaign using airpower, Special Forces, CIA paramilitary officers, and indigenous militia fighters. CENTCOM's innovative methods had unanticipated success as Afghan opposition forces captured key cities, including the capital of Kabul, soon after combat operations began. With the Taliban government defeated, American battlefield priorities shifted to killing or capturing al-Qaeda terrorists in Afghanistan, which led to engagements at Tora Bora and Shahi Kot during December 2001 and March 2002, respectively. The latter battle, also known as Operation ANACONDA, was the first battle in the Global War on Terrorism to involve American and coalition conventional units.

Although an unbroken string of Afghan and American tactical successes forced the al-Qaeda leadership to flee Afghanistan in 2002, the failure to kill or capture bin Laden, coupled with Pakistan's willingness to grant sanctuary to the defeated Taliban, guaranteed a lengthier commitment to the region than originally envisioned. Faced with the need to remain in Afghanistan longer than anticipated, the United States committed itself to a multiyear effort focusing on rebuilding infrastructure, supporting the formation of a democratic central government, and maintaining internal security in a war-torn country. The Taliban's ability to cloak its activities from Western intelligence agencies as it regenerated strength in Pakistan thus set the stage for a protracted conflict that bore little resemblance to the initial campaign planned and waged by CENTCOM.

CHAPTER ONE

The American Response to 11 September 2001

On 11 September 2001, nineteen al-Qaeda members took control of four airliners that had departed Washington, D.C.'s Dulles Airport and Boston's Logan Airport, and rammed the planes into the North and South Towers of New York City's World Trade Center complex and the Pentagon in Arlington, Virginia. The fourth hijacked airliner crashed in a field in rural western Pennsylvania, rather than striking its intended target (thought to be the White House), as a result of the passengers' heroic but fatal bid to retake control of the plane. All told, the attacks killed 2,977 people and caused almost $10 billion in property damage.[1]

Intelligence sources laid the blame for the September 11th terrorist attacks on Osama bin Laden's al-Qaeda network, then based in the "failed state" of Afghanistan.[2] President George W. Bush interpreted the attacks as an act of war.[3] Bush, along with key members of his administration, felt that any retaliatory response needed to act against more than the actual perpetrators, targeting a broad range of groups and individuals who supported terrorism. In the administration's view, the September 11th attacks revealed that global terrorism now threatened "the American way of life."[4] Any future attacks had the potential to cripple the American economy and destroy the openness that defined American society. Thus, in his Oval Office address on the evening of 11 September 2001, President Bush told the nation that "our way of life, our

---

1. 9/11 Memorial, Frequently Asked Questions, https://www.911memorial.org/faq-about-911, Hist Files, OEF Study Grp.

2. National Commission on Terrorist Attacks, *The 9/11 Commission Report: Final Report of the National Commission on Terrorist Attacks Upon the United States* (W. W. Norton & Company, 2004), https://www.9-11commission.gov/report/911Report.pdf (hereafter *9/11 Report*), p. 326.

3. According to President George W. Bush, he decided that the attacks were a "declaration of war" when he learned that a third plane had struck the Pentagon. George W. Bush, *Decision Points* (New York: Crown Publishers, 2010), p. 128. On 11 September, President Bush opened the first National Security Council meeting after the attacks with the statement, "We're at war."; *9/11 Report*, p. 326. Pentagon officials independently arrived at the same conclusion with the same speed as the president, agreeing that the attacks "were more than just a law enforcement matter." Douglas J. Feith, *War and Decision: Inside the Pentagon at the Dawn of the War on Terrorism* (New York: HarperCollins, 2009), pp. 4–5.

4. On the significance of this phrase to the U.S. policy response, see Feith, *War and Decision*, pp. 68–71.

Smoke rises over the damaged Pentagon after the building was struck by a hijacked airliner on 11 September 2001.

very freedom" had come under attack that day. He declared that the United States now stood with its allies "to win the war against terrorism."[5]

The Global War on Terrorism

The Bush administration defined the enemy not as any one group, but as a global network. Groups like al-Qaeda could not operate internationally without support from state and nonstate entities, whether that support was a safe haven, direct state sponsorship, or "charitable" contributions from wealthy sympathizers. In September 2001, the relationships among international terrorist groups and their sponsors were far from clear, but the Bush administration assumed the existence of a global terrorist network and set out to dismantle it.[6] By mid-September, President Bush felt comfortable enough with that policy to publicly state: "Our enemy is a radical network

---

5. George W. Bush, "Address to the Nation on the September 11 Attacks"(National Address, The White House, 11 Sep 2001). https://georgewbush-whitehouse.archives.gov/infocus/bushrecord/documents/Selected_Speeches_George_W_Bush.pdf, Hist Files, OEF Study Grp.

6. Concerns (or speculations) regarding the existence of global terrorist networks surfaced long before the September 11th attacks. For example, in 1903 anonymous parties in tsarist Russia fabricated the anti-Semitic *The Protocols of the Elders of Zion* to stoke widespread fear of global Jewish domination. For a Cold War–era interpretation, see Claire Sterling's *The Terror Network: The Secret War of International Terrorism* (New York: Holt & Company, 1981), which argued that the Soviet Union employed terrorist groups as proxies against the United States.

of terrorists, and every government that supports them."[7] To eliminate the terrorist threat, America would not only have to eliminate sanctuaries, but also convince or compel all entities that sponsored, harbored, or otherwise tolerated terrorists to terminate their support.[8] The Bush administration especially feared that "rogue" states such as Iran, Iraq, and North Korea might lend support to terrorist groups in the form of weapons of mass destruction.[9]

By 13 September, President Bush identified four objectives for what he characterized as the Global War on Terrorism: (1) eliminate al-Qaeda, (2) hold the perpetrators of 11 September 2001 accountable, (3) pursue "other lethal anti-US terrorist groups," and (4) eliminate safe havens and support for terrorists.[10] These goals suggested that the war was both about punishment and prevention, and that it would target both states and the nonstate actors who had attacked the United States. On 14 September, the U.S. Congress gave President Bush the authority to pursue such a war, through an Authorization for Use of Military Force that empowered the president to:

> use all necessary and appropriate force against those nations, organizations, and persons he determines planned, authorized, committed or aided the terrorist attacks that occurred on September 11, 2001, or harbored such organizations or persons, in order to prevent any future acts of international terrorism against the United States by such nations, organizations or persons.[11]

---

7. George W. Bush, "Address to a Joint Session of the 107th Congress"(National Address, U.S. Capitol, 20 Sep 2001). https://georgewbush-whitehouse.archives.gov/infocus/bushrecord/documents/Selected_Speeches_George_W_Bush.pdf, Hist Files, OEF Study Grp.

8. Deputy Secretary of Defense Paul D. Wolfowitz made the scope of the mission public at a Pentagon press conference on 13 September: "It's not just simply a matter of capturing people and holding them accountable, but removing the sanctuaries, removing the support systems, ending states who sponsor terrorism." DoD News Bfg, Deputy Sec Def Wolfowitz, 13 Sep 2001, https://archive.defense.gov/Transcripts/Transcript.aspx?TranscriptID=1622, Hist Files, OEF Study Grp.

9. For weapons of mass destruction fears, see Memo, Sec Def Donald H. Rumsfeld for President George W. Bush, 6 Oct 2001, sub: My Visits to Saudi Arabia, Oman, Egypt, Uzbekistan, and Turkey, 6 Oct 2001, NSA GWU, https://nsarchive.files.wordpress.com/2015/01/secret-october-6-2001-memo.pdf, Hist Files, OEF Study Grp.; Interv, Tom Shanker, *New York Times*, with Sec Rumsfeld, 12 Oct 2001, https://archive.defense.gov/Transcripts/Transcript.aspx?TranscriptID=2097, Hist Files, OEF Study Grp; Ron Suskind, *The One Percent Doctrine: Deep Inside America's Pursuit of Its Enemies Since 9/11* (New York: Simon & Schuster, 2006), p. 65.

10. Talking Points for Principals Committee, U.S. Department of State, 13 Sep 2001, NSA GWU, https://nsarchive.gwu.edu/NSAEBB/NSAEBB358a/doc04.pdf, Hist Files, OEF Study Grp; Talking Points for Principals Committee, U.S. Department of State, 14 Sep 2001, NSA GWU, https://nsarchive.gwu.edu/NSAEBB/NSAEBB358a/doc07.pdf, Hist Files, OEF Study Grp.

11. U.S. Congress, Senate, *Authorization for Use of Military Force*, S. Joint Res. 23, 107th Congress (Cong.). (14 Sep 2001), https://www.congress.gov/bill/107th-congress/senate-joint-resolution/23, Hist Files, OEF Study Grp.

From the outset, the Bush administration planned to target threats outside of Afghanistan, including Iraq. Indeed, in the wake of the attacks, the president and Secretary of Defense Donald H. Rumsfeld assumed that Saddam Hussein's regime had been involved in the plot.[12] When Bush met with his war cabinet at Camp David on 15 September, he had them consider three target options: al-Qaeda, the Taliban, and Iraq.[13] Some within the Office of the Secretary of Defense believed that al-Qaeda and Iraq, not the Taliban, posed the greater strategic threats to the United States. However, the president decided that Iraq was not an immediate priority and directed an attack against al-Qaeda's safe haven in Afghanistan first.[14] However, the decision not to strike Iraq first was only a question of timing; in late November—roughly six weeks after the Afghanistan campaign began—Secretary Rumsfeld would order CENTCOM, at the president's request, to update its Iraq war plans.[15]

As planning for Afghanistan got underway, Rumsfeld continued to push the Pentagon to align its planning horizons with the president's global visions. The defense secretary was reportedly disappointed in General Tommy R. Franks' draft campaign plan, briefed on 20 September, because of its limited "focus on al-Qaida [sic] in Afghanistan."[16] In a 30 September memo to the president, Rumsfeld laid out several political objectives for the war on terrorism, including: "new regimes in Afghanistan and another key State (or two) that supports terrorism," "Syria out of Lebanon," the "dismantlement or destruction of WMD [weapons of mass destruction] capabilities" in two classified locations, and the "end of many other countries' support or

---

12. On the afternoon of 11 September, Defense Secretary Donald H. Rumsfeld told General Richard B. Myers that his instinct was to strike Saddam Hussein at the same time as al-Qaeda; *9/11 Report*, pp. 334–35. Also that afternoon, he directed General Counsel William J. Haynes II to speak with Deputy Secretary Wolfowitz about finding additional support for an Iraq–al-Qaeda connection; Note, Principal Deputy Under Sec Def for Policy Stephen A. Cambone, 11 Sep 2001, NSA GWU, https://nsarchive.gwu.edu/NSAEBB/NSAEBB326/doc07.pdf, Hist Files, OEF Study Grp. On 12 September, President Bush ordered Richard A. Clarke, the National Security Council's national counterterrorism coordinator, to look for Iraqi links to 9/11; *9/11 Report*, p. 334.

13. The "war cabinet" included Vice President Richard B. "Dick" Cheney, Secretary of State Colin L. Powell, Secretary of Defense Donald H. Rumsfeld, Chairman of the Joint Chiefs of Staff General H. Hugh Shelton, Vice Chairman of the Joint Chiefs of Staff General Richard B. Myers, Director of Central Intelligence George J. Tenet, Attorney General John D. Ashcroft, Federal Bureau of Investigation (FBI) Director Robert S. Mueller III, National Security Advisor Condoleezza Rice, White House Chief of Staff Andrew H. Card, and, frequently, Deputy National Security Advisor Stephen J. Hadley and White House Deputy Chief of Staff Joshua B. Bolten; see *9/11 Report*, p. 330.

14. Ibid., p. 335.

15. Bob Woodward, *Plan of Attack* (New York: Simon & Schuster, 2004), pp. 1–4; Tommy R. Franks with Malcolm McConnell, *American Soldier: General Tommy Franks, Commander in Chief, United States Central Command* (New York: Regan Books, 2004), p. 329.

16. Feith, *War and Decision*, p. 63. Feith takes this quote directly from his draft memo for Secretary Rumsfeld, 20 Sep 2001, sub: Briefing President on Operational Plan, Hist Files, OEF Study Grp.

Firefighters search for victims in the World Trade Center ruins on 14 September 2001.

tolerance of terrorism."[17] He appreciated the audacity of this global vision: "If the war does not significantly change the world's political map, the United States will not achieve its aim. There is value in being clear on the order of magnitude of the necessary change."[18] Rumsfeld's radical views on altering the world's political map in order to achieve American aims did not mirror CENTCOM's understanding of the purpose of the upcoming campaign, and made it more difficult for the military to identify the specific standards that it would have to meet to secure a successful outcome.

Rumsfeld continued to espouse his version of national policy by sending a 3 October memo to the combatant commanders and service chiefs. His "strategic guidance for the campaign against terrorism" identified four war "aims," which military planners might call political end states. These end states amounted to the creation of "an international political environment hostile to terrorism," a world in which terrorists could no longer operate.[19]

---

17. Memo, Sec Rumsfeld for President Bush, 30 Sep 2001, sub: Strategic Thoughts, NSA GWU, https://nsarchive.gwu.edu/NSAEBB/NSAEBB358a/doc13.pdf, Hist Files, OEF Study Grp. Feith drafted the memo and Wolfowitz, General John P. Abizaid, and Myers revised it before Rumsfeld made final edits and signed it; Feith, *War and Decision*, p. 81.

18. Memo, Sec Rumsfeld for President Bush, 30 Sep 2001, sub: Strategic Thoughts, Hist Files, OEF Study Grp.

19. Donald H. Rumsfeld, "A New Kind of War," *New York Times*, 27 Sep 2001, https://www.nytimes.com/2001/09/27/opinion/27RUMS.html, Hist Files, OEF Study Grp. See also DoD News Briefing, Sec Def Rumsfeld, 18 Sep 2001, https://archive.defense.gov/transcripts/transcript.aspx?transcriptid=1893. The Office of the Secretary of Defense's strategic guidance called for the "campaign on terrorism" to include "multiple agencies" and "multiple instruments [of national power.]" Even though this responsibility typically belonged to the National Security Council, the

To achieve this ambitious goal, he provided an equally ambitious "strategic concept": "multiple agencies, multiple fronts, multiple instruments, multiple methods and extended duration."[20] In keeping with this concept, he directed his subordinates to "marshal, coordinate and synchronize all instruments of U.S. national power—diplomatic, financial, intelligence, military and other—in the planning, execution and exploitation of a global campaign against terrorism sustainable for the foreseeable future."[21] The 3 October memorandum therefore set highly aggressive goals while promising few additional resources for the military forces charged with obtaining those objectives.

Rumsfeld's global vision also seriously constrained the ability of the Joint Force to plan and execute a successful intervention in Afghanistan. The war in Afghanistan was never meant to be a war in its own right, but the opening campaign of a protracted, global conflict. CENTCOM had to plan not merely to eliminate al-Qaeda's sanctuary in Afghanistan, but also to eliminate terrorist capabilities across its entire area of operations, which at the time included Iran, Iraq, Somalia, Sudan, Syria, and Yemen. In addition, the imperative to fight a global war "sustainable for the foreseeable future" created an unprecedented challenge for the all-volunteer force. Although President Bush told the American public to expect "a lengthy campaign unlike any other we have ever seen," he did not express interest in generating additional warfighting resources and personnel.[22] The war on terrorism's multiple campaigns would therefore be fought by existing military and paramilitary units, and its overall success would depend on rapid victories and equally rapid withdrawals.

Most importantly, the Global War on Terrorism's broad strategic goals made it difficult for military planners to develop clear and feasible termination criteria. In Afghanistan (as in other projected theaters of operation), the core goal was not simply to remove al-Qaeda's sanctuary but to prevent its reemergence.[23] The latter was a fundamentally political goal that necessitated state-building. By definition, terrorist safe havens exist in ungoverned spaces,

---

Department of Defense (DoD) outlined the nonmilitary components of the war's strategy in this document. Memo, Sec Def Rumsfeld, for Deputy Sec Def, Secs Mil Departments, Chairman of the Joint Chiefs of Staff (CJCS), Under Secs Def, Combatant Cdrs, Asst Sec Def for Command, Control, and Communications, and General Counsel, 3 Oct 2001, sub: Strategic Guidance for the Campaign Against Terrorism, p. 6, NSA GWU, https://nsarchive.gwu.edu/NSAEBB/NSAEBB358a/doc15.pdf, Hist Files, OEF Study Grp.

20. Memo, Rumsfeld, for Deputy Sec Def, Sec Mil Departments, CJCS, Under Secs Def, Combatant Cdrs, Asst Sec Def for Command, Control, and Communications, and General Counsel, 3 Oct 2001, sub: Strategic Guidance for the Campaign Against Terrorism, p. 9.

21. Ibid., p. 7.

22. Bush, "Address to the Joint Session of the 107th Congress" (20 Sep 2001).

23. In November 2001, Secretary of State Powell told the UN Security Council that the war would "be fought with increased support for democracy programs, judicial reform, conflict resolution, poverty alleviation, economic reform and health and education programs. All of these together deny the reason for terrorists to exist or to find safe havens within those borders." Colin L. Powell, "Remarks to United Nations Security Council" (Remarks, New York, 12 Nov 2001), Hist Files, OEF Study Grp.

either in a remote location or failed state.[24] It follows, then, that to prevent safe havens, a legitimate government would have to be present and capable of providing order and justice. A sober assessment of existing resources at the time reveals that the American government was ill-equipped to undertake such a task. As a result, American military leaders faced the uncomfortable fact that they would need outside assistance to accomplish many of their goals.

THE BUSH DOCTRINE

The Bush administration faced two significant diplomatic challenges for its Global War on Terrorism. The first consisted of building the international coalition needed to ensure success in achieving ambitious strategic goals, and the second involved convincing unfriendly nation-states to stop supporting terrorism. On the evening of 11 September, President Bush took what he hoped would be the first step in resolving the latter challenge. In his address from the Oval Office, he declared a new foreign policy: from now on, the United States would "make no distinction between the terrorists who committed these acts and those who harbor them."[25] The president restated the new policy more bluntly in his 20 September address to Congress: "Every nation, in every region, now has a decision to make. Either you are with us, or you are with the terrorists. From this day forward, any nation that continues to harbor or support terrorism will be regarded by the United States as a hostile regime."[26] The Bush Doctrine, as it became known, gave countries the world over a stark choice: in the coming war, they would be either friends or enemies of the United States; there was "no neutral ground."[27]

The Bush administration soon put this new policy to the test with the country that had the closest relationship to the Taliban: Pakistan. The administration believed Pakistan's cooperation would be essential to the success of a military campaign in Afghanistan and the broader war on terrorism for three reasons. First, Islamabad offered a diplomatic channel to the Taliban, through which it might be able to convince Mullah Mohammed

---

24. The Intelligence Reform and Terrorism Prevention Act of 2004 would define a terrorist safe haven as an ungoverned and lawless location in a remote region or failing state; see *Intelligence Reform and Terrorism Prevention Act of 2004*, PL 108–458, 108th Cong., 1st sess. (17 Dec 2004) sec. 7102(a). Military doctrine did not define terrorist safe haven in 2001; Lt Col Marc Jamison, *Sanctuaries: A Strategic Reality, an Operational Challenge*, U.S. Army War College Strategy Research Project, 15 Mar 2008, p. 17, Hist Files, OEF Study Grp.

25. Bush, "Address to the Nation on the September 11 Attacks" (11 Sep 2001). President Bush proclaimed this new policy without consulting his vice president, secretary of state, or secretary of defense. Peter Baker, *Days of Fire: Bush and Cheney in the White House* (New York: Doubleday, 2013), p. 131; Bob Woodward, *Bush at War* (New York: Simon and Schuster, 2002), p. 30.

26. Bush, "Address to the Joint Session of the 107th Congress" (20 Sep 2001)

27. "In this conflict, there is no neutral ground. If any government sponsors the outlaws and killers of innocents, they have become outlaws and murderers, themselves." George W. Bush, "Presidential Address to the Nation" (National Archives, The White House, 7 Oct 2001), https://georgewbush-whitehouse.archives.gov/news/releases/2001/10/20011007-8.html, Hist Files, OEF Study Grp; Bush, *Decision Points*, pp. 396–97.

Omar's regime to cease harboring al-Qaeda. Pakistan historically had supported the Taliban and even fostered them into power, and was one of three countries to officially recognize the regime. Conversely, if the Taliban refused to cooperate and pressure from Washington forced Islamabad to cut ties, then the Taliban's leadership would be diplomatically isolated.[28] Second, Pakistan's intelligence agencies, especially the Directorate General for Inter-Services Intelligence, knew Afghanistan and their own Pashtun tribal areas better than anyone. The U.S. government had lost much of its Afghan expertise since disengaging from the region in the early 1990s, and it needed help understanding the enemy. Finally, Pakistan's location made it the best option to gain access to landlocked Afghanistan. The geographical alternatives were worse for various reasons: Iran would never cooperate with American military operations; India had a longstanding policy of nonalignment, and even if this changed, it could not serve as a base for operations in Afghanistan without risking war with Pakistan; and the Central Asian republics were just as landlocked—and therefore just as expensive to transport through for military equipment and humanitarian aid—as Afghanistan.

Deputy Secretary of State Richard L. Armitage delivered the president's ultimatum to Lt. Gen. Mahmud Ahmed, the director of the Inter-Services Intelligence, at a meeting in Washington on 12 September. "Pakistan faces a stark choice," he said. "Either it is with us or it is not."[29] Ambassador Wendy J. Chamberlin delivered the same message to President Pervez Musharraf in Islamabad the next day. While Musharraf tried to distance Islamabad from the Taliban regime, he also noted that Pakistan questioned "how to deal with the Taliban," hinting that it would prefer a nonmilitary solution.[30] After some additional discussion, Musharraf assured Chamberlin of his country's support. Musharraf later framed his decision as a question of whether the Taliban were worth committing suicide over; the answer was "a resounding no."[31]

---

28. The other two were the United Arab Emirates and Saudi Arabia. The former would end relations with the Taliban on 22 September. Saudi Arabia had frozen relations in 1998 over Osama bin Laden's guest status in Afghanistan and would cut ties completely on 25 September 2001. Warren Hoge, "United Arab Emirates Cuts Ties with Afghanistan," *New York Times*, 22 Sep 2001, https://www.nytimes.com/2001/09/22/international/middleeast/united-arab-emirates-cuts-ties-with-afghanistan-20010922933132643342.html, Hist Files, OEF Study Grp; John F. Burns with Christopher Wren, "Saudi Arabia Cuts Ties with Taliban," *New York Times*, 26 Sep 2001, https://www.nytimes.com/learning/teachers/featured_articles/20010926wednesday.html, Hist Files, OEF Study Grp.

29. U.S. Dept of State Cable, Sec State to Ambassador Chamberlin, 12 Sep 2001, sub: Deputy Secretary Armitage's Meeting with Pakistan Intel Chief Mahmud: You're Either With Us or You're Not, NSA GWU, version 1: https://nsarchive.gwu.edu/NSAEBB/NSAEBB358a/doc03-1.pdf, version 2: https://nsarchive.gwu.edu/NSAEBB/NSAEBB358a/doc03-2.pdf; Cable, U.S. Embassy Islamabad to Sec State, 13 Sep 2001, sub: Musharraf: "We Are With You in Your Action Plan in Afghanistan," NSA GWU, https://nsarchive.gwu.edu/NSAEBB/NSAEBB358a/doc02.pdf, Hist Files, OEF Study Grp.

30. Ibid.

31. Pervez Musharraf, *In the Line of Fire: A Memoir* (New York: Simon & Schuster, 2006), p. 202.

The diplomatic exchange shifted from obtaining a broad understanding to engaging specific issues on the following day when Deputy Secretary Armitage presented seven demands for General Ahmed to pass to Islamabad.[32] The list itemized what Pakistan had to do to show it was "with" the United States:

1. Stop al-Qaida [sic] operatives at your border, intercept arms shipments through Pakistan and end all logistical support for bin Laden.
2. Provide the United States with blanket overflight and landing rights to conduct all necessary military and intelligence operations.
3. Provide as needed territorial access to United States and allied military intelligence, and other personnel to conduct all necessary operations against the perpetrators of terrorism or those that harbor them, including use of Pakistan's naval ports, airbases, and strategic locations on borders.
4. Provide the United States immediately with intelligence, [excised] information, to help prevent and respond to terrorist acts perpetrated against the United States, its friends and allies.
5. Continue to publicly condemn the terrorist acts of September 11 and any other terrorist acts against the United States or its friends and allies, [excised].
6. Cut off all shipments of fuel to the Taliban and any secret other items and recruits, including volunteers enroute [sic] to Afghanistan that can be used in a military offensive capacity or to abet the terrorist threat.
7. Should the evidence strongly implicate Usama bin-Laden [sic] and the Al Qaida [sic] network in Afghanistan and should Afghanistan and the Taliban continue to harbor him and this network, Pakistan will break diplomatic relations with the Taliban government, end support for the Taliban and assist us in the aforementioned ways to destroy Usama bin-Laden [sic] and his Al Qaida [sic] network.[33]

On 14 September, Musharraf met with his corps commanders and top generals, and laid out the case that Pakistan would be branded a terrorist state and stigmatized internationally if it refused to join America's war on terrorism. Several of his generals, including Ahmed, nevertheless opposed cooperation. Ultimately, they agreed to accept the demands only because

---

32. Deputy Secretary of State Richard L. Armitage and Powell had developed this list on their own despite its obvious military implications, a move that later irked Rumsfeld, but in fact merely reflected his own willingness to address diplomatic issues. Interv, PBS *Frontline*, with Richard L. Armitage, Deputy Sec State, 20 Jul 2006, https://www.pbs.org/wgbh/pages/frontline/taliban/interviews/armitage.html, Hist Files, OEF Study Grp; Feith, *War and Decision*, pp. 14–15.

33. U.S. Department of State Cable, Sec State to Ambassador Chamberlin, 13 Sep 2001, sub: Deputy Secretary Armitage's Meeting with General Mahmud: Actions and Support Expected of Pakistan in Fight Against Terrorism, NSA GWU, https://nsarchive.gwu.edu/NSAEBB/NSAEBB358a/doc05.pdf, Hist Files, OEF Study Grp.

they feared that delay on their part would push the United States closer to India.[34] At the same time, cooperation with Washington risked provoking a domestic backlash from Pakistanis who held Islamist and anti-American views.[35]

When Musharraf met with Ambassador Chamberlin later that same day, he said that "he accepted the points without conditions and that his military leadership concurred."[36] At the same time, he raised a number of still-classified concerns over their implementation.[37] As these details were worked out in the coming weeks, the United States did not hold Pakistan to its demand for unlimited basing and overflight rights. Rather, it accepted a limited flight corridor and basing rights at Shamsi and Jacobabad, as well as Pakistan's stipulation that no attacks could be launched from its soil.[38]

The Bush administration's demands did not alter Pakistan's strategic calculus, which continued to revolve around India. Pakistan would support the American war on terrorism only insofar as it furthered this core interest. Musharraf made this clear to his constituency in a televised, Urdu-language speech on 19 September. According to Musharraf, this was the only way he could preserve the country's "main cause" in Kashmir: India was trying to woo America to its side, have Pakistan declared a terrorist state, "and thus damage our Kashmir cause."[39] He implied that Pakistan's alignment with America was a temporary, lesser evil, speaking by analogy of how the Prophet Muhammad once had to ally with the Jews of Medina to fight his enemies in Mecca before being able to defeat those same Jews in battle six years later. He also noted his continued efforts to spare Afghanistan and the Taliban from an American attack.[40]

---

34. Hassan Abbas, *Pakistan's Drift into Extremism: Allah, the Army, and America's War on Terror* (Armonk, N.Y.: M. E. Sharpe, 2005), p. 220; Rory McCarthy, "Dangerous Game of State-Sponsored Terror that Threatens Nuclear Conflict," *Guardian*, 24 May 2002, https://www.theguardian.com/world/2002/may/25/pakistan.india, Hist Files, OEF Study Grp.

35. Shuja Nawaz, *Crossed Swords: Pakistan, Its Army, and the Wars Within* (New York: Oxford University Press, 2008), p. 541.

36. Cable, U.S. Embassy Islamabad to Sec State, 14 Sep 2001, sub: Musharraf Accepts The Seven Points, NSA GWU, https://nsarchive.gwu.edu/NSAEBB/NSAEBB358a/doc08.pdf, Hist Files, OEF Study Grp.

37. Ibid.

38. Howard B. Schaffer and Teresita C. Schaffer, *How Pakistan Negotiates with the United States: Riding the Roller Coaster* (Washington, D.C.: United States Institute of Peace, 2011), pp. 138–39; Musharraf, *In the Line of Fire*, p. 206.

39. The geographical area of Kashmir between India and Pakistan has been the main area of conflict between the two nations since the establishment of Pakistan as an autonomous nation in 1947. Pervez Musharraf, "Text: Pakistan President Musharraf" [televised speech to the people of Pakistan], *Washington Post*, 19 Sep 2001, https://www.washingtonpost.com/wp-srv/nation/specials/attacked/transcripts/pakistantext_091901.html, Hist Files, OEF Study Grp.

40. Ibid.; Selig S. Harrison, "Bush Needs to Attach Strings to Pakistan Aid," *USA Today*, 23 Jun 2003, https://usatoday30.usatoday.com/news/opinion/editorials/2003-06-23-oplede_x.htm, Hist Files, OEF Study Grp.

Thus, the Bush administration erred in believing that Islamabad would serve as their most important ally in the coming war in Afghanistan, even though the two countries had divergent interests there. That misplaced faith, sustained for several years by pro-Pakistani voices within the CIA, DoD, and State Department, ultimately placed a large swath of the Taliban's traditional base of support—the Pashtun tribal belt that straddled both sides of the Pakistan-Afghanistan border—off limits to American attack. For the foreseeable future, U.S. ground forces would not be able to pursue their opponents into the sovereign territory of its new friend and ally without risking the logistical and intelligence cooperation on which the military campaign depended.

The diplomatic reset with Islamabad also opened a communications channel that the Bush administration leveraged to deliver its ultimatum to the Taliban. By 14 September, the State Department had developed a list of demands for Omar's regime, which included: (1) turn over Osama bin Laden and his lieutenants; (2) "tell us everything they know" about bin Laden and his associates, "including their whereabouts, resources, plans for future terrorist attacks, and access to WMD [weapons of mass destruction] materials"; and (3) "close immediately all terrorist training camps and expel all terrorists."[41] The State Department entertained the possibility that the Taliban regime would cooperate, either by using their own forces to expel al-Qaeda or allowing U.S. forces to operate freely. If Taliban leaders did not "take decisive action" in twenty-four to forty-eight hours, then—in keeping with the Bush Doctrine—the United States would "take all necessary means to see that terrorist infrastructure is destroyed despite them" and begin to work "to remove the Taliban leadership from power."[42]

General Ahmed delivered a version of the U.S. demands to Omar personally on a 17 September visit to Afghanistan. He reported back to Armitage that he had "framed the decision to Omar and the other Afghans as essentially choosing between one man and his safe haven versus the well-being of 25 million citizens of Afghanistan," and that the Taliban's response was "not negative."[43] According to later reports, Ahmed either did not bring up bin Laden at all, did not push Omar to extradite him, or actively encouraged Omar to resist the United States, even advising him on military strategy.[44] Whatever the case, the Taliban leadership did not agree

---

41. Memo, U.S. Department of State, 14 Sep 2001, sub: Gameplan for Polmil Strategy for Pakistan and Afghanistan, p. 1, NSA GWU, https://nsarchive.gwu.edu/NSAEBB/NSAEBB358a/doc06.pdf, Hist Files, OEF Study Grp.

42. Ibid.

43. U.S. Department of State Cable, Sec State to U.S. Embassy Islamabad, 18 Sep 2001, sub: U.S. Department of State: Deputy Secretary Armitage–Mamoud Phone Call Sept. 18, 2001, p. 2, NSA GWU, https://nsarchive2.gwu.edu/NSAEBB/NSAEBB358a/doc09.pdf, Hist Files, OEF Study Grp.

44. Michael Zielenziger and Juan O. Tamayo, "U.S. Finds Itself Relying on Information from Former Taliban Allies," Knight Ridder/Tribune News Service, 3 Nov 2001, Hist Files, OEF Study Grp; Kathy Gannon, *I is for Infidel: From Holy War to Holy Terror: 18 Years Inside Afghanistan* (New York: PublicAffairs, 2005), pp. 93–94; Nawaz, *Crossed Swords*, pp. 542–43.

to the U.S. demand for action against bin Laden, announcing instead that a grand council of Islamic clerics would decide bin Laden's fate.[45] For Omar, the sticking point seems to have been his responsibility to his Arab Muslim guests under *pashtunwali*, the ancient Pashtun code of conduct that included a strong tradition of hospitality, or specifically *melmastiia*. Under the code of melmastiia, Omar felt he must offer protection to his guest and did not believe he could give up bin Laden—especially to non-Muslims—without losing all honor and legitimacy as a Muslim and Afghan leader.[46]

Although the decision effectively sealed the Taliban leadership's fate, diplomatic efforts continued for another two weeks. In a 24 September meeting with Ambassador Chamberlin, General Ahmed warned that removing the Taliban would leave Afghanistan at the mercy of warlords once again, and that a strike would "produce thousands of frustrated young Muslim men" and "be an incubator of anger that will explode two or three years from now."[47] Four days later, Ahmed traveled to Kandahar—after the first CIA team had already infiltrated Afghanistan—in a last-ditch effort to change Omar's mind. This time Ahmed brought with him eight Pakistani clerics who had instructed several Taliban officials as students, but even they failed to persuade Omar to give up bin Laden.[48] Although it did not oppose Ahmed's mission, the United States now believed that the time for negotiation had passed.[49] The Taliban's failure to surrender bin Laden and his lieutenants would make them the target of a U.S. military campaign in less than two weeks' time.

Once again, the policies adopted by the Bush administration threatened to create as many strategic challenges as it solved. The post–September 11th American approach to global terrorism effectively fused an international terrorist group (al-Qaeda) and a national insurgency (the Taliban) together and made them "the enemy" in Afghanistan. That viewpoint did not take into account that, as CENTCOM planners recognized, the two groups

---

Another version has a Pakistani cleric, Mufti Nizamuddin Shamzai, encouraging Mullah Mohammed Omar to start a jihad against the United States if it attacked Afghanistan; see Abbas, *Pakistan's Drift into Extremism*, p. 221.

45. "Taliban to Decide Fate of Bin Laden," 18 Sep 2001, CNN, https://www.cnn.com/2001/WORLD/asiapcf/central/09/18/afghan.taliban.0430/, Hist Files, OEF Study Grp; Luke Harding, Ewen MacAskill, and Richard Norton-Taylor, "Defiant Taliban Ready for War," *Guardian*, 18 Sep 2001, https://www.theguardian.com/world/2001/sep/18/politics.september11, Hist Files, OEF Study Grp.

46. In a September 2001 interview with Voice of America, Mullah Omar cited "Islam's prestige" and "Afghanistan's tradition" as the reasons why he could not give up bin Laden. Transcript, "Mullah Omar – In His Own Words," *Guardian*, 26 Sep 2001, https://www.theguardian.com/world/2001/sep/26/afghanistan.features11, Hist Files, OEF Study Grp; Nawaz, *Crossed Swords*, p. 542.

47. Cable, U.S. Embassy Islamabad to Sec State, 24 Sep 2001, sub: Mahmud Plans 2nd Mission to Afghanistan, NSA GWU, https://nsarchive.gwu.edu/NSAEBB/NSAEBB358a/doc11.pdf, Hist Files, OEF Study Grp.

48. Ibid.

49. Ibid.

had distinct strategic and operational interests.[50] Nor did it account for the DoD's position that the Taliban did not pose a strategic threat to the United States, or allow for the possibility that the Taliban's "control" over al-Qaeda may have been less than complete.[51] It also was not clear that, within the framework of international law, the Taliban bore legal responsibility for the 11 September 2001 attack.[52] Finally, removing the Taliban from power did not necessarily eliminate al-Qaeda's sanctuary. Rather, by creating a power vacuum, it gave rise to separate strategic challenges that could not be solved militarily. Ironically, the administration's preferred course of action risked trading one ungoverned space (the Taliban's failed state) for another (a power vacuum), and constrained the ability of American military commanders to pursue the enemy into the ungoverned spaces of neighboring Pakistan.

COALITION BUILDING

The remaining major diplomatic challenge for the Bush administration was to secure the international coalition necessary to prosecute the Global War on Terrorism. By 13 September, President Bush had spoken with Russian president Vladimir Putin, British prime minister Tony C. Blair, French president Jacques R. Chirac, German chancellor Gerhard F. Schröder, and Canadian prime minister Joseph Jacques "Jean" Chrétien; Secretary of State Colin L. Powell had spoken with UN Secretary General Kofi A. Annan, European Union leaders, and his counterparts in many countries.[53] They continued to work the phones in that pivotal first week, and in his 20 September speech before Congress, President Bush asked "every nation to join us" in what he called "civilization's fight."[54]

---

50. Theater Campaign Plan, Operation ENDURING FREEDOM, U.S. Central Command (CENTCOM), 26 Nov 2001, p. 9, Hist Files, OEF Study Grp.

51. Alex Strick van Linschoten and Felix Kuehn, *An Enemy We Created: The Myth of the Taliban–Al Qaeda Merger in Afghanistan* (New York: Oxford University Press, 2012). Compare with the State Department's assessment shortly after the attacks: "Tuesday's attacks clearly demonstrate that UBL [Osama bin Laden] is capable of conducting terrorism while under Taliban control—something the Taliban had repeatedly assured us was not the case." Memo, U.S. Department of State, 14 Sep 2001, sub: Gameplan for Polmil Strategy for Pakistan and Afghanistan, p. 1. U.S. Central Command (CENTCOM) planners similarly emphasized "the Taliban's close association with UBL and Al Qaida [sic]" and identified bin Laden as the primary financial backer of the Taliban. Theater Campaign Plan, Operation ENDURING FREEDOM, CENTCOM, 26 Nov 2001, pp. 10–11

52. Helen Duffy, *The 'War on Terror' and the Framework of International Law*, 2d ed. (New York: Cambridge University Press, 2015), pp. 83–89.

53. Ibid.; Jane Perlez, "After the Attacks: The Diplomacy; Powell Says It Clearly: No Middle Ground on Terrorism," *New York Times*, 13 Sep 2001, https://www.nytimes.com/2001/09/13/us/after-attacks-diplomacy-powell-says-it-clearly-no-middle-ground-terrorism.html, Hist Files, OEF Study Grp.

54. Bush, "Address to the Joint Session of the 107th Congress" (20 Sep 2001).

These efforts resulted in an immense outpouring of international support for the United States.[55] On 12 September, NATO agreed to invoke Article 5 of its charter—which required all member states to consider an attack on one member an attack on all—for the first time in its history, provided that the United States could prove that the attacks originated from outside its borders.[56] On 21 September, the European Union condemned the attacks and announced an action plan to fight terrorism.[57] A strong majority of the public in countries such as France and Britain supported their own participation in the anticipated U.S. military actions.[58] This support continued and even increased after the start of operations.[59]

Insofar as they backed a military response by the Americans, however, most allies supported it only in Afghanistan. The Bush Doctrine soon raised concerns that the United States was planning to attack Iraq, which France and Germany (among others) adamantly opposed. The Bush administration's pre–September 11th reputation for "unilateralism"—based largely on its rejection or undermining of major international agreements—exacerbated these fears.[60] These tensions between the Bush administration and NATO would come to a head when the United States invaded Iraq in 2003, and they would strain the coalition effort in Afghanistan.

American efforts at coalition-building also suffered from philosophical differences between the Department of State and DoD. The former wanted to build as broad a coalition as possible to bolster the legitimacy of military action against terrorists and their sponsors. Secretary Powell's talking points

---

55. Warren Hoge, "After the Attacks: West; Outpouring of Grief and Sympathy for Americans Is Seen Throughout Europe and Elsewhere," *New York Times*, 14 Sep 2001, https://www.nytimes.com/2001/09/14/us/after-attacks-west-outpouring-grief-sympathy-for-americans-seen-throughout.html, Hist Files, OEF Study Grp.

56. Tom Lansford, *All for One: Terrorism, NATO, and the United States* (Burlington, Vt.: Ashgate, 2002), pp. 73–74; Suzanne Daley, "After the Attacks: The Alliance; For First Time, NATO Invokes Joint Defense Pact with U.S.," *New York Times*, 13 Sep 2001, https://www.nytimes.com/2001/09/13/us/after-attacks-alliance-for-first-time-nato-invokes-joint-defense-pact-with-us.html, Hist Files, OEF Study Grp.

57. Council of the European Union, Conclusions and Plan of Action of the Extraordinary European Council Meeting on 21 September 2001, https://www.consilium.europa.eu/uedocs/cms_data/docs/pressdata/en/ec/140.en.pdf, Hist Files, OEF Study Grp.

58. Gallup poll, "L'opinion publique internationale et la riposte américaine aux attentats du 11 septembre" [International public opinion and the U.S. response to the September 11 attacks], 14–15 Sep 2001, Association Française de Science Politique [page discontinued], http://www.afsp.info/omasp/agregation/archives/ri/opinionpubliqueinternationale.pdf, Hist Files, OEF Study Grp.

59. Philip H. Gordon, "NATO After 11 September," *Survival* 43, no. 4 (Winter 2002): 3, https://www.tandfonline.com/doi/abs/10.1080/00396330112331343145, Hist Files, OEF Study Grp.

60. These included the Comprehensive Nuclear-Test-Ban Treaty, the Kyoto Protocol on Climate Change, the Anti-Ballistic Missile Treaty, the Biological Weapons Convention verification protocol, the International Criminal Court, and a UN small arms trade agreement; Ibid., p. 2. Also see William Drozdiak, "EU Leaders Back Attacks on Afghanistan," *Washington Post*, 20 Oct 2001, https://www.washingtonpost.com/archive/politics/2001/10/20/eu-leaders-back-attacks-on-afghanistan/fb12b220-966b-4829-ad55-52e0c1fdad2f/, Hist Files, OEF Study Grp.

from 13 and 14 September show diplomatic efforts to have included not only traditional partners like the UN, NATO, Israel, and Japan, but also Iran, Sudan, the Palestine Liberation Organization, the Organization of the Islamic Conference, plus Central, South, and Southeast Asian countries. The State Department identified Saudi Arabia and Egypt as "key priorities for closer cooperation in all possible tracks," and described "moderate Arabs" as "key to the coalition."[61] The State Department opposed striking Iraq in the first phase of the war on terror in part because they feared such action would alienate coalition partners.[62]

By contrast, senior civilian officials in the Pentagon did not want the political sensibilities of other nations to restrict U.S. military options. In fact, Rumsfeld believed that the American position should be the bellwether for the world: "The legitimacy of our actions does not depend on how many countries support us. More nearly the opposite is true: the legitimacy of other countries' opinions should be judged by their attitude toward this systematic, uncivilized assault on a free way of life."[63] He envisioned a coalition of coalitions, recognizing "that coalition members may support aspects of our war effort and not support (or even oppose) other aspects."[64] He encapsulated his philosophy on alliances with the maxim: "The mission must determine the coalition; the coalition must not determine the mission."[65] As Under Secretary Douglas J. Feith observed: "Whereas [Secretary] Powell stressed the importance of respecting the views of allies and friends abroad, we encouraged the President to act, with due respect, to *shape* those views."[66]

The DoD's uncompromising stance guided the Bush administration's response to NATO's Article 5 invocation. Although the U.S. delegation sought the invocation of Article 5, and the North Atlantic Council confirmed it in

---

61. First quotation: Talking Points for Principals Committee, U.S. Department of State, 13 Sep 2001; second and third quotations: Talking Points for Principals Committee, U.S. Department of State, 14 Sep 2001.

62. *9/11 Report*, p. 335.

63. Feith, *War and Decision*, p. 56. Feith takes this quote directly from a memo, no subject, dated 19 September 2001, from Secretary Rumsfeld to Director of Central Intelligence George Tenet, Chief of Staff to the Vice President I. Lewis "Scooter" Libby, and Counselor to the President Karen P. Hughes.

64. Memo, Rumsfeld for Deputy Sec Def, Sec Mil Departments, CJCS, Under Secs Def, Combatant Cdrs, Asst Sec Def for Command, Control, and Communications, and General Counsel, 3 Oct 2001, sub: Strategic Guidance for the Campaign Against Terrorism, p. 11.

65. The maxim appears in different variations in multiple memos: Rumsfeld for Bush, sub: Coalitions, 22 Sep 2001; Rumsfeld for Powell, sub: Coalitions, 18 Oct 2001; Rumsfeld for Bush, sub: Decisions, 19 Jan 2002, Hist Files, OEF Study Grp. Rumsfeld's strategic guidance for the war on terrorism also directed the DoD to "partner, as appropriate, with the people or institutions of other states on particular elements of this campaign, recognizing that our missions should determine the composition of multinational efforts and operations." Memo, Rumsfeld, for Deputy Sec Def, Sec Mil Departments, CJCS, Under Secs Defense, Combatant Cdrs, Asst Sec Def for Command, Control, and Communications, and General Counsel, 3 Oct 2001, sub: Strategic Guidance for the Campaign Against Terrorism, p. 7.

66. Feith, *War and Decision*, p. 59.

early October, they also made clear that the United States neither required collective action from the alliance nor wanted it to form a counterterrorism Combined Joint Task Force (CJTF). Rather, the Bush administration wished to maintain maximum flexibility and lean on NATO as the cornerstone of its coalition of coalitions.[67] Rumsfeld in particular was skeptical of NATO involvement for two reasons. First, he shared the view of some senior defense officials and generals that NATO structures had compromised operational security and interfered with the U.S. military's ability to conduct an efficient campaign in Kosovo.[68] Second, Rumsfeld held a dim view of allied military capabilities. With the exception of Great Britain, NATO allies could not move their assets to the Afghan theater without American assistance.[69]

The secretary of defense's diplomatic efforts ensured NATO played a supporting role in the early stages of the Afghan intervention with only British Special Forces participating in combat operations. NATO's clear support meant that after the cessation of hostilities the United States could lean on member nations to contribute to the peacekeeping and reconstruction missions. This allowed the Bush administration to retain flexibility in the use of its own military to strike terrorists and their sponsors in other theaters.[70] Ultimately, the invocation of Article 5 laid the groundwork for NATO's formal entry into the conflict years later.

Planning for OEF-Afghanistan

Planning for a military intervention in Afghanistan began even before the Bush administration decided that the Taliban regime would be the first target in its war on terrorism. The CIA initially took the lead in planning the intervention, in part because CENTCOM had no contingency plans for Afghanistan, and in part because the CIA had already developed a covert plan to overthrow the Taliban.[71] Indeed, just one day before 11 September, the National Security Council Deputies Committee approved a plan to

---

67. Lansford, *All for One*, pp. 91–93.

68. Dana Priest, "France Played Skeptic on Kosovo Attacks," *Washington Post*, 20 Sep 1999, https://www.washingtonpost.com/wp-srv/national/daily/sept99/airwar20.htm, Hist Files, OEF Study Grp; Interv, PBS *Frontline* with Lt Gen Michael C. Short, Cdr, 16th Air Force and Allied Air Forces Southern Europe Air Component, 22 Feb 2000, https://www.pbs.org/wgbh/pages/frontline/shows/kosovo/interviews/short.html, Hist Files, OEF Study Grp; Gordon, "NATO After 11 September," p. 4; James F. Dobbins, *After the Taliban: Nation-Building in Afghanistan* (Washington, D.C.: Potomac Books, 2008), p. 44.

69. Rebecca Johnson and Micah Zenko, "All Dressed Up and No Place to Go: Why NATO Should Be on the Front Lines in the War on Terror," *Parameters* (Winter 2002-2003): 51–52.

70. The Office of the Secretary of Defense remained wary of involving U.S. forces in international command and control structures that might limit their ability to carry out the counterterrorism mission: "Engaging U.N. diplomacy beyond intent and general outline could interfere with U.S. military operations and inhibit coalition freedom of action." Draft memo, Ofc of the Sec Def, 16 Oct 2001, sub: U.S. Strategy in Afghanistan, NSA GWU, https://nsarchive.gwu.edu/NSAEBB/NSAEBB358a/doc18.pdf, Hist Files, OEF Study Grp.

71. Franks with McConnell, *American Soldier*, p. 266.

increase pressure on the Taliban regime to move against al-Qaeda, and, if those measures failed, to provide covert assistance to topple the regime from within.[72] The plan involved providing assistance to the United Front, a loose alliance of five Taliban opposition groups consisting of the "Panjshir Front," a Tajik group under the command of Mohammed Qasim Fahim after its long-time leader, Ahmad Shah Massoud, died at the hands of al-Qaeda assassins on 9 September 2001; the "Uzbekistan Front" led by Abdul Rashid Dostum; the "Herat Front" in the west, commanded by Ismail Khan, a Tajik with connections to Iran; the "Bamian Front" in the central highlands, led by Shia Hazara chieftain Karim Khalili; and a fifth front in Ghor Province consisting of 2,000 Shia fighters under various commanders.[73]

At a National Security Council meeting on the day after 11 September, Director of Central Intelligence George J. Tenet and Chairman of the Joint Chiefs of Staff General H. Hugh Shelton raised the possibility of adopting this unconventional warfare approach, using CIA paramilitary teams and SOF to partner with the local opposition.[74] At a Security Council meeting on 13 September, Director of the CIA's Counterterrorism Center J. Cofer Black briefed the concept, garnering the support of President Bush and Secretary Rumsfeld.[75] At the Camp David meetings of 15–16 September, Tenet further developed the plan to combine American and United Front forces against the Taliban.[76]

---

72. *9/11 Report*, pp. 205–06.

73. Lester W. Grau and Dodge Billingsly, *Operation Anaconda: America's First Major Battle in Afghanistan* (Lawrence, Kans.: University Press of Kansas, 2008), pp. 33, 44–45. The full title of the organization was the United National and Islamic Front for the Salvation of Afghanistan. The pro-Taliban Pakistani government sought to portray the United Front as an isolated organization representing a discontented minority by referring to it as the "Northern Alliance." There is some truth to that perception, given that its members were organized along ethnic lines that effectively prevented them from collectively agreeing on anything in all but the most extreme circumstances. The motivation levels within the United Front varied widely, with Uzbeks and Hazaras viewing their Pashtun opponents as blood enemies, while Sunni Tajiks disliked Shia Hazaras almost as much as Pashtuns. The United Front's military tactics and capabilities also differed greatly because its leadership had a broad spectrum of professional credentials, ranging from Abdul Rashid Dostum serving with the Soviet and Afghan communist armies to Massoud emerging as the most successful of the irregular mujahideen commanders during the Afghan-Soviet conflict.

74. Unconventional warfare is defined as: "Activities conducted to enable a resistance movement or insurgency to coerce, disrupt or overthrow a government or occupying power by operating through or with an underground, auxiliary and guerrilla force in a denied area." Jeffrey Hasler, "Defining War 2011," *Special Warfare* (Jan-Feb 2011), http://www.soc.mil/swcs/swmag/archive/SW2401/SW2401DefiningWar.html, Hist Files, OEF Study Grp. On the National Security Council meeting, see Shelton with Levinson and McConnell, *Without Hesitation*, p. 441.

75. Tenet with Harlow, *At the Center of the Storm*, p. 175; Shelton with Levinson and McConnell, *Without Hesitation*, p. 443; Feith, *War and Decision*, pp. 16–17.

76. Shelton with Levinson and McConnell, *Without Hesitation*, p. 444; Gen (Ret.) Richard B. Myers with Malcolm McConnell, *Eyes on the Horizon: Serving on the Front Lines of National Security* (New York: Threshold Editions, 2009), p. 167.

The Bush administration saw several advantages to embracing an unconventional warfare approach during the opening phases of a military campaign in Afghanistan. First, utilizing indigenous opposition fighters to gather information would lessen American reliance on Cold War–era intelligence collection systems optimized for use against Soviet-style mechanized forces. Afghanistan possessed very few identifiable "high-value" targets, such as military airfields, air defense sites, oil refineries, dams, and electrical power stations, necessary to support the daily operations of a nation-state.[77] SOF, partnering with the Afghan opposition, stood to improve the effectiveness of preparatory air strikes by identifying and pinpointing discreet assets essential to the Taliban regime's survival.[78]

Harkening back to the Gulf War and Balkans experiences, Rumsfeld had concerns that air strikes carried the risk of inflicting "collateral damage that would be used against us from a religious standpoint," as it might create "images of Americans killing Moslems."[79] In contrast, "equip-and-train activities with local opposition forces coupled with humanitarian aid and intense information operations" would "set the political stage that the people we are going after are the enemies of Moslems themselves."[80] In fact, an unconventional warfare approach had the potential to create a successful model of regime change for the broader war on terrorism. Rumsfeld argued that:

> the U.S. strategic theme should be aiding local peoples to rid themselves of terrorists and to free themselves of regimes that support terrorism. U.S. Special Operations Forces and intelligence personnel should make allies of Afghanis [sic], Iraqis, Lebanese, Sudanese and others who would use U.S. equipment, training, financial, military and humanitarian support to root out and attack the common enemies.[81]

Perhaps the most important requirement that the proposed unconventional approach met was President Bush's demand for swift action. Military logisticians estimated it required several months or more to position sufficient conventional ground forces for an invasion of Afghanistan, but this projected timeline did not satisfy Bush's desire to respond decisively sooner rather than later.[82] In part, this attitude stemmed from the president's outrage at the 11 September 2001 attacks. In his role as a national leader he felt compelled to deliver swift justice to the perpetrators.[83] Yet the administration also desired

---

77. Ibid., p. 65.

78. Memo, Deputy Sec Wolfowitz for Sec Rumsfeld, 23 Sep 2001, sub: Using Special Forces on "Our Side" of the Line, https://library.rumsfeld.com/doclib/sp/267/2001-09-23%20from%20Wolfowitz%20re%20Using%20Special%20Forces%20on%20Our%20Side%20of%20the%20Line.pdf, Hist Files, OEF Study Grp.

79. Feith, *War and Decision*, pp. 55–56.

80. Ibid., pp. 81–83.

81. Ibid., p. 83.

82. Woodward, *Bush at War*, pp. 43–44, 72.

83. Bush, *Decision Points*, p. 128.

immediate military action for strategic reasons. As a later paper from the Office of the Secretary of Defense noted, an early victory could deter other nation-states from supporting terrorist attacks by "making an example of the Taliban."[84] Such a success could "build U.S. public confidence for action in other theaters" and "maintain the support of key coalition members."[85] Thus, when General Franks asked for two months to devise a draft campaign plan, Rumsfeld told him he had only a few days.[86]

Adopting an unconventional warfare approach offered many advantages and would utilize a wide variety of military capabilities to deliver a decisive victory in the shortest time possible. Conventional ground forces likely would be needed in light of intelligence estimates stating the United Front lacked the capability to defeat the Taliban, even with American SOF and air support.[87] Further discussion resulted in a concept combining both conventional and unconventional methods, which General Shelton introduced at the 15 September Camp David meeting.[88] Planners anticipated that, in just a few months' time, the Afghan winter would bring military operations to a near halt.[89] Between the weather and the amount of time it would take to deploy large ground units, CENTCOM did not envision deploying conventional forces in adequate numbers until the spring of 2002.

The amount of ground forces necessary to defeat Taliban and al-Qaeda forces remained an open question, but the Bush administration sought to commit as few U.S. conventional units as possible. The reasons for this "light footprint" approach were complex. Because of the Soviet experience in Afghanistan, members of the administration believed that a large ground force could not succeed there. Afghans were, in Rumsfeld's words, "anti-foreigner," which meant that a military occupation on the model of Japan or Germany was out of the question.[90] Deputy Secretary of Defense Paul D. Wolfowitz believed that putting SOF in the lead would send the important message that the United States was not "heading for a long-term occupation of Afghanistan with all of the potentially catastrophic consequences, which

---

84. Draft memo, Ofc of the Sec Def, 16 Oct 2001, sub: U.S. Strategy in Afghanistan.

85. Ibid.

86. Donald H. Rumsfeld, *Known and Unknown: A Memoir* (New York: Penguin Group, 2011), p. 370.

87. Information (Info) Paper, Defense Intelligence Agency, 15 Oct 2001, sub: Prospects for Northern Alliance Forces to Seize Kabul, NSA GWU, http://nsarchive.gwu.edu/NSAEBB/NSAEBB358a/doc17.pdf, Hist Files, OEF Study Grp.

88. Shelton with Levinson and McConnell, *Without Hesitation*, pp. 444–445; Col. Nathan S. Lowery, *U.S. Marines in Afghanistan, 2001–2002: From the Sea, U.S. Marines in the Global War on Terror* (Washington, D.C.: United States Marine Corps [USMC] History Division, 2011), p. 25.

89. Draft memo, Ofc of the Sec Def, 16 Oct 2001, sub: U.S. Strategy in Afghanistan.

90. Memo, Rumsfeld for Bush, 19 Jan 2002, sub: Decisions, http://library.rumsfeld.com/doclib/sp/743/2002-01-19%20To%20President%20George%20W%20Bush%20re%20Decisions-%20Memo%20Attachment.Bush%20re%20Decisions-%20Memo%20Attachment%2001-19-2002, Hist Files, OEF Study Grp. See also Bush, *Decision Points*, p. 194.

that entails."[91] The logistical challenge of moving large numbers of ground troops into landlocked Afghanistan also presented a powerful argument for going light.[92]

As discussed, the Global War on Terrorism reflected many of these assumptions, and its call for simultaneous operations in multiple theaters precluded U.S. forces from undertaking protracted stability operations in any one place. But perhaps more than any other reason, the Bush administration wanted to minimize the U.S. footprint in Afghanistan because it was opposed to using American troops for nation building. Although nation building is a notoriously ill-defined concept, in the 1990s it became attached—with significant political baggage—to the contingency operations ordered by President Clinton in Somalia, Haiti, Bosnia, and Kosovo.[93] When then-Governor Bush campaigned against nation building in 2000, he was expressing his opposition to using the American military to conduct humanitarian and peacekeeping missions. The president and his advisers believed that such interventions degraded American military capabilities, tied up forces indefinitely, and created economic dependency in the host nation.[94] Compounding this opposition to nation building was the administration's general pessimism about Afghanistan's future prospects. According to Richard N. Haass, who participated in National Security Council meetings in the fall of 2001 as the administration's coordinator for the future of Afghanistan, "the consensus was that little could be accomplished in Afghanistan given its history, culture, and composition, and that there would be little payoff beyond Afghanistan even if things there went better than expected."[95] Thus, President Bush stuck to his position in the wake of

---

91. Memo, Wolfowitz for Rumsfeld, 23 Sep 2001, sub: Using Special Forces on "Our Side" of the Line.

92. Interv, Lynne Chandler Garcia, Combat Studies Institute (CSI), with Gen Victor G. Renuart Jr., former (frmr) CENTCOM Director of Opns, 31 May 2007, p. 7, Hist Files, OEF Study Grp.

93. The term has been used variously to refer to state-building, peace-building, stabilization, reconstruction, democratization, and modernization efforts in postconflict environments. Two RAND studies openly embrace this multiplicity of meaning: see James F. Dobbins et al., *America's Role in Nation-Building: From Germany to Iraq* (Santa Monica, Calif.: RAND Corporation, 2003), p. 1; James F. Dobbins et al., *After the War: Nation-Building from FDR to George W. Bush* (Santa Monica, Calif.: RAND Corporation, 2008), p. 2. For a different take, see Francis Fukuyama, "Nation-Building and the Failure of Institutional Memory," in Francis Fukuyama, ed., *Nation-Building: Beyond Afghanistan and Iraq* (Baltimore: Johns Hopkins University Press, 2006), pp. 4–8.

94. Michael R. Gordon, "The 2000 Campaign: The Military; Bush Would Stop U.S. Peacekeeping in Balkan Fights," *New York Times*, 21 Oct 2000, https://www.nytimes.com/2000/10/21/us/the-2000-campaign-the-military-bush-would-stop-us-peacekeeping-in-balkan-fights.html, Hist Files, OEF Study Grp; Condoleezza Rice, "Campaign 2000: Promoting the National Interest," *Foreign Affairs*, (Jan-Feb 2000), https://www.foreignaffairs.com/articles/2000-01-01/campaign-2000-promoting-national-interest, Hist Files, OEF Study Grp; Donald H. Rumsfeld, "Beyond Nation Building," (Speech, Intrepid Sea-Air-Space Museum, New York City, 14 Feb 2003), http://archive.defense.gov/Speeches/Speech.aspx?SpeechID=337, Hist Files, OEF Study Grp.

95. Richard N. Haass, "Time to Draw Down in Afghanistan," *Newsweek*, 18 Jul 2010, https://www.newsweek.com/haass-time-draw-down-afghanistan-74467, Hist Files, OEF Study Grp.

11 September, declaring on 25 September: "We're not into nation-building; we're focused on justice."[96]

Under these policy constraints and with only basic strategic guidance from Washington, CENTCOM's staff worked furiously to prepare a draft campaign plan for General Franks in the eight days following 11 September. Because it effectively was being asked to plan operations for immediate execution, CENTCOM brought members of its planning and operations staffs together under the leadership of the chief operations officer (J-3), Air Force Maj. Gen. Victor G. Renuart Jr.[97] Renuart also relied upon subordinate components, including Third U.S. Army/U.S. Army Central Command (ARCENT), Fifth Fleet/U.S. Navy Central Command, Ninth Air Force/U.S. Central Command Air Forces, and Special Operations Command Central for additional expertise. While the Marines lacked permanent representation, U.S. Marine Forces Pacific soon transformed itself into U.S. Marine Forces Central Command.[98] In addition to providing insight into unique capabilities resident within their parent service, the subordinate air and naval commands planned and executed strategic sealift and airlift, while ARCENT oversaw theater-wide civil engineering, detainee operations, communications, bulk petroleum management, and Special Forces logistical support.[99]

Although the State Department had succeeded in gaining concessions from Pakistan, other regional diplomatic hurdles constrained military options. Uzbekistan, Turkmenistan, and Tajikistan, all of which had recently gained independence from the Russian Federation, needed Moscow's tacit approval before they could host U.S. troops. In addition, the United States had to convince regional leaders to lend their full support. In some cases, the challenge of persuading smaller nations to accept the presence of U.S. troops proved more difficult than obtaining the backing of America's former Cold War adversary. For example, while Uzbekistan's President Islam A. Karimov agreed to allow CIA and U.S. military personnel to transit his country and survey facilities for possible use, he denied requests to launch air and ground attacks from his nation.[100] Karimov's unwillingness stemmed in part from Uzbek security service reports of U.S. Special Forces personnel talking to known opponents of his regime during a joint training exercise in 2000.[101]

---

96. George W. Bush and Junichiro Koizumi, "International Campaign Against Terror Grows," (Remarks, The White House, 25 Sep 2001), https://georgewbush-whitehouse.archives.gov/news/releases/2001/09/20010925-1.html, Hist Files, OEF Study Grp.

97. Interv, Chandler Garcia with Renuart, 31 May 2007, p. 3.

98. Lowery, *U.S. Marines in Afghanistan*, p. 27.

99. Department of the Army (DA) Field Manual (FM) 1, *The Army*, 14 Jun 2001; DoD Dir 5100.1, 1987, sub: *Functions of the Department of Defense and Its Major Components*.

100. David J. Gerleman et al., *Operation Enduring Freedom: Foreign Pledges of Military & Intelligence Support*, Rpt for Cong. 31152 (Washington, D.C.: Congressional Research Service 17 Oct 2001), p. 9.

101. The fact that the U.S. soldiers were Special Forces personnel resonated with Islam A. Karimov because those types of units often led forcible regime changes of Soviet-era satellite states. Interv, Mark J. Reardon, OEF Study Grp, with Col (Ret.) Gilberto Villahermosa, frmr Central Asian Br Ch, CENTCOM CJ–5, 13 Mar 2015, Hist Files, OEF Study Grp.

CENTCOM planners did not have the luxury of concentrating solely on Afghan issues. General Franks decided that U.S. forces would participate—as planned before 11 September 2001—in BRIGHT STAR, a multinational exercise taking place in Egypt from 8 October to 2 November. Although his staff recommended opting out, Franks viewed BRIGHT STAR as an opportunity rather than a distraction. First, he sought to leverage the momentum created by personnel and equipment flowing into the region for the past several weeks. After BRIGHT STAR concluded, key personnel and units could remain in theater to provide security and build or improve port facilities, billeting, airfields, and command and communications nodes rather than return to their home stations. Second, Franks saw BRIGHT STAR as a means of deceiving al-Qaeda about the timing of impending military operations. Finally, American participation demonstrated to regional allies that the United States would not abandon them during a crisis.[102]

Working under these constraints, Renuart's staff quickly produced a draft plan for General Franks to brief Secretary Rumsfeld and the Joint Chiefs on 20 September. The brief did not satisfy the senior military leaders who received it. As Air Force General Richard B. Myers, who would succeed General Shelton as chairman of the Joint Chiefs on 1 October, recalled: "The operation was too light, too dependent on SOF; heavier forces were needed—but such units were difficult to sustain. Others recommended more air power."[103] By the end of the presentation, Franks believed his audience was focusing too narrowly on promoting their own service's parochial interests.[104] Although he did not voice his misgivings, Rumsfeld was also concerned by the early reliance on air strikes and the lack of actionable intelligence. Nonetheless, he recognized that the "requirement to initiate military strikes within a very short time" had been a key limitation to CENTCOM's planning, and he allowed the draft plan to go forward to the White House.[105]

General Franks briefed his plan to the president and vice president at the White House the next day, accompanied by Secretary Rumsfeld, Generals Shelton and Myers, and a senior Special Operations commander, Army Maj. Gen. Dell L. Dailey. Rumsfeld opened by informing Bush and Vice President Richard B. "Dick" Cheney that the plan was a work-in-progress.[106] Franks began by providing an overview of the operational challenges he faced before progressing to a step-by-step explanation of how he envisioned the campaign unfolding, making "it clear the mission in Afghanistan would not be easy."[107] Franks also informed Bush that the Uzbek defense minister, Kodir Ghulomov,

---

102. Wright et al., *A Different Kind of War*, p. 60.

103. Myers with McConnell, *Eyes on the Horizon*, pp. 175–76.

104. Interv, Mark J. Reardon, Col E. J. Degen, and Maj Matthew Smith, OEF Study Grp, with Gen (Ret.) Tommy R. Franks, frmr CENTCOM Cdr, 4 Dec 2015, Hist Files, OEF Study Grp.

105. Feith, *War and Decision*, p. 63. Feith takes this quote directly from a memo he drafted for Secretary Rumsfeld, sub: Briefing President on Operational Plan, 20 Sep 2001.

106. Rumsfeld, *Known and Unknown*, p. 371.

107. Bush, *Decision Points*, p. 194.

was willing to let the United States use the former Soviet Karshi Khanabad Air Base in southern Uzbekistan. This offer did not come free. The Uzbeks wanted not only compensation in the form of military equipment and money, but also assurances that the Americans would target Islamic Movement of Uzbekistan fighters working with the Taliban.[108] President Bush ended the meeting by asking General Franks when the plan could be executed. Franks replied that, "in about two weeks we'll have the required support from the nations in the region."[109] Despite the unfinished state of the plan, Bush ordered the military to launch an air campaign and insert SOF simultaneously in two weeks' time.[110]

The Pentagon originally named the planned campaign INFINITE JUSTICE, following the precedent of previous efforts in Afghanistan. The 1998 cruise missile strike on al-Qaeda training camps—in retaliation for the bombings of U.S. embassies in Kenya and Tanzania—had been dubbed INFINITE REACH; a proposed follow-on strike was named INFINITE RESOLVE.[111] The name did not last, as the Pentagon soon learned it might offend allies whose Muslim populations believed that only God is capable of dispensing infinite justice.[112] On 24 September, General Franks proposed Operation ENDURING FREEDOM (OEF), which pleased Secretary Rumsfeld and earned White House approval.[113] OEF would refer to both the imminent actions in Afghanistan and to operations in the Global War on Terrorism as a whole. Operations in specific theaters were to be named OEF-Afghanistan, OEF-Philippines, OEF-Horn of Africa, and so forth. Only after Operation IRAQI FREEDOM began in 2003 did OEF become synonymous with the war in Afghanistan.

Even as the president approved CENTCOM's initial course of action, the CIA continued to plan for its role in unconventional warfare operations. On 21 September, the same day the White House hosted General Franks, Director Tenet hosted a brainstorming session at Langley to provide updated guidance to CIA teams preparing to depart for Afghanistan. The attendees shared Secretary Rumsfeld's concerns that the United States had to avoid the appearance of waging a war against Islam or being an occupying force like the Soviets. They also feared that the collateral effect of U.S. strikes against the Taliban could cause tens of thousands of Afghans to flee eastward into Pakistan, where their presence would potentially destabilize the Musharraf regime.[114] CIA officials further agreed that it was important to unite opposition groups that historically had competed against each other, and to leverage the

---

108. Myers with McConnell, *Eyes on the Horizon*, pp. 176–77.

109. Franks with McConnell, *American Soldier*, pp. 280–81.

110. Baker, *Days of Fire*, pp. 158–59. For progression, see Myers with McConnell, *Eyes on the Horizon*, pp. 180–81; Shelton with Levinson and McConnell, *Without Hesitation*, pp. 447–48.

111. *9/11 Report*, p. 336 and endnote p. 85.

112. Elizabeth Becker, "A Nation Challenged; Renaming an Operation to Fit the Mood," *New York Times*, 26 Sep 2001, https://www.nytimes.com/2001/09/26/us/a-nation-challenged-renaming-an-operation-to-fit-the-mood.html, Hist Files, OEF Study Grp.

113. Myers with McConnell, *Eyes on the Horizon*, p. 181.

114. Woodward, *Bush at War*, pp. 114–15.

traditional Afghan distrust of outsiders against the Arabs who constituted al-Qaeda's ranks. Finally, they hoped to capitalize on Afghan resentment toward the Taliban, especially among ethnic and religious minorities such as the Shia Hazara, whom the Taliban actively persecuted.[115]

However, the meeting also exposed differences of opinion within the agency. On the one hand, officers familiar with the United Front noted that near-term results could only be achieved by supporting organized Uzbek and Tajik opposition groups in the north. On the other hand, the Islamabad station chief, Robert L. Grenier, argued that the CIA should invest time and effort in establishing dissident Pashtun groups in the south. A keen student of the centuries-old ethnic tensions dominating the region, Grenier believed that civil war would result if the Tajiks and Uzbeks seized control of Kabul. Rather than aid the United Front, Grenier felt that a lengthy bombing campaign aimed at weakening the Taliban, while CIA and Special Forces teams organized Pashtun dissident groups, was the only logical course of action.[116]

The discussions held at Langley prompted Director Tenet to propose an alternative course of action at a 23 September Security Council meeting. Tenet raised the possibility that U.S. actions should focus on splitting the Taliban from al-Qaeda. By holding off against the Taliban during the opening air attacks and focusing on al-Qaeda's highly trained Brigade 055 instead, the United States might be able to pit moderate Taliban leaders against Omar. This approach elaborated on an earlier State Department proposal to find "subtle ways to encourage splits within the leadership" of the Taliban, and received Secretary Powell's support in the meeting.[117] However, Tenet's proposal raised the possibility of disconnects between the Security Council's goals and the plan taking shape at CENTCOM. As a result, General Shelton asked Franks to synchronize the military's plans with the new approach suggested by the CIA.[118]

On 24 September, Station Chief Grenier participated in a three-way teleconference with General Franks and Director Tenet. After stating his concerns about how Pashtuns would react to the United Front overthrowing the Taliban with American support, Grenier asked Franks to revise the proposed targeting list to ensure that the opening attacks devastated the morale of the Taliban leadership. General Franks agreed to hit Taliban political centers of gravity—the enemy's source of strength—during the initial air attacks, with the caveat that the target set would be expanded if the strikes did not quickly generate visible fissures in the Taliban leadership. General Franks also seemed amenable to holding off

---

115. Wright et al., *A Different Kind of War*, p. 12.

116. Grau and Billingsly, *Operation Anaconda*, p. 51.

117. Woodward, *Bush at War*, pp. 123–25; Memo, U.S. Department of State, 14 Sep 2001, sub: Gameplan for Polmil Strategy for Pakistan and Afghanistan.

118. Robert Grenier, *88 Days to Kandahar: A CIA Diary* (New York: Simon & Schuster, 2015), p. 93.

The mountainous terrain known as the Hindu Kush, which runs directly through the center of Afghanistan, increased the complexity of operations in the area. The Afghan mountain range shown here is near the Pakistan border, just south of Tora Bora.

on sending U.S. conventional troops inside Afghanistan until the CIA signaled that their presence was needed.[119]

This last point led to discussions between Secretary Rumsfeld and Director Tenet to determine how operational command and control would migrate from the CIA to the military as the campaign progressed in Afghanistan. Although the agency depended on U.S. military air power from the onset, the paramilitary teams deployed to Afghanistan and Pakistan would initially have the lead in coordinating with Afghan opposition forces. That responsibility would shift to Franks and his CENTCOM headquarters once growing numbers of Special Forces personnel and conventional military units arrived.[120] Secretary Rumsfeld remained engaged on this issue by continually promoting close cooperation between CENTCOM and the CIA.[121]

CENTCOM continued to refine its campaign plan after the president's initial approval and even after the first CIA team arrived in Afghanistan on 26 September. On 30 September, Special Operations Command Central

---

119. Ibid., pp. 95–96.

120. Although the former secretary of defense does not pinpoint the exact date, he discusses it just before talking about a chance meeting with California's Rep. Dana Rohrabacher on 26 September. Rumsfeld, *Known and Unknown*, pp. 374–75.

121. Interv, Mark J. Reardon and Maj Colin J. Williams, OEF Study Grp, with Gen (Ret.) Richard B. Myers, frmr CJCS, 14 Mar 2015, Hist Files, OEF Study Grp. Myers noted that Secretary Rumsfeld expended significant effort to ensure that U.S. Central Intelligence Agency (CIA) efforts were aligned with plans being developed by General Tommy R. Franks.

briefed a more aggressive unconventional warfare approach to Franks aimed at removing the Taliban from power. They acknowledged the CIA's conflicting views on opposition groups by presenting a range of options that included (1) placing the main unconventional warfare effort in the south, (2) weighting the main unconventional warfare effort in the north, (3) placing equal emphasis in the north and south, and (4) limiting U.S. involvement to indirectly aiding indigenous opposition groups from bases outside Afghanistan. Franks approved the northern option because the main opposition groups were located in that region and the Special Forces units tentatively slated to deploy there were very familiar with implementing unconventional warfare.[122] The Special Forces teams, however, would not enter Afghanistan until CIA officers laid the groundwork for their arrival.[123]

A week later, on 7 October 2001, American and British warplanes began combat operations before CENTCOM had a full, four-phase campaign plan in place. Nevertheless, strategy development continued in Washington and at the CENTCOM headquarters in Tampa even as operations unfolded. This later became known as adaptive planning.[124] On 16 October, the National Security Council approved a strategy for Afghanistan that had been drafted by Rumsfeld's staff within the Office of the Secretary of Defense. Although the strategy called for integrating military, diplomatic, covert, humanitarian, and financial efforts, the strategy clearly emphasized using military force to "eliminate Al-Qaida [sic] leadership and forces" and "terminate the rule of the Taliban and their leadership."[125] The Security Council especially emphasized the antipersonnel focus of the campaign: "Al-Qaida's [sic] and the Taliban's main assets are people. They must be destroyed."[126] To this end, the strategy prescribed using "incentives and disincentives—money, food, military equipment, supplies; air strikes, etc." to get "any and all Afghan tribes and factions" to eliminate enemy personnel and military capabilities.[127] At the strategic level, the Bush administration hoped that military success in Afghanistan would produce intelligence "for the worldwide campaign against terrorism" and show that "harboring terrorism will be punished severely."[128]

Operationally, the strategy sketched a northern-focused approach like that previously approved by General Franks. It called for ground liaison teams to encourage their northern Afghan partners to establish a land bridge to Uzbekistan, clear enemy forces, surround Kabul, and sever Taliban lines of command north of the capital, in that order. The paper also outlined a diplomatic message for the United Front: respect human rights in the conduct of the campaign, and allow the future of Kabul—and by implication, the post-

---

122. Eric Blehm, *The Only Thing Worth Dying For: How Eleven Green Berets Forged a New Afghanistan* (New York: HarperCollins, 2010), p. 40.

123. Rumsfeld, *Known and Unknown*, p. 375.

124. Interv, Chandler Garcia with Renuart, 31 May 2007, p. 3.

125. Draft memo, Ofc of the Sec Def, 16 Oct 2001, sub: U.S. Strategy in Afghanistan.

126. Ibid.

127. Ibid.

128. Ibid.

Taliban government—to be decided by a political process that represented the interests of all Afghans, not merely the Pashtun majority. In the Pashtun south, where the United States did not yet have adequate intelligence or partners, it was "critical that CIA and Defense Department accelerate the process of establishing on-the-ground contacts." The National Security Council paper identified Pakistan and the exiled Afghan king Zahir Shah as possible channels for influencing Pashtuns. It also proposed the following message for the Pashtun tribes: the United States was prepared to give them the same support it was lending the United Front, the United States was "committed to preserving Kabul as a capital for all Afghans," and they (the tribes) needed to join the U.S. coalition to balance the United Front.[129]

The Security Council paper also laid out the American intentions for post-Taliban Afghanistan. In principle, President Bush understood that stability was necessary to prevent Afghanistan from becoming "yet again a haven for terrorist criminals," and that Afghanistan's recent history showed "that we should not just simply leave after a military objective has been achieved."[130] Yet the paper argued that "[t]he U.S. should not commit to any post-Taliban military involvement, since the U.S. will be heavily engaged in the anti-terrorism effort worldwide."[131] Thus, the administration supported deploying an international peacekeeping force to Kabul, but nowhere else in the country and not with U.S. troop contributions. Similarly, it would provide near-term humanitarian relief and long-term "economic support for reconstruction within an all-Afghan political framework," but not take charge of any state-building mission.[132] Although the administration decided on a broad-based coalition government for Afghanistan as early as 14 September, Washington decision makers felt America lacked the influence to mandate a solution, preferring instead to consider the wishes of its international supporters.[133] Therefore, the administration argued that "U.S. preference for a specific outcome ought not to paralyze U.S. efforts to oust Al-Qaida [sic] and the Taliban." As a result, the initial strategic goal for the post-conflict environment remained vague and limited: "Take steps to contribute to a more stable post-Taliban Afghanistan."[134]

---

129. Ibid.

130. President Bush, "Prime Time News Conference" (Remarks, East Room, 11 Oct 2001), https://georgewbush-whitehouse.archives.gov/news/releases/2001/10/20011011-7.html, Hist Files, OEF Study Grp. On the significance of these comments, see David E. Sanger, "A Nation Challenged: News Analysis; A New, Uneasy Burden," *New York Times*, 12 Oct 2001, https://www.nytimes.com/2001/10/12/world/a-nation-challenged-news-analysis-a-new-uneasy-burden.html, Hist Files, OEF Study Grp.

131. Draft memo, Ofc of the Sec Def, 16 Oct 2001, sub: U.S. Strategy in Afghanistan.

132. Ibid.

133. The State Department set out this goal as early as 14 September: "bring together non-Taliban Afghans and [the] Northern Alliance to form [a] broad-based coalition government with broad appeal across geographic and ethnic lines." Memo, U.S. Department of State, 14 Sep 2001, sub: Gameplan for Polmil Strategy for Pakistan and Afghanistan.

134. Draft memo, Ofc of the Sec Def, 16 Oct 2001, sub: U.S. Strategy in Afghanistan.

In rugged Paktiya Province, near the border with Pakistan, the high peaks rapidly descend to create severe valleys running north and south of the Hindu Kush.

As the first Special Forces teams entered the country on 19 October, the Office of the Secretary of Defense and the National Security Council returned to their efforts to update existing guidance focusing on near-term events. In response, by 1 November CENTCOM refined planning for Phase II, which broadly aimed to "destroy, disrupt, [and] degrade Taliban and Al Qaida [*sic*]."[135] The operational objectives for Phase II now included maintaining the internal stability of regional partners, building a coalition to conduct military operations in Afghanistan, significantly reducing the threat posed by al-Qaeda, compelling the Taliban to cease harboring terrorists, providing humanitarian relief to innocent Afghans, and setting the conditions for Phase III.[136] Given that three of the five objectives were independent of U.S. military forces and required diplomatic coordination beyond General Franks' scope of responsibilities, the plan reflected CENTCOM's optimistic opinion of its likely success.

As air strikes continued to pound a dwindling number of Taliban targets, CENTCOM now envisioned Phase II unfolding in three stages. Stage 1, "Initial Strike Operations," had consisted of air operations designed to "to eliminate air/air defense threats, disrupt Taliban planning and communications, and set conditions for follow-on targeting of Taliban and Al Qaida [*sic*] leadership." It also referred to the insertion of CIA teams when noting "an embedded direct action operation to gain actionable intelligence and display U.S. capabilities and resolve." Stage 2, referred to as "Continued Operations," marked the

---

135. Combined Forces Command (CFC) Operation Order (OPORD) 02–02, Phase II-Stage 2 Continued Operations, CENTCOM, 1 Nov 2001, sec. 1.B, Hist Files, OEF Study Grp.

136. Ibid., sec. 3.A.

introduction of SOF tasked with conducting unconventional warfare and "direct action against the Taliban and Al Qaida [sic] centers of gravity in Afghanistan," as well as aerially delivered humanitarian assistance. Although CENTCOM deferred detailed examination of Stage 3 until developments warranted such an effort, Franks' planners began looking more closely at setting conditions for Decisive Operations in Phase III and "expanding counter terrorist operations AOR [Area of Responsibility] wide."[137] Likewise, fruitful Phase IV planning would have to wait for the convening of an internationally recognized conference chartered to determine Afghanistan's post-Taliban political future.

The eight primary operational tasks set out for the Afghanistan campaign at this stage reflected a mix of conventional and unconventional approaches to warfighting. The former received top priority with U.S. military, coalition troops, and proxy military forces alike focusing on degrading and destroying al-Qaeda and the senior Taliban leadership. CENTCOM deemed the latter necessary in order to eliminate the Taliban as a battlefield opponent and pave the way for a new form of Afghan government. Five of the remaining seven tasks were directly or indirectly related to the United Front. These included CENTCOM plans to employ the United Front to secure a land corridor from Mazar-e Sharif to Uzbekistan, the northern cities of Taluqan and Kunduz, Afghanistan's capital city of Kabul, and the eastern city of Jalalabad. CENTCOM also sought to create "operationally viable" opposition groups in southern Afghanistan. The final pair of tasks focused on the civil-military realm, which included delivering sufficient humanitarian assistance to meet the immediate needs of the Afghan people and initiating efforts to promote post-conflict stability and the establishment of a friendly Afghan government.[138]

Thus, as U.S. SOF entered Afghanistan, CENTCOM expected to wage a rapid campaign in comparison to what transpired after Soviet troops invaded in 1979. Instead of being tied up fighting al-Qaeda for years on end, General Franks anticipated a campaign that opened in late fall 2001, followed by an operational pause lasting several months due to severe winter conditions, before resuming full bore in spring 2002. Although U.S. military leaders did not prefer to slow operations during the winter months, they felt it would take some time to provide the United Front with additional training and develop anti-Taliban partners in the Pashtun. By implication, they also believed the winter months provided more time to "cultivate attitudes" among local partners who favored U.S. and international interests. As it happened, events began unfolding in dizzying succession beginning in mid-November, CENTCOM soon found itself scrambling to adjust its campaign plan to reflect battlefield realities.

---

137. Ibid.
138. Ibid., sec. 3.B.2.

The September 11th Attacks and the U.S. Army

The sudden and unexpected nature of the September 11th terrorist attacks severely tested the Army's existing readiness and force management framework. As news of the terrorist strike spread, Army personnel from all three components flocked to both the World Trade Center and the Pentagon to provide security and assist civilian first responders. In stricken New York City, 1,500 Army National Guard soldiers made their way directly to the site of the shattered World Trade Center—soon to be known as Ground Zero—before nightfall.[139] The active duty and reserve forces partnership and affiliation programs leading up to 11 September 2001 were built around a framework of overseas, active-duty-led operations, not the need to react to a major domestic attack. As a result, Joint Forces Command at Norfolk, Virginia—the joint force headquarters responsible for resourcing military units for operations—did not formally respond to the World Trade Center attack until 13 September 2001.[140] On that same day, eighty-five Army Reserve soldiers from 1st Lt. Hector S. Martinez's 311th Quartermaster Company (Mortuary Affairs) deployed to Fort Myer, Virginia, from Aguadilla, Puerto Rico, to aid the 54th Quartermaster Company of Fort Lee, Virginia, with recovering and processing human remains at the Pentagon.[141]

Developments in the aftermath of 11 September inexorably propelled the entire Army toward war. In New York City, 8,000 National Guardsmen were activated before nightfall on 11 September.[142] By the following morning, thousands more National Guard and Army Reserve soldiers, knowing that phone lines were inoperable and transportation was difficult, began to muster at their armories. National Guard soldiers stationed at key airports provided many Americans with the first visible indication of heightened security. The term "Force Protection" also took on real meaning at Army installations as commanders took steps to safeguard soldiers, their families, equipment, and supplies from a follow-on terrorist strike.

On 14 September, President Bush declared a National State of Emergency, "by Reason of Certain Terrorist Attacks." In doing so, he signed Executive Order 13223 invoking Section 12302 of Title 10 of the United States Code which enabled the federal government's right to call into service any reserve unit, and any individual member of the Ready Reserve not assigned to a unit, for a period not to exceed twenty-four months.[143] The Joint Chiefs estimated

---

139. John S. Brown, *Kevlar Legions: The Transformation of the U.S. Army, 1989–2005* (Washington, D.C.: U.S. Army Center of Military History, 2011), p. 212.

140. Joint Forces Command , Execution Order , 131800RSEP01, sub: EXORD for DoD Support to FEMA for Consequence Management in Response to Terrorist Attacks in NYC, Hist Files, OEF Study Grp.

141. Kathryn Roe Coker et al., *The Role of the Army Reserve in the 11 September Attacks: The Pentagon* (Ft. McPherson, Ga.: Office of Army Reserve History, 2003), pp. 124–32.

142. Brown, *Kevlar Legions*, p. 212.

143. "Executive Order 13223 as of 14 September 2001," *Federal Register* 66, no. 181 (18 Sep 2001), https://www.govinfo.gov/content/pkg/FR-2001-09-18/pdf/01-23359.pdf, Hist Files, OEF Study Grp.

the need to activate 50,000 reservists for the purpose of providing "port operations, medical support, engineer support, general civil support, and homeland defense."[144]

The mobilization requirements were based on the personnel needed for improved homeland defense. The declared State of Emergency did not set limits on the mobilization or employment of troops other than those outlined under existing U.S. Code, which authorized up to one million reservists for up to twenty-four months. Although the National State of Emergency expired annually, the president could renew it as many times as the strategic situation dictated, which gave him sustained access to the reserve forces and the supplemental war funding it enabled. This declaration of emergency, written with homeland defense in mind, would become the baseline document that authorized the mobilization of more than 900,000 reservists over the next fifteen years for combat.[145]

The sight of growing numbers of guardsmen and reservists patrolling airports, harbors, and other high-value sites provided a visible reassurance to the American public as CENTCOM initiated planning for a retaliatory strike against al-Qaeda bases in Afghanistan. The call up of reservists and guardsmen, initially conducted under the auspices of the Global War on Terrorism, were consolidated on 25 September as Operation NOBLE EAGLE. The majority of domestic operations were sourced from the National Guard, since Title 32 of the U.S. Code allowed for the National Guard to respond to potential civil disorder without violating the Posse Comitatus Act of 1878.[146] Indeed, nearly 28,000 reserve component soldiers—about the size of two divisions—were mobilized and deployed by November 2001.[147] Although many mobilized reservists and guardsmen were released after intelligence analysts later indicated a reduction of immediate post-attack threat levels, missions such as the New York National Guard's EMPIRE SHIELD, designed to

---

144. At a 14 September 2001 press briefing, the military services identified requirements for 35,500 reservists: 13,000 Air Force, 10,000 Army, 3,000 Navy, 7,500 Marine Corps, and 2,000 Coast Guard. DoD, "Partial Mobilization of National Guard, Reserve Authorized," Press Opns News Release 426-01, 14 Sep 2001, Hist Files, OEF Study Grp; "Military to Call up 50,000 Reservists," CBS News, 26 Sep 2001, https://www.cbsnews.com/news/military-to-call-up-50000-reservists/, Hist Files, OEF Study Grp.

145. DoD Mobilization Rpt, 31 March 2015, http://www.defense.gov/Portals/1/Documents/Mobilization-Weekly-Report-150331.pdf [page discontinued], Hist Files, OEF Study Grp. Sydney J. Freedberg Jr., "Active vs. Guard: An Avoidable Pentagon War," Breaking Defense, 28 Jun 2013, https://breakingdefense.com/2013/06/active-vs-guard-an-avoidable-pentagon-war/, Hist Files, OEF Study Grp.

146. *Posse Comitatus Act of 1878*, 18 U.S.C. § 1385(1878), original at 20 Stat. 152(1878). The act prevents the federal government from using the Title 10 active military in a domestic law enforcement role within the territorial borders of the United States.

147. News Call, "The Army Responds to Terrorist Attacks," *Army Magazine* (Nov 2001): 59; Interv, Lt Col Victor Sundquist, OEF Study Grp, with Lt Col Kelly A. Lelito, 9 Jul 2015, Hist Files, OEF Study Grp; Interv, Lt Col Victor Sundquist, OEF Study Grp, with Col (Ret) Stewart Brown, 10 Jul 2015, Hist Files, OEF Study Grp; Interv, Lt Col Victor Sundquist, OEF Study Grp, with Maj (Ret.) James Larry Kendrick Jr., 6 Apr 2015, Hist Files, OEF Study Grp.

prevent terrorist attacks in New York City, remained in force indefinitely.[148] These sustained commitments, however, created competition between domestic requirements, rotational peacekeeping commitments, and combat rotations for the Global War on Terrorism within a force pool of finite size.

PREPARING FOR BATTLE

The United States could not address the possibility of further al-Qaeda attacks effectively by adopting a wholly defensive stance. On 16 September, the Joint Staff issued a warning order to the Department of the Army alerting the XVIII Airborne Corps, consisting of the 3d Infantry Division (Mechanized), 10th Mountain Division, 82d Airborne Division, and 101st Airborne Division (Air Assault), to be prepared to take part in "an imminent combat mission."[149] The Joint Staff selected the XVIII Airborne Corps because all of its subordinate elements maintained specially designated units, from a company to a full brigade, ready to deploy on little or no notice.

In addition to using XVIII Airborne Corps, CENTCOM envisioned a central role for SOF in Afghanistan. General Franks relied on Air Force General Charles R. Holland, commanding the United States Special Operations Command located adjacent to Franks' headquarters in Tampa, Florida, to spearhead the upcoming campaign. In addition to his other responsibilities, Holland oversaw General Dailey's dedicated counterterrorist command, also located at MacDill Air Force Base. Drawing from special operators provided by the Army, Air Force, and Navy, elements from the Army's 160th Aviation Regiment (Special Operations)—commonly referred to as the 160th Special Operations Aviation Regiment, or 160th SOAR—and the 75th Ranger Regiment, along with National Security Agency and CIA elements, Dailey's Florida-based headquarters transformed itself into a joint element designated as Task Force (TF) SWORD. The responsibilities of TF SWORD included neutralizing weapons of mass destruction and eliminating or capturing high-ranking al-Qaeda and Taliban leaders.[150]

Holland's other assets consisted of U.S. Army Special Operations Command at Fort Bragg, North Carolina; Air Force Special Operations Command at Hurlburt Field, Florida; and the Naval Special Warfare

---

148. "New York National Guard Joint Task Force Empire Shield," New York Division of Military and Naval Affairs, https://dmna.ny.gov/press/NY_JTFES_Fact_Sheet.pdf, Hist Files, OEF Study Grp.

149. Thomas E. Ricks, "Pentagon Issues Order to Elite Units in Infantry," *Washington Post*, 17 Sep 2001, http://jime.ieej.or.jp/htm/extra/2001/09/13/20010917/wp-05.html, Hist Files, OEF Study Grp.

150. Ballard, Lamm, and Wood, *From Kabul to Baghdad and Back*, pp. 55–56; Fred J. Pushies, *Night Stalkers: 160th Special Operations Aviation Regiment (Airborne)* (St. Paul, Minn.: Zenith Press, 2005), p. 123; Backgrounder, Lt Col Pete Blaber, Cdr, Advanced Force Opns, Opn ANACONDA, 1 Mar 2012, p. 2, American Enterprise Institute, https://www.aei.org/press/operation-anaconda/, Hist Files, OEF Study Grp.

Command at Naval Amphibious Base Coronado, California.[151] All of these headquarters interacted with CENTCOM through Special Operations Command Central Command headed by Rear Admiral Albert J. Calland.[152] Lt. Gen. Bryan D. Brown's U.S. Army Special Operations Command provided the bulk of Special Operations Command Central's available resources. In particular, the 5th Special Forces Group, 1st Special Forces Command, commanded by Col. John P. Mulholland, would become Brown's primary force provider. In addition to the 5th Special Forces Group and 160th SOAR at Fort Campbell, Kentucky, U.S. Army Special Operations Command began preparing the 75th Ranger Regiment, 4th Psychological Operations Group, 528th Support Battalion (Special Operations), 112th Signal Battalion, and 96th Civil Affairs Battalion for ENDURING FREEDOM.

Some Special Operations units were already in theater as a result of the decision to go forward with BRIGHT STAR. Holland supported U.S. Army Special Operations Command participation in NATURAL FIRE, a joint United States—Jordanian Special Operations exercise held during the same timeframe. Forces in this exercise included Lt. Col. David G. Fox's 2d Battalion, 5th Special Forces Group; Company A, 2d Battalion, 75th Ranger Regiment from Fort Lewis, Washington; a Navy SEAL (Sea Air and Land) platoon, and elements of the Fort Campbell–based 3d Battalion, 160th SOAR. In addition to personnel in Jordan, elements of Lt. Col. Christopher K. Haas' 1st Battalion, 5th Special Forces Group, were in Kuwait as part of a regularly scheduled force rotation.[153]

CENTCOM's Special Operations Command began making major decisions affecting the upcoming campaign before CENTCOM settled on a specific course of action. On 13 September, Mulholland learned that 5th Special Forces Group would deploy as a Combined Joint Special Operations Task Force (CJSOTF) rather than a service-component headquarters.[154] His unit, designated as CJSOTF-North, had responsibility for Afghanistan north of the prominent Hindu Kush. Calland planned to form a second Joint Special Operations Task Force (JSOTF) to oversee operations south of the Hindu Kush once the Taliban were forced out of Kabul.[155] His decision to

---

151. John Partin et al., *U.S. Special Operations Command History, 1987–2007* (MacDill Air Force Base, Fla.: U.S. Special Operations Command History and Research Office, 2007), pp. 18–20. The Marine Corps did not establish a Special Operations Command until 2006.

152. Dana Priest and William M. Arkin, "'Top Secret America:' A Look at the Military's Joint Special Operations Command," *Washington Post*, 2 Sep 2011, https://www.washingtonpost.com/world/national-security/top-secret-america-a-look-at-the-militarys-joint-special-operations-command/2011/08/30/gIQAvYuAxJ_story.html, Hist Files, OEF Study Grp.

153. Interv, Terry Beckenbaugh, CSI, with Lt Col Donald Bolduc, frmr Ops Ofcr, 2d Bn, 5th Special Forces (SF) Grp, 23 Apr 2007, pp. 19–20, Hist Files, OEF Study Grp; Charles H. Briscoe et al. *Weapon of Choice: ARSOF in Afghanistan* (Fort Leavenworth, Kans.: Combat Studies Institute Press, 2003), p. 58; Interv, John McCool, CSI, with Maj David King, frmr Intel Ofcr, 3d Bn, 160th Special Opns Avn Rgt, 6 Oct 2005, pp. 3–4, Hist Files, OEF Study Grp.

154. Interv, Peter Connors, CSI, with Brig Gen John Mulholland, frmr Cdr, 5th SF Grp, 7 May 2007, p. 4, Hist Files, OEF Study Grp.

155. Briscoe et al., *Weapon of Choice*, p. 54.

The canalized terrain of Afghanistan's lush agricultural valleys had few suitable entry and exit points for ground combat vehicles.

defer the creation of a second JSOTF meant that 5th Special Forces Group would "command all SOF that would fight inside Afghanistan" for an indeterminate period.[156] Colonel Mulholland afterward admitted that the unprecedented responsibility was "worrisome to me because we had never trained to operate at what [was] an operational level of warfare."[157] The Special Operations Command, Joint Forces Command, of Norfolk, Virginia, addressed his concerns by sending a dozen instructors to teach Mulholland's staff how to function as a CJSOTF.[158]

FLESHING OUT THE THEATER FRAMEWORK

Lt. Gen. Paul T. Mikolashek's headquarters, based in Fort McPherson, Georgia, acted as both ARCENT and Third United States Army, reflecting the inherent dual-hatted nature of the commands working for General Franks. As the commanding general of ARCENT, Mikolashek served as Franks' primary ground-component headquarters. As the commanding general of Third Army, he reported to his immediate superiors at U.S. Army Forces Command (FORSCOM), also located on Fort McPherson. FORSCOM was the conduit for the Army to provide personnel and equipment to all CENTCOM components, including ARCENT.

---

156. Ibid., p. 53.

157. Interv, John D. Gresham, Defense Media Network, with Lt Gen John F. Mulholland, frmr Cdr 5th SF Grp, 25 May 2010, http://www.defensemedianetwork.com/stories/interview-lt-gen-john-f-mulholland-jr-usa/, Hist Files, OEF Study Grp.

158. Briscoe et al., *Weapon of Choice*, pp. 54–56.

Although Third Army/ARCENT numbered 1,100 personnel during the 1991 Gulf War, it gradually shrank to 246 active component spaces following several downsizing initiatives implemented during the Clinton administration.[159] Within twenty-four hours following the September 11th attacks, Army Chief of Staff General Eric K. Shinseki authorized an increase in Third Army/ARCENT to 510 officers and enlisted personnel.[160] Translating authorizations to on-hand personnel would take several months due to constraints imposed by the existing assignment system and reserve mobilization process.

General Mikolashek faced the pressing task of creating an infrastructure to sustain the campaign well in advance of his own headquarters deploying into theater. Elements from the 377th Support Command (Theater) and the 335th Signal Command (Theater) initiated that process when they arrived at Camp Doha, Kuwait, in October 2001 to augment ARCENT's forward headquarters and the active component 54th Signal Battalion.[161] The deployment of these reserve units enabled military leaders to shape the network and logistical footprint of the region and to properly set the theater for future operations.

The U.S. military split this logistical and communication framework into two regional approaches—northern and southern—to provide multiple avenues for sustaining the effort in Afghanistan. The two logistical nodes would prove indispensable to the Army's ability to build and sustain combat power in Afghanistan and later in Iraq. They also enabled American and coalition forces to redeploy troops and equipment quickly and efficiently once the wars ended. To establish the southern logistical approach, the 377th Support Command (Theater) formed Combined/Joint Logistics Over-the-Shore sites.[162] By leveraging the formidable capabilities available at Kaiserslautern Army Depot and Ramstein Air Base, Germany, the 21st Support Command (Theater) established a northern logistical route consisting of air and rail corridors designed to funnel both humanitarian relief and combat support to CENTCOM forces in Afghanistan. During the first six months of ENDURING FREEDOM, transport planes hauled 2.2 million humanitarian rations, about 770 metric tons of wheat, nearly 69,000 blankets, and over 2,500 precision-guided container delivery systems to Afghanistan using the northern route.[163]

---

159. Presentation, Third Army/U.S. Army Central Command (ARCENT), sub: Command and Control Enhancement Program, slides 4–9, Hist Files, OEF Study Grp.

160. Presentation, Third Army/ARCENT, 121800Z Sep 2001, sub: Personnel Status, Hist Files, OEF Study Grp.

161. John A. Bonin, U.S. Army Forces Central Command in Afghanistan and the Arabian Gulf during Operation Enduring Freedom: 11 September 2001–11 March 2003, Monograph 1–03 (Carlisle, Penn.: Army Heritage Center Foundation, 2003), p. 11.

162. Annual History (Hist) Rpt, 377th Theater Support Command, p. 3, Hist Files, OEF Study Grp.

163. Sue Harper and Gregory Jones, "Supporting Afghanistan from Europe: U.S. Army Europe's 21st Theater Support Command," *AUSA Army Magazine* (Aug 2002): 1, Hist Files, OEF Study Grp.

While the 377th and 21st Support Commands (Theater) assumed responsibility for the twin logistical footprints, the 335th Signal Command (Theater) took control of the Coalition Forces Land Component Command (CFLCC) and ARCENT-centralized network management responsibilities in theater. At the same time, the 335th also assumed responsibility for Third Army's command, control, communications, and computers operations in Afghanistan.[164] The 335th's initial deployment package included fifty augmentees for ARCENT's forward-stationed 54th Signal Battalion, but it would grow to several hundred reserve soldiers by the end of 2002.[165] The 335th would accept ongoing operational responsibility for "managing the telecommunications infrastructures for Southwest Asia and the Horn of Africa—an area of responsibility covering twenty-five countries from Kenya to Kazakhstan, and Egypt to Pakistan."[166]

Initial Deployment of Conventional Forces

Although CENTCOM envisioned using conventional ground forces in the opening phase of the campaign, the Army found itself providing infantry units to secure Special Operations bases in theater long before combat operations commenced. The 10th Mountain Division from Fort Drum, New York, led by Maj. Gen. Franklin L. "Buster" Hagenbeck, learned on 21 September that Lt. Col. Paul J. LaCamera's 1st Battalion, 87th Infantry, would take part in the security force mission.[167] LaCamera's battalion remained behind when the bulk of the 1st Brigade, along with part of Hagenbeck's staff, deployed several weeks earlier to Kosovo under Hagenbeck's deputy, Brig. Gen. Keith M. Huber.[168] In addition, the 1st Brigade detached its 2d Battalion, 22d Infantry, to Bosnia and Herzegovina. The division's 2d Brigade, under which LaCamera's unit temporarily served, sent its 2d Battalion, 87th Infantry, to the United Nations' Multinational Force and Observers mission in Sinai.

The 101st Division's commanding general, Maj. Gen. Richard A. Cody, faced a similar situation upon learning his unit would also fill security force requirements. Given that the 101st Airborne Division rotated brigades through installation support, training, and deployment-ready cycles, it possessed only one available brigade combat team. Cody alerted Col. Francis J. Wiercinski's 3d Brigade for the mission. Wiercinski's 2d Battalion, 187th Infantry, commanded by Lt. Col. Charles A. Preysler, was already getting ready to assume the Multinational Force and Observers mission in the

---

164. Annual Hist Rpt, 2003, 335th Theater Signal Cmd, p. 9, Hist Files, OEF Study Grp.

165. Bonin, U.S. Army Forces Central Command in Afghanistan and the Arabian Gulf During Operation Enduring Freedom, p. 11.

166. Annual Hist Rpt, 2003, 335th Theater Signal Cmd, p. 9; Mobilization and Deployment Database, G-3 Opns and Contingency Planning Div, Hist Files, OEF Study Grp.

167. Interv, John McCool, CSI, with Maj Roger A. Crombie, frmr Cdr, Co A, 1st Bn, 87th Inf, 10th Mountain (Mtn) Div, 30 Mar 2006, p. 3, Hist Files, OEF Study Grp.

168. Presentation, Coalition Forces Land Component Command (CFLCC) (Forward) Transition Bfg, slides 2–3, 25 Jan 2002, Hist Files, OEF Study Grp.

Sinai.[169] In early October, the Army mobilized the Arkansas Army National Guard's 2d Battalion, 153d Infantry, to assume the Sinai tasking, enabling the 3d Brigade to deploy all three of its infantry battalions to Afghanistan.[170]

In October, as the magnitude of the challenge facing the Army after 11 September became more apparent, General Shinseki assembled key commanders to discuss the difficulties of creating a force prepared to fight an extended campaign in multiple theaters. Following the conference, Shinseki began crafting a set of instructions that would take the Army from its peacetime footing and transform it into a wartime force. All of the Army's plans and programs now had to reflect the fact that the United States was at war. It would take time to reorient both national policy and the Army bureaucracy's mindset, which meant that for the foreseeable future other units would encounter the same hurdles facing the 10th Mountain Division and 101st Airborne Division's 3d Brigade.

OPENING MOVES

The process by which U.S. forces moved into position to execute CENTCOM's campaign plan began soon after General Renuart's staff started work on that document (*Map 1.1*). On 14 September, the DoD sent two tankers carrying 235,000 barrels of maritime diesel fuel to the British atoll of Diego Garcia in the Indian Ocean, along with the transfer of 28,000 tons of jet fuel from NATO stockpiles in Greece to Morón Air Base in southern Spain, where it would be available to tanker and transport aircraft en route to the Middle East.[171] Several days later, President Bush ordered B–52H Stratofortresses and B–1B Lancers, along with their supporting tanker aircraft, to Diego Garcia.[172]

The incoming aircraft would be controlled by the Coalition Air Operations Center located on Prince Sultan Air Base near Riyadh, Saudi Arabia. In accordance with a long-standing agreement with the Saudi government, U.S. strike and reconnaissance aircraft were not permitted to operate from

---

169. Interv, Steven Clay, CSI, with Col Charles A. Preysler, frmr Cdr, 2d Bn, 187th Inf, 8 May 2007, p. 2, Hist Files, OEF Study Grp.

170. "Tribute to Task Force 2-153, Arkansas National Guard," *Congressional Record* 148, pt. 4, 11–24 Apr 2002 (Washington, D.C.: Government Printing Office, 2002), p. 4874.

171. Michael Smith, "Attack 'Could Come This Weekend,'" *Telegraph*, 15 Sep 2001, http://www.telegraph.co.uk/news/worldnews/northamerica/usa/1340597/Attack-could-come-this-weekend.html, Hist Files, OEF Study Grp.

172. The bomber contingent sent to Diego Garcia, designated as the 40th Expeditionary Bombardment Wing, consisted of two squadrons of B–52s from the 2d Bombardment Wing at Barksdale Air Force Base, Louisiana, and the 5th Bombardment Wing at Minot Air Force Base, North Dakota. The B–1B Lancer component was drawn from the 37th Bombardment Squadron at Ellsworth Air Force Base, South Dakota, and the 34th Bombardment Squadron of Mountain Home Air Force Base, Idaho, to form the 28th Expeditionary Bombardment Squadron. See Bill Yenne, *B–52 Stratofortress: The Complete History of the World's Longest Serving and Best Known Bomber* (Minneapolis: Zenith Press, 2012), pp. 149–50; Thomas Withington, *B–1B Lancer Units in Combat* (Oxford: Osprey Publishing, 2007), p. 50; Ellsworth AFB, MilitaryBases.us, http://www.militarybases.us/air-force/ellsworth-afb/, Hist Files, OEF Study Grp.

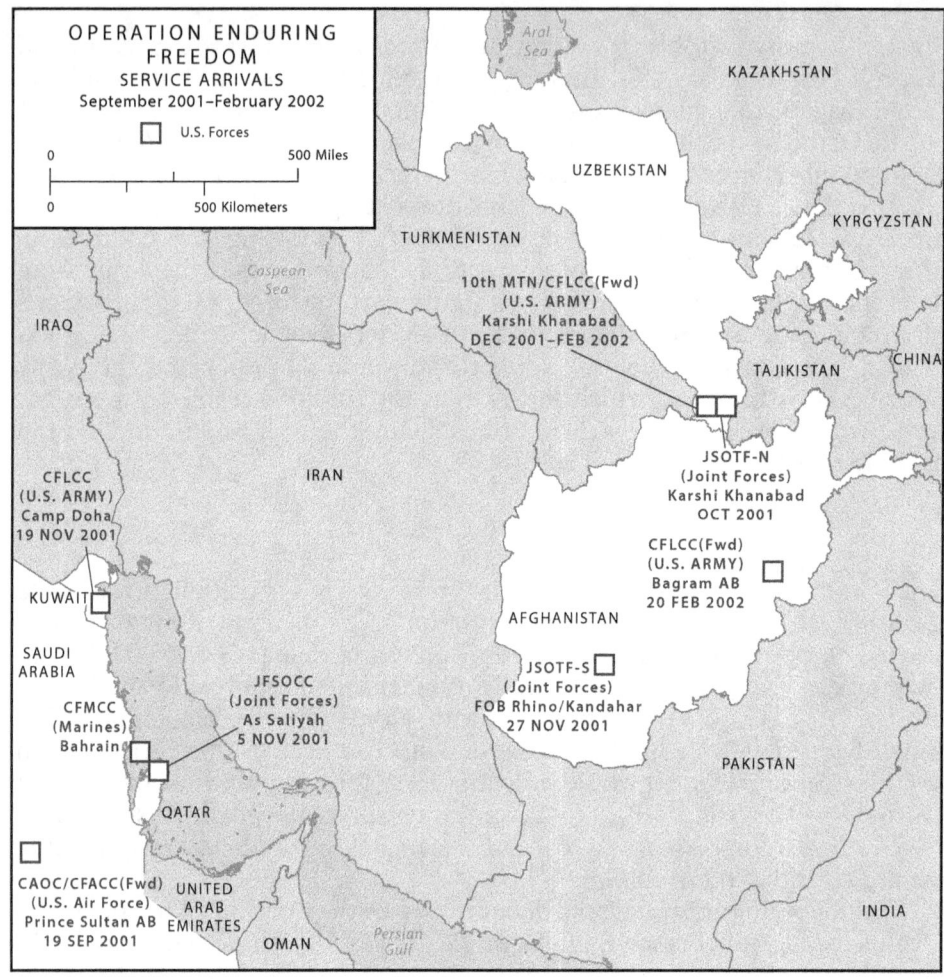

Map 1.1

Prince Sultan Air Base.[173] Although Pakistan granted basing and overflight rights, and Uzbekistan promised the same in the near future, neither country authorized the Americans to launch strike missions from their soil. Until those restrictions were loosened, the B–1B Lancers and B–52H Stratofortresses at Diego Garcia, as well as B–2 Spirit stealth bombers from Whiteman Air Force Base, Missouri, were the only land-based aerial platforms available for the bombing attacks.[174]

The initial deployment orders for conventional army units were issued in late September when Joint Forces Command received a directive to be prepared to send light infantry, explosive ordnance disposal technicians, and logisticians to establish a forward operating base at a yet to be determined

---

173. Tim Ripley, *Middle East Airpower in the 21st Century* (Barnsley, U.K.: Pen and Sword, 2010), p. 341.

174. Benjamin S. Lambeth, *Air Power Against Terror: America's Conduct of Operation Enduring Freedom* (Santa Monica, Calif.: RAND National Defense Research Institute, 2005), p. 250.

A B–52 Stratofortress provides the unaccustomed role of providing close air support to ground forces in early ENDURING FREEDOM operations.

location in Uzbekistan. Those troops would soon be joined by signal, logistics, and aviation support from U.S. Special Operations Command.[175] The growing collection of military assets being assembled in the Gulf also led to the deployment of additional security personnel, including light infantry slated for Camp Doha in Kuwait and potentially Prince Sultan Air Base in Saudi Arabia as well.[176]

Two carrier battle groups, formed around the USS *Carl Vinson* and USS *Enterprise*, were already deployed in the CENTCOM area of operations when the September 11th attacks occurred. On 17 September, Pacific Command passed control of the 15th Marine Expeditionary Unit, commanded by Col. Thomas D. Waldhauser, to General Franks.[177] A third carrier group, formed around the USS *Theodore Roosevelt*, departed Norfolk Naval Base, Virginia, on 19 September. A second amphibious readiness group led by USS *Bataan*, carrying 2,100 officers and enlisted personnel of the 26th Marine Expeditionary Unit, sailed from Norfolk on the following day to take part in BRIGHT STAR.[178] On 30 September, the carrier USS *Kitty Hawk* departed Yokosuka, Japan, for the Middle East to serve as an afloat forward staging

---

175. Wright et al., *A Different Kind of War*, pp. 60–62.

176. Andrew Exum, *This Man's Army: A Soldier's Story from the Front Lines of the War on Terrorism* (New York: Gotham Books, 2004), pp. 76–86.

177. Lowery, *U.S. Marines in Afghanistan, 2001–2002*, pp. 27–31.

178. "Rumsfeld: US Must Drain the Swamp – Roosevelt Carrier Group Headed to Sea," CNN, 19 Sept 2001, http://edition.cnn.com/2001/US/09/18/ret.defense.rumsfeld/, Hist Files, OEF Study Grp.

The U.S. Air Force's C–17 Globemaster was a critical support tool for ENDURING FREEDOM operations in Afghanistan's canalized and restricted terrain.

base for TF SWORD helicopters.[179] Diplomatic considerations proved far less restrictive for U.S. carriers operating in international waters, which ensured naval and marine aircraft would play a major role in the opening air attacks.

As U.S. naval and air assets converged on the Persian Gulf region, a seven-man CIA paramilitary team led by veteran operative Gary C. Schroen linked up with United Front chieftain Mohammed Qasim Fahim approximately 160 kilometers northeast of Kabul at 1440 on 26 September.[180] In addition to disbursing funds to bolster Fahim's commitment and increase his military strength, Schroen's team assessed United Front capabilities, pinpointed the location of opposition fighters and Taliban units, and compiled intelligence for future air strikes. Schroen's operatives also learned that the opposition groups had no intention of acting together against the Taliban until the United States military entered the fray.

Advance parties surveying Pakistani and Uzbek airfields arrived soon after the CIA personnel made contact with Fahim. The 15th Marine Expeditionary Unit established a forward operating base at Shahbaz Air Force Base on the outskirts of Jacobabad, Pakistan, as well as a second airfield at Pasni, located on the Pakistani coast. The Marines also gained approval from the Pakistani military for incoming Special Operations units

---

179. Memo, Commanding Ofcr, USS Kitty Hawk, to Director of Naval History, Ofc of the Ch of Naval Opns, 8 May 2002, sub: USS Kitty Hawk Command History for Calendar Year 2001, https://www.history.navy.mil/content/dam/nhhc/research/archives/command-operation-reports/ship-command-operation-reports/k/kitty-hawk-cv-63-ii/2001.pdf, Hist Files, OEF Study Grp.

180. Gary C. Schroen, *First In: An Insider's Account of How the CIA Spearheaded the War on Terror in Afghanistan* (New York: Ballantine Books, 2005), p. 77.

to utilize smaller airfields at Shamsi and Dalbandin as forward operating and logistical bases.[181] On 29 September, two C–130s carrying an airlift control element of fifty troops departed Germany bound for Karshi Khanabad Air Base, Uzbekistan.[182] Its arrival was the first tangible step to converting the Soviet-era Uzbek airbase into a platform capable of supporting intratheater airlift, Combat Search and Rescue, and the covert insertion of CIA and Special Operations personnel.

Acquisition of the Uzbek air base triggered the flow of Army Special Operations units into the northern part of the theater. Elements of 160th SOAR arrived at Karshi Khanabad within forty-eight hours of the Air Force personnel. Over the next several days, aviation mechanics from the U.S. Army reassembled four MH–47E Chinook and two MH–60L Black Hawk helicopters delivered to Karshi Khanabad via C–17 transport aircraft. The aviators were joined by Company A of the 528th Support Battalion (Special Operations) on 4 October. On 7 October, the 3d Battalion, 75th Ranger Regiment flew out of Fort Benning, Georgia, bound for the Middle East.[183] TF SWORD elements were temporarily bedded down on Jazirat Masirah off the Omani coast awaiting the arrival of the USS *Kitty Hawk*, which would serve as their launching pad for heliborne assaults into southern Afghanistan.[184]

Although Uzbek President Karimov granted basing and overflight rights to the United States, he did not publicly disclose the presence of U.S. personnel in his country until 5 October. The announcement spurred the near-simultaneous departure of almost every U.S. transport plane impatiently waiting at multiple bases across Europe for Karshi Khanabad. Incoming aircraft immediately clogged the limited ramp and taxi space at Karshi Khanabad, creating a huge traffic jam. Air traffic controllers were overwhelmed as offload teams struggled to keep up using the limited equipment they had. This increased activity meant that coalition military personnel on the Uzbek base grew from 100 to more than 2,000 in a week.[185]

On 5 October, the initial elements of a task force from the 10th Mountain Division's 1st Battalion, 87th Infantry, deployed to Karshi Khanabad as some of the first conventional units in theater. The 10th Mountain Division contingent consisted of key personnel from the unit operations section; Capt. Roger A. Crombie's Company A, with attached personnel from the 3d Battalion, 6th Field Artillery; 3d Battalion, 62d Air Defense Artillery;

---

181. Lowery, *U.S. Marines in Afghanistan*, pp. 46–49.

182. Lambeth, *Air Power Against Terror*, p. 86.

183. Capt Brent W. Clemmer, "Raid on Objective Rhino, Helmand Province, Afghanistan, 19–20 October 2001" (Personal experience paper [PEP], Maneuver Capts Career Course, U.S. Army Inf School, n.d.), pp. 6, 19, Hist Files, OEF Study Grp.

184. Pushies, *Night Stalkers*, p. 55; Memo, Commanding Ofcr, USS *Kitty Hawk*, to Director of Naval History, Ofc of the Ch of Naval Opns, 8 May 2002, sub: USS Kitty Hawk Command History for Calendar Year 2001."

185. Wright et al., *A Different Kind of War*, p. 61.

and the 110th Military Intelligence Battalion.[186] The remainder of Colonel LaCamera's battalion arrived soon afterward, assuming responsibility for a larger share of the base perimeter as well as dedicating one rifle company as a quick reaction force. LaCamera's chief logistical officer, Capt. William T. Rodebaugh III, recorded his initial impressions of Karshi Khanabad: "There were some hardstands, some old hangars that we were able to move into, but there were questions about food and potability of water."[187] M. Sgt. Jorge O. Soriano, a senior noncommissioned officer from the 2d Battalion, 160th SOAR, recalled, "[T]here were no porta-potties or buildings to use [as] latrines. We had to dig our own sanitation holes. . . . sleeping was initially under the stars, then we were able to occupy some old, dirty, dusty Russian bunkers. . . . Tents were not used, because we did not own any."[188]

Two days later, the first detachment of Air Force HH–60 Black Hawk helicopters dedicated to Combat Search and Rescue duties arrived at Karshi Khanabad.[189] On that same day, the advance party from 5th Special Forces Group, now known as Task Force DAGGER, arrived. The group included fifteen augmentees from the Special Operations Command of U.S. Joint Forces Command out of Norfolk, Virginia. The first echelon of newly arrived Special Forces personnel took care to maintain a low profile while travelling due to Uzbek government sensitivities. Colonel Mulholland and his staff arrived three days later. The base's inability to accept more than a limited number of inbound aircraft each day, coupled with the lack of housing and life support, constrained the number of Special Operations personnel at Karshi Khanabad until infrastructure improvements could be made. The 5th Special Forces Group ultimately required seventy-two C–17 sorties spread over six weeks to deploy from Fort Campbell, Kentucky, to Uzbekistan.[190]

Despite some internal shortages, the U.S. military deployed sufficient aviation, Special Operations, and logistical units by the end of the first week of October to support the initiation of Phase II. In fact, CENTCOM accelerated this process by proactively assigning key tasks to early-arriving forces. The 528th Support Battalion (Special Operations), for example, gained responsibility for Army sustainment operations at Karshi Khanabad in spite of the prospect that it would receive little or no outside assistance. This unorthodox arrangement prepared units based at Karshi Khanabad

---

186. 1–87th Battalion History, accessed 2 Nov 2011, https://www.drum.army.mil/1stBCT/Pages/I-87_BattalionHistory_lvl3.aspx, Hist Files, OEF Study Grp; Interv, McCool with Crombie, 30 Mar 2006, p. 4.

187. Interv, Jenna Fike, CSI, with Maj William T. Rodebaugh III, frmr Ch Logistics Ofcr, 1st Bn, 87th Inf, 10th Mtn Div, 23 Feb 2010, p. 9, Hist Files, OEF Study Grp.

188. M Sgt Jorge O. Soriano, "TF DAGGER, Uzbekistan and Afghanistan, 09/11/2001 to 03/26/2002, (15P5P) Company First Sergeant, 2–160th Special Operations Aviation Regiment (Airborne) (Student Experience Paper [SEP], U.S. Army Sergeants Major Academy, 5 Oct 2006), p. 12, Hist Files, OEF Study Grp.

189. Lambeth, *Air Power Against Terror*, pp. 85–86.

190. M Sgt Dale G. Aaknes, "Operation Enduring Freedom, Afghanistan, 09/11/2001 through 04/01/2002, 92Y5S2S, Task Force Dagger J-4 NOCIC" (SEP, U.S. Army Sergeants Major Academy, 29 Sep 2006), p. 6, Hist Files, OEF Study Grp.

for Phase II operations well in advance of conventional logistical assets.[191] Likewise, sending the 15th Marine Expeditionary Unit ashore to provide force protection for bases in Pakistan acclimatized its personnel for decisive combat operations in Phase III.

Keenly aware that additional troops and equipment placed a growing burden on the undeveloped support infrastructure in the region, CENTCOM also closely managed the projected arrival dates of Phase III forces. Some units, such as the 101st Airborne Division's 3d Brigade and 507th Support Battalion provided by XVIII Airborne Corps, were not immediately called forward in order to permit logisticians sufficient time to build up stocks. The early November release of BRIGHT STAR participants, including Third Army/ARCENT, the 26th Marine Expeditionary Unit, the 5th Special Forces Group's 2d Battalion, and 160th SOAR's 3d Battalion, also was a critical milestone. By synchronizing the end of BRIGHT STAR with the arrival of conventional units from the United States, CENTCOM not only enhanced General Mikolashek's ability to transform a disparate group of units into a team, but also gave those units time to prepare for combat.[192]

---

191. Wright et al., *A Different Kind of War*, p. 61.
192. Interv, Reardon, Degen, and Smith, with Franks, 4 Dec 2015.

Chapter Two

Initial Combat Operations

General Richard B. Myers assumed the position of chairman of the Joint Chiefs of Staff from General H. Hugh Shelton on 1 October 2001. On the following day, he attended a National Security Council meeting where President George W. Bush expressed his willingness to approve air strikes before Combat Search and Rescue units were in place. Secretary of Defense Donald H. Rumsfeld agreed with Bush, offering a compromise in which B–2 stealth bombers would hit targets in the north before Karshi Khanabad reached full operational capability.[1] The attendees agreed that bombing could start on 6 October with air strikes by the Navy carriers and Air Force heavy bombers based at Diego Garcia and in the United States, as well as Tomahawk missiles launched from warships and submarines sailing in international waters.

On 3 October, Henry A. Crumpton, the CIA counterterrorism special operations chief, met with General Tommy R. Franks at MacDill Air Force Base, Florida, to lay out how the agency planned to work with CENTCOM in the coming weeks. Over the next two to three weeks, the CIA would send several more teams under the leadership of Gary Berntsen, a senior intelligence officer with experience in the region. Berntsen's teams would operate under the codename of JAWBREAKER. Rather than ask Crumpton to provide updates at regular intervals, Franks formalized the future exchange of information by assigning R. Adm. Albert J. Calland as the primary liaison between the agency and the military. However, Franks passed on the first piece of critical information to Crumpton himself by informing the CIA official that American planes were preparing to strike Taliban and al-Qaeda targets any time after 6 October.[2]

THE FIRST SHOTS

Phase II of Operation ENDURING FREEDOM began at 2045 local time on 7 October 2001 when manned aircraft and Tomahawk missiles launched from four American warships in the North Arabian Sea struck thirty-one targets in and around Kabul, Herat, Shindand, Shibirghan, Jalalabad, Mazar-e Sharif, and Kandahar. Before the attacks began, President Bush provided

---

1. Woodward, *Bush at War*, pp. 188–89.
2. Ibid., pp. 193–94.

advance notice of American intentions to key world leaders.³ Shortly afterward, he announced the start of air strikes in a nationally broadcast address: "More than two weeks ago, I gave Taliban leaders a series of clear and specific demands: Close terrorist training camps. Hand over leaders of the al-Qaeda network, and return all foreign nationals, including American citizens unjustly detained in our [sic] country. None of these demands were met. And now, the Taliban will pay a price."⁴

The heaviest attacks were conducted by ten B–52 bombers raining hundreds of Mk–82 500-pound unguided bombs on al-Qaeda training camps around Jalalabad in eastern Afghanistan. A combination of other aircraft, including Diego Garcia–based B–1B heavy bombers, twenty-five Navy F–14 and F/A–18 fighters from the USS *Carl Vinson* and USS *Enterprise*, and two B–2 stealth bombers from Whiteman Air Force Base, Missouri, struck Mullah Mohammed Omar's residence and the airport at Kandahar; the Defense Ministry and airport in Kabul; armored units and two divisional headquarters near Mazar-e Sharif; MiG fighters and transport aircraft at Herat airport; and surface-to-surface missile launchers, air defense sites, and early warning radars across the country.⁵ Although Taliban antiaircraft artillery vainly attempted to down the aerial attackers, the American pilots did not encounter surface-to-air missiles or enemy interceptors.

Determined to demonstrate that the American military could do more than launch air strikes, Rumsfeld also sought to commit Special Forces teams to the fight as soon as possible.⁶ The arrival of additional 5th Special Forces Group personnel at Karshi Khanabad broadened the available tactical options. By 10 October, sufficient resources were in Uzbekistan to support the deployment of Special Operations teams into neighboring Afghanistan. However, a combination of imposing terrain, mechanical issues with the CIA's Soviet-built Mi–8 helicopters, and deteriorating weather stymied TF Dagger's initial attempts to link up with Gary C. Schroen's team at Mohammed Fahim's headquarters.⁷

---

3. Michael Hirsch and John Barry, "Behind America's Attack on Afghanistan," *Newsweek* Web Exclusive on NBC News, 7 Oct 2001, https://www.nbcnews.com/id/3067589/t/behind-americas-attack-afghanistan/, Hist Files, OEF Study Grp.

4. "Text: Bush Announces Strikes Against the Taliban," *Washington Post*, 7 Oct 2001, https://www.washingtonpost.com/wp-srv/nation/specials/attacked/transcripts/bushaddress_100801.htm, Hist Files, OEF Study Grp.

5. Lambeth, *Air Power Against Terror*, pp. 78–82; "Afghanistan Wakes after Night of Intense Bombings," CNN, 7 Oct 2001, https://www.cnn.com/2001/US/10/07/gen.america.under.attack/, Hist Files, OEF Study Grp; "Defense Officials: Air Operation to Last Several Days," CNN, 7 Oct 2001, https://www.cnn.com/2001/US/10/07/ret.attack.pentagon/, Hist Files, OEF Study Grp.

6. DoD News Brfg, Sec Rumsfeld and General Myers, 15 Oct 2001, https://archive.defense.gov/Transcripts/Transcript.aspx?TranscriptID=2108, Hist Files, OEF Study Grp.

7. Gary Berntsen and Ralph Pezzullo, *Jawbreaker : The Attack on Bin Laden and Al-Qaeda: A Personal Account by the CIA's Key Field Commander* (New York: Crown Publishers, 2005), p. 214.

Initial Combat Operations

Into the Heart of Taliban Country

The USS *Kitty Hawk* provided CENTCOM with an additional means of striking the Taliban and al-Qaeda in mid-October. Steaming at high speed, the aircraft carrier traversed the 5,800 kilometers from the Strait of Malacca to Oman in six days, anchoring near Jazirat Masirah on 13 October. Before sailing out of sight a few hours later, the carrier embarked a 600-strong contingent from TF Sword and twenty helicopters.[8] The Special Operations elements on the USS *Kitty Hawk*, as well as their compatriots now on Masirah, were selected to carry out simultaneous strikes against three objectives in southern Afghanistan codenamed Rhino, Gecko, and Badger.

Rhino was an airfield, owned by the United Arab Emirates minister of defense, located around 150 kilometers southwest of Kandahar. Along with gathering intelligence and eliminating any Taliban present at the location, the raiders were ordered to evaluate its feasibility as a future base for U.S. troops.[9] Gecko pinpointed Omar's presidential palace situated several kilometers north of Kandahar. In addition to gathering any intelligence they could find, with particular emphasis on determining whether al-Qaeda possessed weapons of mass destruction, both strike elements were instructed to kill or capture any senior enemy leaders they encountered. Badger's initial target was an electrical power line connecting Kandahar with Herat. After a high-level debate, however, CENTCOM decided Badger did not warrant being labeled a target.

General Franks approved a version of the plan calling for a two-pronged night attack against Rhino and Gecko. The opening assault on Rhino consisted of Oman-based MC–130s airdropping two companies of Rangers onto the desert airstrip. A team of Air Force combat controllers accompanied the Rangers to determine if the airstrip could accommodate American aircraft. After delivering the Rangers, the MC–130 transports were tasked to land at Rhino in order to act as stationary refueling points for the Gecko helicopters. As a result, the Rangers not only had to clear their designated objective, but also had to secure the airstrip until the refueling operation ended.

The second assault force consisted of helicopters launched from the USS *Kitty Hawk* carrying TF Sword special operators and Rangers to Kandahar. The Ranger component provided outer security while Special Forces personnel assaulted Omar's presidential compound. Although the helicopters planned to stop for additional fuel at Rhino on their return trip, the rotary-wing aircraft could divert to the Pakistani base at Dalbandin if they incurred battle damage. Special Operations helicopters would position a platoon from Company B, 3d Battalion, 75th Ranger Regiment, to secure the Dalbandin site. Preparatory fires from fighter-bombers, AC–130 gunships, or

---

8. Memo, Commanding Ofcr, USS Kitty Hawk, to Director of Naval History, Ofc of the Ch of Naval Opns, 8 May 2002, sub: USS Kitty Hawk Command History for Calendar Year 2001. p. 7.

9. Interv, PBS *Frontline* with Gen Tommy R. Franks, Commanding Gen (CG), CENTCOM, 12 Jun 2002, https://www.pbs.org/wgbh/pages/frontline/shows/campaign/interviews/franks.html, Hist Files, OEF Study Grp.

Black Hawk MH–60L armed helicopters preceded the insertion of ground troops into Afghanistan. The dual raids also received dedicated support from CIA Predator drones.

On the evening of 19 October, elements of Ranger Companies A and C of the 3d Battalion, 75th Ranger Regiment, departed Masirah aboard four MC–130 transport aircraft bound for RHINO. The transport planes entered Afghan air space without being detected by Taliban air defenses. Just before the MC–130s arrived, strike aircraft targeted two buildings suspected of housing security personnel on the objective with 2,000-pound laser-guided bombs. The explosions startled a third group of guards into running away, prompting an orbiting AC–130 gunship to engage the fleeing enemy with 105-mm. and 40-mm. shells. Moments later, the quartet of MC–130s carrying the assault element appeared overhead. As the Rangers exited the transports, the pilots released flares designed to decoy man-portable surface-to-air missiles. The pyrotechnic display only angered the Rangers, as the light from the flares revealed their positions while they were still more than a hundred meters above the ground.[10] The enemy did not take advantage of the Rangers' temporary misfortune, however, and only two soldiers sustained injuries, both from landing on rocky ground. The Rangers fanned out, meeting no resistance as they cleared buildings and established a defensive perimeter. The orbiting MC–130s landed once experts on the ground confirmed the runway's suitability. After touching down, the MC–130 flight crews prepared to refuel the helicopters that were en route to the USS *Kitty Hawk* from Kandahar.

As the Rangers occupied RHINO, helicopters deposited a mixed force of Rangers and TF SWORD operators near the Taliban's presidential compound. During the flight to GECKO, the formation encountered a Taliban antiaircraft position, but an armed CIA Predator drone eliminated it before the enemy could fire a shot.[11] As the pilots prepared to touch down, they struggled to identify the landing zone through the dust raised by their churning rotor systems. Although one Chinook aborted its first attempt to land, it struck the side of a hill and sheared off part of its landing gear.[12] Despite the damage, the pilots made a second attempt to deliver their passengers. The Chinook hovered close to the ground as the crew chief helped the assault team exit through a partially open rear ramp. The damaged helicopter then made its way to Jacobabad in Pakistan where it landed safely.[13]

While the Rangers established a security cordon, the TF SWORD personnel entered the compound. The air strikes had reduced half of the buildings to piles of bricks and masonry, which complicated the task. Omar's house,

---

10. Cpt Brent W. Clemmer, "Raid on Objective Rhino, Helmand Province, Afghanistan, 19–20 October 2001" (PEP, U.S. Army Inf School, n.d.), pp. 28–34.

11. Henry A. Crumpton, *The Art of Intelligence: Lessons from a Life in the CIA's Clandestine Service* (New York: Penguin Books, 2015), p. 221.

12. DoD News Bfg, Asst Sec Def for Public Affairs Victoria Clarke and Rear Adm John D. Stufflebeam, 23 Oct 2001, https://archive.defense.gov/Transcripts/Transcript.aspx?TranscriptID=2155, Hist Files, OEF Study Grp.

13. Dick Camp, *Boots on the Ground: The Fight to Liberate Afghanistan from Al-Qaeda and the Taliban, 2001–2002* (Minneapolis: Zenith Press, 2011), p. 252.

with its four-meter-thick reinforced concrete roof, remained largely intact.[14] In sweeping the compound, several Americans were accidentally wounded by fragments from grenades thrown into rooms thought to be occupied by Taliban. Although the task force failed to locate any top-ranking Taliban, the Americans scooped up documents and computers. With information and equipment in hand, the raiders departed without making contact with the enemy. The MH–47E Chinooks flew southwest, where they touched down near the MC–130s at RHINO. Once their helicopters were refueled, the Kandahar raiding force departed, followed by the Rangers of Companies A and C, who reboarded the MC–130s and returned to Oman.[15]

Until the twin raids, the Taliban had considered the Pashtun tribal areas to be secure. They had fixed their attention on containing any United Front attempt to advance in conjunction with the ongoing air strikes. The Americans not only appeared from an unexpected direction, but also used ground troops, helicopters, and fixed-wing aircraft with speed and precision at night. As one senior CIA official observed, "Our HUMINT [human intelligence] reporting covered the Taliban's shock and outrage that U.S. soldiers should penetrate so deeply, so quickly, into the heart of their safe haven."[16] General Franks boasted that the raid succeeded in spreading "shock and awe" among the Taliban beyond all expectations.[17] Despite the CENTCOM commander's enthusiasm and attendant publicity, however, the raid's true impact on the Taliban was little more than a temporary psychological setback.

Although no Americans were seriously injured by enemy action, two Company B Rangers died in a related helicopter mishap in Pakistan. The helicopters ferrying them to the refueling and repair site were directed to land on specific points pre-treated with oil to limit the chances of dust obscuring the pilots' view. Unfortunately, one MH–60K from Company C, 1st Battalion, 160th SOAR, rolled over after touching down. The pilots had approached at the wrong angle, raising enough dust to prevent them from realizing that they were alighting on sloping ground.[18] Spec. John J. Edmunds and Pfc. Kristofer T. Stonesifer, the first American service members to give their lives in ENDURING FREEDOM, received mortal injuries after being ejected from the stricken Black Hawk. Both Rangers were evacuated from the crash site aboard an MH–53 PAVE LOW helicopter and died en route to medical care.[19]

---

14. Jon Lee Anderson, "Letter from Afghanistan: After the Revolution," *The New Yorker*, 21 Jan 2002, https://www.newyorker.com/magazine/letter-from-afghanistan, Hist Files, OEF Study Grp.

15. "Objective Rhino and Gecko," American Special Ops, https://www.americanspecialops.com/operations/rangers-delta-afghanistan-2001/, Hist Files, OEF Study Grp.

16. Crumpton, *The Art of Intelligence*, p. 222.

17. Interv, Mark J. Reardon, OEF Study Group, with Col Brian J. Mennes, frmr Special Opns Forces planner 2001–2002, 27 Apr 2015, Hist Files, OEF Study Grp.

18. Interv, John McCool, CSI, with Maj Robert Bowers, frmr 75th Ranger Rgt Judge Advocate General, 1 Feb 2006, p. 8, Hist Files, OEF Study Grp.

19. Darrell D. Whitcomb, *On a Steel Horse I Ride: A History of the MH–53 PAVE LOW Helicopters in War and Peace* (Maxwell Air Force Base, Ala.: Air University Press, 2012), p. 513.

Bringing the United Front into the Fight

A second CIA paramilitary team, known as Team ALPHA, entered Afghanistan during the early hours of 17 October courtesy of the 2d Battalion, 160th SOAR. The CIA officers departed Karshi Khanabad just before midnight on 16 October bound for a meeting with militia chieftain Abdul Rashid, who went by the nom de guerre Dostum (Uzbek: friend) in the Suf River Valley about 100 kilometers south of Mazar-e Sharif.[20] After a flight lasting almost two and a half hours, the CIA team safely disembarked at the appointed rendezvous. The Americans carried personal weapons, but their real power consisted of cases of money intended to persuade Dostum to fight and to encourage the Taliban to defect.

Although the CIA team provided noticeable American support, Dostum required more than money and promises. To provide the United Front with more tangible evidence of U.S. commitment, General Franks authorized additional bombing missions in the north. However, the CENTCOM air planners hesitated, because CIA officials had voiced concerns about this plan, fearing that providing substantial aid to the Tajiks, Uzbeks, and Hazaras would antagonize potential Pashtun allies.[21] In addition, CENTCOM targeting cells still lacked detailed information on the location of enemy ground units, even though Schroen's CIA operatives had made every effort to collect this information. Secretary Rumsfeld publicly confirmed the latter dilemma. In response to a reporter's comment that Taliban troops in the north felt safe from air attack, he admitted, "At the moment, we have had less than perfect targeting information in the areas I think people are speculating about."[22]

An unequivocal demonstration of American aerial capabilities would be needed to convince the United Front to go on the offensive. To rapidly collect enough information to justify the use of massed airpower against Taliban ground units, CENTCOM ordered Special Operations teams equipped with laser designating devices capable of guiding precision munitions into Afghanistan. After two abortive insertions, six helicopters from the 2d Battalion, 160th SOAR, departed Karshi Khanabad carrying two Special Forces Operational Detachment Alpha (ODA) twelve-man teams on the evening of 19 October. The formation had three separate elements: two MH–47Es carrying ODA 555, one MH–47E and a pair of armed MH–60L Black Hawks bearing ODA 595, and a single MH–47E loaded with extra fuel. ODA 555, led by CWO2 David W. Diaz, would rendezvous with Schroen's CIA team accompanying General Mohammed

---

20. Brian Glyn Williams, *The Last Warlord: The Life and Legend of Dostum, the Afghan Warrior Who Led US Special Forces to Topple the Taliban Regime* (Chicago: Chicago Review Press, 2013), p. 103.

21. Schroen, *First In*, pp. 162–63.

22. DoD News Bfg, Rumsfeld and Myers, 15 Oct 2001.

ODA 595 of the 5th Special Forces Group "Horse Soldiers" ride with General Dostum's forces south of Mazar-e Sharif.

Qasim Fahim. The second detachment, ODA 595 under Capt. Mark D. Nutsch, would join Team Alpha and Dostum.[23]

Although the Chinooks carrying Diaz's team touched down in different locations several kilometers apart at 0300 on 20 October, ODA 555 linked up with Schroen's team before daylight. On the following day, Diaz met with General Bismillah Khan Mohammadi, the United Front's deputy minister of defense and a trusted lieutenant of General Fahim. On 22 October, Diaz relocated to Bagram Air Base, where dug-in Taliban and United Front troops faced each other across the open runway. The move afforded ODA 555 a golden opportunity to demonstrate what the newcomers could accomplish.[24] Four U.S. soldiers made their way to the shattered control tower. Using their elevated vantage point to pinpoint numerous camouflaged targets, the Americans called in devastating air strikes against the Taliban. Further burnishing their newly won battlefield credentials, ODA 555 repeated that feat several times, directing forty to fifty planes on each occasion against enemy troops who remained in place despite the punishing assault.[25]

---

23. Briscoe et al., *Weapon of Choice*, p. 119.

24. Camp, *Boots on the Ground*, p. 120.

25. John D. Gresham, "Triple Nickle at Bagram," *The Year in Special Operations: 2011–2012 Edition: Operation Enduring Freedom – Ten Years Later* (Tampa: Defense Media Network, 2012), pp. 105–06.

Captain Nutsch's ODA 595 landed near the designated landing zone in the Suf River Valley at 0200 on 20 October.[26] Within six hours of its arrival, General Dostum met with the CIA operatives and Captain Nutsch to devise a mutually agreeable course of action for the coming days. At the end of the discussion, half of ODA 595 mounted horses to accompany Dostum to his forward headquarters while the remainder stayed behind to establish a base camp. The mounted group led by Nutsch accompanied the United Front leader to a forward position where the Americans put on a convincing demonstration of the lethality of aerially delivered precision munitions.

Dostum faced a foe that both outnumbered and outgunned his own force. The Taliban deployed local militia in forward positions, backed by fortified positions containing machine guns, mortars, and truck-mounted antiaircraft guns. They had armored vehicles and tanks in reserve so as to deliver counterattacks and recover any lost terrain. Although the Taliban defenses would have proven costly to defeat by a ground force lacking close air support, ODA 595 provided the ever-aggressive Dostum with a significant edge. To provide Dostum with the tactical flexibility he needed to maneuver against the dug-in enemy fighters, Captain Nutsch split his forward element into three smaller teams, each with a trained combat controller. Over the next several days, the Uzbek fighters launched a succession of slashing cavalry charges against their foes immediately after the Americans had directed air strikes against every visible Taliban defensive position.[27] In quick succession, Dostum's forces captured Bishqab on 21 October, Chobaki on the following day, and Chapchal on 25 October.[28]

Soon afterward, the DoD circulated photographs showing Army SOF and Air Force personnel riding horses into battle alongside Uzbek fighters. Although only a few SOF operators relied on equine transport for a limited period, these dramatic images were intended to reassure Americans that the U.S. soldiers battling the Taliban would not find themselves in an unwinnable predicament similar to the Soviet experience in Afghanistan. The photographs offered equally compelling proof that a few well-trained and well-led Green Berets, fighting with indigenous militia, could influence a campaign as significantly as conventional forces.[29]

---

26. Pushies, *Night Stalkers*, pp. 57–58.

27. Camp, *Boots on the Ground*, pp. 132–36.

28. William M. Knarr Jr. and John Frost, *Operation ENDURING FREEDOM Battle Reconstruction: Battle Site Survey and Ground Force Data Reconciliation* (Alexandria, Va.: Institute for Defense Analysis, 2010), pp. V-6–V-9.

29. Warner Bros. Pictures would later produce a feature-length film, *12 Strong*, dramatizing those events. See Justin Kroll, "Chris Hemsworth, Michael Shannon to Star in Afghan War Drama 'Horse Soldiers,'" *Variety*, 30 Sep 2016, https://variety.com/2016/film/news/chris-hemsworth-michael-shannon-horse-soldiers-1201875049/, Hist Files, OEF Study Grp. The film was released in early 2018.

INITIAL COMBAT OPERATIONS

An ODA 595 Forward Air Controller calls in close air support of United Front forces near Kunduz. Timely and accurate close air support from B–52s and other strategic bombers prevented Taliban attempts to halt the advances of the United Front.

THE UNITED FRONT

Concerns about the unfolding campaign now surfaced as other United Front leaders hesitated to follow Dostum's example. The suitcases of cash delivered by CIA operatives in recent weeks had not erased the long-held conflicting agendas of the United Front's disparate elements. Bound only by a common hatred of the Taliban, some opposition leaders refused to cooperate with rivals while others were more interested in postconflict spoils rather than taking on the Taliban in open battle. Dostum, the most aggressive of the faction leaders, aimed to recapture Mazar-e Sharif and expand his dominion to the Uzbek-Afghan border. Fahim, by contrast, sought to push west to seize the cities of Taluqan and Kunduz before veering south to Kabul. Ismail Khan, the exiled governor of Herat, also planned an offensive to the west with the ultimate goal of recapturing his former city, and Hazara leader Karim Khalili wanted to gain control of Bamyan and the area west of Kabul.[30] None of the United Front factions expressed any interest in operating south of Kabul, which meant that before venturing into the Pashtun homelands of the Taliban, the Americans would have to ally themselves with a new collection of Afghan warlords.

On a positive note, additional Special Forces personnel had arrived to work with a growing number of United Front military efforts. At 0200 on

---

30. Henry A. Crumpton, "Intelligence and War: Afghanistan, 2001–2002," in *Transforming U.S. Intelligence*, eds. Jennifer E. Sims and Burton Gerber (Washington, D.C.: Georgetown University Press, 2005), p. 166.

26 October, a pair of MH–47E helicopters delivered M. Sgt. Armand J. "John" Bolduc's ODA 585 to Dasht-e Qal'ah in northeast Afghanistan.[31] A mixed group of Afghan fighters and several CIA operatives greeted the Green Berets. Bolduc's men were taken to General Bariullah Khan near Taluqan. At the same time, Diaz's team added needed weight to CIA efforts to convince Fahim to initiate offensive operations by relocating to the Tajik leader's headquarters.[32] In addition to Bolduc's team, 160th SOAR helicopters delivered Operational Detachment Charlie 51, composed of headquarters personnel from the 1st Battalion, 5th Special Forces Group, led by Colonel Haas, to Samangan Province approximately 160 kilometers south of Mazar-e Sharif. From that central location, Haas could oversee the ODAs in the Mazar-e Sharif and Taluqan areas as well as the SOF teams in the Bamyan region.[33] (*See Map 2.1.*)

On 31 October, General Franks flew to Dushanbe in Tajikistan for a meeting with Fahim and his intelligence chief, Mohammed Arif Sarwari, also known as "Engineer Arif." Other participants included Admiral Calland, CIA counterterrorism chief Henry Crumpton, Col. John P. Mulholland, and Gary Berntsen, the last of whom had been chosen as Schroen's replacement.[34] After listening to Fahim's impassioned pitch for taking Kabul as soon as possible, Franks explained that, after securing Mazar-e Sharif, "Dostum's forces would then take a hard right and march east to support [United Front] Tajik forces, commanded by [Bariullah] Khan, for an all-out assault on Taloqan [Taluqan]. General Fahim's army, further [*sic*] south on the Shomali plains, would maneuver westward to cut off retreating Taliban troops and trap them in a large kill box. Once trapped, the Taliban army of the North could either surrender or be decimated by repeated U.S. bombing runs."[35] Franks also informed Fahim that the United Front would soon receive significantly more air support.[36]

A lively discussion followed before Fahim agreed to follow the plan outlined by Franks. When Franks asked Fahim to pressure the Taliban at Bagram, Henry Crumpton recorded that Fahim demanded "an outrageous sum of cash in monthly payments."[37] General Franks uttered an expletive before walking out of the meeting. With the general out of earshot, Crumpton and Berntsen admonished Fahim, explaining that Franks considered it unprofessional to haggle for money. After ten or fifteen minutes, Franks returned to the meeting where he defused lingering tensions by predicting that Kabul would fall before 25 December. Before the meeting ended, the CENTCOM commander made

---

31. HQDA, GO 10, 25 Sep 2006, sub: Units Credited with Assault Landings, p. 2, Hist Files, OEF Study Grp.

32. Camp, *Boots on the Ground*, pp. 149–50; Schroen, *First In*, pp. 264–65.

33. Berntsen and Pezzullo, *Jawbreaker*, pp. 108–09; GO 10, p. 2, Hist Files, OEF Study Grp. When arrival dates and units in any source differ from General Orders 10, the latter will be used.

34. Berntsen and Pezzullo, *Jawbreaker*, pp. 89–93; Crumpton, *The Art of Intelligence*, pp. 228–30.

35. Berntsen and Pezzullo, *Jawbreaker*, p. 91.

36. Schroen, *First In*, p. 305.

37. Crumpton, *The Art of Intelligence*, p. 230.

Fahim promise that Tajik fighters would obtain American permission before entering Kabul in force.[38]

More Special Forces teams departed from Karshi Khanabad bound for Afghanistan over the next several days. One flight of helicopters delivered Operational Detachment Charlie 53, consisting of headquarters personnel from Lt. Col. Max Bowers' 3d Battalion, 5th Special Forces Group, to Dostum's encampment on 2 November.[39] A second insertion deposited Capt. Dean S. Newman's ODA 534 at a landing zone about fifty kilometers southwest of Mazar-e Sharif.[40] The Americans linked up with twenty opposition fighters who led them to Tajik chieftain Ustad Mohammed Atta Nur.[41] Newman knew little about Atta Nur, except that he had battled Dostum on numerous occasions over the past two decades.[42] In addition to ODA 534, several members of the CIA's Team Alpha were also working with Atta Nur.[43] Early the next morning, a flight delivered ODA 553 to Naylor, a small town about 200 kilometers due south of Mazar-e Sharif, where they linked up with the CIA's Team Delta and Khalili's Hazara fighters. Khalili planned to support the upcoming assault on Mazar-e Sharif by seizing Bamyan in order to prevent the Taliban from threatening Dostum's rear.[44]

During this period, Dostum met with the Americans and other Afghan opposition leaders to plan the attack to seize Mazar-e Sharif. The planning benefited from up-to-date intelligence on the Taliban defending Mazar-e Sharif passed to Dostum by a senior enemy commander.[45] The proposed offensive called for simultaneous attacks by Atta Nur through the Balkh River Valley in the west and Dostum through the Suf River Valley in the east. After rendezvousing where the two valleys met, Dostum's 2,500 horsemen and Atta Nur's 1,000 fighters would push northward toward the Tiangi, a well-defended gap. A third force under Hazara commander Mohammed Mohaqiq would conduct supporting attacks in the mountainous area of Safed Kotal to screen Dostum's right flank. All three opposition groups would combine to assault the Tiangi. Once through the gap, they would be only forty kilometers south of Mazar-e Sharif.[46]

The combined offensive by Atta Nur and Dostum began on 5 November, with the former meeting little opposition for the first several days. Captain

---

38. Franks with McConnell, *American Soldier*, p. 313.

39. Wright et al., *A Different Kind of War*, p. 77; GO 10, p. 2.

40. Briscoe et al., *Weapon of Choice*, p. 98.

41. Camp, *Boots on the Ground*, p. 143.

42. Interv, PBS *Frontline* with U.S. SF Operational Detachment Alpha (ODA) 534, https://www.pbs.org/wgbh/pages/frontline/shows/campaign/interviews/534.html, Hist Files, OEF Study Grp.

43. Schroen, *First In*, pp. 228–29.

44. Camp, *Boots on the Ground*, 155–56; GO 10, p. 2.

45. Knarr and Frost, *Operation ENDURING FREEDOM Battle Reconstruction*, pp. III-35–III-36.

46. Camp, *Boots on the Ground*, p. 141; Knarr and Frost, *Operation ENDURING FREEDOM Battle Reconstruction*, pp. III-2–III-4.

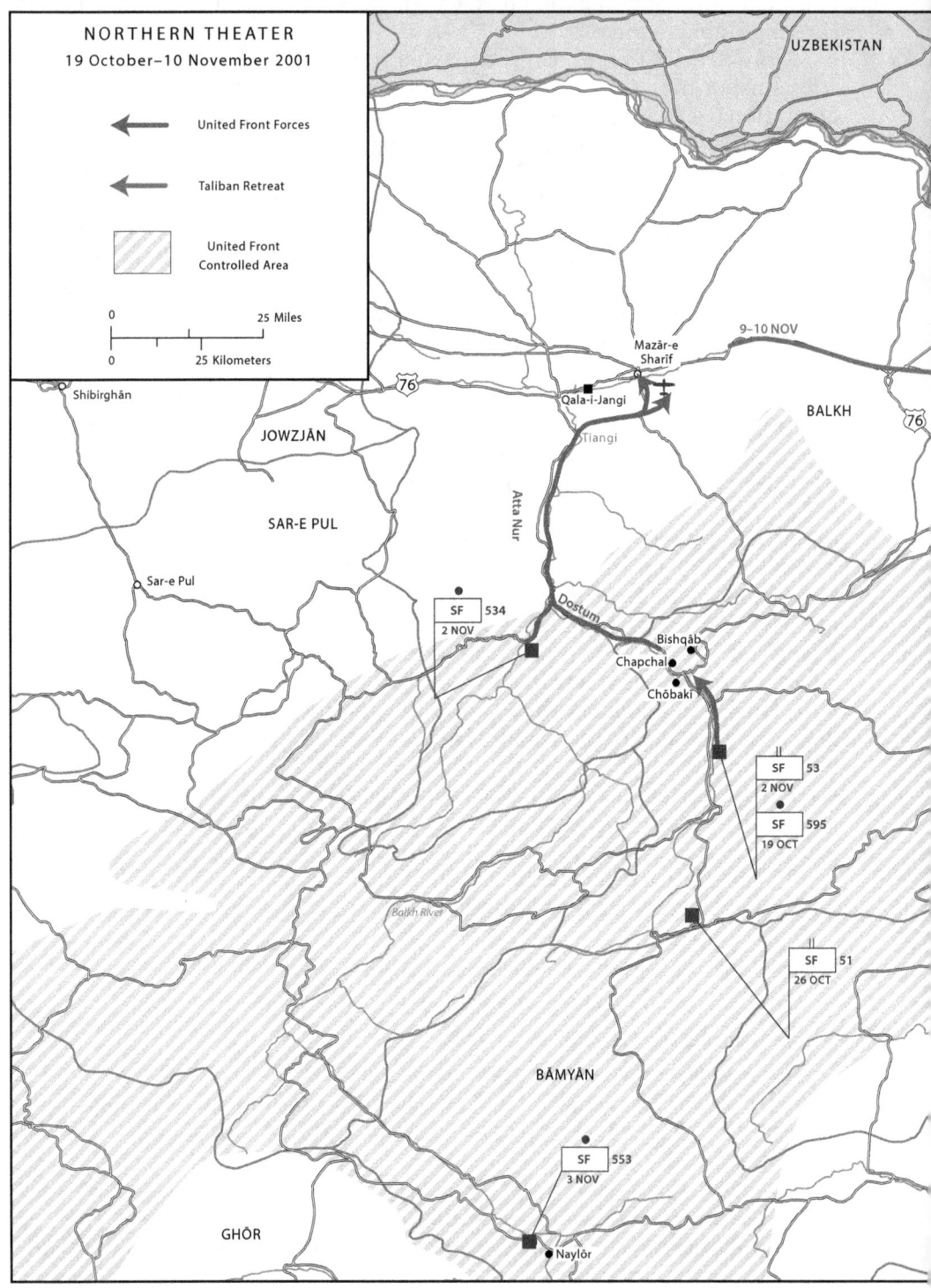

Map 2.1

Newman called in air strikes whenever he encountered Taliban defensive positions, with one or two bombs usually sufficing to convince the enemy to retreat. In sharp contrast, Dostum's troops launched a two-pronged attack from the southwest and southeast pitting 2,300 Uzbek horsemen against 2,000 entrenched Taliban foot soldiers. In a series of mounted charges preceded by air strikes, Dostum's men overran enemy positions on six successive ridgelines, killing hundreds of Taliban and capturing 300 to 400 more, mostly ill-trained Pakistanis. Enemy opposition totally collapsed by the late afternoon.[47] By the end of U.S. and United Front operations in northern Afghanistan, numerous senior opposition leaders would be killed or captured. The fatalities included Juma Namangani, leader of the Islamic Movement of Uzbekistan, and the captives included Taliban leaders Abdul-Razzaq Nafiz and Abdul-Qahir Usmani (both of whom were wounded), as well as Fazil Mazloom and Nurullah Nuri.

After reaching the southern end of the pass on 8 November, Dostum met with Atta Nur and Mohaqiq to finalize plans for an attack on the Tiangi the next day. The renewed advance succeeded in capturing the pass as the Taliban, who suffered numerous losses from air strikes directed by ODA 595, made preparations to retreat. During the night of 9–10 November, the Americans directed air strikes against hundreds of Taliban vehicles streaming eastward out of Mazar-e Sharif toward Kunduz. Although both Atta Nur and Dostum put aside their rivalries during the advance on Mazar-e Sharif, the former's troops claimed the airport on the city's eastern outskirts as a prize of war by advancing before the agreed-upon time. Captain Newman noted that "access to air then had to be approved by Atta Noor [sic]."[48] Dostum rode into Mazar-e Sharif to a hero's welcome as the inhabitants stood by the road cheering.

Part of Dostum's force occupied the Qala-i-Jangi fortress located just northwest of Mazar-e Sharif while the remainder searched the city for Taliban stragglers. That afternoon, Dostum's men located a group of 300 to 400 Pakistani Taliban hiding in a girls' school. When emissaries went forward to negotiate their surrender, the holdouts opened fire. Dostum asked ODA 595 to coordinate an air strike against the building. In an impressive display of airpower, Navy F/A–18s destroyed it without inflicting civilian casualties or collateral damage.[49] All of the enemy holdouts were killed or wounded by the air strike. This signaled the end of the struggle for Mazar-e Sharif, the first Afghan city to be liberated from Taliban rule. Fortunately for the Taliban forces, Sufi Mohammed, the leader of the Pakistan fighters who had been killed or captured in the school building, escaped and slipped back into Pakistan just before the allied forces arrived.

Soon after the capture of Mazar-e Sharif, CENTCOM designated the city as the initial distribution hub for humanitarian assistance flowing

---

47. Camp, *Boots on the Ground*, pp. 145–46; Knarr and Frost, *Operation ENDURING FREEDOM Battle Reconstruction*, pp. III-18–III-23.

48. Camp, *Boots on the Ground*, p. 148.

49. Knarr and Frost, *Operation ENDURING FREEDOM Battle Reconstruction*, p. V-32.

into Afghanistan from Uzbekistan and Germany. TF DAGGER dispatched engineers to repair the local airport and teams from the 96th Civil Affairs Battalion to assess what supplies needed to be delivered first. The civil affairs teams would also provide limited direct aid to show the Afghans that the Americans were liberators and not occupiers. The Americans also found themselves in the midst of a power struggle within the newly liberated city as Atta Nur, Dostum, and Mohaqiq sought to amass as much influence as possible. Admiral Calland and TF DAGGER responded by brokering an agreement assigning responsibility for specific services, rather than geographic areas, to each group.[50]

MORE AMERICANS JOIN THE FIGHT

While the dramatic victory achieved by Atta Nur and Dostum's fighters convinced American officials that CENTCOM could rely on indigenous allies, General Franks continued to plan to deploy U.S. conventional forces to Afghanistan. His actions did not indicate a lack of faith in the Afghan opposition as much as lingering concern that the enemy would retreat into urban sanctuaries rather than continue fighting in open terrain. Although the United Front had considerable experience with fighting on open terrain, it lacked the experience and equipment necessary to fight in Afghan cities. The CENTCOM deputy commander, Marine Lt. Gen. Michael P. "Rifle" DeLong, echoed that concern: "After Mazar-i-Sharif fell, we thought we'd have long, hard battles ahead of us for the remaining cities."[51]

CENTCOM already had laid the foundation for U.S. ground troops to build upon the initial successes of the United Front. Two weeks before Mazar-e Sharif fell, General Franks asked naval headquarters to plan a series of amphibious raids into southern Afghanistan. On 1 November, V. Adm. Charles W. Moore, Commander, U.S. Naval Forces Central Command, directed Brig. Gen. James N. Mattis, Commanding General of 1st Marine Expeditionary Brigade, to conduct "a minimum of three to five raids into Afghanistan over a thirty-day period."[52] For this purpose, Mattis established Naval Expeditionary Task Force 58 (TF-58), which consisted of the 15th and 26th Marine Expeditionary Units (Special Operations Capable). Both units were organized around reinforced infantry battalions (respectively, the 1st Battalion, 1st Marines, and 3d Battalion, 6th Marines) augmented with additional logistical elements plus dedicated rotary and fixed-wing assets.

While Mattis' staff developed a number of different concepts, CENTCOM ultimately settled on directing him to seize and hold a forward operating base at RHINO.[53] Mattis assigned the task of securing RHINO to the 15th

---

50. Briscoe et al., *Weapon of Choice*, p. 102.

51. Lt Gen Michael DeLong, Noah Lukeman, and Tony Zinni, *Inside CENTCOM: The Unvarnished Truth about the Wars in Afghanistan and Iraq* (Washington, D.C.: Regnery Publishing, 2004), p. 51.

52. Native Sum, Opn ENDURING FREEDOM, Combined Task For ce (CTF) 58, Operations in Afghanistan, 27 Oct 2001 to 26 Feb 2002, pp. 7–13, Hist Files, OEF Study Grp.

53. Ibid., pp. 19–22.

Marine Expeditionary Unit, while elements of the 26th Marine Expeditionary Unit conducted raids from the forward operating base into the surrounding countryside.[54]

Lt. Gen. Paul T. Mikolashek accelerated the preparatory measures needed to transform his headquarters into a CFLCC as the Marines were planning for an incursion into southern Afghanistan. Rather than deploy separately from Egypt and Fort McPherson, Georgia, Mikolashek decreed that BRIGHT STAR personnel and equipment would rejoin the Third Army/ARCENT staff at Fort McPherson before returning to the Middle East. The Third Army/ARCENT commander also enjoyed considerable support from senior Army leadership as he prepared CFLCC for deployment. After learning that the CFLCC advance party now planned to depart for Kuwait within the week, followed by the rest of the staff shortly before mid-November, Vice Chief of Staff of the Army, General John M. "Jack" Keane promised to adjust the projected flow of additional personnel and equipment to Mikolashek to fit the accelerated timeline.[55]

General Mikolashek's land component command inserted itself into the existing chain of command immediately upon its arrival at Camp Doha in mid-November.[56] In response to General Franks' orders to send humanitarian aid and security forces to Mazar-e Sharif, Mikolashek's staff began working with TF DAGGER to overcome the challenges of transferring civil affairs, engineers, explosive ordnance disposal, and logistical assets to the newly liberated city.[57] To coordinate ongoing efforts at Mazar-e Sharif, while lightening the burden shouldered by TF DAGGER, Mikolashek sought CENTCOM approval to send a division assault command post to Uzbekistan.[58]

While Franks considered Mikolashek's proposal, Colonel Mulholland prepared for the arrival of his 2d Battalion and logistical assets dispatched by the XVIII Airborne Corps. Several teams from Lt. Col. David G. Fox's battalion, including ODA 553 and ODA 555, were already working with Afghan opposition forces. The advance party from the 2d Battalion, 5th Special Forces Group, departed from Jordan via a commercial airline in early November. They were followed several days later by two companies plus the battalion headquarters and the battalion's support company, all of which flew to Germany on military aircraft with a second stop at Vicenza, Italy, before completing the final leg of the journey.[59] The 2d Battalion's arrival

---

54. Maj Michael L. Valenti, "The Mattis Way of War: An Examination of Operational Art in Task Force 58 and 1st Marine Division," Masters of Military Art and Science Monograph, U.S. Army Command and General Staff College, Fort Leavenworth, Kansas, 2014, pp. 26–27.

55. Memo, Col Eshelman for Third Army/ARCENT Cmd Grp and Staff, 15 Nov 2001, sub: ARCENT Update 15 Nov 01, 1829 hrs, Story CFLCC Collection, OEF Study Grp.

56. Ibid.

57. Ibid.; Memo, Col Eshelman for Third Army/ARCENT Cmd Grp and Staff, 16 Nov 2001, sub: ARCENT Update 16 Nov 01, 1748 hrs, Story CFLCC Collection, OEF Study Grp.

58. Memo, Eshelman for Third Army/ARCENT Cmd Grp and Staff, 16 Nov 2001, sub: ARCENT Update 16 Nov 01.

59. Interv, Peter Connors, CSI, with Col David G. Fox, frmr Cdr, 2d Bn, 5th SF Grp, 30 Nov 2006, p. 3, Hist Files, OEF Study Grp.

infused TF DAGGER with sufficient forces to deploy ODAs simultaneously into both northern and southern Afghanistan if the situation demanded.

An ad hoc logistical group, consisting of the Headquarters and Headquarters Detachment from Lt. Col. Edward F. Dorman III's 530th Supply and Service Battalion and the 7th Transportation Battalion's 58th Maintenance Company arrived at Karshi Khanabad soon afterward.[60] The two companies, designated as Logistical Task Force 530, could provide a wide range of support to American ground forces. In addition to the logistical task force, sorely needed construction expertise and earth-moving equipment appeared in the form of Company B of the 92d Engineer Battalion.[61] Although Company A, 528th Support Battalion (Special Operations), sustained all needs at Karshi Khanabad over the past month, the arrival of additional assets allowed Colonel Mulholland to deploy logistical support to locations other than Karshi Khanabad as needed.

During this same period, Lt. Col. Ronald E. Corkran's 1st Battalion, 187th Infantry, deployed from Fort Campbell, Kentucky, to Jacobabad, Pakistan, to replace the marines securing Shahbaz Air Force Base. Corkran initially learned of the movement from the brigade commander, Colonel Francis J. Wiercinski on 5 November. Seven days later, the aircraft assigned to ferry Corkran's unit to Pakistan began arriving at Fort Campbell, where loading operations occurred during darkness for security reasons.[62] A portion of Corkran's headquarters, along with two rifle companies (B and C) each reinforced with an antitank platoon mounted on High Mobility Multipurpose Wheeled Vehicles (HMMWVs), took over security within forty-eight hours after their arrival.[63] During the handover, the marines informed Corkran that in addition to securing the air base perimeter, his troops were expected to help retrieve downed CIA drones.[64]

CATASTROPHIC SUCCESS

The lavish support provided to Dostum and Atta Nur convinced all but the most skeptical opposition commanders to work closely with the Americans. To link these geographically and operationally disparate bands with the U.S. operational plan, TF DAGGER dispatched additional Special Forces teams into north-central and northwestern Afghanistan. Capt. Glenn R. Thomas' ODA 594 arrived in Bagram on 8 November to augment the advisory team already in place with Fahim. Thomas' arrival permitted Chief Warrant Officer Diaz's

---

60. Kenneth Finlayson, "Not Just Doing Logistics: LTF 530 in Support of TF Dagger," *Veritas : The Journal of Army Special Operations History* 3, no. 2 (2007): 45.

61. Interv, Laurence Lessard, CSI, with Maj Kevin J. Lovell, frmr Cdr, Co B, 92d Engr Bn, 24 Aug 2007, p. 3, Hist Files, OEF Study Grp.

62. Interv, Steven Clay, CSI, with Lt Col (Ret.) Ron Corkran, frmr Cdr, 1st Bn, 187th Inf, 9 May 2007, pp. 3–4, Hist Files, OEF Study Grp.

63. Interv, Laurence Lessard, CSI, with Maj Greg Ford, frmr S-2, 1st Bn, 187th Inf, 23 May 2007, pp. 4–5, Hist Files, OEF Study Grp.

64. Interv, Jenna Fike, CSI, with Maj Joseph Claburn, frmr Air Movement Ofcr, 1st Bn, 187th Inf, 13 Sep 2011, p. 7, Hist Files, OEF Study Grp.

ODA 555 to return to Bagram and prepare to direct air strikes against Taliban fighters in that area. That same morning, Capt. Patrick O'Hara's ODA 586 joined General Douad Khan near Kunduz. Two days later, ODA 554 under CWO3 James P. Newman linked up with Ismail Khan at Den Berenj Qal'ah, located northeast of Herat in western Afghanistan.[65] The deployment of these ODAs expanded TF DAGGER's presence across Afghanistan north of the Hindu Kush.

The growing number of Special Operations teams, when added to greater cooperation by the United Front and CENTCOM's commitment of substantial air power in support of indigenous allies, presaged a major change in the campaign. As a result, events accelerated dramatically as the United Front set into motion the plan discussed earlier by General Franks and General Fahim. On 11 November, a simultaneous push by all Afghan opposition groups, aided by air strikes, resulted in the capture of Taluqan, the capital of Takhar Province, located 61 kilometers east of Kunduz and Bamyan in the heart of the Hazara region of central Afghanistan, 130 kilometers northwest of Kabul. Bamyan controlled the valley of the same name that served for centuries as a vital link on the key trade route, known as the Silk Road, linking China with India via Afghanistan. The provincial capital of Herat, located approximately 500 kilometers south-southwest of Bamyan and home to 1.7 million Afghans, fell soon after Taluqan. The seizure of Herat was a major positive development because the city sat astride the Ring Road linking Kandahar in the south with Mazar-e-Sharif in the north. The tide of battle had turned so suddenly that hundreds of Taliban foot soldiers switched allegiance to the United Front.[66]

Replacing his horses with tanks, personnel carriers, and artillery pieces abandoned by the Taliban, Dostum advanced from Mazar-e Sharif in pursuit of retreating Taliban units attempting to regroup in the provincial capital of Kunduz, about 150 kilometers to the east. Kunduz, home to a quarter-million Afghans, was the last northeastern city still in Taliban hands. General Bariullah Khan's forces at Taluqan sought to envelop the Taliban in Kunduz from the west without assistance from Master Sergeant Bolduc's ODA. Given the uneven American relationships with participating United Front commanders and the presence of Pakistani military and intelligence service personnel advising the Taliban in the city, the two-pronged push on Kunduz promised to be a complicated affair.[67]

Following the capture of Herat, Taluqan, and Bamyan, CENTCOM switched the priority of aerial effort to Bismillah Khan Mohammadi at Bagram. After twenty-four hours of unrelenting bombardment of the Shomali Plain, which cost the enemy twenty-nine tanks and several thousand

---

65. Yaniv Barzilai, *102 Days of War: How Osama bin Laden, Al-Qaeda, & The Taliban Survived 2001* (Washington, D.C.: Potomac Books, 2013), p. 72; Camp, *Boots on the Ground*, pp. 153, 159, 209; GO 10, p. 2.

66. Satinder Bindra, "Afghan Rebels Report Taliban Defections," CNN, 11 Nov 2001, https://edition.cnn.com/2001/WORLD/asiapcf/central/11/11/ret.satinderbindra.otsc/index.html, Hist Files, OEF Study Grp.

67. Camp, *Boots on the Ground*, pp. 152, 156, 161; Barzilai, *102 Days of War*, p. 72.

casualties, Bismillah Khan's fighters shattered the Taliban's defenses, astride the highway that led to the Kotal-e Tonal-e Salang, a tunnel linking Bagram and the northern Afghan cities with Kabul. By the end of the day, the United Front fighters pushed within several kilometers of the Afghan capital. The capture of Bagram and the subsequent rapid advance on Kabul was a critical decision point for both the U.S. government and CENTCOM.

Although the Bush administration did not expect Kabul to fall so rapidly, senior American leaders never doubted that it would. Several weeks previously, the National Security Council discussed in detail what steps should be taken when the Taliban abandoned Kabul. The State Department argued that the administration ought to turn Kabul over to an international body, in order to avoid accusations that the United States was creating a puppet government in Afghanistan.[68] Bowing to Secretary of State Colin L. Powell's logic, the attendees agreed that a UN-sponsored international security force, rather than U.S. troops or United Front fighters, should maintain order in the Afghan capital following its liberation. However, the plan depended on the United Front acquiescing to an American request to remain outside Kabul until the international security force arrived.[69]

Powell followed up the National Security Council discussion with a visit to the United Nations, where he suggested reconvening the dormant "Six plus Two" group—a committee of Afghanistan's six neighbors (China, Iran, Pakistan, Tajikistan, Turkmenistan, and Uzbekistan), plus the United States and Russia, which had been assembled in the mid-1990s to broker ceasefires between warring Afghan factions—to map out a path for a post-Taliban Afghanistan. Working in conjunction with UN Secretary-General Kofi Annan, the group sought to establish broad-based international support for any emergent non-Taliban government in Afghanistan. Ambassador James F. Dobbins, representing the United States, played a leading role in this effort along with the UN Special Representative of the Secretary-General for Afghanistan, Lakhdar Brahimi.

With the United Front on the northern outskirts of Kabul, the Six plus Two group sought to establish key parameters for Afghanistan's future by issuing a Declaration on the Situation in Afghanistan.[70] The UN declaration affirmed the U.S. State Department's original position that a political solution to the Afghan crisis should entail a "broad based[,] multi-ethnic, politically balanced, freely chosen Afghan administration representative of their aspirations and at peace with its neighbours."[71] It also stated that rather than dictating what should be accomplished, the Six plus Two group should support "the efforts of the Afghan people" to reach a suitable political solution, and that its members welcomed the opportunity to assist "the

---

68. Woodward, *Bush at War*, pp. 229–34.

69. Ibid., pp. 306–08.

70. Dobbins, *After the Taliban*, p. 39.

71. "Declaration on the Situation in Afghanistan by the Foreign Ministers and Other Senior Representatives of the 'Six plus Two,'" United Nations (UN), 12 Nov 2001, https://www.un.org/News/dh/latest/afghan/sixplus.htm, Hist Files, OEF Study Grp.

Afghan people in developing a political alternative to the Taliban regime."[72] In addition, Brahimi suggested that an international multilateral security force be deployed immediately to the Afghan capital.[73]

Discussions about an international security force seemed prescient as Taliban units evacuated Kabul during the night of 12–13 November. Although Fahim promised the Americans that his forces would not occupy Kabul until an agreement for a broad-based government was in place, his troops entered the city on the following morning. Ironically, television pictures of their triumphant entry were not broadcast globally because an errant American bomb demolished the Kabul office of the Qatar-based Al-Jazeera television network.[74] Although United Front leaders later explained to the Americans that to do otherwise would have chanced a complete breakdown of law and order in the capital, their actions demonstrated that Afghan agendas would always trump the U.S. agenda.

The relatively few enemy fighters remaining in Kabul were able to slip away undetected, but 10,000 or more Taliban in the northern city of Kunduz were surrounded by the United Front. Unwilling to loosen his hold on Kabul in order to help Dostum, Fahim limited further operations to pushing eastward, in concert with local tribal allies, toward the mountainous region along the Afghan-Pakistan border. A former mujahideen commander who joined the United Front cause, Younis Khalis, took control of the strategic city of Jalalabad astride the main road from Kabul to Pakistan on 14 November. Any Taliban not surrounded in Kunduz appeared to be regrouping around Kandahar in the south. The situation in the south now posed CENTCOM's biggest challenge given that United Front forces could not move south without inflaming its Pashtun inhabitants.

Although most Taliban hailed from the Pashtun region of southern Afghanistan, the Americans were in a position to exploit divisions between tribes that supported the Taliban, and those that did not. Unlike in northern Afghanistan, the United States needed to establish a firm foothold in the south before CENTCOM could rally Pashtun groups that opposed the Taliban. Accordingly, General Franks tasked TF DAGGER to send ODAs to link up with these potential Pashtun allies. Departing from the operational model he employed in the north, Franks envisioned a mixture of U.S. Special Forces and conventional troops operating together in southern Afghanistan. These forces included elements of TF DAGGER, the soon to be created CJSOTF-South, and Marine amphibious groups sailing off the Pakistani coast.

International political considerations grew increasingly important as CENTCOM reshaped its campaign priorities. On 13 November, UN Special Representative Brahimi hosted a meeting to discuss the creation

---

72. Ibid.

73. Sean Maloney, "The International Security Assistance Force: The Origins of a Stabilization Force," *Canadian Military Journal* 4, no. 2 (Summer 2003): 4.

74. Muhammed Najeeb, "NA in Control of Kabul, Taleban Confirms Fall," Rediff.com – India Abroad, 13 Nov 2001, https://www.rediff.com/us/2001/nov/13ny2.htm, Hist Files, OEF Study Grp.

of a transitional political authority in Afghanistan.[75] Although Brahimi wanted United Front leaders to attend, he balked at their request to hold the meeting in Kabul because of security concerns. On the following day, the UN Security Council issued Resolution 1378, exhorting Afghans to accept an invitation to establish a transitional administration that would lead to the formation of a new "broad-based, multi-ethnic and fully representative" government. In addition to the appeal for Afghan involvement, the resolution urged UN member states "to support efforts to ensure the safety and security of areas of Afghanistan no longer under Taliban control, and in particular to ensure respect for Kabul as the capital for all the Afghan people." It also called on member states to support the economic and social rehabilitation of Afghanistan through a combination of "quick-impact projects" and "long-term assistance."[76]

While Kabul monopolized the UN's attention, CENTCOM looked at Bagram with equal interest. Although he knew its facilities were damaged and surrounded by uncharted minefields, General Franks envisioned Bagram as an ideally located operational and logistical hub. With improvements and added capabilities, Bagram could decrease the United States' dependence on Uzbek and Pakistani facilities. As a result, CENTCOM directed TF DAGGER to survey the airfield. Answers to critical questions such as which U.S. and coalition forces could deploy there and what fixes were required to support rotary- and fixed-wing aircraft, depended on Colonel Mulholland's findings.[77] Mulholland passed that mission to Colonel Dorman of Logistical Task Force 530. Accompanied by engineers, maintenance specialists, and airfield repair experts, Dorman conducted a thorough examination of Bagram. He reported to Mulholland that Bagram would suffice as a forward operating base for coalition forces and an entry point for aerially-delivered humanitarian aid.[78]

SECOND FORAY INTO THE TALIBAN'S HEARTLAND

After Kabul's fall, Special Operations Command Central directed TF DAGGER to send ODAs to connect with influential Pashtuns opposed to Taliban rule. The CIA strongly recommended sending a Special Forces team to contact Gul Agha Sharzai, a member of the Barazaki tribe and son of a prominent mujahideen leader. After the collapse of the Afghan communist regime, Sharzai served as governor of Kandahar Province until ousted by the Taliban. Sharzai and his followers fled to Pakistan, where they awaited an opportunity to return to Kandahar.[79] The American team selected to

---

75. UN Security Council, 4414th Meeting, S/PV.4414, 13 Nov 2001, http://www.un.org/en/ga/search/view_doc.asp?symbol=S/PV.4414, Hist Files, OEF Study Grp.

76. UN Security Council, Resolution 1378, S/RES/1378, 14 Nov 2001, http://unscr.com/en/resolutions/doc/1378, Hist Files, OEF Study Grp.

77. Memos, Col Eshelman for Third Army/ARCENT Cmd Grp and Staff, 18 Nov 2001, sub: ARCENT Update 18 Nov 01, 1516 hours, Story CFLCC Collection, OEF Study Grp.

78. Finlayson, "Not Just Doing Logistics," pp. 46–47.

79. Grenier, *88 Days to Kandahar*, pp. 148–49.

work with Sharzai initially knew nothing of the Afghan leader's past, and this reflected poorly on the ability of the U.S. intelligence community to collect such information on short notice. The Special Forces captain chosen to work with him later remarked, "The initial report on Sharzai was horrible. I received a power point slide with an old picture of him. . . . At the top of the slide the name Karzai had been scratched out in pen and Sharzai written in." Fortunately, a face-to-face discussion with newly arrived CIA officers a few days later succeeded in clearing these misconceptions and discerning Sharzai's personality.[80]

The CIA also suggested a Popalzai tribal leader named Hamid Karzai, about whom it had mixed opinions.[81] He was the son of Abdul Ahad Karzai, a prominent Afghan politician from the precommunist years. In the mid-1990s, the Taliban offered Hamid Karzai an ambassadorship, but Karzai refused because of his misgivings about excessive Pakistani influence over the new regime. Karzai then moved to Quetta, Pakistan, where he lobbied for the return of the former Afghan monarch, Mohammed Zahir Shah. In 1999, Taliban assassins killed Abdul Ahad Karzai, which prompted his son to openly support the United Front. Although Karzai had garnered an international reputation as a vocal opponent of Taliban rule, he had no military experience or armed followers. Nonetheless, American Special Forces personnel could easily evaluate Karzai, who resided at the U.S. compound on Shabaz Air Force Base.[82]

Colonel Mulholland selected ODA 574 under Capt. Jason L. Amerine to work with Karzai while assigning Capt. Hank E. Smith's ODA 583 to Sharzai. The decision to send ODAs south of the Hindu Kush merited some changes in task organization. Rather than risk committing scarce assets in an uncertain environment for little or no gain, Mulholland refrained from deploying full ODAs until Karzai or Sharzai gathered at least 300 fighters.[83] In addition, CIA paramilitary operatives and translators would infiltrate with the ODAs rather than precede them. Once Amerine and Smith established good relationships with their respective Pashtun opposition groups, Mulholland planned to send a detachment from Colonel Fox's 2d Battalion headquarters to southern Afghanistan to improve coordination between the multiple efforts in the south.[84]

Gary Berntsen, the newly arrived head of the CIA paramilitary contingent, decided to send two teams, ECHO and FOXTROT, with the ODAs bound for southern Afghanistan. He originally planned to send ECHO to Asadabad, a small town in the Pech River Valley in Kunar Province. Success in the north spurred Berntsen to discard that plan in favor of capturing the Taliban stronghold of

---

80. Email Interv, Dr. Terry Beckenbaugh, CSI, with Maj Hank Smith, frmr Cdr, ODA 583, 18 Apr 2007, p. 4, Hist Files, OEF Study Grp.

81. Grenier, *88 Days to Kandahar*, p. 145; Blehm, *The Only Thing Worth Dying For*, p. 79.

82. Blehm, *The Only Thing Worth Dying For*, pp. 67–68.

83. M Sgt Nick S. Nowatney, "SF NCOs in Afghanistan," (PEP, U.S. Army Sgts Maj Academy, 22 Apr 2004), p. 4 https://server16040.contentdm.oclc.org/cdm4/item_viewer.php?CISOROOT=/p15040coll2&CISOPTR=6260&CISOBOX=1&REC=1, Hist Files, OEF Study Grp.

84. Blehm, *The Only Thing Worth Dying For*, p. 65.

Kandahar. Berntsen's vision meshed perfectly with CENTCOM's emerging concept for southern Afghanistan, which called for Pashtun opposition groups to simultaneously advance on Kandahar from multiple directions.[85] As a result, Team ECHO deployed with Amerine's ODA 574 while Team FOXTROT accompanied Smith's ODA 583.

Captain Amerine flew down from Karshi Khanabad to Shabaz during the first week of November. He met with Hamid Karzai several days before being inserted in Afghanistan. After lengthy discussions with the Afghan leader, Amerine informed Mulholland that Karzai had promised that anti-Taliban fighters would flock to him, but only if he arrived in the company of American soldiers. As a result, Amerine received permission to deploy his entire detachment rather than a few select individuals. The ODA 574 detachment commander also arranged for Special Forces helicopters to ferry a group of Afghan tribal leaders from Jacobabad to Uruzgan Province to prepare for the arrival of Karzai, the American soldiers, and CIA officers.

Karzai, Amerine's ODA, and half of Team ECHO departed Shabaz Air Force Base aboard two Special Operations helicopters during the night of 14 November, arriving safely in a remote part of Uruzgan Province several hours later. Soon after landing, Amerine realized that an impromptu uprising against the Taliban in the nearby town of Tarin Kot had rendered his plan for building supplies and training troops over the next several weeks impracticable. Amerine knew that the Taliban would react by sending a punitive expedition against the townspeople. The Americans relocated to Tarin Kot at Karzai's urging, where Navy and Marine planes from the USS *Theodore Roosevelt* later destroyed a sizable motorized force approaching the town.[86] The American victory over the Taliban, which the entire population of Tarin Kot witnessed, garnered a massive outpouring of local support for Karzai.[87]

Meanwhile, the ODA 583 advance party led by Captain Smith and including several CIA paramilitary operatives, arrived in southern Afghanistan on 19 November. The remaining personnel joined the ODA three days later. Smith's team did not have as dramatic an introduction to combat as ODA 574 because Sharzai initially wanted to negotiate with the Taliban rather than fight, believing that "[t]hese were his people and if he was ever to be governor of Kandahar again, he would later need support from these people."[88] After a misguided attempt to force the Taliban into submission ended with Sharzai's men being ambushed, fighting finally began. The Americans called in air strikes against the Taliban, which enabled Sharzai to capture Takhtah Pul Kelay by 23 November. Western media later

---

85. Barzilai, *102 Days of War*, p. 75.

86. Tony Holmes and Jim Laurier, *F-14 Tomcat Units of Operation ENDURING FREEDOM* (Oxford: Osprey Publishing, 2008), p. 62.

87. Blehm, *The Only Thing Worth Dying For*, pp. 130–54.

88. Nowatney, "SF NCOs in Afghanistan," p. 5.

reported that the Americans were unable to prevent Sharzai from executing 160 Taliban, including some Pakistanis, who refused to surrender.[89]

In addition to the reverses inflicted on Taliban forces by TF DAGGER at Tarin Kot and Takhtah Pul Kelay, TF SWORD carried out a number of forays into southern Afghanistan on 13 November to persuade the Taliban that American ground forces were attempting to interdict the main highway linking Kandahar with Kabul. These operations involved a series of raids with ground and heliborne elements delivered by MC–130s at night to remote desert landing strips. A team of Rangers secured the landing sites during the day while MC–130s inserted Special Operations MH–6 Little Bird helicopters and TF SWORD operators to conduct attacks on the Taliban each night, departing before dawn.[90] The highly successful forays ended on 17 November after participating TF SWORD units learned that they were relocating to Bagram to join the hunt for Osama bin Laden.

The fall of Kabul added considerable momentum to Special Operations Command Central plans to form a second Special Operations task force. In mid-November, CJSOTF-South (also known as Task Force K-BAR) headed by Navy Capt. Robert S. Harward stood up at Jazirat Masirah, Oman. Harward's command initially consisted of Navy SEALs; coalition SOF from Canada, Norway, Denmark, Germany, Australia, New Zealand, and Turkey; and Company A, 1st Battalion, 5th Special Forces Group. Over the next several months, Harward received additional forces, including the 3d Battalion, 3d Special Forces Group, 1st Special Forces Command, and elements of the 528th Support Battalion (Special Operations).[91] Harward gained responsibility for southern Afghanistan from Colonel Mulholland, with the exception of the ODAs working with Karzai and Sharzai. The new command would operate from Oman until Kandahar fell to Pashtun opposition fighters.

ADAPTING TO A DYNAMIC OPERATIONAL ENVIRONMENT

When CFLCC declared itself "mission ready" on 20 November at Camp Doha, it assumed responsibility for a battlespace that had doubled in size over the past two weeks. During that period, General Mikolashek's priorities were adjusted frequently before settling on coordinating the movement of international and U.S. forces into Bagram and Mazar-e Sharif, adjusting

---

89. "160 Taliban Fighters Executed," *Telegraph*, 28 Nov 2001, https://www.telegraph.co.uk/news/1363706/160-Taliban-fighters-executed.html, Hist Files, OEF Study Grp.

90. Briscoe et al., *Weapon of Choice*, p. 144; ibid., pp. 122–36.

91. Combined Joint Special Operations Task Force (CJSOTF)–South began operations on 22 November 2001, supporting the insertion of Marine Corps elements into Objective RHINO. Briscoe et al., *Weapon of Choice*, pp. 205, 216; John D. Gresham, "OEF-Afghanistan: The Campaign Plan," in *The Year in Special Operations 2011–2012 Edition*, p. 98; Austin Mansfield, "Enduring Freedom Task Force Earns Presidential Unit Citation," Naval Special Warfare Command Public Affairs, 8 Dec 2004, https://www.navy.mil/submit/display/asp?story_id=16216, Hist Files, OEF Study Grp; "United States Navy President Unit Citation for 1 NZSAS Regt," *New Zealand Defence Force*, 2 Oct 2014, https://www.nzdf.mil.nz/about-us/nzsof/usnpu-citation.htm, Hist Files, OEF Study Grp.

Defense Secretary Rumsfeld and General Franks hold a press conference at the Pentagon shortly after the September 11th attacks. The two would set the early policy and strategic objectives for operations in Afghanistan.

humanitarian efforts to match the growing American footprint, making final coordination for the marines' raid into southern Afghanistan, and standing up a forward headquarters in Uzbekistan.[92] Although not formally tasked to do so, CFLCC sought to better its overall awareness of United Front actions through interacting closely with TF DAGGER.[93] Senior commanders created ad hoc liaison methods by working around paltry pre–September 11th doctrine, and by relying on the practical experience of integrating Special Operations and U.S. conventional forces on the battlefield. Further complicating matters, the activities of some Special Operations units were considered so sensitive that they were forbidden to coordinate with other Special Operations units or conventional forces.

Creating workable means of exchanging information with TF DAGGER was only one of the numerous challenges facing Mikolashek's headquarters on the eve of major combat operations. With the United Front conduit established, the CFLCC commander turned next to building closer ties with the amphibious forces tabbed to go ashore in Afghanistan. On 21 November, he met with Admiral Moore to discuss what would take place once the Marines established a forward operating base at RHINO. Moore explained that TF-58 under General Mattis required six days to build defensive positions and logistical stocks before it could expand its initial lodgment. In addition to

---

92. Memo, Col Eshelman for Third Army/ARCENT Cmd Grp and Staff, 23 Nov 2001, sub: ARCENT Update 22 & 23 Nov 01, 1350 hours, Story CFLCC Collection, OEF Study Grp.

93. Memo, Col Eshelman for Third Army/ARCENT Cmd Grp and Staff, 20 Nov 2001, sub: ARCENT Update 19 & 20 Nov 01, 1616 hours, Story CFLCC Collection, OEF Study Grp.

serving as a forward operating base for TF-58, Mikolashek envisioned Rhino being utilized by SOF. As a result, the CFLCC commander directed TF-58 to provide common-item logistics support for all collocated SOF. In addition to determining basic logistical relationships, Moore and Mikolashek also agreed that devising an effective coordination system took top priority as the Marines might find themselves in close proximity to CJSOTF-South elements, ODAs deployed by TF Dagger, and their respective Afghan counterparts.

Both commanders examined potential future missions for the marines, including the option of using Rhino as a base for attacking Taliban forces throughout southern Afghanistan and overseeing the start of humanitarian aid operations in Kandahar once Afghan opposition groups secured the city. Mikolashek, aware that the Marine Expeditionary Units did not have a robust civil affairs component, promised Moore that he would send Army personnel capable of coordinating humanitarian aid operations.[94] The CFLCC commander qualified that statement by explaining that, with the exception of a single active-duty battalion, Army civil affairs units belonged to the reserve component and had to be mobilized before deploying to theater.

General Franks arrived at Doha on 23 November to discuss the campaign with Mikolashek. Franks approved Mikolashek's plan to use a division headquarters provided by the XVIII Airborne Corps to establish a forward command post at Karshi Khanabad. He expressed no misgivings about Mikolashek's priorities for Bagram, which were to get the airfield operational and pay locals to build key facilities while still maintaining a small footprint. Mikolashek assured Franks that he would coordinate all movement into the air base through Mulholland. Franks conceded that a sustained U.S. presence might be required at Bagram, but he did not see Mazar-e Sharif in the same light. The CENTCOM commander concluded by telling Mikolashek that he wanted to confine direct U.S. involvement in the upcoming fight for Kandahar to Special Forces teams aiding indigenous militia forces.[95]

That same day, General Franks flew to Bagram for a second meeting with General Fahim. He greeted Fahim before launching into a discussion on how CENTCOM planned to send additional personnel to Afghanistan to support humanitarian relief operations. Franks also explained that U.S. forces were preparing to push south and east in order to apprehend fleeing al-Qaeda and Taliban. He then ended the conference by asking Fahim for "an assessment of combat operations in various parts of the country, including those led by Dr. Karim Khalili in Bamian, [Ustad] Muhammad Atta Noor in Mazar-i-Sharif, and Ismael Khan in Herat."[96]

Believing that victory in the north lay on the horizon, neither commander devoted much time to discussing Kunduz. The city's situation was not static, however. CIA operative Berntsen recounted that United Front sources

---

94. Memo, Col Eshelman for Third Army/ARCENT Cmd Grp and Staff, 21 Nov 2001, sub: ARCENT Update 21 Nov 01, 1724 hrs, Story CFLCC Collection, OEF Study Grp.

95. Memo, Eshelman for Third Army/ARCENT Cmd Grp and Staff, 23 Nov 2001, sub: ARCENT Update 22 & 23 Nov 01.

96. Berntsen and Pezzullo, *Jawbreaker*, pp. 234–38.

claimed two Pakistani planes landed in Konduz [sic] under the cover of darkness to extract key Pakistani advisors to the Taliban and several high-ranking Taliban officials. I had no way to confirm this, but wasn't surprised. Pakistan's Inter-Service Intelligence Directorate had been a close ally [of the Taliban] for years.[97]

Ahmed Rashid, a respected international journalist, offers additional detail by stating that President Bush granted the Pakistani Air Force unimpeded access to Kunduz at the request of President Pervez Musharraf:

> The request was made by Musharraf to Bush, but [Vice President] Cheney took charge—a token of who was handling Musharraf at the time. The approval was not shared with anyone at State . . . until well after the event. Musharraf said that Pakistan needed to save its dignity and its valued people. . . . Hundreds of ISI [Inter-Services Intelligence] officers, Taliban commanders, and foot soldiers belonging to the IMU (Islamic Movement of Uzbekistan) and al-Qaeda personnel boarded the planes. What was sold as a minor extraction turned into a major air bridge.[98]

In addition to Rashid's exposé, contemporary media reports offered glimpses of what transpired in northern Afghanistan during the last week of November. Reports of an aerial evacuation from Kunduz first appeared in the Indian press, quoting intelligence sources citing unusual radar contacts and an airlift of Pakistani troops out of the city. On 24 November, the *New York Times* featured a front page article describing a two-day airlift by Pakistani aircraft, complete with eyewitness accounts of large numbers of armed men lined up along the runway awaiting evacuation.[99] The DoD subsequently took great pains to discredit those reports, leading General Myers on 26 November to state that "the runway [at Kunduz] is not usable. I mean, there are segments of it usable, but they're usually—they're too short for your standard transport aircraft. So we're not sure where the reports are coming from."[100] Secretary Rumsfeld told American television viewers that "to my knowledge, we have not seen a single airplane or helicopter go into Afghanistan in recent days or weeks and extract people and take them out of Afghanistan to any country, let alone Pakistan."[101] With numerous

---

97. Ibid., p. 241.

98. Ahmed Rashid, *Descent into Chaos: The U.S. and the Disaster in Pakistan, Afghanistan, and Central Asia* (New York: Viking Press, 2008), p. 92.

99. Michael Moran, "The 'Airlift of Evil': Why Did We Let Pakistan Pull 'Volunteers' Out of Kunduz?," NBC News, 29 Nov 2001, https://www.nbcnews.com/id/3340165/ns/world_news-brave_new_world/t/airlift-evil/, Hist Files, OEF Study Grp.

100. Bfg, Sec Def Donald H. Rumsfeld and Gen Richard B. Myers, 26 Nov 2001, DoD, https://archive.defense.gov/Transcripts/Transcript.aspx?TranscriptID=2460, Hist Files, OEF Study Grp.

101. Interv, Tim Russert, NBC News' *Meet the Press*, with Donald H. Rumsfeld, Sec Def, 2 Dec 2001, DoD Press Operations, https://archive.defense.gov/Transcripts/Transcript.aspx?TranscriptID=2585, Hist Files, OEF Study Grp.

journalist reports contradicting those statements, it is no wonder that many of the DoD's assessments of the situation in Afghanistan were greeted with reasonable suspicion by the media.

Although Musharraf justified the airlift by mentioning the presence of Pakistani citizens who recently joined the Taliban, that rationale violated a specific provision in the Armitage-Ahmed agreement demanding that Islamabad "cut off all shipments of fuel to the Taliban and any other items and recruits, to include volunteers en route to Afghanistan."[102] Washington could have offered to have U.S. troops verify the identity of the evacuees, but it approved the request without doing so—a decision that indicated the Bush administration's willingness to make exceptions to the agreement's original terms. As a result, not only were hundreds of Pakistani citizens ferried out by American built C–130 transports, but a number of prominent Taliban were potentially spirited out of the besieged city. From a long-term perspective, the compromise over the evacuation signaled that despite the strong language in Armitage's document, Islamabad could pursue its strategic interests in the region on a case-by-case basis without fear of automatic American repercussions.

Once the Pakistanis and top ranking Taliban were evacuated, the thousands of Afghan and foreign Taliban fighters remaining in Kunduz laid down their arms on 24 November. Although Secretary Rumsfeld signaled the Bush administration's disapproval of any initiative to grant amnesty to enemy combatants, a United Front spokesman in Dushanbe, the capital of Tajikistan, told reporters that the Afghan Taliban would be released while foreign fighters faced possible courtroom prosecution.[103] Once again, Afghan agendas had trumped Washington pronouncements. Rather than go home, thousands of Taliban joined the ranks of the United Front. When a puzzled American journalist asked a veteran mujahideen warrior about the willingness of both sides to accept such an arrangement, the Afghan replied, "In America and other places . . . people have the idea that their countries are important to them. But in Afghanistan the fighters don't have this notion, and the poverty here leads them to join whoever is powerful."[104]

Some Taliban fighters in Kunduz, notably foreigners taking part in what they considered to be a holy war against apostate Shia Hazaras, did not give up peacefully. Although the bulk of the city's estimated 10,000 defenders expressed a willingness to switch sides, more than 3,000 did not. As a result, more fighting ensued as Dostum's forces rooted out diehards within the city.

---

102. Msg, Sec State to U.S. Embassy in Islamabad, 13 Sep 2001, sub: Deputy Secretary Armitage's Meeting with General Mahmud: Actions and Support Expected of Pakistan in Fight Against Terrorism, 140119Z Sep 01, NSA GWU, https://nsarchive.gwu.edu/NSAEBB/NSAEBB358a/doc05.pdf, Hist Files, OEF Study Grp.

103. Nikolai Pavlov, "Confusion Cloaks Konduz Surrender Talks," Afghanistan News Center, 22 Nov 2001 [page discontinued], https://www.afghanistannewscenter.com/news/2001/november/nov22j2001.html, Hist Files, OEF Study Grp.

104. Jon Lee Anderson, "The Surrender: Double Agents, Defectors, Disaffected Taliban, and a Motley Army Battle for Konduz," *The New Yorker*, 10 Dec 2001, https://www.newyorker.com/magazine/2001/12/10/the-surrender, Hist Files, OEF Study Grp.

Many United Front fighters were infuriated that their comrades were being killed and wounded even after the Taliban agreed to capitulate. Survivors of these bitter engagements, both wounded and unwounded, were bundled into metal shipping containers bound for Shibirghan prison. When confronted about media claims that most captives from Kunduz died en route to the prison, Dostum admitted that 270 prisoners perished in the mass movement. The deaths were attributed to lack of medical care, rough roads, poor food, and isolated instances of vengeful guards.

In addition to the foreign fighters in the city who refused to surrender, senior Taliban commanders attempted on two occasions to send troops to Mazar-e Sharif to divert Dostum's attention from Kunduz. The initial attempt involved sending a column of trucks and armored vehicles northwest toward Mazar-e Sharif several days before Kunduz's surrender. American planes destroyed the Taliban vehicles as their drivers attempted to negotiate secondary roads in a remote area near the Afghan-Uzbek border. The second attempt took place just before the mass surrender, when a truck column filled with al-Qaeda and foreign fighters boldly attempted to drive down the main highway from Kunduz to Mazar-e Sharif under the cover of darkness. The enemy leader, Mullah Mohammed Fazl, gambled that American planes would not attack the convoy if it used Dostum's heavily traveled main supply route. His plan failed when a number of trucks broke down during the trip. The al-Qaeda and foreign fighters were still far short of Mazar-e Sharif when dawn broke, and the convoy chose to surrender to Dostum's men rather than face certain destruction from the air.[105]

That afternoon, the foreign fighters loaded themselves onto trucks provided by the United Front. They traveled first to Mazar-e Sharif, where they briefly halted next to the Turkish school housing the administrative and logistical elements of Operational Detachment Charlie 53, designated as Forward Operating Base 53, before continuing to the Qala-i-Jangi fortress eleven kilometers west of the city.[106] During the halt outside the school, Dostum placed a phone call to his men and changed the convoy's final destination from Mazar-e Sharif to the fortress, acting on a well-founded hunch that the foreign fighters were not trustworthy. Dostum suspected that the al-Qaeda fighters were fanatical enough to try to accomplish their original mission even after having surrendered.[107]

The octagonal brick fortress known as Qala-i-Jangi, meaning "house of war" in the local dialect, had been constructed a century earlier. Measuring more than 500 meters in width, Qala-i-Jangi had three-meter-wide perimeter walls anchored on each corner by twelve-meter-high stone towers. Inside, a three-meter wall bisected the fortress, which gave defenders a position to continue fighting even if the enemy succeeded in forcing a breach. A single gate with a metal door connected both halves. The predominantly Uzbek

---

105. Interv, Mark J. Reardon, OEF Study Grp, with Maj (Ret.) Mark D. Nutsch, frmr ODA 595 Cdr, 13 Dec 2015, Hist Files, OEF Study Grp.

106. Briscoe et al., *Weapon of Choice*, p. 159.

107. Kalev V. Sepp, "Uprising at Qala-i-Jangi: The Staff of the 3/5th SF Group," *Special Warfare* 15, no. 3 (Sep 2002): 18.

Qala-i-Jangi Fortress, where General Dostum detained initial enemy prisoners during early operations in northern Afghanistan.

garrison lived in a two-story barracks in the northern half, while the southern half was used as an armory and temporary holding facility for prisoners. A one-story building in the center of the southern compound, along with a series of underground rooms, held captives taken earlier by Dostum (*Map 2.2*).[108]

Guards herded the prisoners into a loose formation within the southern courtyard soon after their arrival. When the guard detail began searching the captives, one of the prisoners detonated a grenade that killed himself and one of Dostum's officers.[109] A second prisoner also committed suicide with a grenade, taking several guards with him. After the guards restored order, one of Dostum's officers informed the detainees that they would be turned over to the UN rather than to the Americans. Mollified by the announcement, the prisoners allowed their guards to herd them into cells.[110]

Guards released the captives from confinement the following morning to wash before prayers. At the same time, two members of Team Echo, CIA officers Johnny Michael "Mike" Spann and David Tyson, arrived at Qala-i-Jangi.[111] The appearance of the Americans, which contravened assurances given the previous evening, sparked a riot among the captives. Spann died fighting, along with a number of Dostum's men, while Tyson battled his way

---

108. Daniel P. Bolger, *Why We Lost: A General's Inside Account of the Iraq and Afghanistan Wars* (New York: Houghton Mifflin Harcourt Publishing Co., 2014), p. 53.

109. Briscoe et al., *Weapon of Choice*, p. 159.

110. Bolger, *Why We Lost*, p. 54.

111. Williams, *The Last Warlord*, p. 264.

INITIAL COMBAT OPERATIONS

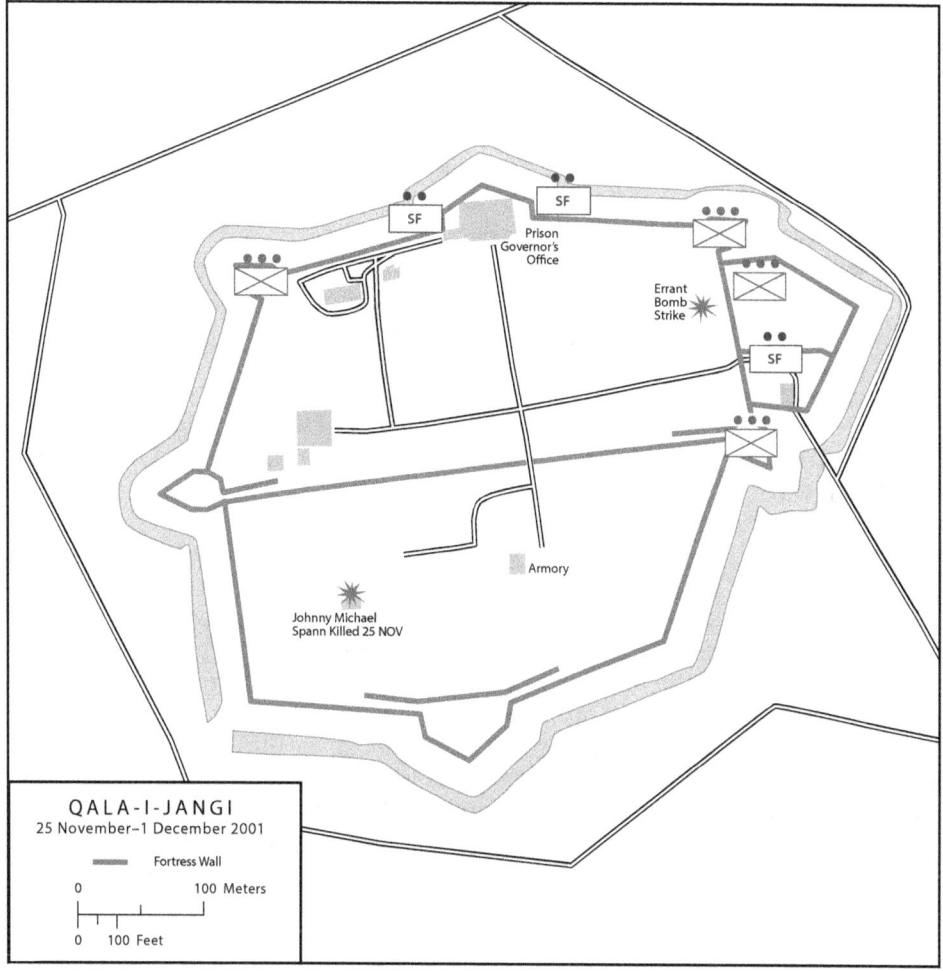

Map 2.2

to safety along with the surviving guards. Tyson relayed a desperate plea for aid through CIA channels, who, in turn, contacted TF DAGGER at Karshi Khanabad. Colonel Mulholland directed Operational Detachment Charlie 53 to send a team to get the CIA officers out of danger.

The rescue party consisted of Colonel Bowers' executive and operations officers, several members of the 3d Battalion, 5th Special Forces Group staff, eight British Special Boat Squadron operators, two Navy SEALs, and a pair of Air Force tactical air support controllers. Colonel Bowers, along with ODA 534 and ODA 595 and his remaining staff, stayed at Kunduz with General Dostum. In addition to mobilizing Operational Detachment Charlie 53, Mulholland sent a quick reaction force from Karshi Khanabad consisting of 1st Lt. Bradley J. Maryoka's 1st Platoon of Company C, 1st Battalion, 87th Infantry, via air to Mazar-e Sharif.[112]

---

112. Williams, *The Last Warrior*, p. 264.

Operating originally on the assumption that one CIA officer had been wounded and a second remained inside the fortress, the rescue force soon learned that the trapped American had died and that the prisoners not only outnumbered the guards, but were as well armed as Dostum's men after ransacking the southern armory. The British commandos directed machine-gun fire against the foreign fighters while the Americans targeted the southern compound with multiple air strikes. The surviving CIA operative and a Western television crew took advantage of the air strikes to make their way out of the fortress. As darkness approached, the rescue force returned to Mazar-e Sharif to await Lieutenant Maryoka's platoon before reentering the fray.[113]

On November 26, the TF DAGGER personnel, reinforced by the soldiers from 10th Mountain Division, resumed their assault at dawn. They were joined by the survivors of the original guard detail and a T–55 tank and several mortar crews sent by Dostum. The Americans, British, and Uzbeks resumed the contest, hurling tank, mortar, and machine-gun fire at the foreign fighters while receiving constant small-arms fire in return. The senior U.S. officer called for air support to break the stalemate. The primary joint tactical air controller, Air Force S. Sgt. Michael A. Scortino, called in the first set of target coordinates to several F/A–18C Hornets orbiting overhead. The pilots complied with the request, releasing a single 2,000-pound JDAM (Joint Direct Attack Munition) that unexpectedly landed alongside the lone United Front T–55 tank. Subsequent investigation disclosed that an F/A–18C pilot inadvertently entered friendly coordinates as the desired target.[114] The blast flipped the armored vehicle over, killing four Afghans and wounding a dozen others.[115] Two British commandos and five Americans were also wounded.[116] The uninjured Americans rendered first aid to their wounded comrades as the joint tactical air controller resumed calling in strikes against the enemy.

Dawn brought a change of tactics on the part of the Special Operations personnel and Dostum's fighters. Rather than rely on air support, the combined Anglo-American and Afghan force began waging a deadly room-to-room battle within the southern compound. Dostum's men retrieved CIA officer Mike Spann's remains after defusing an explosive device placed under his body. The remaining foreign fighters fled into the underground cells, where they held out for several days until driven from hiding by cold water pumped into their refuge. The CIA later discovered two Americans—John Walker Lindh from California and Yaser Esam Hamdi from Louisiana—

---

113. Sepp, "Uprising at Qala-i-Jangi," p. 17.

114. Memo, CENTCOM, 6 Feb 2003, sub: Review of Report of Investigation into Friendly Fire JDAM incident at Mazar-i-Sharif on 26 Nov 2001, Executive Summary, https://www3.centcom.mil/FOIA_RR_Files/5%20USC%20552(a)(2)(D)Records/Friendly%20Fires/26%20Nov%2001%20FF%20Redacted-NAVCENT.pdf, Hist Files, OEF Study Grp.

115. Bolger, *Why We Lost*, p. 62.

116. "Military Awards Ceremony for Service in Afghanistan," CNN.com/Transcripts, 15 Jan 2002, https://cnn.com/TRANSCRIPTS/0201/15/se.03.html, Hist Files, OEF Study Grp.

among eighty-six enemy survivors.[117] Dostum then turned Mohammed Fazl over to the Americans.[118]

The issue of prisoners assumed growing importance following the surrender at Kunduz, the Qala-i-Jangi uprising, and reports of Gul Agha Sharzai's men shooting prisoners at Takhtah Pul Kelay. During a Pentagon press conference, a reporter asked Secretary of Defense Rumsfeld if the continued disintegration of the Taliban's field forces would result in American troops accepting the surrender of enemy combatants. Rumsfeld replied in the negative, stating that "in terms of our actually going out and seeking prisoners or looking for the opportunity to hold prisoners, we're not. [Our Afghan allies] have much larger numbers of people on the ground. They are perfectly capable of doing those kinds of things."[119] Rumsfeld's remarks were consistent with U.S. policy, which sought to minimize the number of American ground troops taking part in the conflict. The Bush administration's preference for finding an Afghan solution to battlefield challenges, which in this case involved the care, feeding, and safeguarding of Taliban prisoners, had been designed to avoid casting the United States in the unwanted role of occupying power.

This policy seemed unambiguous to Washington decision makers, yet the American military's commitment to providing logistical support to the United Front meant that it could not avoid becoming involved. On the day Kunduz fell, General Mikolashek decreed that CFLCC needed to deliver food, water, and other supplies for captives held by the United Front. Humanitarian concerns played a part in that decision, but Mikolashek strongly believed the United Front would balk at the prospect of indefinitely maintaining prisoner-of-war camps without U.S. assistance.[120] Over the past six weeks, the campaign plan successfully weathered several major challenges, but CFLCC soon realized that it could not avoid providing for enemy captives altogether. The need to safely detain and aid prisoners, even to a minor extent, was the first of many unanticipated modifications to the U.S. mandate in Afghanistan.

---

117. Sepp, "Uprising at Qala-i-Jangi," p. 18; Bolger, *Why We Lost*, p. 64.

118. Memo, Cdr, U.S. Forces Southern Cmd, to Cdr, Joint Task Force Guantanamo, 23 Feb 2008, sub: Recommendation for Continued Detention Under DoD Control (CD) for Guantanamo Detainee, ISN US9AF-000007DP (S), "Mullah Muhammad Fazl," *New York Times*, The Guantanamo Docket, https://projects.nytimes.com/guantanamo/detainees/7-mullah-Muhammad-fazl, Hist Files, OEF Study Grp. In May 2014, Mullah Muhammad Fazl was one of five high-ranking Taliban members exchanged for Sgt. Beaudry R. "Bowe" Bergdahl, who had been held captive by the Taliban since he deserted his post in June 2009. See Deb Riechmann, "A Look at the 5 Taliban Figures Exchanged for Sgt. Bowe Bergdahl," *Military Times*, 27 May 2015, https://www.militarytimes.com/news/your-military/2015/05/27/a-look-at-the-5-taliban-figures-exchanged-for-sgt-bowe-bergdahl/, Hist Files, OEF Study Grp.

119. Bfg, Rumsfeld and Myers, 26 Nov 2001.

120. Memo, Col Eshelman for Third Army/ARCENT Cmd Grp and Staff, 24 Nov 2001, sub: ARCENT Update 24 Nov 01, 1319 hours, Story CFLCC Collection, OEF Study Grp.

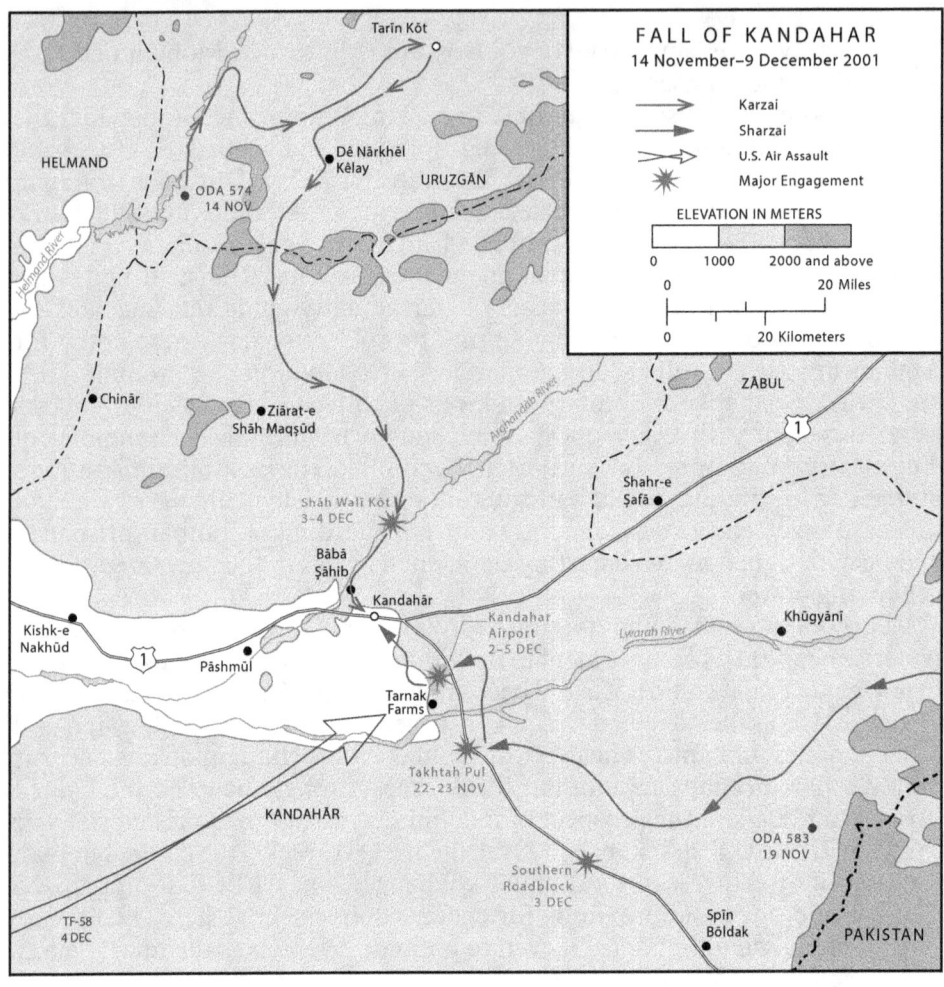

Map 2.3

THE CONFLICT GOES INTERNATIONAL

While the dramatic developments at Qala-i-Jangi drew widespread public attention, CENTCOM remained focused on the city of Kandahar. TF-58 launched its bid to seize Objective RHINO on 25 November after Special Operations teams confirmed that no enemy troops were defending the isolated airstrip southwest of Kandahar. The first wave of troop-carrying CH–53s, bearing sixty-six riflemen and two Interim Fast Attack Vehicles, preceded by three UH–1N utility helicopters and four AH–1W Sea Cobra gunships, arrived at RHINO just before sunset after a four-hour flight from the USS *Peleliu*. Successive flights delivered more troops and equipment until dawn, when the potential threat posed by portable surface-to-air missiles ended helicopter operations until the following evening.[121] Elements of the

---

121. Lowery, *U.S. Marines in Afghanistan, 2001–2002*, pp. 111–16.

Australian Special Air Service's 1 Squadron, led by Lt. Col. Rowan J. Tink, arrived at RHINO from Kuwait aboard leased Ukrainian Antonov transport planes. As the marines improved their defenses, the Australians conducted vehicle patrols in a northwesterly arc centered on Kandahar.[122]

The appearance of the marines coincided with the preparations for Sharzai and Karzai's planned attack on Kandahar (*Map 2.3*). After lengthy discussion, Captain Smith of ODA 583 convinced Sharzai to begin his offensive by establishing roadblocks north and south of Takhtah Pul Kelay on Highway 4. The northern element immediately drew a barrage of rocket fire from Taliban forces while the southern road block detected signs of increasing enemy activity near Spin Boldak. Rather than await a coordinated enemy assault, Captain Smith persuaded Sharzai to attack first. Smith's plan involved an initial push northwest from Takhtah Pul Kelay ten kilometers to the Arghistan Bridge. Sharzai's forces would have to secure the maze of *wadis* (dry riverbeds) and irrigation canals stretching northwest and west from the bridge to Tarnak Farms before they could advance. Tarnak Farms, sited less than three kilometers south-southwest of the airport, had long been known as a major al-Qaeda base in Afghanistan.[123]

To degrade Taliban defenses ahead of Sharzai's main attack, Captain Smith deployed several of his troops, including a joint tactical air controller, atop a commanding ridge ten kilometers southeast of the airport on 26 November.[124] The bombing runs called by the controller would be some of the most dangerous missions of the conflict, as the Taliban greeted incoming planes with antiaircraft artillery and shoulder-fired surface-to-air missiles. The potent combination of broken terrain, persistent antiaircraft fire, and the Taliban's numerical superiority necessitated almost a week of nonstop bombing before Captain Smith notified Sharzai that the attack could begin.[125]

As Sharzai's forces waited for U.S. air power to weaken the enemy defenses overlooking the Arghistan bridge, opposition fighters led by Karzai were preparing to attack Kandahar from the north. In response to rumors that Karzai might be appointed as the future head of an interim post-Taliban government, Colonel Mulholland ordered Colonel Fox's command group to connect with Amerine's ODA before the attack on Kandahar.[126] In yet another example of Americans believing that they could divine Afghan intentions and impressions, the CIA prevailed upon CENTCOM to limit the number of soldiers accompanying Fox because the agency felt that sending a large advisory contingent made Karzai appear overly dependent on U.S.

---

122. Robert Macklin and Clint Palmer, *SAS Insider: An Elite Fighter Inside Australia's Toughest and Most Secretive Combat Force* (Sydney: Hachette Publishing, 2014), pp. 181–82; Ian McPhedran, *The Amazing SAS: the Inside Story of Australia's Special Forces* (New York: HarperCollins, 2007), pp. 164–69.

123. Ben Farmer, "9/11: HQ where Bin Laden Plotted Atrocities," *Telegraph*, 5 Sept 2011, https://www.telegraph.co.uk/news/worldnews/september-11-attacks/8741145/911-HQ-where-bin-Laden-plotted-atrocities.html, Hist Files, OEF Study Grp.

124. Nowatney, "SF NCOs in Afghanistan," p. 4.

125. Briscoe et al., *Weapon of Choice*, pp. 169–71.

126. Grenier, *88 Days to Kandahar*, p. 253.

assistance.¹²⁷ CENTCOM sided with the CIA. As a result, Fox, accompanied only by a communications sergeant and his operations officer, Maj. Donald C. Bolduc, arrived via helicopter north of Tarin Kot on 27 November.¹²⁸

Politics influenced Karzai's advance on Kandahar in other ways. Mullah Mohammed Omar reportedly had departed the city, having handed over control to a pair of subordinates, Mullah Naquib Alikozai and Hajji Bashar, a week earlier.¹²⁹ Alikozai and Bashar telephoned Karzai offering to surrender Kandahar if the United Front turned Kabul over to Pashtun opposition groups. Alikozai also asked for a local cease-fire and a halt to U.S. bombing. Karzai replied that the Taliban had to sever all ties with al-Qaeda before he would agree to a cease-fire or bombing halt.¹³⁰

Given that the terrain between Tarin Kot and Kandahar consisted of "extremely rough and wild country that Karzai said the Soviets learned to avoid after a few devastating ambushes," Colonel Fox suggested the attack take place in several stages rather than one continuous operation.¹³¹ Karzai approved Fox's proposal without hesitation, primarily because a decisive military victory by his troops could tip the balance at the international post-Taliban governance conference called into session in Germany. The conference convened at the Petersberg Hotel in Bonn on the day Colonel Fox arrived at Tarin Kot. Four Afghan delegations were present: the United Front delegation led by Yunus Qanooni, influential expatriates with Iranian ties known as the "Cypress Group," a second band of well-to-do exiles living in Pakistan known as the "Peshawar Group," and representatives of former king Zahir Shah. Although Pakistan lobbied vigorously for allowing Mullah Omar's representatives to participate, the UN did not invite the Taliban.¹³²

Besides the Afghan delegates, representatives from India, Pakistan, Iran, Russia, and European countries attended. Ambassador Dobbins, Afghan-born U.S. envoy Zalmay M. Khalilzad, and Deputy Assistant Secretary of Defense for Near East and South Asian Affairs William J. Luti represented the United States.¹³³ The opening discussions centered on three key issues: the distribution of cabinet positions, security in post-Taliban Afghanistan, and the choice of interim chairman. According to Dobbins, the United States had no preordained position on these matters: "My job was to get an agreement

---

127. Interv, Connors with Fox, 30 Nov 2006, p. 7. The CIA officials involved evidently did not consider the possibility that some good could come from a large number of American troops openly supporting a well-known Pashtun.

128. Blehm, *The Only Thing Worth Dying For*, pp. 175–76.

129. Jane Perlez, "A NATION CHALLENGED: KANDAHAR; Taliban Leader Said to be Yielding Grip on Stronghold to 2 Once-Powerful Supporters," *New York Times*, 17 Nov 2001, https://www.nytimes.com/2001/11/17/world/nation-challenged-kandahar-taliban-leader-said-be-yielding-grip-stronghold-2.html, Hist Files, OEF Study Grp.

130. Grenier, *88 Days to Kandahar*, p. 253.

131. Blehm, *The Only Thing Worth Dying For*, p. 181.

132. "Filling the Vacuum: The Bonn Conference," PBS *Frontline*, https://www.pbs.org/wgbh/pages/frontline/shows/campaign/withus/cbonn.html, Hist Files, OEF Study Grp.

133. Dobbins, *After the Taliban*, p. 70.

Secretary of Defense Rumsfeld meets with Hamid Karzai (left) at Bagram on 1 December 2001.

and almost any agreement would do, so long as it resulted in an Afghan government that would replace the Taliban's, unite the opposition, secure international support, cooperate in hunting down al-Qaeda's remnants, and relieve the United States of the need to occupy and run the country."[134]

The attendees recognized that the best interests of all represented parties would be served by facilitating the reestablishment of security within Afghanistan, while at the same time recognizing that time would elapse before those organizations were "fully constituted and functioning."[135] As a stopgap measure, Bonn Conference attendees called on the UN Security Council "to consider authorizing the early deployment . . . of a United Nations mandated force" to "assist in the maintenance of security for Kabul and its surrounding areas."[136] Attendees also expressed the desire that this force "assist in the rehabilitation of Afghanistan's infrastructure."[137] Crucially, the draft Bonn Agreement left open the possibility that "such a force could, as appropriate, be progressively expanded to other urban centers and other areas."[138] According to Ambassador Dobbins, this provision was a compromise.

---

134. Ibid., p. 85.

135. Agreement on Provisional Arrangements in Afghanistan Pending the Re-establishment of Permanent Government Institutions, Annex I, 5 Dec 2001, https://peacemaker.un.org/sites/peacemaker.un.org/files/AF_011205_AgreementProvisionalArrangementsinAfghanistan%28en%29.pdf, Hist Files, OEF Study Grp.

136. Ibid.

137. Ibid.

138. Ibid.

With the exception of the United Front, the Afghan representatives at Bonn wanted a nationwide peacekeeping force. However, Dobbins and his British counterpart, Robert Cooper, knew that the United States would not commit forces to peacekeeping and that the United Kingdom was the only other country capable of sustaining forces in Afghanistan on its own. They therefore persuaded the Afghans to accept a peacekeeping force—limited, at least for the time, to Kabul.[139]

In comparison to other issues, conference attendees quickly settled on a palatable nominee to lead the provisional government. As Ambassador Dobbins recalled:

> Among the international representatives was a strong consensus in favor of Hamid Karzai. . . . Virtually every foreign official with whom I had met in the past month, including the Pakistani, the Indian, the Russian, the Iranian, the Turkish, and European delegates had mentioned his name unprompted…the unanimity of international support for Karzai was largely Dr. [Abdullah] Abdullah's doing. . . . He knew Karzai as a moderate, personable, conciliatory figure of the sort who might be able to hold a fractious coalition together.[140]

Before the conference concluded on 5 December, the attendees agreed to establish an Afghan Interim Authority with Karzai at the helm as chairman.

The UN Security Council endorsed the conference's political and security pathways on 6 December.[141] The Afghan Interim Authority, slated to assume power in sixteen days, would govern for six months before tribal leaders, meeting in a *loya jirga* (grand assembly, akin to a national convention), would choose its successor. The temporary government approved by the tribal leaders would exist only for the eighteen months needed to draft a constitution and organize national elections.[142] Ensuring that the interim and transitional governments achieved their political milestones—namely, that they completed the Bonn Process on time—became the major focus of coalition efforts in Afghanistan for the next four years.[143]

---

139. Dobbins, *After the Taliban*, p. 88.

140. Blehm, *The Only Thing Worth Dying For*, p. 179. Dr. Abdullah Abdullah, a Kabul born and educated doctor of ophthalmology, was a senior member of the Northern Alliance working as an adviser to Ahmad Shah Massoud. Following the fall of the Taliban, he served as the Afghan minister of foreign affairs from October 2001 to April 2005. He would become the main presidential rival against Hamid Karzai in 2009 and Ashraf Ghani in 2014. Following the disputed 2014 election, a power-sharing agreement was brokered between Ghani and Abdullah, in which Ghani would be the president and Abdullah would be the chief executive of Afghanistan.

141. UN Security Council, Resolution 1383, S/RES/1383, 6 Dec 2001, https://www.securitycouncilreport.org/atf/cf/%7B65BFCF9B-6D27-4E9C-8CD3-CF6E4FF96FF9%7D/AFGH%20SRES1383.pdf, Hist Files, OEF Study Grp.

142. Agreement on Provisional Arrangements in Afghanistan Pending the Re-establishment of Permanent Government Institutions, 5 Dec 2001.

143. Thomas H. Johnson, "The Prospects for Post-Conflict Afghanistan: A Call of the Sirens to the Country's Troubled Past," *Strategic Insights* 5, no. 2 (Feb 2006), https://calhoun.nps.edu/

Initial Combat Operations

All Roads Lead to Kandahar

Karzai and Sharzai launched their respective attacks on Kandahar during the Bonn Conference. Karzai's fighters, along with Colonel Fox and Captain Amerine's team, departed Tarin Kot on 30 November. The convoy reached the village of Petawek by 2200, where it halted for several days to gather recruits and await a scheduled weapons airdrop. The combined U.S.-Afghan force resumed its advance toward Kandahar at noon on 3 December. It moved without incident until reaching a ridge five kilometers north of Shah Wali Kot, a town 16 kilometers from Kandahar overlooking the sole bridge spanning the Arghandab River. When Karzai's fighters reconnoitered the town, the Taliban fired on them. Captain Amerine and the other Americans joined the fight while Colonel Fox and the main body awaited developments. Although the Taliban retained their grip on the town, Amerine and the Afghans of Karzai's reconnaissance element secured vital high ground overlooking the town and bridge before nightfall.

Sharzai's attack had opened the day before Karzai's fighters arrived at Shah Wali Kot. As Captain Smith remembered, "We got our butts kicked and were pushed back to the bridge. It wasn't that the fighting was so intense, though we did take some losses, it was that trying to hold the area around the bridge and advancing to the airport at the same time was too much for that day."[144] The Americans followed Sharzai's men back to the ridge overlooking the bridge and airport. Fighting resumed on the morning of 3 December when a small enemy force probed Sharzai's defensive perimeter. Smith noted, "At this point the Taliban had bugged out and it was mostly AQ [al-Qaeda] we were encountering. They pretty much fought to the death, but there wasn't as many of them as Taliban so it was easier getting around them."[145]

The Taliban defenders of Shah Wali Kot were just as determined to halt Karzai's advance. The evening of 3 December began with an abortive enemy counterattack against Captain Amerine's position overlooking the bridge. Just before noon on 4 December, Amerine launched an assault to seize a second hill overlooking the southern end of the bridge. The attack succeeded in forcing the Taliban away from the bridge but halted after enemy fire wounded an ODA 574 team member.[146] TF Dagger then directed ODA 574 to pull back from the bridge for the night.[147]

Captain Smith received cautionary guidance from TF Dagger. After learning ODA 583 intended to outflank Kandahar International Airport, Colonel Mulholland denied Smith permission to operate west of the city.[148] In

---

bitstream/handle/10945/11226/johnsonFeb06.pdf, Hist Files, OEF Study Grp.

144. Email Interv, Beckenbaugh with Smith, 18 Apr 2007, p. 10.

145. Ibid.

146. Blehm, *The Only Thing Worth Dying For*, p. 246.

147. Interv, Connors with Fox, 30 Nov 2006, pp. 11–12; Interv, Terry Beckenbaugh, CSI, with Lt Col Donald Bolduc, frmr Opns Ofcr, 2d Bn, 5th SF Grp, 23 Apr 2007, p. 12, Hist Files, OEF Study Grp.

148. Briscoe et al., *Weapon of Choice*, p. 178.

turn, Smith convinced Sharzai to limit his activity for the next forty-eight hours to conducting reconnaissance patrols along the city's outskirts.[149] The morning of 5 December found Smith's detachment on the ridge overlooking the Kandahar airport while small groups of Sharzai's fighters circled the city.

To the north of Kandahar, Amerine's troops sorted through newly delivered supplies in preparation for retaking the hill abandoned the previous day. In addition to supplies, 160th SOAR delivered reinforcements and vehicles from TF SWORD, along with personnel from the 2d Battalion, 5th Special Forces command group. The 2d Battalion joint tactical air controller soon found himself pressed into service to aid the Marine F/A–18s in their unsuccessful efforts to lob bombs into a cave serving as a Taliban bomb shelter. Puzzled that the bombs did not land where he intended, the joint controller tried to determine what might be wrong. After the Marine jets departed, he recalibrated the designator according to the user's manual. Noticing a low-power warning after he finished the calibration procedure, he replaced the batteries.

The controller then called in an orbiting B–52 to deliver a Global Positioning System–guided 2,000-pound penetrator against the cave, but instead of hitting the cave, the bomb exploded among friendly troops. Being unfamiliar with the model of designator being employed, the controller had not realized the equipment readings reset automatically to the user's location after replacing the batteries. These default readings remained in the device's memory until the operator lased a target once again. Tragically, twenty Afghans were killed and fifty wounded, while American casualties numbered two dead and nineteen wounded. The blast also knocked Karzai off his feet, inflicting a small head wound as a result of the fall.[150] The uninjured began treating the wounded as a dazed Karzai learned that the Bonn Conference attendees had chosen him to head the Afghan Interim Authority.[151]

Kandahar fell on 7 December after Sharzai's patrols reported that the enemy, with the exception of isolated pockets of foreign fighters, had departed. Captain Smith left part of his team at the airport while the remainder, along with a recently arrived British Special Operations detachment, convoyed into Kandahar accompanied by fighters loyal to Sharzai.[152] The American presence prevented a clash between Karzai and Sharzai. Karzai had promised the governorship of Kandahar to Naquib Alikozai in exchange for surrendering the province while Sharzai single-mindedly pursued his quest to reclaim his former post. Harsh words were exchanged when Karzai arrived to find Sharzai in the governor's residence, prompting Captain Smith and Colonel Fox to intervene in a successful effort to prevent factional fighting.[153]

---

149. Email Interv, Beckenbaugh with Smith, 18 Apr 2007, p. 12.

150. Blehm, *The Only Thing Worth Dying For*, pp. 301–07.

151. Jean MacKenzie, "Karzai's Fall," *The New Republic*, 1 Dec 2009, https://www.newrepublic.com/article/economy/karzais-fall, Hist Files, OEF Study Grp.

152. Email Interv, Beckenbaugh with Smith, 18 Apr 2007, p. 12.

153. Interv, Connors with Fox, 30 Nov 2006, p. 14; Email Interv, Beckenbaugh with Smith, 18 Apr 2007, p. 12.

Expanding the Hunt for al-Qaeda

CENTCOM's operational focus widened beyond Afghanistan's borders as the Bush administration sought to deny al-Qaeda sanctuary in other parts of the region. As early as 21 November, General Myers had been asked to assemble a range of military options focusing on Iraq. General Franks learned of the White House's changing perspective six days later when Secretary Rumsfeld asked him to look again at existing plans for Iraq.[154] Although the Bush administration initiated preparations for a potential conflict with Iraq, it still had no intention of allowing Osama bin Laden to flee Afghanistan. Reports from Afghan sources on bin Laden's whereabouts started pouring in immediately after Kabul's liberation. CIA officer Berntsen investigated the most promising tips from his new headquarters in the Afghan capital while also sending teams to reconnoiter suspected al-Qaeda training camps roughly 120 kilometers to the east in Nangarhar Province and 80 kilometers to the south in Logar Province. Both locations were located in predominantly Pashtun areas, which left Berntsen uncomfortable about using Tajik and Uzbek militia fighters from the United Front. As a result, Berntsen sought and received approval to enlist the aid of additional Pashtun militia groups.[155]

As news of Berntsen's request spread throughout the agency, he received a call from the CIA station in Islamabad suggesting Haji Ghamsharik Zaman, a former mujahideen commander who recently returned to Jalalabad from France, as a potential Pashtun ally.[156] The CIA team chief recruited not only Ghamsharik Zaman and his followers, but also hired groups led by former United Front commander Hazarat Ali and Abdul Zahir, son of the former governor of Nangarhar Province.[157] The three commanders, each of whom claimed to have 700 fighters, were collectively dubbed the Eastern Shura.[158] However, the potential for future problems surfaced when Berntsen learned that Hazarat Ali not only considered Zaman an unreliable battlefield partner but that the militia leaders were all long-time political rivals.[159] Although

---

154. Franks with McConnell, *American Soldier*, p. 329.

155. Peter John Paul Krause, "The Last Good Chance: A Reassessment of U.S. Operations at Tora Bora," *Security Studies* 17 (Dec 2008): 650.

156. Although the specific identity of the station is blacked out in Berntsen's book, the Islamabad CIA station is the likely candidate, as it had a telephone link to Berntsen and unmatched contacts among the expatriate Pashtun community in Pakistan. Grenier, *88 Days to Kandahar*, p. 187.

157. Berntsen and Pezzullo, *Jawbreaker*, p. 238. Journalist Philip Smucker identifies "Babrak" as Hazarat Ali and "Nuruddin" as Haji Zaman; see Philip G. Smucker, *Al-Qaeda's Great Escape: The Military and the Media on Terror's Trail* (Washington, D.C.: Brassey's, 2004).

158. Lutfullah Mashal and Philip G. Smucker, "Afghan Puzzle: Who Shot Qadir?," *Christian Science Monitor*, 8 Jul 2002, https://www.csmonitor.com/2002/0708/p06s01-wosc.html, Hist Files, OEF Study Grp.

159. The CIA suspected Hazarat Ali of being complicit in the murder of Haji Zahir's father in 2002; see Dexter Filkins, "Afghan Official Is Assassinated; Blow to Karzai," *New York Times*, 7 Jul 2002; https://www.nytimes.com/2002/07/07/world/afghan-official-is-assassinated-blow-to-karzai.html, Hist Files, OEF Study Grp.

Berntsen had little choice but to utilize all of the Pashtun militia groups in the region willing to fight for pay, the information highlighted just how little U.S. officials knew about the rivalries and personalities of its Afghan proxy allies.

Despite the potentially fractious nature of the newly formed Eastern Shura, the CIA team chief felt he had collected enough information by the end of November to ask Colonel Mulholland for personnel to work with Pashtun militia groups. The TF DAGGER commander considered the request premature because he had received unverified reports suggesting large bands of Taliban and al-Qaeda fighters were operating in the areas suspected of sheltering bin Laden.[160] With tacit approval from his superiors who ostensibly read the same reports, Colonel Mulholland told Berntsen to "send your team in. If in a week they're still alive and operating, I'll send a team to work with them. The same thing goes for the team you send south."[161] Absent aid from TF DAGGER, Berntsen initially deployed an ad hoc group of U.S. intelligence operatives and military personnel, known as Team JULIET, on 18 November.

The Milawa Valley, three hours south of Jalalabad near the Tora Bora cave complex, drew the immediate attention of JULIET.[162] Hazarat Ali agreed to provide guides for the team after the Americans arrived at Jalalabad. The CIA paramilitary operatives planned to rely on a combination of aerial bombing and Eastern Shura fighters to destroy any sizable al-Qaeda force located there. The friendly Afghans would deploy on the eastern and western edges of the valley while JULIET worked its way south toward the Afghan-Pakistan border. With the Eastern Shura fighters positioned on either flank to prevent the enemy from slipping away, al-Qaeda's choices would be reduced. They could die under a hail of American bombs or make a risky trek across a range of mountains up to 4200 meters high that separated Afghanistan from Pakistan's Federally Administered Tribal Areas.[163] In retrospect, some might question the willingness of the United States to expend a tremendous amount of resources to kill or capture a single man hiding among some of the most rugged terrain in the world, but prevailing emotions among most Americans at the time demanded the effort be made.

On 30 November, Team JULIET infiltrated the high ground overlooking the al-Qaeda camp in the Milawa Valley, whereupon Berntsen authorized it to initiate air attacks (*Map 2.4*). Air strikes succeeded in destroying most of the enemy's communications equipment and heavy weapons which, in turn, forced al-Qaeda to rely on unencrypted walkie-talkies and limited their defensive firepower to mortars, small arms, and a few machine guns.[164] After suffering several hundred casualties, the al-Qaeda fighters abandoned the

---

160. Briscoe et al., *Weapon of Choice*, p. 213.

161. Berntsen and Pezzullo, *Jawbreaker*, p. 214.

162. Peter Bergen, "The Account of How We Nearly Caught Bin Laden in 2001," *The New Republic*, 30 Dec 2009, https://www.newrepublic.com/article/the-battle-tora-bora, Hist Files, OEF Study Grp.

163. Barzilai, *102 Days of War*, p. 90.

164. Krause, "The Last Good Chance," p. 651.

INITIAL COMBAT OPERATIONS

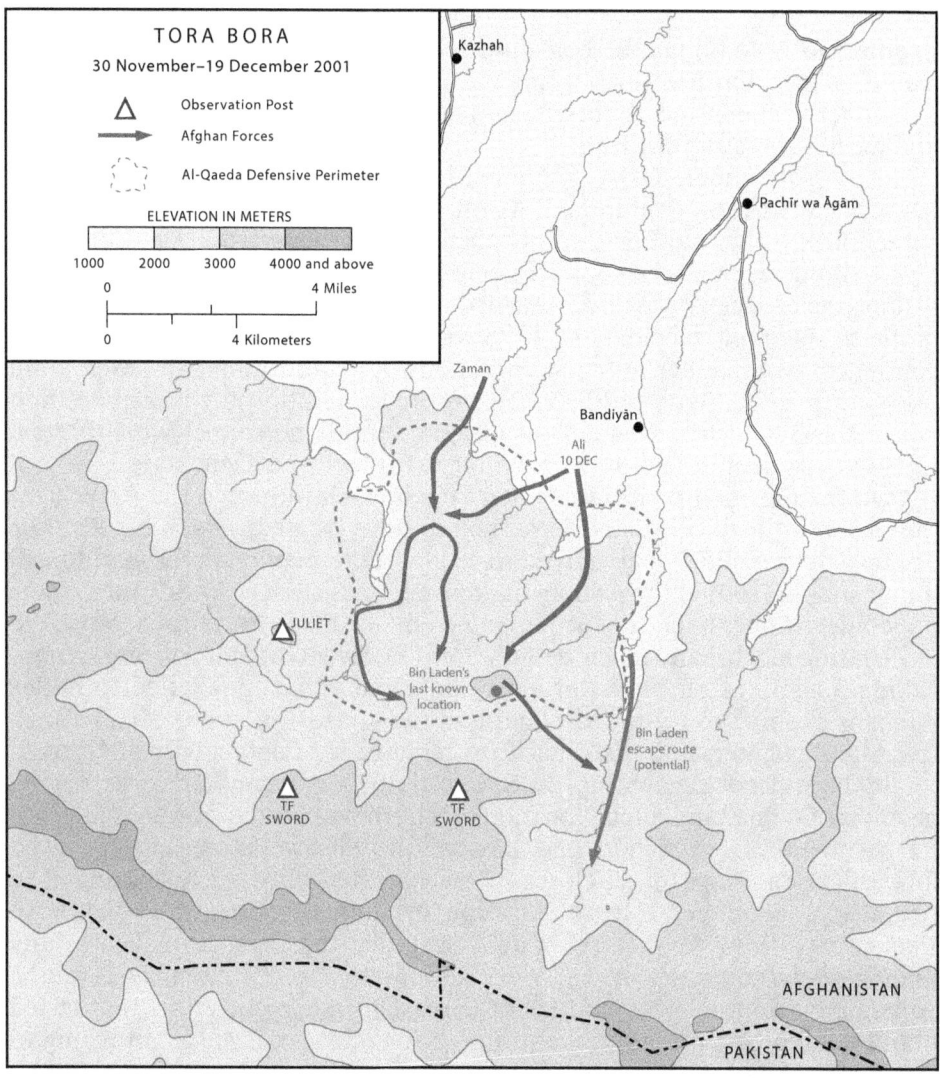

Map 2.4

Milawa Valley for the Tora Bora cave network that had been constructed during the Soviet-Afghan war.

Berntsen took advantage of the successes gained by JULIET to approach TF DAGGER once more for a Special Forces ODA. Given the changed circumstances, Colonel Mulholland agreed to send ODA 572 to Team JULIET. The Special Forces team departed Bagram for Jalalabad via ground convoy on 2 December.[165] After it arrived, the senior Special Operations representative and Berntsen agreed to revise the existing plan. The new concept called for positioning Special Forces teams with close air support controllers on dominating "peaks south and west—one on Tonga mountain,

---

165. Partin et al., *U.S. Special Operations Command History, 1987–2007*, p. 94.

another closer to Slinga further south—while the original post near Milawa would be reestablished further [sic] the east."¹⁶⁶ Once the newly arrived U.S. personnel were in place, Berntsen planned to resume the assault on bin Laden and his followers at Tora Bora.¹⁶⁷

On 6 December, ODA 572 moved from Jalalabad to Hazarat Ali's headquarters near Pachir wa Agam.¹⁶⁸ Over the next two days, the detachment established outposts to the east and west of the 9.5-kilometers-by-10-kilometers mountainous area occupied by al-Qaeda. Before the assault resumed in earnest, JAWBREAKER turned over responsibility for the upcoming battle to incoming elements of TF SWORD on 8 December. The TF SWORD contingent commander initiated operations by establishing two observation posts during the night of 10–11 December. In addition to the observation posts, the TF SWORD element dispatched several personnel with thermal sights to augment each of ODA 572's forward-deployed elements.

On the morning of 10 December, Hazarat Ali informed the Americans that a subordinate commander claimed to have located a weak point in the enemy defenses. TF SWORD agreed to send a three-man team forward to call for air support should the Afghan fighters need assistance. An advance by the mujahideen hours later, now accompanied by the three Americans, provoked devastating mortar and machine-gun fire. The SWORD operators were so busy calling air strikes on a host of emerging targets that they failed to notice Afghans slipping to the rear in ones and twos. As dusk approached, only a few Afghan fighters and the Americans remained in contact with al-Qaeda.

In the midst of the fighting, the SWORD contingent received the electrifying news that Osama bin Laden's location had been pinpointed. Rather than wait for permission from higher headquarters, the TF SWORD contingent moved forward in an effort to get closer to the reported bin Laden sighting. The operators encountered Hazarat Ali's convoy, minus their attached American element, returning to base. After admitting that the chances of successfully finding their comrades in the dark mountains were extremely low, the Americans temporarily abandoned the search. In a hectic effort that lasted until the following morning, the stranded soldiers succeeded in returning to friendly lines without sustaining any casualties.¹⁶⁹

In the seventeen hours separating their departure and return, the isolated TF SWORD operators and members of the easternmost ODA 572 observation post called numerous air strikes on previously undetected targets as al-Qaeda reacted successively to Hazarat Ali's advance, the discovery of Americans in their midst, and SWORD's brief foray onto the battlefield. The bombing missions destroyed almost all of the remaining al-Qaeda crew-served weapons, paving the way for Afghan militia fighters to secure terrain overlooking bin Laden's presumed location. While the U.S. Special Operations Command described

---

166. Berntsen and Pezzullo, *Jawbreaker*, p. 274.
167. Partin et al., *U.S. Special Operations Command History, 1987–2007*, p. 94.
168. Briscoe et al., *Weapon of Choice*, p. 214.
169. Partin et al., *U.S. Special Operations Command History, 1987–2007*, pp. 95–96.

INITIAL COMBAT OPERATIONS

A cave complex in the Tora Bora area of Afghanistan. Cave complexes littered the mountainous terrain near the Pakistan border and made it difficult to find enemy combatants and munitions dumps. Al-Qaeda had spent years in these environments.

the incident as a "comedy of errors," it also noted that those confused hours "proved to be the decisive ones of the operation at Tora Bora."[170]

During the predawn hours of 12 December, the TF SWORD contingent learned that Zaman had entered into negotiations with al-Qaeda. When the Americans attempted to occupy new observation posts, Zaman's men forced them to halt until the negotiations were concluded.[171] By relying on proxy allies, American aims were once more overcome by an Afghan agenda. Some al-Qaeda fighters made good use of this time to reposition while others began trekking south toward the Afghanistan-Pakistan border.[172] Although the U.S. government refused to support his unauthorized initiative, CENTCOM called off planned air strikes for the next eleven hours to ensure Zaman did not turn on his American allies.

Alerted to the possibility that the Eastern Shura forces lacked the same level of motivation as Uzbek fighters under Dostum, Berntsen requested a Ranger Battalion through CIA channels.[173] After querying CENTCOM, Henry Crumpton informed the CIA team chief that "General Franks wants

---

170. Ibid., p. 96. The events at Tora Bora subsequently generated intensive debate, much of it emanating from within the Army. It would seem that the American experience with Dostum was the exception rather than the rule when dealing with Afghan militia leaders. For additional insight into Tora Bora, see Stephen D. Biddle, *Afghanistan and the Future of Warfare: Implications for Army and Defense Policy* (Carlisle Barracks, Pa.: Strategic Studies Institute, Nov 2002).

171. Partin et al., *U.S. Special Operations Command History, 1987–2007*, p. 97.

172. Barzilai, *102 Days of War*, p. 96.

173. Schroen, *First In*, pp. 277–78.

THE UNITED STATES ARMY IN AFGHANISTAN, 2001–2014

Map 2.5

to stick with what has worked, our small teams with our Afghan allies. He also says it will take too much time to plan. Time to deploy Rangers. Too much time."[174] In addition, the CENTCOM commander felt that, unlike the

---

174. The request did not specify the mission envisioned for the Rangers. Crumpton, *The Art of Intelligence*, p. 259.

United Front, militia groups in Nangarhar Province were far less accepting of American troops.[175]

Even if Franks agreed the Rangers could be employed usefully at Tora Bora, the deployment area suggested by the CIA challenged all but the most powerful helicopters operating in good weather, which meant that it could take several days to deploy 600 or more personnel. The lengthy insertion timeframe carried the risk of compromising tactical surprise while also increasing the vulnerability of the helicopters ferrying Ranger units. If the weather worsened during this process, the chances of American personnel being killed or injured in a helicopter mishap grew significantly.

Although the mountains on the Afghanistan-Pakistan border were a formidable barrier that hampered the American use of heliborne troops, al-Qaeda operatives could take advantage of the rugged terrain, using it to escape by hiring locals familiar with well-worn smuggler trails leading into the Federally Administered Tribal Areas (*Map 2.5*). The tribal areas are just across the Durand Line, which designates the internationally recognized border between Afghanistan and Pakistan. The U.S. government asked Islamabad to seal the border to help prevent these escapes, but increased regional tensions following a terrorist attack on the Indian parliament would hamper Islamabad's ability to meet this request. The Indian government mobilized troops after accusing Pakistan of supporting and arming the terrorists. In response, the Pakistani Army redeployed a number of units from its western frontier to new positions opposite Indian military forces massing along the border between both countries. The remaining Pakistani troops near Tora Bora were limited to Frontier Corps paramilitary units whose ranks included many individuals with anti-American or pro-Taliban sympathies.[176]

Bombing recommenced at 1700 on 12 December as U.S. operators resumed their forward movement. Not only did the new observation posts allow the Americans to direct air strikes in areas previously inaccessible to them, but the increased bombing prompted bin Laden to address his wavering fighters via radio more frequently. Although the shrinking battlefield left bin Laden with few options, it also imposed greater burdens on the combatants of both sides. The potential for hypothermia and altitude sickness grew as the battle moved higher into the mountains. Conditions worsened for the American troops, who were heavily burdened and unaccustomed to high altitudes. On the afternoon of 14 December, Afghan militia reported seeing the terrorist chief with several dozen bodyguards. Although the report could not be verified, the Americans directed multiple air strikes against a cave complex allegedly sheltering the enemy force.[177]

---

175. Memo, 6 Jun 2006, sub: TORA BORA, file: TORA BORA_CINCtestimonychg1.docx, CENTCOM History Office folder, Hist Files, OEF Study Grp.

176. Crumpton, *The Art of Intelligence*, p. 258; DeLong, Lukeman, and Zinni, *Inside CENTCOM*, p. 57; Eric Schmitt, "Officer Leads Old Corps in New Role in Pakistan," *New York Times*, 6 Mar 2009, https://www.nytimes.com/2009/03/07/world/asia/07frontier.html, Hist Files, OEF Study Grp.

177. Barzilai, *102 Days of War*, pp. 97–99.

The unconfirmed sighting of Osama bin Laden spurred General Franks to reexamine whether or not U.S. troops could play a part in the fighting. On 17 December, CENTCOM directed CLFCC to assess if conventional forces could be employed at Tora Bora. Mikolashek responded that using a single battalion seemed too risky, suggesting instead that the mission merited sending the 82d Airborne Division's entire ready brigade. CENTCOM rejected that idea, citing its preference for using conventional units already in theater. However, those troops were already protecting Bagram, Kandahar International Airport, and Forward Operating Base RHINO. As a result, Tora Bora would remain the responsibility of U.S. SOF until the fighting concluded.[178]

The Special Operations Command history published six years later recorded "TF 11 [SWORD] departed the battlefield on 19 December . . . without knowing whether or not they had killed UBL [Osama bin Laden] and destroyed AQ [al-Qaeda] in Afghanistan."[179] Although the terrorist leader's fate could not be ascertained, CENTCOM remained determined to eliminate al-Qaeda's surviving enclaves within Afghanistan. In addition to this goal, CENTCOM placed growing emphasis on creating a post-Taliban security environment that prevented other terrorist groups from using Afghanistan as a launching pad for further attacks against the American homeland.

---

178. End of Mission Rpt, CFLCC C–3 Future Opns, Dec 2001, Overview of Future Opns, p. 1, Hist Files, OEF Study Grp.

179. Partin et al., *U.S. Special Operations Command History, 1987–2007*, p. 97.

Chapter Three

Path to Victory

By late December 2001, U.S.-led coalition and Afghan forces had toppled the Taliban regime, helped to establish the Afghan Interim Authority, and removed al-Qaeda forces from all but the most remote areas of the country. Pockets of resistance remained, but U.S. forces would have "unique opportunities to exploit intelligence from materials, documents, and detainees" as they worked to eliminate them. With CENTCOM reporting that it had "succeeded in virtually eliminating Taliban military capability in Afghanistan" and "severely degraded" al-Qaeda's capabilities, the interest of Washington policymakers, military leaders, and intelligence officials began turning elsewhere.[1] Indeed, by late November President George W. Bush had already ordered Secretary Donald H. Rumsfeld to update existing Iraq war plans.[2]

Changing outlooks within the Bush administration were triggered in large part by intelligence reports suggesting roughly 75 percent of the al-Qaeda leadership still remained at large.[3] CENTCOM analysts were already predicting that Osama bin Laden and his surviving lieutenants would "relocate to Pakistan, Yemen, Somalia, or another safe haven to reconstitute C2 [command and control] and continue operations against U.S. interests."[4] In the worst-case scenario, CENTCOM estimated that al-Qaeda might carry out attacks with weapons of mass destruction, or that U.S. adversaries such as Iraq or North Korea might "take advantage of U.S. focus on al-Qaeda activity in Central Asia" by carrying out acts of aggression against Americans, their allies, or U.S. interests.[5]

Thus, with some major objectives accomplished but many enemy leaders still unaccounted for, CENTCOM began transitioning from Phases I (Initial Strike Operations) and II (Continued Operations) toward Phases III (Decisive Operations) and IV (Sustain and Prevent).[6] In anticipation of starting Phase

---

1. CFC OPORD 03, Opns in Afghanistan Phase III and IV, CENTCOM, 22 Dec 2001, sec. 1.B.1, Hist Files, OEF Study Grp. Note: References in subsequent orders date OPORD 03 to 24 Dec 2001.

2. Woodward, *Plan of Attack*, pp. 1–4, 54.

3. Crumpton, "Intelligence and War: Afghanistan, 2001–2002," p. 162.

4. Ibid.

5. CFC OPORD 03, Opns in Afghanistan Phase III and IV, CENTCOM, 22 Dec 2001, sec. 1.B.3.

6. Ibid.

III, CENTCOM issued Operations Order 03 outlining the tasks that would be needed to prevent the reemergence of international terrorist organizations in Afghanistan. These included supporting the Afghan Interim Authority and International Security Assistance Force (ISAF) (which was the incoming UN mission), conducting civil-military operations, and exploiting information gleaned from captured documents and detainees.[7]

Fleshing out Phase IV tasks, which, in theory at least, would begin in the many parts of Afghanistan that had no enemy presence, drew growing interest with the Bonn Conference's creation of an Afghan Interim Authority. Although Phase IV tasks overlapped in some instances with the preceding phase, they included creating post-Taliban Afghan security forces, identifying whether detainees required long-term detention or repatriation, and monitoring Afghanistan for signs of returning al-Qaeda terrorists. As CENTCOM entered Phases III and IV, its desired end state called for the destruction of the al-Qaeda network and other designated terrorist organizations in Afghanistan; retention of sufficient coalition forces in Afghanistan to detect, deter, and either defeat or destroy international terrorist organizations seeking to return there; sustained support of humanitarian assistance efforts; efforts to enhance the legitimacy of the Interim Authority; and a focus on positioning ISAF for future operations.[8] These tasks and end states indicated a shift from unconventional warfare to counterterrorism as the dominant operational approach.

The new emphasis on counterterrorism, when coupled with the transition from Phase II to Phase III along with growing preoccupation with planning for Iraq, made it more difficult to envision how the situation within Afghanistan fit within the changing U.S. strategic vision. Counterterrorism-related directives were clear enough, as was the directive to "establish logistics bases."[9] Yet American efforts to facilitate regime change in Afghanistan were now given equal priority with killing or capturing the enemy. In addition, the concept of what actually constituted a supporting role in regime change was difficult to define. As a result, CENTCOM's orders to support a wide range of entities and operations—including the Afghan Interim Authority, provincial leaders, regional allies, ISAF, other U.S. government agencies, coalition partners, humanitarian assistance operations, and civil-military operations—were subject to interpretation.[10] Most ambiguous of all was the Phase IV task "support setting the conditions to prevent the re-emergence of terrorist organizations with global reach in Afghanistan."[11] The commanders on the ground would have to determine when such support would be appropriate and what form it would take.

---

7. Ibid.

8. Ibid.

9. CFC OPORD 03, Opns in Afghanistan Phase III and IV, CENTCOM, 22 Dec 2001, sec. 3.B.3.J.

10. Ibid.

11. Ibid.

As the Afghan campaign entered its fourth month, few in the international community or U.S. government—to say nothing of the U.S. military—had a common understanding of what the future held. Rumsfeld felt it was in the United States' interest "to be attentive to what kind of government comes along," because "obviously we don't want Afghanistan a year from now to go right back to becoming a place that harbors terrorists."[12] CENTCOM's plans to realize that goal called for a "functioning and stable" Afghan government as part of its end state, and recognized that, after two decades of war, Afghanistan's "economy [was] in shambles, farmland [was] not productive, and large portions of the population [were] displaced and/or in need of sustainment."[13] Without a "functioning and stable" Afghan state, killing or capturing all the terrorists in the country would not necessarily prevent the terrorist safe havens from reemerging. Yet CENTCOM either did not recognize the importance of American military involvement in placing any postconflict Afghan political construct on a stable foundation or decided to downplay its own involvement in that process by stating that initial efforts along those lines would be led by the UN with "minimal military support" from the United States.[14]

With the mission of killing or capturing terrorists and their Taliban supporters in Afghanistan apparently winding down, the public and media alike began seeking insights into the next phase of the Global War on Terrorism.[15] Legitimate questions on that topic laid bare the problems that Washington decision makers were having with articulating the way forward in Afghanistan. Indeed, when a reporter asked him if the United States had an exit strategy, Rumsfeld answered:

> We do. We know what we want to do, and when we've done it, we'll do it someplace else. And what it is we want to do is we want to capture or kill the senior Taliban leadership and see that they are punished. We want to make sure that the Taliban is out of power, which it now is. We want to make sure that the rest of the Taliban are disarmed and/or have become part of various other forces and no longer trying to kill people. And with respect

---

12. Interv, Lally Weymouth, *Washington Post/Newsweek*, with Sec Def Donald H. Rumsfeld, 13 Dec 2001, DoD, Press Opns, https://archive.defense.gov/Transcripts/Transcript.aspx?TranscriptID=2660, Hist Files, OEF Study Grp.

13. CFC OPORD 03, Opns in Afghanistan Phase III and IV, CENTCOM, 22 Dec 2001, sec. 1.B.1.

14. Ibid.

15. Postbattle criticism of U.S. efforts at Tora Bora stems in large part from repeated statements by the Bush administration linking success with the death or capture of Osama bin Laden and his lieutenants. Although these critics often overlook weather conditions, terrain, and other operational constraints, the U.S. military's reluctance to prepare the Rangers or the 82d Airborne units for battle at either Tora Bora or along the Afghanistan-Pakistan border is a legitimate concern. Osama bin Laden's supporters subsequently viewed Tora Bora as a victory rather than a defeat because the United States failed to kill or capture him. Thomas E. Ricks, "Rumsfeld's Hands-on War: Afghan Campaign Shaped by Secretary's Views, Personality," *Washington Post*, 9 Dec 2001, https://www.washingtonpost.com/wp-dyn/articles/A14464-2001Dec8.html, Hist Files, OEF Study Grp.

to the al-Qaeda, we want to capture or kill the senior leadership, and we want to catch and imprison the remainder so that they don't go back to their countries and terrorize people and kill people. . . . When those things have been accomplished, from a military standpoint we will have done our job.[16]

General Tommy R. Franks followed his boss' lead in describing the American exit strategy to the public in similarly general terms. When *PBS NewsHour* anchor Jim Lehrer asked him in early January 2002 if he had termination criteria in mind, Franks replied:

At some point, there'll come a time when I talk to my boss, Secretary Rumsfeld, and when he chooses to talk to the President on this subject. And that time will come when we're able to say, "We have been on the ground, we have been to every place in Afghanistan in a way that satisfies me as the commander-in-chief that we have destroyed al-Qaida [sic] in this country and that we have destroyed the remaining pockets of the Taliban and I would recommend, Mr. Secretary, that you take that to the President." And, Jim, that's a long ways off in the future because we still have a lot of dangerous ground to cover. But that's how it will happen.[17]

THE U.S. ARMY ENTERS IN FORCE

The projected deployment of conventional forces into Afghanistan heralded major changes in how CENTCOM addressed basing and logistical issues. General Franks and his team now faced the additional strategic challenges of jump-starting Phase IV, planning for Iraq, and identifying termination criteria for Afghanistan. Air-dropped supplies had previously proven sufficient to meet the combined needs of the United Front and the small U.S. footprint within Afghanistan. Committing conventional forces in numbers necessary to conduct offensive operations signaled a shift from relying on bases outside Afghanistan, and meant that parachuting supplies into ad hoc drop zones would no longer suffice. Transitioning from air-dropped supplies to aerially transported sustainment drove U.S. forces to acquire airfields that could support cargo-hauling aircraft and rotary-wing platforms within Afghanistan. These airfields required specially trained support units to maintain and operate them along with combat units to provide dedicated security. As a result, coalition forces would have to construct bases large enough to house supporting facilities and personnel with defensive positions sited along the entire perimeter. Correspondingly, the acquisition of fixed bases placed more emphasis on civil affairs providing humanitarian aid to nearby communities.

Both Bagram and RHINO could support Phase III operations by U.S. conventional forces. Although Bagram required a sustained demining effort

---

16. Ibid.

17. Interv, *PBS NewsHour* with General Tommy R. Franks, 8 Jan 2002, https://www.pbs.org/newshour/bb/terrorism-jan-june02-franks_1-8/, Hist Files, OEF Study Grp.

to remove unexploded ordnance dating as far back as the Afghan-Soviet conflict, Col. John P. Mulholland sent a forward element there to maintain liaison with the United Front. TF SWORD followed Mulholland's lead by deploying advance elements to Bagram, including command and control assets as well as a reconnaissance element from Jazirat Masirah off the coast of Oman.[18] Local security in the form of a rifle company and headquarters element from 1st Battalion, 87th Infantry, arrived soon afterward.[19] In addition, General Franks dispatched his security director, Army Brig. Gen. Gary L. Harrell, to Bagram to head an interagency task force that would oversee detainee operations, conduct border surveillance, and distribute U.S. humanitarian aid.[20]

CENTCOM had already begun to invest in improving runways and clearing mines at critical entry points into Afghanistan during the Tora Bora fighting.[21] Transforming Bagram into a forward operating base became General Franks' top priority.[22] Even so, clearing the base proved challenging to the explosive ordnance disposal teams and combat engineers. To provide assistance, CENTCOM dispatched Maj. Gen. Franklin L. "Buster" Hagenbeck's 10th Mountain Division headquarters, minus the elements still serving in Kosovo, to Karshi Khanabad instead of Bagram. General Hagenbeck and his staff arrived in early December 2001, declaring themselves fully operational on 7 December.[23] As commander of CFLCC-Forward, Hagenbeck was responsible for virtually all coalition ground forces in Afghanistan, Pakistan, and Uzbekistan, including airfield security and logistics support.[24]

Although explosive ordnance disposal teams and combat engineers were already committed to improving Bagram, CENTCOM acknowledged the need to acquire an airfield in southern Afghanistan other than the remote airstrip at RHINO. Rather than wait for forces outside of Afghanistan to arrive, General Franks directed CFLCC to employ TF-58 to occupy Kandahar

---

18. Backgrounder, Lt Col Pete Blaber, Cdr, Advance Force Opns, Opn ANACONDA, American Enterprise Institute, 1 Mar 2012, p. 2, https://www.aei.org/press/operation-anaconda/, Hist Files, OEF Study Grp.

19. Capt Timothy L. Gittins, "OPERATION ANACONDA: The Lower Shah-I-Khot Valley" (PEP, Inf Capts Career Course 04–03, 5 Feb 2003), p. 4, Hist Files, OEF Study Grp.

20. Brig. Gen. Gary L. Harrell led a joint, multiagency organization in Afghanistan known as Task Force BOWIE. Berntsen and Pezzullo, *Jawbreaker*, p. 213; Matthew Bogdanos with William Patrick, *Thieves of Baghdad: One Marine's Passion to Recover the World's Greatest Stolen Treasures* (New York: Bloomsbury Publishing, 2006), pp. 55–62.

21. Memo, Col Eshelman for Third Army/ARCENT Cmd Grp and Staff, sub: ARCENT Update 14 Dec 01, Story CFLCC Collection, OEF Study Grp.

22. Interv, OEF Study Grp with Gen Tommy R. Franks, frmr CENTCOM Cdr, 4 Dec 2015, Hist Files, OEF Study Grp.

23. Interv, Maj Richard M. Brown, 130th Military History Detachment (MHD), with Maj Gen Franklin Hagenbeck, Cdr, 10th Mtn Div, 15 Mar 2002, p. 1, Hist Files, OEF Study Grp.

24. Wright et al., *A Different Kind of War*, p. 127.

International Airport.²⁵ In addition to ordering the military airfield restored to operational condition, General Franks indicated that he wanted the marines to determine if weapons of mass destruction were being manufactured or stored in abandoned al-Qaeda training camps near Kandahar.²⁶

CFLCC published a warning order on 11 December notifying TF-58 to prepare to deploy an advance party from Rhino to the Kandahar airport within the next forty-eight hours. The advance party would be followed by elements of the 26th Marine Expeditionary Unit and explosive ordnance demolition teams, contracting officers, civil affairs elements, engineers, and a robust command and control element. The move presaged the eventual transfer of all U.S. forces from Forward Operating Base Rhino to Kandahar once an agreement had been reached with Afghan government officials. The marines were also instructed to prepare for a relief-in-place with a brigade-sized Army element.²⁷

On the morning of 14 November, TF-58 successfully established a forward operating base at Kandahar International Airport.²⁸ Brig. Gen. James N. Mattis soon found himself cast in the unfamiliar role of jailor after being directed to construct a 500-person holding facility within his perimeter.²⁹ Lt. Col. Edward F. Dorman III's Logistical Task Force 530 built a similar holding facility at Bagram.³⁰ Media reports of potential war crimes—including dozens of Pakistanis killed at a school in Mazar-e Sharif, summary executions following the Kunduz surrender, claims of Pashtun allies of the United States executing 160 Taliban fighters outside Kandahar, and coverage of the Qala-i-Jangi prison uprising—argued against using Afghan militia as long-term jailors. Although many reports of alleged atrocities were exaggerated and speculative, the news accounts were "sufficiently disturbing and prominent" to capture the attention of Mary Robinson, the United Nations High Commissioner for Human Rights.³¹

Up to this point in the campaign, CIA and Special Forces had been able to collect information by interrogating captured enemy combatants. Unlike Iraq, where U.S. reconnaissance satellites monitored Saddam Hussein's

---

25. Memo, Col Eshelman for Third Army/ARCENT Cmd Grp and Staff, sub: ARCENT Update 7 Dec 01, Story CFLCC Collection, OEF Study Grp.

26. Memo, Col Eshelman for Third Army/ARCENT Cmd Grp and Staff, sub: ARCENT Update 13 Dec 01, Story CFLCC Collection, OEF Study Grp.

27. Memo, Col Eshelman for Third Army/ARCENT Cmd Grp and Staff, 11 Dec 2001, sub: ARCENT Update 11 Dec 01, Story CFLCC Collection, OEF Study Grp.

28. Narrative Sum, Brig Gen James M. Mattis, Opn ENDURING FREEDOM, Naval Support Activity Bahrain, Opns in Afghanistan, 27 Oct 2001–26 Feb 2002, 21 Feb 2002, p. 44, Hist Files, OEF Study Grp.

29. Memo, Col Eshelman for Third Army/ARCENT Cmd Grp and Staff, sub: ARCENT Update 16 Dec 01, Story CFLCC Collection, OEF Study Grp.

30. Finlayson, "Not Just Doing Logistics," p. 47.

31. Serge Schmemann, "A Nation Challenged: HUMAN RIGHTS; Unsure Ground for Fight against Atrocity," *New York Times*, 29 Nov 2001, https://www.nytimes.com/2001/11/30/world/a-nation-challenged-human-rights-unsure-ground-for-fight-against-atrocity.html, Hist Files, OEF Study Grp.

Early detention operations to control enemy combatants were rudimentary but better than those at Qala-i-Jangi Fortress. This Kandahar facility was manned by the 65th Military Police Company. Detention operations would become a major effort in ENDURING FREEDOM.

military activity, Afghanistan offered few opportunities to exploit the capabilities of surveillance technology. Consequently, U.S. officials relied on human sources to learn al-Qaeda's plans and intentions, seeking not only to prevent another September 11th–type attack but also to fully destroy the organization. Until CIA operatives were able to penetrate al-Qaeda's global network, the United States depended on information provided by prisoners taken on the Afghan battlefields.[32]

The ability of the CIA to interrogate prisoners in a timely fashion came into question when representatives from General Harrell's task force visited Shibirghan prison several weeks after the fall of Kunduz. The Americans were confronted with the sight of hundreds of foreign fighters along one wall of the prison's interior while captured Taliban stood near the opposite wall. The latter did not want to be mistaken for foreign fighters because United Front general Abdul Rashid Dostum had promised early release for all local Taliban.[33] CFLCC dispatched Company C, 1st Battalion, 87th Infantry, from Karshi Khanabad to assist a platoon from 65th Military Police Company (Airborne) with processing the foreign fighters at Shibirghan in preparation for transporting them to holding facilities at Bagram and Kandahar.[34]

---

32. Feith, *War and Decision*, p. 159.

33. Interv, Mark J. Reardon, OEF Study Grp, with Maj Mark D. Nutsch, frmr ODA 595 Cdr, 5th SF Grp, 13 Dec 2015, Hist Files, OEF Study Grp.

34. Interv, Laurence Lessard, CSI, with Maj Sarah K. Albrycht, frmr 65th Military Police Co (Abn) Cdr, 13 Mar 2007, p. 6, Hist Files, OEF Study Grp; Capt Nelson G. Kraft, "Lessons Learned from a Light Infantry Company During Operation ANACONDA," *INFANTRY* 91, no. 2 (Summer 2002): 31.

As the number of prisoners in coalition hands exceeded 4,000, it became clear that vital information might remain untapped for too long. Prompted by that revelation, CFLCC identified the detention, processing, handling, and criminal investigation of al-Qaeda and Taliban detainees as one of its top priorities.[35] CENTCOM responded by sending the Army's 202d Military Intelligence Battalion from the 513th Brigade at Fort Gordon, Georgia, to Kandahar. The newly arrived battalion established a Joint Interrogation Center adjacent to the holding facility constructed by the marines.[36] Part of the incoming unit also went to Bagram to assist with interrogations there. Bagram's interrogators were directed to sift through the prisoner population to uncover time-sensitive information and identify detainees worthy of further interrogation. Individuals determined to be senior al-Qaeda and Taliban leaders, non-Afghan Taliban fighters, other personnel deemed as a potential threat to U.S. interests, and individuals subject to prosecution for past terrorist acts remained in American custody after being interviewed.

Although the deployment of Army interrogators signified CENTCOM's ability to address changing circumstances within the theater of operations, the policy for a long-term detainee solution lay with General Franks' superiors. Secretary Rumsfeld agreed with a CENTCOM proposal to create long-term arrangements for certain high-value prisoners, but only if those individuals remained in Afghanistan. CENTCOM deputy commander Marine Lt. Gen. Michael P. DeLong rebutted that caveat by reminding Rumsfeld that "we want to keep our number of troops down, and the ones that are there need to be fighting and looking for al-Qaeda, not guarding prisoners."[37] A subsequent series of lengthy discussions by Bush administration principals eventually led to the creation of a military detention facility under Marine Brig. Gen. Michael R. Lehnert at Guantanamo Bay Naval Base, Cuba, in January 2002.[38]

SUCCESS CREATES GROWING COMPLEXITY

The fall of Kandahar removed the Taliban as a major player from the Afghan scene while ushering in the arrival of international peacekeepers. CENTCOM supported the deployment of ISAF to Kabul in order to safeguard the creation of a new Afghan central government and to allow American troops to concentrate on other tasks and leave for missions outside of Afghanistan. On 19 December, the United Kingdom informed the UN that it was willing to lead the inaugural ISAF deployment. Although British representatives discussed the initiative with CENTCOM before sending the memorandum, the United Kingdom required UN approval before deploying a headquarters

---

35. Msg, Cdr in Ch CENTCOM (CINCCENT), sub: CFC FRAGO 03-005 CFLCC ISO ISAF OPS IN AFG, 030243Z Jan 02, sec. 1, p. 3, Hist Files, OEF Study Grp.

36. Wright et al., *A Different Kind of War*, p. 219.

37. DeLong, Lukeman, and Zinni, *Inside CENTCOM*, p. 59.

38. Karen J. Greenberg, "When Gitmo Was (Relatively) Good," *Washington Post*, 25 Jan 2009, https://www.washingtonpost.com/wp-dyn/content/article/2009/01/23/AR2009012302313.html, Hist Files, OEF Study Grp.

element and appropriate supporting units to Afghanistan. The next day, the Security Council reaffirmed the Bonn Agreement's call to send ISAF to Kabul by issuing Resolution 1386. The UN approved the request, but further discussion led to a Security Council decision that the British commitment would end in April 2002 when another nation would assume the lead for the remaining ninety days of the initial deployment.[39]

Hamid Karzai's appointment as chairman of the Afghan Interim Authority was Afghanistan's first step toward a new political future, but it also signaled a major shift in the dynamics influencing the ongoing campaign. As Karzai began choosing provincial and district administrators, he found himself with limited options and several challenges to overcome. First, the U.S. military was unwilling to get involved in post-Taliban Afghan internal affairs. Next, the candidates for administrative positions in southern and eastern Afghanistan required credentials acceptable to the Pashtun majority, but Kabul was currently occupied by 20,000 ethnic minority Tajik and Uzbek fighters. Many administrative candidates were former militia commanders whose personal fortunes depended on income from various criminal enterprises. A few nominees, including Pacha Khan Zadran in Paktiya Province, proved so unpalatable that they were rejected, while others, such as narcotics kingpin and future Helmand Province governor Sher Mohammed Akhundzada, joined the government.[40]

An even greater complication involved Jalaluddin Haqqani and his tribal following. Haqqani was allied with the Taliban, but he was careful to maintain his autonomy. Although a fervent Islamist, he was tolerant of Sufism (Islamic mysticism) and other Afghan traditions considered heterodox. Just as important, he had local interests separate from the Taliban and perhaps even from al-Qaeda. The Bush administration's policy in the Global War on Terrorism, however, did not tolerate ambiguity. Haqqani rejected an American offer to surrender. He and his sons then attempted to reintegrate in the traditional Afghan way by switching to the winning side. However, warlord entanglements brought American military power against the Haqqanis before reconciliation could be made. The process was complex, but the end result left the Haqqani family with lasting enmity toward Karzai and his American backers.[41]

---

39. Sean Maloney, "The International Security Assistance Force: The Origins of a Stabilization Force," *Canadian Military Journal* 4, no. 2 (Summer 2003): 6.

40. Feith, *War and Decision*, p. 532; Damien McElroy, "Afghan Governor Turned 3,000 Men Over to the Taliban," *Telegraph*, 20 Nov 2009, https://www.telegraph.co.uk/news/worldnews/asia/afghanistan/6615329/Afghan-governor-turned-3000-men-over-to-Taliban.html, Hist Files, OEF Study Grp.

41. Alissa J. Rubin, "Questions Lurk in a Dead Village," *Los Angeles Times*, 8 Jan 2002, https://articles.latimes.com/2002/jan/08/news/mn-21146, Hist Files, OEF Study Grp. For a summary of U.S.-Haqqani interactions following 11 September 2001, the initial attack against the Taliban, and how these relationships may have constructed a war that was not there, see Anand Gopal, "Tomgram: Anand Gopal, How to Lose a War That Wasn't There," TomDispatch.com, 29 Apr 2014, https://www.tomdispatch.com/blog/175837, Hist Files, OEF Study Grp. The book-length treatment on the same topic

On 3 January 2002, a small group of Americans visited Khost to investigate reports that both Osama bin Laden and Haqqani, still viewed as the Taliban's top commander in the southern provinces, were in the area. While in Khost, the U.S. detachment unknowingly stepped into the middle of a feud between Pashtun warlords from the Ghilzai clan when they accepted help from Zakim Khan Zadran, a long-time rival of Pacha Khan Zadran. In an attempt to convince the Americans they should not work with his rival, Pacha Khan staged an ambush that killed Sfc. Nathan R. Chapman of the 1st Special Forces Group, 1st Special Forces Command, and seriously wounded a CIA operative, and then blamed it on his rival.[42] This was just one of many incidents throughout the entirety of Operation ENDURING FREEDOM in which one faction persuaded coalition forces that its competitors backed the Taliban in order to eliminate a rival with American assistance.

Recognizing that security could not remain indefinitely in the hands of a diverse collection of warlords, CENTCOM accepted the mission of creating security forces loyal to the Afghan Interim Authority on 23 January.[43] An incident the next day highlighted the unsuitability of current arrangements. New Zealand Special Air Service and 5th Special Forces Group, 1st Special Forces, personnel targeted two compounds near Hazarqadam, a small village about 150 kilometers northeast of Kandahar. As the Special Forces soldiers approached the first compound, guards began shooting, wounding one American. The second compound's occupants also opened fire, sparking a melee that resulted in fourteen Afghan deaths. The Special Forces personnel were surprised to learn their opponents had sworn allegiance to Karzai two weeks previously.[44] An investigation disclosed that locals falsely identified the compound's occupants as al-Qaeda and Taliban fighters in a bid to gain control of weapons caches buried nearby. In the raid's aftermath, General Franks told media representatives that, "I've asked everybody be sure that our coordination is O.K. . . . since we're operating inside Afghanistan, we've got to be sure to coordinate our activities with their government."[45]

PLAYING THE "LONG GAME"

The early American presence in Afghanistan included sending a Coalition Joint Civil-Military Operations Task Force to Kabul. Lt. Gen. Paul T.

---

is Anand Gopal, *No Good Men Among the Living: America, the Taliban, and the War through Afghan Eyes* (New York: Metropolitan Books, 2014).

42. John F. Burns, "A Nation Challenged: A Soldier's Story; U.S. War Victim Rode into Afghan Turf Fight," *New York Times*, 9 Feb 2002, https://www.nytimes.com/2002/02/09/international/asia/09SOLD.html, Hist Files, OEF Study Grp.

43. Fragmentary Order (FRAGO) 03-028, Modified CFC Guidance Phase III Afghanistan Theater of Opns, 232201Jan02Z, sec. 1, pp. 3–5, Hist Files, OEF Study Grp.

44. Briscoe et al., *Weapon of Choice*, p. 241.

45. Eric Schmitt, "A NATION CHALLENGED: THE MILITARY; After January Raid, Gen. Franks Promises to Do Better," *New York Times*, 8 Feb 2002, https://www.nytimes.com/2002/02/08/world/nation-challenged-military-after-january-raid-gen-franks-promises-better.html, Hist Files, OEF Study Grp.

Mikolashek chose Army Brig. Gen. David E. Kratzer, deputy commanding general of the 377th Support Command (Theater), to head the new organization. The civil-military organization consisted of a few active component soldiers from Third Army/ARCENT and National Guardsmen assigned to the 122d Support Detachment (Rear Tactical Operations Center), commonly referred to as the 122d Rear Area Operations Center, led by Col. Cassel J. Nutter.[46] Virtually all of the reserve component soldiers, including Kratzer, were chosen because they were available and not because they had specific job skills. General Kratzer recalled, "[General Mikolashek] told me I would probably have a pretty free hand because it was a notional organization that had never been fielded and I couldn't get it wrong in that there wasn't that much to measure against at that point."[47]

Kratzer, whose career included service in the armor, signal, and logistics branches, faced a steep learning curve. The joint doctrinal reference in effect at the time stated that "civil-military operations are to be conducted to minimize civilian interference with military operations, to maximize support for operations, and to meet the commander's legal and moral obligations to civilian populations within the commander's area of control."[48] Company D of the 96th Civil Affairs Battalion was the only readily available unit capable of performing that mission in Afghanistan. Kratzer and his staff were expected to assist that unit while working with international and nongovernmental humanitarian organizations as well as the nascent Afghan government. The greatly accelerated pace of the campaign gave Kratzer only four days to prepare his command to depart Fort McPherson for Afghanistan.[49]

Kratzer recognized that CENTCOM envisioned the American military facilitating civil affairs in the early phases of the campaign while the U.S. Agency for International Development assumed responsibility for the overall humanitarian effort. General Franks therefore expected the new civil-military affairs command to achieve operational control of ongoing humanitarian assistance operations in the CENTCOM area of responsibility in order to integrate available coalition forces, provide rapid and appropriate responses to requests for military support to humanitarian assistance operations, and demonstrate U.S. and coalition commitment to prevent human suffering and death.[50]

CENTCOM's approach in Afghanistan was a major departure from recent civil affairs deployments. Civil affairs in support of peacekeeping operations during the Clinton administration were founded upon an expectation of a long-duration commitment, mobilization of reserve component units, and

---

46. Interv, Maj John Warsinske, 47th MHD, with Maj Gen David Kratzer, frmr Cdr, CJCMOTF, EFIT-047-039, 16 Jul 2002, p. 2, Hist File, OEF Study Grp.

47. Interv, Dennis Van Wey, CSI, with Maj Gen (Ret.) David Kratzer, frmr Cdr, Coalition Joint Civil-Military Opns Task Force (CJCMOTF), 5 Jul 2007, p. 3, Hist File, OEF Study Grp.

48. Interv, Warsinske with Kratzer, 16 Jul 2002, p. 2.

49. Interv, Van Wey with Kratzer, 5 Jul 2007, p. 3.

50. Msg, CINCCENT, 280846ZOCT01, sub: Frag 038, sub: Establishment of JCMOTF, para. 1.E.(2), p. 2, Hist Files, OEF Study Grp.

extensive cooperation with both partner nations and nongovernmental organizations. As a result, the United States almost always gravitated toward a central role, which subsequently made it difficult to extricate itself from nation-building missions or downsize its peacekeeping commitments. To emphasize the different approach being taken in Afghanistan, Franks forcefully informed Kratzer: "[W]e are not going to [re]create Bosnia. We were going to come in with a little bit of money for a short period of time to be the bridge between war and peace and to help the Afghan people [with] whom we are not at war."[51]

In accordance with Phase IV of the campaign plan, CENTCOM allocated a growing amount of resources to ensuring that terrorists could not regain a foothold in Afghanistan following the capture of Kabul. These efforts were intended to support ongoing operations as well as garner domestic support for the Afghan Interim Authority. CENTCOM still intended to give long-term responsibility for humanitarian efforts to other agencies as soon as possible. However, the risks associated with depending on outside agencies emerged when U.S. military forces initially received little help from international and nongovernmental organizations consumed with the challenges of relocating from Pakistan to Afghanistan. Ironically, the early success of the military's civil affairs efforts worked against building a closer relationship between the U.S. military and humanitarian organizations. Early press reports showcasing American military personnel helping Afghan villagers overshadowed coverage of similar nongovernmental and international efforts. The uncoordinated efforts of these other organizations contrasted so sharply with the results achieved by the U.S. Army civil-military efforts that a UN official admitted to Kratzer that, "I really don't want this repeated [to] the non-governmental organization community, but will you share with us where you're thinking about going because you're moving faster than we are, so we will follow you."[52]

The emergence of General Kratzer's organization as a lead player in humanitarian efforts led some nongovernmental aid organizations to view it as a competitor rather than a partner. Within a few short weeks, Kratzer noticed that the corporate offices of several major U.S. agencies were exerting significant effort to find fault with the military's civil affairs programs.[53] Even after humanitarian organizations finally arrived in Kabul, they often hesitated to cooperate with the American military openly for fear of compromising their image of neutrality. As a result, Phase IV opened more tentatively than CENTCOM had hoped, requiring leadership to revisit how the U.S. military would manage the transition from decisive operations to postconflict reconstruction. Adjusting operational plans in light of the dramatic successes of past weeks, however, consumed most of the time and interest of Franks' headquarters.

---

51. Interv, Warsinske with Kratzer, 16 Jul 2002, p. 8.

52. Ibid., p. 11.

53. Ibid., p. 9.

The Bonn Conference's decision to impose a centralized government on post-Taliban Afghanistan presented further unanticipated challenges to the Coalition Joint Civil-Military Operations Task Force. General Kratzer found himself shouldering the responsibility of teaching governance skills to interim authority representatives because the nongovernment and international aid organizations were unable to do so. Rather than confine his efforts to humanitarian missions, he remembered, "I ended up having at least an officer and sometimes a team working as advisers to almost all of the twenty-seven ministries of the Karzai government and doing what we could to help them stand up and help them be successful."[54]

The first significant success for civil-military task force efforts came when Kratzer, Secretary of State Colin L. Powell, and U.S. Special Envoy Zalmay M. Khalilzad attended a donors conference in Tokyo from 20 to 22 January 2002.[55] A preliminary needs assessment, provided by Afghan officials with considerable assistance from Kratzer's organization, formed the basis for determining how to distribute reconstruction funding and prioritize humanitarian projects. After opening pledges of almost a billion dollars by the European Union and Japan, contributions by Iran ($560 million), the United States ($291 million), Saudi Arabia ($220 million), India ($100 million), Pakistan ($100 million), and Kuwait ($30 million) raised the overall amount of pledges to rebuild Afghanistan to more than $4.5 billion. It is important to note that the U.S. contribution at Tokyo was only the first year's total, whereas the amounts pledged by other nations reflected the amount to be contributed over several years.

Hamid Karzai met with President Bush in Washington, D.C., less than a week after the Tokyo Conference on 28 January. The two leaders focused on security issues. The private talks ended with the American president publicly expressing his willingness to train new police officers and help establish and train an Afghan national military rather than support a broader mandate for ISAF.[56] Although Karzai did not present Bush with a formal plan for training Afghan security forces during their meeting, Defense Minister Mohammed Qasim Fahim passed a proposal for a new national army to Secretary of State Powell a week earlier. It called for an initial force of 200,000, including 140,000 enlisted soldiers and 60,000 officers, to be drawn from the estimated population of 700,000 armed Afghans. Priority would be given to recruiting soldiers from militia groups that "played a significant part in the defeat of the Taliban and al-Qaeda."[57] After meeting with Bush, Karzai visited the Pentagon where he endorsed Fahim's plan.[58]

---

54. Interv, Van Wey with Kratzer, 5 Jul 2007, p. 13.

55. Ibid., pp. 26–27.

56. "Bush Meets with Afghan Head Karzai," *Columbia Daily Spectator* 126, no. 6 (29 Jan 2002): 3, https://spectatorarchive.library.columbia.edu/, Hist Files, OEF Study Grp.

57. Memo, Sec Rumsfeld for Gen Franks, 28 Jan 2002, sub: Afghan National Army, Attachment, https://library.rumsfeld.com/doclib/sp/436/To%20General%20Franks%20re%20Afghan%20National%20Army-%20Memo%20Attachment%2001-28-2002.pdf, p. 2, Hist Files, OEF Study Grp.

58. Feith, *War and Decision*, p. 150.

Powell had already forwarded Fahim's plan to the DoD, where Secretary Rumsfeld's staff scrutinized it. The proposed program included $144 million for salaries paid to 60,000 officers, equating to an average annual pay of $2,400 each, and $33.6 million for the $240 annual salaries of 140,000 enlisted soldiers. The price tag for feeding 200,000 officers and men for a year totaled an impressive $182 million. In sharp contrast, Fahim placed the first year's cost of rehabilitating infrastructure and paying for operating costs of the new Afghan army's six main bases at a mere $67.47 million.[59]

Rather than sit down with the Afghans to determine how much it would cost to reconstitute their army, Rumsfeld tasked General Franks to assess what size army Afghanistan really needed, what missions it should pursue, how militia members should be integrated, and what it would cost.[60] CENTCOM reported to the secretary of defense that the Afghan National Army (ANA) needed only $4 million in startup costs.[61] Although the United States contributed $79.2 million to rebuilding the Afghan army during fiscal year 2002, the DoD's share was a paltry $4.3 million.[62] Even procuring this modest sum required legal and financial gymnastics on the part of DoD accountants because the State Department had statutory authority for all foreign security assistance, including train-and-equip missions. Melding the two sources of money led to General Kratzer's appointment as head of the U.S. Embassy's Office of Military Cooperation–Afghanistan while he was also serving as the commander of the Civil-Military Operations Task Force.

In retrospect, it is clear the DoD viewed the ANA's reconstitution through a near-term budgetary lens rather than a long-term strategic one. By passing responsibility for the inaugural ANA funding estimate to CENTCOM rather than negotiating with Afghans, the United States signaled to Kabul that it did not consider the Afghan Interim Authority competent to determine its own needs. The DoD's course of action reflected a commendable sense of fiscal propriety, but it neglected the potential impact on Afghan and international opinion. In addition, limited early investment in Afghan security institutions placed far more vulnerable and costly nation-building initiatives at risk of Taliban interference. Without Afghan forces to secure the construction of new schools, clinics, and wells, American troops would have to perform those tasks. Finally, the DoD's fiscal conservatism during this period demonstrated that its leadership had yet to absorb the concept that money also could be an effective tool in the U.S. wartime arsenal.

Funding questions aside, Mikolashek sent a small group of CFLCC operations and planning officers, headed by Col. Michael B. Weimer, to

---

59. Memo, Sec Rumsfeld for Gen Franks, 28 Jan 2002, sub: Afghan National Army, Attachment, pp. 5–6.

60. Feith, *War and Decision*, p. 150.

61. Ibid., pp. 150–51.

62. The State Department provided the bulk of the funding. Feith, *War and Decision*, p. 151; Rpt to U.S. House of Representatives, Congressional Committee on International Relations, U.S. Government Accountability Ofc, *Afghanistan Security: Efforts to Establish Army and Police Have Made Progress, But Future Plans Need to Be Better Defined* (Washington, D.C.: U.S. Government Accountability Office, Jun 2005), p. 17, Hist Files, OEF Study Grp.

Kabul in mid-February to assist Kratzer. Discussions began on 18 February 2002 to determine the composition, armament, and deployment of the new force. At the onset, the Americans decreed that certain restrictions would be placed on prospective volunteers. Recruits had to have fought with the United Front, fled their homes in avoidance of Taliban rule, or resisted the Taliban. In all other matters, the Office of Military Cooperation–Afghanistan solicited Ministry of Defense input on creating a new Afghan military. The discussions consumed much of General Kratzer's day, which led him to concentrate on security issues while his deputy, Colonel Nutter, assumed the duties of de facto Coalition Joint Civil-Military Operations Task Force commander.

New Boots on the Ground for Evolving Missions

The Bush administration's expectations that the United States could transfer responsibility for security and reconstruction to the international community were enhanced by the arrival of ISAF in Kabul. Its commander, British Maj. Gen. John C. McColl, initially sought permission to deploy 8,000 ISAF personnel, including a sizable combat element. Representatives of the Tajik-dominated defense ministry vetoed that proposal while calling for no more than 1,000 personnel. Subsequent meetings produced a Military Technical Agreement, signed by McColl, Yunus Qanooni, and Kratzer on 4 January 2002, which capped the incoming international force at 4,500 soldiers with no more than 1,000 combat personnel.[63] Although no provisions were made to withdraw United Front warriors from Kabul, Fahim agreed to confine his troops to their barracks after ISAF arrived.[64] Following news of the signing, CENTCOM and CFLCC issued directives explaining the ISAF mission, how it would flow into Afghanistan, what facilities it would occupy upon arrival, and what support would be furnished to it.[65]

Recognizing the importance of working closely with ISAF, General Mikolashek dispatched a liaison officer, Col. Wayland E. Parker, to Kabul several days after McColl's arrival. CFLCC would send forty officers and enlisted personnel over the next several weeks, enough to create self-sufficient signal communications, intelligence, and administrative sections. In addition to maintaining a constant flow of information to CFLCC and CENTCOM, the liaison cell provided ISAF with both secure and open communications channels to their national representatives at Mikolashek's and Franks' headquarters. Colonel Parker's liaison cell also provided ISAF

---

63. Maloney, "The International Security Assistance Force," p. 7; Interv, Van Wey with Kratzer, 5 Jul 2007.

64. "Gurkhas Poised for Afghan Mission," *BBC News*, 9 Jan 2002, https://news.bbc.co.uk/2/hi/uk_news/1751037.stm, Hist Files, OEF Study Grp.

65. Memo, Col Eshelman for Third Army/ARCENT Cmd Grp and Staff, sub: ARCENT Updates 20 and 27 Dec 01, Story CFLCC Collection, OEF Study Grp.

with ready access to information collected by U.S. intelligence, surveillance, and reconnaissance systems.[66]

Other U.S. military organizations also were arriving in Afghanistan during this period. Some of the incoming units were slated to replace forces departing for anticipated missions elsewhere, while others augmented ongoing efforts, such as civil affairs operations, that required different skills or more resources. The most significant changeover involved a relief-in-place between Col. Francis J. Wiercinski's incoming 3d Brigade, 101st Airborne Division, and General Mattis' TF-58. The relief-in-place mainly turned over security functions and flight operations at Kandahar International Airport as well as missions such as sensitive site exploitation and security for remote CIA and Special Forces outposts.[67] Given that several major al-Qaeda training camps were located in southern Afghanistan, the incoming Army brigade undoubtedly would play a major role in Phase III operations.

Initially scheduled for 10 January, the transfer began several days later due to unexpected difficulties moving Wiercinski's brigade combat team by air from Fort Campbell, Kentucky, into theater.[68] The delays reflected the fact that many aircraft in the Air Force's transport fleet were developing maintenance problems after three months of nonstop usage.[69] Given the challenges facing the overworked strategic airlift fleet, CFLCC decided to transfer Capt. Patrick C. Aspland's Company C, 1st Battalion, 187th Infantry, from Pakistan to Kandahar on 15 January.[70] Upon disembarking, Captain Aspland's men joined other early arrivals, including Wiercinski's brigade headquarters and Lt. Col. Charles A. Preysler's 2d Battalion, 187th Infantry.

Although Wiercinski's brigade combat team left behind the 3d Battalion, 187th Infantry; most of the 3d Battalion, 320th Field Artillery; and its habitually supporting air defense battery, the units it did bring roughly matched TF-58 in combat power. Wiercinski's headquarters company and other attached units, such as Lt. Col. Thomas L. Pirozzi's 626th Forward Support Battalion and Capt. Micah R. Duke's Company D, 311th Military Intelligence Battalion, departed Fort Campbell with slightly less than their full complements. To the brigade's benefit, Capt. Mark C. Quander's

---

66. Interv, Maj John Warsinske, 47th MHD, with Col Wayland E. Parker, CFLCC International Security Assistance Force (ISAF) Liaison Ofcr, 10 July 2002, pp. 23–24, Hist Files, OEF Study Grp.

67. Narrative Sum, Opn Enduring Freedom, CTF 58, Opns in Afghanistan, 27 Oct 2001–26 Feb 2002, p. 62, Hist Files, OEF Study Grp.

68. TF Talon helicopters were transported in roundabout fashion to California, Hawaii, and Guam on C–5s before reaching Diego Garcia, where they were reloaded onto C–17 aircraft that took them to Kandahar. Several C–5s broke down en route to Diego Garcia. Interv, Laurence Lessard, CSI, with Maj Paul E. Berg, frmr Bn Personnel Ofcr, 7th Bn, 101st Avn, 5 Feb 2008, p. 4, Hist Files, OEF Study Grp.

69. Interv, Steven Clay, CSI, with Col Charles A. Preysler, frmr Cdr, 2d Bn, 187th Inf, 8 May 2007, p. 3, Hist Files, OEF Study Grp.

70. Capt Peter Aspland, "1-187 INF Comments," Rakkasan Rpt No. 1, 3d Bde Family Readiness Grp Newsletter 1, Issue 1 (13–19 Jan 2002): 2, https://www.angelfire.com/ns/yourwizard/stogransheroes/rep1-2.html, Hist Files, OEF Study Grp.

Company C, 326th Engineer Battalion, deployed with more personnel and equipment than normally authorized. Quander needed the extra troops to maintain Kandahar Airfield.[71] Although not part of Wiercinski's brigade, the 519th Military Police Battalion commanded by Lt. Col. Paul K. Warman also arrived during this period to assume the mission of securing the detention facility.[72]

Army rotary-wing assets appeared at Kandahar during the third week of January in the form of Lt. Col. James M. Mayre's Task Force TALON. Mayre's unit deployed with the 7th Battalion, 101st Aviation headquarters and headquarters company plus Company A, equipped with CH–47 Chinook medium lift helicopters, as well as attached companies of UH–60L Black Hawk assault helicopters (A/4–101st Aviation), AH–64 Apache attack helicopters (A/3–101st Aviation), aviation maintenance (A/8–101st Aviation), air traffic control (C/1–58th Aviation), and a forward support medical evacuation (medevac) team (50th Medical Company).[73] While the bulk of the rotary-wing aircraft remained at Kandahar to support Wiercinski's brigade, a number of UH–60Ls and several Chinooks were soon transferred to Bagram.

One of the final components of Wiercinski's force, the light infantrymen from Company B, 3d Princess Patricia's Canadian Light Infantry, arrived on 1 February. Company B began ten days of training on U.S. tactics and equipment in anticipation of working with Wiercinski's brigade while simultaneously assuming responsibility for defending a portion of the Kandahar Airfield perimeter. The remainder of the Canadian battalion led by Lt. Col. Patrick B. Stogran—including two additional infantry companies, reconnaissance and mortar elements of the combat support company, an armored reconnaissance squadron, an engineer company, and logistical elements—arrived piecemeal over the next several weeks.[74]

PLANNING FOR THE SHAHI KOT

Reports about al-Qaeda remnants hiding in the eastern reaches of Afghanistan led to the first significant engagement of Phase III taking place in the Shahi Kot Valley in early March 2002. Planning and preparation for a foray into that region began more than a month earlier when information obtained by ODA 594 from Afghans convinced Colonel Mulholland to send more reconnaissance assets into the Khost-Gardez region. These initial efforts failed when several Afghan scouts dispatched to the area by Capt. Robert S. Harward's TF K-BAR never returned. On 7 February, a concerned

---

71. Interv, John McCool, CSI, with Maj Mark Quander, frmr Cdr, Co C, 326th Engr Bn, 7 Mar 2007, p. 1, Hist Files, OEF Study Grp.

72. Lowery, *U.S. Marines in Afghanistan, 2001–2002*, p. 201.

73. Lt Col Jim Mayre, "TF 7–101st AVN Comments," Rakkasan Report No. 2, 3d Brigade Family Readiness Grp Newsletter 1, Issue 2 (20–26 Jan 2002): 3, https://www.angelfire.com/ns/yourwizard/stogransheroes/rep2-3.html, Hist Files, OEF Study Grp.

74. "3 PPCLI [Princess Patricia's Canadian Light Infantry] Battlegroup in Afghanistan, January–July 2002," Stogransheroes.com, 4 Feb 2002, https://www.angelfire.com/ns/yourwizard/stogransheroes/index.html, Hist Files, OEF Study Grp.

Afghan civilian provided TF DAGGER with more specific information about a sizable group of enemy fighters in the Shahi Kot Valley.[75] Rather than continue to rely only on Afghan sources, TF SWORD prepared to dispatch its own reconnaissance teams into the valley.[76]

Like Tora Bora, the 150 square kilometers of the Shahi Kot, with its two valleys, the Upper Shahi Kot and the Lower Shahi Kot, made for a potentially difficult operating environment. The Lower Shahi Kot, located 1,500 meters above sea level, was eight kilometers long and four kilometers wide. Up to 1,000 Afghan civilians were reported to live on the valley floor in the villages of Marzak, Babul Khel, and Sher Khan Khel. A prominent ridgeline, soon nicknamed "the Whale" by U.S. forces because it resembled a well-known geographic landmark of the same name at Fort Irwin National Training Center in California's Mojave Desert, dominated its western side.[77] The eastern ridgeline, Takur Ghar, appeared even more foreboding, reaching 3,200 meters at its highest point. A narrow secondary ridgeline, dubbed "the Finger," protruded into the southeastern end of the valley. Whoever controlled the decisive terrain along the ridgelines, specifically those on the Whale, the Finger, and the eastern ridge, held an important tactical advantage.

The reports of massing enemy fighters in that area had surfaced as Captain Harward's command reached full operating capability and Colonel Mulholland's headquarters prepared to turn over its responsibilities to the incoming 3d Special Forces Group, 1st Special Forces Command. Keenly aware that his own staff had far more combat experience and greater insight into working with Afghan militia forces, Mulholland agreed to help Harward devise a plan to destroy the rumored enemy concentration. The initial concept jointly developed by planning cells collocated at Bagram between 6 and 13 February mirrored TF DAGGER's proven method of pairing a small number of Special Forces with Afghan militia fighters and massive air support to overcome enemy forces in rugged terrain.[78]

When updated information placed the estimated number of al-Qaeda fighters in the Shahi Kot Valley at 150 to 200 strong, Colonel Mulholland and Captain Harward decided to solicit assistance from General Hagenbeck. All agreed that the 10th Mountain Division should have overall command of any major operation. Hagenbeck and Mulholland prepared a recommendation along those lines for General Mikolashek, who also agreed the idea had merit. CFLCC directed Hagenbeck to relocate to Bagram to enhance his ability to oversee the upcoming operation.[79] Mikolashek's staff tentatively redesignated

---

75. Wright et al., *A Different Kind of War*, p. 132; Briscoe et al., *Weapon of Choice*, p. 279.

76. Although TF SWORD was renamed Task Force 11 in January 2002, this account will use the original designation to avoid confusing readers.

77. Briscoe et al., *Weapon of Choice*, p. 280.

78. Rebecca Grant et al., "Operation Anaconda: An Airpower Perspective," HQ, U.S. Air Force, ATTN: [Office of the Air Force Lessons Learned], 7 Feb 2005, p. 22. This study presents the Air Force version of events following a lengthy published interview by Maj. Gen. Franklin Hagenbeck in which he discussed fire support problems that appeared in the September–October 2002 issue of the U.S. Army's *Field Artillery Journal*.

79. Wright et al., *A Different Kind of War*, p. 132.

Hagenbeck's new command as Combined Joint Task Force–Afghanistan (CJTF-Afghanistan) before renaming it CJTF-Mountain several days later.[80]

The new title could not disguise the fact that the 167 officers and enlisted personnel of CJTF-Mountain were only a fraction of the staff normally allocated to the 10th Mountain Division headquarters. Digital technology might have offset the personnel shortfall, but as General Myers noted during a visit to Bagram, "The Army had equipped Buster Hagenbeck's Tactical Operations Center so that it looked like something out of a World War II movie, with paper maps instead of interactive screens. CENTCOM had not provided Hagenbeck the facilities he needed to command and maneuver his forces in a rapid and flexible manner."[81]

Although bad weather delayed the 10th Mountain Division's movement from Karshi Khanabad, Hagenbeck's staff began refining existing plans upon arriving at Bagram. Mulholland's planners, led by Lt. Col. Mark D. Rosengard, offered to assist their CJTF-Mountain counterparts headed by Hagenbeck's chief operations officer, Lt. Col. David Gray, and deputy fire support coordinator, Lt. Col. Christopher F. Bentley.[82] The TF Sword reconnaissance element also began liaising informally with CJTF-Mountain.[83] The fact that representatives from the Combined Forces Air Component Command (CFACC) were not present at Bagram at this point did not disturb the other organizations involved. In fact, the projected threat estimate did not seem to warrant making different air support arrangements. The information from various sources—some not fully verified—indicated that the concentration of fighters in the Shahi Kot were the security detail for low- and mid-level al-Qaeda leaders who would flee rather than stand their ground.[84]

Even though conventional forces were entering the fight, which arguably added a new dimension to tactical operations, CENTCOM did not mandate that CFLCC or its Air Component Command review existing policies, plans, and procedures. If that had occurred, CFLCC might have realized General Hagenbeck faced greater wartime command and control challenges than perhaps any other U.S. division commander in recent memory. Not only did Hagenbeck lack organic engineers, artillery, aviation, and reconnaissance assets, but his skeletonized division staff also formed the core of a combined joint task force, responsible for planning, conducting, and supporting the full range of coalition conventional and special forces operations and also for coordinating with theater headquarters.[85] While Hagenbeck could now

---

80. Interv, Brown with Hagenbeck, 15 Mar 2002, p. 2.

81. Myers with McConnell, *Eyes on the Horizon*, p. 211.

82. Grant et al., "Operation Anaconda," p. 22.

83. Backgrounder, Blaber, p. 6.

84. Presentation, Maj Francesca Ziemba, sub: Operation Anaconda: CJTF-Mountain C2 Plans, "Threat Summary" slide, n.d., Hist Files, OEF Study Grp. The presentation's PowerPoint file was entitled "TRADOC [U.S. Army Training and Doctrine Command] Roadshow," intimating that it was intended for internal professional development purposes and disseminated to U.S. Army audiences at training and instructional centers within the continental United States.

85. Wright et al., *A Different Kind of War*, pp. 132–133.

draw upon the resources of several other organizations, many of the parties involved had little or no experience working with their counterparts. In fact, during the post–Cold War era, conventional forces were rarely afforded the opportunity to work with Special Operations elements and vice versa. The various Special Operations elements, ranging from Navy SEALs to Army Green Berets to the multiservice counterterrorist forces of TF SWORD to the Australian Special Air Service, also were not used to working together on an operational level. Finally, Hagenbeck's staff had little or no experience coordinating with the CIA's paramilitary arm, which meant that they had to rely on Special Operations intermediaries to do so.

Impending combat operations led CENTCOM to designate General Harrell and the intelligence community's top military liaison, Brig. Gen. Michael D. Jones, as Hagenbeck's deputies. That move permitted Hagenbeck to interact with TF SWORD elements and the CIA.[86] Having deputies familiar with many of the other organizations aided Hagenbeck, but their presence did not solve the issues created by inserting a partially staffed conventional headquarters within ongoing planning efforts involving the CIA and three different Special Operations elements. All of these elements were expected to participate in the upcoming operation, which resulted in each demanding a say in the planning. Although many of those involved with coordinating the upcoming operation knew of the problems within the new command and control arrangements, the fact that intelligence reports indicated the enemy fighters were more likely to flee than fight quelled their concerns.

As the new operational plan began to take form, its authors christened it Operation ANACONDA in deference to the similarly named Union plan to blockade, encircle, and crush the Confederacy during the American Civil War. The 10th Mountain planners opposed a TF DAGGER proposal to use air power to blast a path for Green Berets and Afghan militia entering the valley from all sides. Representatives from each organization sought to convince their counterparts of the merits of their respective proposals. Ironically, the lack of an Air Force coordination cell magnified rather than decreased the challenges facing General Hagenbeck, as all of the Army and Special Operations plans relied on massive close air support. Hagenbeck settled on a compromise version involving near simultaneous assaults by a combined U.S.-Afghan ground force and American conventional forces inserted via helicopter. The use of helicopters exerted tremendous influence on ongoing planning efforts, which included determining the overall timing, composition of conventional forces, and numbers of U.S. troops involved.[87]

Unlike in Tora Bora and earlier operations, the potential presence of numerous innocents complicated fire support planning. In addition to several hundred enemy fighters, intelligence sources estimated that 1,000 to 1,500

---

86. Backgrounder, Maj Gen Franklin "Buster" Hagenbeck, Cdr, TF Mtn, Opn ANACONDA, 1 Mar 2012, American Enterprise Institute, https://www.aei.org/press/operation-anaconda/, Hist Files, OEF Study Grp.

87. Interv, Brown with Hagenbeck, 15 Mar 2002, pp. 3–4.

Left to right: Wiercinski, Hagenbeck, Smith, Harrell, and Mulholland oversee early moves during Operation ANACONDA.

Afghans were living in the Shahi Kot region.[88] Concern for the valley's civilian inhabitants led CJTF-MOUNTAIN to restrict the use of preparatory fires and to task Afghan irregular forces, rather than American troops, to clear a trio of villages within the objective area. Intelligence assessments also predicted the enemy would fight only long enough to allow its leadership to seek sanctuary in Pakistan. Hagenbeck therefore defined success as preventing enemy leaders from escaping by establishing "three [concentric] circles around the Shah-i-Khot Valley to block off the primary escape routes."[89] The "circles" (which resembled arcs rather than full circles) would be created, beginning with the outermost circle, three days before the start of ANACONDA.[90]

Keenly aware that Cold War–era intelligence collection systems were ill-suited to provide real time information about diffuse threat arrays, CJTF-MOUNTAIN deployed more than two dozen TF K-BAR reconnaissance teams furnished by U.S. Navy SEAL Teams 2, 3, and 8; 3d Special Forces Group; Canada's Joint Task Force 2; New Zealand Special Air Service; Norway's Jegerkommando; Denmark's Jaegerkorpset; and the German Kommando Spezialkräfte along the northern half of the outer circle to maintain constant surveillance over east-west trails and roads. Lt. Col. Rowan J. Tink's Australian Special Air Service, now designated as TF-64, was responsible for the southern half. Despite unfavorable weather during the week before the planned assault, most teams were inserted successfully by helicopter atop

---

88. Capt Glen T. Helberg, "OPERATION ENDURING FREEDOM: Eyes of the Eagle," (PEP, Inf Capts Career Course 04-02, 6 Feb 2003), p. 7, Hist Files, OEF Study Grp.

89. Interv, Brown with Hagenbeck, 15 Mar 2002, p. 3.

90. Wright et al., *A Different Kind of War*, p. 139.

prominent terrain across the north and south of the Shahi Kot. The teams were prepared to remain for as long as necessary in order to target enemy personnel fleeing toward Pakistan with close air support.[91]

The middle circle around the Shahi Kot Valley included two Afghan militia contingents supported by ODAs from the 3d and 5th Special Forces Groups that would move into place one day before the operation's start. Dubbed TF ANVIL, these Afghan fighters were supposed to split up to establish two northern blocking positions dubbed CHEVY and FORD as well as another pair in the south designated as JEEP and OLDSMOBILE.[92] The group led by Kamel Khan Zadran, consisting of 500 militiamen from Khost as well as ODAs 571 and 572, was responsible for the northern roadblocks. A second group led by Zakim Khan Zadran consisting of 300 to 500 fighters from the Urgun region supported by ODAs 542 and 381 had responsibility for the southernmost blocking positions.[93] To preserve operational security, the attached ODAs did not reveal details of the upcoming mission to their Afghan counterparts until just before it began.[94]

The villages of Marzak, Babul Khel, and Sher Khan Khel in the center of the valley were collectively designated as Objective REMINGTON (*Map 3.1*). The innermost circle, consisting of heliborne elements from Colonel Wiercinski's 3d Brigade, 101st Airborne Division, would be inserted at dawn on D-Day to occupy positions AMY, BETTY, CINDY, DIANE, EVE, GINGER, and HEATHER, which were oriented north to south along the eastern edge of REMINGTON. In addition to his own personnel, Wiercinski received Lt. Col. Paul J. LaCamera's 1st Battalion, 87th Infantry. Colonel Preysler's 2d Battalion, 187th Infantry, and LaCamera's unit were selected to conduct the air assault. Preysler's troops were responsible for AMY, BETTY, CINDY, and DIANE, while LaCamera's force established EVE, GINGER, and HEATHER. Lt. Col. Ronald E. Corkran's 1st Battalion, 187th Infantry, remained in reserve at Bagram. Wiercinski, Corkran, and three members of the 1st Battalion staff planned to observe the initial assault into the valley from a command and control helicopter orbiting overhead.[95]

The concentric circles were only useful if the assault force pushed defenders out of the valley. Lacking sufficient American troops for the task, CJTF-MOUNTAIN assigned the task of pushing the enemy eastward out of the valley toward waiting American troops to Afghan militia fighters. This force consisted of 500 fighters led by Hazara commander Zia Lodin accompanied by Capt. Glenn R. Thomas' ODA 594 and Captain Matthew M. McHale's ODA 372. Two other groups of Afghan fighters, one led by a Pashtun commander named Khoshkeyer and the other by Zia Abdullah, agreed to cooperate with Zia Lodin.

---

91. Briscoe et al., *Weapon of Choice*, p. 281.
92. Wright et al., *A Different Kind of War*, p. 139.
93. Briscoe et al., *Weapon of Choice*, pp. 281–82.
94. Wright et al., *A Different Kind of War*, p. 141.
95. Ibid., pp. 139–40.

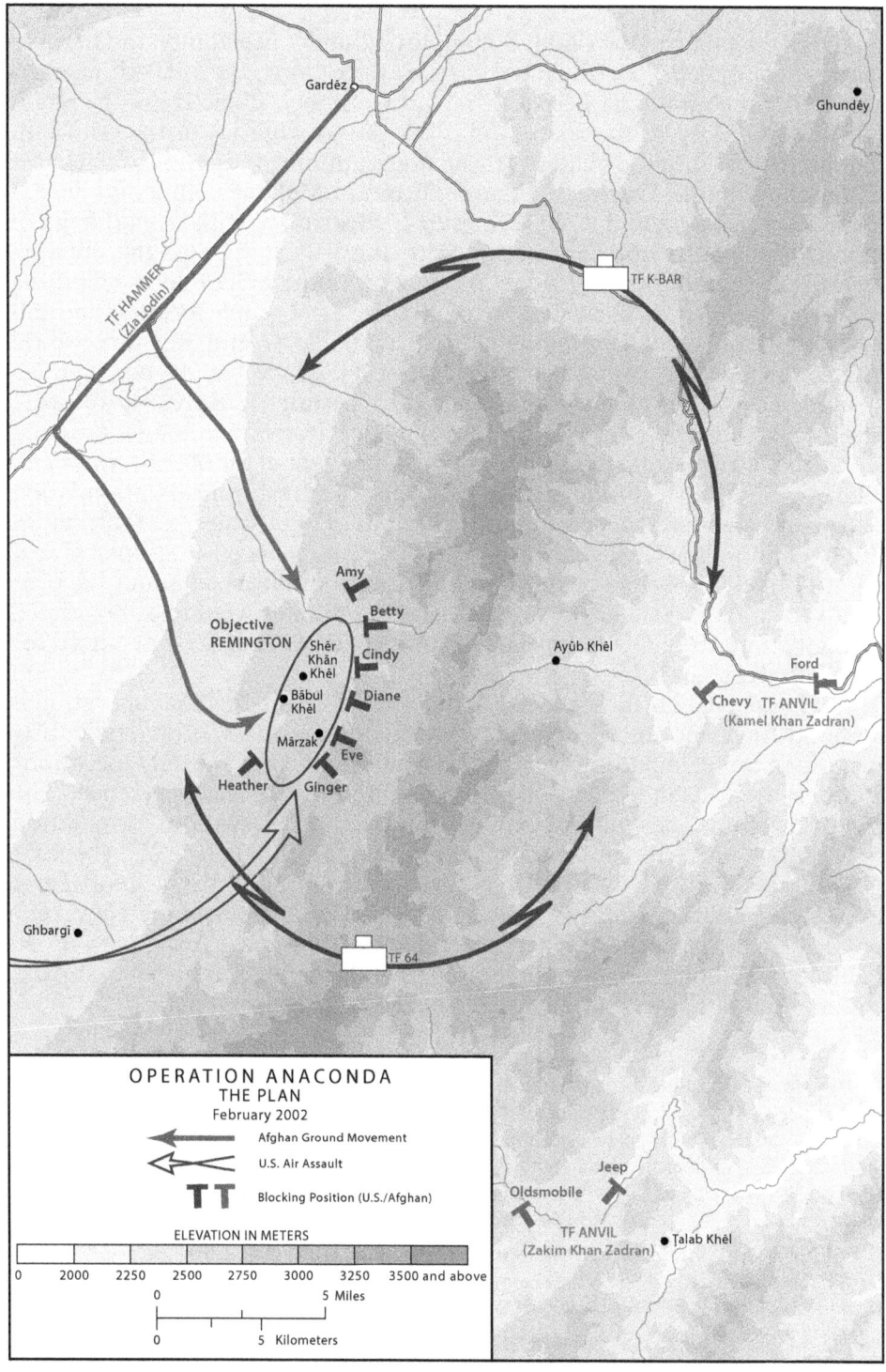

Map 3.1

Afghan participation added complexity and uncertainty to the plan because it entailed a lengthy night road march of more than 150 kilometers, separating the militia gathered at Gardez from their objective in the Shahi Kot. The final leg of the route would tax the capabilities of the militia to the utmost because they had to travel along unimproved roads in darkness and without lights. During the march, Captain McHale planned to detach his second-in-command, CWO2 Stanley L. Harriman, with a small Afghan force to block the northern entrance to the valley prior to the opening assault on the dominating ridgeline known as the Whale located on the western edge of the valley. The remainder of Zia Lodin's force, supported by the bulk of both ODAs along with all available 82-mm. mortars, would attack through the valley's southern entrance. Once the Afghan fighters cleared the Whale, they were instructed to assault Objective REMINGTON, pushing the enemy to the west toward the Americans.[96]

Although the Afghan force was a key component of the overall American plan, CJTF-MOUNTAIN did not include their leadership in its pre-mission rehearsals and intelligence updates. Despite TF DAGGER's confidence in the Afghan fighters, Hagenbeck's staff strongly believed that operational security likely would be compromised if Zia Lodin learned about the plan in advance. As a result, both he and his subordinates would not be briefed by their supporting ODAs until a few hours before his fighters departed for the Shahi Kot.[97]

General Mikolashek received the final version of the operational plan at Bagram on 17 February.[98] All commanders of participating American units, including General Hagenbeck and his Special Operations counterparts, attended in person or through video teleconference. The CFLCC commander did not express any serious reservations, stipulating only that, while he did not want the operation to begin before 25 February, it had to be initiated within thirty days to forestall any al-Qaeda attempt to launch a counteroffensive timed for the onset of the Islamic New Year on 21 March. As a result, Hagenbeck decided to launch ANACONDA on 28 February. Mikolashek also suggested that Hagenbeck give the CFACC commander at Prince Sultan Air Base a copy of the final plan.[99]

---

96. Conducting a night road march under blackout conditions over this distance with little or no notice would be extremely difficult for even the best-trained American units. The Afghans, moreover, had received almost no training to sharpen their night driving or convoy skills before the attack. It is difficult to understand why Combined Joined Task Force (CJTF)MOUNTAIN attempted to synchronize this type of operation with an air assault requiring split-second timing unless it had no other options. Briscoe et al., *Weapon of Choice*, pp. 282–83.

97. CJTF-MOUNTAIN factored the loss of surprise into its calculations because planners were certain the Afghans would notify the enemy of the impending assault. Presentation, Ziemba, sub: Operation Anaconda: CJTF-Mountain C2 Plans, "D-6 to D-1" slide, n.d.

98. Lt. Gen. Paul T. Mikolashek also received an update from Hagenbeck on 21 February 2002 before returning to Camp Doha. Memo, Col Eshelman for Third Army/ARCENT Cmd Grp and Staff, sub: ARCENT Update Kabul Trip 17–22 Feb 02, 24 Feb 02, 1129 hours, Story CFLCC Collection, OEF Study Grp.

99. Grant et al., "Operation Anaconda," pp. 25–26.

As the start date for ANACONDA neared, the TF SWORD reconnaissance detachment supporting CJTF-MOUNTAIN shifted its priorities to pinpointing likely enemy locations. At sundown on 27 February, TF SWORD dispatched three teams—JULIET, INDIA, and MAKO–31—into the Shahi Kot to establish observation posts overlooking key terrain in the valley. INDIA took up position where it could observe the route being used by TF HAMMER while JULIET set up overlooking the helicopter landing zones. However, MAKO–31 halted just short of its intended destination when daylight threatened to expose its presence.[100] After holing up in a hide position for the day, the team resumed its trek at sundown on 28 February. Zero visibility produced by driving snow forced MAKO–31 to suspend the effort once again. Several minutes later, CJTF-MOUNTAIN informed the TF SWORD liaison that unsafe flying conditions would result in ANACONDA being postponed until 0620 on 2 March 2002.

When dawn broke on 1 March, MAKO–31 discovered an enemy antiaircraft position within fifty meters of its hiding place. After reviewing digital photographs of the heavy machine gun sent by MAKO–31, Special Operations liaison personnel at Bagram realized that the enemy occupied the high ground, not the villages, and seemed ready to defend rather than beat a hasty retreat. The liaison team asked CJTF-MOUNTAIN not to land troop-carrying helicopters on the valley floor. Facing the prospect of cancelling the entire operation just before it began, Hagenbeck's chief of staff replied, "I know [we shouldn't land the helicopters there], but it's too late to do anything about it."[101]

INTO THE SHAHI KOT

Operation ANACONDA opened with a pair of AC–130 Special Operations gunships surveying the Shahi Kot Valley during the night of 1–2 March. One gunship confirmed that no enemy troops were in position to contest the movement of the Afghan assault force. The second gunship reported that its thermal sights detected no activity at AMY, BETTY, CINDY, and DIANE, with the exception of a few people walking near some buildings. Owing to mechanical problems, that same gunship returned to base before conducting a similar prebattle reconnaissance of EVE, GINGER, and HEATHER.[102] This development proved singularly unfortunate as Taliban reinforcements were in the process of occupying fighting positions near the southern landing zones after receiving a tipoff from one of the TF HAMMER militia commanders. The tipoff not only triggered the Taliban's arrival, but also alerted between 300 and 400 Uzbek fighters located in that area. Unfortunately, the senior al-Qaeda leaders also

---

100. Backgrounder, Blaber, p. 6.
101. Ibid., p. 7.
102. Grant et al., "Operation Anaconda," p. 61.

heeded the warning by leaving the valley through the southern passes before the Americans even appeared.[103]

The convoy carrying Zia Lodin's fighters departed Gardez as scheduled, but vehicle breakdowns and poor march discipline soon caused problems. The convoy's main body split in two following a truck rollover that injured a dozen or more Afghan militia.[104] When the lead elements reached a point just west of the Shahi Kot before dawn, Chief Warrant Officer Harriman's blocking force headed for the northern valley entrance. As the vehicles neared their designated objective, an explosion destroyed the lead HMMWV, mortally wounding Harriman and injuring two other Special Forces soldiers. Additional hits killed and wounded more than a dozen Afghans.[105] An outbound CH–47 picked up the wounded several hours later, but Harriman died soon after arriving at Bagram.[106] Several weeks elapsed before CENTCOM confirmed that an orbiting AC–130 gunship had mistakenly identified the convoy as an enemy unit following a navigational system failure.[107]

During the early hours of 2 March, Mako–31 made preparations to destroy the nearby antiaircraft machine gun position. The Americans planned to wait until one hour prior to the scheduled arrival of the helicopters before engaging the enemy troops. However, when an enemy soldier exited his tent at 0400 to urinate, he spotted the Americans. The Mako–31 team leader fired the first shots of Anaconda a split second later, killing the enemy fighter. The team killed two more al-Qaeda fighters while a fourth and fifth were eliminated by an orbiting AC–130H gunship.[108]

Commander Zia Lodin's column had halted while the northern element treated its wounded. Once word arrived that the casualties were on their way to Gardez or Bagram, Captain Thomas persuaded his Afghan counterparts to resume their advance. The first rays of daylight were appearing when Zia Lodin's column resumed movement toward the southern entrance. As they neared the valley, the Afghans hesitated. Special Operations historians later explained that mounting Afghan concerns stemmed from assurances that American aircraft would unleash fifty-five minutes of bombing against enemy positions before the assault force entered the Shahi Kot:

---

103. Presentation, Ziemba, sub: Operation Anaconda: CJTF-Mountain C2 Plans, "D-1 to D" slide, n.d.

104. Wright et al., *A Different Kind of War*, p. 141.

105. Ibid.

106. Capt James K. Gadoury, "Eleven Days in the Valley: Operation Anaconda from the Eyes of the A/2-187 Company Executive Officer," (PEP, Inf Capts Career Course 05 -03, May 2003), p. 5, Hist Files, OEF Study Grp.

107. DoD Pentagon Bfg, Gen Franks, 29 Mar 2002, http://archive.defense.gov/Transcripts/Transcript.aspx?TranscriptID=3382, Hist Files, OEF Study Grp; Maj Sean P. Larkin, "Air-to-Ground Fratricide Reduction Technology: An Analysis" (Master's thesis, U.S. Marine Corps Command and Staff College, n.d.), p. 13, https://www.dtic.mil/cgi-bin/GetTRDoc?AD=ADA506423, Hist Files, OEF Study Grp.

108. Backgrounder, Blaber, p. 7.

That promise and CAS [close air support] had been key in persuading the Afghans to participate. Expecting a massive allied bombing attack as the Americans had done against the Taliban in November and December, and then to al-Qaeda around Tora Bora, Commander Zia [Lodin] was surprised to observe and hear only seven explosions in the distance along the "Whale."[109]

In retrospect, it is surprising that the Special Forces personnel with the Afghan assault force did not foresee major adjustments to the plan as a result of the delayed arrival of Zia Lodin's force. CJTF-MOUNTAIN knew that many hours would be needed to regenerate the intricately choreographed air assault following a last-minute cancellation. If the helicopters aborted their approach, TF HAMMER would have to either retreat or initiate an assault before the blocking positions could be occupied. In any event, the ultimate responsibility for that decision fell on Colonel Wiercinski.

If the defenders had any doubts about the tip-off being accurate, the AC–130 engagements and bombing attack must have dispelled them. TF HAMMER reached the southern entrance only to encounter a punishing barrage delivered by artillery hidden in a gully on the reverse slope of the Whale. Dragging their wounded with them, Zia and Khoshkeyer's men retreated out of range. The ODA team leaders were trying to reorganize the Afghans when the American helicopter formation appeared. Recognizing that further air support would not be forthcoming, the ODA team leaders and Afghan commanders called off the assault. Thus, the elements considered to be the main effort of ANACONDA played little or no role in the start of the battle.[110]

As the heavily laden CH–47 and UH–60 helicopters neared the southern entrance of the valley, the air force liaison officer accompanying Wiercinski reported that "not all the targets have been struck. We are fifteen minutes from touchdown and it's obviously your call." Colonel Wiercinski replied, "[S]hut off the air strikes. We're going in. I want to get the guys on the ground, and then we can worry about bombing targets." The brigade air force liaison officer responded by broadcasting, "This is a *global knock it off!* The helicopters are five minutes out, and there will be no more air strikes until we get everybody on the ground."[111] That single call had sufficed to bring all bombing to a halt temporarily.

The initial air assault element led by Colonel Mayre of TF TALON, consisting of two UH–60L Black Hawks, five AH–64A Apache gunships, and six CH–47 Chinooks, entered the Shahi Kot Valley from the south just before dawn. The AH–64 Apaches preceded the troop-carrying helicopters by fifteen minutes to clear the valley of unforeseen threats. The Chinooks bearing Capt. Franklin F. Baltazar's Company C, 2d Battalion, 187th Infantry, passed a short distance from the antiaircraft position silenced by MAKO–31.

---

109. Briscoe et al., *Weapon of Choice*, p. 286.

110. Ibid.

111. Lester W. Grau, "The Coils of the Anaconda: America's First Conventional Battle in Afghanistan" (Ph.D. diss., University of Kansas, 2009), pp. 260–61 (emphasis in original).

Neither the Apaches nor Chinooks provoked an enemy reaction. Hagenbeck recalled:

> As the [sic] Al-Qaeda and Taliban were patting themselves on the back for their great victory of turning Zia [Lodin] away right at dawn, our helicopters went streaming in to the Shah-i-Khot Valley behind them onto the East Ridge. . . . In fact, [in] six of the seven landing zones from north to south, we were able to secure not only the landing zones but the designated battle positions [objectives] within two hours.[112]

Two of the leading CH–47s deposited Baltazar's third platoon near DIANE and his first platoon near CINDY. Captain Baltazar later observed, "Initially, when I landed, there was no contact. Everyone rushed off the helicopter and kind of waited until the Chinooks left. Then, I would say, within a minute, we heard small arms fire."[113] Another minute or so passed before Baltazar's 3d Platoon informed the company commander it had made contact with enemy troops. A third CH–47 dropped off Preysler's battalion tactical command post, along with Company C's 2d Platoon, near a walled compound located between AMY and BETTY.[114] The Americans encountered resistance from isolated gunmen and mortar fire, but a combination of Apache support and air strikes soon silenced the enemy. Preysler then ordered Company C to occupy its designated blocking positions, which it accomplished without loss despite several more brushes with enemy defenders. With the mounting successes, it seemed that the rugged terrain was more a formidable opponent than the enemy was.[115]

The 10th Mountain soldiers bound for the southernmost landing zones included the headquarters and a platoon from Capt. Roger A. Crombie's Company A, 1st Battalion, 87th Infantry, along with members of the battalion scout platoon; Capt. Nelson G. Kraft's Company C with its headquarters and two platoons; seven members of Colonel LaCamera's tactical command post accompanied by two Australian Special Air Service liaison personnel; and the crew of a 120-mm. mortar with forty-eight rounds of mortar ammunition.[116] Three-man intelligence and translator teams from TF DAGGER accompanied each company.[117] All told, Crombie's contingent

---

112. Interv, Brown with Hagenbeck, 15 Mar 2002, p. 5.

113. Wright et al., *A Different Kind of War*, p. 146.

114. Interv, Clay with Preysler, 8 May 2007, p. 4.

115. Helberg, "OPERATION ENDURING FREEDOM," pp. 10–11.

116. Interv, John McCool, CSI, with Maj Roger A Crombie, frmr Co Cdr, Co A, 1st Bn, 87th Inf, 10th Mtn Div, 30 Mar 2006, p. 7, Hist Files, OEF Study Grp; Grau, "The Coils of the Anaconda," p. 257. Grau mistakenly states that two platoons of Crombie's company were part of the first lift.

117. Capt Travis Patriquin, "Operation ANACONDA, March 2d to 5th, 2002," (PEP, Inf Capts Career Course 05 -03, May 2003), p. 3, Hist Files, OEF Study Grp.

numbered forty-three officers and men, while Kraft's and LaCamera's combined force totaled eighty-two personnel.[118]

The CH–47 ferrying Crombie's company headquarters, rifle platoon, and the TF DAGGER liaison team led by Capt. Travis L. Patriquin hovered over the designated landing zone only to find it was unsuitable. The pilot reversed the helicopter to drop the soldiers atop a bare, snow-covered hilltop slightly to the west. Rather than remain where the CH–47 had left them, Captain Crombie ordered his men to occupy a larger hilltop nearby. Covered by Patriquin's team, which had the group's only long-range rifle optics, Crombie's men headed toward their new objective. The Americans were briefly opposed by a single al-Qaeda fighter who subsequently lost his life to an alert M–203 grenadier. Soon after reaching the new location, Crombie could observe at least a hundred al-Qaeda fighters on the valley floor but could not call for fire on them because the 3d Brigade tactical operations center did not know where all the SOF teams were located. Crombie's unit hunkered down atop the hill for the rest of the day, trading shots with al-Qaeda fighters as the sound of fighting to the south steadily increased.[119]

The swelling volume of small arms fire in the southern part of the valley emanated from enemy combatants swarming toward the helicopter landing zones in that area. It turned out that intelligence analysts had correctly predicted that the passes leading southeastward out of the valley would be used by the enemy to escape. However, neither the analysts nor the planners anticipated that the defenders would deploy most of their troops in that area to maintain control of those passes for as long as possible. Later events would reveal that around 500–600 enemy fighters, mostly Uzbek Islamists, defended the southern end of the lower Shahi Kot.[120] Unlike the attackers, the enemy fighters had enough insight into how the battle would unfold to weight their defense in the most critical sector.

In addition to superior numbers, the enemy had antiaircraft cannon and machine guns, several dozen 120-mm. and 82-mm. mortars, nine 122-mm. howitzers, and a 76-mm. cannon.[121] The artillery pieces, which played a key role in repelling the combined U.S.-Afghan assault from the west, had not been pinpointed in advance.[122] Reports of Afghan civilians living in the objective area were erroneous; al-Qaeda had forced the inhabitants out months earlier. While that knowledge might have convinced CJTF-MOUNTAIN to utilize

---

118. DoD News Bfg, Cmd Sgt Maj Frank Grippe at al., Interview with U.S. Soldiers who Participated in Operation Anaconda, 7 Mar 2002, https://archive.defense.gov/Transcripts/Transcript.aspx?TranscriptID=2914, Hist Files, OEF Study Grp; Macklin and Palmer, *SAS Insider*, p. 12.

119. Patriquin, "Operation ANACONDA, March 2d to 5th, 2002," pp. 5–6; Interv, McCool with Crombie, 30 Mar 2006, pp. 7–8.

120. Presentation, Ziemba, n.d., sub: Operation Anaconda: CJTF-Mountain C2 Plans, "Post-Anaconda View of What Was Actually There: D-6 to D-1" slide.

121. Grau and Billingsly, *Operation Anaconda*, pp. 118–121.

122. These included two recoilless rifles of unknown caliber, two unconfirmed 12.7-mm. antiaircraft machine guns, one antiaircraft cannon of unknown type, and one of the hidden artillery pieces. Presentation, Ziemba, n.d., sub: Operation Anaconda: CJTF-Mountain C2 Plans, "Known Locations, OBJ" slide.

significantly more preparatory fires, it ultimately made little difference given that most enemy defensive positions and heavy weapons were not located. The intelligence failures in the opening stages of ANACONDA were numerous.

The unanticipated enemy resistance almost led to the loss of the 3d Brigade tactical command post. Colonel Wiercinski had planned to remain aloft during the initial air assault in order to maintain better situational awareness, but after hearing multiple reports of enemy contact, he directed the pilot of his Black Hawk to land on a ridge just southwest of GINGER. The other Black Hawk in the command and control flight also unloaded its passengers, including Colonel Corkran, on the same ridge. From his new perch, the 3d Brigade commander gained an excellent view of the valley's north-south axis. Although Wiercinski did not know it, he had disembarked only a few hundred meters from MAKO–31.

Within a few minutes, Wiercinski's group had two sets of visitors, one welcome and the other unwelcome. The nearby TF SWORD operators decided to join the 3d Brigade command group rather than remain in place. The other set of interlopers consisted of a group of nine enemy fighters. After an air strike and an Apache gunship failed to eliminate the approaching fighters, Wiercinski's command group and MAKO–31 organized a hasty ambush that inflicted several casualties in the initial volley. The Americans then rose from their positions to hunt down and eliminate the stunned enemy troops. Enemy personnel did not approach Wiercinski's position for the remainder of the day, but tried unsuccessfully to blast the Americans with mortar fire.[123]

The five Apache gunships under Capt. William A. Ryan's Company A, 3d Battalion, 101st Aviation, were increasingly hard-pressed to answer all the calls for support they received. As the AH–64s circled overhead, mortar rounds impacted among the 10th Mountain soldiers on the southern valley floor. The mountainous terrain, coupled with the scattered disposition of both friendly troops and enemy personnel, forced the Apaches to employ running attacks while traversing along the length of the valley in full view of the enemy.[124] An infantryman recalled, "the enemy changed their focus from shooting at us, which I considered a good thing, and then started focusing on the helicopters."[125]

One by one, the Apaches received crippling hits and were forced to abort. Within thirty minutes of the first shots being fired, no American helicopter gunships remained in the air over the valley. Efforts to obtain close air support to replace the Apache gunships proved frustrating and disappointing. The Air Support Operations Cell that stood up at Bagram just prior to the air assault experienced overwhelming challenges on the first day of operations,

---

123. Interv, Steven Clay, CSI, with Lt Col (Ret.) Ron Corkran, frmr Cdr, 1st Bn, 187th Inf, 9 May 2007, pp. 16–17, Hist Files, OEF Study Grp.

124. Wright et al., *A Different Kind of War*, p. 151.

125. Interv, Clay with Preysler, 8 May 2007, p. 8.

including problems created by untested communications systems, tactical air controllers competing for limited resources, and a crowded airspace.[126]

Reports of fierce enemy resistance throughout the day convinced General Hagenbeck to delay sending in more helicopters until nightfall.[127] As darkness approached, CJTF-MOUNTAIN reinforced the northern blocking positions with Capt. Kevin J. Butler's Company A, 2d Battalion, 187th Infantry, rather than reinforcing LaCamera.[128] Hagenbeck also directed Crombie's Company A, holding the hilltop near EVE, to exfiltrate seven kilometers northward to the closest helicopter landing zone. It took all night and most of the following morning for the 10th Mountain soldiers to link up with Preysler's scout platoon.[129] Finally, Hagenbeck ordered the withdrawal of the southernmost blocking position due to the number of wounded requiring evacuation and the distinct possibility of losing a helicopter delivering reinforcements. The retrograde took place in two stages, with nine critically wounded soldiers being evacuated at 2000.[130] The remainder of LaCamera's command group and Captain Kraft's company, including lightly wounded soldiers, was airlifted out at midnight. Black Hawks also retrieved personnel from Colonel Wiercinski's tactical command post during this period.[131]

DAY TWO AND BEYOND

By dawn on the second day, the Americans faced a far different fight in the Shahi Kot than their planners originally envisioned. The Afghan militia fighters were essentially out of the picture for the time being, leaving the American conventional forces to carry on the fight. For their part, the infantrymen of the 10th Mountain Division and 101st Airborne were singularly ill-positioned to assume the role of both assault and blocking forces. Not only were there more defenders than anticipated, but the village of Marzak and the Takur Ghar ridge also appeared to be heavily fortified. In fact, video from a Predator unmanned aerial vehicle showed the enemy reinforcing the defenders rather than preparing to retreat.

General Hagenbeck had several priority tasks on 3 March 2002. First, he had to decide whether to reinforce Colonel Preysler in preparation for a push southward or instruct him to remain on the defensive. Second, the extraction of LaCamera's troops presented Hagenbeck with the unexpected

---

126. American planes dropped 177 Joint Direct Attack Munitions during the first day of ANACONDA. In addition, B–52s dropped seventy-nine Mk–82 weapons. Grant et al., "Operation Anaconda," pp. 66–70.

127. Interv, Brown with Hagenbeck, 15 Mar 2002, p. 7.

128. Gadoury, "Eleven Days in the Valley," pp. 6–7.

129. Interv, McCool with Crombie, 30 Mar 2006, pp. 8–9.

130. HQ, Dept of the Air Force, SO G-0063, n.d., sub: Capt Edward J. Lengle, Silver Star Awarded for Action During Global War on Terror, https://valor.militarytimes.com/recipient.php?recipientid=7443, Hist Files, OEF Study Grp.

131. Grant et al., "Operation Anaconda," p. 65; Kraft, "Lessons Learned from a Light Infantry Company During Operation ANACONDA," p. 29.

Soldiers with the 1st Battalion, 187th Infantry Regiment, 101st Airborne Division (Air Assault), scan the nearby ridgeline for enemy movement during Operation ANACONDA.

challenge of finding a new way to bring supporting fires to bear on enemy fighters operating in the southern part of the valley. As General Hagenbeck recalled, "We had watched from aerial surveillance platforms, to our great frustration, a continuous infiltration of enemy reinforcements coming up from the south. . . . We really needed eyes there in the daytime to direct fire."[132] This gap in coverage meant that the strategic concentric circles were not as restrictive on enemy movement as originally planned.

TF SWORD reacted to the unforeseen coverage gap by alerting two SEAL teams for insertion atop Takur Ghar. Soon afterward, Maj. Gen. Dell L. Dailey's deputy commander, Brig. Gen. Gregory I. Trebon, radioed from Oman to direct the reconnaissance element leader to exfiltrate JULIET, INDIA, and MAKO–31 after the SEALs arrived.[133] At the same time, Harward ordered a patrol from 1 Squadron of the Australian Special Air Service, accompanied by a U.S. Air Force combat controller, to establish an observation post on a prominent ridgeline three kilometers south of Takur Ghar overlooking GINGER.[134] While the Special Operations elements were reacting to Hagenbeck's

---

132. Interv, Brown with Hagenbeck, 15 Mar 2002, p. 8.

133. Backgrounder, Blaber, p. 8.

134. Sgt. Matthew H. Bouillaut of the Australian Special Air Service received the Distinguished Service Cross for heroism in this action. Craig Skehan, "Defence Lifts Lid on Hero's Actions," *Sydney Morning Herald*, 17 Apr 2002, https://www.smh.com.au/articles/2002/04/17/1018333551671.html, Hist Files, OEF Study Grp; Ron Laurenzo, "Predator Was 'Point Man' During Operation Anaconda," *Defense Week*, 23 Sep 2002, https://www.freerepublic.com/focus/news/756273/posts, Hist Files, OEF Study Grp; Bradley Graham, "A Wintry Ordeal at 10,000 Feet," *Washington Post*, 25 May 2002,

concerns with commendable speed, the various directives risked generating a detectable level of activity as multiple teams were repositioned, inserted, or extracted within a compressed window of time.

Finally, Hagenbeck continued to have reservations about close air support arrangements. He viewed them as very unsatisfactory given the high number of combat controller teams competing for the attention of orbiting aircraft. He also felt there was an overreliance on precision-guided weapons that required either a ground-forward air controller or an Air Force enlisted terminal attack controller to employ. Hagenbeck's concerns led the CFACC to deploy five A–10 Thunderbolt IIs—a rugged, ground-attack platform that was optimal for strafing runs and low-level unguided ordnance delivery—from Ahmad al-Jaber Air Base in Kuwait across the 2,300 kilometers to Bagram. Not only did the A–10s add to the spectrum of close air support options, but they also could be called in by Army personnel.[135] Plus, unlike the AC–130s, the attack planes were authorized to conduct daylight operations in the face of enemy opposition. In addition, CFACC repurposed U.S. Air Force personnel at Bagram to form an Air Support Operations Center to provide CJTF-MOUNTAIN with expert planning assistance and a dedicated conduit to timely air support.[136]

Efforts to reinforce Preysler received high priority on the second day. Fortunately for the 101st Airborne Division personnel, enemy mortars were far less effective than the previous day, wounding only a single soldier. Rather than allow the enemy an opportunity to improve with practice, Colonel Wiercinski arranged for a morning air assault by the 1st Battalion, 187th Infantry, to eliminate the opposing mortar teams located east of AMY. The troops taking part in the air assault consisted of Colonel Corkran's command group; Canadian snipers; Captain Aspland's Company C; a platoon from Company D armed with .50-caliber machine guns removed from their HMMWVs; and Capt. Christopher Cornell's Company B, 1st Battalion, 87th Infantry.[137]

Lacking the element of surprise, the second major air assault of ANACONDA did not unfold as anticipated. Although the helicopters made the journey from Bagram to the Shahi Kot without incident, arriving by noon on 3 March, the leading Chinooks received fire as they approached the landing zone, prompting them to turn away while the trailing flight braved the incoming rounds to offload Captain Cornell's company and part of Aspland's unit in

---

https://www.washingtonpost.com/archive/politics/2002/05/25/a-wintry-ordeal-at-10000-feet/f2dd16f6-cc53-40e6-9ec9-f1d9ab9a89ac/, Hist Files, OEF Study Grp.

135. Lt Col Christopher F. Bentley, "Afghanistan: Joint and Coalition Fire Support in Operation Anaconda," *Field Artillery Journal*, HQDA PB6-02-4 (Sep–Oct 2002): 10–14.

136. The A–10s, which belonged to the 74th Expeditionary Fighter Squadron, temporarily operated from a classified forward location in theater until repairs on the Bagram runway were completed on 5 March. Col Matthew D. Neuenswander, "JCAS in Operation Anaconda – It's Not All Bad News," *Field Artillery Journal*, HQDA PB6-03-2 (May–Jun 2003): 2–4.

137. Interv, Clay with Corkran, 9 May 2007, pp. 17–20.

The A–10 Thunderbolt II, or "Warthog," shown here flying near Kandahar, was a vital close air support weapon of choice for ENDURING FREEDOM ground forces.

accordance with the plan.[138] News of those developments prompted General Hagenbeck to postpone the operation until nightfall, whereupon the lead helicopters returned to Bagram with troops still on board.

The Chinooks carrying Corkran's men returned to Bagram as SEAL teams MAKO–21 and MAKO–30, ordered to establish observation posts atop Takur Ghar, waited at the TF SWORD reconnaissance element compound in Gardez. Once again, the profusion of close air support platforms proved to be less helpful than desired. Before teams could be inserted, the helicopters transporting the SEALs returned to Gardez to await a B–52 strike.[139] The Special Operations helicopters remained grounded until Colonel Corkran's task force returned to the northern end of the valley at midnight. Colonel Wiercinski arrived via helicopter at the same time to establish the brigade command post within Preysler's perimeter.[140] Concerned that the arrival of additional Army units might have alerted the enemy, MAKO–30's team leader asked to delay the insertion for twenty-four hours, which TF SWORD in Oman denied. General Hagenbeck at Bagram knew nothing of these developments.[141]

---

138. Capt Joseph T. Dickerson, "Untitled Paper" (PEP, Inf Capts Career Course 05–04, n.d.), pp. 10–11. Then Lt. Dickerson was the 2d Platoon leader in Company C, 1st Battalion, 187th Infantry, during ANACONDA.

139. Briscoe et al., *Weapon of Choice,* pp. 296–97.

140. Wright et al., *A Different Kind of War,* p. 156.

141. Backgrounder, Blaber, pp. 7–9.

The Chinooks carrying the SEALs finally took off shortly after 0230.[142] As the helicopter transporting Mako–30 approached Takur Ghar, a rocket-propelled grenade exploded on its left side, knocking out electrical and hydraulic power. PO1 Neil C. Roberts slipped on hydraulic fluid on the rear ramp, tumbling out of the helicopter to the ground below. The damaged MH–47E fluttered downward to perform a forced landing approximately 600 meters from Preysler's command post.[143]

Over the next eighteen hours, efforts to rescue Petty Officer Roberts consumed virtually all close air support dispatched to the Shahi Kot Valley. The first effort involved Roberts' comrades from Mako–30. The SEALs landed atop the mountain for a second time, but enemy fire killed their radio operator, Air Force Tech. Sgt. John A. Chapman, and wounded several others.[144] The MH–47E carrying the SEALs also suffered significant damage, rendering it non-mission capable. TF Sword then dispatched a quick reaction force from Bagram: two MH–47Es carrying twenty-two Rangers, an enlisted Air Force controller, and a three-man search and rescue team led by Army Capt. Nathan E. Self. Radio problems arising from an ill-timed frequency change resulted in the MH–47E carrying Self and eight Rangers flying directly to Takur Ghar while the other helicopter carried the remaining thirteen Rangers to Gardez.[145]

The MH–47E loaded with Self and his Rangers set down at 0614 only meters from where Mako–30 had attempted to land. The insertion lacked immediate fire support after an AC–130 gunship orbiting overhead departed at dawn per standard operating instructions. Within seconds of the MH–47E touching down, enemy fire tore through the helicopter, killing or wounding most of the crew and several Rangers. The surviving Americans exited the shattered airframe, seeking cover among nearby rocks. In a brief but intense engagement, the Rangers killed the enemy personnel near the downed Chinook. With the immediate threat neutralized, the Americans were able to treat their wounded while making preparations to take the fight to the other enemy personnel atop the mountain.[146]

The second MH–47E, loaded with Rangers and a senior SEAL, eventually departed Gardez. It landed 300 meters from Mako–30, whereupon the SEAL officer joined his isolated team while the Rangers ascended the Takur Ghar

---

142. Briscoe et al., *Weapon of Choice*, pp. 298–99; Wright et al., *A Different Kind of War*, p. 157.

143. Wright et al., *A Different Kind of War*, p. 157.

144. The Air Force submitted Sergeant Chapman for the Medal of Honor after reviewing enhanced Predator video suggesting that he continued to fight after Mako–30 retreated down the mountainside. See Sean D. Naylor and Christopher Drew, "SEAL Team 6 and a Man Left Behind for Dead: A Grainy Picture of Valor," *New York Times*, 27 Aug 2016, https://www.newyorktimes.com/2016/08/28/world/asia/seal-team-6-afghanistan-man-left-for-dead.html, Hist Files, OEF Study Grp.

145. Briscoe et al., *Weapon of Choice*, pp. 298–99.

146. Nate Self, *Two Wars: One Hero's Fight on Two Fronts – Abroad and Within* (Carol Stream, Ill.: Tynedale House Publishing, 2008), pp. 160–64. For a critical and widely accepted account of these events by an *Army Times* reporter in Afghanistan at that time, see Sean D. Naylor, *Not a Good Day to Die: The Untold Story of Operation Anaconda* (New York: Dutton Caliber, 2006).

Soldiers from the 10th Mountain Division, participating in Operation ANACONDA, prepare to dig fighting positions after a day of reacting to enemy fire.

summit. The next several hours passed slowly, with the enemy attempting to destroy the downed Chinook using mortar fire. The surviving Rangers, led by Captain Self, launched a counterattack that revealed the defenders were fighting from well-camouflaged bunkers.

The two Ranger groups joined forces to launch a successful coordinated assault on the enemy position. There they found the remains of Petty Officer Roberts and Sergeant Chapman, as well as several dead al-Qaeda fighters. As Self began evacuating his force, the enemy launched the first of several counterattacks. The al-Qaeda fighters spent the afternoon trying to overrun the small band of Americans, exposing themselves to fire from the Rangers and close air support strikes. The Rangers prevailed, but Senior Airman Jason D. Cunningham died of his wounds during that interval. Three MH–47Ds carrying fifty-nine Rangers to the scene were finally able to retrieve the dead, wounded, and living from Takur Ghar. A fourth MH–47D picked up MAKO–30 and the senior SEAL officer.[147] The fight for Takur Ghar, the northernmost peak on what is now called Roberts Ridge by American forces, ended when the last U.S. service member departed at 2000. Sergeant Chapman and the SEAL team leader, SCPO Britt K. Slabinski, would be awarded the Medal of Honor for their actions on Roberts Ridge. Chapman was the first airman to earn the honor since the conflict in Vietnam.

---

147. Briscoe et al., *Weapon of Choice*, pp. 311–18.

Pushing South

The 4 March 2002 fighting on Roberts Ridge demonstrated the strides that Bagram's Air Support Operations Center had made in providing what CJTF-Mountain needed in terms of air support. Improvements took the tangible form of more Mk–82 bombs and CBU–87s (cluster bomb units), which were useful against area targets. In addition, the first A–10 Thunderbolt II aircraft, performing in the dual role of airborne forward air controller and strike platform, arrived from Kuwait.[148] At the same time, CJTF-Mountain received rotary-wing reinforcements from AH–1T Sea Cobra helicopter gunships and CH–53E heavy lift helicopters from the 13th Marine Expeditionary Unit.

The possibility of renewed fighting around Takur Ghar drove CJTF-Mountain to recalibrate existing plans. To revive the attack on Ginger, Hagenbeck planned to send Colonel LaCamera's battalion—consisting of Captain Kraft's company bolstered by two platoons from Company A; Capt. Robert B. Kuth's Company B from 1st Battalion, 187th Infantry; and Capt. Glenn E. Kozelka's Company C, 4th Battalion, 31st Infantry, 10th Mountain Division, into the Shahi Kot once more. The latter two companies, arriving from Pakistan and Kuwait respectively, would accompany LaCamera's soldiers into the valley at 1615 on 5 March.[149]

At 1630, helicopters deposited LaCamera's force just west of Diane without incident. As the newly arrived Americans dispersed into the valley, they discovered six abandoned 122-mm. artillery pieces in the low ground covering the southern entrance to the Shahi Kot. The howitzers were camouflaged in a wadi with sights mounted, firing tables posted, and prepared ammunition stacked nearby. Engineers with LaCamera's force disabled the artillery pieces by placing explosive charges in their breeches. The destruction of the cannons meant that CJTF-Mountain could send ground forces through the southern valley entrance without being targeted by enemy indirect fire.[150]

Once his entire force arrived, LaCamera ordered Captain Kozelka's company and Captain Kraft's company to ascend Takur Ghar. The final element flown in, Captain Kuth's company, occupied an intermediate ridgeline overlooking Eve.[151] Starting at 1800, the two companies moved out toward the objective. Darkness fell soon afterward, making travel more difficult despite night vision goggles. As the lead platoons stumbled over jagged rocks and boulders ascending Takur Ghar, soldiers began to succumb to altitude sickness. Unable to continue without risking more soldiers' lives, LaCamera halted the advance at 0300. On a positive note for LaCamera, Colonel Preysler detached Captain Crombie's Company A, which began

---

148. Grant et al., "Operation Anaconda," pp. 78–82.

149. The order of battle is drawn from Wright et al., *A Different Kind of War*, p. 162. However, first person accounts from 1st Battalion, 187th Infantry, members indicate a 5 March arrival at Bagram. See also CFLCC (Forward) Sitrep cited in Grant et al., "Operation Anaconda," p. 85.

150. Grau, "The Coils of the Anaconda," p. 424.

151. Capt Samuel Edwards, "OPERATION Anaconda: A Rifle Platoon Leader's Perspective" (PEP, Inf Capts Career Course 02 -04, 9 May 2004), p. 7, Hist Files, OEF Study Grp.

moving south at dawn on 6 March to link up with the remainder of the 1st Battalion, 87th Infantry.[152]

The situation on 6 March differed significantly from the opening day of battle. Coordination problems between coalition air and ground elements operating in the Shahi Kot largely had been overcome. American conventional forces in the valley increased by a factor of four, although units recently transferred from Kuwait and Pakistan had difficulty acclimating. The defenders had lost most of their mortars and artillery pieces. Nonetheless, Uzbek fighters and their Afghan allies were still being supplied with men and equipment through Objective GINGER.

In what can be interpreted as either an impressive demonstration of strategic airlift or the strategic fallacy of CENTCOM maintaining a limit on U.S. troops in Afghanistan even after the start of Phase III, sixteen AH–64s of the 3d Battalion, 101st Aviation, commanded by Lt. Col. James M. Richardson, deployed to Bagram from Fort Campbell.[153] The return of Apache helicopters to the fight, reinforced by Marine Corps AH–1T Sea Cobra gunships, meant that daylight operations by cargo- and troop-carrying helicopters could resume. Although many factors now favored the Americans, the weather did not. Increasing snowfall prevented Wiercinski's brigade from patrolling the foothills of the eastern ridgeline. The snow and lack of American activity also persuaded the defenders that it was time to depart the southern Shahi Kot.[154]

As the weather cleared on 8 March, CJTF-MOUNTAIN found itself with few options other than seizing the villages on the valley floor. Takur Ghar continued to attract attention, but the snow and a lack of climbing gear prevented Wiercinski from sending Colonel LaCamera's battalion to occupy the summit. Conceding defeat in the face of the mountain's impassable slopes, Hagenbeck ordered LaCamera to resume moving southward to GINGER. Bombing attacks against Takur Ghar were more successful, setting off secondary explosions that continued for hours after striking stored munitions.[155] Given the evidence that enemy troops were located in Babul Khel, on the Whale, and in Takur Ghar, the Americans still did not suspect that most of the enemy forces in the southern valley were now gone.

The remaining Uzbek and Taliban fighters began pulling off the ridges east of REMINGTON on 9 March as the Americans belatedly detected signs of a withdrawal from GINGER. In response, TF K-BAR ordered Australian Special Air Service patrols to move closer to the Shahi Kot's southern passes. LaCamera's task force advanced on GINGER that evening, halting twice to await air strikes by B–52s. Given that "[o]nly the rear guard on the Whale, the slow, and uninformed were left," rough terrain turned

---

152. Grau, "The Coils of the Anaconda," p. 425.

153. 1st Sgt P. McGuire, TF Rakkasan, 3-101st Avn, 03/02–08/02, "Long Hard Road: NCO Experiences in Afghanistan and Iraq" (PEP, U.S. Army Sgts Maj Academy, 2007), p. 20. Hist Files, OEF Study Grp.

154. Grau, "The Coils of the Anaconda," pp. 435–38.

155. Ibid., pp. 448–54.

A soldier with the 1st Battalion, 187th Infantry Regiment, 101st Airborne Division (Air Assault), scans the countryside for enemy targets during Operation ANACONDA.

out to be more of an impediment to the 10th Mountain soldiers than the conspicuously absent enemy.[156]

WINDING UP ANACONDA

Lessening enemy resistance, mounting logistical requirements, and the impending commitment of Afghan militia forces prompted CJTF-MOUNTAIN to begin pulling U.S. troops from the valley. By this stage of the fight, Lt. Col. Patrick L. Fetterman's 3d Battalion, 187th Infantry, had arrived in Kandahar, allowing Hagenbeck to deploy the 3d Princess Patricia's Canadian Light Infantry to Bagram to take part in ANACONDA. The Canadian unit, whose sniper team, along with Corkran's 1st Battalion, had inflicted numerous casualties on the enemy during the recent fighting, deserved an opportunity to make a greater contribution.[157] The move did not surprise the Canadian commander, as Colonel Wiercinski had informed him earlier that his unit might be sent into the valley.[158]

The Canadians would have to wait until Afghan militia reentered the fight to subdue the Whale and clear villages on the valley floor. By this time, however, few personnel from the 5th Special Forces Group remained with the Afghans to help control their actions on the battlefield. Just before the attack,

---

156. Ibid., p. 459.

157. Ibid., p. 463.

158. Ron Corbett, *First Soldiers Down: Canada's Friendly Fire Deaths in Afghanistan* (Toronto: Durden Press, 2012), p. 98.

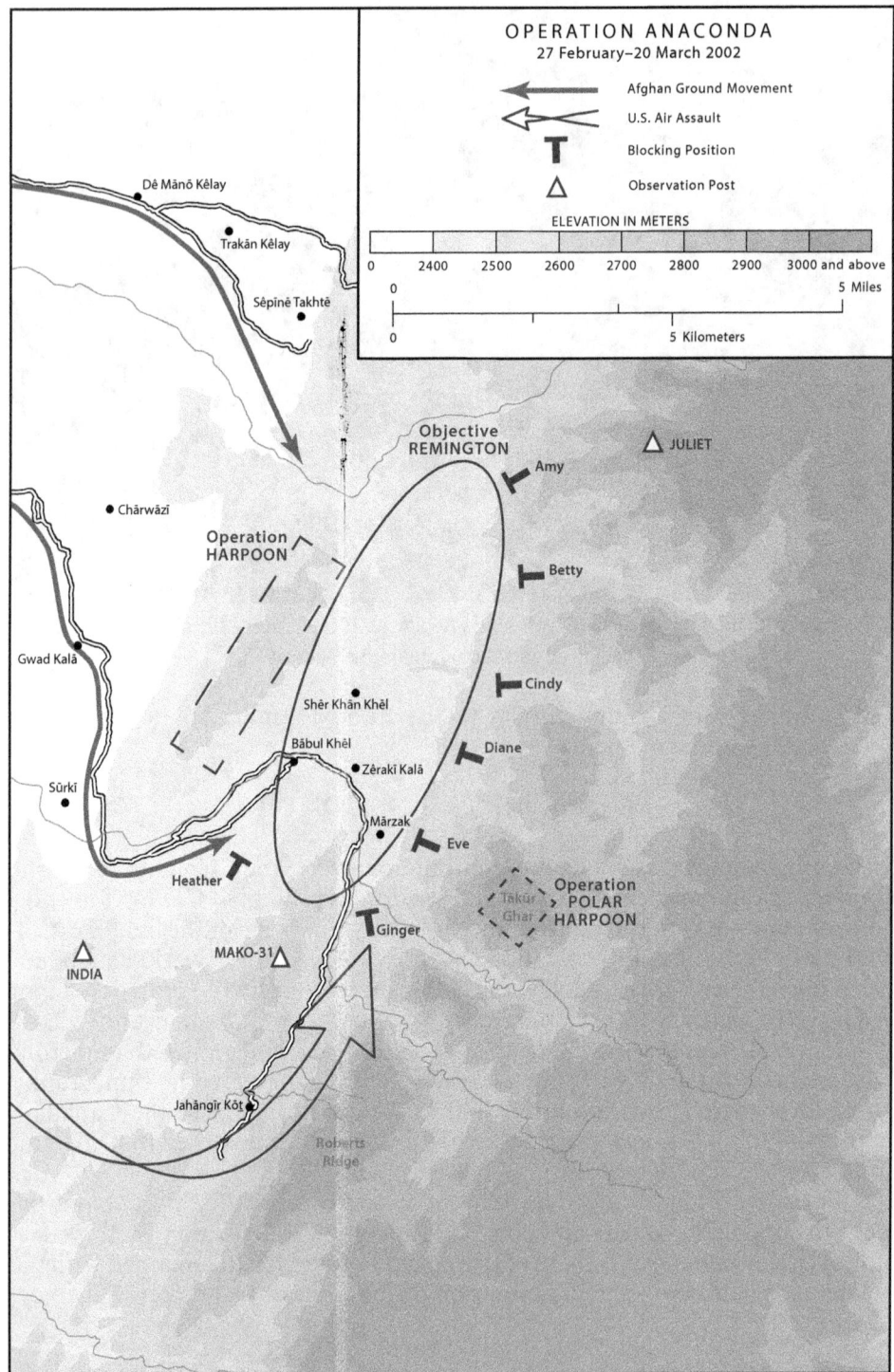

Map 3.2

A soldier with the 1st Battalion, 187th Infantry Regiment, 101st Airborne Division (Air Assault), mans a .50-caliber machine gun during Operation ANACONDA in the Shahi Kot mountain range in eastern Afghanistan.

scheduled for 0500 on 11 March, ODA 372 would establish an observation post on terrain that allowed it to observe the Shahi Kot and call in close air support as needed.[159] Both militia bands were instructed to hold in place until the Air Force dropped a massive 15,000-pound BLU–82 bomb on the Whale, signaling the start of the attack (*Map 3.2*).

Once again, Afghan reality did not match American plans. Ignoring instructions to wait until the following morning, the militia fighters seized the northern tip of the Whale during the evening of 10 March. The Afghans climbed up to the top of the ridge without meeting substantial resistance, whereupon they settled down around a roaring bonfire to await coming events. A second group of militia did not join the unauthorized advance, remaining just outside the northern entrance to the valley. The belated discovery of friendly militia atop the Whale forced Colonel Haas to cancel the BLU–82 strike.

Nevertheless, confident that the Canadians and Afghan militia could get the job done, the Americans started to airlift their troops out that evening, beginning with Captain Crombie's Company A, 1st Battalion, 87th Infantry. Colonel Wiercinski decided to leave one company from each battalion behind while everyone else returned to Bagram. Colonel LaCamera volunteered to remain with the composite task force, which consisted of Company C from each of the four battalions.[160] Redeployment decreased the daily logistical support required by American forces in the Shahi Kot while freeing up

---

159. Briscoe et al., *Weapon of Choice*, p. 322.
160. Grau, "The Coils of the Anaconda," p. 465.

additional capability to support the Afghans. In addition, TF TALON began cycling the CH–47 fleet through much needed maintenance in anticipation of future operations.

The militia attack began at dawn the following morning as scheduled, but it quickly degenerated into a melee as the Afghans exhibited little interest in following the agreed-upon plan. The dismounted troops formed a line atop the Whale in preparation for a north-to-south advance along the spine but soon abandoned that operation in favor of streaming down into the valley to loot abandoned villages. Zia Lodin's column encountered scattered resistance as it pushed through the southern entrance before turning north to join the militiamen holding the villages on the valley floor.[161]

SECURING THE HIGH GROUND

With the valley floor in coalition hands, General Hagenbeck tasked Col. Kevin V. Wilkerson's Karshi Khanabad–based 2d Brigade, 10th Mountain Division, now designated as TF COMMANDO, with clearing the towering ridges overlooking the Shahi Kot. With most of his organic and supporting units in the Balkans or at Fort Drum, Wilkerson would conduct the mission using Colonel Stogran's Canadian battalion, with Capt. Jonathan A. Stevens' Company A of the 4th Battalion, 31st Infantry, attached, and Marine Medium Helicopter Squadron 165, equipped with three CH–53E Sea Stallion heavy lift helicopters; six Army CH–47s from Company B, 2d Battalion, 159th Aviation; and five Marine AH–1T Sea Cobra attack helicopters in support. In addition to Canadian infantry and Marine helicopters, Wilkerson gained the tactical command post from Lt. Col. Stephen J. Townsend's 4th Battalion, 31st Infantry, which allowed Townsend's detached companies to revert to their parent headquarters.[162]

Task Force COMMANDO planned to conduct an air assault, fittingly named Operation HARPOON, onto the Whale. (*See Map 3.2.*) Although clearing the ridge had been the responsibility of Afghan militia, Hagenbeck doubted how well they had accomplished the task. As senior ground commander, Colonel Stogran developed the tactical plan. Stogran decided that the Americans would sweep the spine of the Whale from northeast to southwest while his own Company A scoured the terrain immediately to the east. Company C of the 3d Princess Patricia's Canadian Light Infantry supported the leading companies; while Company B served as Colonel Stogran's reserve. The western slopes of the Whale were so steep and rocky that Stogran settled for tasking his reconnaissance platoon and the Americans of Stevens' Company A with observing the area rather than ordering foot soldiers to negotiate the treacherous terrain.[163]

The combined force air-assaulted onto the Whale on the morning of 13 March with Stogran's Companies A and B, along with part of Stevens'

---

161. Briscoe et al., *Weapon of Choice*, pp. 323–24.
162. Wright et al., *A Different Kind of War*, p. 166.
163. Ibid., p. 167.

Company A, in the first lift. Before the remainder of the 3d Princess Patricia's Canadian Light Infantry arrived the following day, Stogran dispatched his Company B to the northeast to search for the enemy. After Medium Helicopter Squadron 165 delivered the rest of the force on 14 March, Stogran executed the operation as planned. With little time to acclimate after being sent to Afghanistan from Camp Doha in Kuwait, soldiers from Stevens' company experienced acute altitude sickness. Although the soldiers collected documents and destroyed several weapons caches, the sole enemy contact occurred when Stevens' 2d Platoon encountered a bunker held by several al-Qaeda fighters. Antitank rockets destroyed the position and its occupants.[164] Captain Stevens' Company A then returned to Bagram to prepare for Operation POLAR HARPOON. On 18 March, Medium Helicopter Squadron 165 airlifted Stogran's battalion from the Whale after he reported mission completion.

OPERATION POLAR HARPOON

General Hagenbeck still placed a high priority on clearing Takur Ghar and the valley immediately to the east. The arrival of Colonel Townsend's tactical command post permitted Colonel Wilkerson to launch POLAR HARPOON using a two-company task force to clear all enemy off the Whale. In addition to Company A, Wiercinski directed Colonel LaCamera to return Captain Kozelka's Company C to Townsend. Townsend's plan called for inserting Kozelka's unit atop Takur Ghar approximately 800 meters north of Roberts Ridge while Chinooks transported Captain Stevens' Company A immediately east of Takur Ghar onto lower ground in the Nikeh Valley. Both companies were aided by U.S. Army Criminal Investigative Division experts, combat engineers and ordnance disposal experts, a military working dog team, and an Air Force tactical air controller team.[165]

POLAR HARPOON began as scheduled with Townsend's task force lifting off from Bagram on 18 March. After an uneventful flight, the lead helicopter deposited the battalion command group and a platoon from Kozelka's company on a landing zone so small that the front two wheels of the Chinook were not touching the ground. After the troops disembarked without serious mishap, the second Chinook deposited the remainder of Kozelka's company onto the ridge. A few minutes at 2,600 meters altitude convinced Townsend that the heavily burdened soldiers would have to shed most of their gear to climb the remaining 460 meters to the summit. He ordered Kozelka to leave the company mortars and unneeded equipment behind before setting off toward Roberts Ridge.[166]

In a rapid string of successes, the 10th Mountain soldiers discovered dead al-Qaeda fighters, abandoned trenches, crew-served weapons, and

---

164. Capt Gregory Darling, "OPERATION HARPOON" (PEP, Inf Capts Career Course 04-05, Seminar 1, n.d.), pp. 6–8, Hist Files, OEF Study Grp.

165. Dennis Steele, "The Valleys," *ARMY* 52, no. 6 (June 2002): 35–36.

166. Wright et al., *A Different Kind of War*, p. 171.

hidden bunkers honeycombing the mountain peak. In the valley below, Stevens' company similarly cleared each crevasse, cave, and manmade rock shelter. Lt. Andrew Exum's 3d Platoon of Company A encountered and killed an al-Qaeda member who was armed with an M–249 machine gun he had taken from a fallen American on Roberts Ridge. The searchers also recovered equipment left behind by the SEALs and Rangers. In all, Captain Stevens' company destroyed 3,000 mortar and recoilless rifle rounds as it cleared dozens of caves and bunkers.[167] Together, the companies established a defensive position overnight before being airlifted out the following day. The successful clearing of Takur Ghar marked the end of ANACONDA.

The outcome of the Shahi Kot fighting satisfied neither combatant. CJTF-MOUNTAIN had made some questionable decisions, which included relying on Afghan militia and weighing the opening air assault insertions equally. These errors allowed the defenders to mass, forced the Americans to abandon their southernmost blocking position, and thus opened an escape route once the fighting turned against them. Despite the attackers' awkward tactical plan, al-Qaeda and foreign fighters failed to force their opponents to retreat, even though they had received advanced warning and held terrain and numerical advantages throughout much of the fight.

The American failures stemmed from a number of factors: a lack of accurate intelligence during the planning process, complacent air-ground coordination, employment of unconventional warfare methods when the situation dictated otherwise, and the involvement of far too many organizations—all of whom had little experience working with each other—in both the planning and execution process. Most of these problems can be traced to the fact that, based on CENTCOM guidance, the Army deployed into combat a division that lacked a full two-thirds of its force structure. After redeploying from Uzbekistan to Afghanistan on short notice, General Hagenbeck had to assemble additional combat power from a bewildering variety of sources. Although the additional troops and equipment theoretically provided Hagenbeck with greater capabilities, the unfamiliar challenge of building a team from such disparate forces was an overwhelming task. The shortcomings of ANACONDA are attributable to planning and execution miscalculations at the tactical level, but the root cause stems from CENTCOM's inexperience determining what policies and approaches required adjustment during the transition from Phase II (Shaping Operations) to Phase III (Decisive Operations).

---

167. Steele, "The Valleys," p. 40.

Chapter Four

A Campaign in Transition

Most of Col. John P. Mulholland's 5th Special Forces Group, 1st Special Forces Command, departed Uzbekistan and Afghanistan just before the start of Operation ANACONDA. CENTCOM replaced TF DAGGER with Col. Mark V. Phelan's 3d Special Forces Group, 1st Special Forces Command, to form CJSOTF-Afghanistan.[1] Lt. Col. Mark D. Rosengard, former 10th Special Forces Group deputy commander and recent TF DAGGER operations chief, volunteered to stay behind to provide continuity. Assuming the mission on 30 March, Phelan shouldered a wide range of responsibilities that included overseeing warlord militias, completing al-Qaeda's destruction, searching for weapons of mass destruction, and tracking down Taliban remnants. The 3d Special Forces Group was augmented by a battalion headquarters and one company from the National Guard's 20th Special Forces Group; 3d Battalion, 3d Special Forces Group; Company B, 2d Battalion, 3d Special Forces Group; coalition SOF; and a composite battalion of three companies from the Army National Guard's 19th Special Forces Group.[2] Phelan remained under CENTCOM's Special Operations Command operational control while CJTF-MOUNTAIN exercised tactical control over Phelan's command to coordinate and synchronize conventional and SOF operations.[3]

In addition to the northernmost Special Operations task force, the civil affairs component in Afghanistan was slated to transition during this timeframe. The Coalition Joint Civil-Military Operations Task Force staff and 96th Civil Affairs Battalion assessment teams were identified to be replaced by two Army Reserve units, the 352d Civil Affairs Command and 489th Civil Affairs Battalion. Although the United States now had free access to virtually all of Afghanistan, the incoming civil affairs units were deemed sufficient in number to temporarily preside over an effort destined to be downsized by mid-summer from a Coalition Joint Civil-Military Operations Task Force and supporting battalion to a cell working for the U.S. ambassador to Afghanistan.[4]

---

1. "Combined Joint Special Operations Task Force – South (CJSOTF-South) (Afghanistan) 'Task Force K-Bar,'" Global Security, n.d., https://www.globalsecurity.org/military/agency/dod/cjsotf-s-af.htm, Hist Files, OEF Study Grp.

2. Briscoe et al., *Weapon of Choice*, pp. 256–57.

3. Maj Richard G. Rhyne, "Special Forces Command and Control in Afghanistan" (Master's thesis, U.S. Army Command and General Staff College, 18 Jun 2004), , p. 42.

4. Memo, Col Eshelman for Third Army/ARCENT Cmd Grp and Staff, sub: ARCENT Update, 22 Mar 2002, 1420 hours, Story CFLCC Collection, OEF Study Grp.

U.S. Navy SEALs conduct sensitive site exploitation operations in Afghanistan's Dzadzi Mountains.

Recognizing that efforts by nongovernmental and international aid entities were not as effective as originally estimated, Lt. Gen. Paul T. Mikolashek contemplated abandoning the minimalist approach espoused by President George W. Bush and his administration. On 19 April, he asked the CFLCC chief civil affairs officer to prepare a worst-case estimate on nation building in Afghanistan. In sharp contrast to the vague goal of "preventing the reemergence of terrorism," Mikolashek wanted his staff to prepare a revised Phase IV plan listing what the United States hoped to accomplish, how long it would take, and what it would take to meet those goals. The proposal did not garner much support from more senior headquarters, which forced CFLCC to abandon Mikolashek's attempt to identify the resources and goals needed to achieve a stable post-Taliban Afghanistan.[5]

CENTCOM's plans to transfer responsibility for humanitarian efforts made little progress as nongovernmental and international relief organizations continued to demonstrate reluctance to work with the U.S. military. When the Coalition Joint Civil-Military Operations Task Force asked several organizations to distribute aid to the inhabitants of Khost, their leadership refused, stating that they would not do so because of the lack of representation

---

5. Memo, Col Eshelman for Third Army/ARCENT Cmd Grp and Staff, 19 Apr 2002, sub: ARCENT Update, 19 Apr 2002, 1614 hrs, Story CFLCC Collection, OEF Study Grp.

from the International Committee of the Red Cross, suggesting that the area was not sufficiently secure for them to operate. General Mikolashek vented his frustration with the situation: "[T]hey criticize the military when convenient to them and yet fail to act where we've made it safe to do so."[6] In response, CFLCC directed Brig. Gen. David E. Kratzer to expand the Coalition Joint Civil-Military Operations Task Force's footprint by sending teams from the 489th Civil Affairs Battalion to areas where aid organizations refused to go, while continuing to pressure, cajole, or convince recalcitrant civilian agencies to support a coordinated countrywide effort.[7]

Creating the Afghan National Army

Talks about the future of Afghan security forces began when Ministry of Defense representatives met with General Mikolashek and the Office of Military Cooperation–Afghanistan on 18 February. Many issues defied simple resolution because the parties were focused on different goals. An Office of Military Cooperation planner, Lt. Col. Steven D. Russell, noticed that the Afghans were more interested in broader, long-range milestones. Russell's counterparts were frank:

> [T]hey needed everything. They wanted everything. They had to have all their buildings rebuilt. They had to have all their uniforms replaced, all of their weapons replaced. . . . And then, when we looked at the types of needs that they had, we learned something that we had not considered before and that was they had military industry. . . . [they used to have] military meat packing plants, military wool producing plants that benefited not only the military and raised revenue for them but also provided wool and meat to the community. . . . It was the Soviet model.[8]

The Americans, by contrast, were far more interested in how the first four battalions would be trained and where the first nine ANA battalions would be quartered.

The Americans were also surprised to learn that the Afghans did not see Taliban remnants as their greatest security threat. Their top concern was securing their national borders, particularly to the east and southeast, from unfriendly powers seeking to unseat the interim authority. As a result, the Ministry of Defense prioritized creating 300-man border guard battalions over the 600-man light infantry battalions the Americans preferred. Seeking to avoid a lengthy delay, General Kratzer supported fielding a mix of border and infantry battalions until a force structure agreement could be reached.

---

6. Memo, Col Eshelman for Third Army/ARCENT Cmd Grp and Staff, sub: ARCENT Update, 18 Apr 2002, 1619 hours, Story CFLCC Collection, OEF Study Grp.

7. Memo, Col Eshelman for Third Army/ARCENT Cmd Grp and Staff, 4 May 2002, sub: ARCENT Update, 4 May 2002, 1632 hrs, Story CFLCC Collection, OEF Study Grp.

8. Interv, Maj John Warsinske, 47th MHD, with Lt Col Steve Russell, frmr Plans Ofcr, CFLCC C-5, 8 Jun 2002, pp. 5–8, Hist Files, OEF Study Grp.

Both parties agreed that the ANA initially would consist of seven major units, known as "regional corps," of nine infantry battalions apiece. In addition, a "central corps" would be stationed in Kabul. Both parties also agreed on the need to train and field border troops. In addition, the Afghans approved the ten-week training program proposed by Kratzer's staff. That said, the Office of Military Cooperation–Afghanistan did not commit the U.S. Army to training all of the regional corps. The Americans agreed to train only the first nine infantry and six border units. At that point, the Office of Military Cooperation stood prepared to either hand training over to the Afghans or remain involved for a second year.[9]

While the talks were underway, Office of Military Cooperation–Afghanistan representatives toured former Afghan military installations in order to identify potential training sites. The 1960s-era Kabul Military Academy, which survived relatively intact despite a B–52 strike that destroyed its power plant, was the most likely candidate. Though local residents had stripped most buildings of doorknobs, light fixtures, and windows, the survey team estimated that the academy could be refurbished once funding became available.[10] Finding the money to renovate the building, however, was a challenge: by law, Congress could not use security assistance dollars to fund the training of indigenous troops unless American troops provided the instruction. Given the Office of Military Cooperation–Afghanistan's request for a full battalion of Special Forces or light infantry, Joint Staff planners needed time to align projected operational requirements before a specific unit could be provided. Special Forces or infantry units already in country could not be redirected to the training mission because they were already funded by the DoD.[11] As a result, security assistance funds would not be forthcoming until an American unit received the order to train Afghan soldiers. In effect, the bureaucracies and legalities of funding would not allow a fluid transition of the mission.

Efforts to rebuild the ANA faced yet another challenge, albeit from an unexpected quarter, when General Kratzer learned that he had been promoted to major general. Kratzer learned the news from General Mikolashek, who explained that the additional rank meant that Kratzer was leaving the Office of Military Cooperation to take command of the 377th Support Command (Theater). Although Kratzer recommended Colonel Rosengard as his replacement at Military Cooperation, Brig. Gen. John H. Kern, commander of the Army Reserve's 352d Civil Affairs Command, assumed this role as well as the role of commander of the Coalition Joint Civil-Military Operations Task Force.[12] Rosengard replaced Kratzer's deputy, Col. Michael B. Weimer,

---

9. Ibid., pp. 5, 25–26, 65, 75–76.

10. Ibid., pp. 23–24.

11. Interv, Peter Connors, CSI, with Lt Gen (Ret.) Paul T. Mikolashek, frmr Cdr, CFLCC, 13 Dec 2006, p. 14, Hist Files, OEF Study Grp.

12. Interv, Mark D. Sherry, Contemporary Ops Br, U.S. Army Center of Military History (CMH), with Maj Gen (Ret.) David Kratzer, frmr Cdr, CJCMOTF, 10 Apr 2012, pp. 92–94, Hist Files, OEF Study Grp.

who also departed during this period, while serving as interim commander until Kern's arrival.

In early April 2002, a second donors' conference was held in Geneva, Switzerland, to discuss funding options to rebuild Afghanistan's military. The U.S. delegation included both Kratzer and Kern, as well as Colonel Russell. The Tokyo donors' conference had shown the international community's initial reluctance to fund the rebuilding of the ANA, but during the Geneva conference Kratzer discovered that the offers of assistance he received were influenced as much by internal political agendas as by an altruistic interest in post-Taliban security reform. The French, for example, wanted to train several battalions to show voters in their upcoming elections that the incumbent party, led by President Jacques Chirac, had made a material contribution to the fight against terror.[13] Regardless of motivation, all of the international offers of security assistance were valuable, but the conference was yet another cautionary reminder about depending on international venues to achieve U.S. strategic goals. After almost a week of meetings to discuss Afghan-related security issues, the United States, Germany, Italy, Great Britain, and Japan agreed respectively to oversee army; police; judiciary; counternarcotics; and disarmament, demobilization, and reintegration efforts.[14] The conference attendees left Geneva without agreeing on detailed milestones or a way to synchronize individual efforts.[15] As a result, the Office of Military Cooperation–Afghanistan had to devote significant effort to integrating individual pledges of trainers, equipment, and weapons for future Afghan military training.

Soon after Kratzer and Russell returned to Kabul, CENTCOM received word that Lt. Col. Kevin M. McDonnell's 1st Battalion, 3d Special Forces Group, had been selected to train the ANA. Preparations to begin funding the training mission began concurrently with McDonnell's deployment preparations. Funding would not become available for several weeks, during which time McDonnell could not airlift any of his unit's equipment or send an advance party. Learning of McDonnell's predicament, Colonel Phelan sent a team of nine soldiers, headed by his group executive officer, Maj. James S. Burnside, to help prepare the Kabul Military Academy for its first recruits by the 1 May 2002 start date established by General Tommy R. Franks.[16]

The small group of Military Cooperation staffers whose job it was to open the academy welcomed the newcomers with open arms. They arranged to have Spanish engineers clear some drainage ditches, while the Special Forces and Military Cooperation personnel performed most of the renovation work, which included fixing water pipes, replacing fixtures, and filling sandbags. Emergency funding from CENTCOM allowed the Office of Military Cooperation–Afghanistan to purchase bullhorns, tables, chairs, and bedding from local vendors. A contingent of forty-five French soldiers

---

13. Interv, Warsinske with Russell, 8 Jun 2002, p. 84.
14. Dobbins, *After the Taliban*, pp. 122–24.
15. Feith, *War and Decision*, pp. 154–55.
16. Interv, Warsinske with Russell, 8 Jun 2002, pp. 93–98.

who arrived during this period managed all administrative aspects of the training. Colonel Rosengard took temporary charge of the organization just as the commander of the first Afghan battalion, Lt. Col. Najibullah Sadiqi, reported along with his staff and company commanders.[17]

The initial contingent of Special Forces trainers, along with essential equipment needed for their mission, were aboard the first C–17 to land at Kabul International Airport on the evening of 30 April. ISAF provided material-handling equipment to offload the aircraft and buses used to ferry personnel from the 1st Battalion, 3d Special Forces Group, to their barracks. The Americans were able to deposit their gear just before the first recruits appeared at the military academy's newly renovated reception station. Although it took several more days before intratheater airlift could ferry the 500 recruits in Colonel Najibullah's ethnically mixed unit, the course of instruction began as scheduled.[18]

CFLCC Prepared to Hand Over

Plans to redeploy Special Forces units in Afghanistan had been put into motion long before ANACONDA began, but arrangements for rotating out the land component headquarters were placed on hold until fighting in the Shahi Kot Valley ended. During a 22 March video teleconference examining future requirements for ENDURING FREEDOM, General Franks disclosed to Mikolashek that Lt. Gen. Dan K. McNeill, commanding general of the XVIII Airborne Corps, would assume Mikolashek's Afghanistan duties as early as 1 May 2002 but possibly not until 1 July. Franks noted that, in addition to Special Forces elements, a conventional brigade formed around two or three infantry battalions with associated combat support and combat service support assets, including rotary-wing aviation, would be available to Mikolashek's successor. The new force would be known as Combined Joint Task Force 180 (CJTF-180). Navy Capt. Robert S. Harward's headquarters would leave soon after the newcomers arrived. Franks directed Mikolashek to do all he could to prepare the new headquarters to oversee combat operations throughout Afghanistan, rebuild the ANA, support humanitarian aid and civil affairs operations, work closely with ISAF, and remain capable of adjusting to major changes in the tactical situation.[19]

General McNeill learned of the decision to send his XVIII Corps headquarters to Bagram during a March 2002 training exercise hosted by Joint Forces Command in Norfolk, Virginia. The news did not come as a surprise because ISAF commander Maj. Gen. John McColl had informed McNeill during a visit to Kabul in February that several ISAF members had made their future participation conditional on the XVIII Airborne Corps deploy-

---

17. Ibid., pp. 95–96.
18. Ibid., pp. 108–15.
19. Memo, Eshelman for Third Army/ARCENT Cmd Grp and Staff, sub: ARCENT Update, 22 Mar 2002.

A Campaign in Transition

U.S. Navy SEALs interact with local villagers during an operation in the Dzadzi Mountains. Operations such as these were conducted not only to exploit sensitive sites but also to better understand the environment.

ing to Afghanistan.[20] The decision to send the XVIII Airborne Corps to Bagram forced McNeill to ship almost everything he needed from Fort Bragg to Afghanistan instead of using CFLCC facilities in Kuwait. In keeping with previous efforts to maintain the smallest possible U.S. footprint in Afghanistan, General Franks told McNeill to restrict the new headquarters to no more than 400 personnel.[21]

General Franks issued the order authorizing the deployment of the XVIII Airborne Corps to Afghanistan in early April 2002. CENTCOM articulated McNeill's mission as synchronizing "land operations to destroy al Qaida [sic] and prevent the reemergence of international terrorist activities within Combined Joint Operating Area–Afghanistan and support humanitarian operations in order to create a peaceful and stable environment in Afghanistan."[22] CENTCOM believed the XVIII Airborne Corps faced "al Qaida [sic] pockets of resistance, al Qaida [sic] and Taliban leadership, and tribal elements who would actively engage in armed opposition to coalition operations in their areas or actively defend al-Qaeda elements." Although

---

20. Interv, Brian F. Neumann and Maj Colin J. Williams, OEF Study Grp, with Gen (Ret.) Dan K. McNeill, frmr Cdr, Combined Joint Task Force (CJTF) 180, 18 Sep 2015, p. 12, Hist Files, OEF Study Grp.

21. Interv, Col Timothy Reese, CSI, with Gen Dan K. McNeill, frmr Cdr, CJTF-180, 16 Jun 2008, pp. 6–7, Hist Files, OEF Study Grp.

22. Concept of Opns, CENTCOM, 4 Apr 2002, CONOPS for the Establishment of Combined Joint Task Force -Afghanistan (CJTF-AFG), final draft,, p. 4, Hist Files, OEF Study Grp.

most low-level Taliban fighters had been integrated into the United Front or returned to their tribes, CENTCOM felt that some were still holding out in Helmand, Kandahar, Uruzgan, and Zabul Provinces while the Taliban leadership was hiding in northern Helmand and Uruzgan.[23]

On Franks' recommendation, Secretary of Defense Donald H. Rumsfeld invited McNeill to a one-on-one session at the Pentagon soon afterward. Before the meeting, the XVIII Airborne Corps commander called on the senior Army leadership and the chairman of the Joint Chiefs of Staff. General Erik K. Shinseki told McNeill to "do nothing that looks like permanency," while General John M. "Jack" Keane declared, "We are in and out of there in a hurry, Okay? . . . No more Camp Bondsteels," referring to the prohibitively expensive mega-base that U.S. forces had constructed in Kosovo during the Balkan peacekeeping operations in the 1990s. General Richard B. Myers echoed Keane's words when McNeill visited the Joint Staff.[24]

When McNeill arrived for his appointment with Rumsfeld, he found the secretary of defense prepared to offer detailed guidance. During the discussion, Rumsfeld admonished McNeill not to engage in nation building or allow American troops to become involved in Afghan internal politics. Rumsfeld wanted McNeill to remain focused on two primary missions: building the ANA and killing or capturing terrorists. McNeill departed the Pentagon with little doubt that security assistance and counterterrorism were the secretary of defense's sole priorities for CJTF-180. Several months later, on his own initiative, McNeill added assisting the Karzai government with extending its reach and helping with the disarmament, demobilization, and reintegration process to his growing list of priorities.[25]

The transfer process was slated to begin on 23 April with the arrival of the XVIII Airborne Corps' predeployment site survey team. CFLCC would host the survey team to ensure its members learned what they needed to know in order to smooth out the transition. Although both staffs could work side by side at Camp Doha, the transition would not be complete until the XVIII Airborne Corps established itself at Bagram. Fortunately for CJTF-180, the transition did not require the XVIII Airborne Corps to assume all Third Army/ARCENT responsibilities. While McNeill's corps assumed command and control over ENDURING FREEDOM, Mikolashek's headquarters retained its Title 10 service responsibilities. As a result, units such as the 513th Military Intelligence Brigade and 11th Signal Brigade remained behind to provide support after Third Army/ARCENT returned to Fort McPherson.[26]

With the formal changeover set for 30 May, McNeill would start with a virtually clean slate as both the Afghan Interim Authority and ISAF handed the reins to their successors in June. The Bonn Conference had mandated that an Emergency Loya Jirga, a nationwide convention of 1,450 delegates

---

23. Ibid., p. 2.

24. Interv, Reese with McNeill, 16 Jun 2008, pp. 6–7.

25. Ibid., p. 8.

26. Memo, Col Eshelman for Third Arm/ARCENT Cmd Grp and Staff, sub: ARCENT Update, 20 Apr 2002, 1135 hours, Story CFLCC Collection, OEF Study Grp.

General McNeill engages with Governor Hakim Taniwal in the critical border province of Khost.

representing all communities and tribes, be held in Kabul from 11 to 19 June 2002 in order to form a transitional administration. Among other goals, the loya jirga would select a new leader for Afghanistan who would rule until the presidential elections slated for 2004.[27] It also provided the Pashtun majority with a chance to assume a greater role in the new government, which to date had been dominated by United Front Tajiks and Uzbeks. As a result, McNeill did not know before deploying if he would be working alongside Karzai or any of the interim administration's officials beyond CJTF-180's first three weeks at Bagram. As it would turn out, Hamid Karzai would remain in office.

The United Kingdom planned to relinquish command of ISAF to Turkey on the day after the end of the Emergency Loya Jirga. Although CENTCOM encountered few obstacles assembling the initial ISAF contingent, both the United Kingdom and the United States had to meet several conditions imposed by the Turkish government before it agreed to appoint Maj. Gen. Hilmi Akin Zorlu as General McColl's successor. The first indicator that Ankara viewed the mission differently than the United States came in early April after media representatives reported that UN officials were entertaining Afghan suggestions to deploy peacekeepers beyond Kabul. Secretary Rumsfeld welcomed international peacekeepers taking on a larger role in Afghan stabilization, as long as the United States did not have to fund

---

27. International Crisi Group, "The Loya Jirga: One Small Step Forward?," Asia Bfg 17, 16 May 2002, https://www.crisisgroup.org/asia/south-asia/afghanistan/loya-jirga-one-small-step-forward, Hist Files, OEF Study Grp.

their operations, but the Turkish government reacted by immediately making clear that it did not support ISAF expansion.[28]

Even though the Turkish government tentatively agreed to run Kabul International Airport, staff the ISAF headquarters, train a battalion of Afghan recruits, and contribute 1,500 troops between June 2002 and February 2003, final approval remained contingent on financial incentives and improved living conditions for Turkish soldiers.[29] The United States met the former stipulation by adding $28 million in foreign military financing and $200 million in economic support funds for Turkey in the March 2002 emergency supplemental request submitted to Congress. British troops already deployed to Afghanistan accomplished the latter task, which led British government official Steve Brooking to note: "UK soldiers found it somewhat ironic that they were constructing brick buildings in the ISAF headquarters for the Turks, while they themselves were living in tents."[30] It remained to be seen how General Zorlu would view his day-to-day relationship with CJTF-180.

THE LAST ENCLAVE: MOUNTAIN LION

Although President Bush campaigned fiercely against the Clinton administration's enthusiasm for committing U.S. troops to nation-building missions, his remarks at the George C. Marshall Reserve Officer Training Corps Award ceremony at the Virginia Military Institute in Lexington, Virginia, on 17 April 2002 indicated otherwise. He did not specifically commit CENTCOM to a greatly expanded mission, but he did convey the impression that more resources would be allocated to Phase IV of the campaign plan by reminding his audience of the long and costly American program to rebuild post–World War II Europe. Bush also linked a peaceful and democratic Afghanistan to ongoing rebuilding efforts. On the following day, the *New York Times* proclaimed, "President Bush today embraced a major American role in rebuilding Afghanistan, calling for a plan he compared to the one George C. Marshall devised for Europe after World War II, and vowed to keep the United States engaged in Afghanistan until 'the mission is done.'"[31] The speech would have considerable effect on future policy development.

The president also unveiled the last major operation to be planned and executed in Afghanistan before the XVIII Airborne Corps arrived. He noted in his public remarks that "the battles in Afghanistan are not over. American and allied troops are taking risks today in what we call Operation MOUNTAIN

---

28. Feith, *War and Decision*, p. 157; Carol Migdalovitz, Turkey: *Issues for U.S. Policy*, RL31429 (Washington, D.C.: Congressional Research Service, 22 May 2002). p. 12.

29. Migdalovitz, *Turkey*, p. 12.

30. Steve Brooking, "Early ISAF: 'The Good Old Days,'" Afghan Analysts Network e-Book, Jul 2012, http://www.afghanistan-analysts.org/wp-content/uploads/downloads/2012/9/8_Brooking_Early_ISAF.pdf, Hist Files, OEF Study Grp.

31. James Dao, "A Nation Challenged: The President; Bush Sets Role for U.S. in Afghan Rebuilding," *New York Times*, 18 Apr 2002, https://www.nytimes.com/2002/04/18/a-nation-challenged-the-president-bush-sets-role-for-us-in-afghan-rebuilding-html, Hist Files, OEF Study Grp.

LION, hunting down the Al-Qaeda [sic] and Taliban forces, keeping them on the run."[32] Planning for MOUNTAIN LION began in late March after intelligence analysts informed Maj. Gen. Franklin L. "Buster" Hagenbeck that survivors from Tora Bora and the Shahi Kot Valley were gathering in a village about ten kilometers south of Zhaware Kelay in Khost Province.[33] In response, Hagenbeck directed his staff to devise a plan to prevent them from disrupting the Emergency Loya Jirga in June.[34]

Located in a canyon only four kilometers from the Pakistani border, Zhaware Kelay had been a major logistics transfer point for the mujahideen during the Soviet-Afghan war. Supplies and weapons traveled from Pakistani ports and overland routes to Zhaware Kelay, where they were stored in eleven tunnel systems carved into the southeastern face of Shediyaki Ghar.[35] SEAL Team 3 originally investigated the tunnels on 6 January and found documents, radios, inoperable Stinger man-portable surface-to-air missiles, and several mass graves. In addition, the team identified more than sixty buildings and three dozen caves for further investigation in an area measuring five by six kilometers.[36] To continue the search, Captain Harward extended the original mission for another eight days. Using captured al-Qaeda vehicles, the SEALs combed the entire area, destroying newly discovered caches with their own explosives and calling in air strikes against others. On 14 January 2002, helicopters extracted the SEALs and marines without incident.[37]

Capitalizing on the buildup of logistical support and the arrival of Task Force JACANA, a brigade-sized infantry unit led by British Brig. Gen. Richard Lane consisting of 1,700 personnel from the Royal Marine 45th Commando, CJTF-MOUNTAIN planners determined that the optimal means of safeguarding the Emergency Loya Jirga was to sustain pressure against known and suspected enemy forces in eastern and southeastern Afghanistan for several months.[38] The 10th Mountain Division's concept of operations now called for revisiting Shahi Kot and Tora Bora, sending conventional forces to Zhaware Kelay, and launching other operations based on new

---

32. President George W. Bush, "President Outlines War Effort," (Remarks, George C. Marshall ROTC Award Seminar on National Security, Virginia Military Institute, Lexington, Va., 17 Apr 2002), p. 3, Hist Files, OEF Study Grp.

33. Capt Timothy B. McCulloh, "Operation Mountain Lion: Combat Monogram" (PEP, Inf Capts Career Course, n.d.), pp. 6–7, Hist Files, OEF Study Grp.

34. Wright et al., *A Different Kind of War*, p. 185.

35. Mir Bahmanyar, *Afghanistan Cave Complexes 1979–2004: Mountain Strongholds of the Mujahideen, Taliban and al-Qaeda* (Oxford: Osprey Publishing, 2004), p. 51.

36. DoD press conferences hosted by Tori Clarke and R. Adm. John D. "Boomer" Stufflebeem also confirm the air strikes that took place after the operation. Transcript, "Pentagon Briefing: Zawar Kili Buildings Searched, Destroyed," R Adm John D. Stufflebeem and Victoria Clarke, DoD, CNN, 14 Jan 2002, http://edition.cnn.com/TRANSCRIPTS/0201/14/se.04.html, Hist Files, OEF Study Grp.

37. Brandon Webb, *The Red Circle: My Life in the Navy SEAL Sniper Corps and How I Trained America's Deadliest Marksmen* (New York: St. Martin's Press, 2012), pp. 255–92.

38. "Last Marines Arrive in Afghanistan," BBC News, 20 Apr 2002, https://news.bbc.co.uk/2/hi/south_asia/1941370.stm, Hist Files, OEF Study Grp.

intelligence.[39] MOUNTAIN LION faced an unfamiliar challenge in the form of diminishing access to intelligence, surveillance, and reconnaissance assets as they were being redirected to Iraq.[40] MOUNTAIN LION thus depended far more on Afghan sources—which often had their own agenda—rather than U.S. technical means.

In the opening action of MOUNTAIN LION, Lt. Col. Ronald E. Corkran's 1st Battalion, 187th Infantry, departed from Kandahar on 3 April onboard CH–47 Chinooks to seize and clear the Zhaware Kelay tunnel complex. Corkran's plan called for two rifle companies to establish blocking positions while Company A cleared a series of small valleys immediately north of the tunnels. Over the next two days, Company A worked its way south toward the main concentration of caves and tunnels. Although they destroyed caves and buildings with demolition charges, the Americans discovered little of interest. As the battalion prepared to return to Kandahar, storms and high winds forced the troops to remain in place before helicopters finally were able to venture safely once more into Zhaware Kelay on 7 April.[41]

In the wake of Corkran's sweep through Zhaware Kelay, CJTF-MOUNTAIN ordered the Canadians and British into the fray. On 16 April, TF JACANA initiated Operation PTARMIGAN for the purpose of sweeping through the recent Shahi Kot battlefield.[42] Approximately 1,000 British personnel, aided by 500 Afghan militia, took part in the operation, which did not encounter the enemy. A tragic mishap delayed 3d Princess Patricia's Canadian Light Infantry's participation in MOUNTAIN LION when a U.S. Air Force F–16 pilot erroneously identified Canadian troops conducting a live-fire training exercise near Kandahar as enemy troops firing on his aircraft. Despite instructions from a controller aboard an orbiting Airborne Warning and Control System E–3A aircraft not to release any ordnance, the pilot dropped a 500-pound bomb on a Canadian infantry platoon, killing four and wounding eight.[43] The incident played a major role in the Ottawa government's decision not to send more ground troops to Afghanistan after Lt. Col. Patrick B. Stogran's battalion rotated home.[44]

---

39. Bfg, CJTF-Mountain, HQ, 10th Mtn Div, n.d., sub: Afghanistan and Operation ANACONDA, slides 41–42, Hist Files, OEF Study Grp; Wright et al., *A Different Kind of War*, pp. 184–85.

40. Interv, Reese with McNeill, 16 Jun 2008, p. 3.

41. McCulloh, "Operation Mountain Lion," pp. 8–12; Wright et al., *A Different Kind of War*, p. 186.

42. Wright et al., *A Different Kind of War*, p. 186.

43. Corbett, *First Soldiers Down*, pp. 131–34.

44. Both the U.S. Air Force and Canadian militaries separately investigated the incident. As a result of the American investigation, the pilot who released the bomb received a letter of reprimand questioning his judgment and integrity, and was pulled from flight status permanently. The flight leader received a written admonishment for failing to exercise proper control over his wingman's actions. Canadian public opinion believed that the pilot who dropped the bomb should have been jailed rather than reprimanded. Canadian soldiers who served in Afghanistan felt little bitterness toward their American counterparts in general, but harbored strong feelings against the pilot who killed their comrades. John Hendren, "Charges Dropped in 'Friendly Fire'

Colonel Stogran's unit reentered the fight to conduct Operation TORI II in the Tora Bora area. The Canadians were ferried from Kandahar to Bagram aboard U.S. Air Force C–17s in late April, whereupon they waited for eight days before receiving their mission. On 4 May, Chinooks airlifted Companies A and C of the 3d Princess Patricia's Canadian Light Infantry, along with Stogran's tactical command post, snipers, and a reconnaissance platoon, to Spin Ghar in the Tora Bora cave complex. American Special Forces personnel, Afghan militia guides, and a team of U.S. forensic scientists also took part. The combined force examined dozens of caves and exhumed twenty-three graves near the village of Ali Khel, but a week of searching disclosed no information about bin Laden's fate.[45]

During the first week of May, TF JACANA launched Operation SNIPE into southeastern Afghanistan. While the British marines encountered no enemy fighters, they destroyed four caves filled with tons of mortar ammunition, artillery shells, and surface-to-surface rockets.[46] General Lane returned to Bagram on 13 May to declare the campaign against al-Qaeda and the Taliban "all but won." He elaborated on that statement:

> It is true to say that we did not encounter the enemy during this operation. But from a strategic perspective, this is an encouraging sign. The fact that al-Qaeda had been forced to abandon one of the most strategically well-placed and easily defended location[s] in Afghanistan speaks volumes for the military and psychological impact of the operation.[47]

Lane's subordinates, however, complained privately to reporters about the failure of the Pakistanis to seal the border, prompting media representatives to observe, "British officers now talk openly of al-Qaeda having sanctuaries in tribal areas of Pakistan that are off limits to attack because of 'political considerations.'"[48] Public enthusiasm within the United Kingdom for British troops taking part in ENDURING FREEDOM waned in the wake of these revelations.

MOUNTAIN LION may have helped secure the success of the Emergency Loya Jirga, but it failed to find, fix, and destroy the enemy even though it employed an unprecedented number of conventional combat units. Looking back on

---

Deaths," *Los Angeles Times*, 20 Jun 2003, https://articles.latimes.com/2003/jun/20/nation/na-pilots20, Hist Files, OEF Study Grp; Pieter M. O'Leary, "Friendly Fire during the War on Terror: The Law, Procedure, and Likelihood of Recovery Based on the Tarnak Farms Incident," *Gonzaga University Journal of International Law* (2 Feb 2008), https://blogs.law.gonzaga.edu/gjil/2008/02/friendly-fire/, Hist Files, OEF Study Grp.

45. Stephen J. Thorne, "The Caves and Graves of Tora Bora," *Legion Magazine* (1 Sept 2003), https://legionmagazine.com/en/2003/09/the-caves-and-graves-of-tora-bora/, Hist Files, OEF Study Grp.

46. "Al-Qaeda Arms Dump Destroyed," BBC News, 11 May 2002, https://news.bbc.co.uk/2/hi/south_asia/1982059.stm, Hist Files, OEF Study Grp.

47. "Marines' Mission Ends in Frustrating Success," *The Scotsman*, 14 May 2002, https://www.scotsman.com/news/world/marines-mission-ends-in-frustrating-success-1-567010, Hist Files, OEF Study Grp.

48. Ibid.

this phase of the campaign, General Mikolashek rightfully characterized the wholesale removal of intelligence assets as one of his greatest concerns. American estimates on the intentions of their elusive foe depended increasingly on intelligence gleaned from captives and friendly Afghans as technical collection assets were transferred from Afghanistan in anticipation of future operations in Iraq. This situation forced MOUNTAIN LION planning efforts to rely on a worst-case assessment of enemy capabilities rather than verified intelligence.[49] Because the American forces lacked accurate intelligence, they wasted considerable effort in their operation and had to release a growing number of apprehended Afghans after they discovered that their erstwhile captives were not Taliban.[50]

The formal handover between CJTF-MOUNTAIN and CJTF-180 took place at Bagram on 30 May 2002. The Bush administration's interest in assembling general purpose forces for upcoming campaigns, coupled with a pervasive belief that U.S. gains would not be seriously challenged in the near term, triggered tremendous turnover within CJTF-180 soon afterward. The original contingent of U.S. active component, general purpose forces departed, and were replaced either by reserve component organizations that lacked comparable training, equipment, and experience or (in the case of Canadian and British infantry contingents) by no one at all. Although ISAF remained in Afghanistan, General McNeill found himself working with new coalition leaders when the Turks replaced General McColl's staff in June 2002.

The turnover occurred in part because the Bush administration felt McNeill faced a far more permissive operating environment than his predecessor. As a result, CJTF-180 needed less access to resources, including intelligence, surveillance, and reconnaissance systems, than CFLCC. Although the White House considered the environment in Afghanistan as more permissive, McNeill still had to abide with operational limitations prohibiting employment of CJTF-180 forces in neighboring Pakistan. That restriction was logical only if the government of Pakistani president Pervez Musharraf could prevent the Taliban from reconstituting within the Federally Administered Tribal Areas. The Bush administration's efforts to limit long-term investment in post-Taliban Afghanistan thus confined McNeill's antiterrorism efforts to securing the Bonn Process, fielding the ANA, and mentoring key officials as Afghans learned how to exercise political power within a centralized government framework. Given the minimal near-term risk, this limited approach seemed feasible, but success would be far less certain if the Taliban proved resilient enough to challenge the new government in Kabul.

---

49. Interv, Connors with Mikolashek, 13 Dec 2006, p. 14.

50. During the third week of May, for example, U.S. forces detained fifty-five people at a compound west of Kandahar, only to discover that one man was a former junior Taliban official. See News Bfg, Sec Donald Rumsfeld and Vice CJCS Gen Peter Pace, 30 May 2002, https://archive.defense.gov/Transcripts/Transcript.aspx?TranscriptID=3469, Hist Files, OEF Study Grp.

Conclusion

Senior Bush administration officials established the Global War on Terrorism policy before the shock generated by the September 11th attacks had subsided. Their approach differed from past experiences by seeking to eliminate stateless terrorist groups and coerce nation-states to end their support of such organizations. Their deliberations suffered, however, from a lack of information and existing plans for a conflict in Afghanistan. The initial concept developed by CENTCOM influenced cabinet discussions, which drove General Tommy R. Franks to refine draft plans to match changing guidance from his superiors. That cycle forced the military to discard deliberate planning for a more dynamic, adaptive approach. In addition, the DoD advocated a warfighting style that promoted transformational initiatives and was championed by senior administration officials. These factors, combined with a joint planning doctrine that placed greater emphasis on the opening rather than the closing phases of a campaign, produced a constantly evolving war plan that in some respects had been examined meticulously and yet in other respects was severely underdeveloped.

Although a small circle of key individuals successfully produced strategic guidance for the opening campaign in a remarkably short time, the lack of detailed information and preexisting plans hobbled CENTCOM's ability to visualize what might occur after hostilities began. Key elements required by military planners, such as the termination criteria—"specified standards approved by the President and/or the Secretary of Defense that must be met before a joint operation can be concluded"—were not immediately forthcoming.[1] Once hostilities began on 7 October 2001, the relentless pace of events ensured that key administration figures had to amend the initial plan in response to unforeseen developments rather than deliberately refine it in an effort to shape the trajectory of the campaign. After the first bombs dropped, White House strategy sessions focused more on near-term developments than on charting a broader path toward a sustainable end-state.

In an impressively brief period of time and with few casualties, U.S. Special Forces, airpower, and allied indigenous militias dominated the battlefield in Afghanistan. Conventional forces followed up by reducing the remaining al-Qaeda strongholds in the Shahi Kot Valley before expanding

---

1. This topic had been discussed in military academic circles since the end of the Gulf War in 1991. The president's senior military advisers are responsible for pressing for this information if the collaborative decision-making forum fails to do so. Joint doctrine from that period, however, does not mention this critical requirement to any extent. See Lt Col Robert S. Soucy et al., "War Termination Criteria and JOPES: A Dangerous Omission in U.S. Crisis Action Planning," Armed Forces Staff College Intermediate Program, Class 94-1, 25 Mar 1994, https://www.dtic.mil/doctrine/doctrine/research/p180.pdf, Hist Files, OEF Study Grp.

their scope of operations to encompass all of southern Afghanistan. Those dramatic developments, when combined with the premature decision to begin planning for operations against Iraq, obscured the need to reexamine the Global War on Terrorism's trajectory. A sober re-evaluation at this point in the campaign would have revealed that only one of its three main goals—ending Taliban rule—had been achieved.

Even though CENTCOM expelled the Taliban government and al-Qaeda from Afghanistan, both organizations had sufficient transnational support to survive elsewhere. With U.S. interest fixed on al-Qaeda, the Bush administration did not place enough emphasis on denying Taliban leaders sanctuary in nearby Pakistan. As a result, although General Dan K. McNeill was charged with preventing the reemergence of terrorism until the Afghan Interim Authority demonstrated its own capability to do so, he could only delay the Taliban's eventual return. A large number of rank-and-file Taliban remained in the relative safety of their home villages to await developments. In this instance, U.S. forces in Afghanistan could not achieve the desired level of success because strategic guidance did not reflect the realities of post-Taliban Afghanistan.

For the most part, the unexpected issues that emerged at the end of what was characterized as one of the most successful military campaigns in recent history did not stem from deliberate decisions. Neither the Bush administration, nor the U.S. military, nor the CIA had detailed knowledge of Afghan personalities, customs, or tribal dynamics, and had not fully considered the economics of the failed state at this point in the campaign. These shortcomings surfaced in unanticipated ways following the surprising successes of mid-November 2001, which meant that the original CENTCOM plan envisioning the start of the main effort in May 2002 was no longer valid. As a result, the DoD did not appreciate the fact that the United Front could not readily transition itself into the primary military defense force of post-Taliban Afghanistan.

The Bush administration's faulty assumption that indigenous allies could assume a large share of security responsibilities in post-Taliban Afghanistan would have long-term detrimental effects on the country's security. When Tajik and Uzbek militias proved reluctant to operate in southern regions of the country, the XVIII Airborne Corps deployed its forces in Pashtun-dominated areas rather than accept a security vacuum in that vital region. Lacking indigenous support comparable to that available to TF DAGGER, Special Operations task forces supporting the XVIII Airborne Corps had to rely on irregular militias with uncertain loyalties and motives. The rising number of irregulars working with U.S. Special Forces, when combined with Tajik and Uzbek reluctance to contribute fighters to the new Afghan Army, undermined the authority of the nascent Kabul government over time. The DoD, focused on marshaling its resources for the upcoming campaign in Iraq, did not see the need to immediately remedy this situation, thus necessitating a greater investment several years later.

Because of this combination of recognized and unacknowledged factors, the United States unwittingly surrendered the strategic initiative to the Taliban—who, unlike the Serbians in the Balkans, did not interpret their early defeats as an end to the struggle. By focusing primarily on avoiding a long-term commitment of U.S. forces, the administration discounted the potential need for a robust post-Taliban U.S. presence. Even though the defeated Taliban forces were not a near-term threat, the risk they posed increased when their reconstitution efforts in Pakistan began to outpace the growth of Afghan government security forces. The United States had two options to deal with this situation: devote more resources to increase the capacity and capability of the Afghan security forces, or interfere with the Taliban's rearmament efforts. Cost concerns made the former option undesirable, and the latter proved difficult as the Taliban's leadership and support elements remained within Pakistan.

SECTION II

SEARCHING FOR A SOLUTION

Section II

Introduction

Events in Afghanistan between November 2001 and May 2002 appeared to validate the unconventional approach to warfighting advocated by CENTCOM and supported by the Bush administration. The initial campaign had been conceived in a matter of weeks and executed months earlier than envisioned, though many al-Qaeda leaders remained at large and Phase IV remained to be completed. The overthrow of the Taliban regime also produced several unanticipated changes in policy that affected the course of the campaign. The most significant change involved recognizing the Bonn Conference timetable for introducing democracy to Afghanistan. This would culminate with national parliamentary and provincial council elections in September 2005. Although the DoD accepted that some American troops needed to remain in Afghanistan throughout the process, its strategic focus shifted to planning for a preventative conflict aimed at deposing Iraq's Saddam Hussein.

A second change occurred in April 2002 when President George W. Bush pledged to implement a "Marshall Plan" program to help Afghans return to a semblance of normalcy following two decades of conflict. Just as President Harry S. Truman understood in 1945 that nation building was the most effective means of preventing the spread of communism among war-weary populations in postwar Europe, the Bush administration realized that Afghanistan required a long-term commitment of energy and resources to prevent militant Islam from once again taking root within its borders.[1] That policy shift not only was a major departure from Bush's presidential campaign rhetoric against using military forces for nation building, but it also heralded the fact that major changes needed to be made to Phase IV of the CENTCOM campaign plan.

The Army itself entered the first full year of the Global War on Terrorism with 180,000 soldiers deployed or forward-stationed in 120 countries, amounting to 17 percent of the Army's 1,044,302 officers, warrant officers, cadets, and enlisted soldiers. The overall end strength included 486,542 soldiers in the active component, 206,682 Army Reservists, and 351,078 in the Army National Guard. Those figures reflected an increase over the previous year of 5,741 active component personnel and 1,054 National Guardsmen,

---

1. John A. Smith, "Afghanistan's Marshall Plan," *New York Times*, 19 Apr 2002, https://www.nytimes.com/2002/04/19/opinion/afghanistan-s-marshall-plan.html, Hist Files, OEF Study Grp.

balanced in part by a decrease of 751 Army Reservists.[2] All components met or exceeded their retention and recruiting goals during 2002, thus assuring the Army's ranks would remain filled, at least for the near term, as the Global War on Terrorism progressed.[3]

As of October 2002, the Army's senior leaders ranked their three most critical tasks as follows: (1) helping to win the Global War on Terrorism, (2) transforming to meet future challenges, and (3) securing the resources needed to simultaneously fight terrorism and transform the Army. The war itself was a formidable challenge, given that the Army was a core component of America's military response to the September 11th attacks. Soldiers taking part in that mission were serving both in the United States and overseas, with approximately 14,000 soldiers deployed in the CENTCOM area of responsibility as part of Operation ENDURING FREEDOM, while more than 32,000 Army Reserve and National Guard personnel protected the United States from subsequent terrorist attacks. The latter figure did not include more than 11,000 National Guardsmen called up by state governors for similar tasks, such as securing airports, dams, seaports, and power plants. In addition, more than 5,000 Army personnel took part in securing the 2002 Winter Olympic Games in Salt Lake City, Utah. Thousands of Army personnel continued other security-related missions, which included a presence in Kuwait to deter Iraqi aggression and long-term peacekeeping operations in Bosnia, Kosovo, Macedonia, and Sinai.[4]

Transformation continued along an unwavering, pre–September 11th trajectory during 2002, in large part because senior Army leaders viewed involvement in Afghanistan as a reason to accelerate existing efforts rather than reexamine their basic premise. The May 2002 cancellation of the Crusader 155-mm. self-propelled howitzer program was an exception to that trend, but the program was cancelled only at the insistence of Secretary of Defense Donald H. Rumsfeld. However, the Army continued to invest in the Future Combat System, which had been designed to replace Cold War–era combat vehicles. The Future Combat System program sought to produce a lighter, rapidly deployable family of manned and unmanned vehicles with a common design linked by a state-of-the-art digitized communications architecture beginning in 2010. The development of the first Stryker-equipped medium-weight brigade, slated to be fully operational by May 2003, continued in 2002 as the unit successfully completed exercises that tested its deployability and digitized command and control network. The Army planned to field a total of six Stryker brigades by 2007.[5]

---

2. William M. Donnelly, *Department of the Army Historical Summary, Fiscal Year 2002* (Washington, D.C.: U.S. Army Center of Military History, 2011), p. 13.

3. Ibid., p. 14.

4. The peacekeeping missions involved a mix of active and reserve component elements. The Pennsylvania National Guard's 28th Infantry Division assumed responsibility of the Bosnia mission for six months near the end of 2002, providing all deploying elements including aviation support. Thomas E. White Jr., "The Army Is Dedicated to Delivering Victory," *Army Green Book 2002–2003* (Oct 2002): 17.

5. Ibid., p. 18.

Introduction

The strategic landscape changed following the March 2003 invasion of Iraq, where the Army overcame scattered resistance from an overwhelmed conventional opponent unable to cope with the tempo of operations imposed on them by U.S. ground forces. Although that effort culminated with the capture of Baghdad on 9 April, postcombat operations increasingly focused on countering an insurgency that rapidly expanded in scope and level of violence by spring 2004. Troop levels in Iraq during 2003 and 2004 reached 67,700 and 130,600 respectively, with casualties totaling 2,279 killed and wounded in 2003 and 4,886 during the following year. By comparison, operations in Afghanistan resulted in 96 casualties in 2003 and 189 in 2004 while involving approximately 85 percent fewer troops (10,500–15,200).[6] The Iraqi insurgency increasingly monopolized the attention of the Bush administration, DoD, CENTCOM, and the Army. That conflict would also steer Army transformation in unanticipated directions.

In 2002, the Bush administration continued to believe it did not need to mobilize the nation for the Global War on Terrorism. CENTCOM had to monitor the allocation of military power and other resources destined for Afghanistan while ensuring that it had sufficient resources to attack Saddam Hussein's forces. Finally, the swiftness and perceived decisiveness of the initial campaign in Afghanistan convinced the administration of the wisdom of embracing transformation. However, when the DoD repositioned most of the existing high-tech assets to support the impending conflict with Iraq, it left U.S. forces in Afghanistan with far fewer capabilities than they originally possessed.

While American troops remained in Afghanistan to oversee the installation of a democratic central government, the Bush administration realized that some of the Afghan warlords recruited to defeat the Taliban did not necessarily share that vision. It would take years before the Bush administration realized that a number of prominent Afghans within the Kabul government placed personal, tribal, and ethnic goals above the formation of a democratic, fully representative central government. For the time being, the administration focused on building a nonsectarian ANA capable of defeating threats to the democratization of Afghanistan, which included not only recalcitrant warlords but also extremist groups seeking to take advantage of the Taliban's ouster.

American commanders also committed much of their limited available resources to fulfilling President Bush's pledge to rebuild Afghanistan. The original mandate for Provincial Reconstruction Teams focused on building goodwill by providing aid and services to Afghans living near American bases while setting the conditions for the arrival of international humanitarian organizations. Beginning with task forces such as CJTF-180, these teams worked with Afghans in order to build popular support for the nascent

---

6. Although soldiers did not represent 100 percent of the troop levels for Iraq or Afghanistan, they constituted the overwhelming majority for both countries during the period in question. The casualty figures are exclusively Army personnel. Sezgin Ozcan, "Casualty Profile of the United States Army in Afghanistan and Iraq" (student thesis, Naval Postgraduate School, 2012) https://www.dtic.mil/dtic/tr/fulltext/u2/a562838.pdf, pp. 5–6, 14, Hist Files, OEF Study Grp.

democratic government in Kabul. Although U.S. military humanitarian efforts indicated the Bush administration's desire to associate itself closely with Hamid Karzai and the Afghan Interim Authority, Karzai's willingness to ally with regional strongmen in an effort to offset the political domination of Tajiks and Uzbeks from the United Front made that relationship an uneasy one.

American troops in Afghanistan also faced operational challenges that differed from those of the initial phase of ENDURING FREEDOM. The United Front's Tajik and Uzbek militias, which played a significant role at the onset, were unable to provide Lt. Gen. Dan K. McNeill's CJTF-180 and subsequent headquarters with similar aid given the unwillingness of their commanders to operate in the Pashtun-dominated south. Additionally, the primary focus of Special Forces elements changed from unconventional warfare to foreign internal defense as they sought to replace the United Front's militias with indigenous militia proxies that would operate within their local areas. Conversely, CENTCOM adopted a bifurcated approach to creating indigenous security forces as U.S. conventional forces assumed the mission of training the ANA.

As the United States struggled to understand Afghan culture and politics, popular goodwill toward Americans began to dissipate as U.S. forces continued to rely on air- and space-based assets during postconflict operations. From the start of the conflict through July 2002, on eleven occasions, American air strikes killed or wounded approximately 400 innocent Afghans. As long as the bulk of the bombs were aimed at Taliban military targets, most ordinary Afghans could accept the collateral damage, but that attitude changed as U.S. air strikes continued to kill innocents following the Taliban's defeat. The deadliest of these incidents resulted in 54 deaths and 120 wounded on 1 July 2002 when an AC–130 gunship mistakenly identified a group of civilians in Uruzgan Province as Taliban fighters.[7] As a result, even when air strikes inflicted damage on enemy forces, collateral civilian casualties rekindled support for the Taliban and eroded enthusiasm for the presence of foreign troops and the democratic regime taking shape in Kabul.

POLITICAL SETTING AS OF MAY 2002

Success for the United States after Operation ANACONDA hinged on how well the Afghan government could serve as an effective counterterrorism partner. In 2002, the United States' chief partner in this process, Hamid Karzai, was in a precarious situation. As interim head of state, he had no army or revenue of his own. He struggled even to exert influence in his capital. At the time, the "Panjshiri Troika" of Mohammed Qasim Fahim, Yunus Qanooni, and Abdullah Abdullah—Tajik protégés of Ahmad Shah Massoud, who served as defense minister, interior minister, and foreign minister, respectively—

---

7. Dexter Filkins, "Flaws in U.S. Air War Left Hundreds of Civilians Dead," *New York Times*, 21 Jul 2002, https://www.nytimes.com/2002/07/21/world/flaws-in-us-air-war-left-hundreds-of-civilians-dead.html, Hist Files, OEF Study Grp.

dominated Kabul. Outside the capital, warlords reigned—and because some were employed by American units, Karzai could not touch them.

Faced with these realities, the Bush administration sought to publicly maintain its distance from Kabul's internal politics by focusing instead on reconstruction and respect for Afghan sovereignty. "I want to do what people there want to do," Rumsfeld told the press in April 2002. "The last thing you're going to hear from this podium is someone thinking they know how Afghanistan ought to organize itself."[8] Privately, however, Rumsfeld was convinced the United States should "decide what ought to happen" in Afghanistan, and he quietly asked how the United States could "get control of the levers."[9] The United States sought to do just that at the Emergency Loya Jirga in June 2002. At this first milestone of the Bonn Process, Afghan delegates were to elect an interim president of the Afghan Transitional Authority that would govern Afghanistan until a constitution could be written and national elections held. According to reports, the United States—with UN approval—manipulated the election process to keep Hamid Karzai as the head of state instead of restoring the Afghan monarchy under the former king, Zahir Shah.[10] Washington believed that Karzai was the only leader in Afghanistan who represented the country's Pashtun plurality and had the anti-Taliban bona fides to work with, or around, the Tajik ministers holding important government posts.

Having secured Karzai's transitional presidency, the Bush administration then demonstrated that its support would remain covert. When a southeastern warlord named Pacha Khan Zadran challenged Karzai's authority over

---

8. DoD News Briefing, Sec Def Donald H. Rumsfeld with Gen Richard B. Myers, 22 Apr 2002, https://archive.defense.gov/Transcripts/Transcript.aspx?TranscriptID=3410, Hist Files, OEF Study Grp.

9. Memo, Sec Donald H. Rumsfeld for Under Sec Douglas J. Feith, 17 Apr 2002, sub: Afghanistan, NSU GWU, https://nsarchive2.gwu.edu/NSAEBB/NSAEBB358a/doc23.pdf, Hist Files, OEF Study Grp.

10. Tomsen, *Wars of Afghanistan*, pp. 641–42; Anders Fänge, "The Emergency Loya Jirga," in *Snapshots of an Intervention: The Unlearned Lessons of Afghanistan's Decade of Assistance (2001–11)* eds. Martine van Bijlert and Sari Kouvo (Kabul: Afghanistan Analysts Network, 2012), p. 15; Laura Secor, "The Pragmatist," *The Atlantic* (July–August 2004), https://www.theatlantic.com/magazine/archive/2004/07/the-pragmatist/302992/; S. Frederick Starr and Marin J. Strmecki, "Afghan Democracy and Its First Missteps," *New York Times*, 14 Jun 2002, https://www.nytimes.com/2002/06/14/opinion/afghan-democracy-and-its-first-missteps.html, Hist Files, OEF Study Grp; Omar Zakhilwal and Adeena Niazi, "The Warlords Win in Kabul," *New York Times*, 21 Jun 2002, https://www.nytimes.com/2002/06/21/opinion/the-warlords-win-in-kabul.html, Hist Files, OEF Study Grp; Carlotta Gall, "Former Afghan King Rules Out All but a Symbolic Role," *New York Times*, 11 Jun 2002, https://www.nytimes.com/2002/06/11/world/former-afghan-king-rules-out-all-but-a-symbolic-role.html, Hist Files, OEF Study Grp; Carlotta Gall, "Traditional Council Elects Karzai as Afghan President," *New York Times*, 14 Jun 2002, https://www.nytimes.com/2002/06/14/world/traditional-council-elects-karzai-as-afghan-president.html, Hist Files, OEF Study Grp. Zalmay Khalilzad, then a member of Afghanistan's National Security Council, thought that resistance came from the king's inner circle, not the king himself. Zalmay Khalilzad, *The Envoy: From Kabul to the White House, My Journey through a Turbulent World*, advance copy (New York: St. Martin's Press, 2016), p. 144.

Gardez, the capital of Paktiya Province, in May 2002, the Americans informed Karzai that they wanted him to rely on "political methods" to consolidate power. As Under Secretary of Defense for Policy Douglas J. Feith put it: "In Rumsfeld's view, Karzai should learn to operate as the mayor of Chicago did, forging coalitions through consultations, flattery, jobs, and other types of patronage."[11] In January 2003, the CIA began delivering bags of cash monthly to the presidential palace—one month after learning that the Iranians had started to do so—in order to provide Karzai with greater "political" influence. This off-the-books aid program continued throughout ENDURING FREEDOM and reportedly funded the same warlords, opium trade, and corrupt officials that other elements of the United States were trying to eliminate in Afghanistan.[12]

The Bush administration's preference for maintaining a low public profile to avoid being accused of meddling in Afghan affairs meant that its early assistance efforts lacked focus, were poorly coordinated with both recipients and donors, and could not be accounted for in terms of either expenditures or results.[13] Congress was slow to fund aid on the scale the president implied was needed in his April 2002 speech at the Virginia Military Institute. A divided Senate took eight months to pass the Afghanistan Freedom Support Act that the House of Representatives had approved months earlier.[14] By the time Bush signed the bill in December 2002, most of the appropriations it contained would not be available until after October 2003, when the next fiscal year started. Moreover, the act authorized just $450 million in nonmilitary funds for each of the next four fiscal years, well short of Afghanistan's estimated needs.[15] International assistance hardly fared better. In particular, Finance

---

11. Feith, *War and Decision*, p. 143.

12. Matthew Rosenberg, "With Bags of Cash, CIA Seeks Influence in Afghanistan," *New York Times*, 28 Apr 2013, http://www.nytimes.com/2013/04/29/world/asia/cia-delivers-cash-to-afghan-leaders-office.html, Hist Files, OEF Study Grp; Matthew Rosenberg, "C.I.A. Cash Ended Up in Coffers of Al Qaeda," *New York Times*, 14 Mar 2015, http://www.nytimes.com/2015/03/15/world/asia/cia-funds-found-their-way-into-al-qaeda-coffers.html, Hist Files, OEF Study Grp.

13. General Accounting Office, *Afghanistan Reconstruction: Deteriorating Security and Limited Resources Have Impeded Progress; Improvements in U.S. Strategy Needed*, Jun 2004, pp. 2–5, https://www.gao.gov/assets/250/242726.pdf, Hist Files, OEF Study Grp. For the challenges facing the U.S. reconstruction effort, see Dov S. Zakheim, *A Vulcan's Tale: How the Bush Administration Mismanaged the Reconstruction of Afghanistan* (Washington, DC: Brookings Institution Press, 2011).

14. The House introduced the bill in March 2002 (H.R. 3994) and passed it in May, but the Senate could not muster the votes to pass it. The Senate introduced a new version in July 2002 (S. 2712) and did not pass it until 14 November 2002. The House passed it one day later, and the president signed it into law on 4 December 2002. "H.R. 3994, Afghanistan Freedom Support Act of 2002," 107th Cong., GovTrack, 21 May 2002, https://www.govtrack.us/congress/bills/107/hr3994, Hist Files, OEF Study Grp; and "S.2712, Afghanistan Freedom Support Act of 2002," 107th Cong., GovTrack, 14 Nov 2002, https://www.govtrack.us/congress/bills/107/s2712, Hist Files, OEF Study Grp.

15. *Afghanistan Freedom Support Act of 2002*, PL 107-327, 107th Cong., 2d sess., 4 Dec 2002, sec. 108(a), https://www.gpo.gov/fdsys/pkg/PLAW-107publ327/pdf/PLAW-107publ327.pdf, Hist Files, OEF Study Grp. See also Asian Development Bank, UNDP, and World Bank, *Afghanistan*

Minister Ashraf Ghani struggled to convince aid organizations to support his ministry's National Solidarity Program.[16] Instead, international donors routed money directly to organizations that implemented programs across Afghanistan, effectively taking the nascent Afghan government out of the loop. Donors were slow to deliver on the pledges made in Tokyo and reluctant to coordinate with leaders in the new Afghan government.

As part of the Bonn Process, Germany, Italy, Japan, the United Kingdom, and the United States agreed to implement security sector reforms, real progress remained elusive because no nation assumed overall responsibility. To address Afghanistan's most urgent need, Germany instituted a police academy in Kabul and taught a few hundred officers in multiyear courses.[17] However, the German plan did not approach the vision outlined in the Afghan Interim Authority's National Development Framework, which would have trained 25,000 police a year.[18] Under the British counternarcotics program, poppy cultivation rebounded from a historic low of 8,000 hectares in 2001, when the Taliban banned it in response to low opium prices, to 74,000 hectares in 2002, on par with the levels seen in the mid-1990s.[19] Italy did not send advisers to reform Afghanistan's judiciary.[20] Delays and program design flaws hindered Japan's effort to disarm, demobilize, and reintegrate warlord forces.[21] The American-led effort to build and train the ANA, though slightly more successful, produced only 1,800 troops by January 2003.[22]

Slow security-sector progress led Rumsfeld to observe, "We are never going to get the U.S. military out of Afghanistan . . . unless we take care to see that there is something going on that will provide the stability that will be necessary for us to leave."[23] However, he also opined that "the critical problem in Afghanistan is not really a security problem. Rather, the problem that needs to be addressed is the slow progress that is being made on the civil

---

Preliminary Needs Assessment for Recovery and Reconstruction, Jan 2002, https://reliefweb.int/sites/reliefweb.int/files/resources/748E9C42622856FBC1256B430045B74C-undp-afg-15jan.pdf, Hist Files, OEF Study Grp.

16. Jack Fairweather, *The Good War: Why We Couldn't Win the War or the Peace in Afghanistan* (New York: Basic Books, 2014), pp. 61–74.

17. Seth G. Jones, *In the Graveyard of Empires: America's War in Afghanistan* (New York: W. W. Norton & Company, 2010), pp. 164–65; Feith, *War and Decision*, pp. 54–55.

18. Afghan Interim Authority, *National Development Framework*, draft, version 2 Apr 2002, p. 48, https://unpan1.un.org/intradoc/groups/public/documents/APCITY/UNPAN016262.pdf, Hist Files, OEF Study Grp.

19. UN Office for Drug Control and Crime Prevention, "Afghanistan Opium Survey 2002," 2002, https://www.unodc.org/pdf/publications/afg_opium_survey_2002.pdf, p. 4, Hist Files, OEF Study Grp.

20. Feith, *War and Decision*, p. 155.

21. Caroline A. Hartzell, *Missed Opportunities: The Impact of DDR on SSR in Afghanistan*, Special Report 270 (Washington, D.C.: United States Institute of Peace, April 2011), pp. 1, 8.

22. James Dao, "Threats and Responses: Afghanistan; Wolfowitz, in Kabul, Calls for Rebuilding," *New York Times*, 16 Jan 2003, https://nytimes.com/2003/01/16/world/threats-and-responses-afghanistan-wolfowitz-in-kabul-calls-for-rebuilding.html, Hist Files, OEF Study Grp.

23. Memo, Rumsfeld for Feith, sub: Afghanistan, 17 Apr 2002, Hist Files, OEF Study Grp.

side."²⁴ Rumsfeld worried that security would deteriorate if reconstruction aid did not flow.²⁵ In response, he tried to refocus governmental attention on reconstruction, explaining that overemphasizing the security challenge facing Afghanistan would force the United States to deploy more troops, pointing out to Bush that the Soviets "had over 100,000 troops [in Afghanistan] and failed."²⁶

Although Rumsfeld recognized Afghanistan needed some foreign troops to offset the influence of the United Front, the Pentagon wanted to conserve resources for future conflicts in the Global War on Terrorism. Beginning in March 2002, both CENTCOM and the CIA had begun diverting assets from Afghanistan and Pakistan to the Middle East and undertaking "preparatory tasks" for invading Iraq.²⁷ A year before Operation IRAQI FREEDOM officially began, Saddam Hussein's dictatorial government already was the newest "central front" in the Global War on Terrorism. Operations in Afghanistan would have a lesser priority even as the Bonn Process continued to unfold.

THE OPERATING ENVIRONMENT

The commanders of ENDURING FREEDOM from May 2002 to September 2005 were expected to create their own campaign plans, but there was much that they could not control. Policy from Washington, the collateral impact of events in Iraq, and the reemergence of an enemy that had changed significantly since

---

24. Rumsfeld continued: "Karzai needs the institutions of government, a budget that is funded and resources from the international community, so he can develop political strength in the regions. He needs to be able to show the Afghan people that he is delivering for them and that it is in their interest to help keep the Taliban out. Only with progress on the civil side will Karzai gain the strength and leverage he needs with the regional political leaders (warlords)." Memo, Sec Rumsfeld for President Bush, sub: Afghanistan, 20 Aug 2002, https://library.rumsfeld.com/doclib/sp/439/To%20 President%20George%20W%20Bush%20et%20al.%20re%20Afghanistan%2008-20-2002.pdf, Hist Files, OEF Study Grp.

25. Ibid.

26. Ibid.

27. Woodward, *Plan of Attack*, pp. 136–37; Dave Moniz and Steven Komarow, "Shifts from bin Laden Hunt Evoke Questions," *USA Today*, 29 Mar 2004, https://usatoday30.usatoday.com/news/world/2004-03-28-troop-shifts_x.htm, Hist Files, OEF Study Grp; Philip James, "Running Scared," *The Guardian*, 26 Mar 2004, https://www.theguardian.com/world/2004/mar/26/uselections2004.comment, Hist Files, OEF Study Grp; Barton Gellman and Dafna Linzer, "Afghanistan, Iraq: Two Wars Collide," *Washington Post*, 22 Oct 2004, https://www.washingtonpost.com/wp-dyn/articles/A52673-2004Oct21.html, Hist Files, OEF Study Grp; Thom Shanker and Eric Schmitt, "Pentagon Says a Covert Force Hunts Hussein," *New York Times*, 7 Nov 2003, https://www.nytimes.com/2003/11/07/world/pentagon-says-a-covert-force-hunts-hussein.html, Hist Files, OEF Study Grp; Interv, PBS *Frontline* with Gary Schroen, 20 Jan 2006, https://www.pbs.org/wgbh/pages/frontline/darkside/interviews/schroen.html, Hist Files, OEF Study Grp; Bob Graham, *Intelligence Matters: The CIA, the FBI, Saudi Arabia, and the Failure of America's War on Terror* (New York: Random House, 2004), pp. 124–26; David Rohde and David E. Sanger, "How a 'Good War' in Afghanistan Went Bad," *New York Times*, 12 Aug 2007, https://www.nytimes.com/2007/08/12/world/asia/12afghan.html, Hist Files, OEF Study Grp; Rashid, *Descent Into Chaos*, pp. 133–34.

the campaign's beginning belonged in this category. So too did the staffing, training, organization, and equipping of their commands, as well as the Afghan personalities with whom they interacted and the actions that their allies took. Finally, the geography presented obstacles impossible for senior American commanders to ignore and difficult for them to overcome.

The Bush administration's decision to maintain a small footprint in Afghanistan had operational-level consequences after major combat operations ended. Without enough U.S. conventional troops to deploy throughout the country, Maj. Gen. Franklin L. "Buster" Hagenbeck initially relied on U.S. Special Forces partnered with local paramilitaries for protection, intelligence collection, and combat power. Before General McNeill's headquarters arrived, the U.S. Special Forces elements in theater rotated back to the United States in anticipation of operations in Iraq. The United Front militias, which had been invaluable early in the campaign, would not fight outside of their traditional areas of influence. In addition, fewer Special Forces personnel were projected to deploy to Afghanistan because of the perception that the Taliban had been defeated. These developments meant that Special Forces units arriving during this period were expected to perform the same missions as before but with fewer numbers while simultaneously forging ties with unfamiliar militia commanders in a totally different operating area.

Unencumbered by the now-deposed Taliban government, the warlords leading the militias working with U.S. Special Forces gained unprecedented power despite the fact that their presence weakened the Afghan Interim Authority and invalidated attempts at land reform, economic development, and anticorruption measures. In lieu of sufficient U.S., ISAF, or Afghan government troops, American commanders had to rely on warlords to protect local Afghans. Karzai also found himself embracing selected warlords, albeit for different reasons. With no effective control over residents outside Kabul, the chairman of the Afghan Interim Authority used his access to American military and financial power to convert warlords into proxies for his government.

After being appointed interim president of the Afghan Transitional Authority by the Emergency Loya Jirga in June 2002, Karzai began placing warlords in potentially lucrative positions such as provincial governors and government ministers to solidify his influence beyond the capital. They were personally beholden to him but often acted in their own narrow interests. In some cases, appointees who lacked strong personal or financial support took extraordinary measures to ensure their own (and their clients') survival. One of the worst of these opportunists was Sher Mohammed Akhundzada, Karzai's fellow Pashtun and governor of Helmand Province.[28] Akhundzada

---

28. For Akhundzada, see Rajiv Chandrasekaran, *Little America: The War Within the War for Afghanistan* (New York: Vintage Books, 2013), pp. 44–45. For Helmand Province's share in opium production, see United Nations Office of Drugs and Crime, *The Opium Economy in Afghanistan: An International Problem* (New York: United Nations, 2003), p. 213 and United Nations Office on Drug Control and Crime, "Afghanistan Opium Survey 2004," 2004, https://www.unodc.org/pdf/afg/afghanistan_opium_survey_2004.pdf, p. 3, Hist Files, OEF Study Grp.

oversaw the revitalization of the drug trade in his province, fueling social and political conflicts and enhancing his own power. Even before the XVIII Airborne Corps arrived in Afghanistan, strongmen such as Akhundzada were ensuring that tribal affiliations determined patronage, clientage, loyalty, and obligation.

This new elite withheld customs revenues, promoted smuggling and the drug trade, clashed with each other, and plotted against perceived competitors.[29] They propagated patronage down to villages, and institutionalized the bribery of civil servants, executives, and police officials. Even in the Pashtun south, where Karzai's personal and family connections gave him the greatest sway, warlordism became the norm. The Taliban's defeat also freed armed leaders to profit from opium cultivation and heroin production. Unfortunately for the Afghan Interim Authority, for many Pashtun farmers poppy cultivation became the sole deciding factor between economic sufficiency and destitution. The drug trade worked against land reform, economic development, communal security, and governance. It undermined local economies, disrupted justice, and supplemented the incomes and resources of militia warlords—even those who ostensibly were working with the coalition.

Americans sent to Afghanistan after Operation ANACONDA expected to face articulated opposition from al-Qaeda and Taliban remnants, not warlord intransigence. Unsure how to collect intelligence against an enemy who "waged primarily a guerilla war," intelligence officers struggled to brief their commanders on the enemy intentions.[30] Because they found it hard to identify the exact source of the threat, they chose to ascribe the attacks to anticoalition militias such as the Taliban, the Haqqani Network, and Gulbuddin Hekmatyar's HIG, and directed their military power against these supposed targets.[31] Without a deep knowledge of the opposition, American forces identified their opponents using little more than their battlefield locations. When units operated in Khost, Paktika, and Paktiya Provinces, U.S. leaders assumed they faced the Haqqani Network. In the northeastern provinces of Kunar, Laghman, Logar, and Nuristan, the purported opposition was HIG. Everywhere else, American forces branded all enemy forces as the Taliban.[32]

---

29. Martine Van Bijlert, "The Battle for Afghanistan: Zabul and Uruzgan," Afghan Analysts Network, https://www.afghanistan-analysts.org/publication/other-publications/the-battle-for-afghanistan-zabul-and-uruzgan/, p. 8, Hist Files, OEF Study Grp.

30. Rpt, Joint Center for Lessons Learned, 10th Mountain Division (Light Infantry), 6 Jun 2003, sub: Operation ENDURING FREEDOM, Afghanistan, p. 8, Hist Files, OEF Study Grp.

31. Most recent operational use: OPORD 04–07, Lt Gen David W. Barno, Cdr, CFC-A, to Maj Gen Eric T. Olson, Cdr, CJTF-76, copied Maj Gen Craig P. Weston, Ch, OMC-A. See also "Operation ENDURING FREEDOM III, Tactics, Techniques, Procedures," CALL Handbook, No. 05-6, Ft Leavenworth, Kans., Jan 2005. When the Southern European Task Force took the CJTF-76 mantle in May 2005, it initially referred to enemy forces as al-Qaeda Associated Movements, using language borrowed from the March 2005 National Military Strategy Plan for the War on Terrorism.

32. Interv, Peter Connors and Lisa Mundey, CSI, with Lt Gen (Ret.) John R. Vines, frmr CJTF-180 Cdr, 27 Jun 2007, p. 12, Hist Files, OEF Study Grp; Interv, Lynne Chandler Garcia,

INTRODUCTION

Although these labels often accurately described which forces were involved, this oversimplified template blinded the military to differences in enemy tactics and motivation. The American forces also assumed that the anticoalition militias were united in their resistance to the interim government. Although it is believed that sometime in 2003, Gulbuddin Hekmatyar, Jalaluddin Haqqani, and al-Qaeda made a tactical alliance to fight American forces in Afghanistan, the Afghan government and U.S. forces were to some extent responsible for their enemies loosely banding together, as they had treated all three opponents as equal threats to Afghan and American security.[33]

Geography was an equally uncontrollable environmental factor. Tactically, the biggest impediments were spatial: the heights of mountains and the distances between urban and rural areas. Operationally, the terrain determined how military force in Afghanistan could be employed. Because airpower was the main means of striking enemy forces, U.S. forces had to establish, activate, and deactivate engagement zones so as to prevent fratricide and limit collateral damage to civilians. The long distances required to traverse objectives and the poor roads in Afghanistan meant that troops and supplies had to be airlifted, putting a heavy burden on a limited helicopter fleet.

Constrained by geography, operating with incomplete knowledge of Afghan politics, and relegated to secondary priority in the Global War on Terrorism, American commanders in the post-ANACONDA period faced serious challenges in securing Afghanistan. Although they were free to design their own campaigns, they could not predict, stop, or influence certain events. American and coalition forces were not able to prevent the Taliban from regenerating by drawing upon the ranks of disaffected Afghan Pashtuns and foreign volunteers eager to fight Western interlopers. This problem became more apparent throughout the Bonn Process and further complicated American attempts to maintain the military initiative after Operation ANACONDA.

ENEMY SITUATION AS OF MAY 2002

Operation MOUNTAIN LION demonstrated that ENDURING FREEDOM units faced little organized resistance from either the Taliban or al-Qaeda in the immediate wake of ANACONDA. Although survivors from both the Taliban and al-Qaeda fled to neighboring Pakistan, the ties that had existed between these organizations before 2001 were now broken. Free from Arab, Pakistani, and American interference, Mullah Mohammed Omar and his colleagues established an enclave in the Baluch capital of Quetta where they began preparing to return to power. A few al-Qaeda fighters chose to remain in Afghanistan, but most of Osama bin Laden's followers went to Yemen to

---

CSI, with Brig Gen William B. Garrett, III, frmr 1st Bde, 10th Mtn Div Cdr, 5 Jun 2007, p. 14, Hist Files, OEF Study Grp.

33. Carlotta Gall, *The Wrong Enemy: America in Afghanistan, 2001–2014* (Boston: Houghton Mifflin Harcourt, 2014), pp. 67–73.

reestablish training camps and logistical sites, while bin Laden himself took up unobtrusive residence in Pakistan.

Al-Qaeda's departure from Afghanistan lent credence to coalition assessments that at least eight of the twenty top al-Qaeda leaders were killed by United Front militia, U.S. bombing, or during the Tora Bora assault. Two more had been reported captured. With significant help from the United Front, eleven training camps and many other al-Qaeda facilities had been destroyed or overrun. Contemporary estimates suggested that 8,000 to 12,000 Taliban troops died in battle, captivity, or by aerial bombardment, with twice that number wounded and incapacitated.[34] Counting the thousands of prisoners taken at Kunduz and other locations, the Taliban lost nearly half of its 60,000 rank-and-file members.[35] Among the dead were also perhaps as many as 600 to 800 fighters affiliated with al-Qaeda (out of an original total of 2,000 to 3,000).[36]

The Taliban leadership, which had been guilty by association and not directly complicit in the September 11th attacks, found sanctuary in Pakistan's Federally Administered Tribal Areas as American interest in their destruction subsided following the liberation of Kabul, Jalalabad, and Kandahar. Cultural, ethnic, and tribal linkages, not to mention a common history as mujahideen in the anti-Soviet jihad, propelled many surviving Taliban fighters into Pakistan. Although some of the Afghan Taliban castigated Mohammed Omar for refusing to surrender bin Laden—a policy that guaranteed the destruction of his regime—Omar's own intransigence solidified his reputation in Pakistani tribal circles as a selfless, religiously pure, and transcendent figure. Comfortably ensconced in Quetta, Omar and his assembled followers began planning their return within days of their arrival in Pakistan.

The Pakistani government viewed the Taliban collapse and United Front ascendance with alarm. When the United Front captured Kabul, President Pervez Musharraf called together his senior Army commanders to announce "Pakistan would henceforth look after its interests more 'carefully' and not trust anyone."[37] Historically, Pakistan's regional preoccupation had been with India and, by extension, the ongoing low-grade civil war in Kashmir. The Pakistani Inter-Services Intelligence had spent substantial resources supporting the Taliban in order to train and recruit for the Kashmir jihad in a way that would not directly implicate Pakistan. The intelligence agency's commanders felt no pressure to turn over their protégés. On the contrary, elements within the agency provided money, logistical support, medical

---

34. Michael E. O'Hanlon, "A Flawed Masterpiece," *Foreign Affairs* 81, no. 3 (May–June 2002): 47. O'Hanlon quotes casualty estimates from *New York Times* correspondent Nicholas Kristof, who placed Afghan civilian deaths at less than 1,000. No figures for United Front losses during this period have been located.

35. Council on Foreign Relations, "The Taliban," CFRInfoguide, n.d., https://www.cfr.org/interactives/taliban#!/#islamic-emirate, Hist Files, OEF Study Grp.

36. Carl Conetta, *Strange Victory: A Critical Appraisal of Operation Enduring Freedom and the Afghanistan War* (Cambridge, Mass.: Project on Defense Alternatives, January 2002), p. 4.

37. Abbas, *The Taliban Revival*, p. 79.

treatment, and political cover to Mohammed Omar.³⁸ To complicate matters, India moved troops to the Line of Control (the de facto border between India and Pakistan in the disputed Kashmir region) shortly after the start of ENDURING FREEDOM, asserting its right to act against Pakistan-based militants and terrorists. Pakistan responded with a major deployment of forces to the Kashmir border. Unfortunately, this redistribution of Pakistani forces coincided with the American counterterrorism operations at the porous Afghanistan border, where the United States had been hoping for Pakistan's assistance.³⁹

Even after the crisis with India was resolved, Islamabad took only half-hearted measures to address the rise of Taliban-inspired extremism within the tribal areas.⁴⁰ When the Pakistan Army attempted to suppress the Afghan Taliban or Pakistani Pashtuns—who generally were sympathetic to the ideals of al-Qaeda and each other—results were dismal. A few short months after committing troops in the tribal areas, the Pakistani forces found themselves engaged in heavy combat against foreign extremists supported by two prominent tribes, the Mehsud and the Wazirs. Both tribes were opposed to government intrusion and Musharraf's collaboration with the United States, and neither would willingly surrender its guests. In the end, Pakistan's dysfunctional efforts during 2002 proved more successful at radicalizing Pashtun tribes than weaning them away from supporting the Taliban and other belligerent groups.

Whereas Pakistan earlier sought to use the Taliban to ensure strategic depth against India, Omar now turned the tables; it was the Afghan Taliban that enjoyed strategic depth and stood in a position to call upon its Pashtun brothers for help in a war against the American-backed Karzai government.⁴¹ Taliban efforts to reconstitute their ranks benefited from a combination of self-serving policies instituted by former United Front members within the Kabul government, uncertain economic times, American unwillingness to distinguish between opponents, and the Bush administration's refusal to extend Geneva Convention protections to enemy combatants.⁴² Former Taliban fighters who hoped to retire in peace in Afghanistan faced retaliation;

---

38. Antonio Giustozzi, *Koran, Kalashnikov, and Laptop: The Neo-Taliban Insurgency in Afghanistan, 2002–2007* (New York: Oxford University Press, 2009), pp. 2, 13, 23.

39. Conetta, *Strange Victory*, pp. 13–14, 19, 69n19.

40. Rashid, *Descent into Chaos*, pp. 221, 244; Bergen, *The Osama bin Laden I Know*, pp. 380–81.

41. State Department Cable Islam 09489, "S/P Ambassador Haass' Call on [excised]," 13 Nov 2002, NSU GWU, https://www2.gwu.edu/~nsarchiv/NSAEBB/NSAEBB325/doc12.pdf, Hist Files, OEF Study Grp; Abbas, *The Taliban Revival*, pp. 94–120.

42. In retrospect, it is clear the Bush administration did not view the detainee issue as an information operations opportunity to influence the global Muslim community. Otherwise, it would have taken steps to ensure Americans behaved in a just and compassionate manner toward defeated enemies. In fact, the opposite impression prevailed when photographs were published showing shackled prisoners kneeling before their open-air cells. Although Secretary Rumsfeld attempted to defuse the issue, other Pentagon officials undercut that message by intimating that enemy combatants did not deserve Geneva Conventions protections given the heinous nature of crimes committed on 11 September 2001. O'Hanlon, "A Flawed Masterpiece," pp. 47–51.

many were left with a stark choice: arrest, dishonor, or death on one hand, or resistance on the other.[43] With little genuine effort to promote reconciliation and with civilian casualties from bombings and night-time raids into Pashtun homes being common, many Pashtuns believed that Westerners were targeting them.[44] Without any tangible reason to make peace with the Americans or accept the Tajik- and Uzbek-dominated regime in Kabul, most Pashtuns remained susceptible to calls for resistance delivered by Taliban leaders from the safety of Pakistan.[45]

THE EMERGENCE OF DRONE STRIKES IN PAKISTAN

By spring 2004, a number of militant groups that fled Afghanistan to seek shelter in the Federally Administered Tribal Areas in Pakistan were preparing to reenter the fight. Their agenda included not only restoring Taliban rule in Afghanistan, but also creating a similar regime in Pakistan. The latter development began in July 2002 when Pakistani troops, at the insistence of the Bush administration, launched an abortive attack on militant strongholds in the area's Tirah Valley. The attack failed with significant casualties in the face of heavy resistance, but the careless employment of air and artillery bombardments by government forces infuriated the local tribes. The Pakistani Army did not achieve all of its objectives; worse, it inadvertently played a major role in creating the "Pakistani Taliban," a group determined to overthrow the secular government in Islamabad and replace it with one based on a strict interpretation of Islamic law.

The extremist groups spent the next eighteen months solidifying their control over portions of the tribal areas by killing tribal chiefs who opposed their agenda and terrorizing ordinary citizens into unquestioning compliance.[46] In addition, the militants prepared for another incursion by the Pakistani Army by turning key passes, ridgelines, and villages into fortified strongpoints. Fighting erupted once again in late March 2004 when Pakistani troops unsuccessfully attempted to take into custody al-Qaeda members hiding in South Waziristan.[47] The Pakistani government forces suffered another reversal and numerous casualties, this time at the hands of

---

43. Tomsen, *Wars of Afghanistan*, p. 632; Malkasian, *War Comes to Garmser*, p. 192; Bette Dam, *A Man and A Motorcycle: How Hamid Karzai Came to Power* (Lexington, Ky.: Ipso Facto Publishers, 2014), pp. 190–98.

44. Barfield, *Afghanistan*, pp. 40–42, 73–74; Rashid, *Descent into Chaos*, p. 142; Conetta, *Strange Victory*, p. 27.

45. James Fergusson, *Taliban: The True Story of the World's Most Feared Guerrilla Fighters* (New York: Bantam Press, 2010), p. 153; Giustozzi, *Koran, Kalashnikov, and Laptop*, pp. 206–07.

46. These developments are described in detail by a Pakistani investigative journalist who was later abducted and killed. See Syed Saleem Shahzad, *Inside Al-Qaeda and the Taliban: Beyond Bin Laden and 9/11* (London: Pluto Press, 2011).

47. Pakistani reports of senior al-Qaeda members in that region were not entirely accurate. However, Tohir Abduhalilovich Yuldashev, head of the Islamic Movement of Uzbekistan and a major ally of Bin Laden, was hiding there.

the Pakistani Taliban, prompting Islamabad to negotiate a ceasefire in an effort to defuse the deteriorating situation in the tribal areas.

The ceasefire had been brokered by Nek Mohammed Wazir, a charismatic Pashtun fighter from South Waziristan who fought with the Taliban against the Americans in 2001. Almost immediately after signing the treaty, Wazir declared his intention to wage jihad against not only the Americans, but also Islamabad. An increase in violence immediately followed in May 2004, with suicide bombings by militant groups that killed forty-seven people. Those attacks were followed on 10 June by a failed attack on a Pakistani Army corps commander's convoy, which missed the intended target but resulted in eleven deaths.[48] One week later, a missile strike targeting a South Waziristan compound killed Wazir and four other militants as they ate dinner with an Afghan expatriate friend.[49]

The Pakistani military claimed credit, suggesting that artillery or helicopters equipped with night-vision equipment delivered the attack. However, the Pakistani newspaper *Dawn* ascribed Wazir's death to "a spy drone flying overhead minutes before the missile attack."[50] The strike thus heralded a major development in Operation ENDURING FREEDOM as the Bush administration sought an effective means of attacking Taliban and al-Qaeda fighters ensconced within the tribal areas on Afghanistan's eastern borders. Periodic drone attacks would eliminate other enemy leaders over the next several years, albeit with collateral civilian casualties that reflected the challenges of precisely targeting enemy personnel based only on signals intelligence and overhead imagery. The drone attacks also fueled growing protests from Pakistanis and peace activists across the globe.

---

48. P. Nasir, "Letters: A Failing War on Terrorism," *Dawn*, 30 Jun 2004, https://www.dawn.com/news/1066150, Hist Files, OEF Study Grp.

49. Mark Mazzetti, "A Secret Deal on Drones, Sealed in Blood," *New York Times*, 6 Apr 2013, https://www.nytimes.com/2013/04/07/world/asia/origins-of-cias-not-so-secret-drone-war-in-pakistan.html, Hist Files, OEF Study Grp.

50. Quoted in Brian Glyn Williams, *Predators: The CIAs Drone War on al Qaeda* (Dulles, Va.: Potomac Books, 2013), p. 48; Nek Mohammed Wazir's successor, Haji Umar, sought to carry on his legacy, but he died in similar circumstances in 2010. "Top Militant Leader Killed in Drone Attack," *Dawn*, 2 Jan 2010, https://www.dawn.com/news/847884, Hist Files, OEF Study Grp.

CHAPTER FIVE

Counterterrorism as an Operational Approach

The rapid collapse of first the Taliban government and then the al-Qaeda network forced CENTCOM planners to reassess Afghanistan's future stability. Up to this point, thinking about postwar conditions had been influenced by recent experience in the Balkans and dominated by the need to convince Afghans that Americans were not occupiers.[1] As a result, the initial CENTCOM plan relied on international and nongovernmental aid organizations to provide assistance to the Afghan people. When these organizations were unable to meet American expectations in a timely manner, the Bush administration shouldered a much larger share of that task than originally envisioned. The State Department and the U.S. Agency for International Development, however, were incapable of conducting business in post-Taliban Afghanistan without assistance from CENTCOM. In addition to providing aid to the Afghan people, the U.S. military gained responsibility for training the ANA and overseeing the confinement of enemy combatants. In addition, General Tommy R. Franks tasked Lt. Gen. Dan K. McNeill, the CJTF-180 commander, with defeating all remaining opposition and with conducting civil affairs and setting "conditions to prevent the re-emergence of international terrorist organizations."[2] These requirements substantively reshaped the original Phase IV mission.

The Bush administration's December 2001 decision to plan for possible combat operations in Iraq was another factor influencing CENTCOM's continued involvement in Afghanistan. The timing of that decision meant that General Franks had to plan a campaign against a regional power with conventional military capabilities while maintaining pressure on al-Qaeda and the Taliban. The latter task now involved conducting military operations within Afghanistan while working with the Musharraf regime to apprehend enemy leaders and fighters seeking shelter in Pakistan.

The change of strategic priorities affected CENTCOM's operational focus and had a significant impact on combat operations in Afghanistan. General McNeill initially could call upon 6,533 American troops, reinforced by 2,582 allied soldiers, but many had newly arrived in theater or were slated

---

1. CFC OPORD 03, Opns Afghanistan Phase III and IV, CENTCOM, 24 Dec 2001, part 2, Hist Files, OEF Study Grp.

2. OPORD 07, TOA to CJTF-AFG for Phase III and IV Opns in CJOA AFG, CENTCOM, 28 May 2002, p. 4, Hist Files, OEF Study Grp.

to rotate out of Afghanistan in the coming months.³ For instance, Col. John P. Mulholland's TF DAGGER began redeploying to Fort Campbell, Kentucky, in January 2002. The departing Green Berets were replaced by elements drawn from the 3d Special Forces Group, 1st Special Forces Command, from Fort Bragg, North Carolina. The 10th Mountain and 101st Airborne Division elements that took part in ANACONDA were to be replaced by a brigade from the 82d Airborne Division well before the end of the year. Finally, the Canadian infantry battalion and British Royal Marines also were recalled from Afghanistan in 2002.

McNeill's own staff members were new to the theater, and they faced the added challenge of adapting to the ad hoc facilities allocated to Maj. Gen. Franklin L. "Buster" Hagenbeck's CJTF-MOUNTAIN rather than the more developed and supported environs of Camp Doha, Kuwait.⁴ Camp Doha's state-of-the-art facilities and extensive communications infrastructure would be set aside for use as a key command and control node for upcoming operations in Iraq rather than having the installation continue in its role as CENTCOM's primary conduit for operations in Afghanistan. In addition to working in spartan conditions, McNeill's staff had to adjust to operating with fewer troops because of the personnel ceilings that remained in place for the Afghan effort. The shift in priorities did not mean, however, that CENTCOM would ignore Afghanistan in the coming months. Assigning McNeill, a three-star general—a leader who was capable of planning, changing tactical direction, and synchronizing efforts—to Bagram to oversee the completion of Phase III and transition to Phase IV sent a powerful strategic message to the Afghans, coalition partners, and the international community.

PLANNING COLLIDES WITH REALITY

Counterterrorism took clear precedence over CJTF-180's other missions in late spring 2002. Reflecting the Bush administration's concern with another attack on the United States, CENTCOM commander Franks' guidance to McNeill emphasized the need to remove militarized Islamic fundamentalists from Afghanistan.⁵ According to the original campaign plan, that task involved the application of "continuous pressure against all known nodes of global terrorist organizations, associated terrorist groups, and sponsoring states."⁶ Continuous pressure against the terrorists who had launched the September 11th attacks and the radical Islamic political party that had sheltered them would involve targeted operations against developing threats.

---

3. Presentation, CENTCOM, 17 Apr 2002, sub: Personnel in Afghanistan AOR, slides 3, 5, Hist Files, OEF Study Grp.

4. Assessment, Future Planning Element, CENTCOM, 17 Apr 2002, sub: OEF-Afghanistan, Phase III, p. 50, Hist Files, OEF Study Grp; Concept of Opns, CENTCOM, 4 Apr 2002, sub: Establishment of CJTF-180, p. 1, Hist Files, OEF Study Grp.

5. Concept of Opns, Final Draft, CENTCOM, 16 Apr 2002, sub: Establishment of CJTF-180, p. 4, Hist Files, OEF Study Grp.

6. Theater Campaign Plan, CENTCOM, 26 Nov 2001, sub: Operation ENDURING FREEDOM, p. 29, Hist Files, OEF Study Grp.

As Franks wrote in the order dispatching McNeill's headquarters, "the exploitation of intelligence from sites, detainees, and materials enabling the preemption and disruption of future global acts of terrorism [will be] . . . the most critical product of our [Phase III] operations."[7]

According to this premise, ending combat precipitously in Afghanistan in order to focus on nation building would make it harder for coalition forces to gather information on their elusive enemy. Large-scale engagements, such as at Tora Bora and the Shahi Kot Valley, had been productive, and American troops had collected significant amounts of documents from the battlefield. Both engagements also produced collateral benefits, as large numbers of enemy combatants fled from Afghanistan to Pakistan, where the Pakistani Inter-Services Intelligence apprehended a number of foreigners and turned them over to coalition forces. Pakistani intelligence, however, was far less willing to apprehend Afghan Taliban fighters. That development, coupled with the Taliban's decision to avoid open confrontations with the Americans and the withdrawal of U.S. collection assets, made it far more difficult to acquire vitally needed intelligence with the methods employed by CFLCC.

Lacking a direct means to gain information on the Taliban and al-Qaeda, CJTF-180 relied on assistance from indigenous partners. Although the United Front had been a reliable ally in the opening phase of the recent campaign, after Kabul fell many of its leaders refocused on promoting their ethnic or personal agendas. As the initial complement of Western soldiers rotated home from Afghanistan, some proxy militias furthered their own agendas by taking advantage of coalition and U.S. unfamiliarity with Afghan culture and history. CJTF-180 thus inherited a collection of ideologically diverse proxy forces when compared to the Afghan militias that aided TF DAGGER.

Other factors contributed to the challenges facing CJTF-180 as it assumed responsibility for counterterrorism operations in Afghanistan. The withdrawal of intelligence and surveillance assets, when coupled with the reduction of Special Forces assets and the growing reliance on militias, materially impacted CJTF-180's ability to locate and engage al-Qaeda and Taliban remnants in Afghanistan. The reduced numbers of air- and space-based intelligence collection platforms made it increasingly vital to extract information from captive enemy fighters. That responsibility rested with American troops after the United Front demonstrated on two occasions—the suffocation of detainees transported from Kunduz to Shibirghan prison and the uprising at the Qala-i-Jangi fortress—that it could not process, safeguard, or secure detainees in a consistent manner. This development placed the burden of extracting targetable information from enemy combatants on CIA operatives and U.S. Army interrogators. Unfortunately, the sheer number of prisoners, combined with growing emphasis on the timely collection of information from captives, drew less-qualified personnel to the task, such as U.S. Army Special Forces and military police.

Few Pentagon or CENTCOM officials predicted the degree to which detention and interrogation operations would draw the American-led

---

7. OPORD 07, TOA to CJTF-AFG for Phase III and IV Opns in CJOA AFG, CENTCOM, 28 May 2002, p. 6.

coalition into a lengthy justification of its policy toward captured enemy combatants. These prisoners wore no uniform and had no recognizable military hierarchy, yet an understaffed intelligence apparatus had to determine which of them had information of immediate value, which posed a threat to U.S. forces or the United States itself, which were merely opportunists or misguided youths, and which were innocent civilians caught in the wrong place at the wrong time. A scarcity of vetted translators fluent in Pashto, Urdu, and Dari significantly hindered the collection of information. Further complicating this critical battlefield function, Army intelligence in 2002 was still transitioning from the Cold War model of locating and identifying large conventional maneuver forces to understanding networks, ideological warfare, and individual targeting. An intelligence system that had deemphasized human intelligence collection suddenly had to rely on that very source for actionable intelligence.[8]

The arrival of General McNeill's command did not significantly improve the situation. Detailed detainee operations were not normally part of the peacetime training regimen for a corps headquarters; for that level of command, computer simulations focused solely on combat operations usually were sufficient. Peacekeeping operations in the Balkans, where civilian authorities held jurisdiction over detainees in all instances, had not provided opportunities for practical experience in detaining individuals under military jurisdiction. Subsequent investigations into detention irregularities identified deficiencies such as a lack of standardized techniques, inadequately trained personnel, and scarce assets for facility construction. The pressing need for actionable intelligence, coupled with the limited initial capacity at Guantanamo Bay Naval Base in Cuba, meant that military authorities at Bagram and Kandahar held prisoners for far lengthier periods than anticipated.

Another factor that prolonged detainments was the difficulty in ensuring that terrorist organizations did not reemerge within Afghanistan after the Taliban's defeat and al-Qaeda's flight to Pakistan and Yemen. As tactical operations increasingly relied on information from human sources, interrogations became more important. The personnel who questioned captive enemy fighters used the techniques prescribed in *Intelligence Interrogation* (Department of the Army Field Manual 34–52), published in 1992. The fourteen authorized approaches used when interrogating enemy detainees were designed to break down a prisoner's resistance to questioning and collect information in a manner permitted by the Geneva Conventions. None permitted physical contact, sleep deprivation, or the withholding of food, water, or shelter.[9]

Nevertheless, detainees flown to Guantanamo Bay Naval Base were subject to different rules. In February 2002, Secretary of Defense Donald H. Rumsfeld and President George W. Bush determined that al-Qaeda and Taliban captives were "unlawful combatants" and not entitled to enemy

---

8. Interv, Col Bryan R. Gibby, OEF Study Grp, with Lt Gen Mary Legere, HQDA Asst Ch of Staff G–2, 4 Aug 2015, pp. 2–4, Hist Files, OEF Study Grp.

9. Wright et al., *A Different Kind of War*, p. 221.

prisoner-of-war protections, even though the conflict in Afghanistan would be "consistent with the principals of Geneva."[10] However, lumping the Taliban and al-Qaeda together in the same general category merely obscured intelligence collection priorities, mainly by neglecting to separate actual practitioners of global terrorism from followers of Mullah Mohammed Omar's brand of Afghan-centric Islamic rule.

The Bush administration implied that detainees would receive humane treatment, but its "unlawful combatant" classification was problematic, especially as interrogation techniques approved for high-level strategic detainees held at Guantanamo migrated to the ENDURING FREEDOM theater. Interrogations at Guantanamo included "enhanced techniques," such as sleep deprivation and waterboarding, which had been established by the DoD but were limited to specific individuals and were to be conducted with adequate leadership and safeguards.[11] By contrast, soldiers at the Bagram facility, lacking sufficient guidance and resources, began applying unapproved interrogation methods and techniques to uncooperative detainees in 2002. According to one investigation, a sudden influx of detainees combined with supervisory failure, low unit cohesion, unclear policy, and unfamiliarity with doctrine created an environment in which detainee abuse was likely to occur.[12] Three unapproved techniques alleged to have been employed in Afghanistan—sleep deprivation, threats to family, and physical abuse—were used in incidents leading to the deaths of Mullah Habibullah, the brother of a Taliban commander, and Dilawar, a 22 year-old taxicab driver.[13]

Although there is no direct connection between the abuses committed at the Bagram facility and decisions made by leaders in theater or at the

---

10. James Schlesinger et al., *Final Report of the Independent Panel to Review DoD Detention Operations*, Aug 2004, p. 33, http://www.dtic.mil/dtic/tr/fulltext/u2/a428743.pdf, Hist Files, OEF Study Grp. The topic of Guantanamo is an emotional one for opponents and supporters. For an example of how audiences in Southwest Asia reacted to CIA revelations about interrogation techniques used there, see Ahmad Tariq, "6 Most Horrific Torture Techniques Used by Americans at Guantanamo," *Daily Pakistan Global*, 17 Aug 2016, https://en.dailypakistan.com.pk/opinion/blog/6-most-horrific-torture-techniques-america-used-at-the-guantanamo-bay/, Hist Files, OEF Study Grp. Senior CIA officials characterized a 2014 Senate Select Committee on Intelligence report detailing interrogation techniques at Guantanamo as a "one-sided study marred by errors of fact and interpretation—essentially a poorly done partisan attack on the agency that has done the most to protect America after the 9/11 attacks." See "Ex-CIA Directors: 'Interrogations Saved Lives,'" *Wall Street Journal*, 10 Dec 2014, https://www.wsj.com/articles/cia-interrogations-saved-lives-1418142644, Hist Files, OEF Study Grp.

11. Schlesinger et al., *Final Report of the Independent Panel to Review DoD Detention Operations*, p. 35.

12. Ibid., pp. 29, 37.

13. V Adm A. T. Church, *Review of Department of Defense Detention Operations and Detainees Interrogation Techniques*, Ofc of the Sec Def, 7 Mar 2005, p. 228, http://humanrights.ucdavis.edu/resources/library/documents-and-reports/ChurchReport.pdf, Hist Files, OEF Study Grp; Carlotta Gall and David Rohde, "New Charges Raise Questions on Abuse at Afghan Prisons," *New York Times*, 17 Sep 2004, https://www.nytimes.com/2004/09/17/world/asia/new-charges-raise-questions-on-abuse-at-afghan-prisons.html, Hist Files, OEF Study Grp.

Pentagon, CENTCOM's decision to deploy CJTF-180 without its normal associated military intelligence and military police brigades made McNeill's position more difficult. That decision reflected the difficulty of identifying what changes needed to be made to the campaign plan after the transition from Phase II to Phase III. The requirement to secure, screen, safeguard, and extract useful knowledge from detainees in a timely manner presented CJTF-180 with increasingly complex logistical, administrative, security, and legal challenges. Although the presence of the 202d Military Intelligence Battalion helped mitigate some issues, McNeill still operated under an unofficial and ambiguous cap on the number of soldiers he could deploy, which forced him to weight his force with frontline combat formations and leaders over enablers and supervisors. The cap on the size of his headquarters produced a relatively low ratio of support personnel to combat troops, but it also flattened the chain of command to a point where McNeill's staff became directly involved in tactical missions normally left to subordinate headquarters. The absence of intelligence and military police brigades, therefore, hobbled CJTF-180's capabilities to manage and interrogate detainees during the crucial initial months of its deployment.

Even as the detainee population in Afghanistan continued to grow, CJTF-180 did not receive the interrogators, translators, and trained military police it needed to swiftly process and interrogate prisoners in a safe and timely manner. DoD instructions to hold any detainee who "may pose a threat to U.S. interests, held intelligence value, or may be of interest for U.S. prosecution" further complicated McNeill's position.[14] This shortcoming prevented U.S. forces in Afghanistan from understanding the hierarchies, plans, operations, and personalities of al-Qaeda, Taliban, and others right when such information would be most useful to CJTF-180, as it extended its reach in search of terrorists and their sanctuaries.

Counterterrorism

The XVIII Airborne Corps exercised operational authority over or was the supported command for all American combat units in Afghanistan.[15] Upon arrival, their forces were arrayed with 3,352 service members at Kandahar Airfield, 2,567 at Bagram Air Base, 368 in Kabul, 89 in Khost, and 30 in Mazar-e Sharif.[16] Along with the staff in McNeill's reduced-strength headquarters and coalition soldiers who had deployed under the Enduring Freedom banner, these troops constituted the means the CJTF-180 commander had to conduct counterterrorism. In addition to counterterrorism operations, CENTCOM

---

14. Schlesinger et al., *Final Report of the Independent Panel to Review DoD Detention Operations*, pp. 64–66.

15. Concept of Opns, final draft CENTCOM, 16 Apr 2002, sub: Establishment of CJTF-180, pp. 3, 18; Annex J (Cmd Relationships) to CFC OPORD 07, CJTF-180, CENTCOM, 20 May 2002, pp. 2–4, Hist Files, OEF Study Grp.

16. The remaining 127 service members were dispersed throughout the country, mostly at Operational Detachment Alpha (ODA) safe houses. Presentation, CENTCOM, 17 Apr 2002, sub: Personnel in Afghanistan AOR, slide 3.

Troops from the 3d Battalion, 187th Infantry Regiment, on a search-and-attack mission near Narizah as part of Operation MOUNTAIN LION.

tasked the XVIII Airborne Corps to plan the transition from Phase III to Phase IV. The changeover from intelligence-driven combat operations to a predominantly civil-military approach would formally occur when efforts by coalition forces and their indigenous proxies to prevent international terrorist organizations from reemerging showed consistent signs of progress.[17] To prepare for that change, CENTCOM directed McNeill to plan a "reshaping of the force" and "complete active HA [humanitarian assistance] projects" simultaneously with combat operations.[18] In General Franks' view, initiating civil-military operations in Phase III would pacify the populace, aid the XVIII Airborne Corps' counterterrorism efforts, build support for the Afghan Interim Authority, and set the conditions for disengagement at the end of the Bonn Process.

McNeill did not change how Lt. Gen. Paul T. Mikolashek and General Hagenbeck were operating during his first three months in Afghanistan. Arriving in the middle of Operation MOUNTAIN LION, a multiphased sequel to Operation ANACONDA that lasted until August 2002, he continued existing

---

17. Assessment, Future Planning Element, CENTCOM, 17 Apr 2002, sub: OEF-Afghanistan, Phase III, p. 36.

18. In his concept of operations for the XVIII Airborne Corps headquarters, Franks approved a mission statement that ended with "when directed, transition to FID [foreign internal defense] and security assistance ISO [in support of] international organizations and the emerging government of Afghanistan." OPORD 07, TOA to CJTF-AFG for Phase III and IV Opns in CJOA AFG, CENTCOM, 28 May 2002, secs. 3.C.2.H, 3.C.3.B.7, 3D.1.B.15; Concept of Opns, final draft, CENTCOM, 16 Apr 2002, sub: Establishment of CJTF-180, p. 5.

operations and authorized new ones to remove international terrorists from Afghanistan.[19] McNeill sustained MOUNTAIN LION and launched a new operation, CHAMPION STRIKE, because he recognized that the enemy had either melded into village life or fled to Pakistan. At this stage of his campaign, McNeill sought intelligence by ordering active patrolling by combat units in areas that CENTCOM had designated as terrorist-laden, in hopes that they would make contact with enemy forces (*Map 5.1*).

McNeill's main strength in these efforts came from his own XVIII Airborne formation in Fort Bragg. In August 2002, Col. James L. Huggins' 3d Brigade, 82d Airborne Division (Task Force PANTHER), composed of Lt. Col. Ronald Rice's 1st Battalion, 505th Infantry; Lt. Col. David T. Gerard's 1st Battalion, 504th Infantry; Lt. Col. Martin P. Schweitzer's 3d Battalion, 505th Infantry; Lt. Col. Charles K. Hardy's 1st Battalion, 319th Field Artillery; and a number of supporting units, replaced both Col. Kevin V. Wilkerson's 2d Brigade, 10th Mountain Division and Col. Francis J. Wiercinski's 3d Brigade, 101st Airborne Division.[20]

Operation CHAMPION STRIKE shifted the focus of operations eastward. Like MOUNTAIN LION, it was based on an understanding of the enemy presence in Afghanistan that predated Operation ANACONDA. The operation targeted the valley running between western Pakistan and the Bermal District in Paktika Province thought to be "an alternate route for possible AQ/TB [al-Qaeda/Taliban] reconstitution efforts."[21] After reconnaissance, cordon, and search missions, elements of Colonel Huggins' TF PANTHER executed "search and attack" operations to defeat the enemy.[22] During the course of the operation, Colonel Gerard's 1st Battalion detained eight men, including a suspected al-Qaeda financier. The Americans also seized 150 AK47 rifles, 200 improvised explosive devices (IEDs), a mortar, cases of hand grenades, rocket launchers, heavy machine guns, "a bucketful of satellite phones, passports, a poster of Osama Bin Laden, and Taliban and al-Qaeda documents."[23]

To conduct these operations, CJTF-180 employed a variation of a targeting method known as Effects-Based Operations. Initially devised by Air Force theorists during Operation DESERT STORM before being adopted by Army Special Operations for use during ground operations, this method

---

19. As McNeill reflected in retirement, "It was always my understanding . . . that the goal was to enable the Afghans so that they could take responsibility for their own turf." Interv, Kim Sanborn, CSI, with Gen (Ret.) Dan K. McNeill, frmr ISAF Cdr, 21 Apr 2009, p. 4, Hist Files, OEF Study Grp.

20. Wright et al., *A Different Kind of War*, p. 333. Colonel Huggins also gained additional troops in the form of the 26th Romanian Mechanized Battalion stationed in Kandahar.

21. FRAGO 138 to OPORD 02–03, CJTF-180, 27 Aug 2002, attached to CTF-82 Cmd Rpt, D.1.A.1, Hist Files, OEF Study Grp; Cmd Rpt, CTF-82, A.1.A.3, Hist Files, OEF Study Grp.

22. FRAGO 138 to OPORD 02–03, CJTF-180, 27 Aug 2002, attached to CTF-82 Cmd Rpt, D.1.A.2.

23. Ryan Chilcote, "U.S. Forces Capture 'Al Qaeda Financier,'" CNN, 11 Sep 2002, https://edition.cnn.com/2002/WORLD/asiapcf/central/09/11/ar911.afghan.sweep, Hist Files, OEF Study Grp.

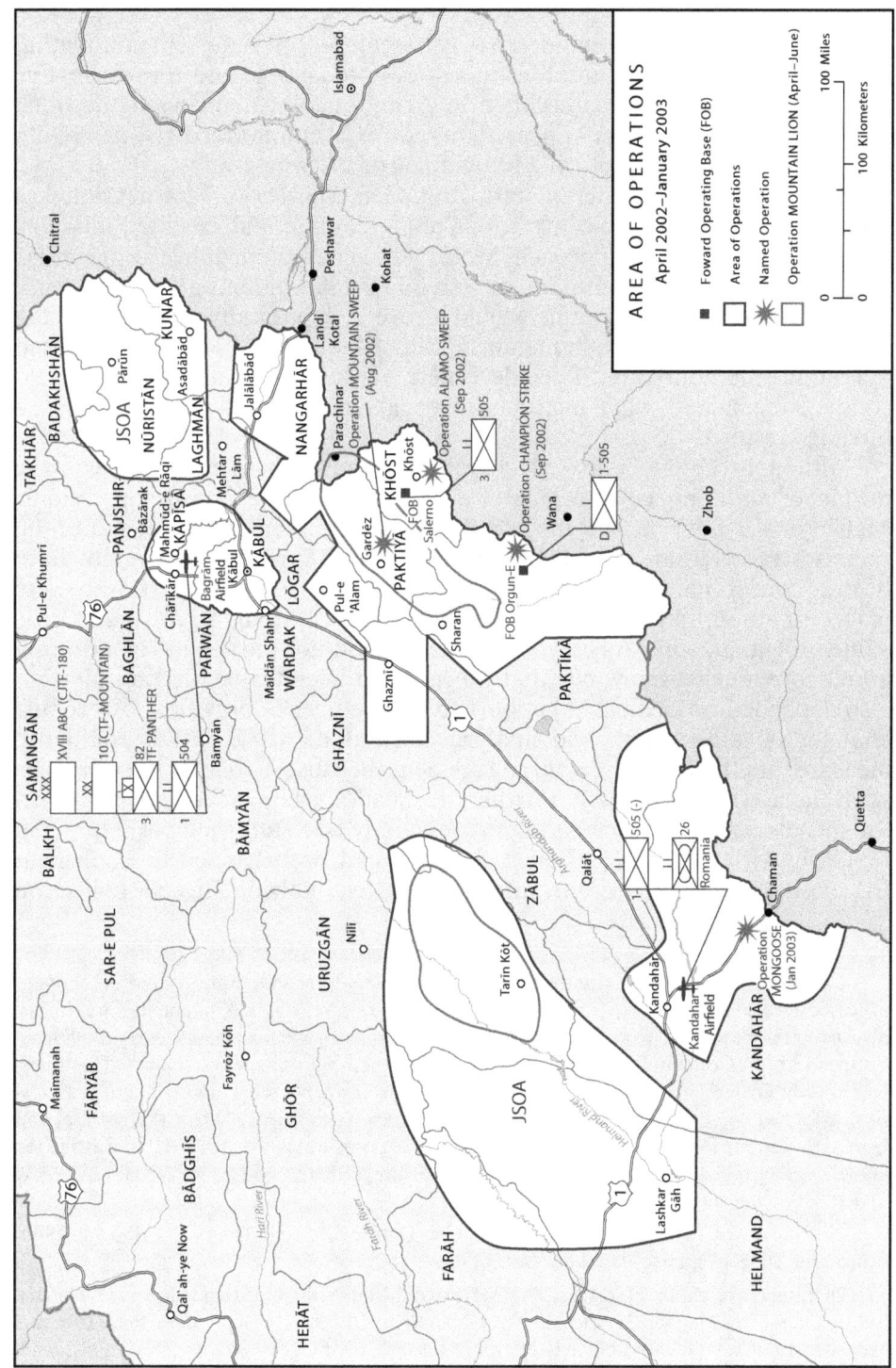

Map 5.1

theoretically offered commanders a way to scale, coordinate, and tailor lethal and kinetic engagements in order to achieve predictable and transformative results.[24] Although not yet codified in Army or joint doctrine at the time, Effects-Based Operations appeared suited for a counterterrorist campaign focusing on killing or capturing individuals or discrete groups.

General McNeill's chief of staff, Brig. Gen. Stanley A. McChrystal, was familiar with how Special Operations units planned and executed missions using this effects-based approach. McChrystal championed the use of similar methods by McNeill's command during CJTF-180's first months in theater.[25] Persuaded that the technique would prove exceptionally effective in the fluid environment of Afghanistan, CJTF-180 planners used effects-based operations methodology to decide which missions to conduct, who should conduct them, and what methods of engagement would best achieve the intended result.[26]

Although the effects-based operational approach seemed like a viable means of utilizing conventional forces for counterterrorism operations, McChrystal's faith in the methodology derived from peacetime training exercises rather than proven battlefield results. The approach might have been a conceptual step in the right direction for Army leaders who were placed in unfamiliar operational environments, but doing so proved of little value in Afghanistan. As conceived, the method not only required thinking about consequences beyond what officers had been trained to consider but also depended on dedicated support from intelligence organizations robust enough to gather, sort, and analyze cultural data. CJTF-180 could not measure the effects of nonlethal engagements because no one on its staff knew what those effects would be. Further, the headquarters lacked the personnel for such an intensive warfighting process; only one staff member interacted regularly with Afghans.[27] Even if the staff had been trained to implement Effects-Based Operations, virtually all of the available intelligence collection

---

24. Military thinkers originally conceived of Effects-Based Operations as a component of Rapid Decisive Operations, the idea that projecting power against an enemy's weakness, if done with speed and from multiple directions, can overwhelm an adversary. J–9 Joint Futures Lab, "A Concept for Rapid Decisive Operations," Whitepaper, v. 2.0, p. 6, Hist Files, OEF Study Group. For other understandings of the concept, see Paul K. Davis, *Effects-Based Operations: A Grand Challenge for the Analytical Community*, Ofc of the Sec Def and United States Air Force (Arlington, Va.: RAND Corporation, 2001), pp. 8–11; and Brig Gen David A. Deptula, "Effects-Based Operations: Change in the Nature of Warfare," *Air & Space Power Journal* 20, no. 1 (Spring 2006): 4–5.

25. Interv, Col Timothy Reese, CSI, with Gen Dan K. McNeill, frmr CJTF-180 and ISAF Cdr, 16 Jun 2008, p. 6, Hist Files, OEF Study Grp.

26. Interv, Maj Philip H. Karns, 49th MHD, with Maj William L. Bialozor, frmr CJTF-180 Future Opns Fires Planner, 31 Aug 2002, p. 4, Hist Files, OEF Study Grp; Interv, Peter Connors and Lisa Mundey, CSI, with Lt Gen (Ret.) John R. Vines, frmr CJTF-180 Cdr, 27 Jun 2007, p. 18, Hist Files, OEF Study Grp.

27. This was British Col. Nick Carter, the head of the corps' planning staff. Interv, OEF Study Grp with Gen Nicholas P. Carter, frmr CJTF-180 Plans Ofcr and Regional Command (RC) South Cdr, 21 Jan 2015, Hist Files, OEF Study Grp.

systems seemed ill-suited to identifying the whereabouts and intentions of both individuals and discrete groups of enemy personnel.

The Effects-Based Operations theory also had other flaws that became apparent over time. The targeting method originally assumed that causality is simple, linear, and immediate. In ENDURING FREEDOM, planners who relied on that assumption soon came to the erroneous conclusion that military action could transform societies in predictable ways. In reality, the changes CJTF-180 was trying to induce were hard to predict, instigate, or measure. Removing Taliban leaders from local communities, although welcome to most Afghans, created power vacuums. Delivering humanitarian assistance provided immediate aid to isolated areas, but this approach was not sustainable and did not improve long-term stability. Even if detained Taliban leaders were replaced by individuals who supported the nascent central government and sustained humanitarian assistance could be provided, the lack of a nationwide communications infrastructure prevented CJTF-180 from advertising those successes in order to influence Afghan opinion. In the end, tactical decisions about how, when, where, and whom to engage had little effect on Afghan willingness to resist a Taliban resurgence.

Decisions about where to conduct missions were just as important to McNeill's counterterrorism approach as decisions about how to operate. CENTCOM had identified more areas of concern than McNeill had troops to patrol. Enemy locations within those areas remained largely unknown by the time CJTF-180 arrived in theater. McNeill responded to this intelligence deficiency in three ways. First, he kept troops at Bagram Air Base and Kandahar Airfield, using them as platforms from which to stage and project combat power. Combined, they provided responsive coverage over most of the area that CENTCOM had identified as being unfriendly to coalition presence. Second, he used helicopters to project companies and battalions on intelligence-gathering missions. This tactic, called air-assaulting, allowed units to surprise, overwhelm, and apprehend individuals in potentially hostile areas in the hope that they would provide actionable intelligence. Third, he relied on Special Forces. Deployed alpha detachments, who often spent weeks living among locals, could learn who the enemy was and who it was not, and the intelligence they provided often was the only information that conventional units received before going out on missions.[28]

Special Forces elements were crucial to the success of early CJTF-180 operations. Soon after TF PANTHER arrived, Australian Special Forces set out to establish a working relationship with their new partners. A pattern quickly developed in which the Australians spent weeks on mission and then informed Huggins' planners what they had learned. Their reports fed effects-based targeting processes used to establish missions.[29] Missions often

---

28. Rpt, Joint Center for Lessons Learned, 10th Mtn Div (Light Inf), 6 Jun 2003, sub: Operation ENDURING FREEDOM, Afghanistan, p. 8; Capt John W. Page, "Operation Viper in the Baghran Valley" (PEP, Maneuver Capts Career Course, Inf Capts Career Course, 9 Feb 2004), p. 2.

29. Interv, Peter Connors, CSI, with Lt Col (Ret.) Ronald M. Stelmasczyk, frmr CTF-82 Ch of Staff, 30 Nov 2006, p. 8, Hist Files, OEF Study Grp.

Soldiers from the 101st Airborne Division secure an area as explosive ordnance and disposal teams deal with a cache of ordnance found during Operation MOUNTAIN LION.

began with reconnaissance by Special Forces and continued with cordon-and-searches, operations in which conventional forces would air-assault into a town or village, secure a perimeter, and methodically search the buildings within the perimeter. These missions, if based on accurate intelligence, would locate the individuals that CJTF-180 wanted to detain without unnecessarily harming or aggravating the local population.[30]

When task forces did not rely on assistance from units familiar with targeted areas, they risked alienating villagers or creating friction between themselves and Special Operations elements already in country. During Operation MOUNTAIN SWEEP (August 2002), the first mission planned by CJTF-180, TF PANTHER entered Zurmat District just south of Gardez, the capital of Paktiya Province, without consulting the two Special Forces detachments in the district.[31] According to a report submitted by ODAs 986 and 314, the brigade initiated the mission with "no intelligence to indicate that any of the targets sought . . . [were] actually in the area."[32] Operating without clear knowledge of who was bad and who was not, soldiers frisked women, destroyed wells, and damaged a house that the ODAs had already cleared.[33]

---

30. Despite efforts to standardize detention procedures, prisoner yields differed greatly across theater. Rpt, Brig Gen Charles Jacoby, 26 Jun 2004, sub: Inspection of CFC-A AO Detainee Operations, p. 948, Hist Files, OEF Study Grp.

31. AAR, Opn MOUNTAIN SWEEP, ODAs 986 and 314, 25 Aug 2002, p. 3, Hist Files, OEF Study Grp.

32. Ibid., p. 5.

33. Ibid., p. 4. According to the ODA, the PANTHER brigade set "U.S. efforts in the region back by 4–6 months." TF PANTHER offers a far different version of events, noting that weapons had

Despite its usefulness to conventional forces, Special Forces' expertise came at a cost. They lacked heavy weapons, which meant they had to siphon heavy mortar teams and mounted machine-gun platoons from deployed conventional forces, thus reducing the latter's numbers and potential scope of operations even further. The widely deployed operational detachments and civil affairs teams depended on armed Afghans for security. ODAs overpaid warlords at the ten firebases they established in Afghanistan, creating employment and financial imbalances that conventional units later had to resolve.[34] Called Afghan Military Forces, Afghan Security Forces, Afghan Guard Forces, or Afghan Security Guards, these armed tribesmen became a source of authority that competed against the Afghan government for influence.[35]

Even though missions during the half year after McNeill established CJTF-180 made it difficult for the Taliban and al-Qaeda to act collectively, sweeps by U.S. troops were not preventing attacks or increasing popular support for the Afghan government created by the Bonn Conference.[36] Operation MOUNTAIN LION "eliminated over 120 sanctuaries, nearly 500 weapon caches and destroyed over 1.2 million pounds of captured ammunition" but did not kill or capture any enemy fighters.[37] TF PANTHER discovered only five weapons and two document caches in MOUNTAIN SWEEP, a sure indicator that preparatory intelligence collection efforts were ineffective.[38] Results did not improve over time as solutions for pervasive intelligence shortcomings remained elusive. When American troops conducted Operation ALAMO SWEEP on 22 September, the same task force cleared two objectives east of

---

been found in a house that belonged to a man personally vetted by the 19th Special Forces Group officer in charge. See Interv, Connors with Stelmasczyk, 30 Nov 2006, p. 11.

34. Rpt, CJTF-180, Sep 2005, sub: Afghan National Police Program, Version 8, p. 90, Hist Files, OEF Study Grp.

35. CENTCOM supported using Afghan Military Forces, which did little to smooth relationships between conventional and Special Forces. Assessment, Future Planning Element, CENTCOM, 17 Apr 2002, sub: OEF-Afghanistan, Phase III, pp. 45–46. Lt. Gen. David W. Barno, who replaced Vines as the senior American commander in Afghanistan, thought the Afghan Military Forces program was a credit to Special Forces ingenuity and retained the program. Interv, Col E. J. Degen, Col Bryan R. Gibby, and Colin J. Williams, OEF Study Grp, with Lt Gen (Ret.) David W. Barno, frmr CFC-A Cdr, 20 Jan 2016, p. 38, Hist Files, OEF Study Grp. U.S. forces in Afghanistan did not decide to disband these groups, now called Afghan Security Forces, until two months after the 2005 parliamentary elections. See OPORD 05–03, ASF Demobilization and/or Transition to GOA ANSF Service, CFC-A, 7 Nov 2005, Hist Files, OEF Study Grp.

36. Memo, Cdr, CJTF-180, 1 Nov 2002, sub: Operational Assessment for Oct 2002, with CJ–3 Info Paper attached, p. 4, Hist Files, OEF Study Grp; Interv, Maj Philip H. Karns, 49th MHD, with Brig Gen Benjamin R. Mixon, Director CJTF-180 Staff, 22 Oct 2002, p. 5, Hist Files, OEF Study Grp.

37. Bfg, CJTF-MOUNTAIN, 13 Jul 2002, sub: Operation MOUNTAIN LION Assessment, slide 5, Hist Files, OEF Study Grp.

38. Operational Sum, OEF II, Task Force (TF) PANTHER, n.d., p. 1, Hist Files, OEF Study Grp.

Soldiers from Company C, 3d Battalion, 505th Infantry Regiment, 82nd Airborne, gather at a safe distance from a local village as the 307th Engineer Battalion destroys a weapons cache during Operation ALAMO SWEEP.

Khost City without making contact with the enemy or seizing significant amounts of documents, weapons, or ammunition.[39]

Throughout this period, CJTF-180 found it difficult to locate the enemy even with the help it received from Special Operations units aided by proxy militia elements. Because Effects-Based Operations required knowledge about targeted populations, commanders often had to conduct operations to gather intelligence instead of letting intelligence drive operations.[40] Existing intelligence systems were ill-suited to meet tactical requirements in Afghanistan. In addition, both CJTF-180 and CENTCOM were slow to acknowledge the extent to which remaining al-Qaeda and Taliban leaders had relocated to Pakistan. As McNeill recalled in a postconflict interview, after the Taliban had gone "to ground" and al-Qaeda had largely perished or fled, CJTF-180 chased "a lot of straws in the wind."[41] McNeill's approach to this problem would evolve over time, but during MOUNTAIN LION, MOUNTAIN SWEEP, and CHAMPION STRIKE (September 2002), it remained centered on launching combat units on forays into CENTCOM-designated areas of interest.[42]

---

39. Ltr, TF PANTHER Opns Ofcr to CTF-82 Opns Ofcr, n.d., sub: TF PANTHER results for ALAMO SWEEP, Hist Files, OEF Study Grp.

40. Interv, Reese with McNeill, 16 Jun 2008, p. 10.

41. Ibid., pp. 8–9.

42. Ibid., p. 10. Before the XVIII Airborne Corps departed Fort Bragg, North Carolina, CENTCOM identified four pockets of resistance for it to address: Paktiya/Paktika/Khost (including Pakistan), Northern Helmand/Uruzgan, Kunar (Pech River Valley), and Kunduz

CJTF-180's continued reliance on intelligence collection systems and information gained through interrogating enemy captives stemmed in part from the limited amount of combat power available to McNeill. American doctrine included the option of employing combat units to aid intelligence collection efforts by conducting operations intended to force the enemy to react, respond, or relocate. CJTF-180's lack of infantry and limited dedicated aviation support constrained its ability to employ those methods. The fierce topography of Afghanistan, with few trafficable roads, placed such a high premium on Army helicopters that McNeill could not afford to dedicate the bulk of those assets to developing the tactical situation through successive air assault operations. As a result, conventional Army rotary-wing assets, and to a lesser degree fixed-wing U.S. Air Force airlift platforms, were involved in myriad everyday tasks such as command and control, close-combat fire support, medical evacuation, reconnaissance, logistics support, transport of ANA recruits to Kabul, counternarcotics support, ballot submission in support of Afghan elections, and movement of detainees to and from interrogation centers.

General McNeill successfully pleaded his case for additional helicopters, which helped to ease the tacit personnel cap that had been in place since November 2001. By summer 2003, one battalion-sized aviation task force operated from Kandahar and one from Bagram. Between them, they had airframes at Khost and fueling points across southeast Afghanistan.[43] In all, seventy-five to eighty helicopters supported both CJTF-180 and CJSOTF-Afghanistan.[44] In comparison, only four helicopters serviced the 5,500 ISAF soldiers, even though ISAF began transitioning from UN to NATO control in April 2003.[45] With only four airframes available for its use, NATO ISAF had only limited ability to help the central Afghan government extend outward.

More helicopters gave CJTF-180 more flexibility, but the additional airframes did not solve McNeill's operational problem. Airframes provided mobility to CJTF-180 at the price of anchoring Army units to airfields. With conventional assets ranging across both CJTF-180 and the Special Operations task force battlespaces, the theater's combat aviation assets

---

Province. Assessment, Future Planning Element, CENTCOM, 17 Apr 2002, sub: OEF Afghanistan, Phase III, p. 5.

43. Interv, Connors and Mundey with Vines, 27 Jun 2007, p. 8.

44. Interv, Charles Stuart Kennedy, United States Institute of Peace, Afghanistan Experience Project, with unidentified Foreign Service Ofcr, frmr member Parwan Provincial Reconstruction Team, 10 Dec 2004, p. 4, Hist Files, OEF Study Grp. Conventional aviation supported Special Forces as well as conventional forces. According to Col. Walter Herd, the CJSOTF commander from summer 2004 to summer 2005, almost all of his aviation support came from the conventional units: "In fact, I did the math and about 95 percent of all our aviation support, like I said, came from the JTF [Joint Task Force], out of either the 10th Mountain Division or the 25th ID [Infantry Division]." Interv, Peter Connors, CSI, with Col Walter Herd, frmr Combined Joint Special Opns Task Force–Afghanistan (CJSOTF-A) Cdr, p. 8.

45. Interv, Kennedy with unidentified Foreign Service Ofcr, 10 Dec 2004, p. 4. The handover from UN to NATO control was completed on 11 August 2003.

regularly traversed lengthy distances.[46] More aviation capability meant more air fields and fuel points, which increased force protection requirements. Constant use of helicopter airframes also necessitated more frequent maintenance, which in turn required additional repair and servicing assets. The influx of additional rotary assets, when combined with the validated need for personnel to satisfy evolving mission requirements, eventually required higher force levels.

FROM CIVIL AFFAIRS TASK FORCES TO RECONSTRUCTION TEAMS

Civil-military affairs presented opportunities and challenges different from combat operations. DoD and CENTCOM strategists originally hoped that relieving Afghan suffering would solidify coalition support and generate favorable world opinion.[47] McNeill agreed. In his view, humanitarian efforts gave coalition forces time and space to complete their mission. He understood that counterterrorism included preventing humanitarian disasters—at least those for which coalition forces could be held responsible—and coordinating reconstruction efforts. Noncombat operations would be an important element of his campaign to secure Afghanistan.

Civil-military operations entailed more than humanitarian assistance. Every interaction between service members and Afghan civilians, from providing medical and dental aid to connecting nongovernmental organizations with indigenous populations, was part of civil-military operations. Once combat operations had diminished in size and frequency, noncombat operations would help prevent Afghanistan from serving as a staging base for future terrorists.

CENTCOM resourced CJTF-180 for civil affairs by establishing the Combined Joint Civil-Military Operations Task Force and deployed it in support of General Mikolashek's Coalition Forces Land Component Command. Led by Brig. Gen. John H. Kern since May 2002, this organization consisted of the Army Reserve's 489th Civil Affairs Battalion, which had replaced the 96th Civil Affairs Battalion, under a brigade-level headquarters.[48] It provided guidance, coordinated with U.S. Civil Affairs Teams–Afghanistan and international coalition humanitarian liaison

---

46. Interv, Connors and Mundey with Vines, 27 Jun 2007, pp. 14–15.

47. One analyst has argued that "ethical foreign policy has become of central importance to . . . [a] government's legitimacy at home." David Chandler, *From Kosovo to Kabul and Beyond: Human Rights and International Intervention* (Ann Arbor, Mich.: Pluto Press, 2006), p. 64. Such policies have become a way of diffusing responsibility for the horrors of intervention, military and otherwise. Ibid., p. 70.

48. The 489th Civil Affairs Battalion, under the impression that it would be in Afghanistan for only a few months, did not deploy at full strength, and operated with reduced personnel until the rest of the unit arrived. As the full scope of its mission became clear, it received individual augmentees from the Army Reserve's New York–based 401st Civil Affairs Battalion.

An Army civil affairs unit fords a river in Uruzgan Province.

cells, and advised the transitional government.[49] Civil Affairs Teams–Afghanistan were small, self-contained teams of civil affairs specialists and Special Operations soldiers who interacted with Afghans in unsecure or less accessible areas. Humanitarian liaison cells were teams of six civil affairs soldiers deployed near selected population centers to coordinate with and assist international and nongovernmental humanitarian organizations seeking to deliver aid to the Afghan people. The humanitarian liaison cells assumed a more direct role over time when other agencies were unwilling or unable to provide needed goods and services to Afghans.[50]

After three months commanding the civil-military task force while overseeing the efforts of the Office of Military Cooperation–Afghanistan to build the nascent ANA, General Kern transferred his civil-military responsibilities to Col. George P. Maughan, the 360th Civil Affairs Brigade commander. Almost immediately, Colonel Maughan established two civil-military operations centers outside Kabul. These centers served as secure sites where military representatives, civilians, the medical community, and aid workers could interact without travelling to the Afghan capital.[51] Working with Special Forces and the UN Assistance Mission in Afghanistan, Maughan posted additional teams and liaisons throughout the countryside.[52]

---

49. Interv, Dennis Van Wey, CSI, with Col Michael E. Stout, frmr CENTCOM Civil-Mil Planner, 24 Apr 2007, pp. 3, 5–6, Hist Files, OEF Study Grp; Interv, Mark D. Sherry, CMH, with Col George P. Maughan, frmr CJCMOTF Cdr, 22 Nov 2002, p. 12, Hist Files, OEF Study Grp.

50. Briscoe et al., *Weapon of Choice*, pp. 251–52; Wright et al., *A Different Kind of War*, p. 194.

51. Interv, Dennis Van Wey, CSI, with Col George P Maughan, frmr CJCMOTF Cdr, 24 Aug 2007, pp. 9–10, Hist Files, OEF Study Grp.

52. Ibid., p. 9.

Although fewer in number and more restricted in scope than he wanted, these organizations provided a rudimentary structure for coordinating humanitarian assistance and identifying candidates for rural reconstruction and development.

By late 2002, the American civil-military effort in Afghanistan involved two operations centers, seven humanitarian liaison cells, and eleven civil affairs teams.[53] One civil-military operations center and its three subordinate humanitarian liaison cells were located north of the Hindu Kush in Uzbekistan; a second civil-military operations center was sited south of the Hindu Kush and tied in with around six humanitarian liaison cells. However, the liaison cells and operations centers, along with Maughan's own staff, numbered only 221 personnel. Recognizing that these resources alone were insufficient to meet the needs of the populace in war-torn Afghanistan, Maughan constantly sought to increase the number of civil-military operations centers in Afghanistan.[54]

Maughan focused on creating more centers because he knew CENTCOM wanted to assist nongovernmental and international aid organizations rather than supplant their efforts using U.S. civil affairs assets. Upon assuming responsibility for Afghanistan, CJTF-180 implemented CENTCOM's guidance by tasking the Combined Joint Civil-Military Operations Task Force "to fix responsibility for humanitarian assistance on UN, UNHCR [United Nations High Commissioner for Refugees], NGO/IO [nongovernmental organizations/international organizations], AIA [Afghan Interim Authority], and OGAs [other governmental agencies]."[55] Like his predecessor, however, McNeill discovered that the U.S. military had only a limited amount of influence over civilian humanitarian organizations, despite having a common purpose. Because American civil affairs teams had been interacting directly with Afghans long before international agencies and civilian humanitarian organizations reappeared, this revelation had little impact on CJTF-180's approach. McNeill continued to employ civil affairs in a manner similar to TF MOUNTAIN's use of humanitarian liaison cells to determine where to "focus combat operations."[56] Civil affairs personnel collected and reported the local Afghans' perceptions of key aspects of the campaign, such as how they felt about coalition forces, enemy strength, and the need for developmental assistance. Unfortunately, the U.S. military had yet to develop an effective fusion process that allowed analysts to combine information collected by

---

53. Interv, Brandi Ershif, CMH, with Col George P. Maughan, frmr CJCMOTF Cdr, 13 Oct 2011, pp. 19, 30, Hist Files, OEF Study Grp. See also Concept of Opns, CENTCOM J–5, 16 Apr 2002, sub: CONOP for establishing CJTF-180, p. 25, Hist Files, OEF Study Grp.

54. Interv, Sherry with Maughan, 22 Nov 2002, pp. 29, 58; Interv, Van Wey with Maughan, 24 Aug 2007, p. 9.

55. Memo, CENTCOM for XVIII Airborne Corps (ABC) (CJTF-180), 6 May 2002, sub: Operation ENDURING FREEDOM, p. 23, Hist Files, OEF Study Grp.

56. Interv, Neil Rogers, CSI, with Col Don Amburn, frmr 489th Civil Affairs Bn Cdr, 7 Dec 2006, p. 6, Hist Files, OEF Study Grp.

civil affairs teams with knowledge gained from Special Forces in order to provide better situational awareness for commanders.[57]

Although CJTF-180 could not use their reporting to the fullest, civil-military operations strove to overcome numerous obstacles to help ordinary Afghans. Metrics gauging the actual benefit of these efforts remained elusive. American authorities highlighted the fact that $296 million in aid "helped avert a famine" in 2002 and 2003, but they did not know whether or not the relief supplies actually went to the parties most in need of assistance.[58] While Maughan reported to CJTF-180 that the civil-military task force approved or was in the process of approving 305 overseas humanitarian disaster and civic aid projects totaling over $14 million by 1 January 2003, he did not differentiate between projects driven by American assessments and those requested by Afghans.[59] The civil affairs effort had other critical flaws. Soon after arriving at Bagram, British Col. Nicholas P. "Nick" Carter, the CJTF-180 planning director, recognized that civil affairs teams and liaisons could project influence on behalf of only the U.S. Army, not the Afghan Interim Authority. Colonel Carter wanted to "connect governance to people" and proposed posting "joint regional teams" in cities other than Kabul for this purpose.[60]

Carter's idea might have remained conceptual if Lt. Col. Michael E. Stout, a reserve civil affairs officer, had not visited Afghanistan with CENTCOM's draft political-military plan for ENDURING FREEDOM.[61] Colonel Stout believed that joint regional teams could transfer theater responsibility from the military to the U.S. Agency for International Development, the agency identified in the plan as the lead for American reconstruction efforts in Afghanistan.[62] In a short time, Stout convinced McNeill not only to convert four civil-military operations centers into what Karzai relabeled as Provincial Reconstruction Teams, but also to give each an infantry platoon for security.[63]

---

57. Daniel Helmer, "Twelve Urgent Steps for the Advisor Mission in Afghanistan," *Military Review* 87, no. 4 (Jul–Aug 2008): 75.

58. This figure is arrived at by adding the value of 434,870 metric tons of wheat funded through two programs ($245 million) with the value of 2,489,880 daily rations dropped from transport aircraft into Afghanistan (about $50.9 million). Rpt to Congressional Committees, U.S. Government Accountability Ofc, *Afghanistan Reconstruction*, p. 16.

59. Memo, Col George P. Maughan, Cdr, CJCMOTF, for Lt Gen Daniel K. McNeill, Cdr, CJTF-180, 5 Jan 2003, sub: OHDACA Status Report as of 1 Jan 2003, p. 3, Hist Files, OEF Study Grp.

60. Interv, OEF Study Grp with Carter, 21 Jan 2015.

61. Interv, Van Wey with Stout, 24 Apr 2007, p. 6.

62. Ibid., p. 8.

63. Colonel Stout's role in finalizing and promoting the Provincial Reconstruction Team concept began in a meeting with CJTF-180 chief of staff Brig. Gen. Benjamin R. Mixon, when he mentioned that CENTCOM's draft political-military campaign assigned leadership of Phase IV to the U.S. Agency for International Development. Stout visited the CJTF-180 joint planning staff after the meeting, learned of the reconstruction concept developed by Colonel Carter, adjusted its organization, and won McNeill's approval of the concept. McNeill had Stout brief the plan in a commander's update, and the combined joint operations

Multiple actors working independently toward common goals made it possible to form these reconstruction teams. The concept had no single progenitor and, in its early development, no agreed purpose. Realizing that current civil affairs entities were few in number and restricted in what they could do, commanders modified organizational structures which, over time, resulted in reconstruction teams replacing operations centers as the accepted instrument for reconstruction, development, and other postconflict missions.[64] Humanitarian liaison cells, which Maughan had placed under civil operations centers, began answering to Provincial Reconstruction Team commanders. Eventually, the Combined Joint Civil-Military Operations Task Force completely subordinated all their operations centers and liaison cells to the reconstruction teams. Constituting one of the most original and adaptive elements of the ENDURING FREEDOM campaign, reconstruction teams emerged in form and importance from well-intentioned efforts to increase the effectiveness of civil affairs operations.

General McNeill's planners designed reconstruction teams as self-contained units capable of influencing populations in strategically important areas of the country. In addition to a maneuver platoon, they ideally included a State Department representative, U.S. Agency for International Development officials capable of funding and overseeing developmental projects, U.S. Department of Agriculture experts, engineers, and an Afghan interior ministry colonel to represent the Afghan government. Although rarely filled to their full complement, teams were designed to house experts capable of improving Afghan communities. Geography was the primary factor in determining their initial locations. The first team established was the Gardez team in Paktiya Province, which began operations on 1 January 2003.[65] The site did not require significant construction and could be established quickly.[66] Reachable by air, it could be supported logistically. Gardez was close enough to Kabul to feel the extended reach of the national government, and close enough to their higher headquarters in Bagram.

---

command subsequently issued orders to staff the first three stations. Stout spent the next few months selling the project to American commanders, who did not want to lose resources or personnel to the effort; to coalition partners, who were reluctant to absorb the expenses of team ownership; to President Karzai, who wanted to direct how U.S. development funding was spent; and to audiences back home, which generally were receptive to the idea. Ibid., pp. 6–9, 10, 12, 13–17.

64. According to Colonel Maughan, "It just so happened that it [the establishment of Civil-Military Operations Centers] coincided with CJTF-180's PRT [Provincial Reconstruction Team] concept. So, basically, it laid out perfect with the PRT concept." Interv, Van Wey with Maughan, 24 Aug 2007, p. 11.

65. Originally, Bamyan was going to be the first Provincial Reconstruction Team established. Memo, Cdr, CJTF-180, 1 Nov 2002, sub: Operational Assessment for Oct 2002, with CJ3 Info Paper attached, p. 10. After Gardez was chosen, Bamyan became the fourth team established. Mazar-e Sharif (Balkh Province) was the second and Maimanah (Faryab Province) was the third, both in July 2003. After Bamyan, Parwan (November 2003), Herat (December 2003), Kandahar (December 2003), and Kunduz (January 2004) followed.

66. Interv, Lynne Chandler Garcia, CSI, with Gen Victor G. Renuart Jr., frmr CENTCOM Dir of Opns, 31 May 2007, p. 13, Hist Files, OEF Study Grp.

The Gardez team and subsequent reconstruction teams soon became many things to many people. Maneuver commanders saw them as a way to strengthen governors; measure support for the interim government; oversee elections; conduct disarmament, demobilization, and reintegration operations; keep the peace among conflicting local factions; and train local police.[67] Their official mandate was as inclusive as their unofficial one. According to a 2003 agreement between the State Department and the DoD, Provincial Reconstruction Teams were to "extend the authority of the Afghan central government, improve security, and promote reconstruction."[68] The multiple expectations for the teams led Stout to refer to them as "Christmas trees": protected enclaves in the Afghan hinterland upon which the goals, actions, and expectations of development, reconstruction, and government agencies were hung like ornaments.[69] As the teams became the default answer for every question about Afghanistan's future stability, they became increasingly difficult for the civil-military task force to coordinate. Even such a basic purpose of the teams—to extend the influence of the central government to the provinces—meant different things to different parties.[70]

The expectations that CJTF–180 had for reconstruction teams grew because Afghanistan did not have an effective central government. In just nine months, operational commanders had begun to expect the teams to produce results that they did not have the civilian expertise, resources, or mobility to accomplish. Although they were supposed to include a Ministry of Interior colonel, the position was largely symbolic; the colonel would represent the Afghan government but would not have a say in whether the coalition decided to initiate reconstruction. Perhaps because of their marginalization, Karzai rarely filled these billets. As with the attempts to connect provinces to Karzai's Afghan Interim Authority, Provincial Reconstruction Team efforts to advance other aspects of their mission depended on the willingness of the Afghan people to accept a centralized political order that few in the country had ever experienced. Without widespread recognition of Kabul's authority, teams could improve security only by sponsoring local militia forces, a practice that complicated disarmament, demobilization, and reintegration of those same forces. Likewise, civil-military operations could not promote stability by themselves. Even if operations were successful, U.S. military leaders did not want to encourage local Afghans to look to the civil-military units for future assistance instead of professing their loyalty to their new national government. The counterterrorist operations McNeill believed would defeat Afghanistan's enemies required a functioning indigenous government, not

---

67. Interv, Kennedy with unidentified Foreign Service Ofcr, 10 Dec 2004, pp. 8–9.

68. Robert M. Perito, *The U.S. Experience with Provincial Reconstruction Teams in Afghanistan: Lessons Identified*, Special Rpt 152 (Washington, D.C.: United States Institute of Peace, Oct 2005), p. 2; Ofc of CJCS, EO to Cdr, CENTCOM, 22 Dec 2003, p. 4, Hist Files, OEF Study Grp.

69. Interv, Van Wey with Stout, 24 Apr 2007, p. 20.

70. Of their three official missions, Provincial Reconstruction Team commanders generally saw promoting Karzai's interim authority as most important. Perito, *The U.S. Experience with Provincial Reconstruction Teams in Afghanistan*, p. 6.

militarized aid organizations. In the meantime, the Afghan authorities would continue to surrender their right to govern at the local and provincial levels as long as the American-led civil affairs organizations offered a viable alternative.

Replacing Warlords with Government Security Forces

Commanders trying to fill security needs with Afghan troops loyal to the nascent central government in 2002 and 2003 soon realized that attempts to solve one problem gave rise to others. The decision to intervene with few troops made it easier to provision units, but the coalition's reliance on indigenous proxies increased. Employing militias to guard bases enabled coalition humanitarian liaison cells to operate independently, but this contravened efforts to invest stature in the Afghan Interim Authority. In a country where civil life was dominated by tribal protectionism, whoever received aid from the U.S. civil affairs soldiers became allies to them, and whoever did not receive their aid distrusted them. Training national security forces, generally recognized as critical for Afghanistan's existence as an independent state, took time and money. Relying on warlord forces until national forces could be fielded weakened Karzai's effective authority. Regional strongmen like Ismail Khan in the west and Sher Mohammed Akhundzada in the southwest held monopolies on security that their appointments as governor condoned and, in some cases, legalized.[71]

Warlord armies had not always dominated Afghan society. According to Ali Ahmad Jalali, an Afghan scholar and future interior minister, "Traditionally the Afghan governments relied on three military institutions: the regular army, tribal levies, and community militias."[72] Following the invasion, coalition forces did not immediately concern themselves with the first of these institutions, in part because the United Front was a suitable alternative. By summer 2002, with independent strongmen proliferating throughout the country and the shortcomings of the United Front option acknowledged, Operation Enduring Freedom's senior military and political leaders began to recognize the necessity of a military force beholden to the central government.[73]

---

71. Although this situation made little sense at the time to Americans unfamiliar with tribal and ethnic rivalries, Karzai embraced a number of questionable characters in order to weaken the influence of his political competitors. Ismail Khan's influence, for example, could be leveraged against Deputy Defense Minister Abdul Rashid Dostum because the latter had forced Khan to flee to Iran during the Afghan civil war. Sher Mohammed Akhundzada, a fellow Pashtun, was able to counterbalance Tajik and Uzbek influences within the government while also providing Karzai with links to the dominant tribe in Helmand Province.

72. Ali Ahmad Jalali, "Rebuilding Afghanistan's National Army," *Parameters* (Autumn 2002): 75, 82. Jalali believed that Green Berets would have to train only 9,600 soldiers for the regular army and 3,000 border forces.

73. For example, see Ambassador Robert P. Finn's State Department correspondence on Under Secretary of Defense Douglas J. Feith's September 2002 visit to Afghanistan. Memo,

Training Afghan forces proved more difficult than CENTCOM first assumed. When General Franks entrusted McNeill with ENDURING FREEDOM in June 2002, he thought Afghan Army units would start replacing American battalions in half a year.[74] However, this estimate did not factor in the need to generate the number of units necessary to force warlord militias to recognize the Afghan Interim Authority's power. As realized by McNeill and his staff, Afghans could not secure their own country until they had enough formations to counter a resurgent Taliban, neutralize potential internal threats to centralized governance, and safeguard their borders. Fortunately for CJTF-180, CENTCOM had already split the Office of Military Cooperation–Afghanistan off from the Combined Joint Civil-Military Operations Task Force. The former was better suited for guiding the interim government in the training and establishment of a national army because it answered both to McNeill and to the State Department representatives responsible for funding.

Afghan leaders originally hoped to field several army corps—each roughly the equivalent of an American infantry division minus supporting artillery, helicopters, and tanks—in Kabul and the provinces simultaneously.[75] This approach offered long-range flexibility by allowing the Afghans to establish government security forces in the potentially restive Pashtun south. Wanting its counterterrorist forces to enjoy freedom of movement throughout the countryside, the coalition disagreed. In a geographically focused approach that placed little emphasis on future threats, the military cooperation headquarters instead planned "to strengthen the center first while working to cement relationships with the regional leaders."[76] That course of action required increasing supplemental funds from $292 million to $350 million in fiscal year 2003. Expenditures would include not only building the ANA but also reconstituting the Ministry of Defense, fielding border guards, and creating an aviation element.[77] Money would also be spent to address systemic problems within existing ANA units. Poor pay, high illiteracy rates, and ethnic friction hobbled ANA recruiting during the second half of fiscal

---

Robert P. Finn, 30 Sep 2002, sub: DOD Under Secretary Feith Discusses National Army Formation, Reconstruction with Afghan and U.N. Officials, Hist Files, OEF Study Grp.

74. Course of Action (COA) Bfg, CENTCOM to CJTF-180, 16 Apr 2002, sub: Phase III, Afghanistan Operation, p. 10, Hist Files, OEF Study Grp. The first three kandaks graduated in July, August, and October 2002 and were sent to the field to partner with ODAs. Although this practice would continue through 2004, it had mixed results, as the kandaks typically rotated out after a two-month operational period, and the Afghan militia working with ODAs initially viewed the kandaks with distrust. Interv, Jenn Vedder, CSI, with Maj David Haskill, 1 Apr 2010, pp. 7–8, Hist Files, OEF Study Grp.

75. Interv, Maj John Warsinske, 47th MHD, with Lt Col Steve Russell, frmr Plans Ofcr, CFLCC C–5, 8 Jun 2002, pp. 5–7, Hist Files, OEF Study Grp.

76. U.S. Congress, Senate, *Operation Enduring Freedom*, Hearing Before the Committee on Armed Services, 107th Cong., 2d sess., S.Hrg 107–801, 7 Feb and 31 Jul 2002 (Washington, D.C.: U.S. Government Printing Ofc, 2002), p. 117.

77. Info Paper, CCJ5-ANA, 14 Nov 2002, sub: Afghan National Army Training Spt, Hist Files, OEF Study Grp.

year 2002. The first and second *kandaks* (Afghan battalion-sized units) of the ANA had entered training with barely 50 percent of the 600 promised inductees per unit. The third and fourth kandaks, which respectively entered training at 61 percent and 68 percent strength, reflected CJTF-180's increased recruiting effort, leveraging radio programs, videos, and leaflets paid for by State Department contributions equating to $450,000.[78]

Reflecting Washington officials' beliefs that factional fighting was more of a threat to the Kabul regime than a resurgent Taliban operating from Pakistan, CENTCOM established a permanent strength of 50,000 soldiers for the ANA. Supported by American funding, the ANA would temporarily grow to 70,000, or one soldier for every militia fighter thought to be in country. Assuming that disarmament, demobilization, and reintegration efforts reduced warlord forces by 50 percent between August 2003 and 2007, the army required only 35,000 troops to maintain the same ratio. By adding another 15,000 as security against an incomplete reintegration effort, the ANA would have excess from which it could make future cuts.[79]

From 24 August to 2 October 2002, a working group convened by the Office of Military Cooperation's newly arrived commander, Army Maj. Gen. Karl W. Eikenberry, developed a more detailed way forward entitled "A Blueprint for the Afghan Military." Unfortunately, restrictive DoD guidance ensured that General Eikenberry's effort adopted the conceptual flaws inherent in earlier studies by focusing on militias belonging to rogue warlords rather than a resurgent Taliban. Like the CENTCOM analysis, the working group pinned recruitment on disarmament, demobilization, and reintegration efforts.[80] As planned, "regional forces [the mujahideen/Afghan Military Forces]" would be "recruited into the National Guard" and incorporated into "seven ANA Regional Corps."[81] This National Guard would both conduct "internal security operations" and protect the central government against external threats.[82] It would help the coalition in two ways. The first corps to be activated would replace the international force stationed in Kabul.[83] Also, it would grow to "have enough combat power

---

78. Info Paper, CCJ5-ANA, 18 Nov 2002, sub: Need ATA Commitment for Quality ANA Recruits, Hist Files, OEF Study Grp.

79. Attachment from Lt Col Michael S. Weaver to Col Jack G. Smith (USA), Col John W. Bullard (USMC), Mr. Michael D. Fitzgerald, Contractor-DPRA (CTR-DPRA), 3 Aug 2004, sub: Extract on History of 70,000 Endstrength for ANA, pp. 2–3, to Msg, CENTCOM, 231306Z, Aug 03, sub: Concept of Operations for the Refinement of Phase IV Operations in Afghanistan (Afg), submitted in response to 242235Z Jul 03 CJCS Planning Order to CDRUSCENTCOM for the Refinement of Phase IV Operations in Afghanistan, Hist Files, OEF Study Grp; Yaqub Ibrahimi, "Army Develops Despite Militia Disarmament Problems," *Institute for War and Peace Reporting*, 29 Sep 2004, p. 2, https://iwpr.net/global-voices/army-develops-despite-militia-disarmament, Hist Files, OEF Study Grp.

80. Rpt, OMC-A, Oct 2002, sub: A Blueprint for the Afghan Military: A Joint Afghan/Coalition Vision to Rebuild the Afghan Military, p. 7, Hist Files, OEF Study Grp.

81. Ibid.

82. Ibid.

83. Ibid.

Colonel Najibullah, ANA, presents the 1st ANA Kandak to President Hamid Karzai at the Kabul Military Training Center during a graduation ceremony on 23 July 2002.

[to] . . . move forward into any area of Afghanistan and impose its will upon any contending factional force."[84]

As originally conceived, the plan ultimately proved too ambitious in the eyes of Eikenberry's superiors.[85] On 2 February 2003, CENTCOM presented CJTF-180 with a modified plan for training the ANA that phased the steps in "A Blueprint for the Afghan Military" over seven-and-a-half years. The ongoing Phase I would conclude by June 2004 when the Afghan Ministry of Defense fielded the Central Corps in Kabul. In addition to two light infantry brigades, the Central Corps included a quick reaction brigade boasting tank, mechanized, and Special Forces kandaks. In Phase II, slated to occur from June 2004 to December 2006, the Afghan government would field ANA corps in northern, western, and southern Afghanistan as well as form an aviation element. Phase III, which would overlap its predecessor for much of 2006, was devoted to generating as much additional force as possible by June 2008. The final phase would occur when the Ministry of Defense assumed full responsibility for employing and sustaining the ANA. As envisioned by CENTCOM, the Ministry of Defense would be ready by December 2009. The CENTCOM plan also embraced the "train the trainer" concept which

---

84. Interv, Lisa Beckenbaugh, CSI, with Lt Gen Karl Eikenberry, frmr OMC-A Cdr, 27 Nov 2006, p. 4, Hist Files, OEF Study Grp; Interv, Col E. J. Degen and Colin J. Williams with Lt Gen Karl W. Eikenberry, frmr CFC-A Cdr and U.S. Ambassador to Afghanistan, 1 Feb 2016, pp. 16–17, Hist Files, OEF Study Grp.

85. COA Bfg, CENTCOM to CJTF-180, 16 Apr 2002, sub: Phase III, Afghanistan Operation, p. 19; COA Bfg, CENTCOM to CJTF-180, 16 Apr 2002, sub: Phase III, Afghanistan Operation, p. 19; Concept of Opns, CENTCOM J–5, 16 Apr 2002, sub: CONOP for establishing CJTF-180, p. 3.

anticipated Afghans incrementally taking over the roles of instructors from American personnel. The number of American and coalition trainers needed to implement the program varied from 600 personnel in 2003 to less than a hundred in 2009.[86]

The DoD, however, rejected CENTCOM's recommended approach. Acknowledging that training structured along the lines of Special Forces Foreign Internal Defense doctrine failed to address future challenges, Pentagon officials transferred that responsibility to the conventional force.[87] The DoD soon settled upon a plan calling for a conventional brigade not only to conduct training, but also to establish school systems, logistics networks, and accelerate the fielding of supporting arms units. Subordinate to the Office of Military Cooperation, this brigade formed the basis of a new organization named Task Force PHOENIX, after the mythical bird that could regenerate itself after burning to ashes. Resourcing the training effort also pushed McNeill's maximum allowable strength up to 10,000 troops.[88]

First to assume the TF PHOENIX mantle was Col. Mark A. Milley's 2d Brigade, 10th Mountain Division. Choosing an active-duty brigade allowed the DoD to implement the new approach faster than sending a reserve component unit that needed to mobilize before deploying. TF PHOENIX trained the ANA from individual to corps level, with the DoD contracting responsibility for ministerial development to a private company, Military Professional Resources Incorporated.[89] The switch from Special Operations to conventional trainers brought attention to new initiatives, including Embedded Training Teams, squads of coalition advisers that joined kandaks two weeks before graduation and mentored them for months afterward.[90] In addition, new kandaks were certified for combat duties after working with U.S. forces in eastern Afghanistan before being returned to Kabul for assignment with the Central Corps. The multinational approach to the training effort—the French still trained Afghan officers and the British still

---

86. Paper, ANA Program, CENTCOM CCJ5-ANA, 5 Feb 2003, pp. 919, Hist Files, OEF Study Grp.

87. Interv, Beckenbaugh with Eikenberry, 27 Nov 2006, p. 29; Interv, Lynne Chandler Garcia, CSI, with Col Timothy Reese, frmr OMC-A Afghan National Army Design Team Ch, 26 Jun 2007, p. 7, Hist Files, OEF Study Grp.

88. By this time, the coalition habitually used the term *kandak* to describe an Afghan battalion-sized element regardless of type. Each kandak numbered around 600 to 800 personnel with a headquarters and several company-sized units of 100 to 150 personnel apiece. The 10,000 number comes from Interv, Col Bryan R. Gibby, Brian F. Neumann, and Colin J. Williams, OEF Study Grp, with Gen (Ret.) John P. Abizaid, frmr CENTCOM Cdr, 10 Feb 2016, p. 29, Hist Files, OEF Study Grp.

89. Special Inspector Gen for Afghanistan Reconstruction, *Reconstructing the Afghan National Defense and Security Forces: Lessons from the U.S. Experience in Afghanistan* (Arlington, Va.: Special Inspector General for Afghanistan Reconstruction, Sep 2017), p. 19.

90. Interv, Lynne Chandler Garcia, CSI, with Col (P) Mark A. Milley, frmr TF PHOENIX Cdr, 6 Jun 2007, pp. 5, 11, Hist Files, OEF Study Grp. Embedded Training Teams had been conceptualized before the 2d Brigade's arrival. See Position paper, "Building the New Afghan National Army," 1 Nov 2002, Hist Files, OEF Study Grp.

trained Afghan noncommissioned officers—and its Kabul focus remained unchanged.

Growing the ANA challenged both the Kabul government and its American sponsors, although some major problems emerged from the latter's unfamiliarity with Afghan history and culture. In short, the effort was about managing three American mandated inputs (trainers, recruits, and resources) to produce three outputs: qualified soldiers, combat-capable units, and societal representation. To ensure no single ethnic faction dominated the Afghan security sector, the Office of Military Cooperation stood by its earlier decision to form units that represented Afghanistan's ethnic tribes proportionately. A recruiting approach that ignored or trivialized centuries of ethnic tension, coupled with the fact that Pashtun soldiers and Hazara officers were particularly hard to find, made this lofty goal difficult.[91] Several times during his command, Eikenberry had to delay training in order to ensure the units were ethnically balanced.[92]

Despite operational and strategic reluctance to increase America's involvement in Afghanistan, the decision to deploy a second maneuver brigade for training swelled ENDURING FREEDOM in scope, troops, and headquarters. Although Colonel Milley's 2d Brigade initially deployed with only two battalion-sized units and a headquarters company, it received reinforcements once in theater. The goal was to grow the ANA rapidly in support of the Bonn Process, which included not only voting for the head of a transitional government but also selecting National Assembly and provincial council members. However, the DoD's decision to have inexperienced conventional forces absorb this training mission while working with indigenous populations demonstrated the DoD's willingness to relegate Afghanistan's near-term needs to a lower priority, thus freeing up Special Forces units for future operations.

THE ARMY ADAPTS TO THE CAMPAIGNS

By the summer of 2003, the Army's senior leaders acknowledged that they had to plan for lengthy combat operations in both Afghanistan and Iraq.[93] Subsequent changes in the Army's institutional strategy were a reaction not only to the immediate pressures of the two ongoing campaigns, but also to the continued demands of Secretary Rumsfeld's vision of transformation. Rumsfeld's Office of Force Transformation, under V. Adm. Arthur K. Cebrowski, championed a vision of agile, network-centric forces, capable of swift and decisive combat operations, based on the critical operational goals outlined in the 2001 *Quadrennial Defense Review*. Those goals were predicated on making joint forces able to command and control operations

---

91. Initially, the Office of Military Cooperation–Afghanistan attempted to balance ethnicity and to mix former communists with former mujahideen and Western-trained officers. Interv, Beckenbaugh with Eikenberry, 27 Nov 2006, pp. 5, 7, 9.

92. Ibid., p. 5; Interv, Chandler Garcia with Reese, 26 Jun 2007, p. 11.

93. Interv, Lt Col Francis J. H. Park, OEF Study Group, with Maj Gen (Ret.) David A. Fastabend, frmr Ch, HQDA Mil Opns Plans and Policy, 1 Jul 2015, Hist Files, OEF Study Grp.

at expeditionary distances from their home bases, even against anti-access and area-denial threats. Those forces would be able to deny sanctuary to enemies by persistent surveillance, tracking, and precision strikes in all terrains and weather.[94]

The conduct of the first four months of Operation ENDURING FREEDOM and the march to Baghdad at the outset of Operation IRAQI FREEDOM in March 2003 seemed to validate the DoD's visions of transformation and Rapid Decisive Operations. What followed, however, did not conform to that vision. Rather than facing an enemy that would capitulate to a tactically and operationally successful combat force, the Army and the DoD found themselves attempting to reestablish order in areas where previous forms of governance had been removed. In the case of Iraq, it was because of the dissolution of the former Iraqi government, whereas in Afghanistan, it was an attempt to create areas that would be under the direct influence of the Kabul government, in many cases for the first time. Doing so, while protecting the force, dramatically increased the demand for ground troops for both security and for the task of delivering basic services to the local population until their own elected leaders could do so.

TOP-DRIVEN CHANGE

General Peter J. Schoomaker, who succeeded General Erik K. Shinseki as Chief of Staff of the Army on 1 August 2003, faced the immediate challenge of sustaining the force required to conduct combat operations in Iraq and Afghanistan. Troops drawn from all eighteen divisions in the active Army and National Guard had already been involved in one or both conflicts. In the two years following 11 September 2001, the Army activated more than 244,000 Army National Guard and Army Reserve personnel, while committing more than 300,000 soldiers in forward-deployed locations, including the combat theaters, peacekeeping in the Balkans and elsewhere, deterrence in Korea, and numerous other missions throughout the world.[95] At the same time, the Army was still transforming along the path Rumsfeld envisioned.[96]

General Schoomaker's first articulation of his intent for the Army emerged in his inaugural meeting with the Army General Staff Council on 14 August 2003. Contrary to the "short war" concept that formed the core tenet of defense transformation, Schoomaker believed that the conflicts in Iraq and Afghanistan would be lengthy, and that sustained employment of the force would be the norm, not the exception. In that meeting, he laid out two core competencies of the Department of the Army: "Train and Equip Soldiers and Grow Leaders" and "Provide Relevant and Ready Land Power Capability to the Combatant Commander and the Joint Team." Schoomaker then outlined

---

94. Ofc of the Sec Def, *Quadrennial Defense Review Report*, DoD, 30 Sep 2001, p. 30, https://archive.defense.gov/pubs/qdr2001.pdf, Hist Files, OEF Study Grp.

95. Hon. Les Brownlee and Gen Peter J. Schoomaker, "Serving a Nation at War: A Campaign Quality Army with Joint and Expeditionary Capabilities," *Parameters* (Summer 2004): 5.

96. "Schoomaker Sworn in as Army Chief," DoD News Release, 1 Aug 2003, https://archive.defense.gov/releases/release.aspx?releaseid=5572, Hist Files, OEF Study Grp.

fifteen focus areas for emphasis in the near-term, while directing the creation of task forces for their implementation.[97]

Not surprisingly, the dialogue among the teams assigned to Schoomaker's focus areas began to reflect a fundamental change in the assumptions governing the near- and long-term employment of Army forces. Before 2003, the Army had anticipated an episodic war where the bulk of the deployed troops would be freed up at the conclusion of the conflict to address other security challenges. With the first major rotation of forces in Iraq after summer 2003, the teams recognized that instead of an episodic war, the Army faced a protracted conflict while supporting existing requirements for maintaining forces in other regions of the globe.[98] The challenge evolved into figuring out how to provide a sustainable rotation of forces trained and equipped to fight insurgencies in two theaters of war while increasing and improving the Army's overall ability to conduct operations across the full spectrum of conflict.[99] The latter focus reflected the Army's worldwide commitments, which included a conventional combined-arms deterrent capability in Korea and missile defense in support of multiple geographic combatant commanders.

General Schoomaker's special operations background made him comfortable working closely with other services and combatant commanders, as well as using a rotational system to sustain a presence in theater.[100] Schoomaker articulated his overarching vision as a "campaign quality Army with a joint expeditionary mindset," and the similarly-named focus area had the guidance of developing "a mindset and program that embraces requirements for modular, capabilities-based Army forces to achieve joint interdependence in support of Combatant Commander[s]."[101] The initial product of that guidance was a white paper bearing not only Schoomaker's signature, but also that of acting Secretary of the Army the Hon. Romie L. "Les" Brownlee. The task of producing the written intellectual underpinning for all focus areas fell to Brig. Gen. David A. Fastabend, the deputy chief of staff for doctrine, concepts, and strategy at U.S. Army Training and Doctrine Command (TRADOC) headquarters at Fort Monroe, Virginia.

Entitled *Serving a Nation at War: A Campaign Quality Army with Joint and Expeditionary Capabilities*, the white paper also appeared as an article in *Parameters*, the journal of the U.S. Army War College, which made it available for study by defense-oriented think tanks and academia.[102] The

---

97. Interv, Park with Fastabend, 1 Jul 2015.

98. Ibid.

99. Gen Peter J. Schoomaker, "The Army: A Critical Member of the Joint Team Serving the Nation at War," *Army* 53, no. 10 (Oct 2003): 25; Lt Col Todd A. Schmidt, "Evolve or Die: The U.S. Army's Darwinian Challenge" (Monograph, U.S. Army School of Advanced Military Studies, 2013), p. 28.

100. Interv, Park with Fastabend, 1 Jul 2015.

101. Ofc of the Deputy Ch of Staff, G–3/5/7, Capabilities Integration Directorate, *Army Planning Priorities Guidance (APPG), 2006–2023* (Washington, D.C.: HQDA, 2004), pp. 16–17.

102. Brownlee and Schoomaker, "Serving a Nation at War," p. 16.

authors of *Serving a Nation at War* built their vision with the expectation of continuous employment of the force. It was a departure from defense transformation in other ways by pointing out that "our current force is engaged, and in ways we could not perfectly forecast." That observation offered a blunt yet persuasive counterpoint to the Rapid Decisive Operations concept's underlying premise that highly networked intelligence, surveillance, and reconnaissance capabilities, combined with precision strikes, would be sufficient to terminate conflicts swiftly.[103] In the realities of Afghanistan and Iraq, Rapid Decisive Operations had transformed one-sided conventional fights into far more complex operational situations.

Force Generation Supply and Demand

With the DoD offering little in the way of immediate assistance, senior Army leaders sought their own resourcing solutions for two land campaigns of undetermined duration without any foreseeable increase in force structure. Up to the beginning of Enduring Freedom, the Army had organized its force along divisional lines, with the expectation that it would fight those units as divisions. Divisions deploying to the Balkans for peacekeeping or peace-enforcement missions did not always deploy in full strength, and those that did not rotated personnel and units internally to replace those rotating out. When operational needs dictated major changes in task organization, they generally were made at the brigade level, such as the attachment of most of the 3d Armored Cavalry to the 49th Armored Division in Bosnia in 2000. In cases where the mission required a brigade of combat power augmented by higher-echelon command and control, those higher elements were pulled from the division headquarters or sister brigades. This practice tended to cause at least two detrimental effects. First, critical leadership was stripped from units left at home station, degrading their readiness. Second, units that were soon to deploy would have to pull critical personnel from the next unit, which would in turn pull people from a third unit, creating a domino effect that degraded readiness across the board.

The choices imposed on CENTCOM, combined with the short lead times, resulted in the Army deploying units to Afghanistan with remarkably different task organizations. The limited number of available airfields, transport aircraft, and helicopters precluded the employment of the 3d Brigade, 82d Airborne Division, which was the full-strength strategic response force in fall 2001. Rather than sending complete brigade combat teams, the Army pieced together the initial conventional maneuver component sent to Afghanistan from available 10th Mountain Division assets, while the other portions of the division were supporting the Kosovo mission. When more troops were needed following the fall of Kandahar, a second incomplete brigade from the 101st Airborne Division was sent.

A far different situation emerged in late 2002 when the Army began preparing for the invasion of Iraq. Following steady improvements in the

---

103. Ibid., p. 8; Ofc of Force Transformation, *Military Transformation: A Strategic Approach*, 18 Nov 2003, pp. 28–34.

logistical facilities in neighboring Kuwait in the decade following DESERT STORM, the United States built up a ground force for the initial invasion totaling more than 100,000 personnel. Although the Bush administration rapidly achieved its goal of deposing Saddam Hussein, combat operations in Iraq transformed into an unconventional fight instead of concluding. By late 2003, the competing demands for forces in Iraq and Afghanistan were so exacting that a full twenty-four of thirty-three active component combat brigades were deployed, while a third of the maneuver battalions in the National Guard's fifteen Enhanced Separate Brigades also served overseas in combat or peacekeeping assignments.[104] Between March and June 2004, the Army rotated 244,000 soldiers in and out of the CENTCOM area of operations, the largest changeover in the U.S. military's history.[105] The Army was neither structured nor prepared to sustain a commitment of that size for one combat zone, let alone two, especially with other operational commitments around the globe and no respite in sight.

REALITIES OF SUSTAINED RESERVE COMPONENT MOBILIZATION

Two underlying assumptions made in the first reserve component mobilizations turned out to have unforeseen long-term implications. First, policymakers thought that the conflict in Afghanistan would be short in duration, as would fit with the Rapid Decisive Operations mindset. Second, they believed that reserve components would not need to mobilize more than once. A critical condition set under the terms of the presidential mobilization was that no service member could be mobilized without their permission for more than twenty-four months, including training time. Twenty-four months was a considerable amount of time on a service member's "clock," providing enough time for a year-long rotation plus training and demobilization. However, two rotations did not fit within a service member's clock. This led to a "one and done" mentality for force-planning and created problems as it became necessary to plan for multiple rotations for reserve forces.[106]

The "without their permission" clause forced the DoD to look to volunteerism as the natural method to circumventing the restrictions outlined in U.S. Code. On 19 July 2002, Undersecretary of Defense for Personnel and Readiness David S. C. Chu issued guidance that volunteerism should be used as the preferred fill method.[107] Volunteering for a mission allowed an exception to the policy, as the mobilization authority only applied the twenty-four-month clock to involuntarily deployed reserve soldiers.[108] However, the

---

104. Hon. Les Brownlee, "A Brave and Determined Army Is Destroying Terrorism Worldwide," *Army* (Oct 2003): 18.

105. Brown, *Kevlar Legions*, p. 251.

106. Michael D. Doubler, *The National Guard and the War on Terror: Operation Iraqi Freedom* (Alexandria, Va.: National Guard Bureau Historical Services Division, 1 Nov 2008), pp. 40–41.

107. AAR, Army National Guard Mobilization, Army National Guard, 10 Sep 2001–31 Dec 2003, p. 20, Hist Files, OEF Study Grp.

108. Dennis P. Chapman, "Manning the Reserve Component Units for Mobilization: Army and Air Force Practice," *The Institute of Land Warfare: The Land Warfare Papers*, no. 74 (Sep

volunteer option was not without its own set of problems. Though policy stated that volunteers from reserve units should not be used "in numbers which would denigrate the readiness standards of their parent reserve units," volunteerism enabled extensive cross-leveling within the reserve components. For example, when the 45th Infantry Brigade of the Oklahoma Army National Guard mobilized and deployed to provide security force assistance under TF PHOENIX in Afghanistan, the mission required volunteers from nineteen states to augment the unit at the required ranks and requisite skills. The preponderance of the volunteers likely would not be available for deployment by their owning units for years after the PHOENIX mission was complete.

Complicating the cross-leveling process was the fact that not every reserve component soldier was immediately available for deployment. Although training requirements often drew the most attention in determining readiness, issues with medical and dental readiness also prevented many soldiers from deploying. Following Operation DESERT STORM, Congress had passed four statutory requirements to monitor the medical and dental readiness of the reserve component: annual medical screenings, dental screenings, selected dental treatment, and examinations for those over age forty every two years and every five years for those under age forty. These measures were underfunded and inconsistently enforced. A 2003 Government Accountability Office survey found that only about 66 percent of reservists had up-to-date medical records.[109] The Uniformed Services University of Health Sciences conservatively estimated that 25 percent of the reservists mobilized in response to the September 11th attacks were nondeployable due to poor dental readiness. A House Armed Services Committee report claimed an even higher percentage by noting that out of 50,594 reservists mobilized from 2001 to 2004, 27 percent, or 13,777, required dental treatment before being released for overseas duty.[110]

The effects of medical and dental issues rippled across the mobilization process, creating a more substantial burden than anticipated. An effort to work around these challenges led force planners to ask for small hybrid units of individuals with critical skills rather than standing reserve organizations such as battalions and brigades. From 11 September 2001 to December 2004, over half of the mobilization orders passed to the Army Reserve were for six or fewer soldiers.[111] The administrative burden to plan, notify, and prepare units for mobilization did not decrease just because smaller units were being sent to Afghanistan or Iraq. For example, a single person with critically needed dental work could have a catastrophic impact on these small tailored units, rendering the entire unit nondeployable until the dental work could be completed or a replacement could be found and trained. Force planners would

---

2009), p. 19.

109. U.S. Government Accountability Ofc, *Defense Health Care: Army Needs to Access the Health Status of All Early-Deploying Reservists*, GAO-03-437 (Washington, D.C.: U.S. Government Accountability Ofc, Apr 2003), Hist Files, OEF Study Grp. .

110. AAR, Dental Care – Installation Mobilization Support Observations and Issues, Army National Guard, 24 Aug 2004, p. 5, Hist Files, OEF Study Grp.

111. Memo, Lt Gen James R. Helmly for Ch of Staff, U.S. Army, 20 Dec 2004, sub: Readiness of the United States Army Reserve, Hist Files, OEF Study Grp.

have to decide whether or not to create another derivative unit identification code or deploy the personnel originally mobilized after the dental issues were solved. A three-person detachment thus demanded the same bureaucratic attention as a 200-strong company. In the National Guard, state commands were forced to mobilize hundreds of soldiers just to handle the growing administrative workload required to send guardsmen to war.[112]

The combined demands of ENDURING FREEDOM and IRAQI FREEDOM were the first real test of the Army's Total Force Policy following its inception after the Vietnam conflict. Reserve component readiness across the force was at a relatively high state as a result of their involvement in numerous peacekeeping missions beginning in the late 1990s. The constant cross-leveling and volunteerism required after 11 September 2001 in order to mobilize these same units caused a domino effect on the reserve mobilizations that followed. By 2004, the reserve components were exhausting what they could provide under peacetime mobilization systems, but the Army's desire to employ reserve component forces to relieve the equally daunting burden on the active component only increased.

Though all Army components were grappling with increased demand, the U.S. Army Reserve was the first to publicly proclaim it. In what became known as the "Broken Force" memorandum dated 20 December 2004, Army Reserve chief Lt. Gen. James R. Helmly notified General Schoomaker that under current policies, procedures, and practices governing mobilization, training, and reserve component staff management, the U.S. Army Reserve would be unable to meet mission requirements for operations in Iraq and Afghanistan or reset and regenerate its forces for future missions. The eight-page memorandum noted that current "capabilities are limited severely by a successive series of [incremental] restrictive mobilization policies and controls" that have "failed to encompass a longer range, strategic view of operational requirements and Army capabilities." It also highlighted a deep concern over the use and abuse of volunteerism as a fill method. The concerns outlined in the "Broken Force" memo were not limited to personnel. The requirement to leave substantial amounts of equipment for other service forces and contractors in theater, policies limiting the training of demobilized soldiers, and failure to modernize retention and personnel-management regulatory policies degraded the Army Reserve's operational stamina. While the memorandum focused on concerns about the Army Reserve's future effectiveness, a National Guard historian observed that it "succinctly summarized many of the same challenges citizen-soldiers faced in the other reserve components, including the National Guard." The Army required both congressional intervention and time to overcome these issues.[113]

---

112. Gary D. Langford, *Power Projection Platforms: An Essential Element of Future National Security Strategy* (Carlisle Barracks, Pa.: U.S. Army War College, 2004), p. 10.

113. Memo, Helmly for Ch of Staff, 20 Dec 2004, sub: Readiness of the United States Army Reserve; Doubler, *National Guard and the War on Terror*, p. 79.

Special Operations Forces Rise to the Challenge

In the years before 11 September 2001, the Army's five active component and two reserve component Special Forces groups had to take unusual measures to counter the effects of tiered readiness while still meeting global commitments. Because of long-standing funding, resourcing, and staff shortages in the 1990s, several groups decided to shutter the doors on two of the seven detachments (or teams) in all nine of their companies in order to pool equipment and fully staff the remaining detachments. These empty "ghost" detachments had to be reestablished in an incredibly short time to meet the long-term needs of the Global War on Terrorism. The civil affairs and psychological operations units within Special Forces also faced personnel and equipment shortages. U.S. Army Special Operations Command would initially delve deeply into the reserves and the National Guard to sustain operations while the active component regenerated. Determining how to rapidly fill, deploy, support, grow, and sustain a continually evolving and diverse force became U.S. Army Special Operations Command's greatest challenge.[114]

The infiltration of Special Forces teams into Afghanistan in 2001, followed by the deployment of two groups to Iraq during 2003, committed the majority of U.S. Army Special Operations Command's assets to the CENTCOM theater for more than a decade. Before combat operations began in Afghanistan, Special Forces groups were regionally aligned and dedicated to a particular geographic command. This design included language and culture training specific to the particular geographic region and its attendant foreign nations. With one Special Forces group rotating to Afghanistan and Iraq every seven months to command the CJSOTFs, four out of the five active Special Forces groups were supporting CENTCOM. The fifth active component group and elements of both National Guard groups contributed a portion of their strength to both Iraq and Afghanistan, while concurrently supporting other counterterrorism efforts in Asia, South America, and Africa. Breaking regionalization in order to provide forces almost exclusively to support CENTCOM raised significant concerns not only within U.S. Army Special Operations Command, but also within other geographic combatant commands.[115]

To address unit staffing issues, which had dipped below 70 percent in some Special Forces groups, and to speed up the two-year training process for special operators (Military Occupational Specialty code 18X), the Army reinstated a pilot program initially used to fill the newly activated 1st and 3d Special Forces Groups in the 1980s. The initiative involved placing civilians directly into the 18X program in addition to drawing on enlisted soldiers from within the Army. Recruiting began in March 2002 to fill understrength

---

114. Charles H. Briscoe, "Factors Affecting ARSOF, Preparation for Operation Iraqi Freedom," *Veritas: Journal of Army Special Operations History* 1, no. 1 (2005), https://www.soc.mil/ARSOF_History/articles/v1n1_factors_affecting_arsof_page_1.html, Hist Files, OEF Study Grp.

115. Ibid.

Army soldiers search cave complexes in eastern Afghanistan for arms caches as part of Operation ALAMO SWEEP.

Special Forces groups. Each 18X candidate would attend infantry basic and advanced individual training, as well as airborne school, before starting the Special Forces Assessment and Selection course. As with all candidates attending assessment and selection, those who passed and were chosen then attended the Special Forces Qualification Course. Following a year or more of training, depending on their specialty, they were awarded their green berets and were placed on alpha detachments as sergeants. All 18X candidates who failed to pass assessment, selection, or any portion of the qualification course were sent to infantry units for the remainder of their enlistment.

The 18X program, in combination with the stop-loss for all Special Forces noncommissioned officers, put Special Forces groups on the path to achieving 100 percent staffing by 2005. The Army examined possible ways to accelerate that process, but few alternatives would be sustainable courses of action. For example, some Special Forces–qualified soldiers were transferred from active civil affairs and psychological operations on a limited voluntary basis, but most returned to their original assignments after one or two deployments. The desire to strip the Generating Force to fill the Operating Force placed the Army's John F. Kennedy Special Warfare Center and School in a difficult position. They had to increase the output of trained personnel while simultaneously reducing their number of qualified instructors. This offered only a temporary respite at a considerable cost to the training force.[116]

---

116. Jared M. Tracey, "Victoria Ex Umbra: Activating 4th Battalion, 1st Special Forces Group (Airborne)," *Veritas: Journal of Army Special Operations History* 14, no. 2 (2018), https://www.soc.mil/ARSOF_History/articles/v14n2_victoria_ex_umbra_page_1.html, Hist Files, OEF Study Grp.

Stop-gap measures designed to alleviate pressures placed on Special Forces groups had little or no impact on other elements of U.S. Army Special Operations Command. Both the 75th Ranger Regiment and the 160th SOAR were integral to the counterterrorism fight. The rapid pace of operations soon outstripped available Ranger forces when their responsibilities expanded first to Iraq, then globally. For the 160th SOAR, the demand placed on their specialized platforms and highly trained aviation crews grew exponentially, because they could deal with rugged, diverse terrain over greatly distributed battlespaces. The challenges facing the Rangers and Special Operations aviators could only be fully addressed through the lengthy process of creating new force structures.[117]

Despite dramatic increases in funding, Army SOF continued to encounter obstacles while seeking to acquire new items and increase existing stocks of equipment. For example, the 5th Special Forces Group, 1st Special Forces Command, received funding from U.S. Special Operations Command in 2001 and 2002 to revamp M1025 HMMWVs to meet unique Special Operations requirements. These modified trucks, known as Ground Mobility Vehicles, had augmented armor kits, additional gun mounts, and improved suspensions. Four of the vehicles were issued to each twelve-man ODA. Initially, only the 5th Special Forces Group in Afghanistan used these vehicles, but others were sent to Iraq after the 2003 invasion.

As more Special Forces groups were tasked to support rotations to Iraq and Afghanistan, the need to field additional Ground Mobility Vehicles became apparent. However, U.S. Army Special Operations Command first had to persuade the Army to authorize vehicles for all groups, then convince the broader U.S. Special Operations Command to fund a much larger vehicle fleet than originally envisioned. Both efforts met with partial success. Although full sets of Ground Mobility Vehicles were sent to Iraq and Afghanistan, Special Operations units not deployed in theater received only the minimum needed for home-station training. As expensive as the Ground Mobility Vehicles had been, increasing the number of the 160th SOAR's rotary-wing platforms, while replacing combat losses and implementing critical airframe and avionics modifications, further strained the finances of the Department of the Army and U.S. Special Operations Command.[118]

In the weeks following the September 11th attacks, Army Special Operations units were constantly deployed to Afghanistan, the Philippines, Africa, Asia, or South America and sent to support security cooperation missions for their assigned theaters between combat deployments. The tempo of deployments increased significantly in 2003 following the invasion of Iraq. The growing number of operational commitments resulted in major efforts to reorganize the force to support sustained combat rotations, including increasing Special Operations force structure. Fortunately for Army Special Operations, the DoD supported efforts to create additional

---

117. Partin et al., *U.S. Special Operations Command History, 1987–2007*, pp. 87–99.

118. "USSOCOM Ground Mobility Vehicle (GMV) Desert Mobility Vehicle (DMV)/'Dumvee,'" Global Security, 27 Oct 2018, https://globalsecurity.org/military/systems/ground/hmmwv-gmv.htm.

forces because it viewed that effort as compatible with transformation. It would take several years to grow the force; in the meantime, existing units would continue their high deployment tempo.[119]

In response to a directive from Secretary Rumsfeld, U.S. Army Special Operations Command took the first steps toward a significant reorganization in late 2004 by reviewing the U.S. Army Civil Affairs and Psychological Operations Command's missions, roles, and functions. After receiving input from all parties involved, Deputy Secretary of Defense Gordon R. England ultimately recommended to Rumsfeld that the new headquarters and its subordinate reserve units be transferred to the U.S. Army Reserve Forces Command rather than remain under U.S. Army Special Operations Command. That decision, which in some circles was called the "Great Divorce," led to U.S. Army Reserve Command gaining responsibility for all reserve unit readiness and mobilization while U.S. Army Special Operations Command retained control of the active component civil affairs and psychological operations units as well as oversight for doctrine and training. At home, the U.S. Army worked to position all three components along with SOF for a long war on terrorism.[120]

Denying Sanctuary in Eastern Afghanistan

About half a year into his command, General McNeill realized that only his civil affairs personnel were positioned where they could develop localized knowledge of Afghanistan. His combat forces, by contrast, "didn't have the intel[ligence]" for "truly enemy-focused operations."[121] Anticoalition militias operated out of Pakistan and, when threatened or pursued, retreated to the country's Federally Administered Tribal Areas. Restricted to areas reachable from Bagram and Kandahar airfields, air assaults by the 3d Brigade, 82d Airborne Division, were inadequate to interdict lines of communication across the Afghanistan-Pakistan border. Recognizing in early November that his forces would continue "to find little evidence of any remaining corporate enemy capability," but still under orders to conduct counterterrorism, McNeill directed Maj. Gen. John R. Vines—commander of the 82d Airborne Division, who had replaced Hagenbeck as Operation Enduring Freedom's tactical commander on 1 September 2002—to focus his efforts on the border and intensify operations in eastern Afghanistan.[122] Starting with Operation Alamo Sweep in September 2002, coalition forces sought to deny the enemy sanctuary in districts west of the Afghanistan-Pakistan border.[123]

---

119. Partin et al., *U.S. Special Operations Command History, 1987–2007*, pp. 87.

120. "Army Civil Affairs and Psychological Operations Command (Airborne)," Global Security, 16 May 2006, https://globalsecurity.org/military/agency/army/ca-psyop.htm.

121. Interv, Reese with McNeill, 16 Jun 2008, p. 10.

122. Memo, Cdr, CJTF-180, 1 Nov 2002, sub: Operational Assessment for Oct 2002, with CJ-3 Info Paper attached, p. 1.

123. OPORD 02-009, Opn Alamo Sweep, CTF-82, 9 Dec 2002, Hist Files, OEF Study Grp.

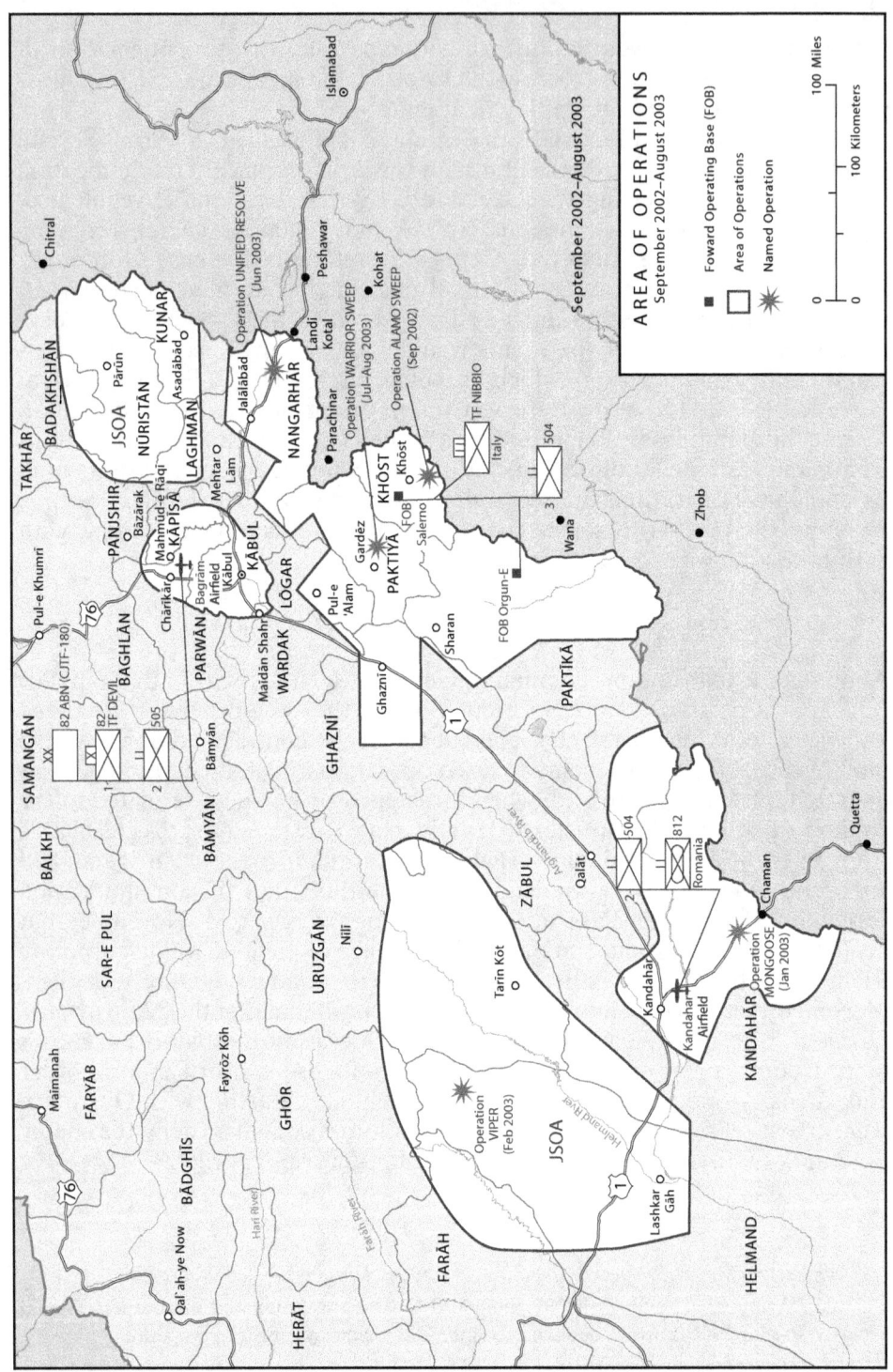

Map 5.2

McNeill wanted Vines to fight a terrain-based battle. Operations MOUNTAIN LION and CHAMPION STRIKE had been launched to reduce terrorist staging platforms and block reconstitution attempts. The primary objective for Operation ALAMO SWEEP, however, was to gather information and generate targets. Unlike the earlier operations, it was meant to secure terrain; for this reason, it had a smaller geographical focus. It signified a shift in how CJTF-180 forces operated. For the rest of his command, McNeill looked to deny militants sanctuary by pushing U.S. troops through towns and over inhabited lands (*Map 5.2*).

McNeill's terrain-based approach differed from that used by the 10th Mountain Division. To position forces where he thought they would be most effective, McNeill constructed four forward operating bases—JALALABAD, GARDEZ, KHOST, and ORGUN-E—close to the Afghanistan-Pakistan border.[124] Units from these bases moved from village to village, "sweeping" anticoalition militia away from their lines of communication. Coalition presence uncovered enemy hideout locations, displaced militants, and engaged them in combat. Col. John F. Campbell's Task Force DEVIL (1st Brigade, 82d Airborne), which replaced TF PANTHER in December 2002, and Col. William B. Garrett III's Task Force WARRIOR (1st Brigade, 10th Mountain), which followed TF DEVIL in August 2003, launched missions from operating bases established by their predecessors. The original forward operating bases thus became semipermanent establishments that expanded the American footprint in Afghanistan.

Colonel Campbell brought with him an airborne combat team comparable to Colonel Huggins' brigade in size and capability. In terms of maneuver and fire support resources, Campbell had Lt. Col. Charles A. Flynn's 2d Battalion, 504th Infantry; Lt. Col. Richard D. Clarke's 3d Battalion, 504th Infantry; Lt. Col. Michael P. Lerario's 2d Battalion, 505th Infantry; and Lt. Col. Dennis D. Tewksbury's 3d Battalion, 319th Field Artillery. In addition, TF DEVIL included the 307th Support Battalion, 307th Engineer Battalion, 50th Signal Battalion, and 307th Finance Battalion.[125]

Like their fellow paratroopers from TF PANTHER, TF DEVIL struggled to find the enemy. In an attempt to improve their own efforts, the 2d Battalion, 504th Infantry, began working with SOF on a regular basis. Operations began with detachments or the battalion's reconnaissance element entering areas where they suspected the enemy to be active.[126] If contact was made, then Colonel Flynn allowed his companies to develop the situation so as to uproot, capture, or kill as many terrorists as possible.[127] The mission ended when the battalion had exploited sites for intelligence that would feed the next mission.

---

124. Hist Narrative, CJTF-180 Provost Marshal, Oct 2002, pp. 6–7, Hist Files, OEF Study Grp. The area encompassed by the plan included two divisions: a northern sector named Area of Operations Bull for conventional forces (U.S. and coalition) and an operating area for the Special Forces.

125. Wright et al., *A Different Kind of War*, p. 333.

126. Page, "Operation Viper in the Baghran Valley," 9 Feb 2004, pp. 6, 8.

127. Ibid.

This sequence occurred unintentionally in Operation Mongoose (January–February 2003) and intentionally in Operation Viper (February 2003).[128]

Conducting an aggressive counterterrorist campaign when enemy contact was infrequent often meant that minor engagements escalated into full-fledged combat. Operation Mongoose began when TF Devil dispatched its quick-reaction force in late January 2003.[129] Enemy personnel engaged helicopters transporting the force to a cave complex in the Ada Ghar region in Kandahar Province between Spin Boldak and Kandahar City. Escorting AH–64s engaged enemy fighters, CJTF-180 ordered the Devil brigade into the fight, soldiers from the brigade identified cave complexes, and planners hastily developed Mongoose to search and seize the complexes. TF Devil soldiers did not find the assailants. Unbeknownst to anyone in the brigade, Special Forces had already seized the enemy who had fired on American aircraft.[130] Although TF Devil cleared cave complexes, the purpose for the mission had already been accomplished.[131]

Operation Viper in February 2003 proved similarly unrewarding. Conventional forces conducted operations at the southern end of the Baghran Valley near Girishk in Helmand Province while SOF operated in the northern end of the valley in Uruzgan Province. The operations targeted the enemy's main supply route through central Afghanistan that originated in Pakistan and ran through southern Kandahar Province into the Baghran Valley. CJTF-180 had coordinated with the Pakistani military to attack the origin of the route simultaneously so as to "deny [identified] anti-coalition elements sanctuary in Afghanistan."[132] Flynn's 2d Battalion, 504th Infantry, conducted more than two dozen cordon-and-search missions during the operation, none of which resulted in sustained engagement, U.S. fatalities, or any measurable effect on the enemy's ability to field combatants and influence populations.[133]

Success came to the battalion only when TF Devil directed it east into the Bagni Valley. In this branch mission, Company B surrounded a suspected Taliban complex and convinced its inhabitants to surrender.[134] Unfortunately, when Company D was removing Taliban captives from the battlefield, a vehicle driven by U.S. soldiers hit a child who later died after being evacuated by American helicopters to a nearby U.S. medical facility.[135] Tragedies such as this erased any goodwill the 2d Battalion, 504th Infantry,

---

128. Ibid.

129. AAR, Opn Mongoose, TF Devil, 1st Bde, 82d Abn, 27 Jan–8 Feb 2003, 18 Mar 2003, p. 16, Hist Files, OEF Study Grp.

130. Ibid., p. 19.

131. Ibid.

132. Capt Dennis Fitzgerald, "Operation Viper" (PEP, Maneuver Capts Career Course, 20 Feb 2004), p. 1, Hist Files, OEF Study Grp; Page, "Operation Viper in the Baghran Valley," p. 4.

133. Fitzgerald, "Operation Viper," pp. 4–5; Interv, Peter Connors, CSI, with Col Charles A. Flynn, frmr 2d Bn, 504th Inf Cdr, 30 Nov 2006, pp. 5, 7, Hist Files, OEF Study Grp.

134. Page, "Operation Viper in the Baghran Valley," pp. 13–14.

135. Ibid., pp. 14–15; PEP, Fitzgerald, "Operation Viper," pp. 9–10.

Operation Alamo Sweep required close coordination between air and ground forces in order to seek out enemy forces and possible arms caches.

had gained by removing enemy fighters from the cross-valley community and made it difficult to rely on the inhabitants for intelligence in the future.

These missions provide a fair representation of what maneuver units did in CJTF-180 during this period. Throughout its seven-month deployment, the battalion conducted multiple missions to "deny sanctuary . . . [and] disrupt the ability of Al-Qaeda [sic] and the Taliban to resource, facilitate, plan, and execute operations."[136] Although its companies sought to destroy enemy forces, contact rarely occurred.[137] With no specific enemy group or location to target, planners designed missions to deter enemies of central Afghan governance. These missions did not advance policy goals—the removal of the Taliban and the establishment of a legitimate government at peace with its neighbors—for three reasons. First, deterrence lasted only as long as the deterring force was nearby. Second, military operations disrupted communities. Unintended consequences such as apprehending a family provider or running over a child negated positive interactions in ways that no military staff could predict, measure, or counter. Third, offensive operations proved that American forces exercised initiative, not that the central Afghan government could control its own dominion. If denying sanctuary meant searching villages, then units clearly succeeded. If it meant preventing counterterrorist forces from mobilizing in eastern Afghanistan, then their long-lasting success was doubtful.

---

136. Interv, Connors with Flynn, 30 Nov 2006, pp. 5–6.

137. Ibid., p. 6.

With no confirmation of progress and an unclear vision of how Operation ENDURING FREEDOM was supposed to end, McNeill did not feel comfortable transitioning away from the tactical fight.[138] In October 2002, he judged ENDURING FREEDOM as still in Phase III, although he expected it to shift to Phase IV (postcombat operations) by February 2003.[139] By February, Afghanistan still faced threats to its existence as an independent state, and McNeill decided not to change his priorities. When Vines took command of CJTF-180 in May 2003, combat operations were all he was resourced or expected to accomplish. In Vines' understanding of counterterrorism, security came before reconstruction.

GENERAL VINES IN COMMAND

Several other factors played a part in CENTCOM's decision not to send another corps headquarters to Afghanistan after McNeill's command left theater in May 2003.[140] The process began months before the end of CJTF-180's deployment when McNeill learned of the pending invasion of Iraq. Rather than take his headquarters completely out of the upcoming fight by replacing his staff at Bagram with personnel drawn from the XVIII Airborne Corps at Fort Bragg, North Carolina, McNeill convinced CENTCOM to give the Afghanistan mission to a division headquarters instead.[141] With attacks by anticoalition militias infrequent, it looked like ENDURING FREEDOM needed fewer combat troops.

Although the XVIII Airborne Corps did not participate in the initial invasion of Iraq, CENTCOM saw no reason to change its original decision to send a division headquarters to Afghanistan. One of the primary considerations behind maintaining that position stemmed from the limited number of available corps headquarters and competing demands of other strategically important regions.[142] Although coalition forces succeeded in

---

138. McNeill looked to Franks for guidance on Phase IV, and Franks looked to the administration. See Interv, Colin J. Williams and Brian F. Neumann, OEF Study Grp, with Gen (Ret.) Dan K. McNeill, frmr CJTF-180 and ISAF Cdr, 18 Sep 2015, pp. 66–71, Hist Files, OEF Study Grp; and Interv, Mark J. Reardon, Col E. J. Degen, and Maj Matthew Smith, OEF Study Grp, with Gen (Ret.) Tommy R. Franks, frmr CENTCOM Cdr, 4 Dec 2015, p. 17, Hist Files, OEF Study Grp.

139. Memo, Cdr, CJTF-180, 1 Nov 2002, sub: Operational Assessment for Oct 2002, with CJ-3 Info Paper attached, p. 10.

140. General Abizaid, who was the director of the joint staff when the decision was made, believed the contraction was part of an effort to reduce the American footprint in Afghanistan. According to him, "There was a period where our orders said to get out . . . [one of our] first principles was that we would not occupy Muslim territory over time." Interv, Gibby, Neumann, and Williams with Abizaid, 10 Feb 2016, pp. 29–30.

141. Interv, Peter Connors, CSI, with Col James H. Huggins II, frmr XVIII Abn Corps Inspector Gen, 4 May 2007, p. 4, Hist Files, OEF Study Grp.

142. There were only four corps headquarters in the active component at this time: I, III, V, and XVIII Airborne Corps. The last named had just returned from a year in Afghanistan, while the V Corps oversaw the initial invasion of Iraq. With the I Corps responsible for potential operations in the Pacific, the III Corps could be considered as the only viable candidate for a

deposing Saddam Hussein in early April 2003, the emergence of an Iraqi insurgency meant that hostilities there would not end anytime soon. In light of the Bush administration's concerns about whether CENTCOM had enough resources to wage two simultaneous wars, Secretary Rumsfeld visited Afghanistan at the start of May 2003 to declare conditions for postcombat operations to have been met.[143] Within thirty days of that announcement, CENTCOM formally directed CJTF-180 to "continue to conduct combat operations to destroy the enemy . . . with an emphasis on Phase IV, sustain and prevent operations."[144] Reconstruction and stability operations became ENDURING FREEDOM's main effort as offensive combat moved to a supporting effort.[145]

General Vines already had nine months of combat experience in Afghanistan, commanding the 82d Airborne Division, before replacing McNeill as the CJTF-180 commander. As the senior American in Afghanistan once McNeill returned to Fort Bragg, Vines sought to gain and maintain contact with the enemy by launching operations into areas thought to be terrorist-dominated, leveraging camera feeds from unmanned aircraft, and reducing the number of decision-makers in the staff process.[146] Vines would have found it difficult to step away from tactical execution even if he had wanted to do so. With experienced corps personnel accompanying McNeill to North Carolina, the new CJTF-180 commander was not staffed to manage political interactions or develop new approaches. In one telling example, his future plans cell decreased from forty people to one person.[147] Although Vines continued to meet the same Afghans with whom McNeill interacted, he had no one like Colonel Carter on his staff to work with Afghan ministries or link operations to civil initiatives.[148] As a result, he had little or no opportunity to create programs, change missions, or redirect his small staff during his short tenure. Judged by what he did and how he did it, Vines found it difficult to stop viewing events through the familiar prism of a division commander.

---

future deployment. As it turned out, the Army deployed a portion of both the I Corps and the III Corps to Iraq in early 2004.

143. Donald H. Rumsfeld, Joint Media Availability with President Karzai, 1 May 2003, https://archive.defense.gov/Transcripts/Transcript.aspx?TranscriptID=2562, Hist Files, OEF Study Grp.

144. FRAGO 07–201, Transition to Phase IV, CENTCOM, 21 Jun 2003, 3.A, Hist Files, OEF Study Grp.

145. Interv, Kennedy with unidentified Foreign Service Ofcr, 10 Dec 2004, p. 3.

146. Interv, Connors and Mundey with Vines, 27 Jun 2007, p. 11; Interv, Christopher N. Koontz, CMH, with Brig Gen Anthony A. Cucolo III, frmr Director CJTF-180 Staff, 17 Jan 2004, pp. 17–18, Hist Files, OEF Study Grp.

147. Interv, Terry Beckenbaugh, CSI, with Lt Col (Ret.) Carl E. Fischer, frmr Deputy CJ–5 CJTF-180, 18 Jan 2007, p. 14, Hist Files, OEF Study Grp.

148. Brig. Gen. Byron S. Bagby, Vines' chief of staff, expressed his staff's limited dealings with the Afghan government when he said in an interview that "we dealt more with the Army and Ministry of Defense than we did other agencies, like the Minister of Finance, and the Minister of Education—we didn't deal with them much." Interv, Christopher N. Koontz, CMH, with Maj Gen Byron S. Bagby, frmr CJTF-180 Ch of Staff, 24 Jan 2007, p. 23, Hist Files, OEF Study Grp.

From the outset, General Vines continued his predecessor's counterterrorist approach and maintained his eastward focus.[149] Realizing that the safe houses from which ODA teams staged were too small for conventional forces, he decided to create a new base close to Afghanistan's border with Pakistan from which battalions could interdict terrorist movement. Large enough to be supplied by aircraft, Forward Operating Base SALERNO in Khost Province extended coalition presence along the border and would remain a key installation for the remainder of ENDURING FREEDOM.[150] Constant activity would make bases in eastern Afghanistan permanent establishments by summer 2003.

Looking for a more effective use of combat power, Vines accepted a request from the Pakistani military for a multination operation.[151] Launched in June 2003, Operation UNIFIED RESOLVE involved 2d Battalion, 505th Infantry, ODA 312, militia forces from an Afghan general named Ali, and Pakistani units in an attempt to close routes between Jalalabad in Nangarhar Province and the Pakistani border.[152] The mission ended in confusion, with unsubstantiated reports of the targets being forewarned, Ali's Afghan troops crossing into Pakistan, Pakistani troops crossing into Afghanistan, armed insurgents of uncertain affiliation escaping capture, and Pakistani smugglers being fired on by unknown assailants.[153] Like McNeill's attempts in Operation VIPER, Vines' efforts to work with the Pakistani military were frustrating and did little to degrade enemy capability.

Vines' next two missions were characterized by inconclusive results. In July and August, CJTF-180 directed Colonel Campbell's brigade combat team to conduct Operation WARRIOR SWEEP, in the Shahi Kot Valley in Paktiya Province with the mission to deny the enemy freedom of movement in the valley. Although TF DEVIL had a good idea of what the mission's targets would be—"organized ACM [anticoalition militia] forces, major caches, and transit bases"—they did not know key enemy personnel, locations of assembly

---

149. McNeill received more troops during his year in Afghanistan. Starting with little more than 8,000 in June 2002, he passed on a command of approximately 11,500 soldiers to Vines. Interv, Reese with McNeill, 16 Jun 2008, p. 6.

150. FRAGO 138 to OPORD 02–003, CJTF-180, 27 Aug 2002, attached to CTF-82 Cmd Rpt, D.1.A.1. Forward Operating Base SALERNO grew out of Forward Operating Base CHAPMAN, a small base constructed by CJTF-180 engineers and 3d Battalion, 505th Infantry, between August and October 2002. Cmd Rpt, version 2, 1 Oct 2002, Maj Philip H. Karns, 49th MHD, Hist Files, OEF Study Grp; Interv, Jenna Fike, CSI, with Maj Daniel Grieve, frmr 3d Bn, 505th Inf Fire Support Ofcr, 22 Nov 2010, p. 8, Hist Files, OEF Study Grp.

151. Bfg, CJTF-180, sub: Opn UNIFIED RESOLVE, 20–26 Jun 2003, slide 4, Hist Files, OEF Study Grp.

152. Although 2d Battalion, 505th Infantry, was habitually part of 3d Brigade, 82d Airborne Division, it was under 1st Brigade for several years after its rotation to Kosovo in 1999. The 3d Battalion, 504th Infantry, replaced the 2d Battalion in 3d Brigade's task organization during that time, which was not readjusted until the 82d Airborne Division began modular conversion in 2005. Wright et al., *A Different Kind of War*, p. 334.

153. Info Paper, CJ–35 Cell, CJTF-180, 24 Jun 2003, sub: Problems Arising during Operation Unified Resolve, pp. 1–2, Hist Files, OEF Study Grp.

Troops on the ground are stacked and prepared to enter a residential compound during Operation ALAMO SWEEP in October 2002.

areas, or possible cache sites.[154] This lack of detail persisted throughout the operation, even though ANA soldiers who could speak the villagers' language served alongside coalition units.[155]

TF WARRIOR, which succeeded TF DEVIL, arrived in country that August to less violence than its commander had expected.[156] Colonel Garrett's brigade consisted of Lt. Col. Michael L. Howard's 1st Battalion, 87th Infantry; Lt. Col. David G. Paschal's 2d Battalion, 87th Infantry; Lt. Col. Joseph DiChairo's 2d Battalion, 22d Infantry; and Lt. Col. Christopher F. Bentley's 3d Battalion, 6th Field Artillery. In addition, TF WARRIOR included the Romanian 151st Mechanized Battalion, an Italian airborne battalion task force, and a French Special Forces element. Garrett also belatedly received a fourth U.S. infantry unit, Lt. Col. Harry C. Glenn III's 1st Battalion, 501st Infantry, in November 2003.[157] Like their predecessors, TF WARRIOR soldiers "encountered relatively few native Afghans involved with Al Qaeda [sic]" and had to search for opposition elements to target and engage.[158]

---

154. COA Decision Bfg, Opn WARRIOR SWEEP, 14 Jul 2003, slide 59, Hist Files, OEF Study Grp.

155. The Afghans contributed six companies, approximately 1,000 troops, to the operation. Hooman Peimani, "Mission Impossible for the Afghan Army," *Asia Times*, 26 Jul 2003; COA Decision Bfg, Opn WARRIOR SWEEP, 14 Jul 2003, slide 62.

156. Interv, Lynne Chandler Garcia, CSI, with Brig Gen William B. Garrett III, frmr 1st Bde, 10th Mtn Div Cdr, 5 Jun 2007, p. 9, Hist Files, OEF Study Grp.

157. Ibid., p. 2.

158. Ibid., p. 9.

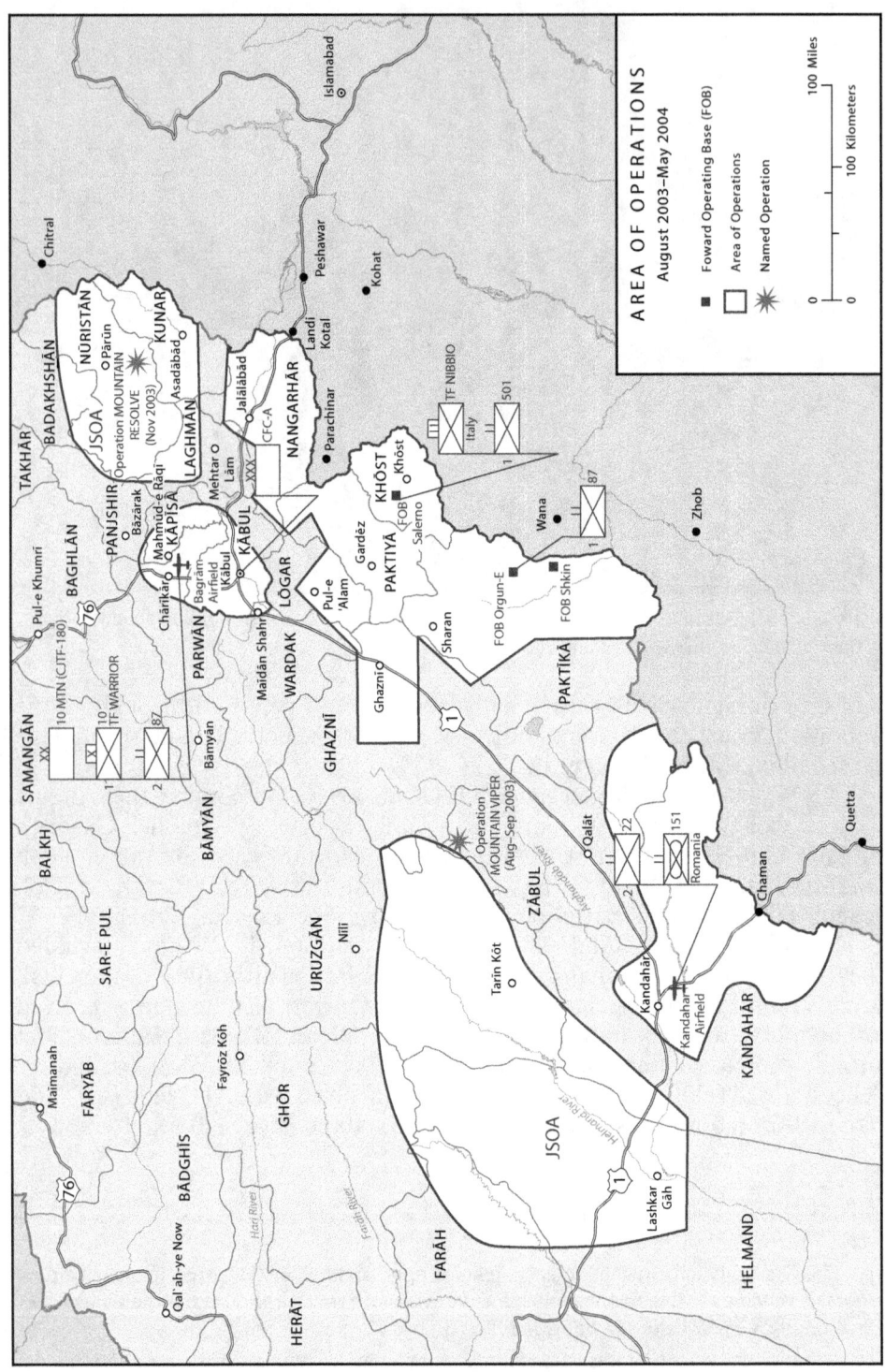

Map 5.3

This development had its advantages and disadvantages. Colonel Howard's 1st Battalion, 87th Infantry, which operated with part of its forces out of Forward Operating Base SHKIN, located six kilometers from the border with Pakistan in Paktika Province, used its proximity to rural Afghans to interact with them in a more sustained and meaningful way than cordon-and-search or civil affairs missions offered. According to the battalion's executive officer, Lt. Col. Paul J. Wille, 1st Battalion, 87th Infantry, "started agriculture and then veterinary care, and then we started looking at road construction, which the follow-on unit, I think, continued and developed."[159] Howard's battalion also established a relationship with ODAs 342 and 344 operating in eastern Paktika near SHKIN. According to Wille, the ODAs provided the unit's best intelligence while the 10th Mountain Division soldiers secured the Special Forces operating base and provided them with a quick reaction force.[160]

TF WARRIOR launched ENDURING FREEDOM's next mission, Operation MOUNTAIN VIPER (July–August 2003), in an area encompassing northwestern Zabul and southeastern Uruzgan Provinces called Daychopan.[161] The operation, initiated to make contact with Taliban fighters, began with a Special Forces reconnaissance, after which Afghan troops accompanied the Americans into Daychopan.[162] A sustained engagement with enemy forces ensued, which led CJTF-180 to insert Colonel DiChairo's 2d Battalion, 22d Infantry, into the fight. Though the Taliban withdrew after suffering losses, its political operatives remained in Daychopan after the Americans left the area to face other threats (*Map 5.3*).

Combat operations provided security for a mission seen as transitioning from peacekeeping to a less lethal peace enforcement. Although Vines pursued a counterterrorist approach, he and his command believed that their efforts were giving Afghanistan the security it needed to become permanently inhospitable to terrorists who threatened the international world order. Vines' command, however, was meant to serve only as a transition to NATO. On 16 April 2003, the North Atlantic Council agreed to assume control of ISAF later in the year.[163]

APPARENT SUCCESS

CJTF-180's tenure in Afghanistan produced far less in the way of concrete results than CENTCOM had envisioned it would. Not only did General McNeill not have enough troops or adequate intelligence on the ground, but Pakistani reluctance, weak Afghan governance, and the Bush administration's

---

159. Interv, Lynne Chandler Garcia, CSI, with Lt Col Paul J. Wille, frmr CJTF-MOUNTAIN C–3 Plans Ofcr and Bn Executive Ofcr, p. 14, Hist Files. OEF Study Grp.

160. Ibid.

161. Cmd Rpt, OEF Rotation IV, Jul 2003–Mar 2004, 130th MHD, p. 4, Hist Files, OEF Study Grp.

162. Ibid.; Interv, Lynne Chandler Garcia, CSI, with Col Joseph DiChairo, frmr 2d Bn, 22 Inf Cdr, 27 Aug 2007, p. 9, Hist Files, OEF Study Grp.

163. Interv, Connors and Mundey with Vines, 27 Jun 2007, p. 24.

fiscal conservatism all hampered CJTF-180 operations. While the enemy avoided decisive engagement, neither Taliban nor al-Qaeda remnants in Afghanistan scored any successes against U.S. troops.[164] Coalition operations had netted prisoners, exerted pressure, and asserted military superiority on the battlefield while avoiding both accidents and fratricide and keeping friendly casualties low. At the same time, Army forces had established four Provincial Reconstruction Teams and initiated many infrastructure projects. Contracting the ENDURING FREEDOM footprint by combining the operational and tactical headquarters in theater reflected the growing tendency of the DoD and CENTCOM to view these developments in a positive light.

The sense of strategic optimism regarding Afghanistan began to emerge long before McNeill's return to Fort Bragg in May 2003. On 1 October 2002, a month after CJTF-180 refocused operations on denying the enemy sanctuary in eastern Afghanistan, General Franks dismissed a pessimistic CIA analysis in a memorandum he wrote to Rumsfeld.[165] Although CENTCOM recognized that al-Qaeda and the Taliban were mobilizing opposition to Hamid Karzai's recently formed Afghan Transitional Authority, its intelligence section assessed their cohesion as "fractious" and the threat as "manageable."[166] Terrorist networks were weak because they lacked the outside support enjoyed by the mujahideen in their fight against the Soviets a generation earlier.[167]

Reports from the Afghanistan theater seemed to bolster the positive views held by senior American military commanders. The counterterrorist campaign that both McNeill and Vines pursued rested on two assumptions. First, CENTCOM assumed that destroying al-Qaeda and the Taliban would bring security to the Afghan people. Yet the country's multiethnic population, plagued by tribal and cultural discord, could not be protected simply by killing those who were attempting to fill a political void. Second, CENTCOM assumed that Afghans with ingrained hatred for each other could be made to realize that they had common interests. Unaware of the depth of Afghan provincialism, McNeill sent Franks an assessment in November 2002 that agreed with the CENTCOM commander's refutation of the CIA's analysis. According to McNeill, operations over the last month were making "Afghans willing and capable of acting responsibly and collectively."[168] He added that almost $5.8 million of the $6 million overseas humanitarian, disaster, and civic aid funds were being spent on national priorities.[169]

McNeill's statement belied several unrecognized problems. Because he was unable to predict if efforts were moving Afghans away from Taliban fundamentalism and toward an acceptance of Karzai's transitional

---

164. Interv, Koontz with Bagby, 24 Jan 2007, pp. 51–52.

165. Memo, Gen Tommy R. Franks for Sec Def Donald Rumsfeld, 1 Oct 2002, sub: Trends in Afghanistan, p. 1, Hist Files, OEF Study Grp.

166. Ibid.

167. Ibid.

168. Memo, Cdr, CJTF-180, 1 Nov 2002, sub: Operational Assessment for Oct 2002, with CJ–3 Info Paper attached, p. 5.

169. Ibid., pp. 5–6.

government, and was not sure what criteria signified a functioning national government, he hesitated to judge the campaign ready for Phase IV operations. Vines was confident that his predecessor's efforts to deny the enemy sanctuary and interdict lines of communication were providing Afghanistan's incipient government with time and space to build anew. He continued to launch aggressive combat missions. While he did so, insufficient intelligence and reluctant participation by the Pakistani government permitted the Taliban and other extremist groups to recover and rearm across the border out of the coalition's reach. To counter this dynamic, McNeill and Vines built bases along the Afghanistan-Pakistan border and established four reconstruction teams. By directing their theater commanders to solve a complex security problem, CENTCOM and the Bush administration, intentionally or not, had allowed Operation ENDURING FREEDOM to expand in size and scope.

Chapter Six

Counterinsurgency as an Operational Approach

In July 2003, General John P. Abizaid assumed command of CENTCOM from General Tommy R. Franks. General Abizaid was not satisfied with how Operation ENDURING FREEDOM was progressing when he assumed command.[1] Wanting a different approach, he established a new three-star command in Afghanistan and nominated Maj. Gen. David W. Barno for the position. Abizaid sent Barno to Afghanistan because he believed consolidating tactical and operational headquarters had been a mistake, and because he thought the counterterrorist approach did little to advance American interests in the region. Barno had been Abizaid's fellow company commander in the 1st Battalion (Ranger), 75th Infantry, during America's 1983 invasion of Grenada, and Abizaid was confident that Barno could handle complex operational problems without being unduly distracted from the broader war on terrorism.[2] As Abizaid made clear, Barno's job was to initiate a new approach for Afghanistan as ENDURING FREEDOM transitioned from a counterterrorism focus to a combined political-military emphasis.[3]

It took time for CENTCOM to prepare written instructions for Barno.[4] Unlike when it had deployed Lt. Gen. Dan K. McNeill and the XVIII Airborne Corps headquarters, the combatant command did not have a ready structure for Barno's political-military command. Instead, the Pentagon had to create one from scratch by constructing a joint manning document. The manning document, along with an official order and strategic analysis,

---

1. Interv, Col Bryan R. Gibby, Brian F. Neumann, and Colin J. Williams, OEF Study Grp, with Gen (Ret.) John P. Abizaid, frmr CENTCOM Cdr, 10 Feb 2016, pp. 29–30, Hist Files, OEF Study Grp.

2. Ibid., pp. 38–39.

3. Abizaid told Barno before he left for Afghanistan that he was "to facilitate integration of POL-MIL [political-military] efforts with chief of mission and GOA [Government of Afghanistan]." EO, CJCS to Cdr, CENTCOM, 22 Dec 2003, p. 4, Hist Files, OEF Study Grp; Interv, J. Patrick Hughes and Lisa Mundey, CMH, with Lt Gen David W. Barno, frmr CFC-A Cdr, 21 Nov 2006, pp. 3–4, 7, Hist Files, OEF Study Grp.

4. It took four months for Abizaid to gain the DoD's agreement on a combined forces command in Afghanistan and two weeks for his staff to write an order for Barno. The CENTCOM commander offered Barno the job on 26 August 2003, and Rumsfeld's office ordered his headquarters established on 22 December 2003. Barno received his orders on 5 January 2004. Jnl, Lt Gen David W. Barno, Afghanistan: Futures/Ops, vol. 1, 8 Aug 2003–26 Oct 2003, p. 53, Barno Papers, Box 1, OEF Study Grp; EO, DoD to CJCS, n.d., sub: Afghanistan Phase IV, para. 4, Hist Files, OEF Study Grp.

were to be ready when Barno arrived in Afghanistan in January 2004. The headquarters would be filled over the next few months by the Army, Air Force, Navy, and Marine Corps.[5]

Given the direction that ENDURING FREEDOM was headed, Abizaid sent Barno to Afghanistan in October 2003. With no staff, no brief from CENTCOM, and his command not yet authorized, the promotable major general devised an approach largely independent of outside influence. Lacking firm, doctrinal guidance with which to plan a campaign, the twenty-seven-year veteran drew on his knowledge of military history for insight into the conflict he was about to oversee.[6] Realizing that the coalition was fighting forces intent on overthrowing Afghanistan's internationally sanctioned government, he developed a counterinsurgency campaign that utilized units in provincial politics and strengthened efforts to build both a central government and a national security apparatus.

Barno may have been the first senior American commander to view ENDURING FREEDOM as a counterinsurgency campaign, but he was not the first to recognize the need for a new approach. Abizaid nominated Barno to lead Combined Forces Command–Afghanistan (CFC-A) to solve the new mission's complex problems.[7] Secretary of Defense Donald H. Rumsfeld, who approved the recommendation, had recognized belatedly that CJTF-180's current methods would not be able to end the conflict. In a memorandum written the month Barno learned of his assignment, Rumsfeld lamented that the detailed information being collected on enemy forces in the country was not "actionable."[8] He wanted targets that would hasten the conclusion of U.S. involvement in Afghanistan, and he expected intelligence to provide them.[9]

Rather than couch the strategic picture in Afghanistan in terms of perceived shortfalls in American warfighting capabilities, Abizaid crafted a

---

5. Except for the six personnel who traveled with him and the leaders he took from deployed units, Barno received all of his staff personnel from the individual ready reserves. Many of these service members had been out of the Army for a decade. According to Barno, "the average age in the ops center dropped ten years when I walked into the room." Interv, Lt Gen David W. Barno in *Enduring Voices: Oral Histories of the U.S. Army Experience in Afghanistan, 2003–2005*, ed. Christopher N. Koontz (Washington, D.C.: U.S. Army Center of Military History, 2008), p. 47.

6. According to Barno, "I actually took to Afghanistan three West Point textbooks that I had as a cadet, dated 1974, Department of History, 'Counter-Revolutionary Warfare,' and they were up on my bookshelf in the embassy in Kabul, because we really had nothing in the way of doctrine." Ibid., p. 18. Barno did not mention the 1986 edition of Field Manual 90–8, *Counterguerilla Operations*, which includes a chapter on counterinsurgency.

7. When Barno met Abizaid on 26 August 2003, the CENTCOM commander told him that "I've voted and you're my choice," although he also reminded his friend that the defense secretary would make the final decision. Jnl, Barno, Afghanistan: Futures/Ops, vol. 1, 8 Aug 2003–26 Oct 2003, p. 53; Interv, Gibby, Neumann, and Williams with Abizaid, 10 Feb 2016.

8. Memo, Sec Def Donald Rumsfeld for Under Sec Def for Intel Steve Cambone, 12 Sep 2003, sub: Intelligence, p. 1, Hist Files, OEF Study Grp.

9. Absent from Donald Rumsfeld's nine-sentence memorandum to Steve Cambone is any recognition that operational approaches are driven as much by political ends as by enemy intelligence. Rumsfeld was seeing a problem he had helped to create. Ibid.

General Barno visits the Transfer of Authority ceremony at the Kunduz Provincial Reconstruction Team in 2004.

more holistic assessment of the situation that he included in the order creating Barno's command:

> [V]iolence is undermining reconstruction, political stability, [and] economic activity. Political tensions include slow security-sector reform, plundering, etc., by regional warlords and efforts by non-Taliban Islamics to form a common front. The Taliban's strategy has shifted to exploiting discontentment within the populace. Other actors, including Fahim's faction, non-Taliban Islamists, and warlords are forging alliances and pursuing goals that are counterproductive to stability and development.[10]

This more pessimistic assessment indicated how dismal Abizaid believed conditions in Afghanistan had become. By giving Barno such an unvarnished evaluation, Abizaid was linking an operational problem-solver to the secretary of defense's frustration with the sluggish pace of developments in Afghanistan.

Political Setting as of September 2003

Increasingly concerned that "things [were not] getting done fast enough," Rumsfeld directed Under Secretary of Defense for Policy Douglas J. Feith and Chairman of the Joint Chiefs of Staff General Richard B. Myers to

---

10. FRAGO 07–234, CENTCOM, 5 Jan 2004, sub: Phase IV Operations in Afghanistan – Part 2 of 2, sec 1.A, Hist Files, OEF Study Grp.

double the pace of ANA training.¹¹ Simultaneously, Rumsfeld asked Marin J. Strmecki, his civilian coordinator for Afghanistan, to propose a new way forward.¹² The latter task resulted in a political-military action plan titled "Accelerating Progress in Afghanistan" (later "Accelerating Success"). The National Security Council deputies approved the program in June 2003; principal members, including the president, endorsed it later that same month. The goal for ENDURING FREEDOM was still disengagement at the earliest defendable opportunity, but the scope of American activity would widen in an attempt to hasten the day when the Afghan government could survive without extensive American troops, money, and political support.

Accelerating Success directed U.S. government agencies to curtail the power of warlords; reform the Afghan interior and defense ministries; accelerate police and army training; stabilize the Pashtun south and east; and build more roads, schools, and health clinics.¹³ The program called for significant short-term investment in Afghanistan: spending more upfront to save money in the long term.¹⁴ This new approach repudiated the fiscal conservatism that had dominated DoD thinking only a few months before. Congress supported Accelerating Success by increasing total spending on Afghanistan from $986 million in fiscal year 2003 to $2.58 billion in 2004, a figure that rose again to $4.9 billion in 2005.¹⁵ The administration's aversion to nation building appeared to be waning.

Accelerating Success was a significant change in the administration's Afghanistan policy. In July 2003, the Joint Staff directed CENTCOM to refine its Phase IV plans in accordance with the new program. To curb warlord influence, CENTCOM was to develop a "political influence" strategy

---

11. "I am concerned that next year will be an election year in Afghanistan, and things aren't getting done fast enough. Roads are not getting built. Schools are not getting built. Too much of what is happening is being done through NGOs [nongovernmental organizations] and AID [U.S. Agency for International Development] in a way that doesn't benefit the central government. We have a big stake in Afghanistan's success. We have to get metrics developed so we can track what is actually taking place in that country. There is not a sufficient sense of urgency on the part of anybody." Memo, Sec Def Rumsfeld for Under Sec Feith and Gen Myers, 2 May 2003, sub: Afghanistan, https://library.rumsfeld.com/doclib/sp/437/to%20Doug%20Feith%20et%20al%20re%20 Afghanistan%2005-02-2003.pdf, Hist Files, OEF Study Grp.

12. Graham, *By His Own Rules*, p. 435. In another telling, Condoleezza Rice asked Strmecki and future ambassador Zalmay Khalilzad to develop a plan. David E. Sanger, *The Inheritance: The World Obama Confronts and the Challenges to American Power* (New York: Harmony, 2009), p. 149.

13. Jones, *In the Graveyard of Empires*, pp. 140–41.

14. "Spending more now will save more money later by advancing U.S. goals and enabling the withdrawal of U.S. forces." Memo, Ofc of the Sec Def, 7 Jul 2003, sub: Principles for Afghanistan—Policy Guidelines, p. 5, https://library.rumsfeld.com/doclib/sp/438/2003-07-07%20re%20 Principles%20for%20Afghanistan-Policy%20Guidelines.pdf, Hist Files, OEF Study Grp. See also, U.S. Congress, Senate, Committee on Foreign Relations, Hearing on the Nomination of Zalmay Khalilzad to be Ambassador to Afghanistan, 108th Cong., 1st sess., 29 Oct 2003, p. 4.

15. Quarterly Rpt to the U.S. Cong., Special Inspector Gen for Afghanistan Reconstruction, Oct 2008, pp. 21–24, https://www.globalsecurity.org/military/library/report/sigar/sigar-report-2008-10.pdf, Hist Files, OEF Study Grp.

for Defense Minister Mohammed Qasim Fahim, plan to demobilize private Afghan militias in Kabul, and prepare responses if the militias resisted demobilization or Hamid Karzai was unable to reduce warlord influence.[16] The order directed CENTCOM to set up a training program for the ANA beyond Phase I (the Central Corps), and develop security options for the upcoming Constitutional Loya Jirga—a grand assembly of senior leaders—and the presidential elections.[17] The Joint Staff expected CENTCOM to fully establish the Provincial Reconstruction Teams no later than 1 December 2003, and plan for additional team coverage in all provinces as soon as possible after 30 June 2004. Crucially, the order also directed CENTCOM to join the embassy in developing a comprehensive political-military plan for the south and east in order to prevent a Taliban resurgence and build support for the coalition and moderates in the central government.[18]

The Office of the Secretary of Defense's new policy guidance for Afghanistan, issued in July 2003 just after the National Security Council approved Accelerating Success, also shaped the campaign. In this guidance, the core goal of the war—eliminating terrorist safe havens—remained the same, despite the administration's newfound enthusiasm for state building.[19] For the first time, the DoD specified a vision for the Afghan government it was trying to build:

> Moderate and democratic, though understanding that Afghans will not simply copy U.S.-style institutions; Representative of all responsible elements in Afghan society and formed through the political participation of the Afghan people; Capable of effectively controlling and governing its territory; Capable of implementing policies to stimulate economic development; and Willing to contribute to a continuing partnership with the Coalition in the global war against terrorism.[20]

It would not be easy to determine how to imbue Afghanistan with these characteristics. Given Afghanistan's political culture and the central government's historically limited role in its social order, this end state made campaign termination unlikely if not unfeasible. Nevertheless, the American-

---

16. Planning Order, CJCS, 19 Jul 2003, sub: PLANORD to CDRUSCENTCOM to Refine Phase IV Plans, secs. 6.B, 6.C, 7.A, Hist Files, OEF Study Grp.

17. Ibid., secs. 6.E, 6.I.

18. Ibid., sec. 6.G.

19. According to the Office of the Secretary of Defense, "Afghanistan was the first arena of the global war against terrorism. Having ousted the Taliban regime, the Coalition is now working to help the Afghans create a stable government and society that will prevent Afghanistan from serving as a base for terrorists. Success could create a model for the region and the Muslim world and an example to other terrorist states. Lack of success—a renewed civil war, a narco-state, or a failed state—would undermine Coalition efforts in the global war on terrorism and could stimulate an increase in Islamist militancy and terrorism." Memo, Ofc of the Sec Def, 7 Jul 2003, sub: Principles for Afghanistan—Policy Guidelines, p. 1.

20. Ibid.

led coalition would try to extend the Afghan government's "effective control" for the remainder of President George W. Bush's time in office.

The new policy expanded America's approach to securing Afghanistan. Secretary Rumsfeld's initial strategy memo from October 2001 had stated that the United States would only end the Taliban's rule, not defeat the entire movement. In July 2003, the Pentagon determined that "[t]he Coalition will defeat and eliminate Taliban, al Qaeda [sic], and Hezb-e-Islami Gulbuddin (HIG) forces seeking to destabilize Afghanistan."[21] This new language signaled that America's war in Afghanistan was undergoing what seemed an imperceptible shift but was in fact a profound change in purpose, from pursuing terrorists to defeating an insurgency. The Office of the Secretary of Defense also made "defending the central government" against armed overthrow an explicit coalition objective, and CENTCOM orders reflected this. Although the coalition would work diligently to avoid intervening militarily in intra-Afghan conflict, it would not rule out using force as a last resort. With continued resistance from Pacha Khan Zadran in Gardez, Ismail Khan's refusal to accept Karzai's interim government in Herat, Abdul Rashid Dostum's unwillingness to demilitarize in northern Afghanistan, and the growing power of Sher Mohammed Akhundzada in Helmand Province, the Bush administration feared seeing its investment in Afghanistan wasted in a coup or, worse, another civil war.

Accelerating Success was not a long-term commitment to Afghanistan. The Pentagon's explicit goal was to complete reconstruction by the end of 2007.[22] Although the program called for more troops, the DoD wanted them in Afghanistan "for as long as necessary to accomplish our goals, and no longer."[23] In practice, this policy translated into a temporary 50 percent increase in U.S. personnel, from approximately 12,000 troops in mid-2003 to roughly 18,000 in 2004, for the coalition to secure the national elections.[24] Notwithstanding his embrace of a larger U.S. role in Afghanistan, Rumsfeld still wished to limit U.S. troop commitments. Iraq was now the "central front" in the war on terrorism.[25] The secretary of defense remained as wary as ever of repeating the Soviet experience or creating "over-dependence," such as he thought the Bosnia and Kosovo peacekeeping missions had done for the United States.[26]

---

21. Ibid.

22. Ibid., p. 5.

23. Ibid., p. 1.

24. Amy Belasco, *Troop Levels in the Afghan and Iraq Wars, FY2001–FY2012: Cost and Other Potential Issues* (Washington, D.C.: Congressional Research Service, 2 Jul 2009), Table D-1, Hist Files, OEF Study Grp.

25. President George W. Bush, "President Addresses the Nation" (National Address, The Cabinet Room, 7 Sep 2003), https://georgewbush-whitehouse.archives.gov/news/releases/2003/09/20030907-1.html, Hist Files, OEF Study Grp; Belasco, *Troop Levels in the Afghan and Iraq Wars, FY2001–FY2012*, Table D-2.

26. Memo, Ofc of the Sec Def, 7 Jul 2003, sub: Principles for Afghanistan—Policy Guidelines, p. 2.

Enemy Situation as of September 2003

A little over one year after being forced to flee Afghanistan, Mullah Mohammed Omar openly resumed his war against the American coalition from his headquarters in Quetta, Pakistan, providing strategic direction, funding, and military planning. Urging all Muslims to join the struggle against the United States, he threatened severe punishment to Afghans who assisted the coalition or served in the Kabul government. Although it is unclear the degree to which other extremist groups agreed with Taliban ideology, it is believed that Gulbuddin Hekmatyar, Jalaluddin Haqqani, and al-Qaeda made a tactical alliance to fight American forces about the same time that Omar began reconstituting his political and military strength. Even though the groups had different strategic objectives, they collaborated to ensure that organized and coherent armed groups would stir up trouble in the border region from Nuristan in the north to Helmand in the south.[27]

Quetta was an ideal base for Omar's campaign. With a secure line of communication extending to the port city of Karachi and hundreds of sympathetic agents throughout South Asia, Saudi Arabia, and the Gulf States, Omar and his subordinates had access not only to cash but also, more importantly, to trucks, motorbikes, arms, ammunition, radios, and satellite phones. As a refuge for Taliban leaders and a conduit for money, personnel, and resources, Quetta became vital to the movement's ideological and military efforts.

Pakistan harbored two other extremist organizations in 2003. Miran Shah in North Waziristan, inside the Federally Administered Tribal Areas, was home to the Haqqani family and served as headquarters for the network bearing the family's name. Under the leadership of the famous anti-Soviet fighter Jalaluddin Haqqani, the Haqqani Network agreed to subordinate itself to the Taliban. Even so, the network maintained its own command and control structure, relationships with other extremist organizations, and lines of operations in Afghanistan. Jalaluddin Haqqani's son, Sirajuddin Haqqani, assumed day-to-day leadership of the network while his brother, Badruddin Haqqani, oversaw combat operations. Ties to al-Qaeda and other foreign extremists in Pakistan likely enabled the Haqqanis to utilize sophisticated IEDs and suicide bombing early on.[28]

The Haqqanis capitalized on their alliance with the Taliban, using its cross-border contacts to operate in greater Paktiya Province. Jalaluddin Haqqani had maintained significant prestige in the region from the Soviet jihad, and his ability to channel money and other resources made him a dangerous adversary. Through new networks, al-Qaeda and other foreign fighters found easy passage into Paktika, Paktiya, and Khost provinces, where they engaged coalition forces with conventional guerrilla tactics. Other foreign fighters used the Haqqani region to train, recruit, and provide logistics. On the Pakistani side of the border, the Haqqanis sponsored a

---

27. Gall, *The Wrong Enemy*, pp. 67–73.

28. Jeffrey A. Dressler, *The Haqqani Network: From Pakistan to Afghanistan* (Washington, D.C.: Institute for the Study of War, 2010), pp. 9, 10.

parallel administration, operating schools, providing social services, and addressing judicial issues. The group also ran criminal enterprises that produced substantial revenues for themselves and the Taliban. According to analyst Jeffrey Dressler, the Taliban's national insurgency would have found it difficult to gain traction without the Haqqani Network.[29]

Having sought refuge in Iran during the Soviet era, Gulbuddin Hekmatyar's HIG returned to Peshawar, the capital of Pakistan's Northwest Frontier Province. Although Hekmatyar had lost much of his former prestige when the Pakistani Inter-Services Intelligence threw its weight behind the Taliban in 1994–1995, he still supported the Taliban elites. As with Haqqani, Hekmatyar had been a ruthless, selfish warlord, which hindered his ability to marshal resources and attract recruits. Consequently, HIG forces had not conducted many operations after September 2001 or when the Taliban reorganized in Quetta, and most had deserted to other extremist groups. Still, after much effort, Hekmatyar was soon fielding recruits from Pakistani refugee camps and local tribesmen.[30] By late 2003, HIG had established significant influence in the eastern provinces of Kunar, Laghman, Logar, and Nuristan. To a lesser extent, HIG groups could also be found in Ghazni, Wardak, and Khost provinces. Though operationally distinct, HIG and Haqqani fighters supported each other when attacking Afghan and coalition forces in the Loya-Paktia region and surrounding provinces.

Even before September 2003, the Taliban had been a coalition of "shifting tactical alliances of convenience."[31] The challenge now facing Mullah Mohammed Omar and his shura was to keep this reconstructed coalition animated. Crucial to his campaign was spreading an ideology that would unite the movement's disparate members. To become a credible insurgency, the Taliban had to give Afghans (and particularly Pashtuns) something for which to fight, in order to recapture the momentum that had elevated it to power. With help from outside sources, the Taliban generated a sophisticated messaging and propaganda strategy that mobilized popular support; recruited locally and internationally; enforced organizational coherence and discipline; and set military strategy, training, and tactics. The goal was to show that the interim government was corrupt, weak, and the servant of Western infidels. Attacks against coalition forces, Afghan security forces, government officials and infrastructure, and high-profile social targets were publicized, recorded, and exported to strike a "severe blow to local perceptions of their new security forces."[32]

Mohammed Omar concentrated on waging political warfare after the Taliban's significant loss to an American infantry patrol at Spin Boldak in eastern Kandahar Province on 27 January 2003. Spin Boldak, located about one hundred kilometers south-southeast of Kandahar, was where the Taliban

---

29. Ibid., pp. 11, 14–15.

30. Rashid, *Descent into Chaos*, p. 221.

31. David Kilcullen, "Taliban and Counter-Insurgency in Kunar," in *Decoding the New Taliban*, ed. Antonio Giustozzi (New York: Columbia University Press, 2009), p. 231.

32. Joanna Nathan, "Reading the Taliban," in *Decoding the New Taliban*, p. 24.

had first enjoyed success eight years earlier. The district was a traditional entry point for supplies and men coming from Pakistan. In the January engagement, eighty Taliban fighters fought against an American patrol backed by air support. The Taliban scattered and withdrew, but the message had been sent: the Taliban had returned.[33]

After Spin Boldak, the Taliban worked quietly in Afghanistan's southern provinces. Zabul, Uruzgan, Kandahar, and Helmand all were open to the Taliban's influence, as the near-total absence of coalition forces had left governing to local warlord militias. Kandahar was of particular importance for the Taliban. It was the Pashtun cultural capital and a significant trading hub; all parties recognized it as the first step to gaining control of the entire country. Taliban cadres infiltrated villages and districts in early 2003, asserted their presence, and reestablished their infrastructure.[34] Foreign aid workers, Afghan officials, militia leaders, and progovernment religious leaders were easy targets during this early phase. Insurgent cadres exploited tribal rivalries, pledging support to those who had been frozen out of government patronage or who had family disputes with Karzai's administration. When infiltrated cadres branded uncooperative tribal elders as collaborators or American agents, these traditional authority figures rarely had the means to resist, especially if local mullahs also had turned to the Taliban.[35]

Opposition to the Taliban in the riverine districts of Kandahar and Helmand Provinces came from local strongmen with private militias, not Karzai's government. Taliban havens usually emerged in these communities following a three-phase template. First, new mullahs entered a region and preached against the government, encouraging young men to join the Taliban's jihad against thieves and foreign infidels. Next, the Taliban cadres organized recruits and led low-level attacks against government authority. One Pashtun elder described this influence as the "time that the Taliban started coming to our homes at night," a reference to the intimidation that accompanied Taliban presence in the village. Finally, the Taliban challenged the legitimacy and commitment of Kabul-appointed politicians by establishing shadow governments—an unelected bureaucracy that supplanted the internationally recognized political apparatus—and sharia courts.[36] The appearance of a pro-Taliban mullah invariably led to local officials departing, finding accommodation, or changing allegiances.[37]

The Taliban insurgency began launching attacks on a regular basis across southern and eastern Afghanistan during this period. Most attacks

---

33. Rashid, *Descent into Chaos*, p. 245; Ballard, Lamm, and Wood, *From Kabul to Baghdad and Back*, p. 119.

34. Abbas, *The Taliban Revival*, p. 24.

35. Fergusson, *Taliban*, pp. 168–69; Giustozzi, *Koran, Kalashnikov, and Laptop*, pp. 46–51; Scott Baldauf and Owais Tohid, "Taliban Appears to Be Regrouped and Well-Funded," *Christian Science Monitor*, 8 May 2003, https://www.csmonitor.com/2003/0508/p01s02-wosc.html, Hist Files, OEF Study Grp.

36. Giustozzi, *Koran, Kalashnikov, and Laptop*, pp. 110–11, 116.

37. Malkasian, *War Comes to Garmser*, pp. 86–98.

were small, but they were the beginning of organized resistance.[38] Mullah Abdul Ghani Baradar, a close associate of Mohammed Omar who came from the same village in Uruzgan Province, reportedly led the military effort. Subordinate to him were Taliban commanders and religious leaders assigned to different territories. Veteran commanders Akhtar Mohammed Osmani, Mullah Abdur Razzaq, and Mullah Dadullah Akhund took charge of operations throughout the south.[39] Recruiting and training drives in Pakistan produced enough fighters to contemplate more significant military operations against coalition forces, which in turn led to an increase in violence during 2004 and 2005.

A New Operational Approach

General Barno saw his critical task as creating "an integrated security structure that extend[ed] the reach of the Afghan government."[40] His approach to achieving this goal was new to ENDURING FREEDOM. In essence, Afghanistan needed a military force to help stabilize its government and economy, even if doing so required soldiers and marines to operate in roles for which they had not trained. To Barno, the "people of Afghanistan" were the enemies' center of gravity, while the coalition's ability to extend "the reach of the central government" was the friendly center of gravity.[41] Barno's challenge was to pull the population toward the Afghan government. To do so, the Afghan government needed to be able to provide reliable services and consistent security to the people, negating their need to turn to the Taliban.

To help connect the Afghan government with the Afghan people, Barno believed CFC-A needed a staff of almost 350 service members. Starting with only six, the rest had to come from CJTF-180 until personnel could be sent from stateside units. Fortunately, the 10th Mountain Division had deployed with an extra layer of senior staff officers. Barno took the colonels who headed the division's G–2 (intelligence) and G–3 (operations) sections, while Brig. Gen. (Promotable) Lloyd J. Austin III, the CJTF-180 commander upon Barno's arrival, kept the lieutenant colonel deputies.[42] When the DoD finally approved CFC-A's joint manning document—several months after Barno was in theater—the services filled it incompletely with unqualified personnel and with many officers recalled from retirement.[43] The Army's Human Resources

---

38. Gall, *The Wrong Enemy*, pp. 67–69.

39. Baldauf and Tohid, "Taliban Appears to Be Regrouped and Well-Funded."

40. Presentation, Lt Col David W. Barno, 18 May 2004, sub: Combined Forces Command-Afghanistan, slides 7, 10, 13, 15, 17, Hist Files, OEF Study Grp; see also Interv, Lynne Chandler Garcia, CSI, with Col Joseph DiChairo, frmr 2d Bn 22 Inf Cdr, 27 Aug 2007, p. 3, Hist Files, OEF Study Grp.

41. Presentation, 15 Mar 2005, sub: CFC-A Update, CG (Commanding General) Final Version Brief to Counterpart, p. 6, Hist Files, OEF Study Grp.

42. Interv, Christopher N. Koontz, CMH, with Brig Gen Anthony A. Cucolo III, frmr Director CJTF-180 Staff, 17 Jan 2004, pp. 18–19, Hist Files, OEF Study Grp; Interv, Christopher N. Koontz, CMH, with Maj Gen Byron S. Bagby, frmr CJTF-180 Ch of Staff, 24 Jan 2007, pp. 13–14, Hist Files, OEF Study Grp.

43. Interv, Hughes and Mundey with Barno, 21 Nov 2006, pp. 10–16.

Command, for example, sent him no graduates from the School of Advanced Military Studies who were trained specifically to plan operations, while ordering quality officers out of his command to attend that same school.[44]

With little staff of his own, Barno relied on projects begun by other organizations. Soon after assuming command, Barno conferred with Lakhdar Brahimi and Jean Arnault, key figures in the UN's mission in Afghanistan. Arnault shared a paper he had written on security in eastern and southern Afghanistan. Barno read the paper, translated its concepts into economic focus areas he called Regional Development Zones, and decided to establish a prototype around Kandahar City.[45] Barno did not just humor Arnault: he used his analysis as the basis of a new campaign. Although the American commander had arrived in Afghanistan with an idea for development zones, he needed both international support and the knowledge that the UN Assistance Mission in Afghanistan had accumulated for it to work.

The biggest step Barno took to ensure unity of effort was to nurture a close relationship with Zalmay M. Khalilzad, the new American ambassador to Afghanistan. Arriving at practically the same time, the two developed a close working relationship.[46] Khalilzad helped align allies, agencies, and agendas behind development zones and other initiatives. Barno supported the ambassador with staff, situated Khalilzad's office next to his, and relied on Khalilzad's negotiating skills to solve disputes among Afghan authorities. Both officials acted on behalf of the American government, both did so aggressively, and both consulted with the other to ensure unity of effort. Khalilzad in particular used his relationships, language abilities, and commission from Bush to help shape Afghanistan's future.[47]

---

44. Ibid., p. 16. The School of Advanced Military Studies offers a year-long course that teaches field-grade officers how to become effective planners who help senior leaders understand the operational environment and then visualize and describe solutions to operational problems.

45. Ibid., p. 44; Presentation, CFC-A, 18 May 2004, sub: Campaign Plan, slide 15, Hist Files, OEF Study Grp. Barno gave his reasoning for Regional Development Zones in a draft directive. According to him, "neither the International Community nor the Coalition has the resources to tackle the security, stability and reconstruction issues within Afghanistan simultaneously. As a result a RDZ [Regional Development Zone] concept has been formulated, in consultation with the UN and ITGA [Islamic Transitional Government of Afghanistan], to address the situation regionally. The aim is to deliver a package of enduring security, good governance, National police, where possible ANA [Afghan National Army] directed Aid and reconstruction, and economic revival into a Region and capitalize on the effects to extend the reach of the Central Government and demonstrate intent to the people." Memo, CFC-A, n.d., sub: Draft (First Cut) CFC Operational Directive, p. 4, Box 2, Barno Papers, Hist Files, OEF Study Grp.

46. Interv, Barno in Koontz, *Enduring Voices*, pp. 23–24.

47. Richard Lugar, chair of the Senate Armed Services Committee, recognized that Khalilzad would hold extraordinary authority in Afghanistan. In the ambassador's confirmation process, the senator told him that "if you're confirmed ambassador from the United States to the country—you're not being designated to be almost an assistant president of the country, yet many of us are going to look to you, because of your extraordinary background and the fact that you have been involved in this diplomacy now for quite a while very successfully, as probably something more than a regular ambassador who simply conveys thoughts." U.S. Congress, Senate, Committee on Foreign Relations, Panel II, Hearing on the Nomination of Zalmay Khalilzad to

Barno believed that it would be advantageous to hold units accountable for defined geographic areas. To him, space had to be owned before it could be controlled. Relationships could be established, situational understanding enhanced, and Provincial Reconstruction Team coordination eased by ensuring that soldiers remained in the same provinces and towns throughout their deployment. Placing soldiers in close proximity to Afghans enhanced intelligence gathering and made it easier to separate insurgents from peaceful locals. While commanders still had to conduct offensive, defensive, stability, and support missions, they knew that the populations they affected would remain constant. Accordingly, Barno divided Afghanistan into battalion areas of operations and, when a second maneuver brigade arrived in February 2004, brigade areas.[48]

Assigning areas of operations unified counterinsurgent efforts. When Barno first visited Afghanistan in late summer 2003, the terrain was essentially one large operations area positioned between a Joint Special Operations Area around Nuristan, Laghman, and Kunar Provinces in the northeast and another around Uruzgan, northwestern Kandahar, and northern Helmand Provinces in the west. The actual areas of control, however, did not extend more than fifteen kilometers from the forward operating bases.[49] The immensity of the joint operations areas meant that Special Forces could conduct only limited foreign internal defense and unconventional warfare in even the most coalition-friendly Afghan regions. The detachments were not robust enough to be placed on guard duty, and so they continued to pay Afghan militias to protect their safe houses and assist on missions, a relationship that empowered locals instead of officials answerable to the interim government.[50] Even though seventeen base camps throughout eastern

---

be Ambassador to Afghanistan, 108th Cong., 1st sess., 29 Oct 2003, p. 9. Senior *Washington Post* correspondent Rajiv Chandrasekaran depicted Khalilzad as far more than an envoy: "By his own account, Khalilzad ate dinner six nights a week at the presidential palace, where he met with Karzai and his advisers into the evening. Karzai made no significant decision in that time without Khalilzad's involvement and sometimes his cajoling and prodding." See Chandrasekaran, *Little America*, p. 91.

48. As expressed in his mission statement, troops were to conduct "full spectrum operations . . . to establish enduring security." Presentation, CFC-A, 3 Mar 2005, sub: Campaign Plan Briefing in Support of Operation Enduring Freedom, slide 12, Hist Files, OEF Study Grp.

49. Interv, Chandler Garcia with DiChairo, 27 Aug 2007, pp. 3–4.

50. Interv, Lynne Chandler Garcia, CSI, with Col Timothy Reese, frmr OMC-A ANA Design Team Ch, 26 June 2007, p. 10, Hist Files, OEF Study Grp. The existence of these militia forces, whose numbers were estimated as high as 60,000 during this period, contributed in no small part to recruiting problems for the Afghan National Army (ANA). The militia fighters were paid an average of $200 per month and could serve near home. ANA recruits were initially paid $30 per month and were often stationed far from home. In addition, the U.S. policy of mixing ethnicities in ANA units encouraged rather than discouraged abuse of minorities by Afghan military officers. Stephen M. Grenier, "UNITED STATES: Examining America's Longest War," in *Coalition Challenges in Afghanistan: The Politics of Alliance*, eds. Gale A. Mattox and Stephen M. Greiner (Stanford, Calif.: Stanford University Press, 2015), p. 61.

COUNTERINSURGENCY AS AN OPERATIONAL APPROACH

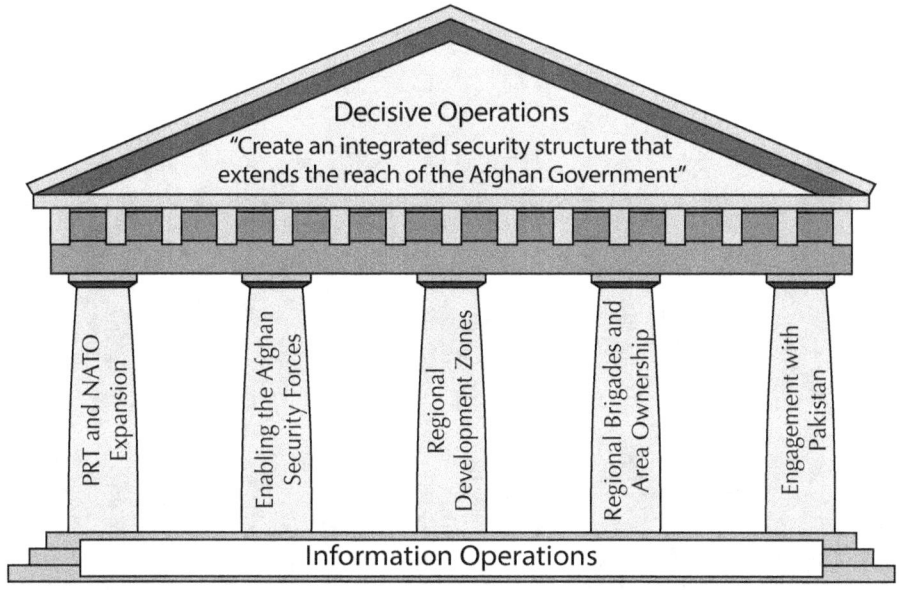

Figure 6.1. Barno's Campaign Model

and southeastern Afghanistan supported operations, the overall structure was too decentralized for the approach Barno wanted to pursue.[51]

Assigned areas supported other elements of Barno's counterinsurgency approach. The CFC-A commander conveyed his operational approach pictorially by showing a Parthenon-like structure with a base labeled "information operations," a pinnacle roof stating the overarching goal as "an integrated security structure that extends the reach of the Afghan Government," and five pillars (*Figure 6.1*).[52] He captured his desire for regional brigades and area-of-operations ownership by making it one of the building's pillars.[53] Reconstruction teams also fit his plan's assigned area of operations. Instead of answering to the civil-military operations task force, reconstruction team commanders (all lieutenant colonels or officers of equivalent military rank) would work for the brigade commander responsible for the areas in which they operated.[54] Barno hoped that such an arrangement would ensure that combat and civil affairs teams worked

---

51. Adrian T. Bogart III, *One Valley at a Time*, Joint Special Operations University Rpt 06-6 (Hurlburt Field, Fla: The Joint Special Operations University Press, 2006), pp. 39–40.

52. Presentation, CFC-A, 18 May 2004, sub: Campaign Plan, slide 15.

53. The other pillars were Provincial Reconstruction Team and NATO expansion, Regional Development Zones, the Afghan security apparatus, and engagement with Pakistan. OPORD 04–07, CFC-A, 7 Nov 2004, sub: Support to National Assembly Elections, p. 15, Hist Files, OEF Study Grp; Presentation, CFC-A, 18 May 2004, sub: Campaign Plan, slide 15.

54. For example, Barno attached the Gardez, Khost, Kandahar, and Sharan Provincial Reconstruction Teams to the TF WARRIOR brigade when he assigned it an area of operations in early 2004. Interv, Lynne Chandler Garcia, CSI, with Brig Gen William B. Garrett III, frmr 1st Bde, 10th Mtn Div Cdr, 5 Jun 2007, p. 3, Hist Files, OEF Study Grp.

General Austin escorts General Abizaid during his visit to Forward Operating Base SALERNO in December 2003.

together on local levels. Subordinate commanders would be responsible for how their soldiers interacted with residents, reconstruction teams would have access to resources, and mission planners would better understand what was happening to whom and why. Under the concept of Regional Development Zones, the third pillar, resources would flow to one area commander and reconstruction team at a time. The same commanders who oversaw other aspects of a province's development would oversee its economic development as well.

It took time for Barno's operational framework to alter how units conducted missions. The 10th Mountain Division had been the tactical force in Afghanistan for only a month when Barno arrived. He had to exercise counterinsurgent operations through General Austin and Col. William B. Garrett's TF WARRIOR. Although the soldiers from the 10th Mountain Division had plenty of experience in Afghanistan, they had deployed to fight terrorists, not to persuade a rural people to accept centralized governance.

Theater responsibility was new to Austin, who had taken command in September 2003, less than a month after leaving Iraq. In Operation IRAQI FREEDOM, he had been the assistant division commander of the 3d Infantry Division (Mechanized) during the drive to Baghdad, but he did not have previous Afghanistan experience or much of an opportunity to study America's involvement there. Being thrust into a complex, unknown environment would have been challenging under any circumstances, but because Maj. Gen. John R. Vines left Afghanistan soon after Austin arrived, the latter's increase in responsibilities was both significant and abrupt. A promotable brigadier general serving in a grade one rank higher, Austin suddenly had theater as well as tactical responsibilities. The decision to send a promotable one-star general speaks highly of the confidence that Army senior leaders had in Austin.

General Austin's experience influenced his outlook. In his view, Afghanistan was a tactical fight in which the mission was "to take away as much capability from the Taliban and al-Qaeda as possible."[55] That belief reflected the reality of the situation facing Austin, who had access to only a fraction of the resources that had been available to the 10th Mountain Division during its initial deployment. Even though Austin was the division commander, most of his soldiers were not deployed in support of ENDURING FREEDOM. As a result, Austin always kept in mind what resources he had when determining tactical options and potential objectives. He had limited means to act, but he believed that Afghanistan's future could only begin when those using violence and intimidation to derail the Bonn Process were stopped.[56]

Although Austin answered to Barno, he continued to receive orders from CENTCOM even after CFC-A's establishment.[57] This dual alignment rearranged traditional relationships for tactics, operations, and strategy, establishing a new form that differed greatly from their usual hierarchical order. CENTCOM issued CJTF-180 (commanded by Austin) tactical guidance and CJTF-180 complied with it.[58] Barno, sent to Afghanistan to interact with Afghan and American diplomats, developed the campaign's operational approach and, with Khalilzad, its political objectives. Thus, policy was set in Kabul by CFC-A based on guidance from Washington, and tactics were sent from Tampa via CENTCOM. This unorthodox practice colored Barno's relationship with CJTF-180 as much as his lack of staff and long transition did. The arrangement worked, but only because the two commanders communicated with each other, not because their responsibilities were nested in a way that logically matched them with assets, experience, and proximity to the fight.[59]

Planning for a move north began in late October 2003 when CENTCOM asked CJTF-180 to support Special Forces operating against high-value targets in Kunar Province. These targets were enemy commanders, planners, and financiers protected by robust security detachments of up to 300 fighters. Austin complied by issuing warning orders notifying selected units at Bagram and Kandahar to prepare to commit aviation, fire support, and maneuver assets to Kunar on short notice in support of the Special Operations teams. At the same time, CJTF-180 also developed courses of action for conventional forces to conduct sensitive site exploitation of weapons caches, thus augmenting Special Operations efforts to do so or to free them up to pursue

---

55. Interv, Lt Col Robert Nye, U.S. Army War College, with Maj Gen Lloyd J. Austin III, frmr 10th Mtn Div and CJTF-180 Cdr, 16 May 2005, pp. 18–19, Hist Files, OEF Study Grp.

56. Ibid., p. 7.

57. Ibid., p. 9.

58. Ibid., p. 7.

59. Interv, Colin J. Williams and Gregory Roberts, OEF Study Grp, with Zalmay Khalilzad, frmr U.S. Ambassador to Afghanistan, 25 Mar 2015, pp. 13, 27–29, Hist Files, OEF Study Group.

the fight against enemy leadership cells.[60] Although Barno's early arrival and lack of staff made it difficult for him to shape the fight, the circumstances freed Austin and his headquarters to plan tactical missions, something at which they excelled.

In order for Barno's counterinsurgency approach to work in this nontraditional command and control relationship, he needed to be able to influence Afghans directly. Because of their convenience and availability, Provincial Reconstruction Teams soon became one of the most important elements in Barno's overall strategy. However, they were not supposed to be the only vehicle through which coalition forces exerted influence. Regional Development Zones, which Barno felt were just as important, were designed to bring the full weight of the international community's development resources to bear on designated areas of the country. If the zones worked as envisioned, resources would flow into one commander's area of operations at a time, creating "economic success stories" by synchronizing security, reconstruction projects, governance support, and the work of nongovernmental organizations.[61] Overwhelming resources and attention would make the targeted zone permanently inhospitable to insurgents, permitting the coalition to shift its focus to a new zone. By progressive steps, Barno hoped to build momentum for a more peaceful Afghanistan.

CFC-A's approach in 2003 differed from those of McNeill and Vines. General Barno rejected the omniscience and control inherent in Effects-Based Operations and addressed operational complexity through a combination of approaches. He became involved in new aspects of Afghanistan's security problem because he felt responsible for the entire intervention. To Barno, a successful counterinsurgency campaign required all actors to focus on extending the Kabul government to the Afghan countryside. Supported by General Abizaid and CENTCOM, Barno adopted a holistic approach to the theater that included both national and local economic and political concerns.[62] Realizing that the temporal phases of the original CENTCOM plan were no longer applicable in Afghanistan, Barno also promulgated the concept that units should be ready to execute a full spectrum of operations in any location throughout their deployment.[63]

Reconstruction teams received most of Barno and CFC-A's time and energy because they enabled military, civilian, international, and Afghan

---

60. Presentation, CJTF-180, 31 Oct 2003, sub: Sensitive Site Exploration, Opn Mountain Resolve, slides 2–5, 18, 22, 30–32, Hist Files, OEF Study Grp.

61. Memo, CFC-A, n.d., sub: Draft (First Cut) CFC Operational Directive, p. 4, Box 2, Barno Papers. Interv, Col E. J. Degen, Col Bryan R. Gibby, and Colin J. Williams, OEF Study Grp, with Lt Gen (Ret.) David W. Barno, frmr CFC-A Cdr, 20 Jan 2016, p. 17, Hist Files, OEF Study Grp. Before consulting with Jean Arnault of the United Nations, Barno had modeled his Regional Development Zone concept on tax-free zones within the United States. Ibid, p. 18.

62. The need for full-spectrum operations was the "big lesson" coming out of an Operation Iraqi Freedom leadership conference that Barno attended in June 2003. Jnl, Lt Gen David W. Barno, CG, U.S. Army Transportation Corps and Fort Jackson, Box 1, Barno Papers, Hist Files, OEF Study Grp.

63. Update, CFC-A, 25 Mar 2005, sub: CG Brief to Counterpart, notes to slide 3, Hist Files, OEF Study Grp.

interaction. No American had served in a similar organization since the Vietnam War. Between 1967 and 1973, the U.S. and South Vietnamese governments had made major military efforts (under the Civil Operations and Revolutionary Development Support program) to improve village life and in so doing gain the support of South Vietnam's rural population, but this program had been wound down as U.S. forces and civilian personnel withdrew from Southeast Asia. Even civil-military operations centers, the base upon which Provincial Reconstruction Teams were formed, had not been codified into Army doctrine until the February 2000 release of *Civil Affairs Operations* (Department of the Army Field Manual 41–10). To Barno, these adaptable counterinsurgency organizations would help secure and stabilize southern and southeastern Afghanistan. However, by prioritizing those regions over less-volatile provinces, Barno set a precedent for future Provincial Reconstruction Team efforts. Teams in contested areas received the majority of available funding and personnel in order to counteract Taliban influence while building ties between the people and Kabul. Regions that supported the Afghan Transitional Authority received less support overall. Although perceptions of reconstruction inequality did not produce noticeable unrest, CFC-A's disproportionate focus reduced the incentive for Afghans in supposedly more stable areas to embrace the coalition or central government over the long term.

General Barno's First Three Months

Barno refined his operational approach during his first three months in theater. Because he was in Afghanistan to oversee but not replace CJTF-180, he used the time to analyze Enduring Freedom, understand its constraints, and plan his operational campaign. Barno did not implement his efforts suddenly. Instead, he sequenced them with previously planned operations and took time to react to unpredicted developments, several of which occurred soon after his arrival. His five-pillar framing of the conflict remained consistent throughout his tenure.

Barno's patience did not dampen his desire for quick victories. As he understood it, the end of the Bonn Process would end America's opportunity to shape and guide Afghanistan's national development.[64] Although al-Qaeda and Osama bin Laden were no longer imminent threats, the Taliban showed signs of increasing activity on both sides of the Afghanistan-Pakistan border. This was evident in the enemy resistance shown to American troops on the border of Zabul and Uruzgan Provinces during Operation Mountain Viper in August and September 2003. With the Constitutional Loya Jirga and a presidential election remaining on schedule for December 2003 and late 2004 respectively, the Taliban's inability to regain a military presence in south and southeastern Afghanistan boded well for the continuing formation of a legitimate Afghan government.

Fortunately for Barno, some units already recognized the discrepancy between the war they were fighting and the insurgency they faced.

---

64. Interv, Degen, Gibby, and Williams with Barno, 20 Jan 2016, p. 20.

According to Colonel Garrett, "the war in Afghanistan had evolved into a counterinsurgency by August 2003."[65] Maj. Dennis S. Sullivan, who served under Garrett as the operations officer for Lt. Col. Michael L. Howard's 1st Battalion, 87th Infantry, credited his unit with recognizing that it was addressing the wrong tactical problem and then adjusting its warfighting methodology halfway through the deployment.[66] According to Sullivan, Colonel Howard switched the battalion's focus from hunting terrorists to securing the local population.[67] As Garrett later reflected, "our challenge was not that the enemy was strong, but that the state was relatively weak."[68]

Other units did not operate in an environment that would help them extend the reach of the nascent central government in Kabul. Soon after Austin's arrival, CENTCOM ordered him to assess Gulbuddin Hekmatyar's HIG activity in Kunar and Nuristan Provinces.[69] Abizaid wanted CJTF-180 to be able to support Special Forces in the region in case they located concentrations of enemy fighters.[70] The underlying premise behind the operation was that by targeting and capturing HIG leadership, the United States would be able to interrogate them to gain knowledge that could lead to the capture of Osama bin Laden and other senior al-Qaeda figures.[71]

The resulting plan triggered Operation MOUNTAIN RESOLVE, a mission that CJTF-180 designed using intelligence gathered from Special Forces.[72] The mission began on 6 November 2003 when two reinforced companies of Colonel DiChairo's 2d Battalion, 22d Infantry, air-assaulted into a landing zone on the outskirts of Mangalam village in Nuristan Province's Pech River Valley. Other troops followed to establish a fire-support base near the landing zone. Once their 105-mm. howitzers and 120-mm. mortars were in place, DiChairo's soldiers advanced northward to push Gulbuddin Hekmatyar, Faqirullah, Haji Ghafour, Kashmir Khan, and Haji Sadiq into the arms of a waiting blocking force.[73] The CJSOTF, aided by three 10th Mountain Division infantry platoons, provided the force that would block the escape of

---

65. Interv, Chandler Garcia with Garrett, 5 Jun 2007, p. 2.

66. Interv, John McCool, CSI, with Lt Col Dennis S. Sullivan, frmr S–3, 1st Bn, 87th Inf, 26 Jun 2006, pp. 3–4, Hist Files, OEF Study Grp.

67. Ibid., pp. 3–5.

68. Interv, Chandler Garcia with Garrett, 5 Jun 2007, p. 13.

69. At the time, only Special Forces F detachments were operating in that region. See Cmd Rpt, Opn ENDURING FREEDOM Rotation IV, Jul 2003–Mar 2004, p. 4, 130th MHD Collection, OEF Study Grp.

70. Interv, Gibby, Neumann, and Williams with Abizaid, 10 Feb 2016, p. 58.

71. Wesley Morgan, *Ten Years in Afghanistan's Pech Valley*, Special Rpt 382 (Washington D.C.: United States Institute of Peace, Sep 2015), p. 4, https://www.usip.org/publications/2015/09/ten-years-afghanistans-pech-valley, Hist Files, OEF Study Grp.

72. Interv, Chandler Garcia with DiChairo, 27 Aug 2007, p. 10; Interv, Gibby, Neumann, and Williams with Abizaid, 10 Feb 2016, p. 59.

73. Sgt Greg Heath, "10th Mtn. Div. Shows Its Mettle in Operation Mountain Resolve," *The Mountaineer Online*, 26 Nov 2003, http://www.drum.army.mil/mountaineer/article.aspx?ID=3423 (page discontinued), Hist Files, OEF Study Grp; FRAGO, CJTF-180, 2 Nov 2003, sub: Opn MOUNTAIN RESOLVE, Hist Files, OEF Study Grp; FRAGO XX to OPORD 03–01, CJTF-180, 2 Nov 2003, sub:

the HIG division leaders. Yet even though the combined Special Forces and infantry teams successfully occupied their designated blocking positions, the insurgents were able to use their intimate knowledge of the area to avoid capture. Rough terrain forced the advancing troops of 2d Battalion, 22d Infantry, to move in single file, which not only slowed their advance but also decreased their chances of detecting the elusive enemy. Several suspicious individuals were detained, but the lightly equipped Afghans were able to stay one to two days ahead of DiChairo's troops. After determining that the enemy had reached sanctuary in Pakistan, the 10th Mountain Division soldiers were airlifted out of the valley.[74]

While planning to move forces into Nangarhar and Kunar Provinces, Barno found his campaign interrupted by a familiar culprit: warlords. He had arrived in Afghanistan in the midst of a spat between Abdul Rashid Dostum and Atta Nur that had the potential to engulf northern Afghanistan in civil war.[75] Fortunately, Interior Minister Ali Ahmad Jalali quieted the dispute by traveling from the capital to Mazar-e Sharif in October 2003 with 400 Afghans and Americans in tow. Backed by such visible support, Jalali announced the arrival of an ANA kandak in the Balkh capital, merged militia commands, and published a schedule for warlords to turn in their heavy weapons.[76] More importantly, he fired the governor, deputy governor, and chief of police of Balkh Province, as well as Mazar-e Sharif's mayor and police chief.[77] For the rest of his command, Barno kept a contingency plan for responding to disputes between Dostum and Atta Nur. The plan spanned degrees of severity and Karzai's willingness to intervene, and included options ranging from face-to-face meetings to a strategy for extracting the reconstruction team from Mazar-e Sharif.[78]

Shutting down a reconstruction team was a significant threat to the well-being of the region. Even though many Afghans regarded the reconstruction teams as an important source of American financial support for their provinces, the teams were conduits for much more than aid money in the summer of 2003. Much like the civil affairs teams they had subsumed, the new organizations were meant to funnel money from nongovernmental and international organizations as well. At first, reconstruction teams did not find it difficult to locate civilian agencies willing to help residents in the war-torn country. According to a list kept by the Combined Joint Civil-Military Operations Command, eighty agencies were willing to provide

---

Planning and Conducting Opn MOUNTAIN RESOLVE Phase IIIB – Continue to Attack, 3.E.1.A.1, Hist Files, OEF Study Grp.

74. FRAGO XX to OPORD 03–01, CJTF-180, 2 Nov 2003, sub: Planning and Conducting Opn MOUNTAIN RESOLVE Phase IIIB – Continue to Attack, 3.B.3.A, 3.B.4.C.

75. Karzai's government had recognized both warlords, labeling Dostum as commander of the 8th Afghan Corps and Atta Nur as commander of the 7th Corps.

76. Rpt, CJCMOTF, Last Week of Oct 2003, p. 1, Hist Files, OEF Study Grp.

77. Ibid.

78. Presentation, CJMOTF, n.d., sub: MeS Master Plan, slide 1, Hist Files, OEF Study Grp.

assistance in Afghanistan through the summer of 2003.[79] Providing security for these organizations was another matter. Since reconstruction teams could protect nongovernmental organizations only if they traveled in their military convoys, few civilian aid organizations wanted to operate in the more hazardous conditions outside Kabul for fear of being too closely associated with the military effort. However, without military protection, aid workers in Afghanistan were all the more vulnerable: in October 2003, for instance, all nongovernmental organizations suspended operations in five southeastern provinces following several attacks on aid workers who were not under the security umbrella of combat forces.[80] To ensure that military and civilian aid efforts could work in tandem and in comparative safety, Barno chose to establish his first Regional Development Zone in Kandahar, one of the more secure areas outside Kabul.[81]

Accelerating Success

Secretary Rumsfeld's office began paying greater attention to reconstruction and ANA formation after hundreds of Afghans in Kabul demonstrated against the continued presence of U.S. troops on 6 May 2003. The gathering included a large number of government workers demanding months of back pay from the cash-strapped Afghan government. The root of that issue appeared to be that warlords were refusing to turn over tens of millions of dollars in customs revenues.[82] Aware of the National Security Council's growing concerns over the training of the ANA and the distribution of aid before the presidential election, Rumsfeld and Marin Strmecki worked with Zalmay Khalilzad, then special assistant to President Bush, to enact Accelerating Success.[83]

Although the situation in Iraq required a significant amount of Rumsfeld's attention, he actively managed Accelerating Success in Afghanistan. As a result, he intervened more in the first half of Barno's command than he had during either McNeill's or Vines' commands. In a demand that proved onerous for Barno's small staff, Rumsfeld wanted weekly briefings focused almost entirely on kandak training, custom revenues, and the dates when U.S. forces could begin withdrawing from theater.[84] Given that Rumsfeld saw

---

79. Rpt, CJCMOTF, Last Week of Oct 2003, pp. 7–10, Hist Files, OEF Study Grp.

80. Rpt, CJCMOTF, Last Week of Nov 2003, p. 14, Hist Files, OEF Study Grp. Although the UN did not name the affected provinces, the likely locations were Nimroz, Helmand, Kandahar, Uruzgan, and Zabul; see "UN Officials Condemn Killing of Aid Workers in Afghanistan," UN News, 28 Sep 2003, https://www.un.org/apps/news/story.asp?NewsID=8388&Cr=&Crl=##WH4Snja7g70, Hist Files, OEF Study Grp.

81. Interv, Degen, Gibby, and Williams with Barno, 20 Jan 2016, p. 14.

82. David Rohde and David E. Sanger, "How a 'Good War' in Afghanistan Went Bad," *New York Times*, 12 Aug 2007, https://www.nytimes/com/2007/08/12/world/asia/12afghan.html, Hist Files, OEF Study Grp; Chris Kaul and Najib Murshed, "Afghan Government Workers Demand Months of Back Pay," *Los Angeles Times*, 7 May 2003, http://articles.latimes.com/2003/may/07/world/fg-afpay7, Hist Files, OEF Study Grp.

83. Jones, *In the Graveyard of Empires*, p. 140.

84. Graham, *By His Own Rules*, p. 501.

Accelerating Success as a means of increasing the resources that America devoted to ENDURING FREEDOM without incurring long-term commitments to Afghan society, he sought to monitor developments to ensure that the program met those expectations.

Even before he had been briefed on Accelerating Success, Barno chose an approach to ENDURING FREEDOM that aligned with the goals of the program.[85] Having been nominated by General Abizaid, who was privy to Rumsfeld's policy intentions, Barno easily assumed oversight of the program when he arrived in theater. His own analysis prompted him to reach out to provinces and work closely with the American ambassador on initiatives that supported the objectives outlined in the program. Barno understood that competent Afghan security forces would obviate the need for future intervention. He also saw the ANA as the primary vehicle for extending the reach of the Kabul government.[86] In his view, a trained force would both defend the state and foster a national identity that he hoped would be professed even by those living in the outer provinces.[87]

Before Accelerating Success, Rumsfeld had wanted Afghanistan to field an army that it could maintain after the coalition departed. In line with the secretary's guidance, CENTCOM planners had envisioned a small, lightly armed force of not more than 50,000 soldiers.[88] Its original near-term mission was to secure Kabul during the Constitutional Loya Jirga in December 2003.[89] Although Afghan officials wanted to deploy troops in other locations, the coalition expected the Taliban to contest the meeting. By setting up checkpoints leading into Kabul, the ANA could play a visible part in thwarting attempts to disrupt the forthcoming national convention.[90]

---

85. Barno first became aware of Accelerating Success on 29 October 2003 but was not fully briefed on the plan until he talked to Khalilzad on 27 November and Abizaid on 29 November. Jnl, Lt Gen David W. Barno, Afghanistan Operations, vol. 2, 26 Oct 2003–18 Jan 2004, 29 Nov 2003, pp. 8, 64, Box 1, Barno Papers, OEF Study Grp.

86. In the order he wrote for the presidential election, Barno tasked the Office of Military Cooperation-Afghanistan to prepare "ANA for sustained presence missions" so as to "extend the reach of the national government throughout Afghanistan." OPORD 04–07, CFC-A, 7 Nov 2004, sub: Support to National Assembly Elections, p. 30, Hist Files, OEF Study Grp.

87. Interv, Degen, Gibby, and Williams with Barno, 20 Jan 2016, p. 22.

88. Attachment from Lt Col Michael S. Weaver to Col Jack G. Smith, Col John W. Bullard, and Michael D. Fitzgerald, Contractor-DPRA, 3 Aug 2004, sub: Extract on history of 70,000 Endstrength for ANA, pp. 2–3, to Msg, CENTCOM, 231306Z, August 2003, Sub: Concept of Operations for the Refinement of Phase IV Operations in Afghanistan (Afg), submitted in response to 242235Z Jul 03 CJCS PLANORD to CDRUSCENTCOM for the Refinement of Phase IV Operations in Afghanistan, Hist Files, OEF Study Grp. As agreed in the Bonn II Conference, 43,000 of the 70,000 soldiers would be ground combat troops. The remainder would be divided among support units, Afghan Ministry of Defense staff, a general staff, and a 3,000-man air element that would fly the president around the country. Rpt to U.S. House of Representatives, Congressional Committee on International Relations, U.S. Government Accountability Ofc, *Afghanistan Security: Efforts to Establish Army and Police Have Made Progress, But Future Plans Need to Be Better Defined* (Washington, D.C.: U.S. Government Accountability Ofc, Jun 2005), p. 6.

89. Interv, Chandler Garcia with Reese, 26 Jun 2007, p. 22.

90. Ibid.

Rumsfeld's focus on reconstruction and development led to the United States adopting a different approach to creating the ANA's force structure and managing its operational deployment. In keeping with the decision made at the Bonn II Conference a year previously, the Joint Chiefs of Staff directed CENTCOM to form an army of 70,000 in December 2003.[91] The DoD supported this directive in January 2004 by approving the Office of Military Cooperation's five-year, $7 billion plan to develop the Afghan defense sector. The effort received a boost later in the year when the sector received $700 million of the $1.76 billion that Congress outlaid for Accelerating Success. This influx allowed them to increase training at the Kabul Military Training Center from two to three kandaks per rotation.[92] By July, the Military Cooperation headquarters was briefing Rumsfeld that it was increasing the rate to five kandaks.[93] Although the number eventually rose to six, space, personnel, and recruitment shortages returned it to five by September.[94]

On paper, the Office of Military Cooperation's efforts to increase ANA growth were successful. According to Barno's talking points for a 4 November 2003 visit by a delegation from the UN Security Council, coalition forces had fielded 5,000 ANA soldiers in eleven kandaks. Four kandaks would start special training in November to support the Constitutional Loya Jirga in December.[95] As more kandaks were fielded, CENTCOM broadened the training program to include command and control functions.[96] General Barno predicted that eighteen infantry and four to six support kandaks would participate in the National Assembly and provincial council elections, alleviating America's reliance on militia forces in the final step in the Bonn Process, expected to be held in late 2004.

As decided the previous December, the ANA existed to provide "security for Afghanistan's new central government and political process, replacing all other military forces in Afghanistan, and combating terrorists and other de-

---

91. Rpt to U.S. House of Representatives, Congressional Committee on International Relations, *Afghanistan Security*, p. 6.

92. Memo, CFC-A, Jan 2004, sub: Key to ANA Acceleration Briefings, pp. 1–2, Hist Files, OEF Study Grp.

93. Ibid.

94. Ibid. The Department of the Army gave Task Force Phoenix additional soldiers but then reduced its strength by replacing the 2d Brigade, 10th Mountain Division, with the Oklahoma National Guard (45th Infantry Brigade). Brig. Gen. Thomas P. Mancino, the 45th Brigade's commander, remembered being jealous that Colonel Milley's 2d Brigade did not have to fight U.S. Army Forces Command (FORSCOM) for each additional soldier that arrived in theater. Interv, Steve Clay, CSI, with Brig Gen Thomas P. Mancino, frmr TF Phoenix Cdr, 12 Sep 2007, p. 4, Hist Files, OEF Study Grp.

95. Memo, CFC-A, n.d., sub: Talking Points for UNSC Delegation, p. 1, Hist Files, OEF Study Grp.

96. The program grew to include an Afghan defense ministry staff adviser and training program, an ANA training assistance group, a doctrine-and-training training assistance team, a Kabul Military Training Center training assistance team, and mobile training teams, among others. EO, CENTCOM, 8 Apr 2003, sub: The Establishment and Training of the Afghan National Army through Completion of Phase 1, p. 3, Hist Files, OEF Study Grp.

The Kajaki hydroelectric plant, if properly refurbished and maintained, would provide much-needed electrical service to many Afghans.

structive elements in cooperation with coalition and peacekeeping forces."[97] By increasing resources, the Bush administration aimed not only to increase the number of kandaks being trained but also to facilitate the drawdown of American forces. "Creating the Afghan Defense Sector," the Office of Military Cooperation's pitch for acceleration, matched reductions in ENDURING FREEDOM battalions to increases in graduated kandaks.[98] The presentation included two timelines: one that assumed an American battalion could leave Afghanistan for every two kandaks fielded, and a second that assumed it would take three new kandaks to replace a single American battalion.[99]

Maj. Gen. Karl W. Eikenberry's Office of Military Cooperation–Afghanistan had staffed a centralized corps first for reasons that were sound from an American viewpoint, but were not without consequences. Recruitment transported young men from rural Afghanistan to the capital, separating them from warlord influence. When these soldiers completed their service, they returned home indoctrinated with a nationalist outlook. More importantly, Karzai worked out of Kabul, and his transitional authority was hosting the Constitutional Loya Jirga in Kabul; both needed protection provided by an indigenous force. Once Kabul's security requirements had been met, Accelerating Success would provide a solid foundation for extending the umbrella of security beyond the Afghan capital by creating regional corps.

---

97. Rpt to U.S. House of Representatives, Congressional Committee on International Relations, *Afghanistan Security*, p. 6.

98. Memo, OMC-A, Jul 2004, sub: Creating the Afghan Defense Sector, Hist Files, OEF Study Grp.

99. Ibid.

Answerable directly to the Ministry of Defense, regional corps were to project national authority by their presence and ability to protect residents. Regional corps also reflected Barno's decision to make American and Afghan military units jointly responsible for critical areas of operations throughout the country, something McNeill and Vines could not accomplish because of the earlier decision to deploy the ANA only in and around Kabul. Just as American areas of operations coincided loosely with Afghanistan's tribal and ethnic divisions, easing the stress on commanders trying to understand local motivations and agendas, regionally aligned ANA boundaries generally coincided with coalition areas of operations. Aligning coalition and ANA footprints not only facilitated potential mentoring or partnership arrangements, but also aided the planning and execution of combined operations.

Despite the progress being made by connecting other areas of Afghanistan to the central government in Kabul through regional corps, Accelerating Success had an uneven impact on the ongoing development of the ANA. The challenges of fielding more kandaks in a shorter time frame undermined unit cohesion, threw ethnic balances out of proportion, and stressed the training headquarters. The leadership of kandaks that were fielded under compressed timelines were uniformly disappointing, which drove U.S. tactical commanders to interact with American advisers rather than the Afghan chain of command.[100] Finally, prioritizing infantry kandaks over support units made it more difficult to sustain ANA troops in outlying Afghan provinces without relying on coalition assistance.

Maj. Richard A. "Rick" Rabe, an adviser at the Kabul Military Training Center, agreed that the Office of Military Cooperation lacked command involvement during Accelerating Success.[101] The only instruction Rabe recalled receiving from higher headquarters during his tour came as a rejection. As part of Accelerating Success, Rabe had asked the Afghan officer in charge of training to devise a plan for pushing multiple kandaks through his facility. An American officer rejected the plan because it did not build force fast enough, leaving Rabe a bit baffled as to the purpose of the advising effort.[102] The teach-coach-mentor approach, which started with a structured, controlled teaching process and ended with a cursory advisory role, was the preferred method of training local forces. However, senior U.S. commanders had not spent enough time with Afghans, or even with U.S. forces interacting with Afghans, to fully understand the limitations of this approach in building the ANA.

Even though Accelerating Success also focused on reconstruction, the policy took little account of the limitations of the Afghan theater. Rumsfeld wanted the United States to launch one reconstruction project big enough to drape the Bush administration with worldwide acclaim. CJTF-180's civil affairs and engineer staffs had studied ideas for such a project, and when

---

100. Interv, Maj Conrad Harvey, CSI, with Maj Thomas Clinton Jr., frmr Embedded Training Team Leader, 1–3 ANA, 12 March 2007, pp. 4, 8, Hist Files, OEF Study Grp.

101. Interv, Charles Dezafia, CSI, with Maj Rick Rabe, frmr TF Phoenix Opns Ofcr, 18 May 2007, p. 6, Hist Files, OEF Study Grp.

102. Ibid., p. 5.

Barno arrived in country they recommended rebuilding the Ring Road—the two-lane highway that connects most of Afghanistan's major cities and population centers. Barno's advocacy was not needed; the Bush administration had already identified road construction as a promising option. By the time Barno took command, President Bush had approved $80 million to rebuild the highway between Kandahar and Herat. Saudi Arabia and Japan had contributed $50 million each to the project. By April 2003, the Louis Berger Group, the firm coordinating the United States portion, reported that $180 million would not suffice to build even the shorter segment from Kabul to Kandahar to the U.S. government's specifications.[103]

Louis Berger's involvement in the road reconstruction would be a debacle. Although the company completed the Kabul to Kandahar road in December 2003, the actual construction costs well exceeded initial estimates. To make matters worse, outside experts described the final result as shoddy work.[104] Afghan authorities were not happy, having been left out of what they deemed an overpriced and inefficient project.[105] Despite cost overruns and upset local Afghans, the project nonetheless won praise from the National Security Council.[106] The U.S. Agency for International Development continued to rely on Louis Berger, and the company continued to disappoint. Awarded $736 million in 2003 to restore the Band-e Kajaki, a major hydroelectric power installation (dam) in Helmand Province, the engineering firm once again failed to meet construction milestones or budget estimates.[107]

In January and February 2004, under pressure from the DoD to "accelerate success," the U.S. Agency for International Development expanded its schools and clinics program. To avoid contracting delays, they initially granted the construction of 314 schools and 219 clinics as a sole-source government contract to the Louis Berger Group, increasing the contract already in place. After Congress raised concerns, the development

---

103. For civil-military operations involvement, see Position paper, "Major Reconstruction Project for Afghanistan," CCJ5-CMO, n.d., Hist Files, OEF Study Grp.

104. Ann Jones, "How U.S. Dollars Disappear in Afghanistan: Quickly and Thoroughly," *San Francisco Chronicle*, 3 Sep 2006, https://www.sfgate.com/opinion/article/How-U-S-dollars-disappear-in-Afghanistan-2488522.php, Hist Files, OEF Study Grp; for a detailed narrative, see Xavier A. Cronin, "The Asphalt Ribbon of Afghanistan: Rebuilding the Kabul-to-Kandahar Highway," Louis Berger Group, 2010, http://www.louisberger.com/sites/default/files/The_Asphalt_Ribbon_of_Afghanistan_webopt4.pdf, Hist Files, OEF Study Grp.

105. Marc Kaufman, "U.S. Role Shifts as Afghanistan Founders," *Washington Post*, 14 Apr 2003, Hist Files, OEF Study Grp.

106. Memo, Condoleezza Rice for Vice President Cheney, Sec Powell, Sec Snow, Sec Rumsfeld, Ch of Staff Andrew Card, Director of Central Intel Porter Goss, CJCS Gen Myers, 18 Jan 2005, sub: Accelerating Success in Afghanistan in 2004: An Assessment, pp. 1, 3, https://library.rumsfeld.com/doclib/sp/440/From%20the%20White%20House%20re%20Accelerating%20Success%20in%20Afghanistan%20in%202004%20an%20Assessment%2001-18-2005.pdf, Hist Files, OEF Study Grp.

107. Chandrasekaran, *Little America*, pp. 317–18; David Voreacos, "Ex-Louis Berger Group CEO Pleads Guilty in USAID Fraud," Bloomberg, 12 Dec 2014, http://www.bloomberg.com/news/articles/2010-11-05/louis-berger-grop-charged-with-fraud-over-contracts-in-iraq-afghanistan, Hist Files, OEF Study Grp.

agency re-awarded 428 facilities to five other U.S. organizations, also as sole-source awards. Even with a reduced number of projects, Louis Berger still struggled to finish them. The international development agency had to push the completion schedule back to September 2004, and then again to the end of the year. By the beginning of October, the program was far behind schedule: only 81 schools and 12 clinics were completed; another 160 schools and 182 clinics were under construction, half of which would not be ready until after the new year; while another 73 schools and 27 clinics had yet to be started.[108] Even with the building of schools and clinics behind schedule, little thought had been given as to whether sufficient teachers and doctors would be available to staff the completed facilities. In retrospect, the initiative suffered not just from gross mismanagement and lack of resources, but also from ineffective interagency coordination. The initiative relied on generalized, Western perceptions of what Afghans needed, rather than on a tailored approach fed by local input.

Regardless, the new construction did little to help Afghan governance. Rushing the construction process in a country without a developed pool of teachers, directors, and bureaucrats wasted effort. If projects did not strengthen and extend Afghanistan's central government, then any goodwill they elicited would be temporary and used only to justify an American withdrawal. Similarly, the DoD's tendency to treat the ANA as an institution that existed primarily to relieve America of its operational responsibilities reduced security to a numbers problem, one that the United State chose to solve by emphasis, additional trainers, and a disregard for standards. The overriding importance given to reducing America's military presence, versus setting Afghanistan's security institutions on a stable footing, led the DoD to establish assistance metrics based on dollars spent rather than Afghan security needs. Ironically, the lack of enthusiasm that Secretary Rumsfeld displayed in January 2002 for investing in the reconstitution of Afghanistan's war-ravaged security infrastructure cost the United States far more money in the long run. The absence of adequate security not only helped the Taliban degrade and disrupt other nation-building programs, but also led to more American troops being deployed to redress that situation.

Barno may have grounded his plans in counterinsurgency principles, but they remained subject to Afghan and American politics. The Bush administration still wanted to reduce its commitment to ENDURING FREEDOM to the point at which it could be maintained with minimal resources and attention. Accelerating Success was not an enduring program of investment and oversight but a sudden influx of resources that would stabilize Afghanistan within a few scant years. Rumsfeld sought outcomes that would justify transferring the operational mission to NATO, which had agreed on 16 April 2003 to assume command of ISAF. Obtaining quantifiable metrics developed with regard to ANA formation and reconstruction programs thus became Accelerating Success's leading effort, and the metrics generated in the form of kandaks trained and money spent were misleading. The administration also

---

108. Ltr, Patrick Fine, 10 Oct 2004, sub: Schools and Clinics Construction Program, http://www.washingtonpost.com/wp-srv/world/documents/USAIDcorrespondence.pdf, Hist Files, OEF Study Grp.

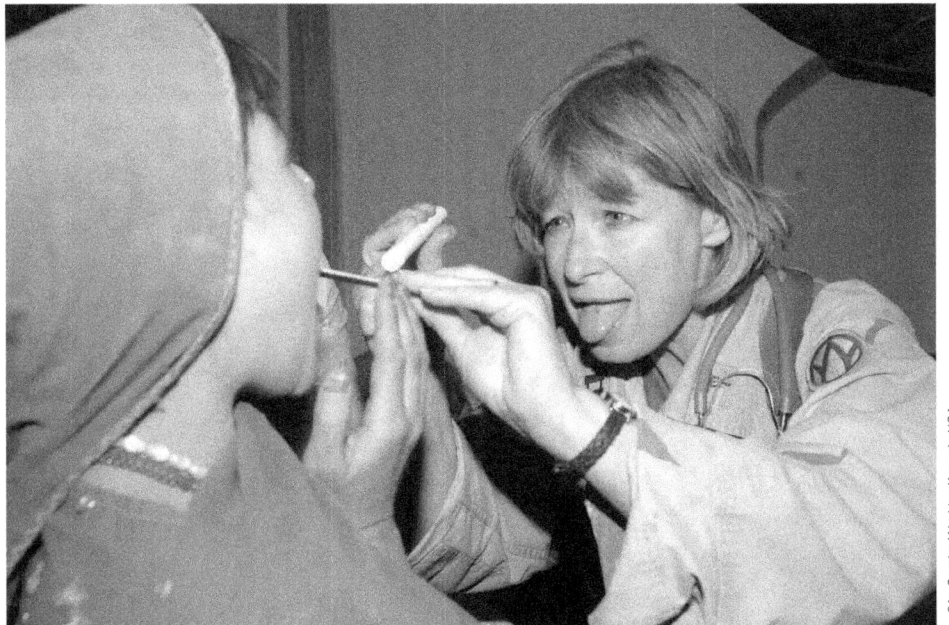

Capt. Denise Wilson examines an Afghan child during a Combined Medical Assistance mission in the Mullayai Suri District of Afghanistan in July 2004.

paid less attention to more complex initiatives that did not lead to quick or easy-to-promote accomplishments, such as transitioning police development from German oversight and establishing unity between conventional and Special Forces.

Barno found himself reacting, as McNeill had, to Afghanistan's new government as well as stateside policy. Beyond his good relationship with Ambassador Khalilzad, Barno had no say in the government framed by the Afghan Constitution Commission and approved by the Constitutional Loya Jirga on 4 January 2004. The new balance of power reflected what the loya jirga delegates thought Afghanistan needed and not how Afghans had exercised power in the past.[109] Authority was centralized in a president who presided over a symbolic legislature, appointed provincial and district governors, and chose ministers whose reach extended only as far as their influence and personality carried them. Working within the political system, Barno adjusted his approach to account for realities he could not control or change.

For his part, Abizaid checked Barno's tendency to involve U.S. forces in efforts which other countries were leading. Ordering him "to relinquish border police training responsibilities" so Germany could retain "the lead for border police training functions with the ministry of interior, supported

---

109. The full history of the Constitutional Loya Jirga has yet to be written. A good contemporary account is International Crisis Group, "Afghanistan's Flawed Constitutional Process," Rpt. 56 (Kabul/Brussels, 12 Jun 2003). See also Thomas Ruttig, "Flash to the Past: Long Live Consensus – A Look Back at the 2003 Constitutional Loya Jirga," Afghanistan Analysts Network, 28 Jan 2014, https://www.afghanistan-analysts.org/flash-to-the-past-long-live-consensus-a-look-back-at-the-2003-constitutional-loya-jirga/, Hist Files, OEF Study Grp.

The United States Army in Afghanistan, 2001–2014

Soldiers assigned to the 307th Engineer Battalion, 754th Explosive Ordnance Disposal, and the 2d Battalion, 505th Parachute Infantry Regiment, 82nd Airborne Division, arrange cases of ammunition and various weapons in a designated area to be destroyed.

by the department of state," Abizaid chose international sensitivity over operational reality in what was proving to be a no-win situation for American military leadership.[110] The need for productive relationships with NATO grew after Barno's appointment as CFC-A commander, as ISAF assumed responsibility for Regional Command (RC) North in October 2004 and RC West in February 2005.

Barno recognized flaws in the coalition's efforts to develop effective police forces.[111] As an operational commander with little time in which to start registering successes, he knew realism would trump idealism in his campaign plan. Once he received orders to stop policing the border, Barno accepted that his authority was limited and concentrated on the efforts he could influence directly. As it was, the U.S. government had not yet set aside enough money to pay ANA salaries in fiscal year 2005.[112] Barno knew that it made little sense for Abizaid and Rumsfeld to ask Congress to support police development when Germany had agreed to absorb costs. He followed

---

110. FRAGO 07–234, CENTCOM, 5 Jan 2004, sub: Phase IV Operations in Afghanistan – Part 1 of 2, sec 3.D.1.J.

111. According to a paper he kept on his computer during his deployment, Barno thought that "the centerpiece of any provincial strategy is the establishment of a credible police force able to stand up to local factional groups." Discussion paper, Lt Gen David W. Barno, 14 Oct 2003, sub: Provincial Strategies, p. 4, Hist Files, OEF Study Grp.

112. See Table 1: U.S. Support for the Afghan Army and Police, Fiscal Years 2002–2006, in Rpt to U.S. House of Representatives, Congressional Committee on International Relations, *Afghanistan Security*, p. 9.

orders but proceeded to look for ways in which coalition forces could help the Germans without robbing them of their authority.[113]

Pressure to focus on the police eventually came from Rumsfeld himself. The defense secretary expressed his dissatisfaction with how the coalition was progressing on police issues in spring 2004, two-and-a-half years after the U.S. invasion.[114] Khalilzad, who was pushing Accelerating Success at the time, also believed Afghanistan needed an effective police force.[115] Although they forced Barno to abide by the international agreement made at the April 2002 donors meeting in Geneva, policy leaders were also among the first to realize that ignoring police development did not bode well for the United States.

Unlike police development, Provincial Reconstruction Teams received significant attention during Accelerating Success. An increase in funding allowed the DoD and the U.S. Agency for International Development to spend twice as much on provincial projects as they did on national projects by summer 2004.[116] Barno's enthusiasm for reconstruction teams surpassed even that of Rumsfeld and his advisers. Realigning civil affairs personnel, the commander established eleven American teams during his command, seven more than originally planned. Although these new formations did not always include representatives from other U.S. government agencies and the Afghan government, their presence in contested provinces put allies of the central government—if not the central government itself—where they could do the most good. This restructuring came at a price, however, as personnel slots required for the enhanced reconstruction team came out of Barno's own staff. It also created a political problem: because reconstruction teams produced wealth for communities, provincial governors considered it an insult if their province did not have one.[117]

Provincial Reconstruction Team commanders generally viewed governance as their most important mission. Lt. Col. Anthony J. Hunter, one of the first officers to command a team, thought that "if we lose districts out here, we lose that connection [with the Afghan people]. We are going to lose the country and it will remain unstable because that influence has to extend out [from Kabul]."[118] Barno, who based his campaign on the need

---

113. Discussion paper, Barno, 14 Oct 2003, sub: Provincial Strategies, p. 4.

114. Ltr, Sec Def Donald Rumsfeld to Gen Dick Myers, Paul Wolfowitz, and Doug Feith, 7 Apr 2004, sub: Afghan Security Responsibility, https://library.rumsfeld.com/doclib/sp/446/2004-04-07%20 to%20Myers%20et%20al%20re%20Afghan%20Security%20Responsibility.pdf#search="Afghan Security Responsibilities," Hist Files, OEF Study Grp.

115. In congressional testimony, Khalilzad stated, "[W]e need Afghan police forces. And I think I have an understanding, given [the] hopefully positive decision that I expect from Congress, that we will produce 16,000 to 18,000 police in the course of the next year." U.S. Congress, Senate, Committee on Foreign Relations, Panel II, Hearing on the Nomination of Zalmay Khalilzad to be Ambassador to Afghanistan, 108th Cong., 1st sess., 29 Oct 2003, p. 9.

116. Rpt to Congressional Committees, U.S. Government Accountability Ofc, *Afghanistan Reconstruction*, p. 13. The U.S. government spent $564 million on provincial-level projects and $283 million on national projects.

117. Interv, Maj Gen Jason K. Kamiya in Koontz, *Enduring Voices*, pp. 237–38.

118. Interv, Lt Col Anthony J. Hunter in Koontz, *Enduring Voices*, p. 498.

to connect central and peripheral governments, could not have expressed the situation better. Agreeing, Lt. Col. Eugene M. Augustine, commander of the Lashkar Gah (Helmand Province) team from 2004 to 2005, thought that his team's greatest achievement was the establishment of a civil-military operations organization.[119]

Not all Accelerating Success projects were successes. Lt. Col. Robin L. Fontes, the Tarin Kot (Uruzgan Province) reconstruction team commander from July 2005 to May 2006, thought the U.S. Agency for International Development's cash-for-work program benefited communities but believed the agency's Alternative Livelihoods Program would not convince farmers to grow wheat instead of poppy (a far more profitable crop that fueled Afghanistan's illicit opium trade).[120] In her view, infrastructure and economic projects were easy for reconstruction teams to oversee, especially when money was plentiful, whereas governance and judicial reform projects were difficult because they lacked material solutions and personnel with the requisite skills.[121] Making matters more difficult, most reconstruction teams did not have a representative from the Afghan interior ministry to symbolize Afghan ownership.

Provincial Reconstruction Teams could not change social behavior. Two of their goals, increasing support for the national government and agricultural reform, would be beyond their capacity. Even though teams registered delegates for the Constitutional Loya Jirga, they could not change Afghan customs or discredit local strongmen.[122] Likewise, the team commander in Herat reported that his psychological and civil affairs teams had visited two villages in the province and reported that "a majority of the farmers do not want to grow any crops for the next harvest because they do not make enough profit. Even [for] their most profitable crops like rice, the fertilizer is still more expensive than the finished product."[123] Without the infrastructure or the financing to support long-term agricultural development across the entire country, Afghanistan's opium economy would continue to flourish in spite of the best efforts of counternarcotics programs.

Even as the reconstruction teams spent money and struggled to support governance, their third mission, promoting security, went unfulfilled. Early in team formation, Barno restricted missions to a fifteen-kilometer radius of the team's bases. Combat operations took precedence over civil affairs missions, sometimes shutting down all reconstruction team activity until troops had departed. Teams also found it difficult to address constabulary issues, especially after Barno removed police training teams from their formations in order to form RC West in 2004.[124]

---

119. Interv, Lt Col Eugene M. Augustine in Koontz, *Enduring Voices*, p. 451.

120. Interv, Lt Col Robin L. Fontes in Koontz, *Enduring Voices*, p. 474.

121. Ibid., p. 475.

122. For example, see Rpt, CJCMOTF to CFC-A, 26 Oct 2003, p. 6, Hist Files, OEF Study Grp.

123. Ibid.

124. Barno pulled military police from units across ENDURING FREEDOM to support the 3d Squadron, 4th Cavalry, the base unit for Task Force LONGHORN, his western response force.

Like other commands, CJSOTF-Afghanistan changed under Accelerating Success. As ground forces transitioned to counterinsurgency operations, operational detachments focused less on foreign internal defense and more on direct action. Reflecting Barno's worry that enemy forces in Pakistan would slip across the border and disrupt the presidential election, CJTF-76 (CJTF-180's replacement in theater as of June 2004) ordered the SOF task force to establish thirteen firebases along the border and move ODAs east from northern Afghanistan to occupy them. Ordered to demobilize the local security forces that guarded their bases and accompanied them on missions, SOF found themselves with few indigenous personnel to train. Although they still worked with the newly graduated kandaks, they did not interact with them closely enough to develop constructive relationships.[125]

Special operations in Afghanistan received public attention after friendly fire killed Spc. Patrick D. Tillman, a former professional football player who was a member of the 75th Ranger Regiment. Tillman's death on 22 April 2004 and his chain of command's subsequent delayed and misreporting of its cause brought negative attention to the Special Operations community, which revealed problems with how special operations were contributing to ENDURING FREEDOM. In a campaign where information operations—the gloss placed on what was or was not accomplished—mattered as much as the events themselves, erroneous reports and an embellished citation for a Silver Star garnered the public's condemnation and weakened efforts to sell ENDURING FREEDOM as a necessary conflict.[126] For his part, Barno understood the incident as a tragic mistake that, for all its domestic impact, did little to change the operational context of the overarching mission.[127]

ELECTION PREPARATIONS

Kabul's inability to support local communities with resources, security, or justice magnified the problems of ineffective governance in Afghanistan. National politics got in the way of good governance, as Karzai often found it advantageous to appoint district and provincial governors who had never resided where they governed. Areas where the Taliban contested Karzai's authority to govern, by contrast, tended to have one common problem: poor security. Barno constantly preached that governance and security were connected: without one, the other was impossible.[128] He understood

---

Interv, Hunter in Koontz, *Enduring Voices*, p. 497.

125. Partin et al., *U.S. Special Operations Command History, 1987–2007*, pp. 112–14.

126. Inspector Gen, DoD, *Review of Matters Related to the Death of Corporal Patrick Tillman, U.S. Army*, Rpt IPO2007E001 (Arlington, Va., DoD Inspector Gen, 26 Mar 2007), p. 1, https://www.npr.org/documents/2007/mar/tillman/tillman_dod_ig.pdf, Hist Files, OEF Study Grp. See also the report's attached memorandum for Acting Secretary of the Army and page 3 of the investigation.

127. Ltr, Lt Gen David W. Barno to Colin J. Williams, 25 May 2016, Hist Files, OEF Study Grp.

128. On Barno and the interrelatedness of security and development, see Interv, Kamiya in Koontz, *Enduring Voices*, p. 221.

that this nexus could be either good or bad. To him, the outcome of the presidential election scheduled for fall 2004 would determine the extent to which Afghanistan could be both secure and governable. If an election free of corruption and interference rallied the country around a single leader, then the new Afghan government would have the authority to combat poor security, nongovernance, bad governance, and other impediments to self-sufficiency.

The upcoming presidential election influenced what districts and provinces Barno believed would benefit most from coalition presence. He did not expect CFC-A units to establish security throughout their entire areas of operations; subordinates could make their own determinations as to where to patrol, who to meet, and what villages to search.[129] With brigade and battalion commanders exercising tactical autonomy, Barno established a border control program that oversaw customs collection while honoring Abizaid's instruction not to interfere with Germany's direction of police development.[130] With the UN Assistance Mission in Afghanistan spearheading voter registration throughout the country, Karzai prompted Barno to operate in as many districts as possible. At the same time, Khalilzad continued to push CFC-A to expand the American footprint north into Pashtun areas in Nangarhar and Kunar provinces.[131]

The need for more indigenous troops to participate in election security forced Barno to apply a provincial focus to Afghanistan's complex tribal and ethnic mosaic. Early in his command, he planned to create a localized Afghan response force that would align the rural male population behind national policies.[132] Called the Afghan National Army Provisional Force, this formation, like attempts before and after it, was to provide a national structure to militias and inculcate a national identity in its recruited members. It was to stand as an interim force "raised, organized and commanded by in-country ODA teams and used to create conditions for enduring security."[133] Barno's goal was to have this force fielded, at least in part, by the presidential election.[134]

---

129. Interv, Lynne Chandler Garcia, CSI, with Lt Col Steven J. Ford, frmr Ghazni Provincial Reconstruction Team Cdr, 14 Sep 2007, p. 10, Hist Files, OEF Study Grp. Barno frequently "found a way around" barriers that segmented Afghan development. Interv, Degen, Gibby, and Williams with Barno, 20 Jan 2016, p. 48.

130. Barno questioned America's involvement in securing Afghanistan's border, writing in one of his notebooks, "[W]hy are we on the border? T[Task]/P[Purpose]? Output? Should we shift to all AMF [Afghan Militia Forces] or ABP [Afghan Border Police]?" Jnl, Lt Gen David W. Barno, vol. 4, 25 Apr 2004–23 Jul 2004, 17 Jun 2004, p. 101, Box 1, Barno Papers, OEF Study Grp.

131. Interv, Williams and Roberts with Khalilzad, 25 Mar 2015, pp. 31–33.

132. Presentation, CFC-A, 18 May 2004, sub: Campaign Plan, slide 11.

133. Memo, CFC-A, n.d., sub: Draft (First Cut) CFC Operational Directive, p. 4, Box 2, Barno Papers, Hist Files, OEF Study Grp.

134. Jnl, Barno, Afghanistan Operations, vol. 2, 26 Oct 2003–18 Jan 2004, 3 Dec 2003, p. 85; Jnl, Lt Gen David W. Barno, 2004 Timeline, Frontispiece (n.d.), vol. 3, 19 Jan 2004–25 Apr 2004, Box 1, Barno Papers, OEF Study Grp.

Barno was not disputing Afghanistan's need for central governance by trying to recruit and mobilize local militaries. Instead, he was trying to ensure a successful presidential election, an event expected to strengthen the national government. Following Khalilzad's argument, Barno thought that both the election and the conflict would be won in the Pashtun countryside. He needed a way to connect this population to Karzai's largely non-Pashtun government. Like McNeill and Vines before him, Barno posted units in eastern and southeastern Afghanistan. Unlike his predecessors, he expected these units to do more than patrol, conduct raids, and oversee developmental projects.

Operation SECURE FUTURE, the first mission Barno and his staff planned, gave coalition units in the Pashtun east and south many methods by which to "set the conditions for future reconstruction and the election process."[135] In addition to promoting the ANA Provisional Force, the order for the operation directed the Combined Joint Civil-Military Operations Task Force to open Provincial Reconstruction Teams at Asadabad, Khost, and Ghazni in RC East.[136] In Kunar and Nangarhar provinces, possible locations for future teams, Barno expected civil-military detachments "to conduct regular bi-weekly operations . . . to include regular MEDCAPS [Medical Civic Action Programs] and VETCAPS [Veterinarian Civic Action Programs] in remote areas."[137] At the same time, SECURE FUTURE was to project a "sustained presence" in eastern, southeastern, and southern regions.[138] Following his commander's lead, General Austin directed maneuver units to support civil-military and Special Forces units during the operation.[139] Conducted in January and February 2004, SECURE FUTURE was the first chance for Barno's multifaceted counterinsurgency mentality to permeate through his land component.

Barno had further ideas for Operation SECURE FUTURE. In addition to establishing reconstruction teams and promoting security, he used the operation to launch a pilot Regional Development Zone program in and around Kandahar City.[140] As part of his comprehensive approach, Barno also

---

135. FRAGO XX to OPORD 03–01, CJTF-180, 6 Dec 2003, sub: Plan and Conduct Operation SECURE FUTURE, p. 1, Hist Files, OEF Study Grp. According to Barno, the order he wrote for Operation SECURE FUTURE directed that the main effort of military operations for 2004 would be to set the condition for a successful presidential election; Interv, Hughes and Mundey with Barno, 21 Nov 2006, p. 36.

136. FRAGO XX to OPORD 03–01, CJTF-180, 6 Dec 2003, sub: Plan and Conduct Operation SECURE FUTURE, p. 6.

137. Ibid.

138. Memo, CJTF-180, 16 Dec 2003, sub: Eastern UNAMA [United Nations Assistance Mission in Afghanistan] Region Sustained Presence Plan, Opn MOUNTAIN RESOLVE, pp. 2–6, Hist Files, OEF Study Grp; Memo, CJTF-180, 18 Dec 2003, sub: Eastern UNAMA Region Sustained Presence Plan, Winter 2003–2004, Opn MOUNTAIN RESOLVE, p. 2, Hist Files, OEF Study Grp.

139. Memo, CJTF-180, 16 Dec 2003, sub: Eastern UNAMA Region Sustained Presence Plan, Opn MOUNTAIN RESOLVE, pp. 2–6.

140. FRAGO XX to OPORD 03–01, CJTF-180, 6 Dec 2003, sub: Plan and Conduct Operation SECURE FUTURE, pp. 1, 2. Barno planned to initiate a second Regional Development Zone for Zabul and

wanted units to learn the "current or future locations of" named individuals, details that CJTF-180 was not staffed to track when it served as the ranking American headquarters in Afghanistan.[141] Coalition forces may have conducted fewer "sweep" and cordon-and-search missions under Barno, but they still engaged enemy targets when they had good intelligence. In addition to creating conditions for a Regional Development Zone around Kandahar City, coalition forces were to conduct area denial missions, preventing enemy fighters from moving freely in areas under coalition control in Jalalabad, Asadabad, and Kantiway-ye Ulya, while Special Forces led Afghan militia forces in unconventional warfare near Ghazni, Qalat, Daychopan, Tarin Kot, Deh Rawud, and Girishk.[142]

With so many concurrent efforts, SECURE FUTURE reflected the reality of full-spectrum operations in a counterinsurgency. Three months in planning, it also reflected Barno's comprehensive, long-term view of his mission. From his perspective, CFC-A was in Afghanistan "to establish enduring security, defeat terrorism and insurgency, and deter its re-emergence in the region by supporting the military, economic, political and social development of Afghanistan."[143] Barno sought to address Afghanistan's problems with activity that ranged the spectrum of military conflict and employed the breadth of available civilian expertise. By pressing simultaneously on multiple fronts, coalition forces would leave the enemy no room to operate.[144]

The arrival of a new headquarters that was prepared to conduct counterinsurgency sped Barno's shift to those methods. Although the 10th Mountain Division had adapted to Barno's operational approach, neither its commander nor its units had trained to fight a political-military campaign before departing New York in August 2003. In order for Barno to fight the conflict in the fashion he wanted to, he needed counterinsurgency practiced at the tactical as well as the operational level of war. Soldiers and commanders would have to learn how to operate within the diverse Afghan population, and beyond that, they would have to be convinced that this approach was a viable way to fight a war.

At the tactical level, this attitude would be adopted by soldiers from Maj. Gen. Eric T. Olson's Hawaii-based 25th Infantry Division, which deployed in May–June 2004. As the 25th Infantry Division headquarters replaced the 10th

---

Uruzgan Provinces after the presidential election. A third zone, covering Paktiya, Paktika, Khost, and Ghazni Provinces, would follow in January 2005. Bfg, Lt Gen David W. Barno, Cdr, CFC-A, 19 Jul 2004, sub: Campaign Plan, Winning the Afghan Counter-Insurgency Fight, p. 24, Hist Files, OEF Study Grp.

141. Included in Barno's priority information requirements were the locations of key enemy figures like Hariz Abdul Rahim, Mullah Omar, Mullah Boradar, Agha, Akhtar Mohammed Osmani, Bashir Noorzai, Mullah Obiadullah Akhund, Mullah Dadullah, Ayman al-Zawahiri, Jalaluddin Haqqani, Mansour, Yuldashev, Al Iraqi, Nek Mohammed Wazir, Elvis, Layth al Libi, and Gul Rahman. FRAGO XX to OPORD 03–01, CJTF-180, 6 Dec 2003, sub: Plan and Conduct Operation SECURE FUTURE, p. 7.

142. Concept Bfg, CJTF-180, n.d., sub: Operation SECURE FUTURE, pp. 3–11, 31, Hist Files, OEF Study Grp.

143. OPORD 04–07, CFC-A, 7 Nov 2004, sub: Support to National Assembly Elections, p. 6.

144. Concept Bfg, CJTF-180, n.d., sub: Operation SECURE FUTURE, p. 32.

Mountain Division as the commanding unit of the combined joint task force, the name also changed from CJTF-180 to CJTF-76. (The "180" designation traditionally had been given to joint task forces led by the Army's XVIII Airborne Corps, and the 25th Division does not traditionally fall under that corps. The choice of "76" called upon imagery from American history, specifically the democratic spirit of 1776.) On 6 May, TF WARRIOR transferred authority to the 3d Brigade, 25th Infantry Division, at Kandahar Airfield. With the additional forces already at Kandahar, 3d Brigade transformed into Combined Task Force BRONCO under Col. Richard N. Pedersen. It initially included Lt. Col. Terry L. Sellers' 2d Battalion, 5th Infantry; Lt. Col. M. Scott McBride's 2d Battalion, 35th Infantry; Lt. Col. Clarence Neason Jr.'s 3d Battalion, 7th Field Artillery; Lt. Col. Robert G. Young's 325th Support Battalion; several ANA battalions; and four Provincial Reconstruction Teams. Containing more than 3,000 soldiers and headquartered at Kandahar Airfield, TF BRONCO had RC South as its area of operations, encompassing Nimroz, Helmand, Kandahar, Zabul, Uruzgan, Paktiya, Khost, Paktika, and Daykundi Provinces (*Map 6.1*).

Responsibility for RC East originally fell to the 6th Marines. The area of operations included Bamyan, Parwan, Kapisa, Nuristan, Kunar, Laghman, Kabul, Wardak, Logar, Nangarhar, and Ghazni Provinces. The 25th Infantry Division Artillery headquarters, commanded by Col. Gary H. Cheek, took over RC East in June 2004. It formed Combined Task Force THUNDER, composed of Lt. Col. Walter E. Piatt's 2d Battalion, 27th Infantry; followed by the addition of Lt. Col. Blake C. Otner's 3d Battalion, 116th Infantry, 29th Infantry Division, in July; Lt. Col. Brian M. Drinkwine's 1st Battalion, 505th Infantry, in September; several ANA battalions; a military police platoon; eight Provincial Reconstruction Teams, including one from New Zealand; and Logistics Task Force 34. The primary mission for TF THUNDER was to stem the growing stream of weapons and Taliban recruits flowing into northeastern Afghanistan from Pakistan. TF THUNDER would be the first ad hoc nonmaneuver brigade to have control of its own battlespace in ENDURING FREEDOM, demonstrating the flexibility of the divisional artillery headquarters.[145]

The newcomers understood Barno's guidance, expected to operate in the assigned areas of operations, and arrived with personnel who were certified to spend the funds from the Commander's Emergency Response Program. TF BRONCO's deployment order reflected Barno's counterinsurgency focus.[146] Deviating from established precedent, Colonel Pedersen stated that he would measure success by "ever increasing" numbers of Afghans persuaded to support Karzai's government and reject the Taliban, a metric in accordance

---

145. Wright et al., *A Different Kind of War*, p. 334.

146. According to the order, TF BRONCO would seek an end state in which "the central government's influence is extended through stabilization and implementation of good governmental practices, delivery of humanitarian assistance, reconstruction, and economic development." OPORD 04–01, CTF BRONCO (3d Bde, 25th Div), 22 May 2004, sub: BRONCO STRIKE (OEF-5 Combat Operations), p. 5, Hist Files, OEF Study Grp.

with CFC-A's goals.[147] Having a tactical command prepared to fight a counterinsurgency helped Barno achieve the unity of effort he had sought to instill since arriving in theater.

Despite their training, it took the 25th Infantry Division time to become comfortable with conducting a counterinsurgency. Although the division did not assume responsibility for the entire country, the newcomers found themselves spread across a large expanse of terrain, with some battalions deployed in the rugged eastern region while the remainder served on the southern plains. In addition to very different types of terrain, unexpected ethnic, tribal, and political factors meant that U.S. forces needed to reconfigure some of their initial subordinate boundaries. When the 2d Battalion, 35th Infantry, first arrived, for example, it operated from Kandahar Airfield and was responsible for parts of three provinces.[148] After strong advocacy from Colonel McBride, CJTF-76 redrew his area of operations. Instead of having to establish relationships with three governors and learn the dynamics of three provinces, McBride could devote his energies to mastering a single province and building a strong relationship with one governor.[149]

Combined Task Force BRONCO soon recognized that the central problem with promoting Afghan governance was the lack of an Afghan government to promote. One challenge that 2d Battalion, 35th Infantry, faced in 2004 was that even its downsized area of operations, Zabul Province, had only enough officials and security personnel to staff four of eleven districts.[150] As one company-grade officer wrote after a mission, "the first lesson taken away from this operation was the need for provincial representation during an operation, whether it's the governor himself, his security chief, an NDS [National Directorate of Security] agent, or a combination of the three."[151] Although the ideal representative may not have existed, somebody was better than nobody.

Rumors of an impending Taliban spring offensive, designed to upset the scheduled Afghan elections, shifted Barno's attention from extending the Kabul government's reach to safeguarding the democratic election. With emphasis from Barno and Olson, election fervor soon permeated the ranks. Commanders and soldiers welcomed this focus not only because the election promised to invest the central government with legal status but also because it justified their deployments. As stated by 1st Lt. Robert S. Anders, a platoon leader with 2d Battalion, 27th Infantry, in Paktika from spring 2004 to spring 2005, "The election itself impacted this counterinsurgency like

---

147. Ibid., p. 12.

148. The 2d Battalion, 35th Infantry's original area of operations spanned Zabul, Uruzgan, and Kandahar Provinces. Chris Barlow, untitled (PEP, Inf Capts Career Course, 20 Jan 2005), pp. 2–3, Hist Files, OEF Study Grp.

149. Ibid., pp. 2–3.

150. Ibid., p. 5.

151. Ibid., p. 7.

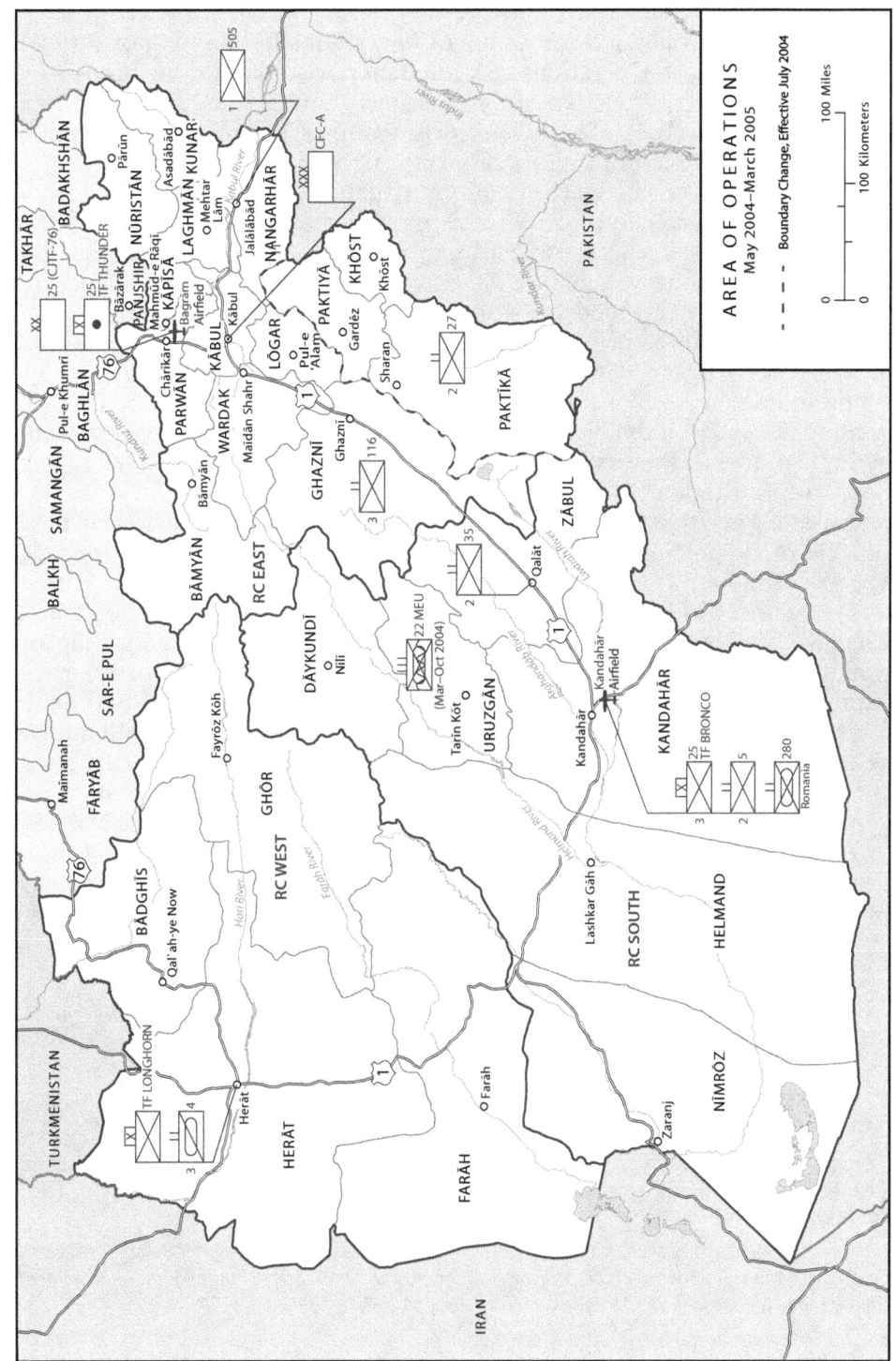

Map 6.1

a nuclear bomb would in a conventional war."[152] In addition to the efforts of CJTF-76, the Special Operations task force supported the election process by conducting Operation TICONDEROGA in eastern, southeastern, and southern Afghanistan as well as a counterterrorist mission, code-named Operation TRENTON, designed to preempt threats to the presidential election.[153]

CENTCOM considered the elections, which had to be rescheduled from July to October owing to security concerns and voter registration difficulties, so important that General Abizaid deployed his theater reserve, the 22d Marine Expeditionary Unit, to Afghanistan amidst growing violence in Iraq.[154] Originally intended for a short stay, the 22d arrived at Kandahar Airfield in late March before travelling north to the predominantly Pashtun province of Uruzgan. Commanded by Col. Kenneth F. McKenzie Jr., its subordinate elements consisted of 1st Battalion, 6th Marines, led by Lt. Col. Asad A. Khan; Medium Helicopter Squadron 266 (Reinforced) commanded by Lt. Col. Joel R. Powers; and the Service Support Group 22 led by Lt. Col. Benjamin R. Braden.[155]

By late May, the marines finished constructing a forward operating base capable of supporting fixed- and rotary-wing flight operations just outside Tarin Kot. Soon afterward, the marines began conducting company-sized forays against Taliban centers of resistance in Daychopan to the east and Chahar Chinah to the west of Tarin Kot that resulted in the killing or wounding of scores of enemy fighters.[156] The 22d Marine Expeditionary Unit's initial efforts were so effective that CJTF-76 placed the 2d Battalion, 5th Infantry, under McKenzie's control. Using the forward operating base as a launching pad, the combined force aggressively targeted suspected enemy concentrations during June and July only to discover the Taliban had departed.[157] Their absence allowed officials from the UN Assistance Mission in Afghanistan to register 44 percent of their goal for Uruzgan Province before the election, and also ensured voters were not intimidated when they went to the polls.[158]

---

152. Robert S. Anders, *Winning Paktika: Counterinsurgency in Afghanistan* (Bloomington, Ill.: AuthorHouse, 2013), p. 319.

153. Bogart, *One Valley at a Time*, p. 62.

154. CJTF-76 Public Affairs Ofc, "Combined/Joint Task Force 76 Deployment Historical Book, 15 April 2004–15 Mar 2005," p. 247, Hist Files, OEF Study Grp.

155. Paul Westermeyer, "MOUNTAIN STORM: Counterinsurgency and the Marine Air-Ground Task Force (Hist Div Landpower Essay, Marine Corps University, n.d.), p. 6, Hist Files, OEF Study Grp.

156. Col Kenneth F. McKenzie, Maj Roberta L. Shea, and Maj Christopher Phelps, "Marines Deliver in Mountain Storm," *U.S. Marines in Afghanistan, 2001–2009: Anthology and Annotated Bibliography* (Quantico, Va.: Marine Corps History Division, 2014), pp. 127–33.

157. Westermeyer, "MOUNTAIN STORM," pp. 8–9.

158. CJTF-76 Public Affairs Ofc, "Combined/Joint Task Force 76 Deployment Historical Book, 15 April 2004–15 Mar 2005," p. 247; Abizaid extended the 22d Marine Expeditionary Unit for thirty days and considered a sixty-day extension. FRAGO 07-275, CENTCOM, 10 Jun 2004, sub: 22d Marine Expeditionary Unit (SOC) Extension, Hist Files, OEF Study Grp.

The 22d Marine Expeditionary Unit's intervention, when combined with sustained preparations by CJTF-76 and SOF elements, enabled the Afghan government to hold a peaceful election with an unambiguous outcome on 9 October 2004. Barno estimated that his brigades, battalions, and reconstruction teams helped the Afghans register more than ten million voters.[159] On the day of voting, ENDURING FREEDOM forces maintained an outer perimeter, letting Afghan security forces protect polling stations so as not to taint the process with overt outside influence.[160] The elections had high voter turnout and few if any disruptions, though there were claims of voter and electoral fraud as well as intimidation at the polls. In spite of these claims, Afghan voters chose Hamid Karzai as the clear winner of the 2004 presidential election. Many American commanders in Afghanistan claimed the election as their unit's most important accomplishment during their deployments.[161]

Although the election elicited both positive press and euphoria in the ranks, it had come at a cost.[162] Worried that coalition forces would be viewed as meddling, the DoD pressured the Office of Military Cooperation–Afghanistan to produce enough kandaks to secure polling sites and counting houses, even though this increased the risk of forming units that would collapse over time through casualties and desertions.[163] Although the election was a milestone for the coalition forces, it could not contribute to security until the Afghan president had a functioning government and proper security forces with which to exercise sovereignty.[164]

The presidential election accentuated how the ENDURING FREEDOM mission had evolved since CJTF-180 had arrived in theater over two years before. General McNeill initially tried to project security by lengthy air insertions in which units traveled from secure locations to areas where the enemy was thought to be active. They responded to whatever resistance they encountered, but stayed only as long as it took to achieve their immediate objectives. As he received more troops, McNeill expanded eastward, building

---

159. Bfg, CFC-A, 22 Oct 2004, sub: Afghanistan: COIN Campaign, p. 3, Hist Files, OEF Study Grp.

160. Interv, Peter Connors, CSI, with Col Walter M. Herd, frmr CJSOTF-A Cdr, 22 Jun 2007, p. 4, Hist Files, OEF Study Grp.

161. For an example of pride in a unit's role in preparing for presidential elections, see Interv, Col Clarence Neason Jr., in Koontz, *Enduring Voices*, p. 368.

162. Barno viewed the election as a "knockout for democracy" that put the Taliban "on the ropes." Interv, Degen, Gibby, and Williams with Barno, 20 Jan 2016, p. 54. According to 1st Lt. Robert Anders, "[A]fter all the celebrations and congratulations, the election slipped quickly into the past." Anders, *Winning Paktika*, p. 327.

163. Eikenberry, commenting about his predecessor's time as commander of Combined Forces Command–Afghanistan, believed that "there was an acceleration of ANA force generation in order to have more Afghan National Army" units protecting election sites in the fall of 2004. Interv, Donald P. Wright, CSI, with Lt Gen Karl W. Eikenberry, frmr CFC-A Cdr, 23 Feb 2012, p. 37, Hist Files, OEF Study Grp.

164. Interv, M Sgt Robert Frazier, CMH, with Lt Col David Volkman, CFC-A CJ-9 Opns Ofcr, 7 Jun 2005, p. 11, Hist Files, OEF Study Grp.

During elections in Khost Province, an Afghan displays the purple ink on his finger, indicating that he has voted.

Provincial Reconstruction Teams and new bases. General Barno began his command believing that he could devote assets and attention to one area—greater Kandahar City was his first choice—and then, once secured, shift focus to another (preferably adjacent) area. After receiving a second maneuver brigade in April 2004, he altered this approach so as to exert influence in multiple areas at the same time. Adding to the operating bases and outposts McNeill and Vines had constructed, Barno grew ENDURING FREEDOM so that, by the October 2004 election, coalition troops were a regular presence in many southern and eastern communities.

Despite the many changes, CFC-A's operational approach during this period still relied heavily on the collection of human intelligence. On Barno's watch, attempts to acquire actionable intelligence from detainees went beyond the approved field manual approaches. Interrogations began to involve sleep deprivation, stress positions, and other techniques similar to those selectively approved for specific detainees under highly controlled interrogation at Guantanamo Bay Naval Base, and not approved for use on any detainees in Afghanistan. Despite employing these unorthodox and unauthorized techniques, the United States had not found an adequate process to obtain timely intelligence from detainees after two years of ENDURING FREEDOM.[165]

Spurred by the sustained public outrage over revelations of prisoner abuse at Abu Ghraib prison in Iraq, Barno requested that CJTF-76 conduct a "top to bottom review" of detention operations in the months leading up

---

165. V Adm A. T. Church III, *Review of Department of Defense Detention Operations and Detainees Interrogation Techniques*, Ofc of the Sec Def, 7 Mar 2005, pp. 80, 196, https://humanrights.ucdavis.edu/resources/library/documents-and-reports/ChurchReport.pdf, Hist Files, OEF Stdy Grp.

to the elections. The findings of the inspecting officer, Brig. Gen. Charles H. Jacoby Jr., suggested that ignorance regarding theater detention operations had "created opportunities for detainee abuse and *the loss of intelligence value* throughout the detention and interrogation process [emphasis added]." Jacoby also found inconsistent standards, uneven leadership, and inadequate tactics for holding, processing, and interrogating detainees for their intelligence value.[166]

Two issues decreased the intelligence value of detention and interrogation, one a condition of the Afghan theater and one a consequence of inadequate training and unclear policies. ENDURING FREEDOM informal force caps drove decisions about facility construction that limited long-term detention centers to Bagram and Kandahar airfields. Moving detainees to these airfields required the use of scarce aircraft or lengthy road movements. Either method of transportation taxed available resources, increasing the chances of untrained or impatient coalition personnel treating enemy fighters improperly during their journey from point of capture to detention facility.[167] Moreover, the use of military police to "set favorable conditions for subsequent interviews"—in essence, to intimidate detainees—merited special criticism. It was not a doctrinal task for military police, and it increased the likelihood of misconduct and abuse.[168] Although Jacoby and other inspectors discovered no evidence of higher officials or military authorities sanctioning abuse, a breakdown in individual discipline, unit order, and theater leadership created conditions under which soldiers felt that they could break rules to obtain the intelligence they wanted from detainees. Jacoby's report was the best-case scenario; the worst case was that soldiers had deliberately abused detainees for personal amusement.[169]

With the presidential election complete and ENDURING FREEDOM avoiding public condemnation for detainee abuse, Barno and his staff shifted resources and attention toward the upcoming National Assembly and provincial council elections.[170] Preparing for elections required planning as intensive as any other operation. To this end, the Joint Staff in the Pentagon directed the services, via the joint manning documents, to provide a robust, consistent flow of individual augmentees to fill Barno's six organizations.[171] Personnel fills for CJTF-76 rose from 61 percent to 75 percent between March 2004 and March 2005.[172] The Office of Military Cooperation received more personnel

---

166. Ibid., pp. 76–77.

167. Ibid., pp. 179, 191.

168. Ibid., pp. 58–59.

169. Ibid., pp. 92, 93–94, 96.

170. OPORD 04–07, CFC-A, 7 Nov 2004, sub: Support to National Assembly Elections, sec. 1.B.1.A.

171. Joint manning documents had been created for CFC-A, CJTF-76, Office of Military Cooperation–Afghanistan, Provincial Reconstruction Teams, CJSOTF-A, and the Joint Logistics Command. These manning documents specifically outline the number, grade, and skills of the personnel on the staff. CENTCOM, 24 Mar 2005, sub: JMD Update, p. 3, Hist Files, OEF Study Grp.

172. Ibid., p. 22.

over the same interval as well, although its fill percentage decreased from 72 percent to 55 percent because it had added 154 billets to its authorized size.[173] The joint staff expanded Barno's headquarters the most, more than doubling it from 50 to 109 personnel.[174]

Barno's strengthened staff pursued several initiatives during this second round of election preparations. While CJTF-76 performed the same support missions that they had for the presidential election, the CJSOTF altered its approach to reflect the new legitimacy of the Afghan government. In particular, ODAs conducted partnered operations to disrupt Taliban networks in the south and to provide reconnaissance and shaping operations in RC East.[175] From July until the calendar year's end, Operation NEWBURGH established a strategic watch over the National Assembly and provincial council elections.[176] As elements of Special Operations Task Force 31 conducted reconnaissance and shaping operations in the south, they included Afghan security forces in the formation to legitimize national governance.[177] Locals provided detachments with the location of anticoalition militia sanctuaries, which resulted in additional missions and the further securing of the voting process.

Meanwhile, CFC-A sought new ways to connect Afghans with the central government. Having already maximized reconstruction team coverage with his available forces, General Barno turned his attention to the most physical of connections between capital and provinces: roads. The first major project consisted of a paved multilane highway from Kandahar City to Tarin Kot designated as National Highway 617, funded by the U.S. Agency for International Development. The project appealed to CJTF-76 because it could provide U.S. forces with improved access to Taliban-controlled areas running from Zabul Province through northern Kandahar, Uruzgan, and Helmand Provinces. Given the escalating frequency of attacks on aid workers, construction could occur only if the U.S. military provided security. As a result, the development agency and CJTF-76 partnered in early 2004, with the former providing technical expertise, project funding, and contracted construction assistance and the latter contributing military engineers and security forces.[178]

Colonel Pedersen's brigade provided security while the 528th Engineer Battalion (Heavy) of Col. Nancy J. Wetherill's 109th Engineer Group (South

---

173. Ibid.

174. Ibid.

175. Michael E. Krivdo, "CJSOTF-A (Combined Joint Special Operations Task Force-Afghanistan): A Short History, 2002–2014" *Veritas: Journal of Army Special Operations History* 12, no. 2 (2016): 12.

176. Ibid.

177. William G. Robertson, ed., *In Contact!: Case Studies from the Long War*, vol. 1 (Fort Leavenworth, Kans.: Combat Studies Institute Press, 2006), p. 104.

178. Maj Nicolas O. Melin, "The Challenge of Access: Using Road Construction as a Tool in Counterinsurgency" (Fort Leavenworth, Kans.: U.S. Army Command and Staff College, 10 Jun 2011), pp. 111–12.

Local Afghan guards secure road construction in Paktiya Province. The Ring Road and many other road construction efforts were critical in linking the population to goods and services.

Dakota National Guard) built the road with commercial assets provided by the aid agency. Barno placed such high priority on the project that he and General Olson sent Pedersen reinforcements in the form of the 25th Infantry Division's 3d Squadron, 4th Cavalry. Pedersen and Wetherill devised a three-phased plan that began with a forty-five-kilometer section from the northern suburbs of Kandahar City through Arghandab District to the village of Dilak in the Shah Wali Kot District. The second phase, which comprised the next twenty-three-and-a-half kilometers of the road, had a forbidding terrain and high probability of enemy attacks. Although the final fifty kilometers of the planned road lay between two known insurgent safe havens, the terrain north of Shah Wali Kot flattened considerably, making it easier to construct the road more quickly and securely. Both Wetherill and Pedersen acknowledged that the entire project would not be completed before the 109th Engineer Group's redeployment. As a result, the 528th Engineer Battalion would also build a forward operating base north of Kandahar City for the incoming engineers to use.[179]

Ambassador Khalilzad, General Olson, and prominent Afghans, including regional powerbrokers Gul Agha Sharzai and Ahmed Wali Karzai, attended the June 2004 highway ground-breaking ceremony. Construction proceeded without interruption throughout the summer, although the need for security limited daily progress to meters rather than kilometers. Progress slowed further after Barno unexpectedly redeployed Lt. Col. Michael J. McMahon's 3d Squadron, 4th Cavalry, to western Afghanistan in response to rising tensions in Herat. To maintain momentum, the aid agency contracted

---

179. Ibid., pp. 114–17.

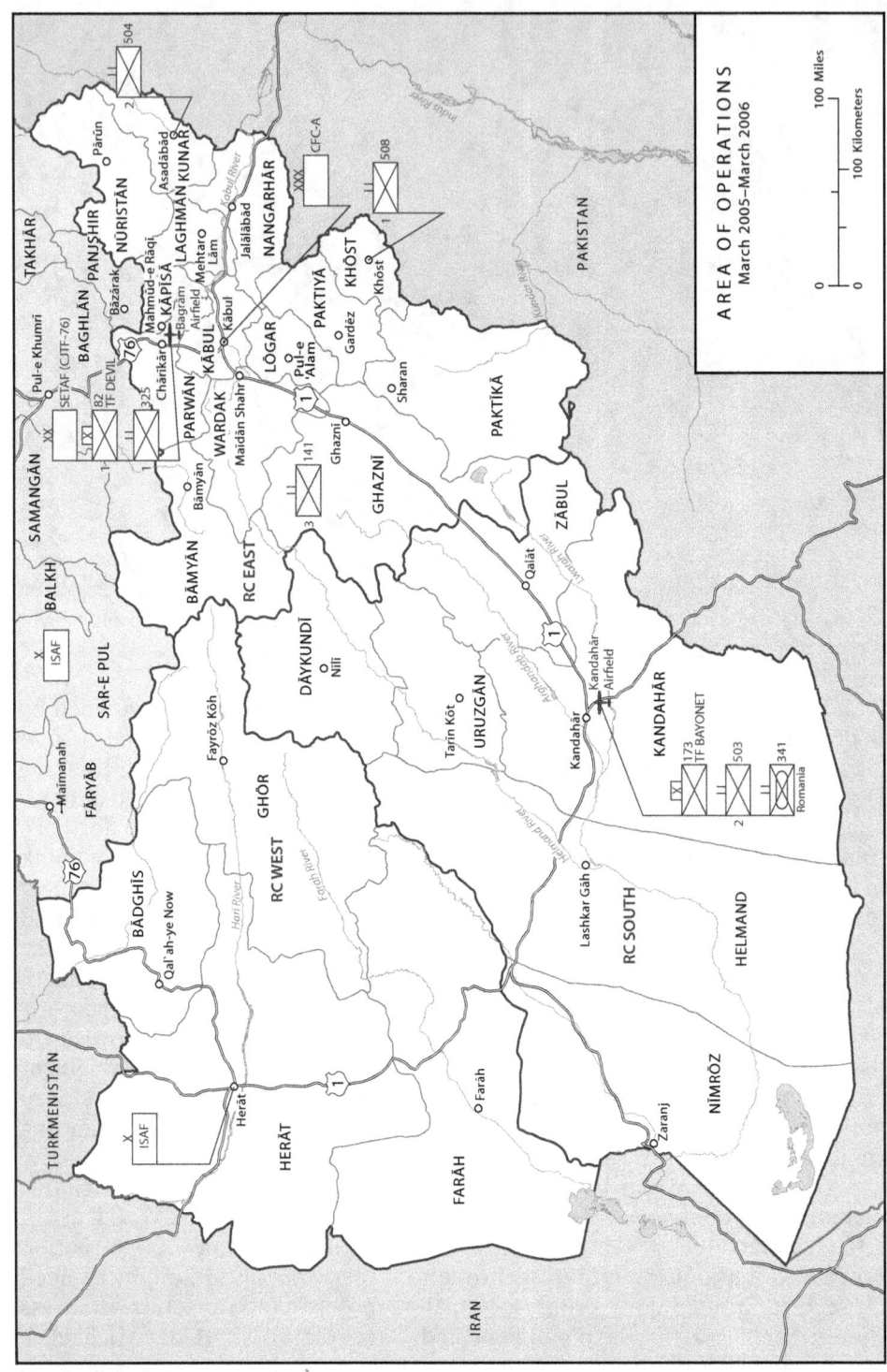

Map 6.2

security from Afghan militia forces. With this help, engineers were able to complete the first section of road and build the forward operating base just before the October 2004 election. In the months following the election, harsh weather began to impede construction, halting it completely by March 2005. Construction resumed in early May 2005 with one team of engineers working southward and another making its way northward through the mountainous Shah Wali Kot.[180]

Transitions in both units and operational priorities combined to divert energies from road building during this period (*Map 6.2*). Maj. Gen. Jason K. Kamiya's Southern European Task Force had taken over as CJTF-76 headquarters in March 2005. Col. Kevin C. Owens' 173d Airborne Brigade, consisting of Lt. Col. Mark R. Stammer's 2d Battalion, 503d Infantry; Lt. Col. Bertrand A. Ges' 3d Battalion, 319th Field Artillery (temporarily detached from the 82d Airborne); Capt. Dirk D. Ringgenberg's 74th Infantry Detachment (Long Range Surveillance); an ANA battalion with French advisers; the 341st Romanian Mechanized Battalion; and Lt. Col. Cynthia Fox's 173d Support Battalion made up half of the ground force for CJTF-76. Col. Patrick J. Donahue II's 1st Brigade, 82d Airborne Division, consisting of Lt. Col. David P. Anders' 1st Battalion, 325th Infantry; Lt. Col. George T. "Tom" Donovan's 2d Battalion, 504th Infantry; Lt. Col. Timothy P. McGuire's 1st Battalion, 508th Infantry (temporarily detached from the 173d Airborne); Lt. Col. James E. Donnellan's 2d Battalion, 3d Marines; and Lt. Col. Orlando Salinas' 3d Battalion, 141st Infantry (Texas Army National Guard), formed the remainder of ground forces under General Kamiya's CJTF-76.[181]

Faced with intelligence that indicated increased insurgent pressure in eastern and northeastern Afghanistan, CJTF-76 focused on RC East rather than RC South following the handover from the 25th Infantry Division. Donahue's brigade, which was responsible for that region, received no fewer than five maneuver battalions from Kamiya. The new CJTF-76 commander also increased the number of Special Forces firebases and checkpoints on the Afghanistan-Pakistan border from twelve to seventeen. As the supporting effort, Colonel Owens' 173d Airborne Brigade had only one infantry battalion, one field artillery battalion, and detachments of Afghan and Romanian units to influence RC South.[182] Despite the reduced level of readily available support, Col. Matthew H. Russell's 18th Engineer Brigade, which replaced Wetherill's unit, received the mission of completing the final ninety kilometers of the road in the southern part of the country before the National Assembly and provincial council elections scheduled for 18 September 2005.[183]

---

180. Ibid., p. 121.

181. Wright et al., *A Different Kind of War*, p. 336; Patrick J. Donahue and Michael Fenzel, "Combating a Modern Insurgency: Combined Task Force Devil in Afghanistan," *Military Review* 88, no. 2 (Mar-Apr 2008): 40. Colonel Ges' battalion task force came to resemble TF THUNDER in miniature, consisting of his organic batteries; Company D, 1st Battalion, 325th Infantry; Company B, 1st Battalion, 508th Infantry; and several ANA companies.

182. Interv, Angela McClain and Steven Clay, CSI, with Col Kevin C. Owens, frmr 173d Abn Bde Cdr, 9 and 10 Dec 2008, pp. 7–8, Hist Files, OEF Study Grp.

183. Melin, "The Challenge of Access," pp. 125–26.

The 18th Engineer Brigade resumed work that summer knowing that a firm deadline loomed in the near future. On 18 August, the southern and northern teams met each other, ensuring the military portion of the project would be completed before the scheduled due date. Although Americans had paved the southernmost and northern third of the route, insurgent activity prevented the 18th Engineer Brigade from using commercial assistance to perform the same task for the middle third. With virtually every American soldier in Afghanistan preparing for the elections, the final phase of the road-building effort would not be completed before the winter of 2005–2006.[184]

Despite minor setbacks, Barno left command believing that roads, elections, and an emphasis on counterinsurgency had improved conditions in Afghanistan. Although he saw ENDURING FREEDOM as undergoing a "consolidation," this phase would end with the National Assembly and provincial council elections.[185] Violence against Afghans, Americans, and ISAF personnel was low. Barno had involved the coalition in all aspects of Afghan governance, as Abizaid had wanted and expected him to do.[186] However, some initiatives championed by Barno produced far different results than envisioned. For example, the central government still did not have enough influence to oversee or secure newly built roads, which led to local warlords and corrupt Afghan security force leaders illegally collecting tolls from drivers. In this instance, a development project backed by the Americans actually contributed to, rather than diminished, the spread of lawlessness within Afghanistan.

MEASURING SUCCESS

Long-standing differences between the perceptions of Washington policymakers and the actual conditions in Afghanistan reappeared in early 2005. The National Security Council had always planned Accelerating Success to be a temporary effort. The program began to wane in late 2004, and was effectively complete by January 2005 when National Security Advisor Condoleezza Rice declared that the effort had brought "transformative changes in governance, security, and reconstruction" to Afghanistan. Rice supported her assertion that Accelerating Success had completed its objectives by listing metrics: leaders persuaded, soldiers and police trained, weapons collected, dollars spent, and positive responses from polled Afghans. With such quantifiable achievements seeming to indicate clear progress, the Bush

---

184. Ibid., pp. 141–49.

185. The second phase, "transition," would change the ENDURING FREEDOM mission from counterinsurgency to reintegrating warlords and disrupting drug networks. In the third phase, "recovery," forces loyal to the Afghan government would replace U.S. units as the primary provider of national security. Bfg, David Lamb et al., CFC-A, 3 Mar 2005, sub: Campaign Plan in Support of Operation Enduring Freedom, p. 17, Hist Files, OEF Study Grp.

186. Interv, Degen, Gibby, and Williams with Barno, 20 Jan 2016, pp. 44, 55.

administration could justify shifting its focus from Afghanistan to other areas of national concern.[187]

In the absence of more traditional metrics showing military success—battlefield victories, terrain liberated, enemy forces eliminated—the administration had to rely on more nuanced evidence to show that the American effort was on track. Rice's statistics were meant to illustrate to the American public, the media, and others within the administration that progress was being made in rebuilding Afghanistan. However, they also created a false narrative by not providing a deeper assessment of the metrics. Highlighting dollars spent, teachers trained, reconstruction teams made operational, and markets opened did not tell the full story. Although accurate, data alone could be misleading. Money had been wasted, teachers were afraid to teach due to insurgent threats, reconstruction teams increased Afghan reliance on foreign aid as easily as they promoted its independence, and markets closed as spontaneously as they opened. Focusing only on metrics that showed progress supported the administration's narrative but it also clouded the view of what was actually happening in Afghanistan.

For the Army, measuring success at the operational level was just as difficult. General Barno's key contribution in Afghanistan was changing the lens through which the American-led coalition viewed the operational problem. In response to pressure from CENTCOM, Barno developed a campaign plan that deviated sharply from the counterterrorism focus of his predecessors. In setting a new purpose for coalition troops in Afghanistan, the CFC-A commander freed himself from doctrinal norms and adopted a broad concept of how power could be exercised, embracing state-building without using that loaded term. To track his campaign, Barno periodically updated a list of CFC-A accomplishments. Some claims made for good talking points: between July 2003 and March 2005, Provincial Reconstruction Teams increased in number from four to nineteen, and Afghan political leaders agreed on a moderate Islamic constitution.[188] Other improvements, such as transitioning from "warlords empowered" to "warlords diminished" were murky and hard to quantify.[189] Still, by the end of his command, Barno believed that CFC-A had achieved the goal of securing Afghanistan, even if the actual definition of "secure" proved elusive.[190]

Unfortunately, Barno's emphasis on CFC-A's purported accomplishments had the same problems as the administration's use of metrics. Moreover, as important as the shift in approach was, Barno was still constrained by the size of his forces. Without sufficient resources to fully implement the new campaign plan, CFC-A was limited in what it could achieve. Compounding

---

187. Memo, Rice for Cheney, Powell, Snow, Rumsfeld, Card, Goss, Myers, 18 Jan 2005, sub: Accelerating Success in Afghanistan in 2004: An Assessment, p. 1.

188. Bfg, CFC-A, 25 Mar 2005, sub: CG Final Version Brief to Counterpart, p. 2, Hist Files, OEF Study Grp. One more Provincial Reconstruction Team would be established at Methar Lam in Laghman Province in April, the last full month of Barno's command. Eleven of the sixteen teams were American-run; NATO countries fielded the other five.

189. Ibid.

190. Interv, Degen, Gibby, and Williams with Barno, 20 Jan 2016, p. 55.

this problem was Barno's belief that having the greatest numbers, most firepower, and deepest pockets made him responsible for the entire coalition effort. Even in areas where other organizations or headquarters led, CFC-A needed to support, coordinate, and sequence the activity on the ground.[191] He instructed staff members to adopt a "we own it all" mentality: he did not want them to ignore other organizations' problems because they did not have the U.S. Army's institutional capacity.[192] This thinking fit well with the Army's focus on full-spectrum operations—the idea that troops under the same commander may have to conduct offensive, defensive, stability, and security operations at the same time and in the same area of operations. Barno's full-spectrum mentality also led him to accept the vision espoused by his stateside command. After securing the National Assembly and provincial council elections—planned for April 2005 but conducted in September 2005—Barno anticipated shifting to a coalition focus on reconstruction, with reconstruction teams serving as the organizational structure through which it would occur.[193] As NATO's influence rose due to its leading role in staffing and operating the reconstruction teams, America's role would diminish accordingly.[194] At the same time, CFC-A would support Karzai's reconciliation with the Taliban and HIG—an idea that American politicians, diplomats, and generals had rejected, more or less consistently, ever since the September 11th attacks.[195]

As important as Barno's shift to a counterinsurgency approach was, it still relied upon the belief that coalition activity could persuade the Afghans as to their new government's legitimacy. Stressing the political nature of the conflict, Barno's approach required reconstruction teams to connect Kabul to the countryside.[196] However, the Afghan government's inability to generate a comparable effort undercut many of CFC-A's initiatives. A strong urban-to-rural connection was important for Afghanistan's future, but American troops alone could not build that connection. Afghan leaders had to convince residents that their central government, and not representatives from a foreign power, was acting in their best interests. Outsiders would find it difficult to convince the people to trust the new government, especially when that message had to be filtered through mullahs, mayors, district governors, provincial governors, and interim national leaders, all of whom had tribal and ethnic agendas as important to them as any attempt to reinforce a largely nonexistent national unity.[197] These complex and unseen motivations made loyalties in this environment hard for military leaders to ascertain.

---

191. Interv, Hughes and Mundey with Barno, 21 Nov 2006, p. 34.

192. Ibid., p. 47.

193. OPORD 04–07, CFC-A, 7 Nov 2004, sub: Support to National Assembly Elections, pp. 12, 14, 18, 29.

194. Ibid., p. 25.

195. Ibid., 3, 18, 30.

196. OPORD 04–01, CTF Bronco, 3d Bde, 25th Div, 22 May 2004, sub: BRONCO STRIKE (OEF-5 Combat Operations), p. 13.

197. Ibid., p. 21.

In fact, the interactions intended to ready Afghans for independence only increased their dependence on the coalition. Building national unity among a people with a history of partisan divisions would be a long and involved process. Barno's political-based counterinsurgency needed time and resources that neither Abizaid nor NATO could provide. Likewise the Taliban-led insurgency would not wait for the coalition or the Karzai government to improve Afghan security and stability. No matter what the reports, memos, and briefings said in Washington or Kabul, based upon the reality on the ground, the United States was no closer to disengaging from Afghanistan at the end of Barno's year and a half in command than it was when he arrived.

THE U.S. ARMY MEETING UNANTICIPATED STRATEGIC NEEDS

As the Afghan theater continued to evolve, the U.S. Army at home needed to adapt to ensure continued support to demanding global missions beyond those of ENDURING FREEDOM. The twenty-first-century Army faced a different set of demands than those anticipated by the Vietnam-era Abrams Doctrine, and the Army would have to rebalance its structure between the active and reserve components in order to respond to those demands. As early as 1 November 2001, Secretary Rumsfeld opined that any situation in which the Army could not perform a key mission without activating the reserves appeared particularly "unwise."[198] As part of transformation-oriented restructuring, Rumsfeld directed the return of capabilities from the reserves that the active component would need in order to perform critical battlefield functions rapidly. A series of subsequent studies by the Army led to an Active Component/Reserve Component Rebalancing briefing on 7 November 2003, out of which came the Chief of Staff of the Army Directive 7. This directive mandated the development of force structure options for a modular army and a revised active and reserve component mix, consistent with "transforming the Army into a campaign quality Army with a joint force and expeditionary mindset."[199]

REBALANCING THE FORCE

Directive 7 led to an Army-wide message on 5 January 2004 directing force structure changes to bring the entire active Army to the highest readiness levels. The document also directed the identification of units and career fields that would be inactivated or downsized in order to fully fill the operating force. It would take considerable funding to provide enough resources to maintain the entire active Army at the highest levels of readiness, but by

---

198. Memo, Sec Def Donald Rumsfeld to Dov Zakheim and Steve Cambone, 1 Nov 2001, sub: Tasks—Reserve Vs. Active Duty, Hist Files, OEF Study Grp.

199. Msg, Ofc of the Deputy Ch of Staff for Opns and Plans, Force Management Directorate, Def Messaging Service Gen Service Msg, 5 Jan 2004, sub: CSA Initiative on ALO and AC/RC Balance, Hist Files, OEF Study Grp.

late 2003, when even rested and fit infantry battalions had become scarce, the Army's mission demands left little recourse.[200] From the standpoint of resourcing and training units, it was far easier to maintain organizations at peak readiness than to reconstitute understrength units that were not fully proficient even with all their required personnel and equipment.

The same message also proposed additional personnel for reserve component units considered "high demand" organizations, especially those responsible for the Army's support to other services and its obligations as an executive agent under Title 10, U.S. Code. Furthermore, it announced the creation of a trainees, transients, holdees, and students account for the reserve component, organized along the same lines as an existing active component account. This account forced reserve unit commanders to maintain nondeployable soldiers on their rolls until they could be formally transferred to the trainees, transients, holdees, and students account for reassignment, training, treatment, or separation.[201]

The scope and the pace of the changes that General Peter J. Schoomaker envisioned led to the first significant change in a loose collection of directives known as the The Army Plan, which would change the way the Army implemented its institutional strategy. On 20 February 2004, Schoomaker authorized the distribution of a new *Army Campaign Plan* that became Section IV (Execution) of The Army Plan, replacing Shinseki's *Army Transformation Campaign Plan*. The new document codified the institutional direction and guidance to the Army's headquarters and staff, its subordinate commands, direct reporting units, and field operating agencies.[202]

The *Army Campaign Plan* published in April 2004 described the Army's actions to address the realities of competing combat operations. It also represented the formal articulation of the assumptions necessary to drive the implementation of a campaign-quality Army. The most significant *Army Campaign Plan* assumption was that the Army's level of strategic commitment would continue at current pace but not necessarily in Afghanistan and Iraq, and that the Army would be able to use supplemental funding to build forces in support of new and ongoing contingency operations. It also assumed that any expansion of the force would have to be coordinated with changes directed by the Defense Base Closure and Realignment Commission, while still maintaining an all-volunteer force. Finally, and perhaps most telling, was the last assumption, which stated that "requirements for RC [reserve component] capabilities in support of global security operations will remain elevated for the foreseeable future," including both combat operations and homeland defense.[203]

---

200. Adams, *The Army After Next*, p. 182.

201. Msg, Ofc of the Deputy Ch of Staff for Opns and Plans, Force Management Directorate, Def Messaging Service Gen Service Msg, 5 Jan 2004, sub: CSA Initiative on ALO and AC/RC Balance.

202. Ofc of the Deputy Ch of Staff, G–3/5/7, *Planning Directive-Army Campaign Plan* (Washington, D.C.: HQDA, 2004), p. 1, Hist Files, OEF Study Grp.

203. Ofc of the Deputy Ch of Staff, G–3/5/7, *Army Campaign Plan* (Washington, D.C.: HQDA, 2004), pp. 1–2, Hist Files, OEF Study Grp.

Modularity

The first sweeping change mandated by General Schoomaker's vision of a campaign-quality force with joint and expeditionary capabilities involved changing the fundamental structure of the forces deploying to combat. The demand for Army forces to support two combat zones within a larger theater of war had emphasized two trends. The first was the importance of brigades in building the force, and the second was the importance of headquarters to employ that combat power effectively. The dramatic reorganization of the Army's forces that became known as modularity would launch the formalized force-management process known as Army Force Generation.

By summer 2003, the staffing demands imposed by the rotational system laid bare the reality that the existing force of thirty-three active and thirty-six National Guard maneuver brigades did not provide enough time to rest and refit those units between successive deployments. A reorganization of the Army would create a larger number of similarly organized brigade combat teams that could sustain the demand on the force over time. On 2 September 2003, General Schoomaker directed both the active and reserve components to take the following steps, with TRADOC as the Army's lead: "Initiate a reset of the Army to a provisional redesign. Reorganize the 3 ID (M) [3d Infantry Division] and 101st AA [101st Airborne Division] into prototype organizations that achieve the near-term modularity needed for the BDE [brigade] and DIV [division] echelons."[204]

Force design and structure debates were not new to the Army. One notable assessment of a possible Army restructuring was Douglas A. Macgregor's *Breaking the Phalanx: A New Design for Landpower in the 21st Century*, published in 1997. In his book, Macgregor makes a powerful argument for a more modular Army that is relevant to modern warfare. Macgregor's earlier work is similar to the Army's modular reorganization efforts under Schoomaker's command. Schoomaker's directive designated the prototype organizations as units of action (UAs), rather than as brigades and regiments. He provided further guidance by making clear his goal to "create modular, capabilities-based units of action . . . to enable rapid packaging and responsive, sustained employment. UAs must be as lethal as current brigade combat teams, be more deployable, and provide more combat forces within the current end strength of the Army."[205] The name change reflected a deliberate effort to avoid tying the new organizations to a particular echelon of command so as not to constrain how those units might be employed.

The Army leadership assembled a group of officers from TRADOC headquarters at Fort Monroe, Virginia, under Maj. Gen. Robert W. Mixon Jr., dubbed Task Force Modularity. The ad hoc study group had the mission

---

204. Presentation, HQ, U.S. Army Training and Doctrine Command, 11 Sep 2003, sub: TRADOC Mission Analysis: CSA Focus Areas vl.8, p. 18, Hist Files, OEF Study Grp.

205. Col Jeffrey R. Witsken, Maj Patrick L. Walden, and Peggy Fratzel, *Task Force Modularity Integrated Analysis Report: Analysis Underpinning Recommendations to the CSA, September 2003–March 2004* (Fort Leavenworth, Kans.: TRADOC Analysis Center, 31 Mar 2004), p. 4.

of formally developing structures to meet Schoomaker's guidance. Mixon drew on organizations across TRADOC for analytical support, as well as retired senior officers such as Lt. Gen. Leonard Donald Holder and Brig. Gen. Huba Wass de Czege, the principal authors of the Army's AirLand Battle doctrine in the 1980s, and Brig. Gen. Thomas R. Goedkoop, who commanded an armored brigade that was the test unit for the Army's Force XXI experiments in the 1990s.[206]

The task force concluded that the Army needed three types of modular brigade combat teams: heavy (armor and mechanized infantry), light (light infantry), and medium-weight Stryker Brigades. Task Force Modularity envisioned each as combined-arms organizations, with permanently organized infantry, armor, cavalry, field artillery, engineers, signal, military intelligence, and logistics capabilities. Schoomaker's units of action were also intended to be self-contained in order to operate independently of a division or corps headquarters if needed. While the aviation, engineer, field artillery, division support commands, and corps support groups were permanently organized around like battalions and separate companies, the modular brigade combat teams absorbed most of the subordinate elements belonging to separate battalions assigned to the division and separate brigades allocated to corps.[207]

One of the most significant changes proposed by Mixon was the presence of only two maneuver battalions in the heavy and light units of action, rather than the three battalions that had been part of the legacy brigade and Stryker brigade structures. The overriding consideration was one of cost. While simulations disclosed that a three-battalion unit of action was more capable than its two-battalion counterparts, the increased personnel bill to staff those units proved infeasible in light of Schoomaker's guidance to increase the number of brigade combat teams without adding to the overall Army end-strength. Even proposals to reduce the size of the battalions in order to create a third maneuver battalion violated the personnel caps that came with that structure. Furthermore, the two-battalion heavy and light unit of action designs included a small cavalry squadron for armed reconnaissance to partly offset the lack of a third battalion, although it was hardly optimal to employ cavalry in lieu of an infantry or armor battalion.[208]

The reorganization efforts mandated by Schoomaker's directive also involved flattening of the force's higher echelons, which shifted responsibilities to the transformed forces. The responsibilities that had been at divisions, corps, and theater armies before modularity were moved to so-called Units of Employment X and Y, which were designated as UEx and UEy respectively. The UEy was responsible for exercising administrative control over all Army forces in the combatant command area of responsibility, regardless of

---

206. Ibid., pp. 4–10.

207. Task Force Modularity, *Army Comprehensive Guide to Modularity (Version 1.0)* (Fort Monroe, Va.: U.S. Army Training and Doctrine Command, 2004), pp. 1-12–1-15.

208. Info Paper, Task Force Modularity, 8 Jan 2005, sub: Analysis of the Heavy and Light Brigade Combat Teams (BCT) with Three versus Two Maneuver Battalions, Hist Files, OEF Study Grp.

geographic location or command relationship.[209] The lower echelon UEx was intended as the Army's primary headquarters for operational and tactical combined arms operations. It would direct the operations of its subordinate units of action and be capable of serving as a joint force land component command, or as a joint task force when augmented for that mission. Unlike the divisions and corps that it would replace, the UEx had no organic forces other than its headquarters.[210]

Aside from the brigade combat teams, Task Force Modularity settled on creating five types of support units of action by taking existing force structure from the corps and division level. These support units included the combat aviation brigade; fires brigade; combat support brigade (maneuver enhancement); reconnaissance, surveillance, and target acquisition (later renamed the battlefield surveillance) brigade, and the sustainment brigade. Unlike their maneuver counterparts, most of these support units of action did not have fixed subordinate units, but instead had an organic headquarters and a pool of units assigned to the brigade. The pool of units did not necessarily deploy with the support unit of action they were organized under in garrison. The support units of action would be tailored to operational requirements before deployment, then would deploy in their task-organized state.[211]

The support units of action were built out of the formerly separate corps-level brigades and separate division-level battalions and squadrons. Similarly, the units of action received the missions that those separate brigades and battalions had previously accomplished. SOF were not affected, nor was the 3d Armored Cavalry—the last organization of its kind at the time.[212] The aviation and fires units of action were not dissimilar in functions from their predecessor aviation, corps field artillery, and division artillery brigades. Because the UEx took the place of the corps and division headquarters, any UEx could employ the combat aviation and fires units of action. Similarly, the sustainment units of action replaced the former division support commands and corps support groups, but were distributed approximately one per UEx.

The most extensive reorganization effort involved the creation of a combat support (maneuver enhancement) unit of action. Divisional and corps engineer brigades were inactivated, and their subordinate companies were placed in the maneuver UAs. Some of the personnel authorizations from the former engineer brigade headquarters were used to create the new organizations, which eventually were retitled as maneuver enhancement brigades. Rather than aligning along a particular branch, the maneuver enhancement brigade was oriented on the force protection function, which

---

209. Task Force Modularity, *Army Comprehensive Guide to Modularity (Version 1.0)*, p. 1-7.

210. Ibid., pp. 1-10–1-11.

211. Ibid., p. 1-16. The term "maneuver UA" refers to an infantry, heavy, or Stryker Unit of Action (UA) in this context.

212. The 11th Armored Cavalry was a unique organization at the National Training Center that converted to a modified heavy brigade, while the 2d Armored Cavalry (Light) was a 1990s-era experiment in lightening the force that ended with its conversion to a Stryker brigade combat team designated as the 2d Cavalry Regiment.

suggested task organization with air defense, engineer, military police, and chemical defense units.[213]

The initial future force transformation plan that emerged in 2005 from modular transformation involved the creation of up to ten additional active component maneuver units of action while increasing combat support and combat service support capabilities throughout the Army. Because the Army wanted to be able to rotate whole and like units regardless of component by fiscal year 2006, it envisioned that five Stryker and twenty-eight other maneuver units of action would have completed modular conversion, six of which would be new active component units. By the end of fiscal year 2009, seventy-seven active and reserve brigades were to have completed modular conversion, creating enough support units of action and other headquarters to support those maneuver units.[214]

The final component of modular conversion involved the permanent designation of the units themselves. Titles such as "Unit of Employment X," "Unit of Employment Y," and "Unit of Action" were useful in conceptualizing the roles and missions for the units, but had little resonance with the force itself. Among the proposed courses of action, one suggested designating the units of action as regiments, while another wanted to elevate the existing structural hierarchy by bestowing corps and divisional shoulder patches on divisions and units of action respectively. In the end, the new monikers for units' designations did not stick, and the Army retained brigades, divisions, and corps. The Army's senior leadership decided to reflag the UEy as theater armies, three-star UEx as corps, two-star UEx as divisions, and units of action as brigade combat teams, brigades, or separate regiments.[215] The decision recognized that corps still retained a requirement to command and control multiple divisions, as was the case with Multinational Corps–Iraq starting in May 2004. What was different was that the new modular divisions and corps were far more capable of acting as joint task forces, which reflected lessons learned in Iraq and Afghanistan.[216] The effort also would provide more combat brigades to better meet the demands of fighting in both theaters of war simultaneously.

ARMY FORCE GENERATION

General Schoomaker's vision of a campaign-quality force with joint and expeditionary capabilities led to his second major initiative and sparked significant changes to the Army Force Generation process by 2003–2004. This process, which involved the repetitive generation of trained and ready

---

213. Task Force Modularity, *Army Comprehensive Guide to Modularity (Version 1.0)*, p. 1-17.

214. Ofc of the Deputy Ch of Staff, G–3/5/7, *Army Campaign Plan, Change 2* (Washington, D.C.: HQDA, 2005), pp. 4–5. The number of "ten active component UA" comes from the *Army Green Books*. The *Army Campaign Plan* postulates up to fifteen additional UAs.

215. U.S. Army Center of Military History, "Unit Designations in the Army Modular Force," 30 Sep 2005, p. 10, Hist Files, OEF Study Grp.

216. Ofc of the Deputy Ch of Staff, G–3/5/7, 30 Sep 2005, "New Army Unit Designations in the Modular Army: Talking Points and Answers to Key Questions," Hist Files, OEF Study Grp.

forces to meet overseas contingency requirements, soon indicated that it would stress the Army in unforeseen ways during a protracted war. As a result, Schoomaker realized that he had to change how the Army provided forces for operational employment.[217]

Before the decision to adopt the new force generation model, and based on the assumption that they would carry out their wartime missions in accordance with their force design, Army units conducted their predeployment training using a mission-essential task list derived from Mission Training Plans specific to their type of unit. This task list became the basis for all individual and collective training plans and their associated resources to train for the unit's wartime mission.[218] However, units deploying to Iraq and Afghanistan found that they had to conduct tasks far removed from the doctrinal missions in their authorization documents. The list of traditional, warfighting, mission-essential training became known as a core mission-essential task list, while the tasks peculiar to a given deployment fell under the domain of a theater mission-essential task list, which later became known as the directed mission-essential task list. This split was particularly pronounced for units such as field artillery or transportation units given "in lieu-of" missions that were far removed from their core missions. Units would train on only one mission-essential task list at a time, so a deploying unit that trained on its directed tasks did not train on its core tasks until after its deployment had ended.[219]

To meet its obligations under Title 10, U.S. Code, the Army functionally divided into what was referred to as the Operational Army and the Institutional Army. Although those terms were not well defined in 2001, they became far better defined by 2005 as the Army provided capabilities to the joint force. The recognition that those capabilities did not cleanly divide along operational and institutional lines led to a shift in terminology, and starting in 2005 the functional divisions became known as the Operating Force and the Generating Force. As the Army leadership saw it, without the Generating Force the Operating Force could not act, and without the Operating Force the Generating Force would not exist.[220]

The Operating Army, and later the Operating Force, consists of units organized, trained, and equipped to deploy and fight as part of the joint force and are mainly under the purview of the Army's FORSCOM. By law, the secretary of defense assigned these units to unified combatant commanders via the Joint Forces Command. The Army provides the largest portion of both conventional ground forces and SOF. The Institutional Army, and later

---

217. Ofc of the Deputy Ch of Staff, G–3/5/7, *Army Campaign Plan, Change 2*, p. 67.

218. The entire process was the subject of HQDA FM 22–100, *Training the Force* (Washington, D.C.: Government Printing Ofc, 1988).

219. HQDA FM 7–0, *Training for Full Spectrum Operations* (Washington, D.C.: Government Printing Ofc, 2008), pp. 4–7.

220. HQDA FM 1, *The Army* (Washington, D.C.: Government Printing Ofc, 2001), p. 27; HQDA FM 1, *The Army* (Washington, D.C.: Government Printing Ofc, 2005), pp. 2-9–2-10; Ofc of the Deputy Ch of Staff, G–3/5/7, *Army Campaign Plan, Change 2*, pp. 9–10; Ofc of the Deputy Ch of Staff, G–3/5/7, *Army Campaign Plan, Change 5* (Washington, D.C.: HQDA, 2007), pp. J-8, J-11, Hist Files, OEF Study Grp.

the Generating Force, provides the Army's functions mandated by federal law to organize, man, train, and equip the forces that were to be provided to combatant commanders. The Generating Force includes the recruiting functions, schools, and soldier training centers. It also includes the organic industrial base, made up of the Army's industrial facilities responsible for producing or maintaining equipment, ammunition, weapons, and other materiel for the Army. Essentially, the Generating Force is the mission of the U.S. Army's TRADOC.

Army Force Generation was a management process intended to focus all active and reserve conventional forces on the missions they could expect to conduct, while retaining the capability to increase the Army's combat power if needed for contingency operations. It explicitly sought to integrate force generation, transformation, force modernization, training, and resourcing in a synchronized process. Rather than focus on events to spur force generation, the process sought to manage the readiness of units for specified deployment timelines, with predictability as the goal.[221]

Units taking part in the force generation process passed through three different "pools" of forces: reset/retrain, ready, and available. Active Army units remained in each pool for one year as part of the three-year cycle, while reserve forces usually applied a five-year cycle. At the onset, FORSCOM, which was responsible for executing the Army's force-provider responsibilities, held a synchronization conference to balance known operational requirements, ongoing operations, war plan requirements, exercises, and transformation experiments. The units identified to fill each of those requirements were assigned to the reset/retrain pool to conduct specific pre-mission training. Units earmarked for ongoing operations were moved into the ready pool, where they organized and trained for their operational missions, then deployed to those operations as they moved into the available pool as part of a Deployment Expeditionary Force. All other forces not intended for immediate employment would train for their core missions as part of the ready pool. Some were earmarked for rapid deployment as part of a Contingency Expeditionary Force, while other units were part of a Ready Expeditionary Force made available for war plans, exercises, and experimentation. After completing their planned training, units would move into the available pool of forces for a year. Active-duty units that did not deploy, whether contingency or not, returned to the reset/retrain pool at the end of that third year (*Figure 6.2*).[222]

What made Army Force Generation more than just another force management construct was the scope of its intended synchronization of resources. Instead of traditionally limiting its oversight to training and equipment, the synchronization process sought to account for facilities, training areas, personnel, and equipment. Given that the DoD was resourcing all National Guard units to the highest readiness levels and implementing Army Force Generation at the same time, the new system was a useful approach to deter-

---

221. Ofc of the Deputy Ch of Staff, G–3/5/7, *Army Campaign Plan, Change 2*, pp. F-1–F-2.

222. Ofc of the Deputy Ch of Staff, G–3/5/7, *Army Campaign Plan, Change 4* (Washington, D.C.: HQDA, 2006), pp. F-3–F-7.

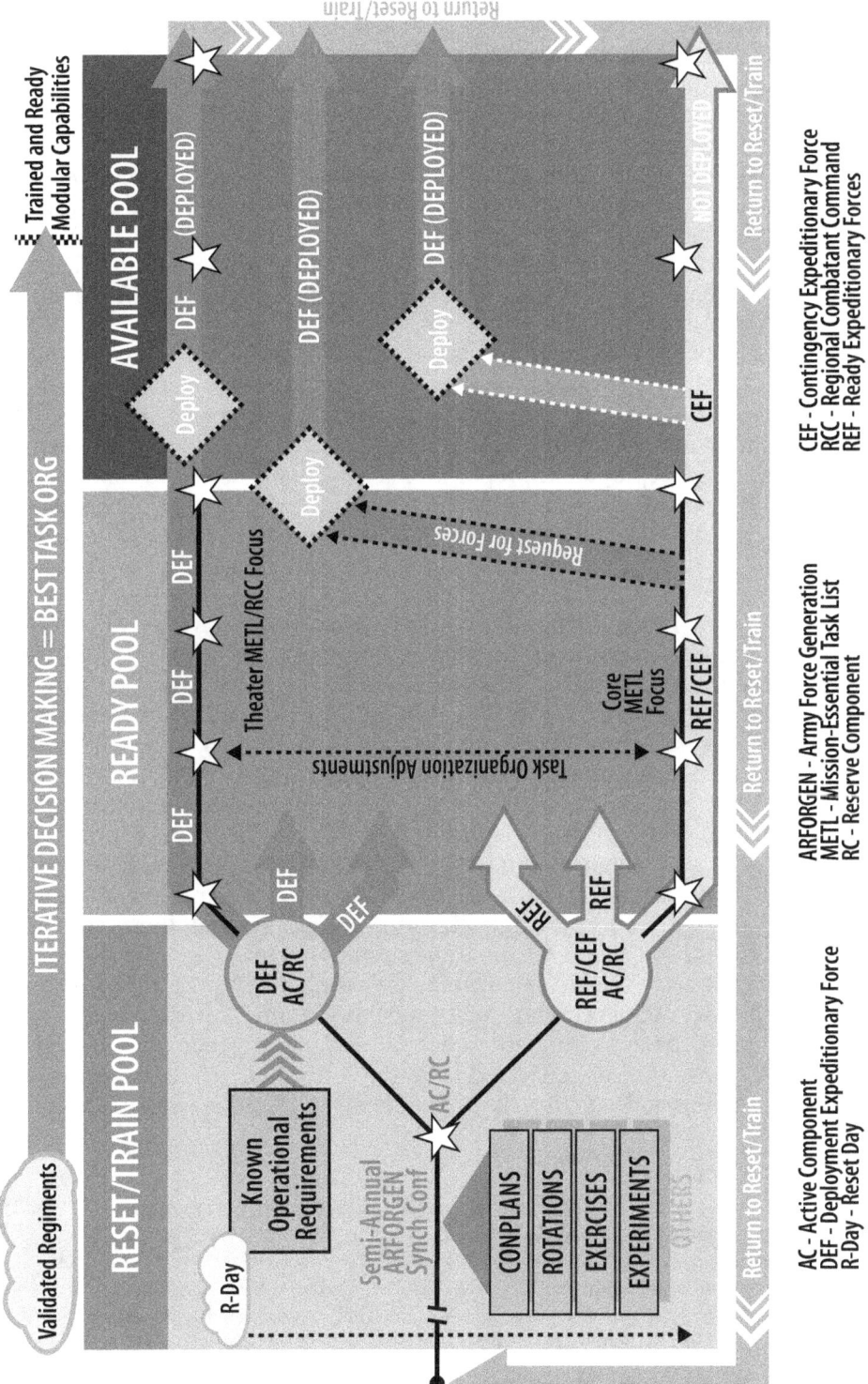

Figure 6.2. Army Force Generation Model

mining which units would be resourced first. As part of the new force generation program, a major policy change allowed reserve component units to validate their own unit premobilization training beginning in 2007. To support that effort, the reserve component was authorized to build or improve training facilities outside of the designated active component training and mobilizations centers known as Power Projection Platforms. In 2008, the Army Reserve established two mobilization centers, called regional training centers, and the National Guard established eight of its own. Within a year of improving its facilities and receiving authorization to validate training ahead of time, the National Guard had reduced the time needed for validation by as much as forty-five days.[223]

The predictability and transparency of Army Force Generation not only eased the mobilization process for the reserve forces, but also reduced tensions between components competing for limited resources. Rather than focus on individual units, force generation grouped them based on their specific stage of predeployment preparation. All reserve units thus entered the cycle as a "donor" to provide personnel to units further along in the deployment process. As that unit's deployment date drew closer, it would be redesignated as a "fill" unit, eligible for personnel siphoned from other units just entering the deployment pipeline.[224]

Army Force Generation allotted up to five years of training and preparation time before reserve component units were mobilized. This allowed units to train individual and collective tasks as part of their predeployment training cycles. However, several factors chipped away at the effectiveness of this approach. During the first two years of the cycle, the unit acted as a donor for mobilizing units, and so many of those who were in training at the beginning of the cycle were not present at the end of the cycle and missed critical training. In addition, attrition within Guard and Reserve units remained a fairly consistent 17 to 22 percent, further degrading unit cohesion and training readiness. While comparable active component statistics differed only slightly, active component soldiers were transferred and retained in a separate holding account (training, transients, holdees, and students) when they left their units for school or change of duty station. This did not degrade active unit readiness, as the units received replacements for vacancies. Reserve soldiers remained assigned to their parent organization until transferred or separated from the service, which meant units could not fill a forecasted vacancy until the departing soldier was actually dropped from the roles.[225]

---

223. A RAND study found units deploying from 2008 to 2010 were able to mobilize 20 to 35 percent faster (depending on unit type) than similar units in 2003–2007; see Pint et al., *Active Component Responsibility in Reserve Component Pre- and Postmobilization Training*. On the National Guard's validation time, see Kathryn Roe Coker, *The Indispensable Force: The Post-Cold War Operational Army Reserve, 1990–2010* (Fort Bragg, N.C.: Office of Army Reserve History, 2013), pp. 378–82.

224. Ibid., pp. 380–84.

225. U.S. Government Accountability Ofc, *Reserve Forces: Army Needs to Reevaluate its Approach to Training and Mobilizing Reserve Component Forces*, GAO-09-720 (Washington, D.C.: U.S. Government Accountability Ofc, 2009), p. 24.

The entire process was the responsibility of FORSCOM, which was the Army service component to U.S. Joint Forces Command, and therefore the Army's agent for providing forces. FORSCOM also oversaw units that were assigned to other unified combatant commands, such as units in Korea or Europe, as well as units across all three Army components.[226] To be fully effective, Army Force Generation relied on the ability to rotate units of like organization, in order to maximize economies of scale in training and resource management. The creation of those units was the focus of Schoomaker's other major initiative.

ARMY FORCE GENERATION'S IMPACT ON TRAINING

Under Army Force Generation, the combat training centers began to focus specifically on predeployment mission preparation, rather than on leader development. Although units conducted individual and crew training at their home stations, the event that validated the brigade's collective tasks in its directed mission-essential task list was a mission rehearsal exercise at a combat training center.[227] However, the available training centers could not support predeployment mission preparation for both active component maneuver brigades as well as the growing number of National Guard brigades. As a result, some Guard brigades had to wait until either a training center became available or they received orders for an abbreviated rotation.[228] To accommodate the larger number of active and reserve component modular brigade combat teams, the DoD changed the policy to reserve space at the combat training centers only for Guard units assigned to control battlespace in Iraq or Afghanistan.[229] In addition, in 2006–2007 the Army began to develop an Exportable Combat Training Center Program to deliver instruction similar to that found at combat training centers.[230] Mission rehearsal exercises for units preparing to deploy to Iraq or Afghanistan remained the norm until 2011.[231]

The limited time between combat rotations, especially during the period when returning brigades had only a year at their home station before preparing for their next deployment, deprived unit commanders of the opportunity and resources to train both core and directed mission-essential tasks. In light of an impending combat rotation to Iraq or Afghanistan, commanders chose to use their available time and resources to focus on deployment-related mission-essential tasks. Because of peak demand for units, when brigade

---

226. Ofc of the Deputy Ch of Staff, G–3/5/7, *Army Campaign Plan, Change 4*, p. F–10.

227. Ofc of the Deputy Ch of Staff, G–3/5/7, *Army Training Strategy: Strategic Training Guidance 2006* (Washington, D.C.: HQDA, 2006), p. 8.

228. U.S. Government Accountability Ofc, *Reserve Forces*, p. 24.

229. Def Science Board Task Force, "Deployment of Members of the National Guard and Reserve in the Global War on Terrorism," Sep 2007, p. 22, Hist Files, OEF Study Grp.

230. U.S. Government Accountability Ofc, *Reserve Forces*, p. 26.

231. Ofc of the Deputy Ch of Staff, G–3/5/7, Directorate of Training, n.d., "CTC Rotation History FY02–FY16," Hist Files, OEF Study Grp.

combat teams were rotating in and out of combat every other year, there was not enough time to complete all home-station training, which required adding those tasks to the mission rehearsal exercises held at a specialized training center. Even though units were still deemed to be trained before their deployment to combat, the decision to make up those shortfalls at a Combat Training Center came at the expense of related battalion- and brigade-level training. In most cases, units did not receive any additional training time after their mission-readiness exercise.[232] The strictly regimented time allotted for training steadily eroded the collective expertise in core, mission-essential warfighting tasks.

THE GUARD SURGE

In late 2004, the DoD published a new directive addressing the reserve's activation, mobilization, and demobilization. Although the document recommended specific roles and mission for the reserves and the use of whole reserve units rather than as individual fillers, and also suggested that reserve mobilizations should be the same length as their active component counterparts, it fell short of mandating these changes. It also neglected to address systemic equipment and medical readiness challenges.[233] In addition, the new directive did not account for the potential impact of Army Force Generation or modularity on the reserve components. Lt. Gen. H. Steven Blum, then chief of the National Guard Bureau, recalled that "to get to the point where it could implement the Army Force Generation and reset some of the active force to put it in a predictable rotation schedule, [General Schoomaker] asked the Guard to assume the bulk of the combat load in Iraq during 2005."[234] Personnel practices that continued to meet near-term overseas needs at the cost of deteriorating long-term readiness, when coupled with a growing number of unit deployments to Iraq, soon stretched the Army National Guard nearly to the breaking point.

Two incidents intensified issues related to the readiness of the National Guard and Reserve. The first, documented in the *New York Times* by Eric Schmitt on 9 December 2004, outlined the friction that arose when Rumsfeld visited a group of Guard units preparing for onward movement into Iraq. Many of the soldiers felt they were not outfitted with the best available equipment before going into combat. When they aired their concerns with the secretary during a question-and-answer session, Rumsfeld said, with some degree of frustration, "You go to war with the Army you have, not the Army you might want or wish to have at a later time." This did little to

---

232. Memo, OEF Study Grp, n.d., sub: Discussion with Mr. Jim Stratton and Mr. Frank Pannocchia, HQDA G–37 Collective Training Division, Hist Files, OEF Study Grp.

233. DoD Dir 1235.10, "Activation, Mobilization and Demobilization of the Ready Reserve," 23 Sep 2004, Hist Files, OEF Study Grp.

234. Bob Haskell, "The Guard Surge in Iraq," *The National Guard* (Mar 2014): 22–27, http://nationalguardmagazine.com/display_article.php?id=1667895&view=202623, Hist Files, OEF Study Grp.

Secretary of Defense Rumsfeld speaks to assembled troops at Bagram on 27 April 2002.

assuage the consternation of the Guard units, but it did much to inflame public opinion at home.[235]

The plight of the Army National Guard came under further scrutiny in late August 2005 when Louisiana officials discovered only 5,700 of their state's national guardsmen were available to respond to a potential natural disaster. As Hurricane Katrina threatened New Orleans, approximately 3,700 Louisiana National Guard personnel were serving in Iraq. In addition, the hundreds of military vehicles that had been shipped with the Guard to Iraq, or had remained behind in theater during previous deployments and were never replaced at their home station, meant that Louisiana had fewer than 200 vehicles for the Guard's emergency response and was critically short on communications equipment and satellite phones.[236] As requests for additional responders reached across the country, it became clear that the Army National Guard was stretched thin. Although 45,000 guardsmen were dispatched to Louisiana within eleven days of Katrina making landfall, the state needed an additional 20,000 active component troops to respond to the natural disaster. The Guard's on-hand equipment status, now at a decade-low 34 percent nationwide, also drew both public and congressional concern.[237]

---

235. Eric Schmitt, "Troops' Queries Leave Rumsfeld on the Defensive," *New York Times*, 9 Dec 2004, https://www.nytimes.com/2004/12/09/world/middleeast/troops-queries-leave-rumsfeld-on-the-defensive.html, Hist Files, OEF Study Grp.

236. Scott Shane and Thom Shanker, "When Storm Hit, National Guard Was Deluged," *New York Times*, 28 Sep 2005, http://www.nytimes.com/2005/09/28/us/nationalspecial/when-storm-hit-guard-was-deluged-too.html, Hist Files, OEF Study Grp.

237. Def Science Board Task Force, "Deployment of Members of the National Guard and Reserve in the Global War on Terrorism," p. 18.

The situation in Louisiana drew attention to the long-overlooked fact that more than half of the Army National Guard's 280,000 deployable personnel were involved in operational deployments.[238] This situation, informally referred to as the "Guard Surge," reflected the combined impact of three things: the Guard's central role in responding to Hurricane Katrina; an unprecedented number of overseas rotations, which allowed active component units to undergo modular transformation; and the higher operational tempo in Iraq. "The Guard Surge" brought to light the Army's unanticipated reliance on the National Guard and the Guard's depleted resources, as well as the degree to which National Guard units within the United States were being degraded by efforts to accommodate overseas combat operations. The belated recognition of the cumulative impact of these developments led to frantic legislative efforts to further codify how often and for what kinds of missions the reserves could be mobilized, and how much of the Army National Guard needed to remain in a state at any given time.[239]

Senator David B. Vitter (R-La.) led the legislative transformation by inserting language into the 2006 National Defense Appropriation Bill to study the Army's use of the Guard and Reserve personnel and units.[240] At the time of the study, standard tour length for a Guard or Reserve unit was sixteen to eighteen months, which included training time and leave. Two Army National Guard brigade combat teams had been mobilized for twenty-one months in order to train with new equipment as part of their transformation. Four brigade combat teams were slated for their second unit deployments, a first in the Global War on Terrorism. Approximately 55 percent of Army Guard and Reserve and 35 percent of active component units had not been previously mobilized for a CENTCOM deployment. Many of these units were not the types needed for the war. The pool of deployable units desired for the Global War on Terrorism was rapidly shrinking because of the short time period between their previous deployments.[241]

---

238. Interv, Steven Clay, CSI, with Lt Gen Clyde E. Vaughn, Director, Army National Guard, 20 Mar 2009, p. 14, Hist Files, OEF Study Grp.

239. Haskell, "The Guard Surge in Iraq," pp. 23–27.

240. Def Science Board Task Force, "Deployment of Members of the National Guard and Reserve in the Global War on Terrorism," p. 4.

241. Ibid.

CHAPTER SEVEN

Afghan and ISAF Expansion as an Operational Approach

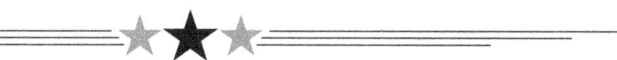

By mid-2005, almost four years into the war in Afghanistan, a pool of experienced senior leaders was available to return there. Lt. Gen. David W. Barno's chosen replacement, newly promoted Lt. Gen. Karl W. Eikenberry, had departed Afghanistan in September 2003 after a tour as the commander of the Office of Military Cooperation–Afghanistan. General Eikenberry arrived in Kabul in May 2005 and assumed command of CFC-A.[1] Instead of turning over command to another American officer at the end of his new assignment, Eikenberry anticipated that he would disband CFC-A headquarters and transfer his political-military responsibilities to the senior ISAF commander.[2] ISAF, which had been run by NATO since August 2003, had assumed responsibility for RC North in October 2004 and was scheduled to assume the other regional commands in the future.

General John P. Abizaid wanted ISAF's expansion to signal the beginning of the end of American combat operations.[3] The CENTCOM commander told Eikenberry that preparing for NATO transition would be his primary mission, and that "internationalizing the fight there was what would be needed over a long term."[4] Along with Afghan security forces capable of defeating armed opposition, NATO leadership would enable the United States to withdraw from counterinsurgency and stability operations. It was Eikenberry's job to turn this possibility into a reality.

Eikenberry received written instructions from CENTCOM in Modification 2 to Fragmentary Order 07–234, "Phase IV Operations in Afghanistan." This order differed from the January 2004 version General Barno had received in two significant ways. First, it conveyed none of the earlier document's pessimism. Second, it officially supported the counternarcotics initiative championed by the United Kingdom and a number of other European coalition members.[5] General Abizaid sanctioned the program, even though

---

1. Interv, Donald P. Wright, CSI, with Lt Gen Karl W. Eikenberry, frmr CFC-A Cdr, 23 Feb 2012, p. 20, Hist Files, OEF Study Grp.

2. Ibid.

3. Interv, Col Bryan R. Gibby, Brian F. Neumann, and Colin J. Williams, OEF Study Grp, with Gen (Ret.) John P. Abizaid, frmr CENTCOM Cdr, 10 Feb 2016, pp. 21–25, 61–62, Hist Files, OEF Study Grp.

4. Interv, Wright with Eikenberry, 23 Feb 2012, pp. 3–4; Interv, Peter Connors, CSI, with Gen (Ret.) John P. Abizaid, frmr CENTCOM Cdr, 10 Jan 2007, p. 6, Hist Files, OEF Study Grp.

5. Christopher L. Elliott, *High Command: British Military Leadership in the Iraq and Afghanistan Wars* (Oxford: Oxford University Press, 2015), pp. 130–131.

he saw it as a distraction, because he wanted NATO to assume control of the theater and therefore needed to factor in British domestic policy in order to secure the participation of the alliance's second-largest troop provider.[6] Whereas Abizaid's planners omitted the narcotics eradication effort in the January 2004 order, they devoted a full five pages to the topic in May 2005.

Central Command's Fragmentary Order 07–234 indicated that America's involvement in Afghanistan would be both limited and lengthy. The document directed the CFC-A commander to stop training border police in customs collection, turning that responsibility over to Germany in full.[7] It also instructed him to "determine [an] organizational structure of CFC-A to meet mission requirements" and "arrange for sufficient housing for U.S. personnel with the post-OEF security footprint in mind," both clear indications that American involvement in Afghanistan would be reduced.[8] Yet the order also broadened the scope of U.S. participation, providing security and helicopters to a counternarcotics effort that heretofore had been Britain's responsibility, stating that the "anticipated length of Phase IV operations" was "undetermined," and remaining silent on the Army's growing role in training police forces.[9] Abizaid thought that increasing influence in some areas while reducing it in others would shape a lasting investment in Afghanistan that would require only a small brigade to sustain.[10] Although his thinking reflected U.S. policy at the time, it did little to help Eikenberry realize termination criteria. In addition, Abizaid's viewpoint discounted the possibility that the Taliban might make an unexpected bid to resume power in Afghanistan at some point in the future.

General Eikenberry faced a deadline. The National Assembly and provincial council elections, now scheduled for September 2005, would complete the Bonn Process and signify Afghanistan's emergence as a sovereign state. In just a few months, Eikenberry had to ensure that the Afghan National Security Forces (ANSF) he had helped build could counter any threats the Taliban and its associated groups posed to Karzai's government.[11] In anticipation of transferring responsibility to ISAF, Eikenberry began to

---

6. Interv, Gibby, Neumann, and Williams with Abizaid, 10 Feb 2016, pp. 65–70; Interv, Col E. J. Degen and Colin J. Williams, OEF Study Grp, with Lt Gen Karl W. Eikenberry, frmr CFC-A Cdr and U.S. Ambassador to Afghanistan, 1 Feb 2016, pp. 3–4, Hist Files, OEF Study Grp.

7. FRAGO 07–234, CENTCOM, modification 2, 27 May 2005, sub: Phase IV Operations in Afghanistan, 3.D.1.J, Hist Files, OEF Study Grp.

8. Ibid.

9. Ibid.

10. Interv, Gibby, Neumann, and Williams with Abizaid, 10 Feb 2016, pp. 17–19; Concept Plan, CFC-A, 31 Jul 2005, sub: Long War Concept Plan, slides 11–12, Hist Files, OEF Study Grp.

11. When he took command, Eikenberry expected to go from two maneuver brigades conducting operations and one training the ANA to one maneuver brigade conducting operations and one training the ANA by no later than the end of the year. Planning Order, CENTCOM, 17 Mar 2005, sub: Posturing for the Long War, 3.C.2.A, Hist Files, OEF Study Grp.

Afghan and ISAF Expansion as an Operational Approach

General Eikenberry and Ambassador Khalilzad address the press in June 2005.

reduce the number of critical tasks that CFC-A needed to perform as the transition process gained momentum.[12]

Political Setting as of May 2005

American strategy for Afghanistan had changed little in the wake of Karzai's election. The Bush administration continued to seek a moderate and democratic Afghan government capable of securing its territory.[13] It looked forward to Afghanistan's upcoming national and provincial elections but remained uncertain about how to terminate military involvement. Concerned that the United States did not have a clear postelection strategy, Secretary of Defense Donald H. Rumsfeld asked Chairman of the Joint Chiefs of Staff General Richard B. Myers in early 2005 to plan the next twelve to eighteen months of ENDURING FREEDOM.[14] He reissued his request a week later, stating that it was "critically important that we, very promptly, have a plan for the

---

12. Col. Mark R. "Tank" Forman, Eikenberry's chief plans officer, recalled that CENTCOM wanted to reduce American forces in Afghanistan from 12,000 in late March 2005 to 3,800 in late summer 2006. A further reduction to 2,000 would occur later. Interv, Steven Clay, CSI, with Col Mark Forman, frmr CFC-A CJ–5, 3 and 5 Mar 2009, p. 10, Hist Files, OEF Study Grp.

13. As expressed nine months later, the strategic end state for U.S. forces in Afghanistan was "a moderate, stable and representative" country, "capable of deterring foreign adversaries with the support of limited but credible international capabilities." Concept Plan, CFC-A, 31 Jul 2005, sub: Long War Concept Plan, 1.B.1.B.4.

14. Memo, Sec Rumsfeld for Gen Myers, 24 Jan 2005, sub: Afghanistan, Hist Files, OEF Study Grp.

rest of this year in Afghanistan. If we announce it and it is a good plan, it can have a positive effect in Iraq."[15]

Rumsfeld spent much of 2005 pushing the United States to support security-sector reform and imploring NATO to increase its military involvement. He understood that withdrawing American forces was contingent upon Afghan security capabilities.[16] Nonetheless, he viewed current troop expenditures as unsustainable with violence mounting in Iraq.[17] In April 2004, he had proposed that CENTCOM assume the police training mission, noting that progress "just isn't happening fast enough there."[18] In February 2005, he made the case to Condoleezza Rice, now the secretary of state, that the condition of the Afghan police was a serious problem, and in March 2005 he complained to Stephen J. Hadley, now the national security advisor, that his agreement with former Secretary of State Colin L. Powell to have the DoD take responsibility for the mission had "unraveled" yet again.[19] Exasperated, he suggested submitting a decision memo to the president to settle the issue permanently. This final push seemed to work: in April 2005, an interagency decision shifted responsibility for the U.S.-funded police-training program from the U.S. Department of State to the DoD.[20]

Meanwhile, NATO had slowly increased its involvement in Afghanistan over the past two-and-a-half years. In the wake of the crisis within the alliance over the invasion of Iraq, the North Atlantic Council began calling for a NATO role in Afghanistan.[21] Germany and the Netherlands had led ISAF in late

---

15. Memo, Sec Rumsfeld for Gen Myers, 31 Jan 2005, sub: Afghanistan, Hist Files, OEF Study Grp.

16. Rumsfeld wrote to National Security Advisor Stephen Hadley in March 2005: "[I]t is our forces that are and will continue to be tied down there until the Afghans can provide their own security," and it was "costing the US taxpayers a fortune as long as the US, instead of the Afghans, continue[d] to provide for Afghan security." Memo, Sec Rumsfeld for Stephen J. Hadley, 4 Mar 2005, sub: Afghan National Police, https://library.rumsfeld.com/doclib/sp/449/2005-03-04%20To%20Stephen%20Hadley%20re%20Afghan%20National%20Police.pdf, Hist Files, OEF Study Grp.

17. Jones, *In the Graveyard of Empires*, p. 245. Indicative of Rumsfeld's cost-cutting concerns is a memo from the DoD comptroller comparing the cost of recruiting, training, equipping, and deploying one U.S. soldier to Iraq or Afghanistan, compared with the cost of training one Afghan or Iraqi soldier. Memo, Under Sec Tina W. Jonas for Sec Rumsfeld and Deputy Sec Wolfowitz, 15 Feb 2005, sub: Cost for a Soldier, Hist Files, OEF Study Grp.

18. Memo, Sec Rumsfeld for Gen Myers, Deputy Sec Wolfowitz, and Under Sec Feith, 7 Apr 2004, sub: Afghan Security Responsibility, https://library.rumsfeld.com/doclib/sp/446/2004-04-07%20to%20Myers%20et%20al%20re%207Afghan%20Security%20Responsibility.pdf, Hist Files, OEF Study Grp.

19. Memo, Sec Rumsfeld for Sec Rice, 23 Feb 2005, sub: Afghan National Police, https://library.rumsfeld.com/doclib/sp/445/2005-02-23%20To%20Condoleezza%20Rice%20re%20Afghan%20National%20Police.pdf, Hist Files, OEF Study Grp.

20. Inspectors Gen of the U.S. Department of State and DoD, *Interagency Assessment of Afghanistan Police Training and Readiness*, Nov 2006, p. 8, https://oig.state.gov/system/files/76103.pdf, Hist Files, OEF Study Grp.

21. Philip Gordon and Jeremy Shapiro, *Allies at War: America, Europe and the Crisis over Iraq* (New York: McGraw-Hill, 2004); Elizabeth Pond, *Friendly Fire: The Near-Death of the*

2002, and in April 2003 the council agreed to take command of it altogether.[22] A month after NATO formally took command in August, the UN Security Council expanded ISAF's mandate to the rest of Afghanistan.[23] Both domestic and alliance politics drove NATO participation. For members that opposed the invasion of Iraq but wanted to maintain the alliance, Afghanistan offered an opportunity to support the Bush administration without losing support at home. German chancellor Gerhard F. Schröder, whose government had campaigned on its opposition to the Bush administration's war plans in a tight election race in September 2002, led this attempt to save NATO from strategic and political irrelevance.[24] With a strong push from German leaders, NATO developed a plan to expand counterclockwise out of Kabul: first north, then west, south, and east.[25] NATO announced this expansion of responsibilities, which included reconstruction team leadership, at the Istanbul Summit in June 2004. In the view of NATO Secretary General Jaap de Hoop Scheffer, nothing less than the alliance's credibility was on the line.[26] Unfortunately for the alliance, attempts to stabilize Afghanistan would soon collide with a reconstruction mission that did not seem to be improving life in the rural provinces and an enemy that could retreat safely to Pakistan sanctuaries whenever pressed.

Rumsfeld wanted NATO to assume combat as well as reconstruction roles in Afghanistan. At a February 2005 meeting in Nice, France, NATO defense ministers discussed merging NATO ISAF and ENDURING FREEDOM into a single command. The desire to combine peacekeeping and counterterrorism reflected growing U.S. confidence that NATO could handle security in

---

Transatlantic Alliance (Washington, D.C.: Brookings Institution, 2003); Terry Terriff, "Fear and Loathing in NATO: The Atlantic Alliance After the Crisis over Iraq," *Perspectives on European Politics and Society* 5, no. 3 (Sep 2004): 419–46; Michael Gordon, "Threats and Responses: Afghan Security; NATO Chief Says Alliance Needs Role in Afghanistan," *New York Times*, 21 Feb 2003, https://www.nytimes.com/2003/02/21/world/threats-responses-afghan-security-nato-chief-says-alliance-needs-role.html, Hist Files, OEF Study Grp.

22. NATO Press Release, "Same Name, Same Banner, Same Mission as NATO Enhances ISAF Role," 4 Apr 2003, https://www.nato.int/docu/update/2003/04-april/e0416a.htm, Hist Files, OEF Study Grp.

23. UN Security Council, Resolution 1510, S/RES/1510, 13 Oct 2003, https://www.nato.int/isaf/topics/mandate/unscr/resolution_1510.pdf, Hist Files, OEF Study Grp. The UN Security Council would continue to reauthorize the International Security Assistance Force (ISAF) mission yearly through the end of 2014.

24. Sten Rynning, *NATO in Afghanistan: The Liberal Disconnect* (Stanford, Calif: Stanford University Press, 2012), pp. 95–97.

25. Ibid., pp. 97–98; Lt Col Steve Beckman, "From Assumption to Expansion: Planning and Executing NATO's First Year in Afghanistan at the Strategic Level" (Strategy research project, U.S. Army War College, 18 Mar 2005), https://handle.dtic.mil/100.2/ADA431768, Hist Files, OEF Study Grp.

26. Jaap de Hoop Scheffer (Speech, National Defense University, 29 Jan 2004), https://www.nato.int/docu/speech/2004/s040129a.htm, Hist Files, OEF Study Grp.

Afghanistan.²⁷ France and Germany responded that NATO was neither equipped nor designed to conduct counterterrorism operations and sought assurances from the United States that it would not hand the mission to NATO. Assurances received, the NATO secretary general asked for the plan to proceed "as soon as it was feasible," perhaps in early 2006.²⁸

Rumsfeld seemed intent on starting to withdraw U.S. forces with or without NATO support. Despite limited progress in the security sector and NATO's uneven commitment to Afghanistan, the Pentagon considered decreasing its approximately 17,500 in-country troops by as much as 4,000 in September 2005.²⁹ Karzai may have sensed wavering American commitment the previous May when he insisted that the United States and Afghanistan agree to a strategic partnership of indefinite duration.³⁰ The joint declaration was more of a symbolic gesture than a substantive commitment.³¹ The United States had long promised to stay in Afghanistan until the mission was complete. Nonetheless, as violence mounted in Iraq, the Bush administration saw that the mission in Afghanistan as shrinking rather than growing.

ENEMY SITUATION AS OF MAY 2005

Unbeknownst to CFC-A and NATO, the Taliban was on the verge of a dramatic comeback. It had rebuilt support in areas where the coalition forces were not present. Zabul Province was largely lost to government control in 2003, Uruzgan and Kandahar Provinces hosted sizable insurgent strongholds, and Kandahar City itself was practically under siege. Helmand Province was likewise teetering. By 2005, Helmand led the world in opium production, the financial engine of the Taliban's resurgence. The movement did not control the drug trade; nonetheless, it profited from compulsory contributions known as *ushr* (a 10 percent tithe, paid in kind) which it collected in exchange for secure transit through territories it controlled.³² By 2005, the Taliban was

---

27. Judy Dempsey, "NATO, US to Merge Afghan Missions," *Boston Globe*, 11 Feb 2005, http://www.boston.com/news/world/europe/articles/2005/02/11/nato_us_to_merge_afghan_missions/, Hist Files, OEF Study Grp.

28. Ibid.

29. Eric Schmitt and David S. Cloud, "U.S. May Start Pulling Out of Afghanistan Next Spring," *New York Times*, 14 Sep 2005, https://www.nytimes.com/2005/09/14/international/asia/14afghan.html, Hist Files, OEF Study Grp; Richard Norton-Taylor, "Allies Rule Out Bigger Afghan Role," *Guardian*, 14 Sep 2005, https://www.theguardian.com/world/2005/sep/15/politics.afghanistan, Hist Files, OEF Study Grp.

30. White House Press Release, Ofc of the Press Sec, 23 May 2005, sub: Joint Declaration of the United States–Afghanistan Strategic Partnership, https://2001-2009.state.gov/p/sca/rls/pr/2005/46628.htm, Hist Files, OEF Study Grp.

31. Ronald E. Neumann, *The Other War: Winning and Losing in Afghanistan* (Washington, D.C.: Potomac Books, 2009), pp. 89–90.

32. Gretchen S. Peters, "The Taliban and the Opium Trade," in *Decoding the New Taliban*, pp. 7–11.

dominant in the province's northern districts and threatened the capital of Lashkar Gah.[33]

The Taliban succeeded during this time by exploiting Afghanistan's tribal disputes and marginalized communities.[34] Operators in cadre cells connected locally raised guerrillas and dedicated fighters who had trained in Pakistan.[35] Once they secured a foothold in one area, Taliban authority spread north to other rural parts of Ghazni, Paktika, Khost, Paktiya, and Farah Provinces. Taliban courts and shadow administrations undermined the nascent Afghan government's authority as effectively as any IED or mortar attack. Residents' fear of the Taliban turned first to sympathy and then to support as the Karzai government failed to check the Taliban's momentum.[36]

Organizationally, the Quetta Shura Taliban recognized four military zones: Kabul, East, Southeast, and South. Each zone had a largely independent commander. As the most experienced militant and a leader with ties to al-Qaeda's training and financial base in Pakistan, Jalaluddin Haqqani served as overall commander.[37] Many Haqqani-linked fighters demonstrated tactical and leadership acumen, prompting one American veteran to call them the insurgents' "version of an NCO [noncommissioned officer] corps."[38] Each zone had "front" commanders who exploited local relationships. To recruit members and capitalize on local grievances, these commanders styled themselves as mujahideen rather than Taliban—a claim meant to contrast their program of respect, security, and sharia authority to Kabul's chaotic government.[39]

By May 2005, Mullah Dadullah Akhund, nicknamed "Lang" or "Lame" for a wartime injury that had cost him a leg, had consolidated power in Afghanistan's southern provinces. His network was vast, encompassing more than a hundred subordinate commanders and a growing contingent of suicide bombers and IED factories. Some reports suggested that he commanded as many as 800 Taliban fighters in Zabul, Nimroz, Helmand, Kandahar, and Uruzgan Provinces. These provinces were permissive enough to allow the Taliban to shelter in mosques by day and emerge "to persuade, bribe, or terrorize farmers into helping them kill U.S. troops" at night. Without a robust coalition or ISAF presence, Zabul and the other four southern provinces remained Taliban country.[40]

---

33. Chandrasekaran, *Little America*, p. 45; Giustozzi, *Koran, Kalashnikov, and Laptop*, pp. 5, 61; Fergusson, *Taliban*, p. 172.

34. Fergusson, *Taliban*, p. 341.

35. Kilcullen, "Taliban and Counter-Insurgency in Kunar," p. 239.

36. Christoph Reuter and Borhan Younus, "The Return of the Taliban in Andar District," in *Decoding the New Taliban*, pp. 110–11.

37. Giustozzi, *Koran, Kalashnikov, and Laptop*, pp. 90–91.

38. John R. Bruning and Sean Parnell, *Outlaw Platoon: Heroes, Renegades, Infidels, and the Brotherhood of War in Afghanistan* (New York: William Morrow, 2012), p. 139.

39. Nathan, "Reading the Taliban," pp. 35–36, 48.

40. Chandrasekaran, *Little America*, p. 47; Rashid, *Descent into Chaos*, pp. 252–53.

Pakistan's purposely limited commitment to combating extremism saved the Taliban from strategic irrelevance. The Pakistan sanctuaries allowed the Taliban to regroup, recruit, and plan without interdiction or arrest. As U.S. government officials in Kabul noted, "Taliban leaders operate with relative impunity in some Pakistani cities, and may still enjoy support from the lower echelons of Pakistan's Inter-Services Intelligence."[41] In this traditional support base, Pakistan's madrassas had a nearly limitless supply of willing recruits. Pakistan appeared unable or unwilling to suppress Taliban-sponsored extremism.[42] Throughout 2005, as it adopted increasingly lethal tactics including suicide bombing, use of IEDs, and assassination campaigns, the Taliban demonstrated resiliency and military competence.

Posturing for a Long War

General Eikenberry arrived in Afghanistan with instructions to transfer operational responsibilities to NATO and strengthen the ANSF, and he set about transforming "the size and shape of U.S. force posture" in anticipation of handing the mission over to ISAF.[43] Pursuing a reductionist agenda, he eliminated many projects begun or expanded by General Barno. In a telling example, Eikenberry prohibited Special Forces operational detachments from hiring local forces for any purpose other than securing outposts.[44] The Americans could no longer use Afghan militia forces, and Afghan security forces could only do what their name implied: provide security. Security became General Eikenberry's overriding concern: any mission, operation, or effort not designed to achieve security for Afghans would be cancelled or suspended.[45] Although Eikenberry understood that Afghans were engaged in a political contest over opposing visions of their future, he did not define his campaign as a counterinsurgency. In fact, he felt that Afghanistan's lack of a preexisting government made counterinsurgency a misguided endeavor.[46] In contrast to his predecessor, General Eikenberry believed that holistic involvement in Afghanistan would protract, not curtail, conflict.

---

41. Info Paper, U.S. Department of State, 9 Dec 2005, sub: Counterterrorism Activities (Neo-Taliban), p. 4, NSA GWU, https://www2.gwu.edu/~nsarchiv/NSAEBB/NSAEBB325/doc14.pdf, Hist Files, OEF Study Grp.

42. Zalmay Khalilzad, whose ambassadorship lasted into the first few months of Eikenberry's command, saw Pakistan as the single reason why U.S. efforts were not more successful. Interv, Maj Colin J. Williams and Gregory Roberts, OEF Study Grp, with Zalmay Khalilzad, frmr U.S. Ambassador to Afghanistan, 25 Mar 2016, Hist Files, OEF Study Grp.

43. Concept Plan, CFC-A, 31 Jul 2005, sub: Long War Concept Plan, slides 4–5.

44. Interv, Steven Clay, CSI, with Lt Col George T. Donovan Jr., frmr Cdr, 2d Bn, 504th Inf, 21 Jan 2009, p. 9, Hist Files, OEF Study Grp. Colonel Donovan approved of Eikenberry's decision, which the general made when he learned that American forces were allowing Afghan militias to collect tolls for road improvements.

45. Interv, Wright with Eikenberry, 23 Feb 2012, pp. 27–28.

46. Ibid., p. 33. See also Karl W. Eikenberry, "The Limits of Counterinsurgency Doctrine in Afghanistan: The Other Side of COIN," *Foreign Affairs* 92, no. 5 (Sep-Oct 2013): 61.

> U.S. Army Doctrine Publication (ADP) 1–02, *Terms and Military Symbols*, presents key definitions, meanings, and implications for specific tactical tasks in military doctrine. The definitions for the following tasks are relevant in the context of the U.S. approach to counterinsurgency described in this chapter:
>
> **NEUTRALIZE** A tactical mission task that results in rendering enemy personnel or materiel incapable of interfering with a particular operation.
>
> **DEFEAT** A tactical mission task that occurs when an enemy force has temporarily or permanently lost the physical means or the will to fight. The defeated force's commander is unwilling or unable to pursue his adopted course of action, thereby yielding to the friendly commander's will, and can no longer interfere to a significant degree with the actions of friendly forces. Defeat can result from the use of force or the threat of its use.
>
> **INTERDICT** A tactical mission task where the commander prevents, disrupts, or delays the enemy's use of an area or route.
>
> **CLEAR** A tactical mission task that requires the commander to remove all enemy forces and eliminate organized resistance within an assigned area.
>
> For more information, see the glossary of military terminology in Appendix A.
>
> Source: HQDA, ADP 1–02, *Terms and Military Symbols*, Aug 2018.

Figure 7.1. Note on U.S. Military Tactical Terminology

To avoid a constant cycle of broadly focused operations, Eikenberry limited what coalition forces did and where they did it (*Figure 7.1*). His intent was to restrict coalition activities to populated areas in which they could exert a positive influence, although he admitted that it was not always easy to determine where these areas were.[47] Soon after assuming command, Eikenberry believed he had identified the delineating factor: roads. Like Barno, he believed that a functioning road network was the closest thing the Army had to a developmental panacea. Unlike his predecessor, Eikenberry also thought that roads would set geographical limits on American military action. He had a number of reasons for initially wanting to prevent activity from extending beyond these lines of communications: his tactical headquarters had been designed more for stability operations than for combat, he was not sure if NATO would be ready to assume RC South from American control, and he was not yet ready to inform Abizaid what America's role under ISAF should be. By following DoD and CENTCOM guidance, he reversed his predecessor's expansive vision of American involvement. Responding to a query from Rumsfeld, Eikenberry briefed Abizaid on a plan to reduce the

---

47. Interv, Wright with Eikenberry, 23 Feb 2012, p. 60.

forty-three bases, Provincial Reconstruction Teams, and other sites housing American troops to twenty-seven by June 2006.[48]

As ordered, Eikenberry also stopped Americans from helping the Afghans collect customs revenue. Under Barno's tenure, CFC-A had created a program that taught Afghans how to collect taxes by watching Americans do it.[49] The effort helped fund the Afghan state and, according to deputy CFC-A commander British Maj. Gen. Peter Gilchrist, it made the new national government more effective.[50] Disagreeing, Ambassador Ronald E. Neumann believed that Barno's desire to satisfy Rumsfeld's intentions had created a poorly-run system that removed Afghans from a critical governmental function.[51] With his ambassador's support, Eikenberry stopped American involvement in Afghan customs activity, intending to replace assistance with a training program run by the U.S. Department of Homeland Security. Unfortunately, the Department of Homeland Security could not deploy experts fast enough or in the numbers needed for the arrangement to work.[52]

Even though Eikenberry was following CENTCOM's instructions to reduce America's involvement in Afghanistan, his approach upset leaders who embraced counterinsurgency.[53] He was not motivated by a desire to distinguish himself from his predecessor, but the new CFC-A commander had instructions to reduce, extend, and redirect coalition efforts. Adapting the long-war concept initially conceived by Barno and his staff, Eikenberry informed Abizaid that America's participation in the Afghan fight would consist of a brigade headquarters for RC East; two infantry battalions; seven reconstruction teams; aviation support; a reduced-strength Special Forces battalion; and intelligence, surveillance, and reconnaissance assets by the end of Eikenberry's command: totaling approximately 3,500 troops by early summer 2005.[54] To him, "it was important to economize and think in terms of handing over essential CFC-A command and control capabilities to NATO in a timely manner according to agreed plans."[55] It made no sense to enlarge a headquarters that would disband at the end of his tour.

General Eikenberry's unwillingness to commit U.S. troops to a sustained counterinsurgency effort did not prevent him from paying attention to

---

48. A further contraction would bring America's base count to thirteen by the time ISAF took operational responsibility for Afghanistan. Bfg, Lt Gen Karl W. Eikenberry, Cdr, CFC-A, to Gen John P. Abizaid, Cdr, CENTCOM, 31 Aug 2005, sub: Afghanistan Force Protection, slides 1, 3–6, Hist Files, OEF Study Grp.

49. Neumann, *The Other War*, p. 47n10.

50. Interv, Maj Gen Peter Gilchrist (UK) in Koontz, ed., *Enduring Voices*, pp. 114–15.

51. Neumann, *The Other War*, p. 47.

52. Ibid., pp. 47n10, 222–23.

53. Interv, Col David W. Lamm in Koontz, *Enduring Voices*, pp. 146–47.

54. Concept Plan, CFC-A, 31 Jul 2005, sub: Long War Concept Plan, slides 11–12.

55. Interv, Wright with Eikenberry, 23 Feb 2012, p. 21.

development.[56] He was especially interested in the Provincial Reconstruction Teams and the Embedded Training Teams designed to mentor Afghan security forces that would remain behind after combat troops departed. In the six weeks before the September elections, the CFC-A commander traveled out of Kabul eight times. These trips typically included meeting a provincial governor, walking in the provincial capital, visiting the province's reconstruction team, and questioning training-team members.[57] They painted Eikenberry a picture of the country's readiness for sovereignty on the eve of the final step in the Bonn Process. Eikenberry became concerned by some of what he heard. Meeting Capt. Dirk D. Ringgenberg, commander of the 74th Infantry Detachment (Long Range Surveillance), Eikenberry learned that the Taliban operated with impunity in areas that reconstruction team soldiers could not traverse. In their initial meeting, Ringgenberg took out a map, identified enemy concentrations, and related an engagement that occurred on 3 May 2005—two days before Eikenberry took command—in which Ringgenberg's troops killed seventy-six Taliban in northern Zabul Province.[58] Presented with clear evidence that enemy forces were massing in a key region, Eikenberry held off from recommending troop withdrawals until after the elections. The elections' security—and their results—would signal the degree and direction of future American intervention in Afghanistan.

Reconstruction team personnel, financing, and logistics were still a significant investment when Eikenberry took command, but he did not believe that they should be a long-term feature of the campaign. Although they were slated to remain even after the combat troops departed, they would reduce in number, activity, and scope under ISAF control. The United States had 1,014 personnel stationed with 13 teams: 996 service members, 17 federal employees, and 1 team member who worked for Britain's Department for International Development.[59] Army logistics also supported teams run by NATO allies, which added long-range staffing, transport, and container-space demands on American forces in theater.

Transferring reconstruction teams to NATO ISAF control was part of Eikenberry's attempt to divest CFC-A of long-term operational

---

56. Eikenberry questioned the effectiveness of developing a country before it was ready to receive and absorb developmental efforts. Ibid., p. 21; Eikenberry, "The Limits of Counterinsurgency Doctrine in Afghanistan," pp. 59–74.

57. Eikenberry's eight trips were to Khost (5–6 August 2005), Herat (8 August 2005), Zabul (12–13 August 2005), Mazar-e Sharif in Balkh Province (15 August 2005), Farah and Helmand (26–27 August 2005), Kapisa (29 August 2005), Ghazni (2–3 September 2005), and Mehtar Lam (Laghman) (16 September 2005). Mtg Notes, Lt Gen Eikenberry, Cdr, CFC-A, 2 Aug–19 Sep 2005 inclusive, folder 20, Hist Files, OEF Study Grp.

58. VTC, Lt Col John Stark, Brian F. Neumann, and Colin J. Williams, OEF Study Grp, with Maj (Ret.) Dirk D. Ringgenberg, frmr Cdr, 74th Inf Detachment (Long Range Surveillance), 24 May 2016; Correspondence, Dirk D. Ringgenberg to E. J. Degen, Director, OEF Study Grp, 31 Dec 2019, Hist Files, OEF Study Grp.

59. Ltr, Donald Rumsfeld to Bill Luti, 15 Apr 2004, sub: PRTs in Afghanistan, https://library.rumsfeld.com/doclib/sp/950/2005-04-20%20To%20Doug%20Feith%20re%20PRTs%20in%20Afghanistan.pdf, Hist Files, OEF Study Grp.

responsibilities. His other attempts occurred during meetings early in his tenure as commander. When not traveling to Pakistan or through Afghanistan in the month and a half before the September elections, Eikenberry held seventeen key-leader meetings in Kabul. Eight of these meetings were with Afghan ministers, eight were talks with ambassadors, and one pertained to elections.[60] Eikenberry clearly understood his political responsibilities. By consulting ambassadors, he was shaping America's transfer of responsibilities to NATO, his primary mission upon assuming command. His secondary mission, readying Afghan security forces for the American withdrawal, was an endeavor about which he had great enthusiasm and strong opinions.

Developing Afghan Government Security Forces

When General Eikenberry returned in May 2005, he increased the attention given to training Afghan security forces. In spite of disarmament, demobilization, and reintegration programs and other efforts to promote national governance, U.S. forces had been relying on local Afghan forces, including the United Front, ever since the invasion. Rumsfeld had directed Special Forces to start training an ANA in May 2002, a month before General McNeill's XVIII Airborne Corps headquarters arrived in country. Aided by ISAF, this moderate investment produced moderate results by January 2003, when the Office of Military Cooperation–Afghanistan (then headed by Eikenberry) assumed responsibility for the ANA mission. Although Accelerating Success had increased the resources and expectations for the Afghan army, security force development competed with the many other efforts Barno viewed as important to conducting a counterinsurgency.

It had been at least a generation since the U.S. Army embarked on a military training project of comparable scale or duration. Although the United States had been investing considerable effort in arming and training foreign militaries since World War II, the U.S. military's experience in the Vietnam conflict had made it far less willing to undertake the challenge of reshaping entire armies in order to maintain the balance of power in key regions. From 1975 onward, American involvement with foreign militaries outside NATO had been confined to special advisory missions conducting training and interacting with the State Department. Growing the Office of Military Cooperation–Afghanistan meant taking an organization designed to be small and subjecting its officers to the confusion that comes from straddling the divide between two federal departments and a number of allied efforts.[61]

Under these conditions, the Army had difficulty finding someone to command an enlarged military cooperation organization. When Eikenberry,

---

60. Mtg Notes, Lt Gen Eikenberry, Cdr, CFC-A, 2 Aug–19 Sep 2005 inclusive, folder 20, Hist Files, OEF Study Grp.

61. The DoD also established a similar organization in Iraq following the fall of Saddam Hussein. Although the initial approach to security cooperation in Iraq mirrored previous efforts in Afghanistan, the emergence of a violent insurgency in April 2004 led to far more resources and funding for the post-Saddam Iraqi Army.

for example, left the organization in September 2003, two months elapsed before his replacement arrived. His successor, Air Force Maj. Gen. Craig P. Weston, considered himself an opportunity hire.[62] An acquisition officer by profession, Weston's expertise in addressing equipment shortages reflected existing views about his assignment rather than a growing awareness of the logistical, doctrinal, and legislative changes needed to realign Afghan security force assistance with projected operational needs.

NEW EXPECTATIONS FOR THE AFGHAN NATIONAL ARMY

In February 2005, Barno briefed Rumsfeld on security force assistance in Afghanistan, to explain how growing the ANA would facilitate an American withdrawal from Afghanistan.[63] Based on the expected production of Afghan security forces, Barno informed Rumsfeld that U.S. forces in country could be reduced from 16,300 to 16,000 by July 2005; 11,500 by July 2006; 10,000 by July 2007; and 5,300 by December 2008. This final total included 1,300 service members providing aviation support to the Afghan government; 1,000 serving in reconstruction teams; 900 in base support roles; 800 providing combat service support; 600 for a headquarters; 400 assigned to combat and combat support missions; and 300 dedicated trainers. As reflected by predicted sustainment costs, this proposed "end state" configuration would remain fixed for at least the next four years, from fiscal years 2009 through 2012. Combat units would leave first, followed by Special Forces and support units.[64] Depending on conditions, this second withdrawal would occur before, during, or after the coalition transferred reconstruction teams to the Afghan government—a process that likely would be completed by December 2008, when CFC-A expected the Afghan government to have built sufficient capacity in the provinces.[65] Barno predicated his original plan on two assumptions. One was that the threat would "remain at current levels."[66] Time would prove otherwise. The second was that one training team–supported ANA brigade equated to one U.S. battalion.[67] The latter point's validity rested on Barno assuming the threat would not increase. In reality, although an ANA brigade theoretically possessed more soldiers and individual weapons than an American battalion, it did not have dedicated access to the combat multipliers available to U.S. troops. These included close air support, helicopter gunships, aeromedevac, responsive logistics, up-armored vehicles, and unmanned aerial vehicles. Although training teams accompanying Afghan troops could call for this support, its availability

---

62. Interv, unknown with Maj Gen Craig P. Weston, Cdr, OMC-A, p. 2, Hist Files, OEF Study Grp.

63. Bfg, CFC-A, prepared 4 Feb 2005, delivered 8 Feb 2005, sub: Afghanistan Security Update to the SECDEF, slide 9, Hist Files, OEF Study Grp.

64. Ibid., slide 10.

65. Ibid.

66. Ibid., slide 9.

67. Ibid.

THE UNITED STATES ARMY IN AFGHANISTAN, 2001–2014

ANA trainees practice marching at the Kabul Military Training Center.

depended on the competing needs of American units and the priority that U.S. commanders accorded to ANA operations.

Eikenberry was less optimistic about the ANA than his predecessor. Concerned that the training effort had accelerated too quickly, he believed that U.S. forces "had to balance quantity with quality."[68] As the leader of the training effort from 2002 to 2003, he had pushed for higher levels of readiness training, thinking that a "standards based army" was the most effective way for "the fourth poorest country in the world" to provide security.[69] The mentality that Eikenberry tried to impart on the ANA did not survive his departure in 2003. With no commander in place when Rumsfeld pushed Accelerating Success through the National Security Council in fall 2003, leaders in Afghanistan responded by turning their training focus to quantity, not quality.

Accelerating kandak production generated unforeseen consequences. For one, it left no time or space to train replacements. Desertions and casualties had thinned the ranks of the first kandaks, and less than a year after graduation they desperately needed more soldiers.[70] More importantly, increasing the graduation rate from four to five kandaks increased the need for embedded trainers "from about 410 to nearly 700."[71] By July 2005, fewer

---

68. Interv, Wright with Eikenberry, 23 Feb 2012, p. 38.

69. Interv, Lisa Beckenbaugh, CSI, with Lt Gen Karl W. Eikenberry, frmr OMC-A Cdr, 27 Nov 2006, p. 29, Hist Files, OEF Study Grp.

70. Ltr, Brig Gen Mitch Perryman to Colin J. Williams, 7 Oct 2015, Hist Files, OEF Study Grp.

71. Rpt to U.S. House of Representatives, Congressional Committee on International Relations, U.S. Government Accountability Ofc, *Afghanistan Security: Efforts to Establish Army*

than 60 percent of Afghan units had training teams.[72] Subsequent Army and Marine Corps efforts to fill training staff positions improved but did not resolve the problem. By December 2005, TF PHOENIX's Embedded Training Teams were only 80 percent staffed.[73]

Eikenberry tried to blend competing needs for quality and quantity. Soon after he returned to Afghanistan, he asked the CFC-A inspector general to devise a "management decision model" to assess the capabilities of kandaks, brigades, corps, and defense ministry organizations before they participated in combat operations.[74] He also formed a study group to help the ANA General Staff, TF PHOENIX, and CJTF-76 determine how to improve ANA readiness. This group's "Afghan National Army Study Phase 1 Report" called for training to replace fielding as the focus of future development but did not map a way for Eikenberry to achieve his desired outcome.[75]

By the summer of 2005, managing training teams had become the overriding mission of TF PHOENIX.[76] When Brig. Gen. John M. Perryman arrived in Afghanistan with his 53d Infantry Brigade (Florida Army National Guard), Army units no longer ran the basic training course. Instead, TF PHOENIX assigned training teams to kandaks a few weeks before graduation so they could get to know the unit they advised.[77]

Transitioning the Embedded Training Team mission to NATO ISAF proved more difficult than transferring Provincial Reconstruction Teams. Although troop-contributing nations fielded advisory organizations called Operational Mentor and Liaison Teams, national caveats—restrictions put on military forces by their national leadership—almost always prevented

---

and Police Have Made Progress, But Future Plans Need to Be Better Defined (Washington, D.C.: U.S. Government Accountability Ofc, Jun 2005), p. 17.

72. Rpt, CFC-A, Ofc of Security Cooperation–Afghanistan, TF PHOENIX, CJTF-76, and Inspector Gen, Department of the ANA General Staff, 14 Jul 2005, sub: Afghan National Army Study Phase 1 Executive Summary, p. 30, Hist Files, OEF Study Grp.

73. Brig Gen (Ret.) John M. Perryman, CSA OEF Study Grp – Survey Questions, n.d., p. 5, Hist Files, OEF Study Grp; TF PHOENIX, 20 Dec 2005, sub: Overview Brief, p. 9, Hist Files, OEF Study Grp.

74. Memo for Inspector Gen, DoD, 26 Jun 2005, Rpt IE2005A004, Appendix A – CFC-A CG Request Ltr in Inspections and Evaluations Directorate, Ofc of Inspector Gen, DoD, Kabul, Afghanistan, 7 Jul 2005, sub: Combined Forces Command–Afghanistan Management Decision Model, Hist Files, OEF Study Grp.

75. Rpt, CFC-A, Ofc of Security Cooperation–Afghanistan, TF PHOENIX, CJTF-76, and Inspector Gen Department of the ANA Gen Staff, 14 Jul 2005, sub: Afghan National Army Study Phase 1 Executive Summary, pp. 2–3.

76. Although Brig. Gen. John M. "Mitch" Perryman retained a Training Assistance Group in his command, it became clear to him that "while the KMTC [Kabul Military Training Center] force generation mission remained a key task, the main effort for the task force has shifted from KMTC to the Embedded Trainer (ET) team forward deployed with ANA operational forces." Perryman, CSA OEF Study Grp – Survey Questions, p. 3.

77. Ibid., pp. 2–3.

them from accompanying Afghans on combat missions.[78] These restrictions would have been less of a concern if the ANA was not facing an active enemy. With Taliban activity rising in almost every regional command, however, the U.S. Army had to send additional teams to help its NATO allies in advising ANA formations.

The adviser deficiency convinced Eikenberry that combat units needed to partner with ANA forces.[79] Experience in Iraq had shown that it was possible to conduct tactical operations using a mix of American and indigenous units. Brigades from the 10th Mountain Division arriving during Eikenberry's command understood that they had deployed not only to conduct "full spectrum military operations" but also to "allow the government of Afghanistan to emplace a security infrastructure."[80] Partnering was one approach to accomplishing this goal.

The Southern European Task Force also arrived prepared to work with Afghans. Maj. Gen. Jason K. Kamiya directed his subordinate units to conduct partnered operations as often as possible.[81] During CJTF-76's first four months in Afghanistan, its mission tasks included "establish ANA presence," "familiarize the ANA with the AO [area of operations] and reassure the populace," and "bolster ANP [Afghan National Police]."[82] By August 2005, CFC-A assessed the ANA's twenty infantry kandaks as capable of operating "side-by-side" with American forces.[83]

Eikenberry realized that unilateral coalition operations could stifle effective Afghan governance. Nonpartnered operations risked making the Americans appear as either an occupying power or the ultimate source of political authority and national security. As late as June 2005, four-and-a-half years after the American-led intervention began, Col. Patrick J. Donahue II's brigade encountered Afghans who still did not understand U.S. soldiers were conducting operations near their villages to ensure the Taliban did not harm them or their families.[84] If Afghans did not believe that American or NATO personnel were conduits of Afghan authority, then the ENDURING FREEDOM mission was not achieving its central purpose. With a shortage of Embedded Training Teams, unit association remained a visible and viable way for Eikenberry to support the Karzai government, even though it was a

---

78. Interv, Jim Bird, CSI, with Maj Gen Richard B. Moorhead, frmr 76th Inf Bde Cdr, 5 Sep 2007, p. 11, Hist Files, OEF Study Grp.

79. Interv, Wright with Eikenberry, 23 Feb 2012, p. 40.

80. Deployment Order 05–05, 10 May 2005, sub: 10th MTN DIV DEPORD ISO OPERATION ENDURING FREEDOM 05-07, pp. 3–4, Hist Files, OEF Study Grp.

81. Examples: Daily Sitrep 163–05, CJTF-76, 13 Jun 2005, Hist Files, OEF Study Grp.; Daily Sitrep 171–05, CJTF-76, 21 Jun 2005, Hist Files, OEF Study Grp.

82. Daily Sitrep 216–05, CJTF-76, 5 Aug 2005, Hist Files, OEF Study Grp; Daily Sitrep 266–05, CJTF-76, 16 Aug 2005, Hist Files, OEF Study Grp; Daily Sitrep 251–05, CJTF-76, 9 Sep 2005, Hist Files, OEF Study Grp.

83. Memo, CFC-A, 29 Aug 2005, sub: Afghan National Security Forces Update, p. 8, Hist Files, OEF Study Grp.

84. Daily Sitrep 100–05, CJTF-76, 10 Jun 2005, Hist Files, OEF Study Grp.

troop-intensive answer to Afghanistan's security problem that hindered his reductionist approach.

INCREASED FOCUS ON THE AFGHAN NATIONAL POLICE

Although ANA training suffered from insufficient resources, it was not the greatest security force challenge facing CFC-A. The United States placed a lower priority on police development because the Germans had lead-nation responsibility. Eikenberry accepted a large part of the blame for the imbalanced focus placed on each type of security force in the past. As commander of the military cooperation headquarters, he had taken great care when choosing senior ANA leaders, a laborious political exercise designed to ensure that the many factions vying for influence and power in Karzai's government would accept the Afghan commanders.[85] Eikenberry regretted not being as involved in selecting leaders for the Afghan National Police (ANP), and regarded it as a missed opportunity.[86]

There were other reasons why American soldiers did not fully emphasize training and equipping police units before Eikenberry arrived at CFC-A. U.S. laws dictated that the State Department, not the DoD, was responsible for funding the ANP's training. Shifting responsibility between agencies required new legislation or a presidential directive. UN money earmarked to develop an Afghan constabulary, known as the Law and Order Trust Fund for Afghanistan and relied upon by American commanders, had not been sufficiently allocated. To correct this deficiency, U.S. military would cover the shortfalls in its outlay for Accelerating Success. According to the action plan, expenditures would cover salaries, training, and equipment.

Afghan domestic politics, in addition to U.S. legal roadblocks and funding scarcity, hindered efforts to form a national police force. Warlords, graft, confusion over responsibilities, porous borders, and a developing insurgency made it difficult to maintain law and order. It should have been easier to create a centrally run constabulary than to form a national army, but the process had become so convoluted that the problem became hard to define and solve.

Coalition forces used multiple national approaches to develop the ANP. Although the Germans were responsible for developing the Afghan police, both Germany and the United States provided training, with each nation employing fundamentally different methodologies. As one study summarized, the German approach was "cautious and rational, building on what already existed and extending outwards," while the American approach was "bold and sweeping, attempting to tackle a number of pressing problems all at the same time."[87] Both methods had merits, but neither provided a

---

85. Interv, Beckenbaugh with Eikenberry, 27 Nov 2006, p. 24.

86. Interv, Wright with Eikenberry, 23 Feb 2012, p. 50.

87. Tonita Murray, "Police-Building in Afghanistan: A Case Study of Civil Security Reform," *International Peacekeeping* 14, no. 1 (Jan 2007): 108–26.

comprehensive vision for linking the police force to a government-backed rule-of-law system.

Organizationally, the Afghan government divided ANP activity into two ministries. The Counter-Narcotics Police totaled approximately 2,250 personnel who worked with international partners to interdict and eradicate production and trafficking. They answered to the Minister of Counter-Narcotics. The majority of the ANP operated under the Ministry of Interior. The largest force under the Ministry of Interior was the Afghan Uniformed Police, with a targeted goal of 31,000 personnel. The second largest was the Afghan Border Police, with a total strength of just under 8,000 personnel at the end of 2005. To enable both of these forces to focus on their primary missions, the ministry had two smaller policing units: the Afghan Highway Police (roughly 3,400 members) to secure major highways, and the Standby Police (at just over 4,000 members) to serve as a rapid-reaction force that could be deployed as needed anywhere in the country.[88]

The Ministry of Interior, however, was unable to exert effective control over the various organizations. The Afghan Police Law, issued in late September 2005, stipulated that "police shall perform their duties under the leadership of the Minister of Interior in the capital, and under the guidance of the governors and district chiefs in the provinces and districts respectively."[89] Dividing oversight made sense, considering that the border and highway police responsibilities transcended district or provincial security; nonetheless, it required a functioning interior ministry to execute the plan. Given that the ministry did not have administrators throughout the country, control of the border and highway police was marginal at best. Both organizations struggled to maintain even basic competency.

By the time he assumed command of CFC-A, Eikenberry had developed a nuanced understanding of how police could help establish and maintain order in Afghan society. He believed police could affect loyalties through their connections to the populace and their embodiment of a law-based judiciary system.[90] His observation, reflecting the prevailing American perspective at the time, was that "a coherent police program didn't really begin until 2006."[91] That viewpoint, however, ignores the fact that the United States, as the acknowledged coalition leader in Afghanistan, did not exercise oversight of police training before Eikenberry's arrival.[92]

---

88. Andrew Wilder, "Cops or Robbers?: The Struggle to Reform the Afghan National Police," Afghanistan Research and Evaluation Unit Info Paper Series (Kabul: Afghanistan Research and Evaluation Unit, Jul 2007), pp. 11–13.

89. Government of Afghanistan, 2005 Afghan Police Law, Article 4, Hist Files, OEF Study Grp.

90. Interv, Wright with Eikenberry, 23 Feb 2012, pp. 46–47.

91. Ibid., p. 49; Bfg, CFC-A, 8 Feb 2005, sub: Afghanistan Security Update to the SECDEF, slide 7.

92. For insight into the German perspective, see Gale A. Mattox, "Germany: The Legacy of War in Afghanistan," in Gale A. Mattox and Stephen M. Greiner, eds., *Coalition Challenges in Afghanistan: The Politics of Alliance* (Stanford, Calif: Stanford University Press, 2015), pp. 96–97.

As reports of poor standards, rampant corruption, and routine equipment shortages reached the Pentagon, Secretary Rumsfeld angled to have the DoD assume greater control over the training mission. When the DoD finally received this authority during Bush's second presidential administration, the task fell to the Office of Military Cooperation. On 12 July 2005, they began the new and expanded mission by changing the organization's name to the Office of Security Cooperation–Afghanistan, now under Air Force Maj. Gen. John T. Brennan.[93] Next, Congress substantiated the expanded mission on a trial basis in the 2005 National Defense Authorization Act and permanently in the 2006 version of the act.[94]

Although these policy decisions gave the security assistance organization a clear mandate, they did not accurately reflect the situation on the ground, nor did they result in more American trainers. Germany maintained its position as lead nation owing to its control over the National Police Academy.[95] Training for rank-and-file patrolmen continued at the Central Training Center in Kabul and seven regional training centers, which now theoretically belonged to the Office of Security Cooperation. The State Department, reluctant to depart from established procedures, also maintained a role in police development.[96] In essence, the new headquarters assumed responsibility for the police

---

93. The rationale behind the DoD's decision to send Brennan to Afghanistan, given the priority placed on building the ANA, is unclear. An exceptionally qualified F–15 fighter pilot with considerable time in command at all levels, as well as a congressional liaison, he lacked experience in security assistance matters or even as a ground liaison officer working with Army units. Brennan became the CIA's associate director of military affairs following his tour in Afghanistan before retiring in 2008. See also Lt Col Frederick Rice, "Afghanistan Unit Takes on New Mission, Name," DoD News Service, 13 Jul 2005, https://www.archive.defense.gov/news/newsarticle.aspx?id=16650, Hist Files, OEF Study Grp; Wright et al., *A Different Kind of War*, pp. 301–02; Fact sheet, Ofc of Security Cooperation–Afghanistan, 21 Sep 2005, sub: Office of Security Cooperation–Afghanistan Fact Sheet, Hist Files, OEF Study Grp.

94. Given the Bush administration's original stance on nation building, this legislation is another example of significant changes to national policy within a relatively short period. Implementing such major policy shifts with little or no notice indicates a lack of long-range planning and makes it more difficult to sustain the momentum of an ongoing military campaign. See *National Defense Authorization Act of 2005*, PL 108–375 (28 Oct 2004), sec. 1208, http://www.gpo.gov/fdsys/pkg/PLAW-108publ375/pdf/PLAW-108publ375.pdf, Hist Files, OEF Study Grp; *National Defense Authorization Act of 2006*, PL 109–163 (6 Jan 2006) sec. 1206, https://www.govinfo.gov/content/pkg/PLAW-109publ163/pdf/PLAW-109publ163.pdf, Hist Files, OEF Study Grp.

95. For more information on this specific program, see Markus Feilke, "German Experiences in Police Building in Afghanistan," Proceedings of the GRIPS State-Building Workshop, Jan 2010, https://citeseerx.ist.psu.edu/viewdoc/download?doi=10.1.1.604.6222&rep=rep1&type=pdf, Hist Files, OEF Study Grp.

96. As CENTCOM chief of staff Maj. Gen. Lloyd J. Austin III commented in October 2006, "Department of State retains lead responsibility for the police program. [Office of Security Cooperation–Afghanistan] directs (and has operational responsibility for) the police training and equipment program, [the Bureau of International Narcotics and Law Enforcement Affairs] manages the contract, and [the] US Ambassador is responsible for policy guidance." Memo, Maj Gen Lloyd J. Austin for Inspector Gen, DoD, 24 Oct 2006, sub: DOS/DOD Interagency Afghan National Police Assessment, reprinted in Appendix

training program, but neither made policy nor oversaw the government contractor, DynCorp International, that staffed and ran the training centers. This disconnection would have detrimental effects for years to come.

The lack of oversight and authority on the contract diluted the Office of Security Cooperation's control and limited its reach. However, the DoD needed the contractors to fulfill the mission: the Office of Security Cooperation did not have enough personnel to run the central and regional training centers on its own, especially considering that it was already responsible for training the ANA. As the main contractor for training police, DynCorp was providing several hundred trainers and mentors under its contract with the State Department, and would continue to be the largest contingent of police trainers in Afghanistan, despite the widespread belief that "the contract['s] management was a nightmare."[97] The main problem with DynCorp's contract was that it included police training in Iraq and Jordan as well as in Afghanistan. Having multiple customers dispersed across three nations weakened the organization's influence over the agreement, with the result that the company was more beholden to those who controlled disbursement payments in Washington than the State Department's representatives in Kabul. As Ambassador Neumann noted, "Our contractual arrangements were distant, rigid, bureaucratic, and terribly ill suited [sic] to fighting a war," because, "a contractor, even the best, is hired to carry out a contract, not to tell the government that the contract's objectives may themselves be wrong, inadequate, or unresponsive to changed circumstances."[98]

Although contracting civilian support in this instance came with challenges and shortcomings, the importance of contractor support in Afghanistan cannot be overstated. The U.S. Army's Title 10 responsibilities for the entire theater of operations in Afghanistan were vast and included major functions such as the intelligence apparatus, logistical support, communications architecture, and medical care. It took inordinate amounts of staffing, money, time, and equipment to provide these services to all U.S. elements, and in many cases to coalition entities. This vast mission to sustain multiple theaters of war could not have been accomplished without contractor support.

By the September 2005 elections in Afghanistan, various agencies had attempted to reform recruitment, training, and payment for the Afghan police. Despite good intentions, little progress was made. With the effort's outcome riding on contractors who worked for a subordinate agency of the State Department and had goals different from those of U.S. and German military trainers (who themselves did not always pursue complementary approaches), problems continued to fester.[99] As Eikenberry looked to give

---

J, Inspectors Gen of the U.S. Department of State and DoD, *Interagency Assessment of Afghanistan Police Training and Readiness*, Nov 2006, p. 95.

97. Neumann, *The Other War*, pp. 119–20.

98. Ibid.

99. An interagency Inspector General report released by the State and Defense Departments in November 2006 illustrated the depths of this confusion. During its visits, the assessment team found that neither the embassy nor the military had a copy of the contract or the relevant

police training the same attention he had given previously to the Afghan army, he struggled to get ahead of the numerous challenges.

THE END OF THE BONN PROCESS

General Eikenberry could not control the events that diverted his attention from transferring operational responsibilities to ISAF. He had not been consulted in the Army's decision to replace the 25th Infantry Division with General Kamiya's Southern European Task Force. The latter, which was originally designed to serve as one component of a larger NATO headquarters, had far fewer capabilities than its predecessor. Among other things, Kamiya's headquarters lacked an organic intelligence section and had difficulty analyzing enemy actions in a timely fashion.[100] Its March 2005 deployment to Afghanistan marked the first time the two-star headquarters, hailing from Vicenza, Italy, assumed a combat mission since its inception in 1955. Its previous deployments were to oversee humanitarian assistance missions in Africa in 1997. Assigning a headquarters that was not designed for sustained campaigning frustrated Eikenberry's efforts to pursue an approach that still included combat.

Taliban activity also made the transition between the 25th Infantry Division and the Southern European Task Force difficult. The enemy intensified operations in spring 2005 for reasons which ran the gamut from the onset of the fighting season—that is, warmer weather—to increased political and military strength. Colonel Donahue, who observed this increase in enemy aggressiveness, thought that the Taliban had become active in an attempt to discredit the forthcoming Afghan national elections.[101] Eikenberry's decision to eschew counterinsurgency practices also may have increased the likelihood of enemy contact. Coalition patrols had initiated most of the engagements with the Taliban in the last few months of the Bonn Process.[102] In keeping with his roads-as-a-barrier thinking, Eikenberry measured every attempt to push troops into areas that coalition forces had never entered by weighing the risks and the rewards.[103] Regardless, the Southern European Task Force, an instrument designed for stability operations, soon found itself engaged in

---

modifications, and DynCorp's representatives in Afghanistan did not have copies of the contract's most recent modifications. In effect, all three parties were operating under a contract to which they did not have clear and ready access. Inspectors Gen of the U.S. Department of State and DoD, *Interagency Assessment of Afghanistan Police Training and Readiness*, Nov 2006, p. 35.

100. Interv, Wright with Eikenberry, 23 Feb 2012, p. 70.

101. Interv, Steven Clay, CSI, with Brig Gen Patrick J. Donahue II, frmr 1st Bde Combat Team, 82d Abn Cdr, 16 Mar 2009, pp. 9–10, Hist Files, OEF Study Grp.

102. Col. Kevin C. Owens estimated that 90 percent of his unit's engagements "were on our terms and [due to] our initiative," including a June 2005 meeting engagement in Mya Neshin District (Kandahar Province) in which the task force killed about forty-five Taliban. Interv, Angela McClain and Steven Clay, CSI, with Col Kevin C. Owens, frmr 173d Abn Bde Cdr, 9 and 10 Dec 2008, pp. 17, 21, Hist Files, OEF Study Grp; Interv, Angela McClain and Ross Steele, CSI, with Maj Greg S. Harkins, frmr 2d Bn, 503d Inf Opns Ofcr, 22 Dec 2008, p. 4, Hist Files, OEF Study Grp.

103. Interv, Stark, Neumann, and Williams with Ringgenberg, 24 May 2016.

A CH–47 Chinook lands on an airstrip near the town of Khost, Afghanistan, to refuel and prepare to transport soldiers to outlying areas to conduct cordon-and-search missions.

missions even more aggressive in nature than the ones its predecessors had been conducting.

Although Eikenberry simultaneously struggled to influence the units he received and to stem enemy activity, he exerted far less control over special operations in Afghanistan. In the three-and-a-half years since Col. John P. Mulholland's TF DAGGER initiated Operation ENDURING FREEDOM, the authority exercised by the senior American commander in Afghanistan over these troops had vacillated between directing operations and coordinating them. By the time Eikenberry arrived for his second tour in country, CFC-A had authority over CJSOTF-Afghanistan but not the counterterrorist forces reporting directly to CENTCOM.[104] Eikenberry believed that all special operations should be coordinated and synchronized with his campaign. In addition to eliminating the use of Afghan militia forces, he wanted to restrain night raids, viewing them as a "train wreck" that would interfere with his planned drawdown schedule.[105] His frustration was essentially a command and control issue, but it was one that he lacked the authority to resolve unilaterally.

Operations over which Eikenberry did not exercise strict control occasionally caused problems as well. Missions conducted to prepare historically hostile provinces for the September elections remained subject to the limitations of rotary-wing aircraft and the aggression of a hard-to-reach enemy. Both factors were present in June 2005 when Operation RED

---

104. Interv, Wright with Eikenberry, 23 Feb 2012, p. 14.
105. Ibid., p. 15.

Wings resulted in the greatest number of casualties in a single incident since Operation Anaconda. The mission started when the 160th SOAR carried out a night insertion of a SEAL reconnaissance team into RC East on behalf of Lt. Col. James E. Donnellan's 2d Battalion, 3d Marines. Donnellan's unit patrolled an area to the west of Asadabad, the capital of Kunar Province. Its mission was to disrupt enemy activity so as to prevent resistance to the national and provincial elections in September.[106] The SEALS were to collect real-time intelligence for the marines who, in turn, were seeking to pinpoint the whereabouts of a strongman who was attempting to ally himself with the Taliban. Unfortunately, local Afghans compromised these special operators, who soon found themselves under heavy assault. An unsuccessful attempt to extract the team led to the loss of all but one SEAL on the ground and resulted in the deaths of sixteen more personnel when enemy fire downed an CH–47 Chinook carrying a Special Operations quick-reaction force.[107] Rugged terrain, a reliance on rotary-wing assets, and a tragic chance encounter had combined to turn a high-risk mission of medium importance into a tragedy. The incident reinforced Eikenberry's intent to approve only missions whose potential benefit outweighed their incurred risk. The CFC-A commander wanted intelligence, not its absence, to drive operations.

Events taking place outside Afghanistan also had a significant impact on how Eikenberry conducted operations. On 29 July 2005, Uzbekistan informed the United States that it would no longer allow the American military to use Karshi Khanabad Air Base.[108] At the time, CENTCOM maintained twelve C–130 aircraft at the airfield and relied on fuel pipelined onto the base to sustain air operations in Afghanistan.[109] In accordance with subsequent CENTCOM guidance, Eikenberry divided Karshi Khanabad's functions between Manas Air Base in Kyrgyzstan and Bagram Air Base in Afghanistan. Manas Air Base easily absorbed the mission of entering and exiting personnel from theater. Bagram Air Base, however, needed new facilities before it could host the additional aircraft and fuel.[110] Since fuel could not be transported via pipeline to Bagram, engineers had to build the storage capacity for 5.6 million gallons of fuel.[111] For someone trying to limit

---

106. Ed Darack, "Operation Red Wings," *Marine Corps Gazette* (Jan 2011): 91–92.

107. Lt. Michael Patrick Murphy was awarded a Congressional Medal of Honor for his bravery in Operation Red Wings. In 2014, a feature-length movie of this incident, entitled *Lone Survivor*, was released. The film focused on the experiences of Navy SEAL Hospital Corpsman First Class Marcus Luttrell, portrayed by actor Mark Wahlberg.

108. OPORD 05–01, CFC-A, 4 Sep 2005, sub: K2 Relocation, p. 1, Hist Files, OEF Study Grp. The decision resulted from strained relations between the U.S. and Uzbek governments following an incident in May 2005 when Uzbek security forces fired on a crowd of protesters in Andijon, Uzbekistan, killing nearly 200 people. In addition to closing the U.S. air base, Uzbekistan's government shifted away from its previous focus on interacting with Western nations by strengthening ties with Russia and China.

109. Ibid.

110. Ibid., paras. 1, 4, 3.A.1, 3.A.2.

111. Ibid., paras. 1–2, 3.A.2., p. 8.

An AH–64 from Company B, 2d Battalion, 211th Aviation Regiment, refuels at Asadabad during a mission to pick up Afghan presidential election ballots at remote locations in October 2004. ANA soldiers provide security in an old Soviet tank in the background.

American involvement in Afghanistan, Eikenberry was not helped by having to convert Bagram into a projection platform.

If Eikenberry could not control decisions made by Uzbekistan, Special Forces, the enemy, or allies, he could at least direct how General Kamiya's combat units supported the upcoming elections. Although U.S. troops in Afghanistan sought to create "a stable and secure state willing to contribute in a continued partnership with the U.S.-led coalition in the global war on terror," Eikenberry placed more emphasis on their efforts to pave the way for Afghan elections than his predecessors had.[112] Successfully run elections may not have automatically triggered a reduction in the number of American troops in Afghanistan, but they at least were a concrete step toward "a stable and secure state." Botched or disputed elections might delay or disrupt the Bonn Process, which in turn might necessitate a more robust or lengthier American commitment.

Eikenberry's election focus reinforced Barno's efforts to involve local Afghans in national politics. Unlike the presidential election, however, the September elections would decide who sat in parliament and on provincial councils: each voter would have to select politicians to fill many different seats. This election would not only complete the last step in the constitutional process outlined almost four years ago at Bonn, but also populate government bodies designed to connect people with national governance. Like Barno before him, Eikenberry wanted the election to serve as a referendum on national authority.

---

112. OPORD 04–07, CFC-A, 7 Nov 2004, sub: Support to National Assembly Elections, para. 1, Hist Files, OEF Study Grp.

An estimated 7,000 polling stations and thirty-four regional counting centers attested to Karzai's desire to reach all of Afghanistan; however, not all of these places could be observed by UN personnel or protected by coalition forces.[113] Eikenberry's command supported the election when and where it could. In addition to providing outer-cordon security, American soldiers helped register voters, and U.S. helicopters flew ballots to counting stations. Even though the election itself was Afghan-run, the U.S. military remained invested in the result. America's exit from theater was predicated on the elections being a transformative event in the lives of Afghans.

The Taliban opposed the September 2005 National Assembly and provincial council elections with more vigor than it had the October 2004 presidential election. Before the elections, Lt. Col. Orlando Salinas' 3d Battalion, 141st Infantry, whose soldiers were divided among several reconstruction teams, identified that election workers were registering children as voters in Andar District, Ghazni Province. When questioned, one registration coordinator admitted that the Taliban had pressured him into allowing this disruption to occur.[114] More importantly, CJTF-76 recorded thirty-two major attacks the day before the election and forty-one on election day, significant increases over the daily average of twelve.[115] Although most attacks were IED strikes or indirect fire incidents—modest responses, given the lucrative targets presented by people funneling into election sites and standing in lines to vote—they indicated the enemy's willingness to slow governmental progress.

As it turned out, the resistance to the September 2005 elections was more a prelude to future aggression than a serious attempt to oppose Karzai's legitimacy. The enemy's measured response was partly attributable to coalition troops making it difficult to attack polling stations, a temporary condition created by an influx of resources and months of preparation.[116] At the same time, with an estimated 1,700 to 3,500 enemy fighters and a historical willingness to engage Westerners, the Taliban was not deterred

---

113. Ibid., para 3.E.1.

114. Daily Sitrep 199–05, CJTF-76, 19 Jul 2005, Hist Files, OEF Study Grp.

115. Daily Sitrep 261–05, CJTF-76 19 Sep 2005, Hist Files, OEF Study Grp. Colonel Donahue, who commanded TF Devil during the elections, recalled twenty-six attacks on election day; Interv, Clay with Donahue, 16 Mar 2009, p. 14. According to the chief of current operations for the 1st Brigade, "[E]lections made for a rough week. We stopped putting information in the computer because we couldn't put our contacts in the computer fast enough. We started setting up white boards so we could track all the incidents." Interv, Laurence Lessard, CSI, with Capt Keller J. Durkin, frmr 1st Bde Combat Team, 82d Abn Opns Ch, 3 Mar 2008, p. 7, Hist Files, OEF Study Grp.

116. For example, the Taliban in Sangin and other districts in northern Helmand Province were attacked preemptively in order to prevent them from being active on election day. Interv, Stark, Neumann, and Williams with Ringgenberg, 24 May 2016. The 1st Battalion, 325th Infantry, which CENTCOM deployed to Afghanistan to support the elections, spent its short deployment targeting known Taliban cells in Wardak and Logar Provinces. Interv, Steven Clay, CSI, with Lt Col David P. Anders, Cdr, 1st Bn, 325th Inf, 14 Jan 2009, pp. 7, 9–10, Hist Files, OEF Study Grp.

by American firepower.[117] However, the Taliban was waging a protracted war, and if the elections held any significance, it was because they offered an opportunity to show Afghanistan's elected leaders as corrupt or feckless. Attacking hard targets such as polling sites was not worth the effort if the same effect could be achieved at far less cost through information operations.[118]

Time favored Mullah Mohammed Omar and the Taliban. The transition from American to ISAF lead in supporting the Afghan government and the continued development of ANSF were painstaking endeavors that required time and resources. Meanwhile, the unstable political climate in Afghanistan and sanctuary in western Pakistan favored the Taliban's efforts to rebuild its strength and influence. With the United States increasingly focused on operations in Iraq and NATO expanding its geographic responsibilities to include regions sympathetic to the Taliban regime, the stage was effectively set for its reemergence as a significant obstacle to the Karzai government and the intended trajectory of Operation ENDURING FREEDOM.

---

117. Tim Bird and Alex Marshall, *Afghanistan: How the West Lost Its Way* (New Haven, Conn.: Yale University Press, 2011), p. 142. However many soldiers the Taliban had, the number appears sufficient to have disrupted the elections more robustly.

118. Colonel Donahue disagreed, suggesting the Taliban did oppose the elections to its fullest extent. In his view, the fundamentalist organization had been embarrassed by its defeat in the presidential election and "made a concentrated effort to try to disrupt" the September election so as to avoid a similar failure. Interv, Clay with Donahue, 16 Mar 2009, p. 9.

Conclusion

The factors that constrained U.S. operations in Afghanistan between May 2002 and September 2005—a lack of resources, poor situational awareness in Washington, D.C., and a distracted senior headquarters in Tampa—all stemmed from insufficient interest among U.S. policymakers. With the Taliban seemingly neutralized and the Bonn Process underway, the Bush administration shifted its attention and resources from Afghanistan to other rogue states that might aid Osama bin Laden and his global terrorism network. Additionally, U.S. policymakers were reluctant to commit to a deeper relationship with the Afghan people. Some cabinet members were concerned that Afghans would view Americans as occupiers like they had the Soviets. Others feared incurring large and expensive peacekeeping obligations similar to recent operations in the Balkans, which had required a multiyear commitment of U.S. forces and resources. As a result, the administration's policy on post-Taliban Afghanistan vacillated for months until Accelerating Success lent belated—and inadequate—clarity to the relationship between America's strategic goals and the war-torn country of Afghanistan.

Forward Deployed in Afghanistan

A greater U.S. commitment to Afghanistan took a back seat to the Bush administration's next goal in the Global War on Terrorism, which was Iraq. CENTCOM deployed another three-star headquarters—built around the XVIII Airborne Corps—that did not have the capabilities and capacity of Lt. Gen. Paul T. Mikolashek's CFLCC, and pulled Mikolashek's headquarters out of Afghanistan in anticipation of subsequent efforts against Saddam Hussein's Iraq. Lacking the ability to develop greater insight into turbulent post-Taliban Afghanistan, General Tommy R. Franks issued CJTF-180 orders based on two assumptions. First, he believed it was essential to maintain a minimal footprint in Afghanistan, despite mounting evidence that Afghans did not understand the U.S. mission and objectives but also did not believe that the Americans harbored territorial ambitions like the Soviets. Second, General Franks and the Bush administration overestimated how much assistance the United States could expect from local allies once the Taliban had been ousted from power. As Operation Iraqi Freedom loomed, Franks sought to free more resources for the pending invasion by converting CJTF-180 from a corps to a division headquarters. This reduction further limited what American commanders could accomplish and whom they could influence. As the Afghan state struggled to assert itself during this formative period, warlords took advantage of the sparse U.S. presence by fomenting violence, hindering reconstruction efforts that did not directly benefit their own interests, and actively working to prevent the young government in Kabul from gaining more power.

When General John P. Abizaid replaced Franks, he sought to address the situation in Afghanistan while remaining attentive to the administration's desire to limit America's long-term commitment to the country. With another war to oversee, the new CENTCOM commander influenced Operation ENDURING FREEDOM most directly by whom he chose to lead the American effort. To fix what he believed were inadequate responses to evolving operational conditions, General Abizaid switched the emphasis of conventional forces from counterterrorism to counterinsurgency. Like Franks with Lt. Gen. Dan K. McNeill, however, Abizaid allowed the campaign plans devised by Lt. Gen. David W. Barno and Lt. Gen. Karl W. Eikenberry to substitute for ambiguous U.S. policy in Afghanistan.

Generals Barno and Eikenberry enjoyed almost as much operational freedom in Afghanistan as had General McNeill and Maj. Gen. John R. Vines. Although Barno had to implement an administration-written plan in Accelerating Success, its primary author, Zalmay M. Khalilzad, accompanied him to Kabul as U.S. ambassador. As an outcome of the friendship between Barno and Khalilzad, American strategy was formulated in theater and not in Washington. General Barno created more reconstruction teams than ordered, established areas of operations for battalions and brigades, melded his version of Regional Development Zones with a similar plan from the UN Assistance Mission in Afghanistan, and navigated around instructions to leave police development to Germany. However, despite receiving more resources than his predecessors, Barno still lacked sufficient staff and funding. As a result, American efforts during this period produced isolated islands of progress within a country that remained largely untouched by his initiatives.

General Eikenberry could not link together those islands of progress because he had received instructions to reduce American involvement in political and developmental affairs. However, Eikenberry did not hesitate to address unfavorable situations that threatened the development of Afghan democracy, as witnessed by the fact that he expanded American participation in police training and, upon orders from Abizaid, supported Britain's counternarcotics campaign. He also recognized the growing competency of the Taliban opposition and ISAF's unwillingness to directly confront this threat. The perceived need to militarily respond to emerging threats made him doubt the propriety of withdrawing resources from Afghanistan to battle the unexpectedly virulent insurgency that sprang up in Iraq following the fall of Saddam Hussein in April 2003.

Although theater commanders in Afghanistan sometimes made decisions with the larger conflict in mind, they directed their experience, energies, and imagination toward the problems at hand. Franks and Abizaid oftentimes allowed their responses to these problems to become the United States' effective strategy for the conflict, not because they intentionally abdicated their campaign planning responsibilities but because they trusted their subordinates and needed time to plan future operations in the Global War on Terrorism. While laudable in retrospect, the relationship that developed between CENTCOM leaders and their subordinates in Afghanistan demonstrates both the U.S. military's abhorrence of a policy vacuum and the administration's abiding belief that it did not have to invest significant resources in a conflict it felt it had already won.

For all of these reasons, a series of unexpected developments—including Afghanistan's weak central government and the Taliban's resurgence—drove the war after Operation ANACONDA, rather than a coherent plan. Ironically, many of the developments that alarmed American policymakers might have been avoided if the administration had adopted a more deliberate approach to both seeking out the next battlefield and consolidating the dramatic gains that the United States had made in its victory over the Taliban. Capping three-and-a-half years in which Franks and Abizaid gave their commanders the latitude to exert tremendous influence on America's involvement to Afghanistan, the National Assembly and provincial council elections on 18 September 2005 signified the beginning of an even more tumultuous phase of Operation ENDURING FREEDOM.

BACK IN THE UNITED STATES

The demands of two active theaters, Afghanistan and Iraq, tested the Army's institutional agility in numerous ways. The biggest challenges were manpower and time. The Army's adjustments to the force structure and readiness models were critical to providing the constant stream of trained and ready forces to meet the requirements. These efforts provided some immediate relief, but the prolonged conflicts would present myriad challenges to the institutional Army in the future.

The DoD's pursuit of transformation in the years before the September 11th attacks generated the need for change of a far different variety than envisioned within the Army. One reason for these changes stemmed from the fact that the Rapid Decisive Operations approach was unable to bring an end to the conflicts the United States had initiated in Afghanistan and Iraq. In both cases, defeated nation-state regimes supporting global terrorism adopted asymmetrical warfighting methods that nullified American advantages. As the Afghanistan and Iraq conflicts displayed few signs of concluding on terms favorable to the United States and its allies, the U.S. Army transformed itself into an organization capable of accommodating multiple campaigns of indefinite duration. Whenever the Army lacked the authority to make necessary changes, it enlisted the help of appropriate legislative or corporate bodies to achieve its desired outcomes.

The unforeseen course of the Afghanistan and Iraq campaigns was not the only factor driving internal adaptation and change. The Army's decision to adopt a brigade-based rotation system, when coupled with the DoD's reluctance to divert funding and resources from its pursuit of transformation-oriented initiatives, promised scant relief to soldiers shouldering the overwhelming share of fighting in Afghanistan and Iraq. That situation sparked sweeping force structure changes within the Army, leading to the creation of modular combat, combat support, and combat service support organizations under modular headquarters organizations.

The Army, however, incurred some strategic risk when implementing modularity. The redesigned organizations were far better suited to battle irregular opponents, as compared to peer competitors—such as Russia and China—who were still waging a conventional fight. Modularity, coupled with the Army's deployment and readiness models, all but ensured that most of a brigade's experienced leadership rotate out upon redeployment to its home station. The Army would have to regenerate the organization for the next deployment. In the years to follow, many of the modularity initiatives would be reversed, giving the impression that modularity was itself a method to deal with the immediate issues as opposed to long-term warfighting challenges. Modularity sacrificed much of the capability and capacity of the divisions' and corps' warfighting teams.

Neither the transformation of doctrine nor force structure could account fully for the stresses endured by the Army through the early years of the Global War on Terrorism. The root cause stemmed from the sustained demand on ground forces, which had to defeat irregular opponents in two significantly different operational environments. The sheer difficulty of achieving near-simultaneous victory in both conflicts eventually would lead the Army to use techniques in Afghanistan that it had used successfully in Iraq. It combined this population-centric counterinsurgency doctrine with a surge of forces to the ongoing campaign in Afghanistan. The consequences of this counterinsurgency effort and the effectiveness of the surge will be examined in depth in the second volume of *Modern War in an Ancient Land*.

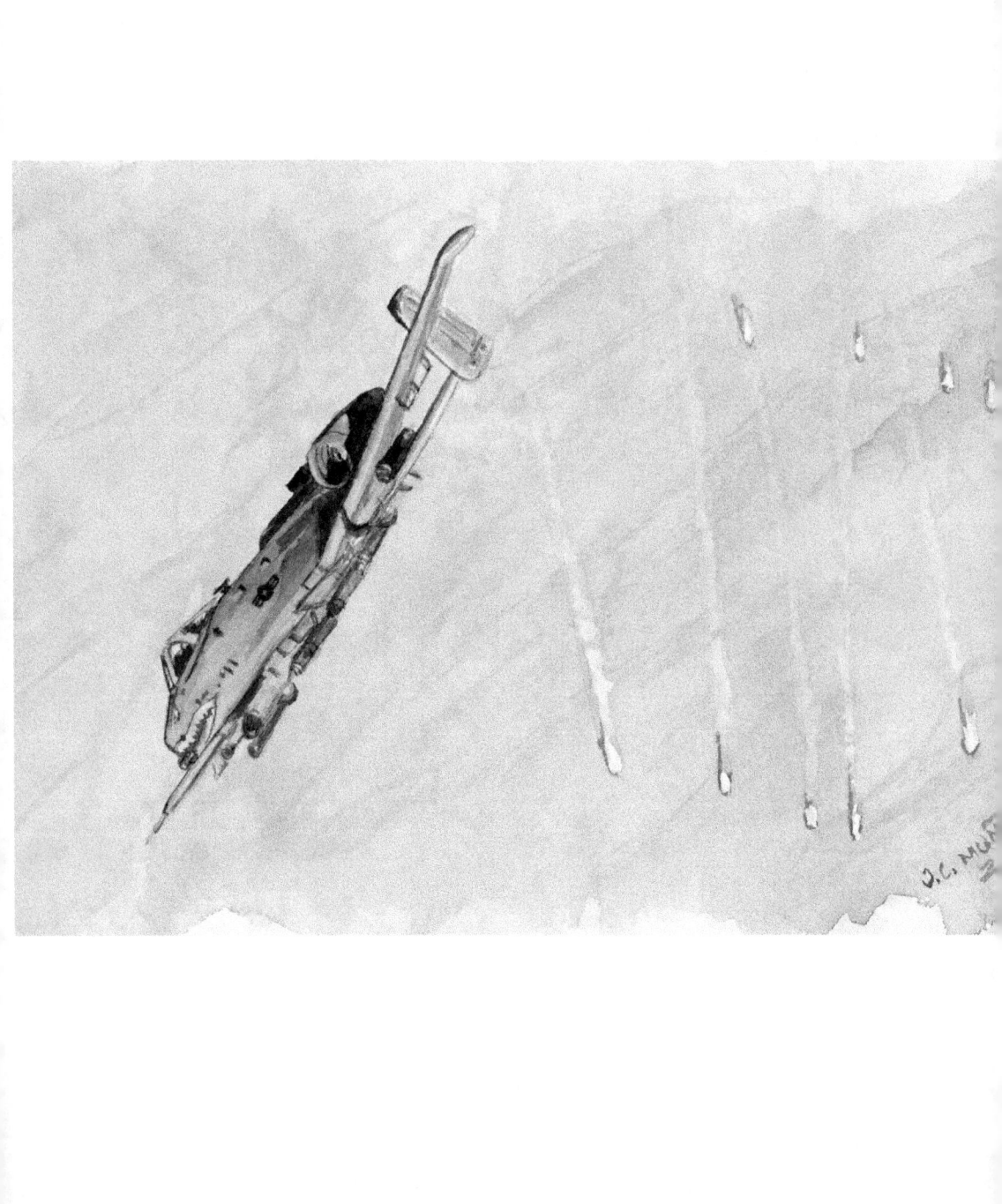

Bibliographical Note

Documents and Publications

The sources for this account by the Chief of Staff of the Army's Operation ENDURING FREEDOM Study Group were campaign plans, daily update briefings, and monthly and weekly reports compiled or composed before, during, and immediately after many of the events described in this account. They were collected in Afghanistan, from CENTCOM files at MacDill Air Force Base in Tampa, Florida, and from archival sources available at the U.S. Army Center of Military History at Fort McNair, D.C. Those caches of electronic documents—virtually all of which remain classified—were created by the headquarters overseeing the operations discussed in this narrative. These include CJTFs MOUNTAIN, 76, 82, 101, and 180; RC East, RC South, and RC Southwest; TF PHOENIX; Office of Military Cooperation–Afghanistan and Office of Security Cooperation–Afghanistan; CFC-A; CSTC-A; and USFOR-A. Operational records from upper-echelon headquarters outside of Afghanistan, such as CENTCOM at MacDill Air Force Base; CFLCC at Camp Doha, Kuwait; and Southern European Task Force at Vicenza, Italy, also were useful sources of information.

Much of the documentation required to write about events happening after 2006 was generated by NATO ISAF and its subordinate commands. However, these records are classified by both U.S. and NATO sources. As a result, few of the NATO records were used because of the lengthy procedures required to declassify NATO material. Even more restrictive measures are in place in regards to the release of information on Special Operations activities after the March 2002 timeframe. However, there are a few online avenues for researchers to access formerly classified materials, including George Washington University's National Security Archive and the CENTCOM Freedom of Information Act Web page. The U.S. material provides strategic-level planning, diplomatic, and policy-making documents generated by the Departments of Defense and State, while material found on the latter site is devoted to declassified reports and investigations covering critical events involving U.S. forces in Afghanistan.

Useful unclassified accounts of Operation ENDURING FREEDOM and the events leading up to that conflict include retired Brig. Gen. John S. Brown's *Kevlar Legions: The Transformation of the U.S. Army, 1989–2005* as well as two books by the U.S. Army Combat Studies Institute: *A Different Kind of War: The United States Army in Operation ENDURING FREEDOM, October 2001–September 2005* and *Weapon of Choice: ARSOF in Afghanistan*. The material in *Weapon of Choice* is amplified by the United States Special Operations Command's unclassified *United States Special Operations Command History*

1987–2007. In addition to these unclassified published accounts, primary source materials used to examine the conflict's impact on the Army as an institution were collected from various staff sections of the Headquarters, Department of the Army; the National Guard Bureau; Office of the Chief of Army Reserve; U.S. Army TRADOC at Fort Eustis, Virginia; U.S. Army Combined Arms Center at Fort Leavenworth, Kansas; and U.S. Army Corps of Engineers headquarters in Washington, D.C.

A number of memoirs dealing with events leading up to the events of 11 September 2001 and the American reaction to the terrorist attacks were consulted. While these accounts often provided a detailed, first-hand perspective of decisions made by senior policymakers and commanders, in some cases they presented differing interpretations of events that required deconfliction by the Study Group. Useful accounts of events leading up to the attacks and the U.S. response include CIA director George J. Tenet's *At the Center of the Storm: My Years at the CIA*, Chairman of the Joint Chiefs of Staff General H. Hugh Shelton's *Without Hesitation: The Odyssey of an American Warrior*, CENTCOM commander General Tommy R. Franks' *American Soldier*, DoD policymaker Douglas J. Feith's *War and Decision: Inside the Pentagon at the Dawn of the War on Terrorism*, and former Secretary of Defense Donald H. Rumsfeld's *Known and Unknown: A Memoir*. For the post-2002 timeframe, the Study Group utilized Chairman of the Joint Chiefs of Staff General Richard B. Myers' *Eyes on the Horizon: Serving on the Front Lines of National Security*, Secretary of Defense Robert M. Gates' *Duty: Memoirs of a Secretary at War*, as well as autobiographies of ISAF commanders, including General Sir David J. Richards' *Taking Command* and General Stanley A. McChrystal's *My Share of the Task: A Memoir*.

In addition to the recollections of senior officials and military officers, American and British soldiers have written a number of eyewitness accounts that convey a human perspective often invisible to operational and strategic-level participants. These include Robert S. Anders' *Winning Paktika: Counterinsurgency in Afghanistan*, Doug Beattie's *Task Force Helmand: A Soldier's Story of Life, Death and Combat on the Afghan Front Line*, Jimmy Blackmon's *Pale Horse: Hunting Terrorists and Commanding Heroes with the 101st Airborne Division*, Ronald Fry's *Hammerhead Six: How Green Berets Waged an Unconventional War Against the Taliban to Win in Afghanistan's Deadly Pech Valley*, Carter Malkasian's incomparable *War Comes to Garmser: Thirty Years of Conflict on the Afghan Frontier*, Dakota Meyer's *Into the Fire: A Firsthand Account of the Most Extraordinary Battle in the Afghan War*, Sean Parnell's *Outlaw Platoon: Heroes, Renegades, Infidels, and the Brotherhood of War in Afghanistan*, Clinton Romesha's *Red Platoon: A True Story of American Valor*, and Stuart Tootal's *Danger Close: Commanding 3 Para in Afghanistan*.

ORAL HISTORY INTERVIEWS AND MANUSCRIPT SOURCES

The OEF Study Group's efforts to interview various notables for the project proved very productive due to the tremendous cooperation it received from virtually everyone contacted. While the roster of prominent civilian

Bibliographical Note

officials and military officers—both American and allied—who agreed to be interviewed is too lengthy to list in its entirety, the Study Group gratefully acknowledges President George W. Bush, Vice President Richard B. "Dick" Cheney, Secretaries of Defense Robert M. Gates, Leon E. Panetta, and Charles T. "Chuck" Hagel; CENTCOM commanders Tommy R. Franks, John P. Abizaid, David H. Petraeus, and Lloyd J. Austin III; Ambassadors Ronald E. Neumann, Zalmay Khalilzad, Karl W. Eikenberry, William B. Wood, and Robert P. J. Finn; ISAF commanders Dan K. McNeill, David D. McKiernan, and Stanley A. McChrystal; RC East commanders James J. Schlosser and Curtis M. Scaparrotti; RC South commanders British General Sir Nicholas P. Carter and Dutch Lt. Gen. Mart De Kruif; senior Marine commanders Lt. Gen. Lawrence D. Nicholson and Lt. Gen. Richard P. Mills; and *Washington Post* reporter Bob Woodward, who provided key insights into the Obama White House. Many other individuals not listed here kindly consented to being interviewed and for that courtesy the Study Group is profoundly grateful.

The authors also made use of unpublished first-person accounts written to satisfy academic requirements in U.S. Army professional development courses. Most prominent were Personal Experience Papers by students attending the Maneuver Captains Career Course at Fort Benning, Georgia's Maneuver Center of Excellence. Several hundred of these accounts have been declassified and posted on Army Knowledge Online and the Fort Benning Donovan Research Library Web site. Similar narratives utilized by the Study Group included those authored by senior noncommissioned officers attending the U.S. Army Sergeant Majors Academy at Fort Bliss, Texas, available online via the U.S. Army Command and General Staff College's Ike Skelton Combined Arms Research Library digital collection. That same collection contains Afghanistan-related interviews conducted by Combat Studies Institute historians for the Operational Leadership Experience series.

Recognizing the need to capture information on key events soon after they occurred, the U.S. Army deployed a number of Military History Detachments to Afghanistan during the opening phase of Operation ENDURING FREEDOM. Maj. Richard M. Brown's 130th Military History Detachment and Maj. John Warsinke's 47th Military History Detachment conducted valuable interviews between March and July 2002. Following the 2001–2002 timeframe, however, most Military History Detachments were deployed to Iraq, and few U.S. Army historians served in Afghanistan between 2003 and 2010. After discovering large gaps in the available Military History Detachment collections, the OEF Study Group conducted a targeted collection effort by compiling multiple terabytes of electronic records from Maj. Gen. John M. Murray's 3d Infantry Division headquarters at Bagram and General John F. Campbell's ISAF headquarters in Kabul.

Secondary Sources

Commercially produced accounts augmented or filled gaps in our primary sources. Although the Study Group drew on information from many publications, several are worth singling out. For a useful general overview, both Peter Tomsen's *The Wars of Afghanistan: Messianic Terrorism, Tribal Conflicts, and the Failures of Great Powers* and Thomas J. Barfield's *Afghanistan: A Cultural and Political History* proved informative. Valuable accounts that shed additional light on extremist influences in the Middle East and Central Asia included not only Barfield and Tomsen, but also Peter Bergen's *The Osama bin Laden I Know: An Oral History of Al-Qaeda's Leader*, Mustafa Hamid and Leah Farrall's *The Arabs at War in Afghanistan*, Ahmed Rashid's *Taliban: Militant Islam, Oil and Fundamentalism in Central Asia*, and Seth G. Jones' *Hunting in the Shadows: The Pursuit of al Qa'ida since 9/11*.

A selection of useful books on U.S. and ISAF conventional units includes Patrick Bishop's *3 Para*, Stephen Grey's *Into the Viper's Nest: Task Force 1 Fury and the Battle of Musa Qala*, Toby Harnden's *Dead Men Risen: The Welsh Guards and the Defining Story of Britain's War in Afghanistan*, Col. Bernd Horn's *No Lack of Courage: Operation Medusa, Afghanistan*, Jake Tapper's *The Outpost: An Untold Story of American Valor*, Gregg Zoroya's *The Chosen Few: A Company of Paratroopers and Its Heroic Struggle to Survive in the Mountains of Afghanistan*, Col. Nathan S. Lowrey's *U.S. Marines in Afghanistan 2001–2002: From the Sea*, and compiler David W. Kummer's *U.S. Marine Corps in Afghanistan, 2001–2009: Anthology and Annotated Bibliography* and its companion volume by Paul W. Westermeyer with Christopher Blaker entitled *U.S. Marines in Afghanistan, 2010–2014: Anthology and Annotated Bibliography*.

There are a similar, if not greater, number of detailed and well-written accounts dealing with special operations in Afghanistan, notable among which are Eric Blehm's *The Only Thing Worth Dying For: How Eleven Green Berets Fought for a New Afghanistan*, Rusty Bradley and Kevin Maurer's *Lions of Kandahar: The Story of a Fight Against All Odds*, Daniel R. Green's *In the Warlords' Shadow: Special Operations Forces, the Afghans, and Their Fight Against the Taliban*, Linda Robinson's exceptional *One Hundred Victories: Special Ops and the Future of American Warfare*, and Mitch Weiss and Kevin Maurer's *No Way Out: A Story of Valor in the Mountains of Afghanistan* by.

The OEF Study Group also relied on published accounts of nation building and coalition warfare, both of which are central to the Afghanistan conflict. A few of the books consulted for reference on these topics include James F. Dobbins' *After the Taliban: Nation-Building in Afghanistan*; Ahmed Rashid's *Descent into Chaos: The U.S. and the Disaster in Pakistan, Afghanistan, and Central Asia*; and *Coalition Challenge in Afghanistan: The Politics of Alliance*, edited by Gale A. Mattox and Stephen M. Grenier.

Think tank papers and government reports frequently contain facts unavailable elsewhere. First and foremost among sources covering the period from October 2008 onward were Special Inspector General for Afghanistan Reconstruction reports submitted quarterly to Congress. Among private institutions, the Santa Monica, California–based RAND Corporation has produced a number of useful studies of Afghanistan, including Terrence K. Kelley, Nora Bensahel, and Olga Oliker's *Security Force Assistance in Afghanistan: Identifying Lessons for Future Efforts*, Seth G. Jones and Arturo Muñoz's *Afghanistan's Local War: Building Local Defense Forces*, and C. Christine Fair's *The Counterterror Coalitions: Cooperation with Pakistan and*

India. Many articles and publications by RAND's competitors—the majority of which are located in Washington, D.C.—not only enlightened OEF Study Group members but also provided valuable insights to senior commanders in Afghanistan. Sources for these pieces include the Center for Strategic and International Studies, the Institute for the Study of War, the Brookings Institution, the Center for a New American Security, and the Foundation for Defense of Democracies. The last named institution also hosts Bill Roggio's informative *Long War Journal* Web site.

Newspapers often can provide historians with perspectives and facts found nowhere else. Useful media sources on events in Afghanistan for the OEF Study Group included the *Los Angeles Times*, *New York Times*, and *Washington Post*; the British newspapers the *Guardian* and the *Independent*; the Pakistani newspaper *Dawn*, and Agence France-Presse. When consulting these sources, the OEF Study Group members normally compared multiple accounts from various publications before settling on an accepted version of events in order to compensate for inadvertent errors introduced by journalists writing under tight deadlines. This precaution, however, did not have to be used as frequently when consulting pieces by reporters on extended assignment in the region.

Operation Enduring Freedom Study Group Biographies

Col. (Ret.) Edmund J. "EJ" Degen, a career field artillery officer, currently serves as the director of the Chief of Staff, Army's Operation ENDURING FREEDOM Study Group. He has commanded artillery units at all levels through brigade, and served as the V Corps (U.S.) chief of plans for the Iraq invasion at the start of Operation IRAQI FREEDOM, chief of future operations for U.S. Forces Korea, and chief of staff for Combined Joint Interagency Task Force 435 in Afghanistan. Colonel Degen was a fellow on the CSA's inaugural Strategic Studies Group and served as the Senior Fellow the following year. He has multiple combat deployments to Iraq and Afghanistan. Colonel Degen has an MMAS (Master of Military Art and Science) from the Army's School of Advanced Military Studies and an MS in Strategic and Operational Planning from the Joint Advanced Warfighting School. He is the coauthor of *On Point: The United States Army in Operation IRAQI FREEDOM* (Annapolis, Md.: Naval Institute Press, 2005), along with numerous journal articles.

Col. Adrian A. Donahoe, a Special Forces officer, enlisted in the Iowa National Guard in 1987. He was commissioned and entered active-duty service in 1993 after graduating from the University of South Dakota. He completed the Special Forces Qualification Course in 1999 and has served in various command and staff positions within Special Operations and the conventional Army. He is a veteran of Operation ENDURING FREEDOM and multiple Operation ENDURING FREEDOM–Philippines deployments. Colonel Donahoe holds an MS from the Naval Postgraduate School and an MMAS from the School of Advanced Military Studies. He is the former director of Special Operations Leadership Development and Education at Fort Leavenworth, Kansas, and the director of the Commander's Action Group for NATO Special Operations Component Command-Afghanistan/Special Operations Joint Task Force–Afghanistan.

Col. Bryan R. Gibby is the chief of the Military History Division in the Department of History, United States Military Academy, West Point. A 1993 West Point graduate, he was awarded master's and doctoral degrees in history from Ohio State University. Colonel Gibby is a career military intelligence officer and has served in command and staff assignments from tactical to strategic levels. His most recent operational experience was as Commander, 707th Military Intelligence Battalion, providing SIGINT (signals intelligence) support to the CENTCOM areas of responsibility. He twice deployed in Operation IRAQI FREEDOM as a brigade (2007–2008) and division (2005–2006) intelligence officer. Following service in Iraq, Colonel Gibby joined Allied Force Command, Madrid, where he served as the chief of intelligence assessments for CJTF UNIFIED PROTECTOR in 2011. He is the author of *The Will to Win: American Military Advisors in Korea, 1946–1953*.

Dr. Brian F. Neumann is a historian at the U.S. Army Center of Military History. He earned his BA in history from the University of Southern California in 1998 and his MA and PhD in history from Texas A&M University in 2001 and 2006, respectively. His academic field is twentieth-century U.S. military history with a focus on World War I. After teaching for four years, he joined CMH in 2010 and began working in the Contemporary Studies Branch, Histories Division, with a focus on Operation ENDURING FREEDOM. He cowrote and edited the center's campaign brochure on Operation ENDURING FREEDOM 2002–2005. After working with the CSA's OEF Study Group for two years, Dr. Neumann became the editor of the "U.S. Army Campaigns of World War One" commemorative pamphlet series in November 2016. He also serves as a member of the CMH World War I Commemoration Committee and as the Center's World War I subject matter expert.

Col. Francis J. H. Park is a historian in the Joint History and Research Office of the Joint Staff. Prior to his current assignment, he was the chief of the Strategy Development Division in the Joint Staff J-5. After commissioning in 1994, he served in command and staff duties primarily in armored cavalry and light airborne cavalry assignments. Designated an Army strategist in 2004, he has served at division, corps, army service component command, and joint task force levels, as well as in the Army Staff and Joint Staff. His service in Operation ENDURING FREEDOM spans 2008–2009 as principal campaign planner for CJTF 101 and RC East, and 2013–2014 as deputy director, Commander's Action Group, ISAF. His other combat experience includes Operations IRAQI FREEDOM and INHERENT RESOLVE. Colonel Park holds a BA in history from the Johns Hopkins University; an MA in international relations from St. Mary's University of San Antonio, Texas; an MMAS from the School of Advanced Military Studies; and a PhD in history from the University of Kansas.

Mr. Mark J. Reardon is a senior civilian historian with the U.S. Army Center of Military History. Before joining the Center in 2006, he served as a regular officer in parachute, reconnaissance, and armor units during a twenty-seven-year career in the Army, and retired as a lieutenant colonel. Mr. Reardon, who recently completed a manuscript for the Center on training the post–Saddam Iraqi Army, has also published four books on World War II and Korea, a history of the initial Stryker Brigade deployment to Iraq, several detailed studies of small-unit actions in Iraq, and three studies on U.S. military innovation in World War II.

Dr. Gregory G. Roberts is a desk officer in the State Department's Office of Afghanistan Affairs. As a Presidential Management Fellow (2014–2016), he served as a historian at the U.S. Army Center of Military History and the

Combat Studies Institute, and as a special assistant to the Chairman of the Joint Chiefs of Staff in the Chairman's Action Group. Prior to entering federal service, Dr. Roberts worked as a research associate in national security studies at the Council on Foreign Relations. In 2013, he earned a PhD in history from Yale University, where his research focused on policing in medieval Italy. He earned an MA and an MPhil in history from Yale in 2010, and a BA in history and a BA in French from Vanderbilt University in 2007. Dr. Roberts has published on OEF in the *SAIS Review of International Affairs* and has a chapter in the forthcoming volume *Makers of Modern Landpower: Post-9/11 Perspectives* (University Press of Kentucky).

Lt. Col. (Ret.) Matthew B. Smith is a graduate of Norwich University where he was commissioned field artillery officer in 1999. His initial assignment was with the 1st Battalion, 94th Field Artillery Regiment, in Idar-Oberstein, Germany. As a battery commander, he deployed with his unit to Iraq and assumed the mission for all surface-to-surface guided MLRS (multiple launch rocket system) fires throughout Multinational Corps–Iraq. Colonel Smith was then assigned as a Fires Observer Trainer with the Mission Command Training Program at Fort Leavenworth, Kansas. Upon graduating the Command and General Staff College, he reported to the 2nd Brigade Combat Team, 10th Mountain Division, in Fort Drum, New York. He deployed to Paktika Province, Afghanistan, in January 2013 and conducted security force assistance with the ANA. Colonel Smith holds an MS in management and business from Webster University.

Lt. Col. (Ret.) John R. Stark retired in 2017 as an armor lieutenant colonel after twenty-five years of service. He graduated as a distinguished cadet from West Point in 1991 and earned an MA (2000) and a PhD (2003) in European history from Ohio State University. He has taught history at West Point and Princeton. While in the Army, he served in Iraq in 2006–2007 as operations officer for the 1st Battalion, 37th Armor "Bandits," in Sinjar and Ramadi and in Afghanistan in 2011–2012 for NATO Rule of Law Field Support Mission in Kandahar and Kabul. He was an Observer-Controller-Trainer at the Joint Military Readiness Center in Hohenfels, Germany, where the Grizzly team trained forces for Afghanistan, Iraq, and Kosovo in 2007–2008. He served at NATO headquarters in 2013–2014 as a liaison officer for Allied Command Transformation, Capabilities Engineering and Innovation. He continues his service to the nation as a diplomat at the Department of State.

Maj. Miranda M. Summers-Lowe is a curator of modern military history at Smithsonian's National Museum of American History and an officer in the District of Columbia National Guard. She enlisted in the Army National Guard in 2002 and served as a supply sergeant in Iraq in 2005 before commissioning through Officer Candidate School in 2009. Other assignments include state public affairs officer, command historian, and intelligence officer in the District of Columbia National Guard. She most recently served as the deputy director of public affairs for CJTF-Horn of Africa in Djibouti and as a public affairs adviser in the Office of the Director, Army National

Guard. She was selected as an Army Congressional Fellow and a nonresident fellow of the Modern War Institute at West Point in 2019. Her work has been published in *Military Review*, War on the Rocks, and the *New York Times*. She has a BA in history from the College of William and Mary and a master's in public humanities from Brown University.

Col. Victor H. Sundquist, an intelligence officer, enlisted with the 7th Infantry Division in 1988. He was commissioned in the Intelligence Branch from the United States Military Academy at West Point in 1995 and transitioned to the Army Strategist Functional Branch in 2014. He holds a MMAS from the School of Advanced Military Studies and an MS in counterterrorism theory from Henley-Putnam University. He is a 2016 graduate of the Army's Senior Service War College, where he served as a Fellow at Georgetown University in the Institute for the Study of Diplomacy under the School of Foreign Service. During his twenty-eight years in the Army, he has served in various intelligence and strategist positions at all levels of command, including assignments in CENTCOM's J–2 staff; the J–2X at ISAF headquarters; the 1st Cavalry Division G–2; the State Department's Provincial Reconstruction Team in Basra, Iraq; deputy director for the Headquarters, Department of the Army's War Plans Division; and most recently as the J–53 plans chief at U.S. Southern Command. He has multiple operational and combat tours, including Operations SOUTHERN WATCH, ENDURING FREEDOM, IRAQI FREEDOM, and NEW DAWN.

Dr. Colin Jay Williams is the command historian for the Defense Logistics Agency. A retired Army officer, he taught military history at the United States Military Academy and has combat experience in both Afghanistan and Iraq. He received a PhD in military history from the University of Alabama and has been published in *Key to the Northern Country: The Hudson River Valley in the American Revolution* (SUNY Press, 2013) and *New York History* (vol. 99, no. 1).

Appendix

U.S. Military Terminology and Definitions

The following terms and definitions, drawn from official Army publications and used in the text of this book, are provided here for the reader's ease of reference.

Department of the Army Field Manual (FM) 3-24.2, *Tactics in Counterinsurgency*, 21 April 2009 (Selected Text)

A *clear-hold-build* operation is a full spectrum operation that combines offense (finding and eliminating the insurgent), defense (protecting the local populace) and stability (rebuilding the infrastructure, increasing the legitimacy of the local government, and bringing the rule of law to the area) operations. Each phase—clear, hold, and build—combines offensive, defensive, and stability operations in varying degrees. In the *clear* phase, offensive operations usually dominate; in the *hold* phase, defensive operations are emphasized; and in the *build* phase, stability operations are preeminent. It is usually a relatively long-term operation and requires the commitment of a large number of forces. Clear-hold-build operations are often preceded by shaping operations to set the proper conditions.

Shape – A shaping operation is an operation at any echelon that creates and preserves conditions for the success of the decisive operation.

Clear – Clear is a tactical mission task that requires the commander to remove all enemy forces and eliminate organized resistance within an assigned area (FM 3-90). The force does this by destroying, capturing, or forcing the withdrawal of insurgent combatants and leaders. This task is most effectively initiated by a clear-in-zone or cordon-and-search operation, as well as patrolling, ambushes, and targeted raids.

Hold – After clearing the area of guerrillas, the counterinsurgent force must then assign sufficient troops to the cleared area to prevent their return, to defeat any remnants, and to secure the population. This is the hold task. Ideally, Host Nation security forces execute this part of the clear-hold-build operation. Success or failure depends on effectively and continuously securing the populace and on reestablishing a Host Nation local government. Although offensive and stability operations continue, this phase uses defensive operations to secure the population.

Build – The build phase of clear-hold-build operations consists of carrying out programs designed to remove the root causes that led to the insurgency, improve the lives of the inhabitants, and strengthen the Host Nation's ability to provide effective governance. Stability operations predominate in this phase, with many important activities being conducted by nonmilitary agencies. During this phase, the Host Nation security forces should have primary responsibility for security. Progress in building support for the Host Nation government requires protecting the local populace. People who do not believe they are secure from insurgent intimidation, coercion, and reprisals will not risk overtly supporting counterinsurgent efforts.

Army Doctrine Publication 1–02, *Terms and Military Symbols*, 14 August 2018 (Selected Text)

aeromedical evacuation – (DOD) The movement of patients under medical supervision to and between medical treatment facilities by air transportation. Also called AE. (JP 4–02)

air assault – (DOD) The movement of friendly assault forces by rotary-wing aircraft to engage and destroy enemy forces or to seize and hold key terrain. (JP 3–18)

airborne assault – (DOD) The use of airborne forces to parachute into an objective area to attack and eliminate armed resistance and secure designated objectives. (JP 3–18)

airdrop – (DOD) The unloading of personnel or materiel from aircraft in flight. (JP 3–17) See ATP 4–48.

air-ground operations – The simultaneous or synchronized employment of ground forces with aviation maneuver and fires to seize, retain, and exploit the initiative. Also called AGO. (FM 3–04)

air movements – (Army) Operations involving the use of utility and cargo rotary-wing assets for other than air assaults. (FM 3–90–2)

all-source intelligence – (DOD) 1. Intelligence products and/or organizations and activities that incorporate all sources of information, most frequently including human intelligence, imagery intelligence, measurement and signature intelligence, signals intelligence, and open-source data in the production of finished intelligence. (FM 3–24)

ambush – An attack by fire or other destructive means from concealed positions on a moving or temporarily halted enemy. (FM 3–90–1)

antiterrorism – (DOD) Defensive measures used to reduce the vulnerability of individuals and property to terrorist acts, to include rapid containment by local military and civilian forces. Also called AT. (JP 3–07.2)

Appendix

area of influence – (DOD) A geographical area wherein a commander is directly capable of influencing operations by maneuver or fire support systems normally under the commander's command or control. (JP 3–0)

area of interest – (DOD) That area of concern to the commander, including the area of influence, areas adjacent thereto, and extending into enemy territory. This area also includes areas occupied by enemy forces who could jeopardize the accomplishment of the mission. Also called AOI. (JP 3–0)

area of operations – (DOD) An operational area defined by the joint force commander for land and maritime forces that should be large enough to accomplish their missions and protect their forces. Also called AO. (JP 3–0)

area of responsibility – (DOD) The geographical area associated with a combatant command within which a geographic combatant commander has authority to plan and conduct operations. Also called AOR. (JP 1)

ARFOR (Army Forces) – The Army component and senior Army headquarters of all Army forces assigned or attached to a combatant command, subordinate joint force command, joint functional command, or multinational command. (FM 3–94)

Army doctrine – Fundamental principles, with supporting tactics, techniques, procedures, and terms and symbols, used for the conduct of operations and which the operating force, and elements of the institutional Army that directly support operations, guide their actions in support of national objectives. It is authoritative but requires judgment in application. (ADP 1–01)

Army personnel recovery – The military efforts taken to prepare for and execute the recovery and reintegration of isolated personnel. (FM 3–50)

Army special operations forces – (DOD) Those Active and Reserve Component Army forces designated by the Secretary of Defense that are specifically organized, trained, and equipped to conduct and support special operations. (JP 3–05)

assign – (DOD) 1. To place units or personnel in an organization where such placement is relatively permanent, and/or where such organization controls and administers the units or personnel for the primary function, or greater portion of the functions, of the unit or personnel. (JP 3–0)

attach – (DOD) 1. The placement of units or personnel in an organization where such placement is relatively temporary. (JP 3–0)

attack – An offensive task that destroys or defeats enemy forces, seizes and secures terrain, or both. (ADRP 3–90)

base camp – An evolving military facility that supports that military operations of a deployed unit and provides the necessary support and services for sustained operations. (ATP 3–37.10)

battalion – A unit consisting of two or more company-, battery-, or troop-size units and a headquarters. (ADRP 3–90)

battalion task force – A maneuver battalion-size unit consisting of a battalion headquarters, at least one assigned company-size element, and at least one attached company-size element from another maneuver or support unit (functional and multifunctional). (ADRP 3–90)

battery – A company-size unit in a fires or air defense artillery battalion. (ADRP 3–90)

biometrics – (DOD) The process of recognizing an individual based on measurable anatomical, physiological, and behavioral characteristics. (JP 2–0)

block – A tactical mission task that denies the enemy access to an area or prevents his advance in a direction or along an avenue of approach. Block is also an obstacle effect that integrates fire planning and obstacle effort to stop an attacker along a specific avenue of approach or to prevent the attacking force from passing through an engagement area. (FM 3–90–1)

brigade – A unit consisting of two or more battalions and a headquarters company or detachment. (ADRP 3–90)

cache – (DOD) A source of subsistence and supplies, typically containing items such as food, water, medical items, and/or communications equipment, packaged to prevent damage from exposure and hidden in isolated locations by such methods as burial, concealment, and/or submersion, to support isolated personnel. (JP 3–50)

campaign plan – (DOD) A joint operation plan for a series of related major operations aimed at achieving strategic or operational objectives within a given time and space. (JP 5–0)

canalize – (Army) A tactical mission task in which the commander restricts enemy movement to a narrow zone by exploiting terrain coupled with the use of obstacles, fires, or friendly maneuver. (FM 3–90–1)

capacity building – The process of creating an environment that fosters host-nation institutional development, community participation, human resources development, and strengthening of managerial systems. (FM 3–07)

casualty – (DOD) Any person who is lost to the organization by having been declared dead, duty status – whereabouts unknown, missing, ill, or injured. (JP 4–02)

Appendix

casualty evacuation – (DOD) The unregulated movement of casualties that can include movement both to and between medical treatment facilities. Also called CASEVAC. (JP 4–02)

center of gravity – (DOD) The source of power that provides moral or physical strength, freedom of action, or will to act. Also called COG. (JP 5–0)

civil affairs – (DOD) Designated Active and Reserve Component forces and units organized, trained, and equipped specifically to conduct civil affairs operations and to support civil-military operations. Also called CA. (JP 3–57)

clear – A tactical mission task that requires the commander to remove all enemy forces and eliminate organized resistance within an assigned area. (FM 3–90–1)

close air support – (DOD) Air action by fixed and rotary wing aircraft against hostile targets that are in close proximity to friendly forces and that require detailed integration of each air mission with the fire and movement of those forces. Also called CAS. (JP 3–0)

close combat – Warfare carried out on land in a direct-fire fight, supported by direct and indirect fires, and other assets. (ADRP 3–0)

coalition – (DOD) An arrangement between two or more nations for common action. (JP 5–0)

collateral damage – (DOD) Unintentional or incidental injury or damage to persons or objects that would not be lawful military targets in the circumstances ruling at the time. (JP 3–60)

combatant command – (DOD) A unified or specified command with a broad continuing mission under a single commander established and so designated by the President, through the Secretary of Defense and with the advice and assistance of the Chairman of the Joint Chiefs of Staff. Also called CCMD. (JP 1)

combined arms – The synchronized and simultaneous application of arms to achieve an effect greater than if each arm was used separately or sequentially. (ADRP 3–0)

command and control – (DOD) The exercise of authority and direction by a properly designated commander over assigned and attached forces in the accomplishment of the mission. Also called C2. (JP 1)

commander's intent – (DOD) A clear and concise expression of the purpose of the operation and the desired military end state that supports mission command, provides focus to the staff, and helps subordinate and supporting commanders act to achieve the commander's desired results without further orders, even when the operation does not unfold as planned. (JP 3–0)

command relationships – (DOD) The interrelated responsibilities between commanders, as well as the operational authority exercised by commanders in the chain of command; defined further as combatant command (command authority), operational control, tactical control, or support. (JP 1)

company – A company is a unit consisting of two or more platoons, usually of the same type, with a headquarters and a limited capacity for self-support. (ADRP 3–90)

concept plan – (DOD) In the context of joint operation planning level 3 planning detail, an operation plan in an abbreviated format that may require considerable expansion or alteration to convert it into a complete operation plan or operation order. Also called CONPLAN. (JP 5–0)

contain – A tactical mission task that requires the commander to stop, hold, or surround enemy forces or to cause them to center their activity on a given front and prevent them from withdrawing any part of their forces for use elsewhere. (FM 3–90–1)

conventional forces – (DOD) 1. Those forces capable of conducting operations using nonnuclear weapons; 2. Those forces other than designated special operations forces. Also called CF. (JP 3–05)

convoy – (DOD) 2. A group of vehicles organized for the purpose of control and orderly movement with or without escort protection that moves over the same route at the same time and under one commander. (JP 3–02.1)

cordon and search – A technique of conducting a movement to contact that involves isolating a target area and searching suspect locations within that target area to capture or destroy possible enemy forces and contraband. (FM 3–90–1)

core competency – An essential and enduring capability that a branch or an organization provides to Army operations. (ADP 1–01)

counterattack – Attack by part or all of a defending force against an enemy attacking force, for such specific purposes as regaining ground lost, or cutting off or destroying enemy advance units, and with the general objective of denying to the enemy the attainment of the enemy's purpose in attacking. In sustained defensive operations, it is undertaken to restore the battle position and is directed at limited objectives. (ADP 1–02)

counterinsurgency – (DOD) Comprehensive civilian and military efforts designed to simultaneously defeat and contain insurgency and address its root causes. Also called COIN. (JP 3–24)

Appendix

countermeasures – (DOD) That form of military science that, by the employment of devices and/or techniques, has as its objective the impairment of the operational effectiveness of enemy activity. (JP 3–13.1)

counterterrorism – (DOD) Activities and operations taken to neutralize terrorists and their organizations and networks in order to render them incapable of using violence to instill fear and coerce governments or societies to achieve their goals. Also called CT. (JP 3–26)

debarkation – (DOD) The unloading of troops, equipment, or supplies from a ship or aircraft. (JP 3–02.1)

decisive action – (Army) The continuous, simultaneous combinations of offensive, defensive, and stability or defense support of civil authorities tasks. (ADRP 3–0)

decisive point – (DOD) A geographic place, specific key event, critical factor, or function that, when acted upon, allows commanders to gain a marked advantage over an adversary or contribute materially to achieving success. (JP 5–0)

defeat – A tactical mission task that occurs when an enemy force has temporarily or permanently lost the physical means or the will to fight. The defeated force's commander is unwilling or unable to pursue his adopted course of action, thereby yielding to the friendly commander's will, and can no longer interfere to a significant degree with the actions of friendly forces. Defeat can result from the use of force or the threat of its use. (FM 3–90–1)

delay – To slow the time of arrival of enemy forces or capabilities or alter the ability of the enemy or adversary to project forces or capabilities. (FM 3–09)

demobilization – (DOD) The process of transitioning a conflict or wartime military establishment and defense-based civilian economy to a peacetime configuration while maintaining national security and economic vitality. (JP 4–05)

demonstration – (DOD) 2. In military deception, a show of force in an area where a decision is not sought that is made to deceive an adversary. It is similar to a feint but no actual contact with the adversary is intended. (JP 3–13.4)

denial operations – Actions to hinder or deny the enemy the use of space, personnel, supplies, or facilities. (FM 3–90–1)

deny – A task to hinder or prevent the enemy from using terrain, space, personnel, supplies, or facilities. (ATP 3–21.20)

deployment – (DOD) The rotation of forces into and out of an operational area. (JP 3–35)

destroy – A tactical mission task that physically renders an enemy force combat-ineffective until it is reconstituted. Alternatively, to destroy a combat system is to damage it so badly that it cannot perform any function or be restored to a usable condition without being entirely rebuilt. (FM 3–90–1)

detainee – (DOD) Any person captured, detained, or otherwise under the control of Department of Defense personnel. (JP 3–63)

deterrence – (DOD) The prevention of action by the existence of a credible threat of unacceptable counteraction and/or belief that the cost of action outweighs the perceived benefits. (JP 3–0)

direct action – (DOD) Short-duration strikes and other small-scale offensive actions conducted as a special operation in hostile, denied, or politically sensitive environments and which employ specialized military capabilities to seize, destroy, capture, exploit, recover, or damage designated targets. (JP 3–05)

direct fire – (DOD) Fire delivered on a target using the target itself as a point of aim for either the weapon or the director. (JP 3–09.3)

disarmament – (Army) The collection, documentation, control, and disposal of small arms, ammunition, explosives, and light and heavy weapons of former combatants, belligerents, and the local populace. (FM 3–07)

disrupt – 1. A tactical mission task in which a commander integrates direct and indirect fires, terrain, and obstacles to upset an enemy's formation or tempo, interrupt his timetable, or cause enemy forces to commit prematurely or attack in piecemeal fashion. 2. An obstacle effect that focuses fire planning and obstacle effort to cause the enemy to break up his formation and tempo, interrupt his timetable, commit breaching assets prematurely, and attack in a piecemeal effort. (FM 3–90–1)

division – An Army echelon of command above brigade and below corps. It is a tactical headquarters which employs a combination of brigade combat teams, multifunctional brigades, and functional brigades in land operations. (ADRP 3–90)

embarkation – (DOD) The process of putting personnel and/or vehicles and their associated stores and equipment into ships and/or aircraft. (JP 3–02.1)

end state – (DOD) The set of required conditions that defines achievement of the commander's objectives. (JP 3–0)

Appendix

enemy combatant – (DOD) In general, a person engaged in hostilities against the United States or its coalition partners during an armed conflict. Also called EC. (DODD 2310.01E)

fix – A tactical mission task where a commander prevents the enemy from moving any part of his force from a specific location for a specific period. Fix is also an obstacle effect that focuses fire planning and obstacle effort to slow an attacker's movement within a specified area, normally an engagement area. (FM 3–90–1)

force projection – (DOD) The ability to project the military instrument of national power from the United States or another theater, in response to requirements for military operations. (JP 3–0)

force tailoring – The process of determining the right mix of forces and the sequence of their deployment in support of a joint force commander. (ADRP 3–0)

foreign internal defense – (DOD) Participation by civilian and military agencies of a government in any of the action programs taken by another government or other designated organization to free and protect its society from subversion, lawlessness, insurgency, terrorism, and other threats to its security. Also called FID. (JP 3–22)

foreign military sales – (DOD) That portion of United States security assistance authorized by the Foreign Assistance Act of 1961, as amended, and the Arms Export Control Act of 1976, as amended. This assistance differs from the Military Assistance Program and the International Military Education and Training Program in that the recipient provides reimbursement for defense articles and services transferred. Also called FMS. (JP 4–08)

fragmentary order – (DOD) An abbreviated form of an operation order issued as needed after an operation order to change or modify that order or to execute a branch or sequel to that order. Also called FRAGORD. (JP 5–0) See FM 6–0.

fratricide – The unintentional killing or wounding of friendly or neutral personnel by friendly firepower. (ADRP 3–37)

governance – (DOD) The state's ability to serve the citizens through the rules, processes, and behavior by which interests are articulated, resources are managed, and power is exercised in a society, including the representative participatory decision-making processes typically guaranteed under inclusive, constitutional authority. (JP 3–24)

human intelligence – (Army) The collection by a trained human intelligence collector of foreign information from people and multimedia to identify elements, intentions, composition, strength, dispositions, tactics, equipment, and capabilities. Also called HUMINT. (FM 2–22.3)

imagery intelligence – (DOD) The technical, geographic, and intelligence information derived through the interpretation or analysis of imagery and collateral materials. Also called IMINT. (JP 2–03)

improvised explosive device – (DOD) A weapon that is fabricated or emplaced in an unconventional manner incorporating destructive, lethal, noxious, pyrotechnic, or incendiary chemicals designed to kill, destroy, incapacitate, harass, deny mobility, or distract. Also called IED. (JP 3–15.1)

indigenous populations and institutions – (DOD) The societal framework of an operational environment including citizens, legal and illegal immigrants, dislocated civilians, and governmental, tribal, ethnic, religious, commercial, and private organizations and entities. Also called IPI. (JP 3–57)

infiltration – (Army) A form of maneuver in which an attacking force conducts undetected movement through or into an area occupied by enemy forces to occupy a position of advantage in the enemy rear while exposing only small elements to enemy defensive fires. (FM 3–90–1)

information operations – (DOD) The integrated employment, during military operations, of information related capabilities in concert with other lines of operation to influence, disrupt, corrupt, or usurp the decision making of adversaries and potential adversaries while protecting our own. Also called IO. (JP 3–13)

institutional training domain – The Army's institutional training and education system, which primarily includes training base centers and schools that provide initial training and subsequent professional military education for Soldiers, military leaders, and Army Civilians. (ADP 7–0)

instruments of national power – (DOD) All of the means available to the government in its pursuit of national objectives. They are expressed as diplomatic, economic, informational and military. (JP 1) See ATP 3–57.60

insurgency – (DOD) The organized use of subversion and violence to seize, nullify, or challenge political control of a region. Insurgency can also refer to the group itself. (JP 3–24)

intelligence – (DOD) 1. The product resulting from the collection, processing, integration, evaluation, analysis, and interpretation of available information concerning foreign nations, hostile or potentially hostile forces or elements, or areas of actual or potential operations. (ADRP 2–0)

interagency – (DOD) Of or pertaining to United States Government agencies and departments, including the Department of Defense. (JP 3–08)

Appendix

interdict – A tactical mission task where the commander prevents, disrupts, or delays the enemy's use of an area or route. (FM 3–90–1)

intermodal operations – The process of using multimodal capabilities (air, sea, highway, rail) and conveyances (truck, barge, containers, pallets) to move troops, supplies and equipment through expeditionary entry points and the network of specialized transportation nodes to sustain land forces. (ATP 4–13)

intertheater airlift – (DOD) The common-user airlift linking theaters to the continental United States and to other theaters as well as the airlift within the continental United States. (JP 3–17)

in-transit visibility – (DOD) The ability to track the identity, status, and location of Department of Defense units, and non-unit cargo (excluding bulk petroleum, oils, and lubricants) and passengers; patients, and personal property from origin to consignee or destination across the range of military operations. (JP 4–01.2)

intratheater airlift – (DOD) Airlift conducted within a theater with assets assigned to a geographic combatant commander or attached to a subordinate joint force commander. (JP 3–17)

isolate – A tactical mission task that requires a unit to seal off—both physically and psychologically—an enemy from sources of support, deny the enemy freedom of movement, and prevent the isolated enemy force from having contact with other enemy forces. (FM 3–90–1)

joint – (DOD) Connotes activities, operations, organizations, etc., in which elements of two or more Military Departments participate. (JP 1)

joint force – (DOD) A general term applied to a force composed of significant elements, assigned or attached, of two or more Military Departments operating under a single joint force commander. (JP 3–0)

joint force air component commander – (DOD) The commander within a unified command, subordinate unified command, or joint task force responsible to the establishing commander for recommending the proper employment of assigned, attached, and/or made available for tasking air forces; planning and coordinating air operations; or accomplishing such operational missions as may be assigned. Also called JFACC. (JP 3–0)

joint force commander – (DOD) A general term applied to a combatant commander, subunified commander, or joint task force commander authorized to exercise combatant command (command authority) or operational control over a joint force. Also called JFC. See also joint force. (JP 1)

joint force land component commander – (DOD) The commander within a unified command, subordinate unified command, or joint task force responsible to the establishing commander for recommending the proper employment of assigned, attached, and/or made available for tasking land forces; planning and coordinating land operations; or accomplishing such operational missions as may be assigned. Also called JFLCC. (JP 3-0)

joint force maritime component commander – (DOD) The commander within a unified command, subordinate unified command, or joint task force responsible to the establishing commander for recommending the proper employment of assigned, attached, and/or made available for tasking maritime forces and assets; planning and coordinating maritime operations; or accomplishing such operational missions as may be assigned. Also called JFMCC. (JP 3-0)

joint force special operations component commander – (DOD) The commander within a unified command, subordinate unified command, or joint task force responsible to the establishing commander for recommending the proper employment of assigned, attached, and/or made available for tasking special operations forces and assets; planning and coordinating special operations; or accomplishing such operational missions as may be assigned. Also called JFSOCC. (JP 3-0)

joint task force – (DOD) A joint force that is constituted and so designated by the Secretary of Defense, a combatant commander, subunified commander, or an existing joint task force commander. Also called JTF. (JP 1)

law of war – (DOD) That part of international law that regulates the conduct of armed hostilities. Also called the law of armed conflict. (JP 1-04)

levels of warfare – A framework for defining and clarifying the relationship among national objectives, the operational approach, and tactical tasks. (ADP 1-01)

line of communications – (DOD) A route, either land, water, and/or air, that connects an operating military force with a base of operations and along which supplies and military forces move. Also called LOC. (JP 2-01.3)

main effort – A designated subordinate unit whose mission at a given point in time is most critical to overall mission success. (ADRP 3-0)

main supply route – (DOD) The route or routes designated within an operational area upon which the bulk of traffic flows in support of military operations. Also called MSR. (JP 4-01.5)

mission – (DOD) 1. The task, together with the purpose, that clearly indicates the action to be taken and the reason therefore. (JP 3-0)

Appendix

mission creep – Tangential efforts to assist in areas of concern unrelated to assigned duties that cripple efficient mission accomplishment. (FM 3–16)

mission-essential task list – A tailored group of mission-essential tasks. Also called METL. (FM 7–0)

mobilization – (DOD) 1. The process of assembling and organizing national resources to support national objectives in time of war or other emergencies. See also industrial mobilization. 2. The process by which the Armed Forces or part of them are brought to a state of readiness for war or other national emergency. Which includes activating all or part of the Reserve Component as well as assembling and organizing personnel, supplies, and materiel. Also called MOB. (JP 4–05)

movement to contact – (Army) An offensive task designed to develop the situation and establish or regain contact. (ADRP 3–90)

multimodal – The movement of cargo and personnel using two or more transportation methods (air, highway, rail, sea) from point of origin to destination. (ATP 4–13)

multinational operations – (DOD) A collective term to describe military actions conducted by forces of two or more nations, usually undertaken within the structure of a coalition or alliance. (JP 3–16)

neutralize – (DOD) 1. As pertains to military operations, to render ineffective or unusable. 2. To render enemy personnel or materiel incapable of interfering with a particular operation. 3. To render safe mines, bombs, missiles, and booby traps. 4. To make harmless anything contaminated with a chemical agent. (JP 3–0)

objective – 1. The clearly defined, decisive, and attainable goal toward which every operation is directed. (JP 5–0) See ADRP 5–0, ATP 3–06.20. 2. The specific target of the action taken which is essential to the commander's plan. See ATP 3–06.20. 3. (Army) A location on the ground used to orient operations, phase operations, facilitate changes of direction, and provide for unity of effort. (ADRP 3–90)

operation – (DOD) 1. A sequence of tactical actions with a common purpose or unifying theme. (JP 1) See FM 3–0, FM 3–09, ATP 3–09.42. A military action or the carrying out of a strategic, operational, tactical, service, training, or administrative military mission. (JP 3–0)

operational art – (DOD) The cognitive approach by commanders and staffs—supported by their skill, knowledge, experience, creativity, and judgment—to develop strategies, campaigns, and operations to organize and employ military forces by integrating ends, ways, and means. (JP 3–0)

operational control – (DOD) The authority to perform those functions of command over subordinate forces involving organizing and employing commands and forces, assigning tasks, designating objectives, and giving authoritative direction necessary to accomplish the mission. Also called OPCON. (JP 1)

operation order – (DOD) A directive issued by a commander to subordinate commanders for the purpose of effecting the coordinated execution of an operation. Also called OPORD. (JP 5–0)

organic – (DOD) Assigned to and forming an essential part of military organization. Organic parts of a unit are those listed in its table of organization for the Army, Air Force, and Marine Corps, and are assigned to the administrative organizations of the operating forces for the Navy. (JP 1)

patrol – A detachment sent out by a larger unit to conduct a specific mission that operates semi-independently and return to the main body upon completion of mission. (ATP 3–21.8)

peace enforcement – (DOD) Application of military force, or threat of its use, normally pursuant to international authorization, to compel compliance with resolutions or sanctions designed to maintain or restore peace and order. (JP 3–07.3)

peacekeeping – (DOD) Military operations undertaken with the consent of all major parties to a dispute, designed to monitor and facilitate implementation of an agreement (cease fire, truce, or other such agreement) and support diplomatic efforts to reach a long-term political settlement. (JP 3–07.3)

platoon – A subdivision of a company or troop consisting of two or more squads or sections. (ADRP 3–90)

port of debarkation – (DOD) The geographic point at which cargo or personnel are discharged. Also called POD. (JP 4–0)

port of embarkation – (DOD) The geographic point in a routing scheme from which cargo or personnel depart. Also called POE. See also port of debarkation. (JP 4–01.2)

propaganda – (DOD) Any form of adversary communication, especially of a biased or misleading nature, designed to influence the opinions, emotions, attitudes, or behavior of any group in order to benefit the sponsor, either directly or indirectly. (JP 3–13.2)

raid – (DOD) An operation to temporarily seize an area in order to secure information, confuse an adversary, capture personnel or equipment, or to destroy a capability culminating with a planned withdrawal. (JP 3–0)

Appendix

Rangers – (DOD) Rapidly deployable airborne light infantry organized and trained to conduct highly complex joint direct action operations in coordination with or in support of other special operations units of all Services. (JP 3–05)

redeployment – (DOD) The transfer or rotation of forces and materiel to support another joint force commander's operational requirements, or to return personnel, equipment, and materiel to the home and/or demobilization stations for reintegration and/or outprocessing. (JP 3–35)

reintegration – The process through which former combatants, belligerents, and displaced civilians receive amnesty, reenter civil society, gain sustainable employment, and become contributing members of the local populace. (ADRP 3–07)

relief in place – (DOD) An operation in which, by direction of higher authority, all or part of a unit is replaced in an area by the incoming unit and the responsibilities of the replaced elements for the mission and the assigned zone of operations are transferred to the incoming unit. (JP 3–07.3)

reserve – (Army) That portion of a body of troops which is withheld from action at the beginning of an engagement, in order to be available for a decisive movement. (ADRP 3–90)

rule of law – A principle under which all persons, institutions, and entities, public and private, including the state itself, are accountable to laws that are publicly promulgated, equally enforced, and independently adjudicated, and that are consistent with international human rights principles. (FM 3–07)

rules of engagement – (DOD) Directives issued by competent military authority that delineate the circumstances and limitations under which United States forces will initiate and/or continue combat engagement with other forces encountered. Also called ROE. (JP 1–04)

secure – A tactical mission task that involves preventing a unit, facility, or geographical location from being damaged or destroyed as a result of enemy action. (FM 3–90–1)

seize – (DOD) To employ combat forces to occupy physically and to control a designated area. (JP 3–18) See ATP 3–06.20. (Army) A tactical mission task that involves taking possession of a designated area using overwhelming force. (FM 3–90–1)

sensitive-site assessment – Determination of whether threats or hazards associated with a sensitive site warrant exploitation. Also called SSA. (ATP 3–11.23)

sequel – (DOD) The subsequent major operation or phase based on the possible outcomes (success, stalemate, or defeat) of the current major operation or phase. (JP 5-0)

Service component command – (DOD) A command consisting of the Service component commander and all those Service forces, such as individuals, units, detachments, organizations, and installations under that command, including the support forces that have been assigned to a combatant command or further assigned to a subordinate unified command or joint task force. (JP 1)

shadow government – Governmental elements and activities performed by the irregular organization that will eventually take the place of the existing government. Members of the shadow government can be in any element of the irregular organization (underground, auxiliary, or guerrilla force). (ATP 3-05.1)

shaping operation – An operation that establishes conditions for the decisive operation through effects on the enemy, other actors, and the terrain. (ADRP 3-0)

signals intelligence – (DOD) 1. A category of intelligence comprising either individually or in combination all communications intelligence, electronic intelligence, and foreign instrumentation signals intelligence, however transmitted. (JP 2-0)

special forces – (DOD) United States Army forces organized, trained, and equipped to conduct special operations with an emphasis on unconventional warfare capabilities. Also called SF. (JP 3-05)

special operations forces – (DOD) Those Active and Reserve Component forces of the Military Service designated by the Secretary of Defense and specifically organized, trained, and equipped to conduct and support special operations. Also called SOF. (JP 3-05)

special operations task force – A temporary or semipermanent grouping of Army special operations forces units under one commander and formed to carry out a specific operation or a continuing mission. Also called SOTF. (ADRP 3-05)

squad – A small military unit typically containing two or more fire teams. (ADRP 3-90)

stability operations – (DOD) An overarching term encompassing various military missions, tasks, and activities conducted outside the United States in coordination with other instruments of national power to maintain or reestablish a safe and secure environment, provide essential governmental services, emergency infrastructure reconstruction, and humanitarian relief. (JP 3–0)

staging – (DOD) Assembling, holding, and organizing arriving personnel, equipment, and sustaining materiel in preparation for onward movement. See also staging area. (JP 3–35)

standard operating procedure – (DOD) A set of instructions covering those features of operations which lend themselves to a definite or standardized procedure without loss of effectiveness. The procedure is applicable unless ordered otherwise. Also called SOP. (JP 3–31)

status-of-forces agreement – (DOD) A bilateral or multilateral agreement that defines the legal position of a visiting military force deployed in the territory of a friendly state. Also called SOFA. (JP 3–16)

strong point – A heavily fortified battle position tied to a natural or reinforcing obstacle to create an anchor for the defense or to deny the enemy decisive or key terrain. (ADRP 3–90)

supporting effort – A designated subordinate unit with a mission that supports the success of the main effort. (ADRP 3–0)

suppress – A tactical mission task that results in temporary degradation of the performance of a force or weapons system below the level needed to accomplish the mission. (FM 3–90–1)

surveillance – (DOD) The systematic observation of aerospace, surface or subsurface areas, places, persons, or things by visual, aural, electronic, photographic, or other means. (JP 3–0)

tactical control – (DOD) The authority over forces that is limited to the detailed direction and control of movements or maneuvers within the operational area necessary to accomplish missions or tasks assigned. Also called TACON. (JP 1)

tactical level of war – (DOD) The level of war at which battles and engagements are planned and executed to achieve military objectives assigned to tactical units or task forces. (JP 3–0)

task organization – (Army) A temporary grouping of forces designed to accomplish a particular mission. (ADRP 5–0)

task-organizing – (DOD) An organization that assigns to responsible commanders the means with which to accomplish their assigned tasks in any planned action. (JP 3–33) See FM 3–98. (Army) The act of designing an operating force, support staff, or sustainment package of specific size and composition to meet a unique task or mission. (ADRP 3–0)

terrorism – (DOD) The unlawful use of violence or threat of violence, often motivated by religious, political, or other ideological beliefs, to instill fear and coerce governments or societies in the pursuit of goals that are usually political. (JP 3–07.2)

theater – (DOD) The geographical area for which a commander of a geographic combatant command has been assigned responsibility. (JP 1)

theater distribution system – (DOD) A distribution system comprised of four independent and mutually supported networks within theater to meet the geographic combatant commander's requirements: the physical network; the financial network; the information network; and the communications network. (JP 4–01)

theater of operations – (DOD) An operational area defined by the geographic combatant commander for the conduct or support of specific military operations. Also called TO. (JP 3–0)

throughput – (DOD) 1. In transportation, the average quantity of cargo and passengers that can pass through a port on a daily basis from arrival at the port to loading onto a ship or plane, or from the discharge from a ship or plane to the exit (clearance) from the port complex. (JP 4–01.5)

training objective – A statement that describes the desired outcome of a training activity in the unit. (ADRP 7–0)

troop – A company-size unit in a cavalry organization. (ADRP 3–90)

unit – (DOD) Any military element whose structure is prescribed by competent authority, such as a table of organization and equipment; specifically, part of an organization. (JP 3–33)

unity of command – (DOD) The operation of all forces under a single responsible commander who has the requisite authority to direct and employ those forces in pursuit of a common purpose. (JP 3–0)

unity of effort – (DOD) Coordination, and cooperation toward common objectives, even if the participants are not necessarily part of the same command or organization, which is the product of successful unified action. (JP 1)

unmanned aircraft – (DOD) An aircraft that does not carry a human operator and is capable of flight with or without human remote control. Also called UA. (JP 3–30)

vehicle-borne improvised explosive device – (DOD) A device placed or fabricated in an improvised manner on a vehicle incorporating destructive, lethal, noxious, pyrotechnic, or incendiary chemicals and designed to destroy,

Appendix

incapacitate, harass, or distract. Otherwise known as a car bomb. Also called **VBIED**. (JP 3–10)

warfighting function – A group of tasks and systems (people, organizations, information, and processes), united by a common purpose that commanders use to accomplish missions and training objectives. (ADRP 3–0)

Acronyms, Abbreviations, and Key Terms

Text Acronyms and Abbreviations

ANA	Afghan National Army
ANP	Afghan National Police
ANSF	Afghan National Security Forces
ARCENT	U.S. Army Central Command
CBU	cluster bomb unit
CENTCOM	U.S Central Command
CFACC	Combined Forces Air Component Command
CFC-A	Combined Forces Command–Afghanistan
CFLCC	Coalition Forces Land Component Command
CIA	U.S. Central Intelligence Agency
CJSOTF	Combined Joint Special Operations Task Force
CJTF	Combined Joint Task Force
CMH	U.S. Army Center of Military History
CSA	Chief of Staff, Army
DoD	Department of Defense
FORSCOM	U.S. Army Forces Command
HIG	Hezb-e-Islami Gulbuddin
HMMWV	High Mobility Multipurpose Wheeled Vehicle
IED	improvised explosive device
ISAF	International Security Assistance Force
JDAM	Joint Direct Attack Munition
JSOTF	Joint Special Operations Task Force
medevac	medical evacuation
MLRS	multiple launch rocket system
MMAS	Master of Military Art and Science
NATO	North Atlantic Treaty Organization
ODA	Operational Detachment Alpha
OEF	Operation ENDURING FREEDOM
RC	Regional Command
RMA	Revolution in Military Affairs
SIGINT	signals intelligence
SOAR	Special Operations Aviation Regiment
SOF	Special Operations Forces
TF	Task Force
TRADOC	U.S. Army Training and Doctrine Command
UA	units of action
UEx	Units of Employment X
UEy	Units of Employment Y
UN	United Nations
U.S.	United States

Foreign Terms

al-Qaeda	the foundation or the base [*organization name*]
Amir al-Mahmunen	Commander of the Faithful
bayat	an oath of personal allegiance

burqa	head-to-toe covering
fatwa	a deliberate call to arms for believers
jihad	struggle, in the sense of a holy war waged on behalf of Islam
kandak	Afghan battalion-sized unit
loya jirga	grand assembly, akin to a national convention
madrassa	religious educational institution
melmastiia	the obligation to offer protection to guests
mujahideen	those who are struggling or striving for a praiseworthy aim
pashtunwali	the ancient Pashtun code of conduct that includes a strong tradition of hospitality
Qala-i-Jangi	house of war [*place name*]
sharia	Islamic religious law
shura	a local consultative council or assembly
talib	individual member of the Taliban
Taliban	students of Islam [*organization name*]
ushr	a 10 percent tithe, paid in kind
wadi	dry riverbed

Selected U.S. Military Staff Designations

C–3	Combined (Coalition) operations
CCJ5-CMO	Combined (Coalition) joint planning–civil-military operations
CCJ5-ANA	Combined (Coalition) joint planning–Afghan National Army
CJ–3	Combined (Coalition) joint operations
CJ–35	Combined (Coalition) joint future operations
G–3/5/7	Army operations, plans, and training
J–2	Joint staff intelligence
J–3	Joint staff operations
J–5	Joint staff planning
J–9	Joint staff civil-military cooperation
S–2	battalion or brigade intelligence
S–3	battalion or brigade operations

Map Symbols and note terms

Map Symbols

Function

Armor	⬭
Brigade Special Troops Battalion	BSTB
Cavalry (Armored)	
Cavalry (Motorized)	
Cavalry (Motorized, Mountain)	
Cavalry (Air Assault, Motorized)	
Cavalry (Rotary Wing, Air)	
Commando	CDO
Field Artillery	•
Field Artillery (Air Assault)	
Infantry	⊠
Infantry (Airborne)	
Infantry (Air Assault)	
Infantry (Air Assault with Organic Lift)	
Infantry (Headquarters or Headquarters Element)	
Infantry (Mechanized, Amphibious)	
Infantry (Mechanized, Armored)	
Infantry (Mountain)	
Infantry (Wheeled, Armored)	
Infantry (Wheeled, Armored with Gun System)	
Maneuver Enhancement	▼
Military Police	MP

The United States Army in Afghanistan, 2001–2014

Reconnaissance (Battlefield Surveillance)	
Reconnaissance (Wheeled, Armored)	
Reconnaissance (Wheeled, Armored with Gun System)	
Special Forces	SF
Rifle/Automatic Weapon (Enemy)	
Light Machine Gun (Enemy)	
Mortar (Enemy)	
Attack by Fire Position	
Support by Fire Position	
Mortar, 60mm or less	
Mortar, greater then 60mm but less than 107mm	
Antitank missle launcher	

Size

Team	ø
Squad	•
Section	••
Platoon or Detachment	•••
Company, Battery, Troop	I
Battalion or Squadron	II
Regiment or Group	III
Brigade	X
Division	XX
Corps	XXX
Task Force	

Map Symbols and Note Terms

Example

3d Battalion, 103d Armor

3d Squadron, 4th Cavalry

2d Squadron, 17th Cavalry

4th Battalion, 320th Field Artillery

Polish Air Assault Infantry

22d Marine Expeditionary Unit

Company A, 1st Battalion, 17th Infantry

504th Battlefield Surveillance Brigade

Special Forces ODA 586

3d Brigade, 205th Afghan National Army

Enemy Infantry Platoon

Country Flag

Australia

Denmark

France

Georgia

Germany

Italy

Poland

Romania

Spain

Turkey

United Kingdom

United States

Note Terms

ANA	Afghan National Army
ARCENT	U.S. Army Central Command
CENTCOM	U.S. Central Command
CFC-A	Combined Forces Command–Afghanistan
CFLCC	Coalition Forces Land Component Command
CIA	U.S. Central Intelligence Agency
CINCCENT	Commander in Chief, CENTCOM
CJCS	Chairman of the Joint Chiefs of Staff
CJSOTF	Combined Joint Special Operations Task Force
CJTF	Combined Joint Task Force
CMH	U.S. Army Center of Military History
DoD	Department of Defense
EO	Executive Order
FM	Field Manual
FORSCOM	U.S. Army Forces Command
FRAGO	Fragmentary Order
GO	General Orders
Grp	Group
Hist Files	Historians Files
ISAF	International Security Assistance Force
MHD	Military History Detachment
NATO	North Atlantic Treaty Organization
NSA GWU	National Security Archive, George Washington University
ODA	Operational Detachment Alpha
OEF	Operation ENDURING FREEDOM
OEF Study Grp	Operation ENDURING FREEDOM Study Group
OMC-A	Office of Military Cooperation–Afghanistan
OPORD	Operation Order
PEP	Personal experience paper
RC	Regional Command
RMA	Revolution in Military Affairs
SEP	Student experience paper
SF	Special Forces
SOF	Special Operations Forces
TF	Task Force
TRADOC	U.S. Army Training and Doctrine Command
UN	United Nations

Index

A–10 Thunderbolt II, 159, 163
Abdul Ahad Karzai. *See* Karzai, Abdul Ahad.
Abdul Ghani Baradar, Mullah. *See* Baradar, Mullah Abdul Ghani.
Abdul Rahim, Hariz. *See* Rahim, Hariz Abdul.
Abdul Rashid Dostum. *See* Dostum, Abdul Rashid.
Abdul Zahir. *See* Zahir, Abdul.
Abdullah Abdullah, 116, 19
Abdullah Azzam. *See* Azzam, Abdullah.
Abdullah, Zia, 148
Abdul-Qahir Usmani. *See* Usmani, Abdul-Qahir.
Abdul-Razzaq Nafiz. *See* Nafiz, Abdul-Razzaq.
Abdur Razzaq, Mullah. *See* Razzaq, Mullah Abdur.
Abizaid, General John P., 258–59, 272, 274, 277, 283–84, 288, 294, 302, 305, 319–20, 327–28, 346–47
Abrams Doctrine, 18–19, 305
Abrams, General Creighton W., 18–19
Abu Ghraib prison, 296
AC–130 gunships, 81–82, 151–53, 159, 161, 194
    40-mm. shells, 82
    105-mm. shells, 82
Accelerating Success, 260–62, 276–80, 282, 285–87, 302, 332, 335, 346
Aeromedevac. *See* Medevac.
Afghan Interim Authority, 116, 118, 128, 135–36, 138, 140, 178, 186, 194, 197, 199–200, 224–25, 227, 229
Afghan National Army (ANA), 140, 173–75, 178, 184, 193–94, 197, 221, 223, 229–33, 251, 261, 275, 277–78, 280, 282, 284, 288–89, 291, 301, 332–34, 338
    central corps, 174, 231, 232, 261
    General Staff, 333
    kandaks, 230, 231–32, 275–76, 278–80, 287, 295, 332–34
    provisional force, 288–89
    regional corps, 174, 230, 279–80
    Study Phase 1 Report, 333
Afghan National Police (ANP), 334–36
Afghan National Security Forces (ANSF), 320, 326, 344
Afghanistan Freedom Support Act, 196
Agha (nom de guerre), 290
Agha Sharzai, Gul. *See* Sharzai, Gul Agha.
AH–1T Sea Cobra gunships, 112, 163–64, 168
AH–64 Apache gunships, 17, 143, 153–54, 156, 164, 246
Ahad Karzai, Abdul. *See* Karzai, Abdul Ahad.
Ahmad al-Jaber Air Base, 159
Ahmad Jalali, Ali. *See* Jalali, Ali Ahmad.
Ahmad Shad Massoud. *See* Massoud, Ahmad Shah.
Ahmed Rashid. *See* Rashid, Ahmed.
Ahmed Wali Karzai. *See* Karzai, Ahmed Wali.
Ahmed, Lt. Gen. Mahmud, 42–43, 45–46
Aideed, Mohammed Farah, 15
Air Force, U.S., 14, 55–56, 66, 72, 74–76, 79–81, 86, 95, 100–101, 105, 109–10, 142, 146, 153, 158–59, 161, 167, 182–83, 214, 221, 258, 331, 337

Air Force units
- 2d Bombardment Wing, 40th Expeditionary Bombardment Wing, 71
- 5th Bombardment Wing, 40th Expeditionary Bombardment Wing, 71
- 34th Bombardment Squadron, 28th Expeditionary Bombardment Squadron, 71
- 37th Bombardment Squadron, 28th Expeditionary Bombardment Squadron, 71
- 74th Expeditionary Fighter Squadron, 159
- Ninth Air Force, 55

Airborne units. *See also* Infantry Battalions.
- 1st Brigade, 82d Airborne Division, 245, 250, 301, 343
- 2d Battalion, 505th Parachute Infantry Regiment, 82nd Airborne Division, 284
- 3d Battalion, 505th Infantry, 82d Airborne Division, 220
- 3d Brigade, 82d Airborne Division, 214, 236, 243, 250
- 3d Brigade, 101st Airborne Division (Air Assault), 70–71, 77, 142, 148, 155–56, 214
- 65th Military Police Company (Airborne), 133
- 507th Support Battalion, XVIII Airborne Corps, 77
- 82d Airborne Division, 22, 24, 66, 126, 129, 208, 214, 220, 236, 243, 245, 249–50, 301, 343
- 101st Airborne Division (Air Assault), 22, 66, 70–71, 77, 142, 148, 157–59, 165, 167, 208, 214, 218, 236, 301, 307
- 173d Airborne Brigade, 301
- XVIII Airborne Corps, 22, 66, 77, 94, 104, 176–78, 180, 186, 200, 212–14, 248, 257, 291, 330, 345

Aircraft, fixed-wing, 17, 83, 93, 99, 221, 294. *See also* A–10 Thunderbolt; AC–130 gunships; B–1 Lancer bombers; B–2 Stealth bombers; B–52 bombers; C–17 Globemasters; C–130s; E–3A Sentry (Airborne Warning and Control System); F/A–18 fighters; F–14 fighters; F–16 fighters; MC–130 Combat Talons; MiG fighters; Predator drones; Unmanned aerial vehicles.

Aircraft, rotary-wing, 81, 93, 99, 130, 143, 163, 176, 221–22, 242, 294, 340–41. *See also* Helicopters.

AK47, 214

Akhtar Mohammed Osmani. *See* Osmani, Akhtar Mohammed.

Akhund, Mullah Dadullah, 266, 325

Akhund, Mullah Obiadullah, 290

Akhundzada, Sher Mohammed, 135, 199–200, 262

Al Iraqi, 290

al Libi, Layth, 290

Alaska, 28

Albania, 17, 26

Ali (Afghan general), 250

Ali Ahmad Jalali. *See* Jalali, Ali Ahmad.

Ali, Hazarat, 119–20, 122

Alikozai, Mullah Naquib, 114, 118

al-Qaeda, 33–35, 37–38, 40, 42, 45–47, 53, 56–58, 62–63, 65–66, 79–81, 104, 107, 113–15, 117, 120–23, 125–28, 132–36, 139, 142, 144–45, 150, 152, 155, 162, 169–70, 177, 181, 183, 185–86, 200–205, 207, 209–12, 214, 219–20, 247, 254, 263, 271, 273–74, 325. *See also* bin Laden, Osama; Taliban.
- beginnings, 8–12
- flight from Afghanistan, 202, 204–05, 210, 220
- sanctuaries, 2, 37, 40, 47, 119, 183, 186, 247
- September 11th attacks, 33, 35, 46, 48, 69, 73, 133, 192, 202, 238, 242, 304, 347
- tactical alliance, 201

Index

training camps, 57, 80, 119, 132, 142, 201–02
al-Zawahiri, Ayman, 9–10, 290
Amerine, Capt. Jason L., 100–101, 113, 117–18
Anders, 1st Lt. Robert S., 292
Anders, Lt. Col. David P., 301
Andijon, 341
Annan, Kofi A., 97
Antonov transport plane, 113
Apaches. *See* AH–64 Apache gunships.
ARCENT. *See* U.S. Army Central Command (ARCENT).
ARFORGEN. *See* Army Force Generation (ARFORGEN).
Arghandab District, 299
Arghandab River, 4, 117
Arif Sarwari, Mohammed. *See* Sarwari, Mohammed Arif.
Armitage, Richard L., 42–43, 45, 106
Armitage-Ahmed agreement, 106
Armored units, 6, 22, 28–29, 80, 86, 107, 110, 143, 308. *See also* Cavalry units.
   1st Armored Division, V Corps, 16
   2d Armored Cavalry (Light), 309
   3d Armored Cavalry, 22, 236, 309
   11th Armored Cavalry, 309
   49th Armored Division, 236
   155th Armored Brigade, VII Corps, 19
Army Directive 7, 305
Army Force Generation (ARFORGEN), 307, 310, 312, 314–16
Army Transformation Campaign Plan, 306
Arnault, Jean, 267
Artillery, 1, 5, 6, 17, 80, 96, 113, 153, 155, 163–64, 183, 204–05, 229
Artillery units, 28, 308–09, 311
   1st Battalion, 319th Field Artillery, 214
   3d Battalion, 6th Field Artillery, 75, 251
   3d Battalion, 7th Field Artillery, 291
   3d Battalion, 62d Air Defense Artillery, 75
   3d Battalion, 319th Field Artillery, 245, 301
   3d Battalion, 320th Field Artillery, 142
   25th Infantry Division Artillery, 291
Ashcroft, John D., 38
Aspland, Capt. Patrick C., 142, 159
Atta Nur. *See* Nur, Ustad Mohammed Atta.
Augustine, Lt. Col. Eugene M., 286
Austin, Maj. Gen. Lloyd J. III, 266, 270–72, 274, 289
Australian Special Air Service, 146–47, 154, 158, 164
Aviation units
   1st Battalion, 160th Aviation (SOAR), 83
   2d Battalion, 159th Aviation, 168
   2d Battalion, 160th Aviation (SOAR), 76, 84
   2d Battalion, 211th Aviation Regiment, 342
   3d Battalion, 101st Aviation, 156, 164
   3d Battalion, 160th Aviation (SOAR), 67, 77
   7th Battalion, 101st Aviation, 143
   58th Aviation, 143
   101st Aviation, 143, 156, 164
   159th Aviation, 168
   160th Aviation (SOAR), 66–67, 75–77, 83–84, 88, 118, 242, 340
   211th Aviation Regiment, 342
Ayman al-Zawahiri. *See* al-Zawahiri, Ayman.
Azzam, Abdullah, 8, 9

B–1 Lancer bombers, 71–72, 80
B–2 Stealth bombers, 72, 79–80
B–52 bombers, 71–72, 80, 118, 157, 160, 164, 174
Badruddin Haqqani. *See* Haqqani, Badruddin.
Bagby, Brig. Gen. Byron S., 249
Bagram, 85, 88, 96–97, 99, 102, 104, 121, 126, 130–34, 143–45, 148,

Bagram—*Continued*
    150–52, 156, 159–61, 164, 167, 169, 176–79, 183–84, 208, 210–11, 217, 221, 225–26, 271, 297, 341
    Air Base, 85, 212, 217, 341
    Air Support Operations Cell/Center, 156, 159, 162
    capture of, 97
    holding facility, and abuses committed at the facility, 132
Balkh Province, 226, 275, 329. *See also* Mazar-e Sharif.
Balkh River Valley, 89
Baltazar, Capt. Franklin F., 153–54
Bamyan Province, 7, 87–89, 96, 226, 291
Baradar, Mullah Abdul Ghani, 266
Bariullah Khan. *See* Khan, Bariullah.
Barksdale Air Force Base, 71
Barno, Lt. Gen. David W., 257–59, 266–73, 275–78, 280–92, 295–99, 302–05, 319, 327–28, 342, 346
Base Closure and Realignment Commission, 306
Base realignment and closure. *See* Base Closure and Realignment Commission.
Bashar, Hajji, 114
Bashir Noorzai. *See* Noorzai, Bashir.
Bayat, 5
Bentley, Lt. Col. Christopher F., 145, 251
Bergdahl, Sgt. Beaudry R., 111
Bergen, Peter, 12
Berntsen, Gary, 79, 88, 100–101, 104, 119–23
bin Laden, Osama, xvii, 8–11, 25, 34–35, 42–43, 45–46, 102, 119–20, 122–23, 125–27, 129, 136, 183, 201–02, 214, 273–74. *See also* al-Qaeda.
Bismillah Khan Mohammadi. *See* Mohammadi, Bismillah Khan.
Black, J. Cofer, 51
Black Hawks, 34, 75–76, 82–84, 143, 153, 156–57. *See also* Helicopters; HH–60 Black Hawks; MH–60 Black Hawks; UH–60 Black Hawks.
Blair, Tony C., 47
Blum, Lt. Gen. H. Steven, 316
Bolduc, M. Sgt. Armand J., 88, 96
Bolduc, Maj. Donald C., 114
Bolten, Joshua B., 38
Bombs, 1, 6, 11, 14, 17–18, 25, 57, 71–72, 79–82, 84, 88, 92, 96, 98, 113–14, 118, 120, 123, 125, 152–53, 163, 164, 167, 182, 185, 194, 202, 204–05, 263, 294, 325–26. *See also* B–1 Lancer bombers; B–2 Stealth bombers; B–52 bombers; CBU–87 (cluster bomb unit); Mk–82 (500-pound) bomb.
    suicide bombers, 25, 205, 263, 325–26
Bonn Conference, 115, 118, 128, 139, 178, 219
    Bonn Agreement, 115, 135
    Resolution 1386, 135
Bonn II Conference, 277–78
Bonn Process, 116, 184, 195, 197–98, 201, 233, 271, 273, 278, 320, 329, 339, 342
Bosnia and Herzegovina, 16, 54, 70, 138, 192, 262
Boston, 35
Bowers, Lt. Col. Max, 89, 109
BRAC. *See* Base Closure and Realignment Commission.
Braden, Lt. Col. Benjamin R., 294
Brahimi, Lakhdar, 97–99, 267
Brennan, Maj. Gen. John T., 337
Brezhnev, Leonid I., 1
Brigade 055, 8, 58
Brigade combat teams, 24, 70, 142, 236, 250, 307, 308–10, 315, 318. *See also* Interim brigade combat teams; Stryker brigade combat teams.
Bright Star, 56, 67, 73, 77, 94
Brooking, Steve, 180
Brown, Lt. Gen. Bryan D., 67
Brownlee, Romie L., 235
Burnside, Maj. James S., 175
Bush, George H. W., 13

INDEX

Bush, George W., 24–26, 33, 35, 37–38, 40–41, 44–46, 48–54, 56–57, 60–61, 64, 97, 105–06, 111, 127, 134–35, 139, 172, 184, 186, 191, 193–96, 198–99, 203, 205, 207, 210–11, 237, 249, 255, 262, 267, 279–82, 302, 323–24, 337
    Bush administration, 12, 24, 33, 38, 41, 44–50, 52–54, 60, 97, 106, 111, 127, 134–35, 141, 184, 186, 191, 193–96, 199, 203, 205, 207–08, 211, 237, 249, 254–55, 262, 279–82, 302, 323–24, 337, 345
    Bush Doctrine, 41, 45, 48
Butler, Capt. Kevin J., 157

C–17 Globemasters, 75–76, 142, 176, 183
C–130s, 75, 106, 341
Calland, R. Adm. Albert J., 67, 79, 88, 93
Cambone, Stephen A., 26
Camp David, 38, 51, 53
Camp Doha, Kuwait, 69, 73, 94, 169, 178, 208
Campbell, Col. John F., 67, 76, 95, 142, 164, 208, 245, 250
Cannons, 155, 163. *See also* Howitzers.
    76-mm., 155
    122-mm. artillery, 163
Card, Andrew H., 38
Carter, Col. Nicholas P., 225, 249
Cavalry units, 28, 308–09
    1st Cavalry Division, 19, 22
    2d Armored Cavalry (Light), 309
    2d Cavalry Regiment, 309
    3d Armored Cavalry, 22, 236, 309
    3d Squadron, 4th Cavalry, 286, 299
    11th Armored Cavalry, 309
CBU–87 (cluster bomb unit), 163
Cebrowski, V. Adm. Arthur K., 27
CENTCOM. *See* U.S. Central Command (CENTCOM).
Central Intelligence Agency (CIA), 33–34, 45–46, 51, 55, 57–62, 66, 74–75, 79–80, 82–84, 86, 88–89, 95, 100–101, 104, 108–11, 114, 119–20, 124–25, 132–33, 136, 142, 146, 186, 196, 198, 209, 254
CFACC. *See* Combined Forces Air Component Command (CFACC).
CFC-A. *See* Combined Forces Command–Afghanistan (CFC-A).
CFLCC. *See* Coalition Forces Land Component Command (CFLCC).
CH–47 Chinooks, 75, 82–83, 85, 143, 152–55, 159–61, 168–69, 182–83, 341
CH–53 Sea Stallions, 112, 163, 168
Chamberlin, Wendy J., 42, 44, 46
Chapman, Sfc. Nathan R., 136
Chapman, Tech. Sgt. John A., 161–62
Cheek, Col. Gary H., 291
Cheney, Richard B., 56
Chinese Embassy bombing, 17
Chinooks. *See* CH–47 Chinooks; MH–47 Chinooks.
Chirac, Jacques R., 175
Chrétien, Joseph Jacques, 47
Chu, David S. C., 237
CIA. *See* Central Intelligence Agency (CIA).
Civil Affairs Task Forces, 222
Civil affairs teams, 93, 219, 222–25, 269, 275, 286
Civil Affairs units, 104
    96th Civil Affairs Battalion, 67, 93, 137, 171, 222
    352d Civil Affairs Command, 171, 174
    360th Civil Affairs Brigade, 223
    401st Civil Affairs Battalion, 222
    489th Civil Affairs Battalion, 171, 173, 222
Clark, General Wesley K., 17–18
Clarke, Richard A., 38
Clarke, Lt. Col. Richard D., 245
Clarke, Victoria, 181
Clinton, William J., 11, 14–17, 21, 24–25, 54
    Clinton administration, 15, 21, 24, 69, 137, 180

Coalition Forces Land Component
   Command (CFLCC), 70, 94,
   103–04, 111, 131–34, 140–42,
   144–45, 150, 172–73, 177–78,
   184, 209, 222
Coalition Joint Civil-Military
   Operations Task Force, 139,
   141, 171–74
Cody, Maj. Gen. Richard A., 70
Combined Forces Air Component
   Command (CFACC), 145, 150,
   159
Combined Forces Command–
   Afghanistan (CFC-A), 258,
   266, 269, 271–73, 284, 288, 290,
   292, 296, 298, 303–04, 320–21,
   328–29, 333–36, 340–41
Combined Joint Civil-Military
   Operations Task Force, 222,
   224, 226, 229, 289
Combined Joint Special Operations
   Task Force (CJSOTF), 67–68,
   98, 102, 104, 221, 274, 287,
   298, 340. *See also* Special
   Operations Command.
   Afghanistan, 171, 221, 287, 297,
      340
   North, 67
   South, 98, 102, 104. *See also* Task
      Force K-Bar.
Combined Joint Task Force (CJTF), 50,
   145, 147–48, 150–51, 153, 155,
   157, 159, 163–64, 170, 178–82,
   184, 193–94, 208–09, 212,
   214–16, 217–22, 224–25, 227,
   229–31, 245–50, 253–54, 258,
   266, 271, 274, 280, 287, 290–92,
   294–98, 301, 333–34, 343
   CJTF-76, 200, 287, 291–92, 294–98,
      301, 333–34, 343
   CJTF-180, 176, 178–80, 184,
      193–94, 207–09, 212, 214–16,
      217–22, 224–27, 229–31,
      245–50, 253–54, 258, 266, 271,
      273–74, 280, 287, 290–91, 295,
      345
   CJTF-Afghanistan, 145
   CJTF-Mountain, 145, 147–48,
      150–51, 153, 155, 157, 159,
      163–65, 171, 181–82, 184, 208
Combined Task Forces
   Bronco, 291–92
   Thunder, 291, 301
Constitutional Loya Jirga. *See* Loya
   Jirga, Constitutional.
Cooper, Robert, 116
Corkran, Lt. Col. Ronald E., 95, 148,
   156, 159–60, 165, 182
Cornell, Capt. Christopher, 159
Corps, I, 248–49
Corps, III, 22, 248–49
Corps, V, 16, 248
Corps, VII, 19
Corps, XVIII Airborne. *See* Airborne
   units.
Crane, Conrad C., 19
Crombie, Capt. Roger A., 75, 154–55,
   157, 163, 167
Crumpton, Henry A., 79, 88, 123
Cunningham, Sr. Amn. Jason D., 162

Dadullah Akhund, Mullah. *See*
   Akhund, Mullah Dadullah.
Dailey, Maj. Gen. Dell L., 56, 66, 158
Daykundi Province, 291
de Hoop Scheffer, Jaap, 323
Defense Department. *See* Department
   of Defense (DoD).
DeLong, Lt. Gen. Michael P., 134
Department of Defense (DoD), 45,
   47–49, 61, 86, 105–06, 140, 174,
   186, 193, 211–12, 227, 230,
   232–34, 237, 242, 260–62, 266,
   278, 281–82, 285, 295, 312, 316,
   322, 327, 335, 337–38, 347
Diaz, CWO2 David W., 84–85, 88, 95
Dilak, 299
DiChairo, Lt. Col. Joseph, 251, 253,
   274–75
Dilawar, 211
Dobbins, James F., 97, 114–16
Donahue, Col. Patrick J. II, 301, 334,
   339
Donnellan, Lt. Col. James E., 301, 341
Donovan, Lt. Col. George T., 301
Dorman, Lt. Col. Edward F. III, 95, 99,

Index

132
Dostum (nom de guerre). *See* Dostum, Abdul Rashid.
Dostum, Abdul Rashid, 84–89, 92–93, 96, 98, 106–11, 123, 133, 262, 275
Douad Khan. *See* Khan, Douad.
Drinkwine, Lt. Col. Brian M., 291
Drones. *See* Predator drones; Unmanned aerial vehicles.
Duke, Capt. Micah R., 142

E–3A Sentry (Airborne Warning and Control System), 182
Edmunds, Spec. John J., 83
Effects-based operations, 214–16, 217, 220, 272
Eighth Army, 28
Eikenberry, Lt. Gen. Karl W., 230–31, 233, 279, 319–21, 326–30, 332–36, 338–43, 346
Elvis (nom de guerre), 290
Embedded Training Teams, 232, 329, 333–34
Emergency Loya Jirga. *See* Loya Jirga, Emergency.
Engineer Arif. *See* Sarwari, Mohammed Arif.
Engineer units
    18th Engineer Brigade, 301–02
    92d Engineer Battalion, 95
    307th Engineer Battalion, 245
    326th Engineer Battalion, 142
    528th Engineer Battalion (Heavy), 109th Engineer Group (South Dakota National Guard), 298–99
England, Gordon R., 243
European Union, 48, 139
Executive Order 13223. *See* Posse Comitatus Act of 1878.
Exum, Lt. Andrew, 170

F/A–18 fighters, 80, 92, 110, 118
F–14 fighters, 80
F–16 fighters, 182
Fahim, Mohammed Qasim, 51, 74, 84–85, 87, 88–89, 96, 98, 104, 139–40, 261
    as defense minister, 139–40, 141, 194, 261
    as United Front general, 74, 84–85, 87, 88–89, 96, 98, 104
Faqirullah, 274
Farah Aideed, Mohammed. *See* Aideed, Mohammed Farah.
Farah Province, 325, 329
Faryab Province, 226
Fastabend, Brig. Gen. David A., 235
FATA. *See* Federally Administered Tribal Areas (Pakistan).
Fatwa, 10–11
Fazil Mazloom. *See* Mazloom, Fazil.
Fazl, Mullah Mohammed, 6, 107, 111
Federally Administered Tribal Areas (Pakistan), 120, 125, 184, 202, 263
Feith, Douglas J., 49, 196, 228
Fetterman, Lt. Col. Patrick L., 165
Field Artillery. *See* Artillery units.
Finance Battalion, 307th, 245
Flynn, Lt. Col. Charles A., 245–46
Fontes, Lt. Col. Robin L., 286
Foreign units
    3d Princess Patricia's Canadian Light Infantry, 143, 168, 182–83
    26th Romanian Mechanized Battalion, 214
    151st Romanian Mechanized Battalion, 251
    341st Romanian Mechanized Battalion, 301
    Royal Marine 45th Commando, 181, 208
Forman, Col. Mark R., 321
FORSCOM. *See* U.S. Army Forces Command (FORSCOM).
Forts
    Benning, 19, 75, 352
    Bragg, 66, 177, 208, 214, 220, 248–49, 254
    Campbell, 67, 76, 95, 142, 164, 208, 245, 250
    Drum, 70, 168
    Gordon, 134

Forts—*Continued*
   Hood, 19
   Irwin, 23, 144
   Lee, 64
   Lewis, 24, 67
   McPherson, 28, 68, 94, 137, 178
   Monroe, 235, 307
   Myer, 64
   Polk, 23
   Riley, 19
   Stewart, 19
Forward Operating Bases, 72, 74–75, 93–94, 99, 104, 131–32, 245, 268, 294, 299, 301
   53, 107
   Gardez, 245
   Jalalabad, 245
   Khost, 245
   Orgun-E, 245
   Rhino, 93, 103–04, 126, 130–32
   Salerno, 250
   Shkin, 253
Forward Support Battalion, 626th, 142
Fox, Lt. Col. Cynthia, 301
Fox, Lt. Col. David G., 67, 94, 100, 113–14, 117, 118
Franks, General Tommy R., 34, 38, 53, 55–60, 62–63, 66, 68, 73, 79, 81, 83–84, 88–89, 93–94, 96, 98–99, 104, 119, 123–26, 130–32, 134, 136–38, 140–41, 175, 176–78, 207–09, 213, 229, 254, 257, 346–47
Future Combat System, 192

Garrett, Col. William B. III, 245, 251, 270, 274
Gentile, Gian, 19
Gerard, Lt. Col. David T., 214
Ges, Lt. Col. Bertrand A., 301
Ghafour, Haji, 274
Ghamsharik Zaman, Haji. *See* Zaman, Haji Ghamsharik.
Ghani Baradar, Mullah Abdul. *See* Baradar, Mullah Abdul Ghani.
Ghani, Ashraf, 116, 197, 266
Ghazni Province, 264, 289–91, 325, 329, 343

Andar District, 343
Ghilzai clan, 136
Ghor Province, 51
Ghulomov, Kodir, 56
Gilchrist, Maj. Gen. Peter, 328
Glenn, John H. Jr., 1
Glenn, Lt. Col. Harry C. III, 251
Global War on Terrorism, 34, 37, 40, 54, 57, 65–66, 129, 135, 186, 191–93, 198, 201, 318, 346, 348
Goedkoop, Brig. Gen. Thomas R., 308
Gorbachev, Mikhail, 1
Gore, Albert A., 24, 25
Gray, Lt. Col. David, 145
Green Berets, 86, 88, 146, 208, 241
Grenier, Robert L., 58
Guantanamo Bay Naval Base, 134, 210, 296
Gul Agha Sharzai. *See* Sharzai, Gul Agha.
Gul Rahman. *See* Rahman, Gul.
Gulbuddin Hekmatyar. *See* Hekmatyar, Gulbuddin.

Haas, Lt. Col. Christopher K., 67, 88, 167
Haass, Richard N., 54
Habibullah, Mullah, 211
Hadley, Stephen J., 322
Hagenbeck, Maj. Gen. Franklin L., 70, 131, 144–47, 150–51, 154, 157–60, 163–64, 165, 168, 169, 170, 181, 199, 208, 213, 243
Haji Ghafour. *See* Ghafour, Haji.
Haji Ghamsharik Zaman. *See* Zaman, Haji Ghamsharik.
Haji Sadiq. *See* Sadiq, Haji.
Haji Umar. *See* Umar, Haji.
Haji Zahir. *See* Zahir, Haji.
Hajji Bashar. *See* Bashar, Hajji.
Hamdi, Yaser Esam, 110
Hamid Karzai. *See* Karzai, Hamid.
Hand grenades, 83, 108, 214
Haqqani Network, 135, 200, 263–64, 325. *See also* Haqqani, Badruddin; Haqqani, Jalaluddin; Haqqani, Sirajuddin.

Index

Haqqani, Badruddin, 263. *See also* Haqqani Network.
Haqqani, Jalaluddin, 135–36, 201, 263–64, 290, 325. *See also* Haqqani Network.
Haqqani, Sirajuddin, 263. *See also* Haqqani Network.
Hardy, Lt. Col. Charles K., 214
Hariz Abdul Rahim. *See* Rahim, Hariz Abdul.
Harrell, Brig. Gen. Gary L., 131, 133, 146
Harriman, CWO2 Stanley L., 150, 152
Harward, Capt. Robert S., 102, 143–44, 158, 176, 181
Haynes, William J. II, 38
Hazara, 58, 89, 96, 148, 233
Hazarat Ali. *See* Ali, Hazarat.
Hekmatyar, Gulbuddin, 3–6, 200–201, 263–64, 274. *See also* Hezb-e-Islami Gulbuddin (HIG).
Helicopters, 74–76, 80–84, 88–89, 101–02, 105, 114, 125, 143, 146–48, 151–57, 159–61, 163–64, 168–69, 181–82, 201, 205, 217, 221–22, 229, 236, 246, 294, 320, 343. *See also* AH–1T Sea Cobra gunships; AH–64 Apache gunships; CH–47 Chinooks; CH–53 Sea Stallions; Chinooks; HH–60 Black Hawks; MH–6 Little Bird; MH–47 Chinooks; MH–53 Pave Lows; MH–60 Black Hawks; Mi–8s; UH–1N Twin Hueys; UH–60 Black Hawks.
Helmand Province, 135, 178, 199, 246, 262, 265, 268, 281, 286, 291, 298, 325. *See also* Lashkar Gah; Sangin.
Helmly, Lt. Gen. James R., 239
Herat Province, 80–81, 96, 104, 262, 281, 286, 299
Hezb-e-Islami Gulbuddin (HIG), 3, 200, 262, 264, 274–75, 304. *See also* Hekmatyar, Gulbuddin.
HH–60 Black Hawks, 76. *See also* Black Hawks.

HIG. *See* Hezb-e-Islami Gulbuddin (HIG).
High-mobility multipurpose wheeled vehicle (HMMWV), 95, 152, 159, 242
Hindu Kush, 67, 100, 224
HMMWVs. *See* High-mobility multipurpose wheeled vehicle (HMMWV).
Holbrooke, Richard C., 16
Holder, Lt. Gen. Leonard D., 308
Holland, General Charles R., 66–67
Howard, Lt. Col. Michael L., 251, 253, 274
Howitzers, 155, 163, 192, 274. *See also* Cannons.
   105-mm., 274
   122-mm., 155
   155-mm. self-propelled, 192
Huber, Brig. Gen. Keith M., 70
Huggins, Col. James L., 214, 217, 245
Hunter, Lt. Col. Anthony J., 285
Hussein, Saddam. *See* Saddam Hussein.

I Corps. *See* Corps, I.
III Corps. *See* Corps, III.
Improvised explosive device (IED), 214, 263, 325–26, 343
Infantry Battalions. *See also* Airborne units.
   1st Battalion (Ranger), 75th Infantry, 257
   1st, 87th Infantry, 70, 75, 109, 131, 133, 148, 154, 159, 163, 167, 251, 253, 274
   1st, 187th Infantry, 85, 95, 142, 148, 158, 159, 163, 165, 167, 182
   1st, 325th Infantry, 301, 343
   1st, 501st Infantry, 251
   1st, 504th Infantry, 214
   1st, 505th Infantry, 214, 291
   1st, 508th Infantry, 301
   2d, 5th Infantry, 291, 294
   2d, 22d Infantry, 70, 251, 253, 274–75
   2d, 27th Infantry, 291–92
   2d, 35th Infantry, 291–92
   2d, 87th Infantry, 70, 251

Infantry Battalions—*Continued*
  2d, 153d Infantry (Arkansas Army National Guard), 71
  2d, 187th Infantry, 70, 142, 148, 153, 157
  2d, 503d Infantry, 301
  2d, 504th Infantry, 245–46, 301
  2d, 505th Infantry, 245, 250
  3d, 116th Infantry, 29th Infantry Division, 291
  3d, 141st Infantry, 301, 343
  3d, 187th Infantry, 142, 165
  3d, 504th Infantry, 245, 250
  3d, 505th Infantry, 214, 250
  4th, 31st Infantry, 163, 168
Infantry Brigades
  3d, 25th Infantry Division, 291
  45th, 238, 278
  48th (Mechanized), 19
  53d (Florida Army National Guard), 333
  256th (Mechanized), VII Corps, 19
Infantry Divisions
  1st (Mechanized), 19
  2d, 22
  3d (Mechanized), 22, 66, 270, 307
  24th (Mechanized), 19
  25th, 221, 290–92, 299, 301, 339
  28th (Pennsylvania National Guard), 192
  29th, 291
Infantry units
  1st, 25
  5th, 291, 294
  22d, 70, 251, 253, 274–75
  27th, 291–92
  31st, 163, 168
  35th, 291–92
  74th, Detachment (Long Range Surveillance), 329
  75th, 257
  87th, 70, 75, 110, 131, 133, 148, 154, 159, 163, 167, 251, 253, 274
  116th, 291
  141st (Texas Army National Guard), 301, 343
  153d, 71
  187th, 70, 95, 142, 148, 153, 157,
    159, 163, 165, 182
  325th, 301, 343
  501st, 251
  503d, 301
  504th, 214, 245–46, 250, 301
  505th, 214, 220, 245, 250, 284, 291, 294
  508th, 301
Interim brigade combat teams, 24
Interim Fast Attack Vehicles, 112
International Committee of the Red Cross, 173
International Security Assistance Force (ISAF), 128, 139, 141, 176, 178–80, 184, 199, 221, 253, 282, 284, 302, 319–20, 322–23, 325, 327, 329, 333, 344, 346
Inter-Services Intelligence (Pakistan), 42, 202, 209, 264, 326
Iran, 40, 42, 49, 97, 114, 139, 264
Iraq, 38, 40, 48–49, 69, 127–28, 132, 182, 184, 186, 193, 198–99, 207–08, 234–40, 242, 248, 262, 270, 276, 294, 296, 306, 310–11, 315–18, 322–24, 334, 338, 344, 346–48
ISAF. *See* International Security Assistance Force (ISAF).
Islamabad, 41–43, 45, 58, 106, 119, 125, 203, 205
Islamic Movement of Uzbekistan, 57, 92
Ismail Khan. *See* Khan, Ismail.
Ismail, Jamal, 9
Israel, 10, 49
Italy, 28, 94, 175, 197, 339

Jacobabad, 44, 74, 82, 95, 101
Jacoby, Brig. Gen. Charles H. Jr., 297
Jaegerkorpset, 147
Jalalabad, 63, 80, 98, 119–22, 202, 245, 250, 290
Jalali, Ali Ahmad, 228, 275
Jalaluddin Haqqani. *See* Haqqani, Jalaluddin.
Jazirat Masirah, 75, 102, 131
Jamal Ismail. *See* Ismail, Jamal.
Japan, 33, 49, 53, 73, 139, 175, 197, 281

Index

Jegerkommando, 147
Jihad, 202, 205, 263, 265
Joint Direct Attack Munition (JDAM), 110
Joint Forces Command, 68, 72, 76, 176, 311, 315
Joint Task Forces, 309–10
    2 (Canada), 147
    EMPIRE SHIELD, 65
Jones, Brig. Gen. Michael D., 146
Jordan, 67, 94, 338

Kabul, 34, 58, 60–61, 63, 67, 74, 80, 88–89, 96–99, 102, 114–16, 135, 138, 140–41, 174–76, 179–80, 184, 186, 193–95, 197–99, 202–04, 209, 221, 223, 225–27, 229–34, 261, 265, 271–74, 276–81, 285, 291–92, 304–05, 323, 325–26, 329–30, 337–38, 346
Kabul Military Academy, 174–75
Kamel Khan Zadran. *See* Zadran, Kamel Khan.
Kamiya, Maj. Gen. Jason K., 301, 334, 342
Kandahar, 46, 80–83, 96, 98, 101–02, 104, 113–14, 118, 126, 131–34, 136, 142–43, 178, 182–83, 202, 210, 217, 221, 236, 246, 264–65, 267–68, 271, 276, 281, 289–92, 294, 296–99, 325
    Airfield, 143, 217, 291–292, 294
    fall of, 6, 134, 236
    International Airport, 117–18, 126, 131–32, 142
    shrine, 5
Kandahar Province
    Ada Ghar, 246
    Arghandab District, 299
    Maywand, 4
    Panjwa'i District, 4
    Shah Wali Kot District, 117, 299, 301
    Spin Boldak, 113, 246, 264–65
Kandaks, 275–76, 332
Kantiway-ye Ulya, 290
Kapisa Province, 291, 329
Karachi, 263

Karim Khalili. *See* Khalili, Karim.
Karimov, Islam A., 55, 75
Karshi Khanabad Air Base, 57, 75–76, 80, 84, 89, 95, 101, 104, 109, 131, 133, 145, 341
Karzai, Abdul Ahad, 100
Karzai, Ahmed Wali, 299
Karzai, Hamid, 100–101, 112, 113–14, 116–18, 135–36, 139, 178–79, 194–96, 199–200, 203, 225–28, 254–55, 261–62, 265, 268, 275, 279, 287–89, 291, 295, 304–05, 320–21, 324–25, 334–35, 342–44
    2004 Afghan presidential elections, 287–88, 295, 321
    2005 Afghan elections, 342–44
    and the Afghan National Police, 335–39
    as chairman of the Afghan Interim/Transitional Authority, 116, 118, 135, 139, 179, 194–96, 199–200, 225, 227, 228, 254–55, 261–62, 265, 275, 279, 289, 291
    as president, 231, 304–05, 320, 324–25, 334
    as tribal leader, 100–101, 113–14, 115, 117
Kashmir, 44, 202–03
Kashmir Khan. *See* Khan, Kashmir.
Kazakhstan, 70
Keane, General John M., 94, 178
Kenya, 57, 70
Kern, Brig. Gen. John H., 174–75, 222–23
Khalili, Karim, 51, 87, 89, 104
Khalilzad, Zalmay M., 114, 139, 267–68, 271, 283, 285, 288–89, 299, 346
Khalis, Younis, 98
Khan Mohammadi, Bismillah. *See* Mohammadi, Bismillah Khan.
Khan Zadran, Kamel. *See* Zadran, Kamel Khan.
Khan Zadran, Pacha. *See* Zadran, Pacha Khan.
Khan Zadran, Zakim. *See* Zadran, Zakim Khan.

Khan, Bariullah, 88, 96
Khan, Douad, 96
Khan, Ismail, 6, 51, 87, 96, 104, 228, 262
Khan, Kashmir, 274
Khan, Lt. Col. Asad A., 294
Khoshkeyer, 148, 153
Khost Province, 136, 148, 172, 181, 200, 220–21, 245, 250, 263–64, 289, 291, 325. *See also* Forward Operating Bases, Provincial Reconstruction Teams.
Kommando Spezialkräfte, 147
Kosovo, 50, 54, 131, 178, 192, 236, 262
Kotal-e Tonal-e Salang, 97
Kozelka, Capt. Glenn E., 163, 169
Kraft, Capt. Nelson G., 154–55, 157, 163
Kratzer, Brig. Gen. David E., 137–41, 173–75
Kunar Province, 100, 200, 264, 268, 271, 274–75, 288–89, 291, 341
    Asadabad, 100, 289–90, 341
Kunduz Province, 63, 92, 96, 98, 104–07, 109, 111, 132–33, 202, 209
Kuth, Capt. Robert B., 163
Kuwait, 67, 69, 73, 94, 139, 159, 163–64, 169, 177, 192, 208, 237
Kyrgyzstan, 341

LaCamera, Lt. Col. Paul J., 70, 76, 148, 154–55, 157, 163–64, 167
Laghman Province, 200, 264, 268, 291
    Mehtar Lam, 329
Lakhdar Brahimi. *See* Brahimi, Lakhdar.
Lashkar Gah, 286, 325
Lane, Brig. Gen. Richard, 181, 183, 281
Law and Order Trust Fund for Afghanistan, 335
Layth al Libi. *See* al Libi, Layth.
Lehnert, Brig. Gen. Michael R., 134
Lehrer, Jim, 130
Lerario, Lt. Col. Michael P., 245
Lindh, John Walker, 110
Lodin, Zia, 148, 150, 152–54, 168
Logar Province, 200, 264, 291

Logistical Task Force 530, 95, 99, 132
Logistics Task Force 34, 291
Louis Berger Group, 281
Loya Jirga, 116, 179, 283
    Constitutional, 261, 273, 277–79, 283, 286
    Emergency, 178–79, 181, 183, 195, 199
Loya-Paktia region, 264
Lugar, Richard, 267
Luti, William J., 114
Luttrell, HM1 Marcus (Navy SEAL), 341

M–203 grenade launcher (grenadier), 155
M–249 machine gun, 170
M1A1 Abrams tank, 17
M270 Multiple Launch Rocket Systems, 17
M2A3 Bradley fighting vehicles, 17
MacDill Air Force Base, 66, 79
Macgregor, Douglas A., 307
Machine guns, 151–52, 155, 169
    0.50 caliber, 159
    12.7-mm. antiaircraft, 155
    M–249, 169
Madrassa, 5, 11, 326
Manas Air Base, 341
Mansour (nom de guerre), 290
Marine Corps, U.S., 55, 73–74, 77, 93–94, 98, 101, 103–04, 113, 118, 132, 134, 164, 181, 183, 208, 258, 291, 294–95, 301, 333, 341
Marine Corps units
    1st Battalion, 1st Marines, 93
    1st Battalion, 6th Marines, 294
    1st Marine Expeditionary Brigade, 93
    2d Battalion, 3d Marines, 301, 341
    2d Marine Division, 23
    3d Battalion, 6th Marines, 93
    6th Marines, 93, 291, 294
    13th Marine Expeditionary Unit, 163
    15th Marine Expeditionary Unit, 73–74, 77, 93–94

Index

22d Marine Expeditionary Unit, 294–95
26th Marine Expeditionary Unit, 73, 77, 93–94, 132
Medium Helicopter Squadron 165, 169
Medium Helicopter Squadron 266 (Reinforced), 294
Martinez, 1st Lt. Hector S., 64
Maryoka, 1st Lt. Bradley J., 109
Marzak, 144, 148
Massoud, Ahmad Shah, 2–3, 6–7, 51, 116, 194
Mattis, Brig. Gen. James N., 93, 103, 132, 142
Maughan, Col. George P., 223–26
Mayre, Lt. Col. James M., 143, 153
Maywand, 4
Mazar-e Sharif, 63, 80, 88–89, 92–94, 96, 104, 107, 109, 132, 275
Mazloom, Fazil, 92
MC–130 Combat Talons, 81–83, 102
McBride, Lt. Col. M. Scott, 291–92
McChrystal, Brig. Gen. Stanley A., 216
McColl, Maj. Gen. John C., 141, 176, 179, 184
McDonnell, Lt. Col. Kevin M., 175
McGuire, Lt. Col. Timothy P., 301
McHale, Capt. Matthew M., 148, 150
McKenzie, Col. Kenneth F. Jr., 294
McMahon, Lt. Col. Michael J., 299
McNeill, Lt. Gen. Dan K., 176–79, 184, 186, 194, 199, 207–10, 212–16, 217, 219–21, 224–27, 229, 232, 245, 248–50, 254–55, 257, 272, 276, 280, 283, 289, 295–96, 330, 346
Medevac, 143, 331
Medical Company, 50th, 143
Melmastiia, 46
MH–6 Little Bird, 102
MH–47 Chinooks, 75, 82–84, 88, 161–62, 169, 341
MH–53 Pave Lows, 83
MH–60 Black Hawks, 75, 82–84. *See also* Black Hawks.
Mi–8s, 80
MiG fighters, 80

Mikolashek, Lt. Gen. Paul T., 68–69, 77, 94, 102–04, 111, 126, 140–41, 144, 150, 172–74, 176, 178, 184, 213, 222, 345
Milawa Valley, 120–22
Military Intelligence units
  110th Military Intelligence Battalion, 76
  202d Military Intelligence Battalion, 134, 212
  311th Military Intelligence Battalion, 142
  513th Military Intelligence Brigade, 134, 178
Military Police units, 143, 209, 212, 286, 291, 297, 310
  65th Military Police Company (Airborne). *See* Airborne units.
  519th Military Police Battalion, 143
Military Technical Agreement, 141
Milley, Col. Mark A., 232–33, 278
Milošević, Slobodan, 17–18
Minot Air Force Base, 71
Mixon, Brig. Gen. Benjamin R., 225
Mixon, Maj. Gen. Robert W. Jr., 307–08
Mk–82 (500-pound) bomb, 80, 157, 163, 182
Modular brigade combat teams. *See* Modularity.
Modularity, 307–09, 316, 348
Mogadishu, 34
Mohammadi, Bismillah Khan, 85, 96–97
Mohammed Akhundzada, Sher. *See* Akhundzada, Sher Mohammed.
Mohammed Arif Sarwari. *See* Sarwari, Mohammed Arif.
Mohammed Atta. *See* Nur, Ustad Mohammed Atta.
Mohammed Farah Aideed. *See* Aideed, Mohammed Farah.
Mohammed Fazl, Mullah. *See* Fazl, Mullah Mohammed.
Mohammed Mohaqiq. *See* Mohaqiq, Mohammed.
Mohammed Najibullah. *See* Najibullah, Mohammed.

Mohammed Omar, Mullah. *See* Omar, Mullah Mohammed.
Mohammed Osmani, Akhtar. *See* Osmani, Akhtar Mohammed.
Mohammed Qasim Fahim. *See* Fahim, Mohammed Qasim.
Mohammed, Sufi, 92
Mohammed Wazir, Nek. *See* Wazir, Nek Mohammed.
Mohammed Zahir Shah. *See* Shah, Mohammed Zahir.
Mohaqiq, Mohammed, 89, 92–93
Moore, V. Adm. Charles W., 93, 103–04
Mortars, 86, 121, 150, 154–55, 159, 164, 169, 274
   82-mm., 150, 155
   120-mm., 154–55, 274
Morón Air Base, 71
Mountain Division, 10th, 25, 66, 70–71, 75, 110, 131, 144–46, 154–57, 163–65, 169, 181, 208, 221, 236, 245, 253, 266, 270–71, 274–75, 290–91, 334. *See also* Artillery units; Infantry Battalions; Infantry Brigades; Infantry Divisions; Infantry units; Military Intelligence units.
Mountain Division, 10th, units
   1st Brigade, 23, 70, 245
   2d Brigade, 70, 77, 168, 214, 232–33, 278
Mountain Home Air Force Base, 71
Mubarak, Hosni, 10
Mueller, Robert S. III, 38
Mufi Nizamuddin Shamzai. *See* Shamzai, Mufi Nizamuddin.
Muhammad, Prophet, 5, 8, 44
Mujahideen, 98, 106, 119, 122, 181, 202, 230, 254, 325
Mulholland, Col. John P., 67–68, 76, 88, 94–95, 99–102, 104, 109, 113, 118, 120–21, 131, 144–45, 171, 208, 340
Mullah Abdul Ghani Baradar. *See* Baradar, Mullah Abdul Ghani.
Mullah Abdur Razzaq. *See* Razzaq, Mullah Abdur.
Mullah Dadullah Akhund. *See* Akhund, Mullah Dadullah.
Mullah Habibullah. *See* Habibullah, Mullah.
Mullah Mohammed Fazl. *See* Fazl, Mullah Mohammed.
Mullah Mohammed Omar. *See* Omar, Mullah Mohammed.
Mullah Naquib Alikozai. *See* Alikozai, Mullah Naquib.
Mullah Obiadullah Akhund. *See* Akhund, Mullah Obiadullah.
Murphy, Lt. Michael Patrick, 341
Musharraf, Pervez, 42–44, 57, 105–06, 184, 202–03, 207
Myers, General Richard B., 56, 105, 145, 178

Nafiz, Abdul-Razzaq, 92
Najibullah Sadiqi. *See* Sadiqi, Najibullah.
Najibullah, Mohammed, 2–3, 9
Namangani, Juma, 92
Nangarhar Province, 119, 125, 250, 275, 288–89, 291
   Jalalabad, 63, 80, 98, 119–22, 202, 245, 250, 290
Naquib Alikozai, Mullah. *See* Alikozai, Mullah Naquib.
National Guard. *See* U.S. Army National Guard.
National Highway 617, 298
National Security Council, Afghanistan, 195
National Security Council, U.S., 51, 54, 60–62, 97, 261, 281, 302, 332
NATO. *See* North Atlantic Treaty Organization (NATO).
NATURAL FIRE (joint exercise), 67
Naval Amphibious Base Coronado, 67
Naval Expeditionary Task Force 58. *See* Task Force 58.
Naval Special Warfare Command, 66
Navy, U.S., 26–27, 33, 43, 55, 65–67, 73–74, 79–80, 92–93, 101–02, 109, 134, 146–47, 158, 161–62, 176, 210, 258, 296, 341
Navy units
   Fifth Fleet, 55

INDEX

SEAL Team 2, 147
SEAL Team 3, 147, 181
SEAL Team 8, 147
SEAL Team Mako–21, 160
SEAL Team Mako–30, 160–62
SEAL Team Mako–31, 151–52, 153, 156, 158
Naylor, 89
Neason, Lt. Col. Clarence Jr., 291
Nek Mohammed Wazir. *See* Wazir, Nek Mohammed.
Neumann, Ronald E., 328, 338
New Orleans, 317
New York City, 64, 66
New Zealand Special Air Service, 136, 147
Newman, Capt. Dean S., 89, 92
Newman, CWO3 James P., 96
Nikeh Valley, 169
Nimroz Province, 276, 291, 325
Ninth Air Force, 55
Nizamuddin Shamzai, Mufi. *See* Shamzai, Mufi Nizamuddin.
Nom de guerre
 Agha. *See* Agha (nom de guerre).
 Dostum. *See* Dostum, Abdul Rashid.
 Elvis. *See* Elvis (nom de guerre).
 Mansour. *See* Mansour (nom de guerre).
Noorzai, Bashir, 290
Norfolk, 64, 68, 73, 76, 176
Norfolk Naval Base, 73
North Africa, 10
North Arabian Sea, 79
North Atlantic Treaty Organization (NATO), 48–50, 221, 253, 282, 284, 304–05, 319–20, 322–24, 327–30, 333–34, 344
North Korea, 127
North Waziristan, 263
Northeast Asia, 22
Northwest Frontier Province, 264
Nur, Ustad Mohammed Atta, 89, 92–93, 95, 104, 275
Nuri, Nurullah, 92
Nuristan Province, 200, 264, 268, 274, 291
Mangalam, 274
Nurullah Nuri. *See* Nuri, Nurullah
Nutsch, Capt. Mark D., 85–86
Nutter, Col. Cassel J., 137, 141

Obiadullah Akhund, Mullah. *See* Akhund, Mullah Obiadullah.
Objectives
 BADGER, 81
 GECKO, 81–82
 GINGER, 164
 REMINGTON, 148, 150, 164
 RHINO, 81–83, 102, 112–13
ODAs. *See* Operational Detachment Alpha (ODA) teams.
Office of Military Cooperation–Afghanistan, 140–41, 174–75, 223, 229–30, 232–33, 278–80, 295, 297, 330, 337
O'Hara, Capt. Patrick, 96
Olson, Maj. Gen. Eric T., 290, 292, 299
Oman, 81, 83, 102, 131, 158, 160
Omar, Mullah Mohammed, 4–7, 10, 41–42, 45–46, 58, 80–82, 114, 202–03, 211, 263–64, 266, 344
Operational Detachment Alpha (ODA) teams, 84, 88, 95–96, 98–100, 102, 104, 148, 150, 212, 218–19, 229, 253, 287, 298, 326
 ODA 312, 250
 ODA 314, 218
 ODA 342, 253
 ODA 344, 253
 ODA 372, 148, 167
 ODA 381, 148
 ODA 534, 89, 109
 ODA 542, 148
 ODA 553, 89, 94
 ODA 554, 96
 ODA 555, 84–85, 94, 96
 ODA 571, 148
 ODA 572, 121–22, 148
 ODA 574, 100–101, 117
 ODA 583, 100–101, 113, 118
 ODA 585, 88
 ODA 586, 96
 ODA 594, 95, 143, 148
 ODA 595, 84–86, 92, 109

401

Operational Detachment Alpha (ODA) teams—*Continued*
    ODA 986, 218
Operational Detachment Charlie teams
    51, 88
    53, 89, 107, 109
Operational Mentor and Liaison Teams, 333
Operations, U.S.
    ALAMO SWEEP, 219, 245
    ANACONDA, 34, 146–47, 150–53, 156, 159, 170, 200–201, 208, 213–14, 340, 347
    CHAMPION STRIKE, 214, 220, 245
    DESERT SHIELD, 13
    DESERT STORM, 214, 237–38
    ENDURING FREEDOM, 57, 67, 69, 83, 136, 178, 183, 192, 194, 196, 203, 205, 211, 217, 225–26, 228–29, 233–34, 239, 248–50, 253, 255, 258, 271, 277, 279, 282, 287, 291, 295–97, 302, 323, 334, 340, 344, 346–47
    ENDURING FREEDOM–Afghanistan, 50, 57
    ENDURING FREEDOM–Horn of Africa, 57, 70
    ENDURING FREEDOM–Philippines, 57, 242
    ESSENTIAL HARVEST, 26
    HARPOON, 168–69
    INFINITE JUSTICE, 57
    INFINITE REACH, 57
    INFINITE RESOLVE, 57
    IRAQI FREEDOM, 57, 198, 234, 239, 270
    MONGOOSE, 246
    MOUNTAIN LION, 180–84, 213–14, 219–20, 245
    MOUNTAIN RESOLVE, 274
    MOUNTAIN SWEEP, 218–20
    MOUNTAIN VIPER, 253, 273
    NEWBURGH, 298
    NOBLE EAGLE, 65
    POLAR HARPOON, 169
    PTARMIGAN, 182
    RED WINGS, 340
    RESTORE HOPE, 14
    SECURE FUTURE, 289–90
    SNIPE, 183
    TICONDEROGA, 294
    TORI II, 183
    TRENTON, 294
    UNIFIED RESOLVE, 250
    VIPER, 246, 250, 253, 273
    WARRIOR SWEEP, 250
Osama bin Laden. *See* bin Laden, Osama.
Osmani, Akhtar Mohammed, 266, 290
Otner, Lt. Col. Blake C., 291
Owens, Col. Kevin C., 301, 339

Pacha Khan Zadran. *See* Zadran, Pacha Khan.
Pachir wa Agam, 122
Panjwa'i District, 4
Pakistan, 34, 41–45, 47, 55, 57, 59, 61, 70, 72, 74, 77, 82–83, 92, 95, 97–98, 100, 105, 114, 120, 123, 125, 127, 131, 138–39, 142, 147–48, 163–64, 183–84, 186–87, 198, 202–04, 207, 209–10, 214, 220, 230, 245–46, 250, 253, 255, 263–66, 273, 275, 287, 291, 301, 323, 325–26, 330, 344
    Federally Administered Tribal Areas, 120, 125, 184, 202, 263
    Islamabad, 41–43, 45, 58, 106, 119, 125, 203, 205
    Jacobabad, 44, 74, 82, 95, 101
    Karachi, 263
    Miran Shah, 263
    North Waziristan, 263
    Northwest Frontier Province, 264
    Pasni, 74
    Peshawar, 114, 264
    Quetta, 100, 201–02, 263–64
    Quetta Shura Taliban, 325
    South Waziristan, 204–05
    Tirah Valley, 204
Paktika Province, 200, 214, 253, 263, 291–92, 325
    Sharan, 269
Paktiya Province, 135, 196, 200, 218, 226, 250, 263, 291, 325
    Gardez, 150, 152, 160–61, 196, 218,

INDEX

226–27, 245, 262
Jaji, 8
Zurmat District, 218
Palestine, 49
Parker, Col. Wayland E., 141
Parwan Province, 291
Paschal, Lt. Col. David G., 251
Pashtun, 42, 45–46, 58, 61, 63, 83–84, 98, 100–102, 114, 119–20, 132, 135–36, 148, 179, 186, 194–95, 199–200, 203–05, 229, 233, 260, 265, 288–89, 294
Pashtunwali, 46
Pasni, 74
Patriquin, Capt. Travis L., 155
Pedersen, Col. Richard N., 291, 298–99
Pennsylvania, 35
Perryman, Brig. Gen. John M., 333
Persian Gulf, 74
Peshawar, 114, 264
Petawek, 117
Phelan, Col. Mark V., 171, 175
Philippines, 57, 242
Piatt, Lt. Col. Walter E., 291
Pirozzi, Lt. Col. Thomas L., 142
Positions
    Amy, 148, 154, 159
    Betty, 148, 154
    Cindy, 148, 154
    Diane, 148, 154, 163
    Eve, 103, 148, 157, 163, 329
    Ford, 148
    Ginger, 148, 156, 158, 163–64
    Heather, 148
    Jeep, 148
    Oldsmobile, 148
Posse Comitatus Act of 1878, 65
    Executive Order 13223, 64
    Title 10, U.S. Code, 64–65, 178, 306, 311, 338
    Title 32, U.S. Code, 65
Powell, General Colin L., 13, 38, 40, 43, 47–49, 58, 97, 139–40, 322
Powers, Lt. Col. Joel R., 294
Predator drones, 82, 95, 157, 161, 204–05. *See also* Unmanned aerial vehicles.
Presidential Decision Directive 25, 15–16
Pressler Amendment, 1–2
Preysler, Lt. Col. Charles A., 70, 142, 148, 154, 157, 159–61, 163
Prince Sultan Air Base, 71–73, 150
Project Standard Bearer, 20
Prophet Muhammad. *See* Muhammad, Prophet.
Provincial council elections, 278, 297–98, 301–02, 304, 320, 343, 347
Provincial Reconstruction Teams, 193, 225–27, 255, 261, 268–70, 272–73, 275–76, 285–86, 289, 291, 295–96, 298, 303–04, 323, 328–29, 333, 343, 346
Psychological Operations Group, 4th, 67
Puerto Rico, 28, 64
Putin, Vladimir, 47

Qala-i-Jangi, 92, 107–12, 132–33, 209
    prison uprising, 107–11, 132–33
Qanooni, Yunus, 114, 141, 194
Qasim Fahim, Mohammed. *See* Fahim, Mohammed Qasim.
Qatar, 98
Quander, Capt. Mark C., 142
Quartermaster units
    54th Quartermaster Company, 64
    311th Quartermaster Company (Mortuary Affairs), 64
Quetta, 100, 201–02, 263–64, 325
Quetta Shura Taliban, 325. *See also* Taliban.

Rabe, Maj. Richard A., 280
Rahim, Hariz Abdul, 290
Rahman, Gul, 290
Ramstein Air Base, 69
Ranger Regiment, 75th, 66–67, 75, 81-82, 242, 287
    2d Battalion, 67
    3d Battalion, 75, 81–82
Rapid Decisive Operations, 234, 236, 347
Rashid Dostum, Abdul. *See* Dostum, Abdul Rashid.
Rashid, Ahmed, 6, 105

Razzaq, Mullah Abdur, 266
Rear Area Operations Center, 122d. *See* Support units, 122d Support Detachment (Rear Tactical Operations Center).
Reconstruction teams. *See* Provincial Reconstruction Teams.
Regional Commands (RCs), 319, 334
    East, 289, 291, 298, 301, 328, 341
    North, 284, 319
    South, 216, 291, 301, 327
    West, 284, 286
Regional Development Zones, 267, 270, 272, 276, 289–90, 346
Renuart, Maj. Gen. Victor G. Jr., Renuart 55–56, 71
Reserves, the. *See* U.S. Army Reserve.
Rice, Condoleezza, 24, 38, 260, 302–03, 322
Rice, Lt. Col. Ronald, 214
Richardson, Lt. Col. James M., 164
Ring Road, the, 96, 281
Ringgenberg, Capt. Dirk D., 301, 329
Riyadh, 71
Roberts Ridge, 162, 170. *See also* Takur Ghar.
Roberts, PO1 Neil C., 161–62
Robinson, Mary, 132
Rocket launchers, 6, 17, 214
Rocket-propelled grenades, 160
Rockets, 6, 17, 113, 169, 183
Rodebaugh, Capt. William T. III, 76
Rohrabacher, Dana, 59
Rosengard, Lt. Col. Mark D., 145, 171, 174, 176
Rumsfeld, Donald H., 14, 26–27, 38–40, 43, 49–53, 56–57, 59–60, 80, 84, 105–06, 111, 129–30, 134, 140, 178–79, 192, 195–98, 210, 233, 243, 249, 254, 257–58, 262, 276–78, 280, 282, 284–85, 316, 322–24, 327–28, 332, 336
Russell, Col. Matthew H., 301
Russell, Lt. Col. Steven D., 173, 175
Russia, 3, 12, 36, 47, 55, 76, 97, 114, 116, 341, 348. *See also* Soviet Union.
Ryan, Capt. William A., 156

SA–3 Goa radar-guided surface-to-air missiles, 6
SA–7 Grail man-portable surface-to-air missiles, 6
Saddam Hussein, 10, 13, 38, 132, 191, 193, 198, 237, 249, 330, 345–46
Sadiq, Haji, 274
Sadiqi, Najibullah, 176
Safed Kotal, 89
Salinas, Lt. Col. Orlando, 301, 343
Sami ul-Haq. *See* ul-Haq, Sami.
Samangan Province, 88
Sangin, 343
Sarajevo, 16
Sarwari, Mohammed Arif, 88
Saudi Arabia, 49, 71, 73, 139, 263, 281
Schmitt, Eric, 316
Schoomaker, General Peter J., 234–35, 239, 306–08, 310–11, 315–16
Schröder, Gerhard F., 323
Schroen, Gary C., 74, 80, 84–85, 88
Schweitzer, Lt. Col. Martin P., 214
Scortino, S. Sgt. Michael A., 110
Sea-Air-Land (SEAL) units. *See* Navy units.
SEAL units. *See* Navy units.
Self, Capt. Nathan E., 161–62
Sellers, Lt. Col. Terry L., 291
September 11th, 33, 35, 46, 48, 69, 73, 133, 192, 202, 238, 242, 304, 347. *See also* al-Qaeda.
    attacks 35, 69, 73, 192, 202, 238, 242, 304, 347
Serbia, 17
Service Support Group 22, 294
Shah Massoud, Ahmad. *See* Massoud, Ahmad Shah
Shah, Mohammed Zahir, 61, 100, 114, 195
Shah Wali Kot, 117, 297–99, 301
Shah, Zahir. *See* Shah, Mohammed Zahir.
Shahbaz Air Force Base, 74, 95
Shahi Kot Valley, 34, 144–45, 147–48, 150–53, 155, 159, 161, 163–67, 170, 181–82, 185, 209, 250
    Whale, the, 144, 150, 153, 164–65,

INDEX

167–69
Shamsi, 44, 75
Shamzai, Mufi Nizamuddin, 46
Sharia, 265, 325
Sharzai, Gul Agha, 99–102, 111, 113, 117–19, 299
Shah Wali Kot, 117, 299, 301
Shediyaki Ghar, 181
Shelton, General H. Hugh, 25–27, 38, 51, 53, 56, 58, 79
Sher Khan Khel, 144, 148
Sher Mohammed Akhundzada. *See* Akhundzada, Sher Mohammed.
Shibirghan, 79
 prison, 107, 133, 209
Shindand, 79
Shinseki, General Erik K., 21, 23, 24, 29, 69, 71, 178, 234, 306
Shura, 119–20, 124, 264, 325. *See also* Quetta Shura Taliban; United Front.
 meaning of, 3
 Eastern Shura (United Front), 119–20, 124
Shomali Plain, 96
Signal units
 11th Signal Brigade, 178
 50th Signal Battalion, 245
 54th Signal Battalion, 69–70
 112th Signal Battalion, 67
 335th Signal Command (Theater), 69–70
Sinai, 21, 25, 70–71, 192
Sirajuddin Haqqani. *See* Haqqani, Sirajuddin.
Slabinski, SCPO Britt K., 162
Smith, Capt. Hank E., 100–01, 113, 117–18
SOAR, 160th. *See* Aviation units.
SOCOM. *See* Special Operations Command.
SOF. *See* Special Operations Forces (SOF).
Solana, Javier, 18
Somalia, 40, 54, 127
Soriano, M. Sgt. Jorge O., 76
South Korea, 28
South Waziristan, 204–05
Southern European Task Force, 301, 334, 339
Southeast Asia, 273
Southwest Asia, 70
Soviet-Afghan War, 121, 131, 181
Soviet Union, 1–4, 6, 8–10, 12–13, 22, 24, 33, 36, 52–53, 55, 57, 63, 75, 80, 86, 114, 173, 198, 202, 254, 262–64, 345. *See also* Russia.
Spann, Johnny Michael, 108, 110
Special Forces Battalions
 1st, 3d Special Forces Group, 175–76
 1st, 5th Special Forces Group, 67, 88, 102
 2d, 3d Special Forces Group, 171
 2d, 5th Special Forces Group, 67, 77, 94, 100, 118
 3d, 3d Special Forces Group, 102, 171
 3d, 5th Special Forces Group, 89, 109
Special Forces Groups
 1st, 136, 240
 3d, 102, 144, 147–48, 171, 175–76, 208, 240
 5th, 67–68, 76–77, 80, 88–89, 94, 102, 109, 118, 136, 148, 165, 171, 242
 10th, 171
 19th, 171, 219
 20th, 171
Special Operations Aviation Regiment, 160th. *See* Aviation units.
Special Operations Command units, 55, 59, 66–68, 73, 76, 102, 123, 126, 240, 242–43
 1st Special Forces Command, 67, 102, 136, 144, 171, 208, 242
 75th Ranger Regiment. *See* Ranger Regiment, 75th, units.
 160th Aviation Regiment (Special Operations). *See* Aviation units.
Special Operations Forces (SOF), 1, 51–53, 56–57, 63, 66, 68, 86, 88, 102, 104, 126, 155, 240, 242–43, 245–46, 287, 295, 309, 311

Spin Boldak, 113, 246, 264–65
Stammer, Lt. Col. Mark R., 301
Stevens, Capt. Jonathan A., 168–70
Stogran, Lt. Col. Patrick B., 143, 168–69, 182–83
Stonesifer, Pfc. Kristofer T., 83
Stout, Lt. Col. Michael E., 225–27
Strmecki, Marin J., 260, 276
Stryker brigade combat teams, 192, 308–10
Strykers, 24, 192, 308, 310
Stufflebeem, R. Adm. John D., 181
Sudan, 40, 49
Sufi Mohammed. *See* Mohammed, Sufi.
Sufism, 135
Sullivan, General Gordon R., 13, 21
Sullivan, Maj. Dennis S., 274
Supply and Service Battalion, 530th, 95
Support Battalions
   173d, 301
   307th, 245
   325th, 291
   507th, XVIII Airborne Corps. *See* Airborne units.
   528th (Special Operations), 67, 75–76, 95, 102
   626th Forward. *See* Forward Support Battalion, 626th.
Support units
   21st Support Command (Theater), 69–70
   122d Support Detachment (Rear Tactical Operations Center), 137
   377th Support Command (Theater), 69–70, 137, 174
Supreme Headquarters Allied Powers Europe, 28
Surface-to-air missiles (SAMs), 80, 82, 113, 181. *See also* SA–3 Goa radar-guided surface-to-air missiles; SA–7 Grail man-portable surface-to-air missiles.
Syria, 38, 40
T–55 tanks, 110
Tajikistan, 55, 88, 97, 106
Takhar Province, 96
   Taluqan, 63, 88, 96

Takur Ghar, 144, 158, 160–64, 170. *See also* Roberts Ridge; Shahi Kot.
Takhtah Pul Kelay, 101–02, 111, 113
Taliban, 34, 38, 41–47, 51–53, 57–58, 60–63, 66–67, 74, 79–86, 88–89, 92, 96–102, 104, 106–07, 111, 113–15, 117–18, 120, 125–26, 128–29, 132–36, 139–41, 164, 172–73, 175, 177–78, 181, 183–84, 186–87, 193–95, 197, 199–205, 207, 209–12, 214, 217, 219–20, 229–30, 246–47, 253–55, 261–66, 271, 273, 277, 282, 291–92, 294, 298, 304–05, 320, 325–26, 329, 334, 339, 341, 343–44, 346–47. *See also* al-Qaeda.
   Afghanistan post-rule, 61, 63, 67, 97–99, 113–15, 126, 128, 134–35, 139, 172, 175, 184, 186–87, 207, 343–45
   defeat of, 183, 186, 191, 199–200, 202, 207, 262, 298
   defined, 2
   and Hamid Karzai, 100, 195, 304
   and Haqqani Network, 135–36, 263
   history of, 2–8
   missions against, 62–63, 74, 79–83, 85–86, 92, 96–97, 101–02, 106–07, 113–14, 117–18, 151–54, 164, 171, 180–81, 194, 209, 246–47, 253–54, 264–65, 294, 329
   and opium production, 197, 200
   and other extremist groups, 263–65
   Pakistani, 92, 106, 203–05, 220, 255, 263, 326, 344
   and Pashtuns, 45, 87, 98, 99, 132, 195, 203, 264
   prisoners, 133–34, 184, 210–11, 246
   resurgence, 201, 229–30, 261, 265, 273, 305, 324–25, 334, 343–44, 347
   ruling in Afghanistan, 10–11, 34, 45–46, 52
   strategy against, 41–43, 46–47, 50–51, 53, 57–62, 66, 84, 87–89, 100, 104–05, 111, 120, 129, 130,

136, 200–201, 209, 217–19, 247, 254, 266, 271–73, 291–92, 320, 334
   threat from, 38
   in Uzbekistan, 57
Tanzania, 57
Tarin Kot, 101–02, 114, 286, 290, 294, 298
Tarnak Farms, 113
Task Forces (TFs), U.S. 58, 93, 103–04, 112, 131–32, 142 64, 147
   Anvil, 148
   Bowie, 131
   Commando, 168
   Dagger, 76, 80, 93–95, 98–99, 102–04, 109–10, 117–18, 120–21, 144, 146, 150, 154–55, 186, 208–09, 340
   Devil, 245–46, 250–51, 343
   Hammer, 151, 153
   Hawk, 17–18
   Jacana, 181–83
   K-Bar, 102, 147, 164. *See also* CJSOTF South.
   Longhorn, 286
   Modularity, 307–309
   Panther, 214, 217–19, 245
   Phoenix, 232, 238, 278, 333
   Sword, 66, 74–75, 81–82, 102, 118, 122–23, 126, 131, 145–46, 151, 156, 158, 160–61
   Talon, 143, 153, 168
   Warrior, 106, 245, 250–51, 253, 270, 291
Teams
   Alpha, 84–85, 89, 217, 241
   Delta, 89
   Echo, 100–101, 108
   Foxtrot, 100–101
   India, 42, 44, 96, 114, 139, 151, 158, 202–03
   Jawbreaker (CIA), 79, 122
   Juliet, 120–21, 151, 158
   ODA teams. *See* Operational Detachment Alpha (ODA) teams.
   SEAL teams. *See* Navy units.

Tenet, George J., 38, 49, 51, 57–59
Tewksbury, Lt. Col. Dennis D., 245
Third Army, 69–70, 77, 94, 178. *See also* U.S. Army Central Command (ARCENT).
Thomas, Capt. Glenn R., 95, 148, 152
Tiangi, the, 89, 92
Tillman, Spec. Patrick D., 287
Tink, Lt. Col. Rowan J., 113, 147
Tokyo Conference, 139
Tomahawk missiles, 18, 79
Tora Bora, 34, 120–23, 125–26, 131, 144, 146, 181, 183, 202, 209
Total Force Policy, 239
Townsend, Lt. Col. Stephen J., 168–69
TRADOC. *See* U.S. Army Training and Doctrine Command (TRADOC).
Training and Doctrine Command. *See* U.S. Army Training and Doctrine Command (TRADOC).
Transportation Battalion, 7th, 58th Maintenance Company, 95
Trebon, Brig. Gen. Gregory I., 158
Turkey, 102, 179–80
Turkmenistan, 55, 97
Tyson, David, 108–09

UAV. *See* Unmanned aerial vehicles.
UH–1N Twin Hueys, 112
UH–60 Black Hawks, 143, 153. *See also* Black Hawks.
ul-Haq, Sami, 11
Umar, Haji, 205
United Arab Emirates, 7, 42, 81
United Front, 51, 53, 58, 60–61, 63, 74, 83–88, 92–93, 96–100, 103–04, 106–07, 110–11, 114, 116, 119, 125, 131, 133, 141, 178–79, 186, 194, 198–99, 202–03, 209, 228
United National and Islamic Front for the Salvation of Afghanistan. *See* United Front.
United Nations, 7, 10, 14–15, 33–34, 48–49, 70, 97–99, 108, 114–15, 128–29, 132, 134–35, 138, 179, 195, 221, 223–24, 267, 272, 276,

United Nations—*Continued*
    288, 294, 335, 346
    Security Council, 7, 40, 99, 115–16, 278, 323
    Security Council Resolution 1378, 99
    Security Council Resolution 1386, 135
Units of action, 307–10
Unmanned aerial vehicles, 157, 192, 249. *See also* Predator drones.
Urgun region, 148
Uruzgan Province, 101, 178, 194, 246, 253, 265–66, 268, 273, 286, 291, 294, 298, 325
    Tarin Kot, 101–02, 114, 286, 290, 294, 298
U.S. Agency for International Development (USAID), 137, 207, 225–26, 260, 281, 285–86, 298
U.S. Air Force. *See* Air Force, U.S.
U.S. Army Central Command (ARCENT), 55, 67–70, 77, 93–94, 137, 178, 320
U.S. Army Civil Affairs and Psychological Operations Command, 240, 241, 243, 286
U.S. Army Forces Command (FORSCOM), 28, 67–68, 72, 76, 102, 118, 136, 144, 176, 208, 243, 258, 278, 311–12, 315
U.S. Army National Guard, 64–65, 71, 191–92, 230, 237–40, 301, 307, 312, 314, 316–18, 333
U.S. Army Pacific, 55, 73
U.S. Army Reserve, 64–65, 69–70, 86, 104, 137, 148, 168, 171, 174, 184, 192, 222, 225, 232, 237–39, 243, 294, 306–07, 310, 312, 314, 316, 318
U.S. Army Special Operations Command. *See* Special Operations Command.
U.S. Army Training and Doctrine Command (TRADOC), 145, 235, 307–08, 312
U.S. Central Command (CENTCOM), 34, 38–40, 46, 53, 55–60, 62–63, 65–67, 69, 73, 76–77, 79, 81, 83–84, 88, 92–94, 96–99, 101, 104, 114, 123–29, 131, 134, 136–38, 140–41, 145–46, 152, 164, 170, 172, 175, 177–79, 185–86, 191–94, 198, 207–09, 212, 214, 217, 220, 222, 224–25, 229–32, 236–37, 240, 248–49, 254–55, 257–58, 260–62, 271–72, 274, 277–78, 294, 303, 318–20, 322, 327–28, 340–41, 346–47
    Afghan elections and, 221, 292, 342
    Afghan National Army and, 140, 175, 178, 193–94, 229–32, 261, 277–78
    Afghanistan war plans and, 38, 127
    initial response to September 11th attacks, 24, 34, 38–40, 46, 53, 55–60, 62–63, 65–67, 69
    International Security Assistance Force and, 128, 141, 178–79, 319–20, 322, 327, 346
    Iraq war plans and, 38, 40, 57, 69, 127–28, 186, 193, 198, 207–08, 236–37, 240, 248, 262, 294, 318, 322, 346–47
U.S. Central Intelligence Agency. *See* Central Intelligence Agency (CIA).
U.S. Civil Affairs Teams. *See* Civil affairs teams.
U.S. Embassies, 11, 140, 261, 338
    bombings in Kenya and Tanzania, 11, 57
    Islamabad, 4
    Kabul, 258
U.S. Marine Corps. *See* Marine Corps, U.S.; Marine Corps units.
U.S. Marine Forces Central Command, 55
U.S. Marine Forces Pacific. *See* U.S. Marine Forces Central Command.
U.S. Navy. *See* Navy, U.S.; Navy units.
U.S. Special Operations Command. *See* Special Operations Command.

USAID. *See* U.S. Agency for International Development.
Ushr, 324
Usmani, Abdul-Qahir, 92
USS *Bataan*, 73
USS *Carl Vinson*, 73, 80
USS *Cole*, 25
USS *Enterprise*, 73, 80
USS *Kitty Hawk*, 73, 75, 81–82
USS *Peleliu*, 112
USS *Theodore Roosevelt*, 73, 101
Ustad Mohammed Atta Nur. *See* Nur, Ustad Mohammed Atta.
Uzbekistan, 55, 57, 60, 63, 72–73, 75–76, 80, 92–94, 97, 131, 170, 224, 341–42

V Corps. *See* Corps, V.
VII Corps. *See* Corps, VII.
Vicenza, 94, 339
Vietnam War, 162, 239, 273, 330
Vines, Maj. Gen. John R., 219, 243, 245, 248–50, 253–55, 270, 272, 276, 280, 289, 296, 346
Virgin Islands, 28
Virginia Military Institute, 180, 196
Vitter, David B., 318

Wahhabi, 7
Waldhauser, Col. Thomas D., 73
Wali Karzai, Ahmed. *See* Karzai, Ahmed Wali.
Wardak Province, 264, 291, 343
Warman, Lt. Col. Paul K., 143
Washington, D.C., 42, 44, 55, 60–61, 67, 106, 111, 129, 139, 195, 230, 271, 302, 305, 338, 346
Wass de Czege, Brig. Gen. Huba, 308
Wazir, Nek Mohammed, 205, 290
Weapons of mass destruction, 38, 45, 66, 81, 127, 132
Weimer, Col. Michael B., 140, 174

West Point, 28, 258
Weston, Maj. Gen. Craig P., 331
Wetherill, Col. Nancy J., 298–99, 301
Whale, the. *See* Shahi Kot.
Whiteman Air Force Base, 72, 80
Wiercinski, Col. Francis J., 70, 95, 142–43, 148, 153, 156–57, 159–60, 164–65, 167, 169, 214
Wilkerson, Col. Kevin V., 168–69, 214
Wille, Lt. Col. Paul J., 253
Wolfowitz, Paul D., 26–27, 37–39, 53

XVIII Airborne Corps. *See* Airborne units.

Yemen, 10, 25, 40, 127, 201, 210
Young, Lt. Col. Robert G., 291
Younis Khalis. *See* Khalis, Younis.
Yuldashev, Tohir Abduhalilovich, 204, 290
Yunus Qanooni. *See* Qanooni, Yunus.

Zabul Province, 178, 253, 265, 273, 291–92, 298, 325, 329
  Qalat, 290
Zadran, Kamel Khan, 148
Zadran, Pacha Khan, 135–36, 195, 262
Zadran, Zakim Khan, 136, 148
Zahir Shah, Mohammed. *See* Shah, Mohammed Zahir.
Zahir, Abdul, 119
Zahir, Haji, 120
Zakim Khan Zadran. *See* Zadran, Zakim Khan.
Zaman, Haji Ghamsharik, 119, 123
Zhaware Kelay, 181–82
Zia Abdullah. *See* Abdullah, Zia.
Zia Lodin. *See* Lodin, Zia.
Zorlu, Maj. Gen. Hilmi Akin, 179–80

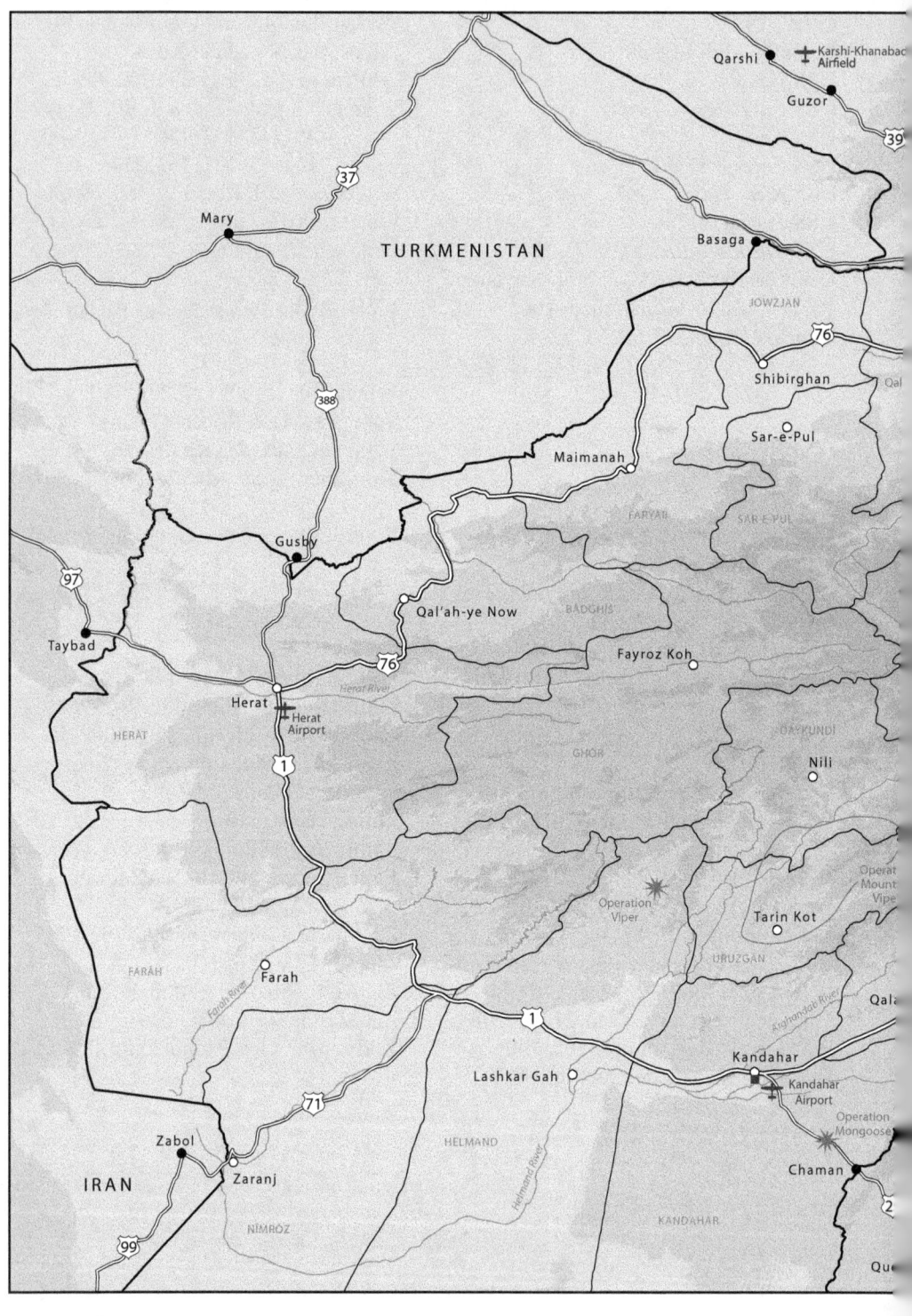

www.ingramcontent.com/pod-product-compliance
Lightning Source LLC
Chambersburg PA
CBHW080722300426
44114CB00019B/2464